THE PROGRESSIVE PUBLICATION OF MATTHEW

Dedicated to Marcus Loane, KBE,
Principal of Moore Theological College
(and, subsequently, Archbishop of Sydney),
where I was one of his students of the Gospels,
who alerted me to the nature of the Synoptic Problem
and the serious difficulties with the Markan Priority view

THE PROGRESSIVE PUBLICATION OF MATTHEW

An Explanation of the Writing of the Synoptic Gospels

B. WARD POWERS

The Progressive Publication of Matthew:
An Explanation of the Writing of the Synoptic Gospels

Copyright © 2010 by B. Ward Powers

All rights reserved.

ISBN: 978-0-8054-4848-1

Published by B&H Publishing Group
Nashville, Tennessee

Dewey Decimal Classification: 226.1
Subject Heading: BIBLE. N.T. GOSPELS—STUDY\BIBLE. N.T. MATTHEW\
BIBLE. N.T.—HISTORY

The Greek New Testament, Third Corrected Edition, edited by Kurt Aland, Matthew Black, Carlo M. Martini, Bruce M. Metzger, and Allen Wikgren in cooperation with the Institute for New Testament Textual Research, Münster/Westphalia, (c) 1983 United Bible Societies. Used by permission.

Scripture quotations are from the Revised Standard Version of the Bible, copyrighted 1946, 1952, © 1971, 1973.

Printed in the United States of America

CONTENTS

1. What This Book Is All About 1
2. One Leg to Stand On 16
3. Explaining Mark's Gospel 53
4. Fleshing Out the Facts and Figures 102
5. The Markan Priority Explanation 156
6. The Markan Dependence Explanation 208
7. Seventeen Impossible Things before Breakfast . . . 257
8. The Relationship Between Luke and Matthew 346
9. Putting Things in Order 382
10. A Quick Look at Some Other Ideas 448
11. Now Take the Case of the Rich Young Man 490
12. In Conclusion 540
    Bibliography 578
    Name Index 587
    Subject Index 591
    Scripture Index 595

1 WHAT THIS BOOK IS ALL ABOUT

An overview of the Progressive Publication of Matthew Hypothesis, with a presentation of the five basic propositions to which the evidence points.

> *The Synoptic Problem is an important matter. . . . When we recognize the solution to the Synoptic Problem to be a central building block in our understanding of how to answer questions about the trustworthiness of the Gospels and the distinctive theologies of each evangelist, we cannot help but appreciate its importance.*
> —Craig Blomberg
> (advocate of Markan Priority),
> in Black and Beck (2001, 40)

A BRIEF DESCRIPTION

This book is about the relationship between the first three Gospels in the New Testament. In the pages to follow I give you two good reasons why it is not worth your while to bother with this book—it is simply a waste of your valuable time. But I also give you a response to those reasons. And you might decide that the response is in fact better than the two good reasons, so that this book *is* worth looking at after all. But first of all, I need to clarify what I am discussing in this book.

The first three Gospels—Matthew, Mark, and Luke—are often called the Synoptic Gospels or simply the Synoptics. The word *synoptic* means "to look at or see together," that is, to compare things side by side. When you do this, you will immediately be impressed by two striking features about the Synoptics: their similarities, the things they have in common; and their differences, the places where they are unlike each other—and occasions where they seem to contradict each other.

These similarities are at times quite remarkable and cry out for explanation. There are places where two and even three Synoptics are identical, ranging from several words to entire sentences. Now when this occurs in a teaching that Jesus gave or a story that he told, then the explanation could simply be that this is indeed what was said (or reported) and thus the authors got it right—whatever their sources. But if it occurs in a piece of narrative, a description that some author has written, then this explanation is not adequate and we need to look for another. The most obvious one that comes to mind is that of a common source: either one Gospel copied from the other, or two of them used a third source, whether written or oral.

But the differences between the Synoptics are also at times quite remarkable and cry out for explanation. If one used another—if A used B—why does A change so much of B? By accident? To make a point? For correction? Because of some external consideration, such as a later church tradition or doctrine? All these possibilities and more have been advocated in the wealth of literature that discusses these matters. This issue is often called the Synoptic Problem, and these Synoptic differences are so great and so varied that a large number of solutions to the Synoptic Problem have been proposed to account for them.

The differences are of three main kinds: (1) differences of points of detail in the stories in which they are found; (2) differences of content in the stories overall, including some stories or units of material—called pericopes—found in only one Gospel, others in two, and still others in all three; and (3) where two or three of the Synoptics do contain the same pericopes, differences in Synoptic order, that is, differences in the sequence of events they record.

An explanation of Synoptic relationships (i.e., a solution to the Synoptic Problem) needs to address all these Synoptic features, and it will be—or ought to be—judged on the basis of its explanatory power. A proposed solution to the Synoptic Problem is valuable only to the extent that it can supply a convincing and satisfactory account of what we observe in these Gospels.

IS THIS BOOK WORTHWHILE?

There are two good reasons for not reading any further in this book. The first of these is that the Synoptic Problem was solved years ago so scholars in general agree on the solution. Thus G. M. Styler said (1962, 223), "After a century or more of discussion, it has come to be accepted by scholars almost as axiomatic that Mark is the oldest of the three Synoptic Gospels and that it was used by Matthew and Luke as a source. This has come to be regarded as 'the one absolutely assured result' of the study of the Synoptic Problem."

The second reason for dismissing the issue is that it doesn't really seem to matter anyway. We can just go on and read the Gospels and use them without bothering with any question of relationships between them. Since all three were inspired by the Holy Spirit, we can just take each one as it stands.

My response to the first reason is that the Markan Priority Hypothesis is widely accepted, not because it explains everything satisfactorily, but because it seems to do a better job than any other alternative. There are indeed many problems with Markan Priority as an explanation of the data and with the traditional reasons given in support of it—reasons going back to B. H. Streeter, who gave it its classic form in 1924.

It deserves to be noted that a substantial volume of literature exists— some from years ago and some of recent origin—that casts grave doubt on the validity of Markan Priority. The individual arguments for Markan Priority have all been tested, assessed, and rebutted by a variety of authors. A string of monographs and detailed studies has exposed the weaknesses of the grounds for the Markan Priority Hypothesis, which has difficulty in explaining observable Synoptic data apart from a resort to subjective opinion or dependence on coincidence. The snag is that while it is pretty easy to find holes in the case for Markan Priority, there have been similar holes in the other explanations that have been offered.

Styler himself recognized that the Markan Priority Hypothesis was not without its problems. But he holds firmly to Markan Priority because it has fewer problems than any other explanation. For example, Styler demolished the view of Bishop B. C. Butler (1951, 90–92), who contended that the order of writing is Matthew-Mark-Luke, and said about this view, "Butler's treatment of this leaves me quite unconvinced" (ibid., 228). In summary, Styler wrote, "Our explanation of *his* favourite cases may be cumbersome; but his explanation of *our* favourite cases is incredible" (ibid.).

Styler concluded, "Until some less incredible explanation is forthcoming, the natural conclusion that Mark is prior to Matthew will continue to hold the field" (ibid., 231). In my judgment Styler's analysis remains valid. Most scholars hold to Markan Priority with or without postulating another source designated Q to explain Matthew-Luke agreements. But this is not because they cannot see the problems with that hypothesis; it is because Markan Priority seems to hold up as a better explanation than any other alternative and can be said to cover more of the observable data.

If we are going to adhere to Markan Priority, honesty demands that we at least be aware of the flimsy and dubious nature of the foundation on which it rests. This book explains all the arguments known to me for Markan Priority and summarizes the rebuttal of those arguments that competent scholars have given over the years. The reader can then judge whether any objective, factual, valid support for this hypothesis remains. I also offer an explanation of Synoptic interrelationships that I believe answers all the problems that exist both with Markan Priority and the other hypotheses, and this explanation accords both with internal observable data and external evidence.

But what about the second objection, that it doesn't really seem to matter? Actually, it matters seriously, for several important reasons.

First, at the academic level this is a significant issue in New Testament research that has had a focus on Gospel scholarship for more than two centuries. If there is now a hypothesis propounded that has greater explanatory power than those offered so far, then it should be examined and assessed and a verdict given on its validity. All kinds of repercussions flow from the explanation one adopts for Synoptic differences. For example, certain variations of the literary interdependence hypothesis will push one toward giving the Gospels a late date, which in turn affects one's approach to questions of authorship, which interacts with one's assessment of how close in time the Gospel writings are to the events they record—which then becomes (for some scholars) a measure of their reliability.

In 2000 D. Black and D. Beck convened a conference at Southeastern Baptist Theological Seminary that gathered together (to quote the conveners) "some of the world's leading experts in the field of New Testament studies" (2001, 13). The purpose was to assess the current state of scholarship relating to the Synoptic Problem. The papers presented at that conference have been published (2001) with the title *Rethinking the Synoptic Problem*, edited by D. A. Black and D. R. Beck. One point of consensus amongst the differing viewpoints expressed at the conference was the crucial nature of this issue in New Testament scholarship. C. Blomberg expressed this consensus when he wrote (Black and Beck 2001, 40) that "the Synoptic Problem is an important matter. . . . When we recognize the solution to the Synoptic Problem to be a central building block in our understanding of how to answer questions about the trustworthiness of the Gospels and the distinctive theologies of each evangelist, we cannot help but appreciate its importance."

Second, at the practical and pastoral level, what are we to make of the Gospel accounts where they differ? For example, when Jairus the synagogue ruler came to Jesus, was his daughter still alive (though close to death), or already dead (Mark 5:23 and Luke 8:42 compared with Matt 9:18)? And regarding the rich ruler who came to Jesus, was he still young, or does his claim to have kept the commandments *from the time of his youth* indicate that he was young no longer (Matt 19:20,22 compared with Mark 10:20 and Luke 18:21)? Did Jesus encounter blind Bartimaeus when entering or leaving Jericho (Luke 18:35 compared with Matt 20:29 and Mark 10:46)?

When teaching from one of these stories, one can avoid these problems by simply choosing one of the Gospel accounts and ignoring the others. While considering two or three accounts of the same event, one could say that all of the accounts are quite independent—there was no literary copying at all, and the differences in the stories are exactly the kind that would be found between the accounts of any two (or three) witnesses of the same event. Fair enough, this "complete independence" view could account for the Synoptic differences, but what about the remarkable similarities of wording and pericope order one often encounters in the Synoptics?

When proposing that the accounts are independent, one has begun seeking an explanation for those similarities and differences. And this is exactly what this present book is about: examining the Gospel material and seeking an explanation that accounts for the observable data.

At the 2000 Synoptic Problem conference referred to above, there were three points of agreement among all participants: (1) the central importance of this issue, as already mentioned; (2) the Complete Independence view of the three Synoptics does not hold up in the light of the data we have; and (3) Mark is clearly the middle factor between the two major Synoptics, so that there are two basic hypotheses that correspond with the data: (a) Mark was written first and was used by Matthew and Luke (i.e., some version of Markan Priority); or Mark was written third and used Matthew and Luke as sources (i.e., some version of Markan Posteriority, or Markan Dependence on the other two Gospels). S. McKnight summed it up this way: "Whether first or third, Mark is the middle factor. . . . We are reasonably confident that Matthew, Mark and Luke are related at the literary level and that it is highly likely that they are mutually dependent, however one might see that relationship or set of relationships" (Black and Beck 2001, 76–77).

McKnight's own position (ibid., 67) is that the so-called proofs of Markan Priority put forward by B. H. Streeter in 1924 are not decisive for Markan Priority as against Markan Dependence, and that either explanation is possible. The choice between them is to be made on the basis of probability. When weighing alternative explanations, he said, "We are dealing with probabilities, not possibilities. I don't rule out the possibilities. I only ask which is more probable" (ibid., 86). McKnight's assessment of the evidence brings him down on the side of Markan Priority, which by his own admission he maintained because of the balance of probabilities.

In fact, McKnight asked in 2000 (see Black and Beck 2001, 80, 83, 89–90, 95), as Styler did in 1962 (ibid., 232), "Where is the more convincing alternative?" I am offering, for your consideration, such an alternative to Markan Priority.

In putting this alternative forward, I draw attention to the way that scholars investigating the Synoptic Problem throughout the years seem to agree on the acceptance of one fundamental presupposition. They differ as to the order and interrelationship of the Synoptics; they differ concerning the nature, scope, contents, language, date, and so forth, of the sources, written and oral, lying behind the Synoptics; but they all seem to accept that Matthew, Mark, and Luke were written (or, at least, were published) in some particular order, and the nature of the Synoptic Problem is to decide, on the basis of the evidence, what that order was.

This presupposition, regarded virtually as axiomatic, was stated explicitly by W. Farmer (1976, 199) in this way:

> However important the part oral tradition and other written sources may have played in the composition of the Synoptic Gospels, the problem of determining which was written first, which second, and which third still persists. One of the three was written before the other two. One was written after the first, and before the third. And one was written after the other two.

But my question would be, "Is this necessarily so?" I suggest that the key to the Synoptic Problem lies in the recognition that *one of the Gospels was written and published in stages, and that Gospel was Matthew*. In other words, Matthew's Gospel had its beginnings in a series of separate documents authored by the apostle Matthew over a period of some years, which thereafter were circulating independently in the churches before being edited and expanded by this same apostle Matthew into the Gospel we now have.

Thus the distinguishing characteristic of the position I am presenting is its proposal of the progressive publication of Matthew. To indicate this and to differentiate this hypothesis from others with which it partly agrees, I have referred to it throughout this book as the Progressive Publication Hypothesis.

It is well worthwhile, then, to see if this new Synoptic hypothesis can do a better job of accounting for the observable data, to see if it has greater explanatory power than the other hypotheses. Indeed, I would contend that when this hypothesis is seriously examined, it will be seen that it meshes well with what we know of the situation in the early church and with the external evidence of church history, and that it explains all the observable data of the Synoptic Gospels.

I intend in this book to indicate how this hypothesis derives from several propositions, which I submit are abundantly supported by the evidence and which together offer the most convincing explanation of all the observable data. This is a new hypothesis in that it has not been presented before in this manner, with its components assembled and defended in these propositions. But almost all of these individual components have in fact been put forward and often advocated vigorously over the decades by competent Gospel scholars, as I have demonstrated in the following pages. My purpose here is to bring these components all together, to show how they interrelate, and to draw conclusions from them.

With this in mind, I have provided an outline of this hypothesis in the remainder of this chapter. I indicate the main areas of observable data with which it interlocks, so that its overall cohesiveness can be seen. Then in the following chapters I look in rather more detail at the evidence on which it rests. I indicate where and how it is superior to other hypotheses, including how it will explain what they do not. I examine several key Synoptic passages that are much more convincingly explained on this basis. I also show how it offers a simple answer to one of the greatest Synoptic enigmas: the order of pericopes in all three Synoptic Gospels.

THE FIVE PROPOSITIONS OF THE PROGRESSIVE PUBLICATION HYPOTHESIS

This section describes the five propositions on which this hypothesis rests. The first proposition is that *Matthew responded to a growing need with initial written accounts of Christ's life.* In Jerusalem, the apostle Matthew produced, between the time of Christ and about AD 60, a series of short accounts of different episodes from the life and teachings of Jesus. Of all the eyewitnesses known to us, Matthew would have been preeminently the best qualified to produce written records of Christ's life. As a former Roman customs official at Capernaum on the Great West Road, the main trade route from Syria and the East to the Mediterranean, he of necessity would have been fluent in Greek and Aramaic, and probably in Latin and Hebrew as well, and he would have been able to read and write—a far from universal accomplishment in those days. Many scholars have recognized these facts (see R. H. Gundry 1975, 174; J. N. Sevenster 1968, 176–91; and the references they give).

Shorthand had been in use for some time in the ancient world, and it would be a reasonable expectation that Matthew knew and used one of the available shorthand systems in his official taxation work. It is not unlikely that Matthew used these skills in making notes of Christ's deeds and teachings at the time they occurred. The development and use of shorthand in the ancient world has been discussed by many scholars (e.g., E. J. Goodspeed 1959, 86ff., 108ff.; Gundry, ibid., 182; W. Hendriksen 1973, numerous places; B. Gerhardsson 1998, 148–56).

In any case it would be highly probable that the apostle Matthew wrote much of the eyewitness material that, according to Luke's account (1:1–4), was circulating at the time when Luke was gathering the content for his own Gospel. Luke 1:2 refers to eyewitness material that had been "handed on" (NRSV) to Luke and others. The term παραδίδωμι in this and similar passages means, "of oral or written tradition: hand down, pass on, transmit, relate, teach" (BDAG 762; of the many who point to both the oral and written implications of this word, see Creed 1953, 4; Ellis 1966, 63; Morris 1974, 66; re the implications of this word in Luke 1:2, see Newman's Dictionary 132; TDNT 1968, 2:171; ISBE 1979, 1:916).

The alternative would be to say that, of the various documents Luke mentioned, *none* at all came from the apostles. Yet these were the very men who were chosen by Christ specifically to be his companions (Mark 3:13–14), and to whom he gave much of his teaching privately (for example, Mark 4:34). They alone would be in a position to record many of the details of what he said and did (John 15:15); they were those whom he designated as his witnesses (Luke 24:48; John 15:27; Acts 1:8).

It is highly improbable that the apostles would have had no connection at all with the production of the accounts of Christ's life and teaching that began (as Luke said) to circulate, or, if it be acknowledged that some of these accounts *did* originate with the apostles, that Matthew had no part in their production.

The circumstances that would have given rise to the writing down of such accounts are easy to envisage. Jewish Christians from the churches of Palestine, coming up to Jerusalem for the feasts, would meet with the Christian congregation there and hear the preaching and teaching of the apostles (Acts 2:42; 6:2–4). All the first Christians were Jews or proselytes. As late as Acts 21:20 reference is made to the thousands of Jewish believers who are "zealous for the law." In accordance with Judaistic practice, the Jewish Christians would go up to Jerusalem regularly for the feasts. In addition, Acts implies that traveling up to Jerusalem by Christians generally was frequent throughout this period (see 21:15–16).

Coming in many cases from congregations where there were few eyewitnesses to Christ's life, and where there was a thirst for more information about him, these pilgrims would be eager to take home from Jerusalem a record of what they heard there. W. F. Albright and C. Mann referred to the "relatively small number of people who had access to the facts of Jesus' ministry," and they add that because of this and other factors they believe "we must reckon with the desire to record the oral tradition at a comparatively early date" (1971, 174ff.). So if a request were made for a written record of teaching that they had heard from the apostles, the logical member of the apostolic band to provide this for those who asked would be Matthew. Thus they went back to their churches with a written account of something Christ did or said: perhaps a few sentences of teaching or a lengthy story of a complete incident.

The first Christian congregations in Palestine would have included some who spoke Aramaic, and therefore material that was produced for them in this way would likely be in Aramaic. Papias's information about the *logia* produced by Matthew (see Eusebius 1999, 3.39.16) indicates the existence of these Aramaic documents written by Matthew. In due course, in view of the number of Hellenist or Greek-speaking Christians in Palestine and nearby areas, there would have arisen a demand for similar material in Greek, and Matthew would soon have found himself asked to meet requests of this kind.

The second proposition is that *these Matthean accounts would not be the only ones that began circulating since Luke said "many have taken in hand to write"* (Luke 1:1). Other eyewitnesses would be motivated to take pen in hand in similar fashion and begin recording the teachings and deeds of Christ of which they were aware. We have the evidence of Luke's prologue to tell us this was so. These accounts would also have been of varying lengths and written in either Aramaic or Greek. They would have circulated side by side with those already written by Matthew and doubtless side by side with oral traditions about Christ.

In the process of time the various churches would have accumulated a significant number of these short accounts and would have added to their own collections by exchanging copies with other churches around them. We know that this occurred in the case of Paul's Epistles, and there is no reason that it would not have also happened in the case of documents containing incidents and sayings from the life of Christ to which Luke refers. In fact the prologue to Luke's Gospel looks like a reference to the very situation that I have just outlined.

An obvious question may strike us. If there were circulating in the churches a host of short documents from the AD 30s to the 50s (as Luke indicates and this present hypothesis now elaborates), how would it happen that none of them survived for us now to find? First of all, none of the original New Testament documents has been preserved, meaning that every manuscript we possess is a copy of a copy. Why should any scribe have wished to copy some partial piece of text once the full Gospels of Matthew and Luke were published? The part would have been absorbed into the whole. Any Gospel segments we may yet find are almost certainly going to be parts of or extracts from the canonical Synoptic Gospels as we have them.

Second, suppose they aren't. Suppose that some family possessing an original document had it copied and passed it down for several generations, and that a copy of that document were to come to light today. If that happened, how would we know? It would simply look like a section of the later Gospel into which it became incorporated. It is an interesting thought, and perhaps worthy of further investigation, whether any of the extant Synoptic Gospel fragments could be a copy, not of part of a complete Gospel, but of a pre-Gospel document of exactly the kind under discussion. If such were the case—if we had any such extract among the multitude of early extant Gospel manuscripts—how would we know? A section of such a document would look the same as a section of a complete Gospel.

The third proposition is that *Luke collected his own material that he eventually incorporated into his Gospel.* During his travels in company with Paul, Luke made notes of the various things said and done, and these, when written up, became the second half of his book the Acts of the Apostles. At some point he also formed the intention of investigating the period before his personal involvement. The opportunity for this came during AD 56 to 58, the years while he was in the Palestine area and Paul was imprisoned in Caesarea (Acts 24:27).

For this work, he was interviewing eyewitnesses and collecting the information that he used in writing the first half of Acts. Similarly, it was also his opportunity to prepare to undertake the second task: to write an account of the ministry and message of Jesus.

In the prologue to his Gospel he relates that he carried out a very thorough and careful investigation of everything connected with the life of Christ. Whatever documents were available to him, he collected at this stage, and perhaps he had begun collecting them even earlier. He took them with him to Rome, managing to keep them safe during his shipwreck on Malta on the way there.

There is widespread agreement with this understanding of the implications of Luke's prologue that I have just given. The distinctive proposition that I am putting is that these documents that Luke collected did *not* (as some people would think) include Mark's Gospel, for this book had not yet been written. However, among the eyewitness material to which Luke himself referred were numerous separate short accounts written by the apostle Matthew.

The fourth proposition is that *the two major Synoptic Gospels, Matthew and Luke, were the first ones published.* While Luke was on his way to Rome with Paul, Matthew was in Jerusalem producing further material where he then decided to issue a "collected edition" of his records of the deeds and teaching of Jesus. He used the basic outline of Christ's life as his framework, but within this he made only a very limited attempt to assemble his material in the order in which the events occurred or the teaching was given. More frequently, the basis on which he arranged his material was *topical* rather than *chronological*. Given the different plan on which Matthew constructed his Gospel by comparison with Luke, it is not surprising to see particular events or sayings being placed differently in these two Gospels.

The evidence from an examination of Matthew's Gospel indicates that Matthew, while compiling his material for his Gospel, used what he had previously written and rewrote it in Greek—as distinct from just translating it—in places that were originally in Aramaic. He also added some extra stories—including his opening chapters and his distinctive material in the Passion Narrative—and provided his "program notes" linking one block of material to the next.

Albright and Mann said, "What we appear to have in Matthew's gospel is a kind of teacher's guide, a collection of blocks of material from the private instruction of Jesus to the inner circle, together with other material from public teaching, and the whole assembled in a rather loose chronological framework" (ibid., 165). The place of publication of Matthew's finished Gospel would have been Jerusalem.

Meanwhile Luke composed his Gospel while in Rome with Paul. He worked from the material he had collected in Palestine, completing and publishing it c. AD 60. (The case for this date is in the next chapter.) So did Luke see Matthew's Gospel as a completed Gospel? No, he did not. The arguments that scholars have put forward against Luke's use of Matthew's Gospel are valid. But Farmer's arguments that Luke knew Matthew, based on passages showing close identity between the two Gospels, are also valid.

Chapter 8 examines in detail the case for the proposition that Luke knew and used Matthew's Gospel, which is central to the Two-Gospel school of Farmer and his supporters, and the evidence against it. Considered in its totality, this apparently conflicting evidence is accounted for by the explanation that *Luke read and used the sections of Matthew that had been in circulation in the churches*, which he had obtained while collecting information.

The evidence indicates that neither Matthew nor Luke saw the completed Gospel written by the other prior to publishing his own, and this points to the publication of both of them in the same year. So AD 60 would also be the publication date for Matthew.

Thus we come logically to conclude that material originally written by the apostle Matthew and circulated during the period between the time of Christ and AD 60 became incorporated independently in *both* the Major Synoptics, Matthew's Gospel and Luke's Gospel, though neither of these writers saw the finished Gospel of the other before the publication of his own.

The fifth proposition is that *Mark produced a special-purpose Gospel*. Mark was not an eyewitness of the life of Christ, but (as Papias and other Fathers have told us) he was an associate of the apostle Peter, and he wrote his Gospel based on Peter's preaching. The early church Fathers identify the writing of Mark as being c. AD 65 in Rome.

By this time also the Gospels of Matthew and Luke had begun to circulate among the churches, and Mark used them both as the basis of his Gospel. We can describe this Synoptic relationship as Markan Dependence: Mark's Gospel was dependent on and derived from the other two. This means that Mark had three sources for his Gospel: what he heard from Peter, and the written Gospels of Matthew and Luke. It is the purpose of this book to demonstrate that this is the explanation of Mark's Gospel to which the evidence points.

Mark is the shortest Gospel, and yet Mark's account of any given pericope is almost always the longest. Exceptions are in places where Mark omitted teaching or speeches that Matthew or Luke (or both) included at certain points, or where Mark gave this teaching in part only. Mark's greater pericope length is because he conflated Matthew and Luke and added a plethora of further points of detail not to be found in the other two Gospels but drawn from his third source, what he had learned from Peter.

Mark consists almost entirely of "action stories" that show Jesus healing, performing miracles, engaged in conflict with his opponents, and so on. Jesus' teachings in Mark either arise out of these situations or are illustrative of the teaching aspect of Jesus' ministry, and in any case they are always related directly to one or more of the main themes of Mark. In his Gospel, Mark did not assume the post-Easter faith, as do Matthew and Luke. Mark traced the journey of the disciples from doubt and disbelief, and he aimed to take his readers and hearers on that same journey. His Gospel is an evangelistic tool—a resource book for evangelists—aimed at introducing Jesus to the interested outsider. It was intended to be used as a source book in evangelistic preaching, and even to be read aloud wherever people gathered.

So Mark had a specific linguistic program and purpose in view. While skillfully conflating the accounts of Matthew and Luke, Mark transformed their more literary wording into clear, simple, everyday language (the language of conversation and preaching), changed some of their vocabulary into the vernacular used by his hearers, and rendered the whole into simple, straightforward sentences. In fact (as Streeter himself has most perceptively noted, 1924, 163), Mark worded his Gospel in the colloquial spoken Greek of the Roman Empire.

Mark was quite consistent in producing his Gospel. He included material in Matthew and Luke that was in accord with his themes, and *he excluded the rest*. Mark's Gospel sets out the *kerygma* being preached to unbelievers. It is "pure" *kerygma,* while Matthew and Luke are combinations of *kerygma* and *didache*. Mark's Gospel climaxes with the cross and with the revelation of Jesus as the Son of God—which Mark does not teach earlier (more on this point later). His motivation in producing his Gospel was exactly the same as that of those Christians today who publish extracts from Scripture in modern speech for use in evangelistic outreach. Like those who do this today, Mark knew that the rest of the Gospel story was readily available in the church for those who became interested.

It is straightforward to explain the order of Mark's Gospel. First, in accordance with his intention to produce a Gospel containing the deeds rather than the teachings of Jesus, Mark therefore adopted a framework that avoided the Sermon on the Mount, the Sermon on the Plain, and Luke's central teaching section (Matt 5–7; Luke 6:17–49; 9:51–18:15). This Markan framework consists of two parts: he followed the order of Luke's Gospel to Mark 6:14, Herod's comment about Jesus; and thereafter the order of Matthew's Gospel.

Second, into the Lukan part of his framework he added four sections from Matthew: Mark 1:16–20; 3:22–35E; 4:30–34; 6:1–6. Into his Matthean framework he added four short sections that he drew from Luke, consisting of material not paralleled anywhere in Matthew. These are Mark 6:30–31;

9:38–41; 11:18–19; 12:41–44E. These insertions were placed into Mark's Gospel at the same point at which they occurred in his source (respectively, Matthew or Luke).

The figure that is customarily given for unique verses in Mark is usually 50 to 56 verses, but I have found on my count that the equivalent of 155 verses of Mark (or 23.5%, just under one quarter of the Gospel) consists of material that could not have been derived from either Matthew or Luke, because it is simply not there. To state this data in the Markan Priority way, these verses consist of Markan material that was not then used either by Matthew or by Luke in their respective Gospels. This comprises for the most part a wealth of small but vivid details not found in Matthew or Luke, details that had lodged in Mark's memory from the preaching of Peter and with which he enlivened his stories.

CONCLUSION

I submit that all of the difficulties, problems, and inadequacies of the Markan Priority view are met completely by the Progressive Publication Hypothesis (including Markan Dependence) as I have outlined it. I contend that there is nothing inherently improbable in any part of this hypothesis, while it is in accord with all the known facts and is compatible with the external traditions about authorship. It provides a framework within which it is readily possible to explain all the observable phenomena of the Synoptic Gospels.

This view that I am putting forward has no need of Q. We can recognize *all* the material in Matthew and Luke that shows evidence of a common literary source as having been based upon documents written by Matthew and progressively circulated over the years. These documents were among all those collected by Luke (to which he refers in his prologue) and that he utilized in writing his own Gospel.

This hypothesis shares with Farmer's Two-Gospel school the belief in Markan Posteriority, that is, Mark's Gospel was written third and used Matthew and Luke as sources. But apart from this one similarity, it is a very different approach. In particular, contrary to the Two-Gospel school, I find the evidence to be strongly against the idea that Luke ever saw Matthew's Gospel in its final form. There are many sections of Luke's Gospel that can be accounted for only on the basis that Luke had *not* seen Matthew's Gospel.

The Progressive Publication of Matthew Hypothesis is not dependent on coincidence, or unproven assumptions, or circular arguments, and it involves a minimum of subjective assumptions. It meets fully the various criticisms that have been leveled in the past against other forms of the Markan Posteriority or Griesbach explanation.

This hypothesis accounts for the interrelationship among the three Synoptic Gospels solely in terms of the three men known to us from the New Testament—Matthew, Mark, and Luke—without hypothesizing other authors in order to account for this interrelationship. But it also recognizes and encompasses the role of the other eyewitnesses/writers, together with Luke's own investigations, to whom and to which Luke referred in his prologue. And it rests also on the well-attested tradition in the early church Fathers that Peter's preaching stands behind Mark's Gospel.

A tremendous amount of New Testament scholarship has proceeded upon the assumption of Markan Priority. The very existence and extent of this body of scholarship tends by itself to create an inertia resistant to the suggestion that we may need to think again about "the one absolutely assured result of the study of the Synoptic Problem" (Styler 1962, 223; cf. Streeter 1924, 157). In this connection there is food for thought in the words of V. Taylor (1966, 76) about other Synoptic research (which he rejected), words that I find quite opposite in relation to Markan Priority (which he accepted): "There is no failure in Synoptic criticism, for, if we reject a particular suggestion worked out with great learning and ability, we are compelled to reconsider the evidence on which it is based and seek a better explanation, knowing that a later critic may light upon a hypothesis sounder and more comprehensive still." That, I suggest, is how we should regard the idea of abandoning the hypothesis of Markan Priority, in the light of the case I present for the Progressive Publication of Matthew's Gospel.

This chapter provides the outline of the Synoptic explanation to which I find the evidence points. The remainder of this book considers in more detail the grounds of support to be adduced for these five propositions—and, in looking at the data, this book also compares the explanatory power of this hypothesis with the alternative hypotheses that have been put forward.

There is a possible misunderstanding of this fivefold thesis that I wish to guard against. The last thing that I would want to suggest is that I consider the Gospel writers to have been no more than compilers who assembled a collection of previous documents, or even editors who carried out the task of editing such material. They were indeed in every sense *authors*, with an aim and a purpose in their work. The evaluation of their purposes, their interests, and their theology is a valid exercise. But in their writing, their authoring, they drew upon documents that they had at hand.

ONE LEG TO STAND ON

This chapter demonstrates how the Progressive Publication of Matthew Hypothesis is based on known first-century evidence.

> *Matthew has written a collection of statements made by Christ which may have been only single proverbs or extended ones, or most probably both. Papias' expression simply cannot mean anything else. . . . The Gospel of Matthew embraces this collection. . . . [T]he reason it bears the name is because it is based on this work by Matthew.*
> — F. E. D. Schleiermacher in 1832,
> cited by H. H. Stoldt (1980, 48)

> *[W]ith admittedly varying degrees of probability, yet without relapse to airy speculation, it is still possible to trace the use by the evangelists, notably Mark and Luke, of short tracts telling of the ministry of Jesus, such as would be required by individual missionaries sent out by the primitive Christian centres, Jerusalem and Antioch. For their work the single pericope with its isolated and often anecdotal character would scarcely be adequate. On the other hand we are not postulating circumstances where the full Gospel story is needed for sustained reading or for liturgical usage. The stage here envisaged was no doubt early. Probably even in the late thirties, and certainly by the early fifties of the first century, shorter tracts of the type postulated would have become the normal type of Christian propagandist literature.*
> —Wilfred L. Knox (1957, 2:139)

INTRODUCTION

This chapter demonstrates how the Progressive Publication of Matthew Hypothesis is based on known first-century evidence. The Progressive Publication of Matthew Hypothesis has two interdependent legs on which it stands.

First, between the time of our Lord's earthly ministry and about AD 60 the apostle Matthew produced numerous short accounts of events and teachings from the life and ministry of Jesus, some in Greek and some in Aramaic, which circulated independently in the church. Some of these documents were collected by Luke and incorporated into his Gospel material, and Matthew subsequently issued a collected and expanded edition of his own material. This is the specific leg of the Progressive Publication of Matthew Hypothesis that accounts for the writing of the two Major Synoptics in the church.

Second, Mark's purpose in writing his Gospel was to meet a specific need in the church by producing a special-purpose "preacher's edition" of Gospel material. He did this c. AD 65 by drawing on three sources: (1) Matthew and (2) Luke, the two Major Synoptics that were by then available in the church; and (3) his own recollections of the preaching of the apostle Peter. This leg of the hypothesis can be termed "Markan Dependence," in contradistinction to Markan Priority.

This chapter examines the support for the first of these two legs of the Progressive Publication of Matthew Hypothesis. But first we need to consider what scholars have said regarding attitudes about writing in the first century, and what bearing this issue may have on further examinations.

THE ROLE OF WRITING IN THE NEW TESTAMENT ERA

Significant differences exist regarding the assumed background for the writing of the Gospels. For example, some writers have drawn attention to the use of writing in the world of the first century, in both Jewish and Greek cultures, while other scholars have stated that the Jews were oriented against recording material in writing, and have found in this an explanation for the "oral period," the gap that they believe lasted several decades between the events in the Gospels and the writing of the Gospel accounts.

The witness of history does contain evidence that there was a preference among the Jews and in the early church for the oral account rather than the written record, the living witness in preference to the impersonal book. Thus the Aramaic translation of the Jewish Scriptures and their commentaries on these Scriptures were transmitted orally for a period of time running into centuries. The books and articles by Riesenfeld and Gerhardsson (see bibliography) are carefully documented accounts of how this was done and why it was preferred. There is some evidence for this same kind of attitude in the early church.

Thus Papias, in a well-known comment (Eusebius, 3.39.4; Maier 1999, 127), indicated that he much preferred to have the comments of a living witness to merely reading about the deeds and sayings of Jesus. Eusebius quoted Papias about reports of what had been said by the "disciples of the Lord" and their immediate followers: "For I did not think that information from books would help me as much as the word of a living, surviving voice." (We will say more about Papias's comments later in this chapter.) But it is an error to take this evidence as indicating either that there was a low level of literacy in the Roman Empire in the first century, or that there was a general antipathy towards writing itself. The evidence indicates the opposite of this.

From the classical periods of Greece and Rome there is an abundance of literature of every kind that shows that writing—and reading—were normal activities for the populace in general. Reading and writing were standard skills taught to the young in schools. When Hellenistic culture was spread throughout the Middle East in the wake of the conquests of Alexander the Great, this included not merely the spoken but also the written use of the Greek tongue. Recent evidence of this has been the papyrus finds in Egypt, which include numerous documents written by ordinary people in the course of their normal lives: shopping lists, accounting records, and an overwhelming wealth of business and private correspondence. The latter includes letters between businessmen and their agents and representatives, and letters between family members, close friends, and casual acquaintances. It is possible to see a close parallel between the ease and frequency with which people in first-century society would make written notes or write letters and the situation in our own society today.

And books, though extremely expensive by today's standards, were widely circulated and widely read. Alexandria was renowned for its library with volumes on every conceivable subject of interest in the ancient world. Carl Sagan has an interesting comment about this library (1980, 20):

> The heart of the library was its collection of books. The organizers combed all the cultures and languages of the world. They sent agents abroad to buy up libraries. Commercial ships docking in Alexandria were searched by the police—not for contraband, but for books. The scrolls were borrowed, copied, and then returned to their owners. Accurate numbers are difficult to estimate, but it seems probable that the Library contained half a million volumes, each a handwritten papyrus scroll.

In addition to formal books and informal notes, writing was used in ancient society in the same ways as it is today: for gravestones and inscriptions on tombs, for notices and announcements (e.g., the inscriptions on the walls of the temple, and Pilate's inscription about Jesus above his head on the cross, John 19:19–20).

People immediately and automatically turned to writing whenever the situation required it. Thus the Tribune Claudius Lysias wrote a formal letter to Governor Felix about Paul's case to accompany Paul (Acts 23:26), and it was taken for granted that a written explanation would also accompany Paul when he was sent to Rome (Acts 25:26).

There was no antipathy towards writing in Christian circles. Papias's comment quoted above indicates his enjoyment of meeting people who had themselves known Jesus or the apostles and early Christian leaders; it certainly does not mean that he was opposed to the use of written records as such. After all, we know what he said about the matter because he himself *wrote it down!*

The clearest evidence for all this is the New Testament itself. Paul resorted promptly and unhesitatingly to writing a letter when he had something to say, and so did the authors of the other New Testament epistles. It is not possible to maintain that this was something he did only when he had no alternative open to him. On at least three occasions Paul sent a trusted colleague *with* the letter, so if he had regarded the writing of a letter as a matter of last resort, only to be employed when no one was in a position to take his message, then the Epistles to Philemon, Colossians, and Ephesians would not have been penned. For Tychicus took these three letters in person, and thus could have delivered Paul's message orally *instead of* taking a letter, if Paul had had a negative attitude to the use of writing. Rather, Tychicus took each of Paul's letters and verbally added his own further comments to it when he arrived at his destinations. Thus Paul said, "Tychicus will tell you all about my affairs; he is a beloved brother and faithful minister in the Lord. I have sent him to you for this very purpose, that you may know how we are and that he may encourage your hearts" (Col 4:7–8). Ephesians 6:21–22 has an almost identical comment. The bearer of the letter would *supplement* Paul's letter with additional information of his own, but Paul did not think that an oral message delivered by his colleague to those Christians was preferable to his sending a message in writing.

This background data becomes relevant to our present investigation because of the common suggestion that the Gospels were written quite late, after a gap of many decades from the events they describe, this delay being due to the antipathy of the Jews and the early Christians to the use of writing for their message. This argument claims that only when the last of the eyewitnesses and their immediate followers were passing away did some men see the need to overcome this antipathy and—with some measure of reluctance but under the necessity of the situation—to sit down and compose the Gospels that have come down to us. The background data of the first century shows that such a picture of the situation in the early church is not an accurate one.

It is also inaccurate to claim that writing was acceptable in *Hellenistic* culture but not in *Jewish* culture, for at least three reasons. First, Paul, the most prolific of letter writers, was a "Hebrew of the Hebrews," and there is not the slightest evidence that he found writing about the gospel an "un-Jewish" thing to do. Second, if this comment were valid, it would not in any case have affected the writing of a Gospel by Luke, who arguably was a Gentile, and those who hold this viewpoint do not also normally regard Luke as the earliest Gospel to be written. Third, the Jewish church leader James had the exact same attitude. His letter is considered by most scholars as one of the earliest of the New Testament epistles, and when he wished his judgment at the Jerusalem Council to be circulated to the churches he sent representatives to report that judgment and he also *recorded it in writing and sent a written letter with them* (Acts 15:19–23,30–31). This is similar to what Paul did in regard to Philemon, Colossians, and Ephesians, as noted above.

Thus all the evidence shows that Christians in the early church were quite ready to accept the use of writing for recording and conveying their message, and there is no evidence at all that gives any grounds for believing that they had any kind of objection to its use. There is consequently no justification for the suggestion that the first Christians would have been slow and reluctant to set down in writing the details of the life and teachings of Jesus.

While all this is true of formal writings, it is even truer of informal, private notes. Gerhardsson's account of the transmission of oral tradition within Judaism shows that this was accomplished by means of a form of written mnemonics akin to shorthand. That is to say, the Jewish tendency towards oral transmission did not *preclude* the use of written notes but in fact *required* it.

A consideration of all these factors reveals the very extensive use of oral transmission by the Jews for their traditions. This practice has implications for the consideration of the transmission of the "Jesus traditions" during the so-called "oral period," as shown in the research and writings of Gerhardsson. But it also prevents us from adopting an unbalanced view of the first-century situation by over-exaggerating this so-called antipathy to written accounts to the point of accepting without justification the belief that the early Christians would have had strong feelings against making any written record of the deeds and sayings of Jesus, feelings that would have required a lengthy passage of time and exceptional circumstances to overcome.

Even if such an attitude had existed in the Jewish section of the church (and the evidence is against this), it would certainly not have influenced the Greek-speaking church—and the New Testament was written in Greek! Moreover, the same Jews who are thought to have had such an attitude also had and venerated their own *written* Scriptures, the record of God's revelation of himself by speaking to humanity.

This data indicates that there was no factor inherent in the first-century situation that mitigated against the writing down of the gospel record at an early date; in fact, to the contrary, there is a strong probability that, in accordance with the custom of the time, written notes (ὑπομνήματα) of Jesus' deeds and sayings would have been made by eyewitnesses at or immediately after the time of occurrence. These private notes would then pave the way for and provide the core for the subsequent fuller writing down of the sayings and deeds of Jesus by the apostle Matthew and other eyewitnesses. The evidence for this is considered next.

PROPOSITION 1:
MATTHEW RESPONDS TO A GROWING NEED

Initial Written Accounts—Tracts, Fragments, and Fly-Sheets

The idea that there were written sources of some description behind our canonical Gospels has a long history. This idea is widely accepted, irrespective of which Synoptic Gospel is considered to be the first written. Thus T. H. Robinson, an advocate of Markan Priority, stated (1960, ix):

> [W]e have no certainty as to the literary processes of the church till we find a book known to us to-day as the gospel according to Mark. . . . Working, no doubt, on material already to hand in written form, at least in part . . .

This idea of written sources has surfaced in numerous different forms, usually being attached to whichever view of Synoptic interrelationship the particular writer espoused.

Much of the later speculation about these documentary sources looks back to comments made by the church Father Papias that Eusebius preserved. The early church Fathers were not very much interested in the order in which the Gospels were written, or in their interrelationships. Eusebius (3.39.15–16; Maier 1999, 127–30) informed us that Papias (c. 110) referred briefly to the writing of John, Mark, and Matthew, but not in a way that gave any information about order of writing, or the slightest hint of any interrelationship. Eusebius recorded Papias's comments about Mark, and then what Papias wrote about Matthew: "These things are related by Papias concerning Mark. But concerning Matthew he writes as follows: 'So then Matthew wrote the oracles [*ta logia*] in the Hebrew language, and everyone interpreted them as he was able.'"

I consider what Papias said about Mark at a later point, but now the focus is on his reference to Matthew's writing *ta logia* in Hebrew (or Aramaic). Initially, this was taken in the eighteenth century (particularly in Germany) to refer to a kind of Proto-Gospel. B. Reicke comments (Orchard and Longstaff 1978, 52):

> [T]he Proto-Gospel Hypothesis . . . stems from a remark of Papias implying that Matthew had compiled the *logia* in Hebrew (Eusebius, *History* 3.39.16). Following this, Epiphanius and Jerome held that there was an older Gospel of Matthew in Hebrew, and claimed that it had reappeared in the Hebrew or Nazarene Gospel of the Syrian Judaeo-Christians. This theory was taken up in 1689 by Richard Simon in Normandy, the pioneer of New Testament text criticism. He asserted that an old Gospel of Matthew, presumed to have been written in Hebrew or rather in Aramaic and taken to lie behind the Nazarene Gospel, was the Proto-Gospel.

When the hypothesis of Markan Priority gained favor, the *logia* became the forerunner of the concept of Q as the source for material common to Matthew and Luke but absent from Mark. But the idea of *logia* written by Matthew in Hebrew/Aramaic during the time prior to the existence of the Gospel that now bears his name is a concept totally independent of any attachment to the Markan Priority Hypothesis. It can well be taken as referring to (primarily teaching) material written by Matthew and subsequently incorporated (in Greek translation) into the Gospels of Matthew and Luke *totally without reference to whether any of that common material became included in Mark.*

Reicke described the Fragment Hypothesis (ibid., 52, 72):

> [T]he Fragment Hypothesis had been conceived in 1783 by Johann Benjamin Koppe in Göttingen. He assumed the existence of a number of shorter and longer accounts in Hebrew and Greek no longer accessible, but which had been used by the Synoptists. . . . He preferred to regard the Synoptic Evangelists as dependent on a plurality of earlier sources, like those alluded to in Luke 1:2. More exactly he supposed that Matthew, Mark and Luke had collected longer and shorter reports, spread among the Christians in oral and written form and moulded into narratives, speeches, parables, sayings of Jesus and other categories. By his assumption of several fragmentary sources Koppe anticipated the so-called Fragment Hypothesis propagated by F. Schleiermacher in 1817; and

by his reference to categories first developed in oral form he anticipated the inauguration of form criticism by M. Dibelius in 1919.

D. Dungan comments (1999, 323) further concerning Koppe that he brought "out a publication in 1782 denouncing the idea that there had been any *direct* literary utilization by the canonical authors of each other's writings. Koppe insisted that the Preface to the Gospel of Luke was proof that the canonical Gospels were based on earlier Greek and Hebrew narratives." Dungan went on to say (ibid., 325–26), "The University of Berlin New Testament scholars W. M. L. De-Wette and Friedrich Bleek adopted the emerging consensus that both Luke and Matthew had made independent and differing use of a mass of earlier written and oral sources."

Kümmel (1972, 84) comments, "Schleiermacher in 1817 . . . advanced the suggestion that a collection of the sayings of Jesus that goes back to the apostle Matthew had been incorporated into this Gospel as an important component." Stoldt (1980, 48) reports that, in a discourse published in 1832, Schleiermacher made these comments about the Papias quotation concerning the *logia* written by Matthew in Hebrew: "Matthew has written a collection of statements made by Christ which may have been only single proverbs or extended ones, or most probably both. *Papias' expression simply cannot mean anything else.*"

In more recent times, other authors have concluded that there is evidence for documents behind and incorporated into our canonical Gospels. In his 1906 Jowett Lectures, F. C. Burkitt (1911, 62–64) considered this question and decided that "the Eschatological Discourse in Mark xiii once circulated, very much in its present form, as a separate fly-sheet." The following year W. C. Allen discusses in his commentary on Matthew the question of the sources for Matthew and Luke and in particular this proposal, "The two Evangelists drew from independent written sources." He then comments (xlvii):

> It is quite unlikely that when these editors drew up their Gospels S. Mark's writing was the only written source before them. So far as S. Luke is concerned, he distinctly implies that there were many evangelic writings. And indeed nothing is in itself more probable than that sayings, parables and discourses of Christ should have been committed to writing at a very early period. Not, of course, necessarily for wide publication, but for private use, or for communication by letter, or for the use of Christian teachers and preachers.

There are numerous scholars who emphasize the oral period of tradition transmission. They carefully argue their position and question the existence of such early written material. But it must be asked whether it is possible to be so certain that all the early sources of the Synoptic Gospels were oral, not written. During the 1950s, extensive work in this area was done, quite independently of each other, by W. L. Knox and H. A. Guy.

Knox died in 1950, but his work *The Sources of the Synoptic Gospels* was published posthumously in 1953 (vol. 1, St. Mark) and 1957 (vol. 2, St. Luke and St. Matthew). Guy's book *The Origin of the Gospel of Mark* appeared between these two dates (1954) and contains one brief reference (p. 47) to Knox's first volume.

Knox forcefully argues for the existence from very early times of written pericopes and pericope clusters and collections (1953, 1:3–4,5,7):

> But the situation of the primitive Church would demand collections of the sayings and doings of Jesus of this kind. We have noticed that mission-speeches of a more or less definite pattern can be found in the New Testament. But a mere summary of the vital facts of the Gospel—that Jesus went about doing good, that he died for our sins and was raised on the third day according to the Scripture—, however bulky the quotation of *testimonia* might be and however full the story of the Passion, would not permanently satisfy the homiletic needs of the Church. Those who had accepted Jesus as Lord for whatever reason, as for instance the hearing of a sermon, the witnessing of a miracle of healing or an outpouring of the Spirit, or again conviction that Jesus was indeed the fulfillment of prophecy, would inevitably seek to know what manner of man the Lord had been....
>
> Converts would certainly ask questions which must needs be satisfied.... For such a view we have the evidence of such passages as Acts 10:37f., where the brief summary of the ministry in the typical primitive *kerygma* is a fairly transparent literary device for avoiding the necessity of a fuller account; the hearers are supposed to know the story and therefore Peter need not repeat it here; but normally the hearers would not know. The similar Pauline *kerygma* of Acts 13:24ff. leaps from the Baptist to the crucifixion; but no body of converts could be permanently content to know nothing of the intervening period....
>
> The rest of their common material—and it must be remembered that "Q" is simply a symbol of the material common to Matthew and Luke which is not found in Mark—may have been derived from the same document; but some at least of the difficulties of the Q hypothesis are more easily explained if it be supposed that both evangelists were drawing on collections of material which in some cases reached them in the same written form, but [which] in others had an independent history behind them.

Knox further states in the epilogue (2:138–39):

> Among the avowed interests of the present study, as of almost all studies of the history of the synoptic tradition in modern times, has been "the quest of the historical Jesus." Yet the questions of historicity and authenticity cannot be usefully discussed before the closest detective work has been done on the synoptic sources. In this book it is claimed that with admittedly varying degrees of probability, yet without relapse to airy speculation, it is still possible to trace the use by the evangelists, notably Mark and Luke, of short tracts telling of the

ministry of Jesus, such as would be required by individual missionaries sent out by the primitive Christian centres, Jerusalem and Antioch. For their work the single pericope with its isolated and often anecdotal character would scarcely be adequate. On the other hand we are not postulating circumstances where the full Gospel story is needed for sustained reading or for liturgical usage. The stage here envisaged was no doubt early. Probably even in the late thirties, and certainly by the early fifties of the first century, shorter tracts of the type postulated would have become the normal type of Christian propagandist literature.

Like Knox, Guy wrote from within the perspectives of Markan Priority and strongly affirmed the written sources behind all three Gospels.

Occasional references have been made by scholars to the proposals of Knox and Guy since their books appeared, but I can find little in the way of careful evaluation of their idea that at an early date, and parallel with the oral transmission of sayings and stories of Jesus, there were numbers of short written records of these in circulation as well.

But C. F. D. Moule (1962, 55) states:

> It is not difficult to imagine how self-contained units of Christian teaching came to be hammered out, first orally, then as written fly-sheets or tracts—often in several differing though related shapes, according to the contexts in which they were used. When therefore John Mark (for example) sharpened his reed pen and dipped it in the ink to write, he had already behind him a considerable tradition of Christian speaking and possibly writing, by Peter and others—recognized patterns of argument and exhortation, of defense and attack, of instruction and challenge—from amongst which he might select his narrative material and his sayings. The earliest Christian writers were probably already heirs to a considerable body of tradition.

Conclusion

The concept of a number of written documents behind the Gospels was first enunciated in 1782–83 and became referred to as the Fragment Hypothesis. In various forms this hypothesis has been held by a string of different scholars for the past two centuries.

What do these data show? They disclose that a number of different scholars—from different centuries and different cultures and backgrounds, and with varying theological outlooks and holding different positions in regard to Synoptic relationships—had this one thing in common: they came to the view that behind the Synoptic Gospels were numerous earlier written documents. These scholars were not in agreement concerning any details about these documents: how many of them there might have been, and what role they played in the writing of the Synoptics, and even which Gospel(s) they can be detected in. They call them tracts, fragments, fly-sheets. They often link them with the predecessors that Luke mentioned in his prologue, compilers busily at work putting together narratives of the events of the life of Jesus. They may or may not identify them with Matthew's *logia*, which they may view as a substantial Proto-Gospel, or may take to be a number of separate accounts of things Jesus said. But they do say that there is good reason to recognize that there were such documents in the period between the ministry of Jesus and the writing of the canonical Gospels. Actually, in their different ways (and with vastly different conclusions) they have taken seriously the evidence for early Gospel fragments and segments.

I cannot find any of them with whom I would closely agree. I consider that in many instances their conclusions go beyond the structure of the evidence. I certainly do not hold the theological attitude to the Synoptics that I detect in many of them. But I wholeheartedly agree with them in the one factor in which they agree: the existence of numerous documents of varying length lying behind the Synoptics.

Luke, Papias, and Matthew's *Logia*

Luke and Papias affirm that there were numerous short documentary records of the life and teachings of Christ in circulation in the first century. Let us consider more carefully what they say.

What exactly did Luke mean in his prologue? He spoke about the early stages in the development of written Gospel material, and on this development Plummer commented: "This prologue contains all that we really know respecting the composition of early narratives of the life of Christ, and it is the test by which theories as to the origin of our Gospels must be judged. No hypothesis is likely to be right which does not harmonize with what is told us here" (*ICC* on *Luke*, 2). Luke 1:1–4 may be translated as follows:

> Seeing that many have set to work putting together a consecutive narrative [ἀνατάξασθαι διήγησιν] covering the things that have been fulfilled among us, exactly as those who from the beginning were eyewitnesses and ministers of the Word delivered to us, it seemed good to me also, after investigating everything thoroughly and accurately from the beginning, to write a chronological account for you, most excellent Theophilus, in order that you may know more fully about the truth, reliability and certainty [all implied by ἀσφάλεια] of the matters of which you have been informed.

The words ἀνατάξασθαι διήγησιν are rendered by A. Plummer (1969, 2) as "to arrange afresh so as to show the sequence of events" (2). It is intriguing that Godet (1870, 1:55) asks concerning these words:

> Did this arrangement consist in the harmonizing of a number of separate writings into a single whole, so as to make a consecutive history of them? In this

case, we should have to admit that the writers of whom Luke speaks had already found in the Church a number of short writings on particular events, which they had simply united: their work would thus constitute a second step in the development of the writing of the gospel history.

Godet (ibid., 55–56) then rejects this idea because it would interpose "intermediate accounts between the apostolic tradition and the writings of which Luke speaks." But when we recognize that these short writings had originated from the apostolic circle itself (that is, *from Matthew*), then Godet's objection is answered. I believe Godet's rejected suggestion is in fact an accurate description of *exactly* what was happening: Luke found that many people were gathering the various eyewitness traditions of the deeds and teachings of Jesus, and were combining them together into a consecutive narrative.

The word Luke uses for the "delivering" or "handing on" (παραδίδωμι) by the eyewitnesses and ministers of the Word can refer to either oral or written tradition (or both). Plummer (ibid., 3) said that Luke "gives no hint as to whether the facts were handed down orally or in writing. The difference between the *polloi* and these *autoptai* is not that the *polloi* wrote their narratives while the *autoptai* did not, but that the *autoptai* were primary authorities, which the *polloi* were not." E. E. Ellis (1966, 63) said the term meant "delivered: i.e. in both oral and written form," and L. Morris agreed (1974, 66). A. B. Bruce said (1897, 459) that "καθώς implies that the basis of these many *written* narratives was the παράδοσις of the Apostles, which, by contrast, and by the usual meaning of the word, would be mainly though not necessarily exclusively oral (might include, e.g., the Logia of Matthew)."

Luke was not criticizing these compilers for what they were doing; in fact, he referenced their activities as a reason (almost a justification) for his doing the same thing ("it seemed good to me also . . . to write"). "Many" persons had begun assembling these eyewitness reports into some kind of narrative account.

Luke saw himself in a position to do this also, and to do it better. He was writing an account that would be comprehensive, thorough, orderly, and trustworthy. He thus stated four characteristics of his own work. It may perhaps be inferred that he was motivated to engage in his project because these characteristics (which he regards as important) are absent from the works of others (in some measure at least).

The apostolic accounts that Luke mentioned were not necessarily in writing, since the word παραδίδωμι could include oral accounts as well. But it would be going well beyond what Luke said to assume that these accounts did *not* include written records. Rightly understood, Luke's explanation says that from the apostles there came numerous accounts of events, and teachings of events, of which they themselves had been eyewitnesses.

This is the most logical thing one would expect. These men were called by Christ and commissioned to be his witnesses (Luke 24:48; John 15:27; Acts 1:8). What Luke said they were doing was precisely what Christ called them to do. What we can glean from Luke's explanation is that this apostolic eyewitness testimony was being written down. Thus the overwhelming preponderance of probability, based on what Luke said in his prologue, is that from the apostolic band there went into circulation various accounts of the things Jesus said and did, and that some of these accounts were written down.

The man at the center of this activity was the man who was called from a secretarial-type appointment as a Roman official to join a group commissioned to become witnesses for Jesus. Luke told us what was happening: the apostles were bearing eyewitness testimony to the events. Papias put a name to this. He said that Matthew wrote down the *logia*. The situation indicates that this is inherently unlikely *not* to be true. Matthew was sufficiently impressed with what he saw of Jesus to follow him. It is necessary to think a bit more deeply about what this bare statement indicates.

Jesus spent some time teaching in the Capernaum area, where Matthew (Levi) had his customs office on the Great West Road. He had an unending stream of travelers passing by and coming to him to pay their taxes. People had congregated from everywhere to hear the teaching of Jesus. They heard what he was teaching, and they saw the miracles he performed. Reports of these deeds and teachings were circulating widely, and in the nature of the case Matthew/Levi was in just the job and the location to hear them all. Then came the day when Jesus approached him and called him to become a follower. The records of this (Matt 9:9//Mark 2:14//Luke 5:27) do not hint at a moment's hesitation. Matthew immediately arose, left everything, and followed Jesus.

Matthew had a lucrative business as a taxation official in the Roman administration. We understand quite a bit, from our knowledge of Roman institutions and practices, about what this meant. This job would not make a man popular, but it would certainly make a man rich. Yet Matthew/Levi left it in an immediate response to the call of Jesus.

This response demonstrates one thing beyond all doubt: Matthew recognized the importance of Jesus—who he was, and what he was doing and teaching. We must not oversell this point. There was still a lot that Matthew had to learn and see. But we do know that Matthew's participation within the band of disciples was such that when Jesus chose 12 of them to be apostles and to have the role above all to be his witnesses, Matthew was one of those 12.

To have this evidence about the apostle Matthew—his background, training, and employment in the Roman administration; his response to the call to follow Jesus; his appointment to the role and responsibility of apostle—and to believe that he would *not* write down what Jesus was doing and teaching requires a far bigger leap of faith than believing that he did. It would be psychologically impossible that such a man as Matthew, trained and experienced in writing records and reports—he was a Roman official and such work was requisite for him since it went with the job—would not have recorded things Jesus said. He had the ability, the means, the opportunity, the motivation, and he wouldn't have done it? Impossible!

What happened after his call? We have no direct evidence for this. But an awareness of Matthew's circumstances and background points unerringly to it: he took down in his notebook what Jesus was teaching. He had been used to writing reports for his Roman employers, he had left this to follow Jesus, he heard the important things that Jesus was saying, and he would not make a record of them? Unbelievable! Rather, he wrote down what Jesus taught—there and then. Logic demands it. Papias confirmed it.

B. Gerhardsson (1961, 154, 156) discusses the use of written notes, especially notes of lectures and rabbinic teaching, in contemporary Judaism in the time of Christ, concerning which he says:

> In order to mark a fact, impress it clearly on the memory and prevent faulty memorization, the Rabbis often provided it with a *siman*.... These *simanim* often serve to prevent mistakes in respect of authors, figures or other facts which are easily confused in the memory....We thus see that these *simanim* are often expressions of a system of abbreviations which has with some justification been compared to shorthand.

It would thus be most natural if this practice of a rabbi's students making notes of his teaching were to be followed by Matthew (in particular) for recording Christ's teachings. Gerhardsson (ibid., 195) describes "the way in which the evangelists copied down and/or edited their work on the basis of material which had long been in use in the work of preaching and teaching, and which had therefore been memorized or—one might suppose—existed in private notebooks." He goes on to discuss the Christian use of the codex rather than the scroll for their writings (ibid., 201):

> It is a known fact that in the Christian church we find the Holy Scriptures in codex form at an unexpectedly early date. This is all the more remarkable when we consider the Hellenistic and Jewish milieus. In the Graeco-Roman world the

scroll enjoyed almost undisputed supremacy as the repository of literary work: a book *was* a scroll. In Judaism, too, the scroll was unchallenged as the vehicle for the written divine Word. With this in mind it is all the more remarkable that as early as the beginning of the second century—and presumably even earlier—the codex was used in the Church. Some scholars have connected this with the possibility that the gospel literature was derived from *notebooks*, which were often in codex form.

R. H. Gundry (1967, 182) attributes the origin of much Gospel material to Matthew's notebook, acknowledging that he was adopting a hypothesis that has been supported by E. J. Goodspeed (*Matthew, Apostle and Evangelist*, 1959), B. F. C. Atkinson (*The New Bible Commentary*, 1954, 771), and A. T. Robertson (*Studies in Mark's Gospel*, 1919, 28). Gundry also recognizes the points of similarity between his views and Gerhardsson, but says (ibid., 183), "My own hypothesis stresses note-taking, whereas Gerhardsson stresses memorization." Gundry (ibid., 181–83) explains his view this way:

> There is but one hypothesis known to the present writer which can meet the requirements of the data which has been discovered in this study. It is the hypothesis that the Apostle Matthew was a note-taker during the earthly ministry of Jesus and that his notes provided the basis for the bulk of the apostolic gospel tradition. The use of notebooks which were carried on one's person was very common in the Graeco-Roman world. In ancient schools outline notes (γράμματα ὑπομνημάτικα) were often taken by pupils as the teacher lectured. The notes became the common possession of the schools and circulated without the name of the lecturer. Sometimes an author would take this material as the basis for a book to be published (γράμματα συνταγμάτικα). Shorthand was used possibly as early as the fourth century B.C. and certainly by Jesus' time. The Oxyrhynchus papyri show that scribes and clerks were often trained in shorthand. Rabbinic tradition was transmitted by the employment of catchwords and phrases which were written down in shorthand notes. Thus, from both the Hellenistic side and the Judaistic side it is wholly plausible to suppose that one from the apostolic band was a note-taker—especially since the relationship of Jesus to his disciples was that of a teacher, or rabbi, to his pupils.
>
> As an ex-publican, whose employment and post near Capernaum on the Great West Road would have required and given a good command of Greek and instilled the habit of jotting down information, and perhaps a Levite, whose background would have given him acquaintance with the OT in its Semitic as well as Greek forms, Mt the Apostle was admirably fitted for such a function among the unlettered disciples [Acts 4:13]. We can then understand how all strands of textual tradition made their way into the whole of the synoptic material, for the looseness and informality of such notes made it possible for Hebrew, Aramaic, and Greek all to appear in them.

Gundry's view is endorsed by W. Hendriksen: "Matthew's *notes* ... could very well account also for" that Gospel material that is found not only in

Matthew but "in all three Synoptics" (1973, 90; see 53f.). A few pages later Hendriksen adds (96):

> Again, as a tax collector Matthew was obliged to make written reports of the moneys he collected. He may even have known shorthand. [That shorthand was well-known and widespread even before Matthew was born is also confirmed by the fact that already in 63 BC Marcus Tullius Tiro, a friend of Cicero, had invented a system of shorthand that was widely taught in the schools of the empire and used by the *notarii* in the Roman Senate to take down the speeches of the orators. And the Greek world was not behind in this, as Milligan and others have shown; p. 96n116.] He was therefore the logical person to take notes on Christ's words and works.

D. Hill cites Gundry's comment above and then adds (1972, 54), "The wide use of shorthand and the employment of note-books in the Graeco-Roman world, the ancient school practice of circulating lecture notes which could be used later in published works, and the later transmission of rabbinic tradition through shorthand notes, support the suggestion." Therefore, in the judgment of quite a few scholars, a case can be made for the proposal that Matthew's Gospel had its origins in notes that Matthew made at the time of Christ's deeds and teachings.

Matthew's accounts began to be copied and to circulate. Two factors contributed to this. First, perhaps these notes were at first intended only for limited private use, or perhaps from the beginning Matthew had in mind their wider circulation. Either way, there was Matthew's own innate perception of the importance of what Jesus was saying and which he was recording. He was aware that those who heard would not remember all of it. (The idea that the Jews of Jesus' day had wonderful memories and perfect recall is an unsubstantiated myth.) And always, as Jesus was teaching, there were untold multitudes who were *not* there on any given occasion to hear him. There would be the inner compulsive response, "Others must hear this also," which would have led Matthew to make some copies for distribution.

Second, Matthew began to receive requests. People who heard Jesus wanted a record of what they heard so they could take Jesus' message back to their villages and their families. People who were not there wanted to learn what Jesus had taught.

Conclusion

Aramaic was the mother tongue of most of Jesus' hearers, so much of his teaching was in Aramaic. Matthew wrote down in Aramaic what Jesus taught in Aramaic, and his record of the sayings and teaching of Jesus was copied and circulated in Aramaic. Did this actually happen? Papias said that it did.

There are certain situations in life where you *can* and therefore you *do*. Matthew was in such a situation. It reveals a distinct failure to understand how people tick to look at Matthew and to say that he would not have done and did not do exactly what church history tells us he did: write down what he heard Jesus teaching—in Aramaic, yes; but in Greek also. Moreover, we ought to recognize that this was part of the divine purpose for Matthew from the time of his call, and even earlier than that—from his training and preparation before his call.

<u>PROPOSITION 2:
MANY HAVE TAKEN IT IN HAND TO WRITE</u>

Luke's Explanation

Matthew was not the only one to write. Luke said, "Many have taken it in hand" (Luke 1:1).

The apostles were not the only eyewitnesses. Hundreds saw and heard one part or another of Jesus' ministry. In his prologue, Luke said that many responded by writing down the things they had heard and seen. Luke further explained that these early documents motivated him to write his own record since others were already doing the same thing. They had collected various accounts, originating with the apostles and other eyewitnesses, that recorded the deeds and teachings of Jesus. "Many" had begun assembling these into some kind of narrative account. Luke saw himself in a position to do this also, and to do it better. He was writing an account that would be comprehensive, thorough, orderly, and trustworthy.

Luke said that "many have set to work putting together a consecutive narrative covering the things that have been fulfilled amongst us, exactly as those who from the beginning were eyewitnesses and ministers of the Word delivered to us" (Luke 1:1–4, author's translation). This undoubtedly refers first and foremost to the apostles. They were *par excellence* the "eyewitnesses and ministers of the Word delivered to us." But Jesus had taught crowds of people over several years and had performed many healings in their midst. So there were quite a few other eyewitnesses of such events in addition to the apostles—many who had themselves become believers and were engaged in witness to their Lord. For instance, there were 70 (perhaps 72) of them who went out on mission for Jesus on one occasion during his years of ministry (Luke 10:1), and there were 120 by the time of the ascension (Acts 1:15). Some of these also were "eyewitnesses and ministers of the Word," and they began to write down their recollections.

Further, there were "many" who had begun assembling this material into "a connected narrative" of what had happened. This was happening before Luke wrote—during the decades of the AD 30s, 40s, and 50s.

Some have objected to this scenario with the claim that the Jews of those times had a prejudice against putting sacred things into writing, and in any case Christian believers were expecting the imminent return of Christ and would not have been motivated to take time to write things down. But Knox correctly states (1953, 1:5):

> It is indeed sometimes urged that the first generation of Christians was so filled with enthusiastic expectations of the immediate return of the Lord that its members had no interest in the details of his life. [Dibelius, *Formgeschichte d. Evang.* 9, 22.2] This seems to me frankly incredible. The missionary could hardly call on men to repent and believe in the Lord Jesus Christ, the Messiah whom the rulers of the Jews had crucified and whom God had raised from the dead, unless they were prepared to vindicate this somewhat startling message by giving an account of the things which Jesus had said and done. And no expectation of the Lord's return, however enthusiastic, is likely to have retained for long an intensity sufficient to stifle the ancient and deep-rooted curiosity of the human mind and its desire to be told a story.

Indeed, a century or so ago, W. C. Allen responded to these assertions (1907, xlvii, xlix):

> The assertions frequently made, that the Christian eschatological doctrine would have acted as a prejudice against writing down the words of Christ, and that the Jewish scruple about committing the oral law or the targums to writing would have transferred itself to the early Christian community and the teaching of their Master, are purely conjectural, and without foundation. We are dealing with a society in which, as the letters of the New Testament show, writing was well known and in common use. In every Christian community there would probably be found individuals who possessed in writing some of the words of Christ. . . .
>
> If there were any good reason for denying the existence of a multiplicity of written sources, the conception of oral tradition as a source for these sayings would be less artificial and more agreeable to the data than the hypothesis of a single written source. In view, however, of the facts . . . it would be arbitrary to assign all the sayings common to Mt. and Lk. to oral tradition. Wherever verbal agreement extends over several verses, it may reasonably be supposed either that Lk. had seen Mt., or that both writers had before them written sources containing, not, indeed, identical, but similar sayings. That amongst these written sources one or more may have been used by both Evangelists is, of course, possible, but can nowhere be proved with certainty so long as the possibility remains that the literary link consists in the dependence of Lk. upon Mt.

These comments by Knox and Allen remain totally valid today. In chapter 8 I have provided a substantial number of convincing reasons for seeing that the literary link between the two Major Synoptics cannot be that Luke used Matthew's Gospel. This removes Allen's caveat and leaves him as a supporter of my basic premise.

These apostolic and other eyewitness remembrances of Jesus' words and deeds were coming to be assembled together into longer narratives or "pericope clusters." It is completely impossible for us to know to what extent this grouping-together of pericopes could have been done by the original author at the point of first issuing them, by that author at a subsequent time, or by some other person (such as those about whom Luke was hinting). But this would be a logical next step. Knox spells this out (1:4–6):

> Moreover the travelling evangelist of the primitive Church would need some material for his work beyond the two elements of the mission-speech with its *testimonia* and the Passion story. For this purpose the individual pericope would be too short; the whole Gospel would be too long. What he would need would be a compilation of sayings or miracles or a mixture of the two, having some general unity either of thought or verbal association to aid his memory.
>
> Thus there would arise a number of "Tracts" containing accounts of the ministry of the Lord on earth, either written or committed to memory; it is at least reasonable to suppose that the great Churches of Jerusalem and Antioch would exercise some supervision of these collections and not leave the individual to compile his own and to introduce matter of his own invention. We know little of the process by which the Church detached itself from Judaism; it would appear from the only evidence available that for some time Christians attended the synagogue but had their own worship as well (Acts 2:46). But we must allow for the possibility that in some places Christians would be expelled from the synagogue quite soon, while elsewhere a particular synagogue might be dominated by a Christian majority, supported by the Elders, even if it were not entirely Christian in its membership; elsewhere again Christians might be allowed to express their opinions quite freely.
>
> These conditions would demand something more than a mere repetition of an outline *kerygma* of the Gospel, backed by a selection of proof-texts from the Old Testament and "prophecies" of an apocalyptic type; it seems quite incredible that in these cases, particularly where Christians had been expelled from the synagogue, there would be no attempt to provide a record of what Jesus had done and taught. . . .
>
> Writings of this kind . . . would be a natural growth, not a literary product. They would be of the sort of length which could easily be committed to memory, and furnish the basis for a sermon to instruct a congregation, to confirm their faith under persecution, or to edify them and emphasize their responsibilities as Christians. They could be used as an addition to the synagogue lessons or as a substitute for them. The practice attested by Justin Martyr of reading the memorials of the Apostles at Christian worship may well go back to the very early beginnings of the Church; it would be extremely perilous to argue from

the absence of any mention of the practice in earlier Christian writers that it cannot have existed, in view of the scanty nature of our records.

The investigative research of Guy mentioned earlier led him to a similar conclusion (1954, 123, 127):

> We know that collections in writing of the sayings of Jesus were made at an early date. . . .
>
> If written collections of the teaching of Jesus were made quite early, it is at least possible that written accounts of incidents also were set down. These first attempts would consist of the stories told by the preachers. . . . The independence and isolation of the episodes would be preserved if each story was first set down on a separate sheet of papyrus.

Guy examines in some detail a simple question that other writers who postulate early documents are slower to address: In what form did these documents circulate? His explanations are worthy of note (ibid., 127): "We have had evidence in recent years of the extent to which the papyrus codex, consisting of a number of sheets bound together, was in use among the early Christians instead of the papyrus roll, which was the more common form for books." He then enumerates (ibid., 128) various examples of early Christian use of papyrus sheets and codices:

> There is thus at least a likelihood that even in the first century the Christians used papyrus sheets, and this becomes a probability when we remember the frequent use of such sheets in ordinary correspondence in the Roman Empire. The letter of Paul to Philemon was probably written on one sheet, both sides perhaps being used. Separate papyrus sheets would also be much cheaper for Christians to use than an expensive roll, some of which was almost bound to be unused. The papyrus roll itself was of course but a number of sheets stuck together. The "rubbish heaps" of Egypt have revealed to us thousands of such sheets in daily use, some of them dating from New Testament times, employed for personal letters, business contracts, bills, receipts and invitations. Leaves in common use varied from 15.5 inches in length to small pieces of only a few inches. A quite frequent size was 9 to 11 inches in height and 5 inches wide. Study of the earliest pieces of Christian writing which we now possess shows that similar sheets were in use in the Church very early in its existence.

Guy sums up the conclusions to which his investigation led him (ibid., 130–32):

> The general conclusion from this investigation is that a sheet of papyrus in use among the Christians of the second century—if not of the first—might be from 2.245 inches to 10 inches in height and from 2.2375 inches to 8 inches in width. With these we may compare the sheets containing the Oxyrhynchus sayings of Jesus, which are 5.75 inches by 2.2375 inches. A page would thus contain from 400 to 800 Greek letters, according to the size of the sheet and the scribe's handwriting.

> There is at least one paragraph in the Gospels which apparently circulated as an independent unit, presumably written on a sheet of papyrus—the story of the adulteress. (This is the only way in which its presence in some MSS. at John 7:53ff., its total omission in others, and its inclusion at Lk 21:38 in the Ferrar Group can be accounted for.) Scribes included it where they thought fit, while some omitted it altogether. In the Westcott and Hort text the paragraph contains 820 Greek letters. There are, however, many words bracketed as doubtful; if these are not counted, the total is 705. This fragment could thus have been contained on a sheet of papyrus approximately the same size as a page of the Chester Beatty codex or the John Rylands fragment of the Fourth Gospel. . . .
>
> There is admittedly no parallel to this practice in the case of disciples of the Jewish Rabbis, who depended on oral instruction and repetition of their teaching. But the Christians would not feel bound by this precedent. Their teaching was not for a select circle of disciples but was an open proclamation of good news for all men. They would desire as wide a circulation as possible for the stories about Jesus. What is more natural than that the preachers or their disciples would use odd pieces of papyrus, instead of embarking on the formidable task of writing a book and using a valuable and expensive papyrus roll?

There is thus substantial support for the view that there were numerous eyewitnesses in addition to the apostles who wrote down what they had heard and seen in Jesus' ministry, and that there was a very definite demand for these written records, both to help Christians learn more about their Lord and in particular as an aid for preachers and leaders in the growing church. And the more widely the church spread during the decades of the AD 30s, 40s, and 50s, the more insistent became this demand.

The materials they wrote include the following:

1. material that had originated from within the apostolic group—and (as already shown) there is solid evidence for attributing this to the apostle Matthew;

2. varied accounts from other nonapostolic eyewitnesses;

3. narratives or clusters of pericopes, either originating from these authors themselves, or being assembled by others (the "many" to whom Luke referred).

What Are We to Think of Q?

Further obvious data in this connection is before us in the passages in Matthew and Luke that have such close correspondence that a common written source seems plausible. This is the material commonly designated "Q."

Obviously, the material common to the two Major Synoptics must be explained. The standard Markan Priority view is that the material of the

Triple Tradition—that is, material closely similar in wording and content that occurs in all three Synoptics—is explained on the basis that it is original in Mark and drawn from that source by the other two. But if (as I am setting out to show) Mark was written third instead of first, then we must now recognize a source that comprises *all* the material common to Matthew and Luke, completely irrespective of whether or not it is also found in Mark. My hypothesis must account for this common material, and it does so on these bases:

1. Where there is such close correspondence between the Major Synoptics as to require literary dependence, the source is an original document written by Matthew in Greek that was copied and circulated and then obtained by Luke when he gathered his material for his Gospel, and it was also incorporated by Matthew when he prepared his Gospel.

2. Where there is such close correspondence between the Major Synoptics as to require literary dependence but with some verbal variation, the source is likely to be an original document written by Matthew in Hebrew/Aramaic that was obtained by Luke when he gathered his material for his Gospel, either already translated into Greek when Luke found it or else translated by Luke himself, and also rewritten in Greek by Matthew when he prepared his Gospel. W. F. Albright and C. Mann comment, "In relation to this version, it may be said that many minor variants in the use of 'Q' material between Matthew and Luke can be ascribed to varying translations of the original" (1971, 51). Similarly, D. Hill writes (1972, 25): "The fact that in many passages in the material common to Matthew and Luke the extent of verbal agreement is considerable although far from total (as it is in other passages) makes it likely that we are dealing, not simply with a common written Greek source, but with alternative translations of earlier Aramaic material as well."

3. There are a number of verses in the two Major Synoptics that record the same incident or that have similar subject matter, but there do not appear (from examination and comparison of the text of these two Gospels) to be adequate grounds for concluding that the two accounts in the two Major Synoptics have been derived from a single document. When it is clearly the same speech being reported or the same incident being described but with significant differences of wording, detail, or perspective, the explanation is that the account in Matthew's Gospel is his own, and the account in Luke's Gospel is sourced by Luke from a nonapostolic eyewitness report of the event.

4. In numerous pericopes, where a teaching is being recorded with significant differences of wording or context between the Gospels, we have

in fact in the two Gospels the record, from two different sources (Matthew and another eyewitness), of *two* distinct occasions. We have only to think of the number of situations in which we could expect Jesus to repeat the use of his stories, his parables, his sayings, to different audiences in different places on different occasions. It is totally gratuitous and unrealistic (and quite opposed to our own normal ministry experience) to decide that Jesus could only have spoken any given teaching on the *one* occasion, and then for us to deduce from this assumption that if any two pieces of teaching (often dubbed "doublets") look similar, they must be variants of something said on that one occasion.

There may be an occasional redaction of a pericope by one author or the other to fit it harmoniously into the setting into which he is placing it, but this has been very much overworked as an explanation for passages that are much more reasonably seen as an occasion of one of the four explanations above. The best that can be said of this redaction approach in a great many instances is that it is an unnecessary hypothesis.

The above explanation points to the existence, behind Luke's Gospel, of a variety of documents of various kinds and sizes, many of them of Matthean authorship, and many of them from other, non-Matthean, eyewitnesses. This fully accords with what Luke himself tells us. And behind the material in Matthew's Gospel is the apostle Matthew. This explanation allows us to dispense with Q altogether. Chapter 8 examines instances of each of these different kinds of situations in the text of the Major Synoptics.

PROPOSITION 3:
LUKE COLLECTS HIS MATERIAL

The Authorship of the Third Gospel

This question is not highly disputed territory, and therefore, as on this point I am in complete agreement with the scholarly consensus, it is not necessary to do more than state this consensus. Luke's Gospel was written by the same author as the Acts of the Apostles, that is to say, the physician who accompanied Paul on his travels for many years. Thus in order to understand the background to the writing of Luke's Gospel, we begin with what we know about this man and with what he said in his opening prologue about the writing of his Gospel.

Luke Seizes His Opportunity

In AD 56 Luke arrived in Palestine in company with Paul. We can recognize from the "we" passages of Acts—which give Luke's firsthand eyewitness accounts of the events that he himself shared in—that by the time he came to Palestine he had already begun the practice of recording material about the spread of the Christian gospel. It seems clear then that he had already formed the intention of writing it up as a connected account. In any case his visit to Jerusalem (Acts 21:17) and the two years he spent in Palestine while Paul was imprisoned in Caesarea (Acts 24:27) provided a perfect opportunity—and, it would appear, his only significant opportunity—for collecting the material that he used in writing the first half of the Acts of the Apostles, which involved events that he himself did not witness.

If Luke was engaged between AD 56 and 58 in discussions with eyewitnesses, and in collecting information to provide the basis for his record in Acts of the events from Pentecost onwards, then it is clear that he would have used the same opportunities and questioned the same people about the life of Christ. He does not say at what time he first learned about the documents in circulation that set forth narratives of the events of the life of Christ. It may have been earlier than his AD 56 visit to Jerusalem and Palestine. In fact, there are good grounds for believing that Paul had in his possession—and used in his ministry—copies of pericopes of incidents and teachings of Christ's life. Paul frequently quoted from Christ's teachings or showed a knowledge of things Christ said. Be that as it may, it is certainly most unlikely that it would have been later than AD 56 or in some other area that Luke first came across the accounts he mentioned. And in his prologue to his Gospel, he stated that he carried out a very thorough and careful investigation of everything connected with the life of Christ.

So it is legitimate to conclude that while Luke was in Palestine he completed the collection of the material for his Gospel and took it with him to Rome, managing to preserve it intact during his shipwreck on Malta on the way there. What then would have been the sources that Luke used for his Gospel? There is evidence for the existence of these different sources:

1. There were numerous pericopes of varying lengths that had originally been written by Matthew, some that Matthew wrote in Greek and some that he originally wrote in Aramaic (i.e., the *logia* to which Papias referred). Of those in Aramaic, many were translated into Greek by Luke himself for inclusion in his Gospel. Other accounts that Matthew originally wrote in Aramaic had already been translated by others into Greek for the use of Greek-speaking Christians, before Luke came across them.

2. There were numerous pericopes of varying lengths written by others, some almost certainly in Aramaic (and translated by/for Luke) and some in Greek. Albright and Mann (1971, 175) made this interesting comment: "In the course of writing this commentary it has become increasingly clear to us that we may well be dealing with material which had been transmitted in Aramaic and occasionally in Hebrew."

3. There were copies of written but unpublished notes made of various teachings and incidents by some who were present at the time. The existence of such eyewitness notes, privately preserved, is conjectural, I acknowledge, but highly probable. Many who were deeply impressed by what they heard and saw during the ministry of Jesus would have been motivated to preserve a record of it. (I consider the argument overstated which says that in the first century people had such excellent memories that even those who could write would not trouble to write down those things that they wanted to remember accurately and permanently.) During his research for his Gospel, Luke would have had ample opportunity to learn about the existence of such private records and to track them down in order to copy them.

4. Oral tradition was available that had not been committed to writing prior to the time Luke himself recorded it.

5. Luke was able to obtain information in Palestine through his own investigation and interviews—including details of time, place, circumstances, responses, and so on.

PROPOSITION 4:
PUBLICATION OF THE TWO MAJOR SYNOPTIC GOSPELS

The Four Characteristics That Luke Claims for His Book

Luke was no mere collector and compiler of documentary information. In his prologue he said that he had personally investigated everything accurately from the beginning and written an orderly account. His statement deserves special attention.

1. The word ἄνωθεν ("from the beginning") indicates that in his investigation he has traced things back to the earliest events connected with the coming of Jesus. Thus his Gospel begins prior to the birth of John. What Luke has said here connects to his earlier comment and suggests that "investigating everything accurately from the beginning" involved him in firsthand discussions with those who were "eyewitnesses from the beginning," both apostles and others.

2. The word πᾶσιν ("everything") shows the scope of Luke's investigation. He wanted to find out all that could be known about Christ's life and teaching. Thus Luke's Gospel commences at an earlier point in time than either of the other Synoptics and carries through to a later point in time; it also includes a great deal of Jesus' teachings (especially in parables) and a number of his miracles and other events that do not occur elsewhere. Luke's interest in tracing the course of everything from the beginning raises a question about the Markan Priority theory. Why would Luke have omitted so much of the detailed information of Mark's Gospel if he used it as his source? And in particular, why would he have left out completely a number of Mark's pericopes, including the entire section Mark 6:45–8:26, often called "the Great Omission"? Advocates of Markan Priority have suggested a number of possible explanations: (a) Luke was not interested in points of detail; (b) he already had stories rather similar to those that he omitted; (c) he cut his Gospel to a length that would fit into a single roll; (d) he considered some of Mark's material irrelevant or theologically objectionable; and (e) the edition of Mark from which he was working lacked the Great Omission. But the question is raised in an even more acute form if one is forced to conclude (as many scholars do) that the most valid explanation of much of the material that Luke shares with Matthew but not with Mark is that Luke had access to Matthew's Gospel. If one seeks to avoid this problem by saying that Luke had access only to *some* portions of Matthew, this is in fact to adopt a view similar in its essentials to the Progressive Publication Hypothesis. But these other explanations virtually amount to a denial of Luke's expressed interest in tracing every aspect of Christ's life.

3. The word ἀκριβῶς ("accurately") draws attention to the fact that Luke was no mere uncritical collector of traditions of untested veracity. He used critical judgment, assessing and weighing the traditions he was able to collect, checking out his information and authenticating his facts before including material in his Gospel. The other compilers of narratives were, as we have seen earlier, engaged in assembling isolated (and frequently quite short) traditions into a connected sequence. It is completely unreasonable to hold that Luke knew of the collections of material that others had made and that he referred thus to this other material, but that he did *not* look at these narratives he mentioned yet still claimed to have checked out "everything." Moreover, in the nature of the case his statement that he investigated *everything* would of necessity mean that he became involved in an evaluation of the *order* into which these others cast their pericopes. That is to say, "an accurate investigation of everything" inevitably involves the question of the *order* in which he is going to assemble his material from

all his sources, and thus of the *order* in which events took place. And this is in fact the next aspect that Luke mentions.

4. The word καθεξῆς ("in order") emphasizes Luke's concern about the *sequence of events*. The commentators are divided as to whether this term indicates *chronological* order or some other kind of order. To a significant extent, their opinion on this point correlates with their overall conclusion as to whether Luke's Gospel places everything in chronological order—or whether, for instance, Mark is to be regarded as more chronologically accurate where it diverges from Luke. I think it is reasonable to say that the word καθεξῆς certainly may mean "chronological order" but does not necessarily do so. The kind of order that is meant is best ascertained by looking at the actual contents of Luke.

Throughout his Gospel, Luke showed a constant concern with issues of time, place, and sequence of events (see details in chap. 4). This is shown in the dating of the commencement of his account (1:5; 3:1–2), his giving of the best estimate of Jesus' age that he had been able to find (1:23), and the way in which virtually every separate incident he records is linked with the previous one by some note of time and place transition. And where he did not determine this information, he said so: "While he was in one of the cities" (5:12); "On one of those days" (5:17); "Now he was teaching in one of the synagogues on the Sabbath" (13:10). All in all, it seems pretty clear that the evidence in Luke's Gospel itself indicates that he *intended* to write in chronological order to the extent to which, in his investigations, he was able to discover what that order was. He may or may not have succeeded in his intention at all points, and this is a matter open for further investigation and discussion. There are a few places where I think Matthew's order is clearly to be preferred. But there is good reason for taking καθεξῆς in 1:3 to indicate Luke's plan to give a *chronological* account (see further in chap. 4).

The significance of Luke's fourfold claim—that he investigated and traced the course of everything accurately from the beginning, and wrote his account of everything in order—is reinforced by his final comment. He wrote so that Theophilus would have been enabled to know for certain (ἐπιγινώσκω) the truth, the reliability, and the certainty (all conveyed by the word ἀσφάλεια) of the λόγοι of which he had been informed. Luke thus assured Theophilus (and, of course, his other readers) that the account that he had produced could be depended on completely to convey the message they had heard. This indicates the measure of Luke's confidence that he had carried through the standards and the program that he had explained in the previous verse. So it is legitimate to conclude that while Luke was in

Palestine he collected all the material for his Gospel and took it with him to Rome.

The Dating of the Synoptic Gospels

The date of the publication of Luke's Gospel is closely tied to that of his sequel, the Acts of the Apostles. Acts commences where the Gospel ends, and in Acts 1:1–5 Luke indicated to Theophilus that this volume is indeed a sequel to his first book. So when was the book of Acts written?

On the usually accepted chronology of Paul's life (with which I completely concur), Paul reached Rome in either February or March of AD 60. In the closing verses of Acts, Luke said that Paul remained (ἐνέμεινεν) there two whole years; thus the account in the book of Acts ends in AD 62.

But Luke's account doesn't *conclude* so much as simply *stop*. This raises the obvious question that numerous scholars have addressed across the years: Why did Luke stop here?

One of the scholars who spent considerable time and labor looking into this question was A. Harnack. He says (1911, 93–94) that his understanding of this issue has been maturing for "more than fifteen years," and then he argues strongly for dating the writing of Acts at the conclusion of the "two years" mentioned in its closing verses. He also says that this is the first impression that one receives from these words, and it "will continue to hold the field against all other possibilities. . . . This also is the significance of the aorist ἐνέμεινεν. . . . [I]t shows that the situation is now changed."

Harnack then considers the possible changes that may have followed those two years and points out that, whatever that change may have been, Luke could not possibly have stopped his account on this note if that account were written some years later. Harnack avers (ibid., 95), "Thus, according to the concluding verses, the Acts was written very soon after the day on which St Paul was condemned to leave his hired lodging." He also states (97):

> The more clearly we see that the trial of St Paul, and above all his appeal to Caesar, is the chief subject of the last quarter of the Acts, the more hopeless does it appear that we can explain why the narrative breaks off as it does, otherwise than by assuming that the trial had actually not yet reached its close. It is no use to struggle against this conclusion. If St Luke, in the year 80, 90, or 100, wrote thus, he was not simply a blundering but an absolutely incomprehensible historian!

Harnack points out that the clear impression, based on the references in Acts to Peter and Paul, is that both apostles were still alive at the time of writing. The only realistic explanation of why the book ends in such a manner is because Luke had brought his account up-to-date. It is clear from the way he finishes ("for two whole years") that it was not written at a later time—Luke could hardly say "two years" if he wrote later and things had continued unchanged for several years further. Similarly, if Paul had come to trial and the outcome was known at the time he wrote, it is inconceivable that Luke would end his account without a mention of this. After further discussion of these issues, Harnack sums up his discussion (99): "We are accordingly left with the result: that the concluding verses of the Acts of the Apostles, taken in conjunction with the absence of any reference in the book to the result of the trial of St Paul and to his martyrdom, make it in the highest degree probable that the work was written at a time when St Paul's trial had not yet come to an end."

Harnack then mentions briefly a number of negative factors that point to this date. In the book of Acts there is a total absence of references to crucial events that affected both Christians and Jews: Nero's persecution of Christians; the rebellion of the Jews against Rome; the destruction of Jerusalem; and the lack of any use or even mention of Paul's epistles, which is especially hard to explain if Acts were written years later. Harnack explains (ibid., 100) that "St Luke's absolute silence concerning everything that happened between the years 64 and 70 AD is a strong argument for the hypothesis that his book was written before the year 64 AD."

Harnack's thesis was written about a century ago. In 1976 J. A. T. Robinson published the fruits of a careful and thorough investigation of the dating of all the books of the New Testament. Robinson spends several pages discussing Harnack's treatment of the dating of Acts and notes the changing and maturing of his views over a period of time, until Harnack himself was forced by his weighing of the evidence to decide for the early date of Acts. Robinson comments (90): "Harnack is still worth quoting, not merely because he is one of the great ones in his field, whose massive scholarship and objectivity of judgement contrast with so many who have come after him, but because on this subject he was forced slowly and painfully to change his mind."

Robinson (ibid., 88) then elucidates and expands on the reasons that led Harnack to change his mind, adding more of his own reasons that point to an early date for Acts, such as the absence in Acts of any reference to "the flight of Christians to Pella prior to the beginning of the [Jewish] war in 66," and the lack of "any hint of the death of James the Lord's brother in 62, which took place at the hands of the Sanhedrin *against* the authority of Rome" (89). Robinson concludes (90) that explanations for the ending of Acts other than the simple one that Luke took his account up to his time of writing are "recourses of desperation." Therefore, if Acts is dated AD 62, this would indicate that Luke's Gospel (his first volume) should be dated a couple of years earlier, AD 60.

But what about the date of Matthew's Gospel? Robinson traces in detail the relevant features in Matthew's Gospel that bear upon the question of dating. In particular he points out (ibid., 103) that "Matthew represents the gospel for the Jewish-Christian church, equipping it to define and defend its position over against the arguments and institutions of the main body of Judaism." He shows (104) that Matthew's manner of writing indicates that "the old *status quo* is still in operation," that is, Matthew's Gospel must be dated before the destruction of Jerusalem in AD 70 and the devastating changes that event brought on Judaism. Matthew's Gospel presupposes a still-operating temple and sacrificial system (e.g., Matt 12:5–7), including payment of taxes for the upkeep of the temple (17:24–27), at a time when there was a stand-off between Jews and Christians but not yet a total and open breach—as distinct from how one would write if speaking of something that had been wiped away by a catastrophic destruction.

After considering all the relevant factors he could identify, Robinson says (ibid., 107), "In this case we have pushed Matthew back at any rate before 62, which is exactly the date to which we were driven by Acts, with Luke a little earlier." He therefore dates the Synoptic Gospels in the period from AD 50 to 60.

It is interesting to see how, again and again, Robinson refuses to base his dates on any particular "solution" to the Synoptic Problem. He considers the issues both from the perspective of Markan Priority and Markan Posteriority, without allowing his conclusions to be determined by either, but by investigations independent of Synoptic hypotheses.

D. Black (2001, 67–68) makes a similar and independent assessment of what can be seen in Matthew that bears on its dating, listing 10 significant features that need to be noted. Black says (68) that this data "indicates that the social milieu of Jesus' time was still intact when Matthew was written (see the phrase 'even unto this day' in Matt 27:8; 28:15)." He concludes (69), "The formation of Matthew's Gospel probably took place in the first decade of the church's life, that is, before 44, and thus not only before 1–2 Thessalonians and Galatians but probably before Paul's second visit to Jerusalem 'after fourteen years' (Gal 2:1; cf. Acts 11:27–30; 12:25)."

When scholars have come to accept AD 65 as the date for Mark's Gospel (largely on the basis of the testimony of the early church Fathers), and they take this Gospel as being prior to the Major Synoptics (because it was supposedly used by them), they are then compelled by their assumptions to reject the evidence that would date Matthew and Luke in c. AD 60.

But when one recognizes the validity of the evidence pointing to the Markan Dependence explanation, then the chronology falls quite smoothly into place. I would agree with Black to the extent that *some portions* of Matthew were written (and in circulation) by AD 44, though not the complete Gospel quite as early as this date. I see the evidence pointing to the conclusion that Matthew and Luke were published in the same year (for they did not see each other's Gospel), and that year was AD 60. Mark used them both in the writing of his Gospel, and this Gospel dates from the period around the death of Peter, as the early church Fathers testified. Thus Mark's Gospel was published in c. AD 65.

The Authorship of Canonical Matthew

A substantial number of scholars reject the Matthean authorship of the First Gospel. Quite a few of these are willing to acknowledge that some Matthean writing lies behind it, particularly the *logia* mentioned by Papias since they often conjecture that this is the basis for how the name of Matthew came to be attached to the entire Gospel. But this question of the authorship of the canonical Matthew needs to be considered more fully.

The apostle Paul ended up (under the guidance and inspiration of the Holy Spirit) writing a significant section of the New Testament. Matthew was called to be with Jesus during the exciting years of his earthly ministry so that he could record them. He was a prepared and chosen vessel just like Paul, and he too was called to have a vital writing ministry. Like Paul, Matthew wrote (under the guidance and inspiration of the Holy Spirit) a significant section of the New Testament.

It is incredible that so many New Testament scholars, without one piece of definite evidence to suggest it, would deny the Matthean authorship of the First Gospel (authorship by the one man so obviously prepared by the Lord for just such a task) and would attribute it instead to some later anonymous person [or persons] writing many years afterwards.

Like Esther (Esth 4:14), Matthew was one who had come to the kingdom for such a time as this. Like Paul, he was prepared and chosen and called and appointed to the ministry that church history affirms he fulfilled: writing his account of the life and ministry of Jesus. Acts 9:15 says of Paul that "he is a chosen instrument of mine to carry my name before the Gentiles and kings and the children of Israel." Paul recounted how Ananias said to him, "The God of our fathers appointed you to know his will, to see the Righteous One and to hear a voice from his mouth; for you will be a witness for him to everyone of what you have seen and heard" (Acts 22:14–15). These things are written about Paul and his call; but every word applies with equal force and relevance to Matthew: how the Lord God was at work in Matthew's life years beforehand, preparing him for this very task, bringing him to his employment in customs work in Capernaum during the period when Jesus was ministering there, moving his heart to respond to the invitation to join Jesus' band of followers. A preparation, all of it, that fitted and equipped him in every way with the training and the skills and the opportunities to participate in, and record, the ministry of Jesus.

Although the First Gospel does not ascribe its authorship to Matthew, church history did—unanimously. But it has become fashionable with a plethora of modern scholars to denigrate the testimony of church history. Thus A. Plummer says (1896, viii) that "it is difficult to believe that it is the work of the Apostle." His explanation (viii–x) is:

> Whoever wrote it took the Second Gospel as a frame, and worked into it much material from other sources. . . . And it is not likely that the Apostle Matthew, with first-hand knowledge of his own, would take the Gospel of another, and that other not an Apostle, as the framework of his own Gospel. There would seem, therefore, to be some error in the early tradition about the First Gospel. . . . When the unknown constructor of the First Gospel took the Second Gospel and fitted on to it the contents of this collection of Utterances, together with other material of his own gathering, he produced a work which was at once welcomed by the first Christians as much more complete than the Second Gospel. . . . The answer, therefore, to the question, Who was the author of the First Gospel? is a negative one. It was not S. Matthew. The writer was an early Jewish Christian, not sufficiently important to give his name to a Gospel, and in no way desiring to do so.

W. C. Allen writes similarly in discussing the tradition in the church Fathers (1907, lxxx–lxxxi):

> This tradition (and inference) is, however, directly contradicted by the testimony of the First Gospel itself, for that work clearly shows itself to be a compilation by someone who has interwoven material from another source or other sources into the framework of the Second Gospel. This renders it difficult to suppose that the book in its present form is the work of the Apostle Matthew. It is indeed not impossible, but it is very improbable, that an Apostle should rely upon the work of another for the entire framework of his narrative. . . . It would therefore seem that . . . the only course open to us is to assert that tradition has here gone astray. . . . The compiler was either unknown, or, if known, a man of second rank within the church.

A. H. McNeile (1915, xxvii) follows suit: "He was certainly not Matthew the apostle. Apart from the characteristics just mentioned, one who could write with the paramount authority of an eyewitness would not have been content to base his work on that of a secondary authority." McNeile dates Matthew's Gospel c. AD 80–100.

Similarly, J. C. Fenton writes (1963, 12):

> Since 1835, when it was first put forward, the view has become widely accepted that Matthew drew upon Mark, and that Mark's is the earlier Gospel. . . . It is usually thought that Mark's Gospel was written about AD 65; and that the author of it was neither one of the apostles nor an eyewitness of the majority of events recorded in his Gospel. Matthew was therefore dependent upon the writing of such a man for the production of his book. What Matthew has done, in fact, is to produce a second and enlarged edition of Mark. Moreover, the changes which he makes in Mark's way of telling the story are not the corrections which an eyewitness might make in the account of one who was not an eyewitness. Thus, whereas in Mark's Gospel we may be only one remove from eyewitness, in Matthew's Gospel we are one remove further still.

Thus Fenton (ibid., 11) dates Matthew's Gospel as written "between about AD 85 and 105."

But enough! I have cited a sufficient number of such writers, and I have on my shelves commentary after commentary and a range of other works that similarly reject Matthean authorship and pronounce the testimony of the church Fathers to this authorship as being mistaken. There is a consistency about their reason for this: they accept the Markan Priority explanation of Gospel interrelationships, and they then pronounce it as unthinkable that an apostle would base his Gospel on that of a non-apostle.

There is one other reason sometimes found, as mentioned by Gundry: "Another objection to Matthean authorship often heard is that Mt's frequent disinterest in the vivid details of Mk shows him not to have been an eyewitness" (1975, 184). T. H. Robinson also writes of this (1928, xiii):

> On other grounds, the gospel does not impress us as being the work of an eyewitness of the events it describes. . . . The First evangelist gives us the impression of relying on the observation of others, and indeed, on earlier documentary sources. The mention of other sources leads us to ask a question as to the material on which the evangelist had to rely. It is obvious at a glance that his mainstay was the gospel of Mark, practically in the form in which we have it to-day.

The question of the authorship of the First Gospel is of considerably greater significance than it is often accorded in the literature about this Gospel. It greatly impacts the authority with which one views this book. One's attitude toward this book (both its authority and divine inspiration) will be different if on solid grounds one accepts that it came from the pen of the apostle Matthew—one of those men who were specifically promised by Christ that they would receive the aid of the Holy Spirit in their ministry (John 14:25–26; 15:26–27; 16:13)—than if the author were just a "compiler," a man of "second rank within the church," who put the book together many years later.

It is a grievous error of the most wretched kind if the decision in this matter is based on the acceptance of a theory of Synoptic interrelationships that claims Mark's Gospel was written first and used in the writing of Matthew, and thus the author of Matthew's Gospel cannot be the apostle. In this present book I give cogent and compelling grounds for seeing that Matthew was written *before* Mark and not afterwards; but even if one were to find this demonstration unconvincing, a view about Gospel sequence is not a valid reason for rejecting apostolic authorship.

As for the second ground mentioned above, primarily that of Mark's "vivid details," this is fully answered when one considers that Matthew wrote a virtual summary of the events he described, while Mark wrote with a different purpose for a different audience. Mark enlivened his narrative with a multitude of eyewitness details fresh in his mind from his recollections of frequently hearing Peter tell these stories. I expand these questions much more fully later when I compare the style, content, and purpose of Matthew and Mark.

In his defense of the validity of Matthew's authorship of the First Gospel, N. B. Stonehouse (1963, 23) mentions one other objection to Matthean authorship:

> A rather different type of argument than the one which has just been under discussion has evidently, however, contributed far more decisively to the rejection of the apostolic authorship of Matthew. Stated in general terms this is the argument that a careful study of this Gospel will disclose historical and theological perspectives which are irreconcilable with what an eyewitness and hearer of Jesus in the days of his flesh would presumably have reported. In somewhat more specific terms, the argument has characteristically taken the form that there are distinctive tendencies in Matthew—whether legalistic, or ecclesiastical, or universalistic, or eschatological—which betray the fact that the evangelist has rather freely interpreted, that is, altered, his sources or has fashioned new material as he addressed the Church of his day.

The weight that one attributes to this objection depends on how much one believes that Jesus had actually taught the apostles while they were with him, how much understanding they came to have during this time, and how much importance one attaches to Luke's words after Christ's resurrection, "Then he opened their minds to understand the Scriptures" (Luke 24:45).

During his earthly ministry, Jesus often rebuked his disciples for their dullness of understanding. Are we to understand that these men, to whom he committed the task of leading and guiding the infant church, remained with this same imperfect understanding after the resurrection? Are we to accept the view that "a careful study of this Gospel will disclose historical and theological perspectives which are irreconcilable with what an eyewitness and hearer of Jesus in the days of his flesh would presumably have reported" (as stated by Stonehouse, ibid., 23)? Is it more plausible that a shadowy, anonymous, later compiler of material for this Gospel could have worked these things out or come to see them after further years of reflection, whereas those who were appointed by Christ to be his witnesses and who were taught by him could not have had these insights by the time Matthew's Gospel was published? This ground for rejecting apostolic authorship is a very subjective and insubstantial one, and reveals more about the commentator than it does about the facts related to the authorship of this Gospel.

If one accepts that Jesus knew he was the Messiah during the period of his earthly ministry, that he came to earth to die on a cross, that he knew it was the reason he came, that he was engaged in revealing this to his chosen apostles as they were able to receive it so that by the time of his ascension they could understand these things, that Jesus did indeed send the Holy Spirit to his apostles as he promised (John 14–16), and that in consequence the writing of the Gospels (and the rest of Scripture) is through the inspiration of the Holy Spirit who enabled the apostles to remember clearly the life and teachings of Jesus (John 14:26), then one cannot find any substance in this kind of argument. And there is no reason to doubt that the apostle Matthew could have composed what is written in the First Gospel. However, if one does not believe any of these things but rather looks at Matthew's Gospel as a purely human production, slightly different from but on a par with the histories written by Greek and Roman authors and their "Lives" of famous people, then one can conclude that Matthew's Gospel is the later work of an anonymous compiler—someone using a few documents from an earlier time on the basis of reflection, speculation, and a certain amount of wishful thinking.

Matthew's Gospel is a major book that helped shape the church, and through the church, helped shape the world. It was written by the apostle who was being prepared for the task by divine providence, both before and after his call to follow Jesus. Of all the apostles, he was the best equipped and the most able to fulfill this role and accomplish this task. This is where both evidence and logic point us. This is what the early church Fathers said. There is no objective data that would lead someone to believe otherwise.

I have cited at some length above those who reject Matthean authorship. But there are other commentators and theological writers who have examined the evidence and have come to the conclusion that the tradition of the early Fathers in this regard was well founded: the apostle Matthew was indeed the author of the Gospel that bears his name.

I am particularly warm to some of the comments on authorship by Albright and Mann (1971, 177–78):

> Traditionally, this gospel was written by Matthew, the tax collector described in 9:9 and 10:3, and further identified with the Levi of Mark 2:14 and Luke 5:27 (properly, as we shall see, "the Levite") . . . the main controversy has always centered around the identification of Matthew with Levi in our present texts. . . . There is a simple solution to the difficulty and one which we believe has the merit of doing justice to all available facts. It is that Levi is not (as usually held) a personal name but the tribal designation of the man who was called by Jesus from his tax collecting. That is to say, the person under discussion is "Matthew the Levite". . . . Everything which we judge to be characteristic of this gospel—its conservatism, its interest in the traditional oral law, in lawyers and Pharisees, its traditional eschatology—all this fits admirably into the background of an author who was a Levite. . . . If Matthew the Levite found a living as a tax collector for the political authorities—and his education would certainly fit him for such responsibility—then his rejection by his fellow Pharisees would follow inevitably. So too would inevitably follow carefully collected reminiscences of Jesus' attitude to the Law and to those who made their living by oral interpretation of that Law.

Albright and Mann (183–84) go on to identify 10 discernible features in or about the First Gospel. The tenth is that if the Gospel were not written in Matthew's day by someone with training and background like Matthew's, it would have to have been by someone "who would have had nothing apart from antiquarianism to inform him, if his work was written or compiled at the end of the first century" (184). This is the conclusion they then draw (ibid):

> The Levite Matthew fulfills the conditions for an author which we have outlined above far better than any other candidate known to us from the New Testament. That there is no certainty to this hypothesis, we readily concede. But it has the merit of taking Papias and those who cite him seriously, and of accepting historical and archeological evidence of chaotic conditions in Palestine between AD 60 and 75. It also saves us from the inherent absurdity of supposing that Palestinian Christians—Jewish Christians at that—would have based the first Palestinian gospel on a recent arrival from Rome. It is very doubtful whether in the thoroughly confused situation which must have immediately preceded the flights of Jewish Christians from Palestine [at the time of the Jewish War], there would have been time or encouragement for composition of a Palestinian gospel . . . We have already stated, in the earlier parts of this Introduction, that we do not find it necessary to accept the notion of dependence of Matthew on Mark.

CONCLUSION

If one decides (as did Albright and Mann) to refuse to allow the issue of the authorship of Matthew to be determined upon the basis of a Synoptic hypothesis of relationships and to judge exclusively on the evidence, there are no valid grounds for doubting the unanimous testimony of the early church Fathers to Matthean authorship.

All the cautions Albright and Mann gave, all the considerations that they raised, all the issues and factors that they pointed out that are to be taken into account—all of these are fully satisfied if we recognize that the First Gospel was published by the apostle Matthew in about AD 60, and that into it he incorporated numbers of documents of varying length that he had previously written and that had had a measure of independent circulation in the churches of that time.

EXPLAINING MARK'S GOSPEL

This chapter examines Mark's Gospel to learn its nature and purpose, and also explains why it was written.

> *Given Matthew, it is hard to see why Mark was needed.*
> —G. M. Styler (1962, 231)

MARK IN RELATION TO THE MAJOR SYNOPTICS

Synoptic Interrelationships

The second leg of the hypothesis I am proposing is that of Markan Dependence. This is the explanation that Mark's Gospel was the third of the Synoptics to be written, and that this Gospel was dependent on both the Gospels of Matthew and Luke, both of which Mark used in his writing.

Here are the seven major hypotheses that have been proposed to explain Mark's relationship to the other two Synoptics.

1. The Complete Independence Hypothesis: the Synoptic Gospels were written independently, and there is no literary relationship between them.

2. The Successive Dependence Hypothesis: the Synoptics were written in the order Matthew–Mark–Luke; that is, their order in the New Testament canon also reflects their order of writing.

3. The Griesbach Hypothesis: the two Major Synoptics were written before Mark, and both were then used by him (Markan Posteriority). There are scholars who support the idea that Luke was first written (see chap. 10), though most who hold a Markan Posteriority position would regard Matthew as first written. (Griesbach himself did not deal in detail with this question, but simply placed Mark after the other two.)

4. The Two-Source Hypothesis: Mark was written first and was then used by both Matthew and Luke (Markan Priority); further, Matthew and Luke also used another source, Q (no longer extant), for sections of Gospel material that these two have in common.

5. The Farrer Hypothesis: Mark was written first (Markan Priority), but there is no Q. The material in common between Matthew and Luke (Q) is explained on the basis that Luke knew Matthew's Gospel.

6. The Multiple-Sources Hypothesis (with a number of variants): there were several other sources in addition to those we now know about, and there would have been various kinds of interaction between them. This means that the factors leading to our Synoptics were quite complex.

7. The Ur-Gospel Hypothesis: in early times there existed an original Gospel, called an Ur-Gospel, now lost, which our canonical Gospels drew upon and eventually replaced.

Thus between them these various hypotheses place Mark as written first, written second, or written third. To which of these does the evidence point? I set out the Synoptic data in chapter 4. I then examine the Markan Priority view in chapter 5, the Markan Posteriority (Griesbach) position in chapter 6, and the others in chapter 10. But the purpose of this chapter is to take a careful look at Mark's Gospel to see what light can be thrown on the evaluation of these hypotheses from this Gospel itself.

As we read it, there are numerous questions that come to mind. If Mark were written first, why does it leave out so much of Christ's life and teaching? We must keep in mind that according to this hypothesis Mark was the only Gospel then in existence. Does it set down everything that Mark knew? And indeed, we must ask the same question even more sharply if Mark were written second or third, using Matthew and Luke. If Mark had such a great deal of other material in front of him, why would he leave out so much?

This question must be asked—and answered—by advocates of each school of thought. And an explanation is called for not only for the pericopes that Mark does not include, but for what he does have that the others do not: mostly a host of small details and expansive comments added into his stories. Then we need to note also his theological perspective, which at times can be seen as different from the other Synoptics. Therefore at an early point in our consideration of the entire field of Synoptic inter-relationships—and particularly in regard to the Synoptic view that I am advocating—we need to examine what this Gospel is like and consider the question: Why Mark?

WHY MARK?

So the first question to consider is: If Matthew and Luke already existed in the church, why on earth would anyone want to produce a Gospel such as Mark is? As Styler famously said (1962, 231), "Given Matthew, it is hard to see why Mark was needed." A serious objection to the view that puts Mark third is that if Matthew and Luke already existed, Mark would be totally pointless. This is indeed a major objection that confronts any Markan Posteriority proponent.

But this objection is basically that proponents of a hypothesis have failed to think of a satisfactory reason for something happening. First of all, I would point out that our failure to understand *why* something happened does not in itself demonstrate that it *did not* happen. Whether or not Griesbach or Farmer—or I—can point to a convincing explanation of what we assert Mark did, Mark still may have done it, even if for reasons not now apparent. The possibility that Markan Posteriority is actually the fact of the matter ought not to stand or fall according to our ability to determine conclusively what would have led to the writing of Mark so many centuries ago.

However, we need to inquire into this matter further. The first thing to do, when seeking to understand why something was made as it is, is to analyze, "What is it designed to do? What is its purpose?" It is a fair guess to say that when you can see what it is designed to do, you will see why it was made.

What will be true in general of things around us will be true also of why books are written—including Mark's Gospel. So then, what do we see when we look at this Gospel? What is it seeking to do that is different from the other Gospels? Three things will stand out from a thoughtful consideration of what Mark contains:

First, Mark only contains the central part of the story of Christ found in the others. There are no stories of events before John the Baptist came and introduced the ministry of Jesus, and there is only a very brief summary of the resurrection appearances if you accept the long ending of Mark—and none at all, if you hold that Mark ends at 16:8. (For discussion of why these appearances would be left out, see chap. 7.)

Second, most of the teachings of Jesus are left out—no Sermon of the Mount or Sermon on the Plain, no mission charge, only a few parables (4 out of a total of 32 in Matthew and Luke between them—but including one that is unique to Mark), and none of Luke's central teaching section. Further (as I say), if the Gospel ends at 16:8, there are no resurrection appearances. There is only the briefest of references to the "young man" who brought the women the message of the risen Christ, and told the disciples to meet him in Galilee (16:5–7).

Third, it is a verifiable fact (chap. 4 gives the actual figures) that in the pericopes which Mark does have in common with the Major Synoptics, Mark is almost always the longest; indeed, in every instance it contains more information than we can glean from Matthew and Luke *put together*!

Why was such a Gospel as Mark ever written? That is, why was Mark's Gospel written, and why does it have the form that it does, containing some things and omitting others? While critics often pose this question as an objection to the Markan Posteriority view, it is a question that any Synoptic hypothesis must answer. The kernel of the problem that requires explanation is twofold. First, Mark lacks a very substantial amount of important material found in the Major Synoptics, so that while there is rather little in Mark that is not also included in either Matthew or Luke (or both), there are many sections of Matthew and Luke that have no parallel in Mark. Second, Mark is by far the shortest Gospel (661 verses compared with 1,067 in Matthew and 1,148 in Luke), but he gives more detail on the material he does cover than do Matthew and Luke.

The proponents of the Markan Priority Hypothesis consider this question as easily answered on the basis of their theory, but believe it poses a problem for the theory of Markan Posteriority. They ask, if Matthew and Luke were already in the hands of the church, why would a Gospel like Mark be written? And if someone *were* going to write a third Gospel with Matthew and Luke in front of him (as the Markan Posteriority position claims that Mark has done), then why would he omit so much material of such great interest and value? This question must have a convincing answer if the Markan Dependence Hypothesis (a version of Markan Posteriority) is to have any real credibility. But so also must an explanation of these matters be given for Markan Priority and for all other hypotheses.

The purpose of this chapter is to explore the nature of Mark's Gospel and from this to consider the reason it was written in terms of its own inner rationale. In other words, what does Mark's Gospel reveal about itself? If an answer can be found to this question, we can then ask what light this throws on the matter of its relationship to the Major Synoptics.

In making this investigation we must operate on the working assumption that Mark—and indeed the other Synoptists also—each accomplished what he set out to do. We have no grounds for thinking that Mark, or any of them, failed in what they intended, so that they produced a document that did not fulfill the purpose that they each had in view. Such a supposition would be completely gratuitous. It follows then that it is a legitimate exercise to ascertain the purpose of the Synoptists by examining what each author in fact did in handling the Jesus traditions that he had. As it proceeds, this investigation considers the nature of the relationship between the Synoptics as this affects their source materials. But initially we can explore a Gospel with any presuppositions about this matter firmly set aside, accepting that the author received the tradition of the church in some form and assessing how he handled what he received.

There is a limit to how far this investigation can legitimately be taken. David Wenham (1972, 10) alerts us concerning this with the well-founded warning that

> it is none the less salutary to be reminded that it will not always be possible for us to read the writers' minds in retrospect; and we shall be wise to speculate on questions of motive and situation only after we have reached conclusions on less subjective grounds. As H. Palmer says, "What we would do if we were the evangelists is just irrelevant. What they would do can be discovered only by inspecting what they did." [See N. H. Palmer, *The Logic of Gospel Criticism* (London: Macmillan, 1968), 121.]

As we inspect what Mark actually did when he wrote his Gospel, we can hope to gain some measure of insight into his purpose in writing.

MARK'S USE OF SOURCES

A fundamental factor in the situation is how much of the Jesus tradition Mark knew when he wrote his Gospel. What is the explanation for the considerable amount of this tradition that is lacking in Mark? There are only three possible explanations of this circumstance. First, Mark did not know any of the material that he omits; i.e., the reason for the omission is Mark's ignorance. Second, Mark did know the material that he omits but left it out by accident; i.e., the reason for the omission is Mark's carelessness. Third, Mark did know this material but decided not to use all of it; i.e., the reason for the omission is Mark's deliberate choice.

The first of these possible explanations appears to be held by a number of scholars. Thus A. Wright (1903, xi) affirms, "We may lay down this as a golden rule, that if a section is not found in an Evangelist, the presumption is that he was not acquainted with it." But he immediately qualifies this (ibid.): "Of course our rule is not absolute; it must be applied (like other rules) with discretion and with full allowance for the evidence in each case." It seems that some scholars would apply this "golden rule" to Mark. Thus R. P. Martin writes (1972, 113), "We see how Mark has arranged what small amount of didactic material he had at his disposal . . ."; and subsequently, concerning Mark 1:12–13, he states (ibid., 128), "Mark knows no explicit detail of the Temptation story such as Matthew and Luke record in full."

One of the most influential attacks on the hypotheses that Mark used Matthew's and/or Luke's Gospels was made by F. H. Woods (1886, 66–67) who says:

> We cannot reasonably account for the remarkable omissions which St. Mark must continually have made, such as the Birth and Childhood of our Lord, the details of the Temptation, the Sermon on the Mount, the full ministerial directions to the Apostles or the Seventy, and above all the accounts of our Lord's appearances after His Resurrection. All these are topics which would have become of increasing interest and importance as the Church grew; and it is extremely unlikely that we should find them in the earlier Gospel, and not in the later.

This argument indicates the assumption that if Mark had known these things he would have included them, so that the absence of this material from Mark demonstrates that he could not have known Matthew or Luke. This argument has been repeated by scholar after scholar. And similar reasoning lies behind Streeter's (1924, 158) well-known judgment that "only a lunatic" would leave out such material if he had Matthew's Gospel in front of him.

We ought to note what this line of reasoning implies. First, it is grounded upon a particular scholar's ability (or inability) to conjecture why a writer such as Mark may have chosen to omit certain material. As Woods (ibid.) puts it, "We cannot reasonably account for the remarkable omissions which St. Mark must continually have made." This argument is saying in effect, "Because I cannot think of a reason why a Gospel writer should do something, therefore he cannot have done it." Thus the measure of the critic's ability 19 centuries later to reconstruct a situation is made determinative as to whether or not something happened in the first century. This is a very subjective argument, if indeed it is reasonable to describe it as an argument at all.

Second, if we accept this argument, it would have repercussions beyond the initial question of Mark's knowledge of the Jesus tradition. It would in particular rule out the possibility that John wrote his Gospel after Matthew and Luke wrote theirs—and that John was aware of them—for he also omits most of these things, and many others as well. But who would assert that the date of John vis-à-vis Matthew and Luke should be settled on such a basis?

Third, if indeed Mark's Gospel contains nothing else because Mark knew nothing else, then this Gospel is a fortuitous, haphazard collection of pericopes: the incidents of Jesus' life that Mark *happened* to learn about—whether from Peter or other sources. If that is the case, then the question of the purpose of Mark's Gospel is solved at this point: Mark's purpose was to record all that he knew of the life and teaching of Jesus, and he did so, and all that our investigation will disclose is what traditions Mark had happened to hear about.

But this viewpoint would not receive very much agreement. Gould asks (1896, xii-xiii), "Is there any evidence that Mark's Gospel was in part a compilation?" and proceeds to assemble evidence to show the wide extent of Mark's knowledge of the Jesus traditions. Gould accepts the tradition of Peter standing behind Mark, but he takes it as beyond question that Mark also drew on other sources. He shows from Mark's treatment of the parables that he must have been familiar with a much larger collection, probably in the same source as that from which Matthew drew his parables, and he applies this also to Mark 13, reckoning the source of sections such as these as being the *logia* to which Papias refers. From this point in his Introduction onwards, Gould writes virtually as if Mark had access to as much as Matthew and Luke did, and as if Mark left out a great deal of material by a deliberate policy of exclusion (see ibid., xiii–xv). He says (xiii):

> Mark has a way of his own of handling his material. Whatever may be his reason, the fact is, that he dwells on the active life of our Lord, the period from the beginning of the Galilean ministry to the close of his natural life. The introduction to this career, including the ministry of John the Baptist, the baptism and the temptation, he narrates with characteristic brevity. But it is not brevity for the sake of brevity; it comes from a careful exclusion of everything not bearing directly on his purpose. The work of John the Baptist is introduced as the beginning of the glad tidings about Jesus Christ, and the material is selected which bears on this special purpose. The baptism is told as the inauguration of Christ into his office, and only the baptism, the descent of the Spirit, and the voice from heaven are narrated. And the temptation is merely noted in passing. All of these things have a value of their own, but they are evidently regarded by the writer as introductory to his theme, the active ministry of Jesus, and are abbreviated accordingly.

Significantly, Gould was as solidly committed to Markan Priority as Woods or Streeter—he begins his preface (p. v) with the statement that he writes his commentary specifically from this point of view. But he was also firmly of the opinion that what is omitted in Mark is not due to Mark's ignorance of that material but rather "comes from a careful exclusion of everything not bearing directly on his purpose."

It would in fact be true to say that the majority of scholars appear to hold the opinion (where they have referred to the matter) that Mark knew more than he recorded. If we may take this point as well founded, it follows that Mark's omission of material was either intentional (as Gould believes) or happened by accident.

It is difficult to exclude entirely the possibility that Mark had no particular reason for omitting something that he knew, but left it out inadvertently, perhaps because he just did not think of it at the time of writing. If such were the fact of the matter then in the nature of the case it is something that it is impossible to prove or disprove, because logical arguments do not enable us to establish an instance of bad memory. However, if the material in question is extensive enough and important enough (and this is certainly the situation with the teaching of Jesus that Mark's Gospel lacks), then it is very difficult to accept that the omission of *all* of this material was a sheer accident on Mark's part.

We are brought then to the entirely reasonable proposition (which has been accepted by adherents of all schools of thought on Gospel interrelationships) that, for reasons consequent to his purpose in writing his Gospel, Mark chose the material that he incorporated into his Gospel from the wider range of Jesus traditions that was available to him. And he deliberately decided against the inclusion of a number of lengthy sections of Jesus' teaching that have been included by one or both of the authors of the other two Synoptic Gospels. C. F. Evans (1968, 54) explains:

> What is involved in this particular selection of teaching by Mark? For while the view that Mark has here arranged all the teaching he was aware of cannot be disproved, it is, in the light of the evidence of the other gospels and of indications elsewhere in the New Testament of a strong catechetical interest, highly unlikely. Mark has presumably chosen to reproduce from a wider stock that particular teaching which served his purpose in writing.

D. E. Nineham agrees (1977a, 34), "Being familiar with a large number of separate stories about our Lord, St. Mark selected those which were specially relevant to the circumstances of his particular community, and he arranged and presented them so as to bring out the truths about Our Lord's life and work which he felt it most vital for his fellow-members in the community to grasp." Similarly, Moule (1962, 55) says, "When therefore John Mark (for example) sharpened his reed pen and dipped it in the ink to write, he had already behind him a considerable tradition of Christian speaking and possibly writing, by Peter and others—recognized patterns of argument and exhortation, of defense and attack, of instruction and challenge—from amongst which he might select his narrative material and his sayings."

The more extensive comments of Trocmé (1975, 39, 43–45, 85) on this point deserve our attention:

> If we think of tradition as an abundant source which fed all catechetical teaching and from which preaching drew part of its content, it becomes likely that the author of Mark knew many more sayings of Jesus of the three types in question than he used. His ignorance is particularly improbable when it comes to the pronouncements and sayings on the subject of the Law and of discipline, given the highly moral character the catechism always possessed, if we are to rely on appearances. It must therefore be supposed that the Evangelist made a choice among the sayings of Jesus known to him. As Matthew and Luke made no similar choice, one is led to ask what the significance of Mark's choice may have been. . . .
>
> Mark certainly used Palestinian traditions formed at a very early date for the few parables he records. . . . Our view is rather that these parables were known to Mark separately or, at most, that he had access to a general collection of them from which he made a strict selection. However this may be, it is striking that Mark should contain so few parables. It is most unlikely that he could have known only so few as ten, since Jesus often taught in parables and the early community based its moral teaching on the parables of our Lord. Whatever the form in which the tradition came to the author of Mark it must be supposed that he made a choice among all the *meshalim* known to him. We shall be enquiring later into the reasons for this selection, which is surprising in a man who must surely have had the greatest respect for all the teaching of Jesus. . . .
>
> The "sayings of Jesus" used by Mark were handed on to him separately. . . . The Evangelist's work consisted partly of arranging this heterogeneous material. . . . It is clear that the author of Mark made a certain selection among the "sayings of Jesus" handed on to him by tradition. . . . Towards [certain] kinds of saying deriving from tradition the Evangelist's attitude is one of reserve and he retails only a small number in his Gospel. This can be seen in the case of the scholastic discussions, the *logia*, the prophetic and apocalyptic utterances, the "canonical" pronouncements, perhaps the passages where the risen Christ speaks of himself, and certainly the parables. The points made [above] . . . are particularly important because they imply an active attitude on the part of the author of Mark to tradition, which was after all his only source for the words of Jesus. . . .
>
> [Mark's] appeal is made by three means: by choosing, among the material offered by tradition, the parts that would best serve his purpose; by adding to this a certain number of popular tales concerning John the Baptist and above all Jesus; and by placing the whole in an artificial framework designed to bring out its ecclesiological significance.

Some of the comments quoted above reveal the view of their respective authors that Mark is the first Gospel written, whereas this of course is the issue under investigation in the present study. But at this stage we are able to note the solid support that is given for the conclusion that Mark's Gospel does not reveal all the Jesus traditions that Mark knew, but that he chose what he put into his Gospel from the wider range of material he had in hand.

On the usual definition of parable, there are four in Mark: the sower (4:3–9), the growing seed (4:26–29), the mustard seed (4:30–32), and the wicked farmers (12:1–12). Using a wider definition of parable, Trocmé (in the above quotation) finds 10 parables in Mark; but on any definition, Mark has far fewer than Matthew or Luke.

In the traditional view of authorship, the author of the Second Gospel was John Mark, a young man whose home was the house where the Jerusalem church met (Acts 12:12–17), and a companion and associate of Barnabas, Paul, and Peter (Acts 12:25; 13:5,13; 15:37–39; Col 4:10; 2 Tim 4:11; Phlm 24; 1 Pet 5:13). It would be very difficult to establish a case that a person like John Mark was acquainted with only four (or 10) of the parables of Jesus out of the 32 that the Synoptics jointly contain—especially since Mark tells us that Jesus customarily taught in parables (4:33–34). Just as difficult to prove is the idea that Mark was completely ignorant of the Sermon on the Mount and all the other teachings of Jesus that he omits.

If the authorship of this Gospel is attributed not to John Mark but to a later writer in the church, then it will be more likely, not less, that such a person would know a greater amount of Jesus' teaching than is contained in the Second Gospel. Moreover, Mark constantly reveals a knowledge of events, sayings, and circumstances far wider than those he actually records, referring in passing to this event or that, recording extracts from a set of sayings, or a few examples of various teachings. Evans states the matter thus (ibid., 48–49):

> What is puzzling is that the sketch is not really filled out like that of the thaumaturge, and what for want of a better word we call the "teaching" of Jesus is limited in scope, and occupies a subordinate place in a narrative of mighty works. Mark may underline the activity of Jesus as preacher and teacher, but it is difficult to discover from his Gospel what exactly the preaching and teaching can have been. Thus Jesus is said (1:14–15) to proclaim in Galilee the gospel of God and to summon men to "believe in" the gospel (a use of "believe" without parallel in the New Testament), which gospel is later coupled with himself as that for which men are to be ready to forsake all possessions and to lay down their lives. But what this gospel is is not specified, except that it involves the near approach of the rule of God. He is then said to teach in synagogues with such authority as to be distinguished from the scribes, but no specimen is given of this teaching, and it is exemplified rather by exorcism. He is said to speak the word to the crowds (2:2), but no content is given to this word, and what follows is the healing of the paralytic.
>
> Again when an enormous mixed crowd gathers from all quarters of Palestine (3:7ff.) he is said to speak the word to them in many parables as they were able

to hear, and not to speak to them apart from parables, but all that is given is the somewhat meagre collection of parables in 4:1–23, which are in any case to be made intelligible only to disciples. Similarly when the Twelve are sent out on mission they are given elaborate instructions as to their behavior, but nothing is said of their message, except that it is a preaching of repentance; and when they report back what they had done and said, the reader knows that the former means exorcism and healing, but he has no inkling of what the latter might have been. Both the gospel and the teaching of Jesus seem to be assumed. What then is the teaching which is recorded, and what purpose is it intended to serve in relation to the whole book and to the gospel in Mark's own day?

Widen Evans's reference to teaching, in his last sentence, to include *all* that Mark has recorded, and this issue is the one to which we now direct our attention. If Mark's Gospel does represent a meaningful selection made from the whole range of tradition known to Mark, then examining what he has chosen to include sheds light on his purposes in writing.

AN OVERVIEW OF MARK'S GOSPEL

John appears suddenly in the wilderness preaching a baptism of repentance for the forgiveness of sins, and proclaiming the coming of the One mightier than he. Jesus appears suddenly and is baptized by John, and the voice from heaven testifies, "You are my beloved Son." Jesus begins preaching the gospel of God and saying, "The time is fulfilled, and the rule of God is at hand; repent and believe in the gospel." He calls four fishermen to follow him, and they do. He teaches with authority. He demonstrates his power over the unclean spirit in the man in the Capernaum synagogue, and the people are amazed. On this and subsequent occasions (1:24,34; 3:11; 5:7) the unclean spirits declare that Jesus is the Holy One of God, the Son of God, and he silences them and will not accept their testimony.

Jesus also demonstrates his power over illnesses of various kinds (Simon's mother-in-law, the sick at nightfall). After a time alone praying, Jesus sets out on a tour through Galilee, preaching and casting out demons. He demonstrates his power over leprosy, which causes such a furor that he can no longer enter a town openly. He shows his power to forgive sins when he cures a man with paralysis. This leads to the stirring of opposition from scribes who ask, "Who can forgive sins but God alone?" Thus at this early stage Mark confronts his readers with the necessity to think through their attitude about Jesus. The story raises this syllogism: "Only God can forgive sins; Jesus forgave sins; therefore Jesus is God." But the scribes did not accept the second proposition, so their syllogism was: "Jesus is not God; Jesus claims to forgive sins (which only God can do); therefore Jesus is a fraud and a blasphemer." But if that is the case, the scribes have to explain how he has power over illness and demons. (Their solution is recorded in Mark 3.) The response of the crowd, however, is less complex: "They were all amazed and glorified God."

The healing of the paralyzed man is the first of a series of conflict stories that now continues. Jesus sees Levi engaged in his work as a tax collector and calls him to follow. Levi responds and, as Jesus sits at a table in his house with many other tax collectors and sinners, the scribes and the Pharisees question the company he keeps. Next, Jesus is asked why he and his disciples are not fasting while others are. This is followed by two stories about conflict with the Pharisees over Sabbath observance: when the disciples pluck grain in the fields, and when Jesus heals the man with the withered hand in the synagogue. Each of these is a pronouncement story: in each case the opposition leads to pronouncements by Jesus that clarify the issues in question. Mark is thus introducing his readers to the inevitability of conflict—and choice—whenever Jesus confronts people. And Mark is giving his readers Jesus' answer to those who opposed him.

In thus moving quickly into the conflict stories, Mark omits material that occurs in Matthew and Luke at this stage. This includes the Sermon on the Mount *in toto*, the miraculous catch of fish, and the healing of two blind men and a dumb demoniac. (Matt 9:27–34 contains these "routine" healings not involving conflict, or pronouncements by Jesus, and they are covered by Mark's general references to Jesus' healing ministry in Galilee, as in 3:10, "For he had healed many." Matthew's reference to the Pharisees' comment about Jesus casting out demons by the prince of demons is taken up later by Mark in another context and covered fully.) This series of conflict stories climaxes in the conference of the Pharisees with the Herodians (Mark 3:6) that results in the unlikely alliance of religious scrupulosity and political expediency in planning to destroy Jesus. Thus at this early stage Mark records the rejection of Jesus by the hierarchy.

Jesus now withdraws from the towns, followed by multitudes whom he heals and teaches. He appoints the Twelve to be with him from that time onward, and (subsequently) to be sent out to preach and to cast out demons. Then he goes home to Capernaum and encounters further opposition: from his family and/or friends (the Greek is ambiguous) who say that he has gone mad, and from the scribes from Jerusalem who explain his power as deriving from the Prince of Demons. Mark records Jesus' answer to this (though incorporating only some of the material that Matthew and Luke include at this point), and follows this immediately with the visit of Jesus' mother and brothers and his pronouncement that "whoever does the will of God" is his true family.

Mark next records that Jesus taught the crowd many things in parables. And, of "many such parables" (4:33), Mark relates three, all connected with seeds growing. The first is the parable of the sower, which is the key to all parables (4:13) and for which Jesus gives the interpretation. The same seed falls on very different kinds of soil. This explains the varied responses to Jesus' ministry, the opposition he encounters, and the necessity for the hearer responding to the Word. Moreover it warns the hearers that "tribulation or persecution arises on account of the Word" (4:17). But a lamp is not lit to be hidden (4:21), and the kingdom of God is seed that *will* grow and produce a harvest (4:26–29). Mark's unique parable, added at this point, is an addendum to the parable of the sower: although response to the Word is varied, and although for a time the response may be hidden, nonetheless the harvest is certain. And although the seed may be small, the kingdom will grow up like the mustard seed "and becomes the greatest of all shrubs" (4:30–32). Mark's trilogy of seed parables shows that Jesus' word will triumph over all opposition, appearances to the contrary notwithstanding, and will be fruitful.

Mark's next sections show Jesus' power over the unclean spirit in Legion—the story shows this demon possession to have been a particularly serious case—followed by Jesus' power over an uncontrollable hemorrhage and then over death itself. After this his tour of Galilee brings him to his own country where he is met with cynicism and unbelief. He continues his tour "among the villages, teaching," and he briefly exhorts the Twelve and sends them out in pairs to preach that men should repent, to cast out demons, and to heal. Jesus' fame has reached Herod's ears, and many are the assessments given of Jesus. Herod's troubled conscience leads him to conclude "John, whom I beheaded, has been raised," and this is followed by the vivid story of the circumstances of John's beheading—doubtless intended by Mark to be proleptic of the fate that lies ahead for Jesus.

The Twelve then return to Jesus and he attempts to take them aside to a deserted place to rest, but the crowds gather and Jesus teaches them. This account leads into two miracle stories that show Jesus' power over creation (the multiplication of the loaves and fishes, and Jesus' walking on the sea) and a summary section about the healing of sick people.

Another conflict story follows about the ceremonial washing of hands, introducing Jesus' pronouncements about "the tradition of the elders" and the nature of defilement. He journeys to the region of Tyre and Sidon where he seeks to have a period in seclusion (7:24), and where he cures the

Syrophoenician's daughter. Then he heals a deaf man with a speech impediment, and again multiplies food to feed 4,000, which leads into a discussion of the leaven of the Pharisees and the two miracles of food multiplication.

In Bethsaida he heals a blind man and travels on to the village of Caesarea Philippi. Here Jesus asks for the assessment of his disciples concerning who he really is. Simon proclaims, "You are the Christ." This marks a transition point in Jesus' ministry to his disciples. Hitherto his aim was to bring them to a realization of who he is. Henceforth his purpose is to help them to see why he came. From this time "he began to teach them" (8:31) of his suffering, death, and resurrection, and to explain to them the full meaning and the cost of following him (8:34–38).

Shortly afterwards some measure of his divine glory shines through in the transfiguration, when the voice from the cloud testifies, "This is my beloved Son; listen to him." Jesus and the three disciples with him come down the mountain, discussing the meaning of the coming of Elijah, and then Jesus cures the demon-possessed boy whom his disciples could not cure.

Jesus now passes through Galilee, seeking to prevent anyone knowing his whereabouts, "for he was teaching his disciples" (9:31). He again explains about his forthcoming death and resurrection, but the disciples can only squabble over which of them is the greatest, so Jesus uses a child to provide a lesson in humility. Then they express their concern about another person who is speaking in Jesus' name, and Jesus points out that "he who is not against us is for us" and proceeds into a discussion about causing little ones to sin and about the seriousness of sin.

At this point in Jesus' life Matthew and particularly Luke record a large number of parables, other teachings, the healing of a cripple on the Sabbath, and various other incidents. Mark records none of this (save only two verses about salt in 9:49–50) but passes straight to the controversy with the Pharisees over divorce, followed by Jesus' blessing the children and challenging the rich young man concerning discipleship. The third prediction of the passion is followed by the request from James and John for places of honor in the kingdom and Jesus' teaching that he came to serve and to give his life a ransom for many—and thus also must it be among his disciples.

They journey towards Jerusalem and at Jericho Bartimaeus calls Jesus "Son of David" and Jesus heals his blindness. Then Jesus rides into Jerusalem on a colt, an implied claim to be the one of whom the prophet Zechariah wrote—which requires the Jews to consider again their attitude to him. But, as has also been the case in so many ways hitherto, the gesture is not explicit; it is a sign that can be recognized by the godly who are expecting the Messiah, and its meaning will be overlooked by the unthinking. The crowds shout with enthusiasm, but it is not clear how much they understand.

Perhaps this vagueness and uncertainty are best exemplified by Jesus' choice of the term "Son of Man" as a self-designation. Jesus' use of this term runs through all the Gospels and through every postulated source into which they may be subdivided. Volumes have been written on the meaning of the term, but there is general agreement on one point: it was ambiguous. Jesus' use of the term could hardly be said by his hearers to constitute a claim to be the Messiah, but it was a term that could be interpreted with Messianic overtones. Thus the hearer's own (perhaps changing and growing) assessment of the person of Jesus would structure his understanding of the term. Similarly, in each level of Jesus' ministry, he avoids making claims for himself and refuses to give any sign for the purpose of authenticating his deeds or words (see 8:11–12) or to give a clear answer to those who demand an explanation of his authority (see 11:27–33). Those who in faith seek for the truth will perceive and understand, but not "those outside"—the spiritually heedless and thoughtless and uncaring (see 4:10–20,33–34).

Thus begins the final week in Jerusalem. For the first three days Jesus engages in daily teaching in the temple. Mark records none of this except the confrontations and disputes: the cleansing of the temple; the question about authority, leading into the parable of the wicked farmers and the questions about paying taxes to Caesar; the resurrection; the great commandment; and Jesus' question about David's son, leading into his denunciation of the scribes. Also included are the cursing of the fig tree and the significance of the widow's gift. This period ends with the apocalyptic discourse, where Mark has much that is also included in Matthew (and to a lesser extent, Luke) about the coming of the Son of Man with great power and glory, and concludes with something of a summary of what he has not given in detail (13:33–37).

From here on, Mark records the Synoptic tradition quite fully: the conspiracy, the anointing at Bethany, the betrayal, preparation for the Passover, Jesus' word about the traitor, the bread and the cup, Gethsemane, Jesus' arrest, Peter's denials, Jesus on trial before Pilate that ends with his being condemned, mocked, crucified, dead, and buried. Then Mark states the fact of the resurrection and his Gospel concludes. (If one accepts the longer ending, Mark ends with a very short summary of Jesus' resurrection appearances.)

MARK'S THEMES: WHO JESUS IS

Mark's presentation of his material constantly confronts the reader from the very beginning with the question of who Jesus is. In his Gospel he shows how the crowds (1:27), the scribes (2:7), the disciples (4:41), the people of Jesus' own town (6:2), and the king himself (6:14) have to face this question. Even when not explicitly mentioned, this wondering and puzzling about him is implicit in the frequent response of amazement that Mark describes. This reaches its climax in the question that the high priest asks Jesus at the trial (14:61). What answers is Mark providing?

Jesus Is a Man

First of all, Mark shows quite clearly that Jesus is a man, a human being. Jesus became tired from the pressures of his ministry and needed to sleep (4:38), and he also sought rest from these pressures (6:31). He needed to eat, and managing to do this became a problem at times (3:20; 6:31). On one occasion Jesus' hunger is mentioned but the food he sought was not available (11:12). Sometimes Jesus could become exasperated at the obtuseness of the disciples (4:13; 8:21; 10:14), or filled with anger and sadness because of the hardness of heart of his opponents (3:5)—or his disciples (10:14). He needed to take precautions to avoid being crushed by the crowd (3:9; 4:1). Jesus could be surprised and saddened by unbelief (6:6), and he responded with love and concern to others (8:2; 10:14,21; 14:6). Jesus felt the full impact of the spiritual pain of the cross (14:33–42).

Jesus Is a Man with Supernatural Power

Second, Mark shows progressively that Jesus is more than an ordinary man. Mark's stories are selected to demonstrate Jesus' power: over nature, unclean spirits, fever, deafness, dumbness, blindness, hemorrhaging, paralysis, leprosy, deformity, and even death itself. Four times Mark refers in general terms to Jesus' ministry of healing the sick and casting out demons (1:32–34,39; 3:7–12; 6:53–56), and 13 times he records the details of a healing. In most cases Mark chose to record only one example of each kind of healing; the exceptions are that he records two cases of Jesus' curing blindness (8:22–26, the man at Bethsaida, which Mark alone gives; and 10:46–52, Bartimaeus at Jericho) and four cases of casting out a spirit (1:21–28, the man in the Capernaum synagogue; 5:1–20, "Legion" and the herd of swine; 7:24–30, the Syrophoenician's daughter; and 9:14–29, the boy with the dumb and deaf spirit).

Each of these cases exhibits special or unusual features that make it distinctive. Mark's stories contain more detail (sometimes much more) than their parallels in Matthew and/or Luke and are told in a much more vivid and dramatic way: comments that also apply to Mark's five stories of other miracles (4:35–41, stilling the storm; 6:30–44, feeding 5,000; 6:45–52, walking on the sea; 8:1–10, feeding 4,000; 11:20–26, withering the fig tree). With the possible exception of withering the fig tree, all Mark's miracle stories are told in such a way as to raise the question, "Who is this who does such deeds?" Mark is concerned to confront the reader with this question, and to provide the evidence that will lead him to reach a conclusion for himself.

All of what Mark records reveals that Jesus possesses some kind of supernatural power. The scribes attribute this to Beelzebul (Satan), but the response of Jesus shows how illogical this is (3:22–30). Mark's readers and hearers are therefore forced to consider the alternative: that Jesus' power comes from God. But this conclusion amounts to recognition and acceptance of the fact that the divine endorsement has thus been placed on Jesus' words and deeds, for God would not grant his divine power to one who was a blasphemer (2:7) and lawbreaker (3:2–4), as Jesus was accused of being. Initially, the reader/hearer is left by Mark to see and ponder for himself the significance of this.

Jesus Is a Prophet

Jesus teaches with an authority that astounds the crowds (1:22). Mark's account portrays him as constantly engaged in teaching and in performing a wide range of miracles, some of which are recorded in detail while others are summarized (1:34,39; 3:10; 6:56). These were the hallmarks of prophets of old. In 6:4 Jesus uses a proverb that refers to himself as a prophet. By the time Herod hears of Jesus, popular opinion has decided (6:14–15) that Jesus is John the Baptist raised from the dead, or maybe Elijah (a prophet who performed miracles and taught authoritatively and challenged the regime of his day), or at least a prophet like the prophets of old.

There were thus varieties of opinion about the details, but Jesus was recognized by all as being a prophet. Jesus asks his disciples (8:27), "Who do men say that I am?" and they repeat the popular opinions, "[Some say] John the Baptist; others, Elijah; still others, one of the prophets." By this stage, then, Jesus is identified with John the Baptist or Elijah (whose coming was prophesied in the Old Testament) or certainly he is a prophet of *some* kind. Thus Mark has brought his readers this far in their understanding of the person of Jesus of Nazareth.

Jesus Is the Messiah

Meanwhile the disciples themselves have been challenged to find an answer to the question they have asked, "Who is this man?" (4:41). They have been chosen to be with Jesus (3:14); they have been sent out with his authority to teach and with his power to heal (6:7–13). Jesus sought unsuccessfully to spend time with them on their own, after their return from their mission (6:30–32), but the persistence of the crowd in following him prevented that (6:33–34). So he led them out of the territory of Israel into the area of Caesarea Philippi (8:27–30) where he asks them what people were saying about his identity and then, "But who do you say that I am?"

Peter responds, "You are the Christ" (Gk. *Christos*, meaning "anointed One" and equivalent to the Hb. *Meshshiach*, "Messiah"). This means that Peter acknowledges Jesus as the Messiah, God's chosen and anointed One foretold in the Old Testament. This means more, much more, than merely a prophet. This is the One for whom all Israel waited. This is the One who was to fulfill the purposes of God as the Scriptures foretold. It is to be noted that in Mark this is the *first time*—apart from Mark's programmatic title for his book in 1:1—that this word "Messiah" ("Christ") has been used.

By contrast Matthew's Gospel uses *Christos* six times before the account of Peter's confession; and Luke's Gospel uses the word four times prior to Peter's confession. Matthew and Luke both reveal very early in their Gospels an acceptance of this designation for Jesus, and they presume a similar acceptance of it on the part of their readers. But Mark does not read back such an acceptance of Jesus as the Messiah into the record of events prior to Peter's confession. This was the event when Peter—and presumably the other disciples as well—were led to the point of recognizing that Jesus was the Messiah, and this is when Mark first reveals it to his readers. There is no indication that Mark has assumed earlier that his readers would already accept such a view of Jesus. But Mark has presented them with a record of the evidence that led the disciples to this conclusion, so perhaps Mark's readers can be encouraged by the record of that confession of faith to share in it.

We need to note, further, that Peter's confession is followed by two teachings from Jesus. First, he charged them to tell no one about it (8:30); and second, he began to teach them that the Son of Man must suffer many things" (8:31).

The implication here is that Jesus does not want this truth concerning himself to be indiscriminately and publicly proclaimed. Jesus himself had not stated it openly, and now that they have come to recognize and accept it, they must accept also this same restraint. In keeping with this policy, Mark continues to be very restrained in his own use of this designation for Jesus. The only place where Mark uses *Christos* of Jesus prior to his trial before the high priest is 9:41 ("whoever gives you a cup of water to drink because of My name, since you belong to the Messiah"), a saying of Jesus that may be taken as prophetic of the disciples' future ministry. (In 12:35 Jesus uses the term with its Old Testament connotation, "How can the scribes say that the Messiah is the son of David?" Then in 13:21–22 Jesus says that in the end times some will say, "Look, here is the Messiah," a warning about false "Christs" who will arise.)

In Mark 14:61–62 the high priest—presumably having heard accounts of who Jesus was believed by his disciples to be—asks him point-blank, "Are you the Messiah, the Son of the Blessed One?" and Jesus replies, "I am." In the only other occurrence of the word *Christos* in Mark, the title is thrown at Jesus on the cross in mockery by his enemies (15:32).

After the resurrection the title *Christos* is regularly used of Jesus: the word occurs about 25 times in Acts (depending on textual variants), approximately 450 times in the epistles (most if not all of these antedate the writing of Mark's Gospel), and 8 times in Revelation. But Mark does not anachronistically read this common usage back into the life of Jesus in his Gospel, for at that time it was *not* a common term for Jesus. Matthew and Luke similarly allow themselves a very limited use of the term *Christos* for Jesus and thus to a considerable extent they follow a policy closely similar to Mark's, but they are willing, as we have noted above, to accept the use of this designation for Jesus by using it themselves editorially (Matt 1:1,16,17,18) and by recording its use by participants in the narrative (Luke 2:11,26): for Matthew and Luke presume that this designation for Jesus is one that their readers will accept. John's Gospel has no direct parallel to Peter's confession, but the term *Christos* does refer to Jesus in 1:17 editorially and in 1:41 by a participant in the narrative (Andrew).

Once the disciples acknowledged Jesus' messiahship, he began to teach them of his coming passion, death, and resurrection—that is, what kind of Messiah he was and what his messiahship meant. Popular expectations of the Messiah looked for a conquering leader to bring military and political victory to Israel. Jesus had before him the formidable task of correcting his disciples' misunderstanding of this matter. At times they failed to understand (Mark 8:31–33; 9:32). Luke explains that after the resurrection the lesson still needed to be repeated—they had thought he was the one to redeem Israel, but now (i.e., after the crucifixion) they refer to him only as a prophet (24:19–21). Jesus explains again the nature of his messiahship

(24:46), but their question on the eve of the ascension (Acts 1:6) suggests that their previous attitudes still persisted. It is likely that here we have the key to why Jesus' messiahship was to be kept secret by the disciples: if this was the measure of *their* understanding of what his messiahship meant, the misunderstanding of Jesus' mission by friends and enemies alike would have been enormous if he had publicly claimed or accepted the designation "Messiah" during the course of his ministry.

Jesus Is the Son of God

There is one other designation for Jesus that is significant in Mark: Son of God. Martin (1972, 99) considers this concept to be substantially more important in Mark than that of Messiah: "At the opposite end of the scale of interest the appellative 'Son of God' carries a much more central significance in this Gospel." Without being persuaded by Martin's low estimation of the importance of *Christos* in Mark, we can agree with his assessment of the significance of "Son of God." It is surprising therefore to find the two designations being regarded by some scholars as identical. For example, Trocmé (1963, 148) says, "As for the title υἱὸς τοῦ θεοῦ, used seven or eight times by Mark, it comes closer to the Evangelist's central ideas. . . . But this title . . . is still for Mark simply a sort of less hermetic variant of the word Χριστός."

The problem here is that the post-resurrection church applied both titles, "Messiah" (*Christ*) and "Son of God," to Jesus without distinction, for both were recognized as describing him, and they appear to be used without any specific difference or variance in shades of meaning. Thus in Acts 8:20–22, "And in the synagogues immediately [Saul] proclaimed Jesus, saying, 'He is the Son of God'. . . . But Saul . . . confounded the Jews who lived in Damascus by proving that Jesus was the Christ."

Both titles are often applied to Jesus together in the Epistles. Such an application of the title "Son of God" to Jesus is an ascription of deity to him and part of the overall doctrine of the Trinity. But this doctrine was not fully developed in the pages of the New Testament and was unknown in Old Testament times, though occasionally anticipated in passages that we can now, with hindsight, interpret from a trinitarian perspective (e.g., Isa 9:6; 42:1; 48:16).

In consequence it needs to be emphasized that when the people of God were looking for the coming of the Messiah, they were *not* expecting that that Messiah would be deity, the Son of God. The nation called God "Father" (Isa 64:8) and Israel was God's "son" (Exod 4:22f.; Hos 11:1: "Out of Egypt I called my son"), and this concept was fulfilled in a special and unique sense in Jesus (Matt 2:15 applies Hos 11:1 to Jesus). The son of King David would be the son of God (2 Sam 7:14)—but that this refers initially to the descendants of David in the kingly line and not directly to Jesus is shown by the words that follow: "When he commits iniquity." The original context for Psalm 2 was the coronation of the Davidic king: "I have set my king on Zion, my holy hill. . . . You are my son, today I have begotten you" (vv. 6,7), but in the New Testament both 2 Sam 7:14 and Ps 2:7 are applied to Jesus in Heb 1:5 (Acts 13:33 and Heb 5:5 also apply Ps 2:7 to him). But in the time of Jesus' ministry, people had no concept that the divine Son of God would come to earth.

Thus for them to recognize Jesus as Messiah is *not* the same thing as recognizing him as Son of God. Understanding that Jesus is not only Messiah but also Son of God would happen in people's minds only gradually. Moreover, the meaning of the term is not self-evidently clear. What would a person in the time of Jesus' earthly life have thought it to mean? What would Mark's audience have made of the term? John 1:34 tells us that John the Baptist bore witness that Jesus is the Son of God. Nathanael accepts that Jesus is the Son of God (John 1:49). Would John's hearers, and Nathanael, have understood by this what the early church later came to accept it to mean?

Mark's Gospel uses the term "Son of God" (or simply "Son") in a very significant way. This can best be seen if we compare the passages in the Synoptics in which it occurs.

MATTHEW	MARK	LUKE
	1:1 The beginning of the gospel of Jesus Christ, Son of God.	
		1:32 The child to be born will be called holy, the Son of God.
2:15 Out of Egypt have I called my Son.		
3:17 This is my beloved Son, with whom I am well pleased.	1:11 You are my beloved Son; with you I am well pleased.	3:22 You are my beloved Son; with you I am well pleased.
4:3 If you are the Son of God . . .		4:3 If you are the Son of God . . .
4:6 If you are the Son of God . . .		4:9 If you are the Son of God . . .
	1:24 You are the Holy One of God.	4:34 You are the Holy One of God.
	1:34 and cast out many demons and he would not permit the demons to speak, because they knew him.	4:41 and demons also came out of many crying, "You are the Son of God." But he rebuked them and would not allow them to speak, because they knew that he was the Christ.
	3:11 You are the Son of God	
8:29 O Son of God	5:7 Jesus, Son of the Most High God	8:28 Jesus, Son of the Most High God
11:27 and no one knows the Son except the Father, and no one knows the Father except the Son and any one to whom the Son chooses to reveal him.		10:22 and no one knows who the Son is except the Father, or who the Father is except the Son and any one to whom the Son chooses to reveal him.
14:33 Truly you are the Son of God	6:51 they were utterly astounded	
16:16 You are the Christ, the Son of the living God.	8:29 You are the Christ.	9:20 The Christ of God.

MATTHEW	MARK	LUKE
17:5 This is my beloved Son, with whom I am well pleased; listen to him.	9:7 This is my beloved Son; listen to him.	9:35 This is my Son, my Chosen; listen to him.
21:37 he sent his son to them	12:6 a beloved son—he sent him	20:13 I will send my beloved son
24:36 nor the Son	13:32 nor the Son	
26:63 Tell us if you are the Christ, the Son of God.	14:61 Are you the Christ, the Son of the Blessed?	22:67 If you are the Christ, tell us. 22:70 Are you the Son of God, then?
26:64 Jesus said to him, "You have said so."	14:62 And Jesus said, "I am."	And he said to them, "You say that I am."
27:54 Truly, this was the Son of God!	15:39 Truly this man was the Son of God!	23:47 Certainly this man was innocent!

Of the Matthean and Lukan references to Jesus as "the Son of God" (or "the Son"), Mark parallels the following: the two occasions when the voice of God acknowledges him as Son (at Jesus' baptism and the transfiguration); two occasions when demons call him "Son of God" and are immediately silenced (3:11; 5:7; cf. 1:24,34); two occasions when Jesus refers to himself as the Son (one of them by implication in a parable); and two occasions when the term appears on the lips of men (the high priest's question and the centurion's affirmation). Mark also uses the term in his programmic title (if we accept the longer reading in 1:1).

In the other instances the tradition that occurs in Matthew and Luke is either absent in Mark, abbreviated, or has a different wording. Thus the declaration at the baptism is immediately followed by the temptation which in Matthew and Luke centers on an iterated "If you are the Son of God," in which the truth of the Father's declaration is called into question by Satan. But Mark gives a greatly shortened version of the temptation that omits this. The worshipful response of the disciples to Jesus' walking to them across the water in the storm, "Truly you are the Son of God" (Matt 14:33) is paralleled in Mark 6:51, "And they were utterly astounded." Peter's confession "You are the Christ, the Son of the living God" (Matt 16:16) appears only as "You are the Christ" in Mark 8:29. The other passages in which the term occurs in Matthew and Luke are absent in Mark.

From the Markan Priority perspective the absence from Mark of any particular occurrence of the term "Son of God" can easily be explained on the basis that the occurrence in question was not known to Mark: it is an editorial comment, it was found in Q or the Synoptist's special source, and thus was not accessible to Mark. An explanation along these lines is less convincing for Matt 14:33//Mark 6:51: why would Matthew want to *insert* such a saying at *this* point (i.e., prior to Peter's confession) if it were not in his source? A similar problem exists with Peter's confession. Where did Matthew get the words "the Son of the living God" to insert at 16:16? Are we compelled to conclude that they derive from the later church, which had invented them, so that they are unauthentic?

Moreover, the number of instances where the term "Son (of God)" is absent in Mark should give us pause. Can it be that Mark knew of *none* of them from church tradition? If Peter's "the Son of the living God" is authentic, how could Mark fail to be aware of it?! Now, if we recognize that it is reasonable to believe that Mark may well have known of one or more of these occurrences of the term, then we are brought to conclude that the absence of that term from his account at that point is the result of *choice* and not *ignorance*, and we must consider the question of a policy on Mark's part.

The voice of the Father speaks at Jesus' baptism, but how many heard this testimony? Mark records it and passes on without comment, but in Matthew and Luke this issue becomes the crux of Jesus' controversy with the Devil in the temptation narrative: "If you *are* the Son of God . . ." Subsequently, demons speak and are silenced. How much value can we place on the comments of a demon? The voice of the Father speaks again at Jesus' transfiguration, but it was heard only by Peter, James, and John. Again, Mark records it and passes on without comment. Neither the reference to the "beloved son" in the parable nor Jesus' "nor the Son" in the Olivet Discourse is fully clear in the nature of its identificatory reference to the person of Jesus, and in any case they both come at the end, during Passion Week.

If we look at the whole of Mark's Gospel, and what Mark is seeking to achieve by what he includes, we can recognize that his purpose is to reveal who Jesus *is* through the record of what he *did*. Jesus is seen progressively as a man, as more than a man, as the possessor of power from God, as a prophet, and then as the Messiah. But Mark's ultimate purpose is to lead his readers beyond even this. As he arouses in his readers the question "Who is this man?", he gives enigmatic hints about the ultimate answer. But—just as Jesus himself did—he leaves people to weigh and meditate on the evidence and reach the conclusion for themselves.

The brief mention of the voice from heaven and the quickly silenced testimony of demons (shown as being part of the response evinced from them by the mere presence of Jesus) are aspects of the evidence. But there is more.

Mark begins his narrative (after his title in 1:1) with an Old Testament citation that also occurs in Matthew and Luke but in a later context (Matt 11:10//Luke 7:27), prefixing this to the quotation from Isaiah with which Matthew and Luke begin the pericope about John the Baptist. The result is the juxtaposition, unique to Mark, of "I send my messenger before your face, who shall prepare your way," and "Prepare the way of the Lord." The "messenger" is clearly John the Baptist. The one for whom he prepares the way is Jesus. But in Mark's juxtaposed verses, the one whose way is to be prepared is the Lord. Thus there is an implication (nothing more, but clearer in Mark than in Matthew and Luke) that identifies "Jesus" as "the Lord."

A similar implication arises in the healing of the paralyzed man. The scribes ask, "Who can forgive sins but God alone?" Jesus claims to forgive sins and to authenticate this by the man's visible healing. The implied term in this syllogism is that God would not grant him the power to perform this miracle if it were to be used to support a blasphemous statement. This is something that the people would have accepted. But the logic of the situation, if followed through to the end, leads to the identification of "Jesus" with "God."

Again the question of Jesus' identity arises with the ambiguous but thought-provoking statement, "The Son of Man is Lord even of the Sabbath" (Mark 2:28). Then Mark 5:19–20 records that Jesus charged the healed man to tell his family circle and friends "how much the Lord has done for you," and the man began to proclaim "how much Jesus had done for him." Again the wording and the juxtaposition sets up the implication (nothing more) that identifies "Jesus" as "Lord"—and "Lord" in this context has the fuller meaning "God" (cf. Luke 8:39).

On Palm Sunday Jesus' words in all three Synoptics are, "The Lord has need of it/them" (Matt 21:3//Mark 11:3//Luke 19:31). Now in Matthew and Luke "Lord" here could refer to Jesus, or it could mean God in the sense, "The animal is needed for something connected with God's service." But only Mark follows it with the words "and will send it back here immediately," which identifies "the Lord" with Jesus.

Thus in Mark's Gospel, up to Jesus' trial, Mark provides the progressive revelation of who Jesus is, leading to the acceptance of him by the disciples as Messiah, followed by the repeated teaching by Jesus about what this will mean. But *no human being* has used the term "Son of God" in reference to Jesus, though there are several hints in the record that raise the implication of Jesus' deity. The climax comes in the events of the crucifixion. The high priest asks point-blank, "Are you the Christ, the Son of the Blessed [i.e., the Son of God]?" and Jesus gives an equally straightforward answer, "I am" (compare the periphrastic wording of the answers in Matthew's and Luke's parallels in the table above). He is thereupon condemned to death for blasphemy. At his death the centurion says, "Truly this man was the Son of God"—a confession of faith defective to the extent that it uses the past tense "was." But then comes resurrection Sunday and the news, "Do not be amazed; you seek Jesus of Nazareth, who was crucified. He has risen" (16:6).

Mark has reached his goal. His purpose was to reveal the person of Jesus. The title of his book (1:1) gives something of a program of where he intends to go: "The beginning of the good news of Jesus Christ, Son of God." Thereafter, assuming nothing initially on the part of the reader, he progressively leads to a higher and higher view of the person of Jesus, until the high priest asks the crucial question that goes to the very heart of the matter. Without hesitation or equivocation Jesus replies "I am." He is thereupon rejected as Messiah and Son of God by the high priest of Israel and his associates, but affirmed as Son of God by an unnamed nonentity, a Gentile and a member of the occupying Roman forces. Finally, the story of Jesus climaxes in the resurrection.

This is (if one wishes to use the term) the "Messianic Secret" in Mark: the fullness of the revelation of who Jesus is. Writing in the light of and from the perspective of the post-resurrection faith of the church, Mark carefully avoids allowing that perspective to intrude too early into his account. Rather, he shows Jesus as gradually allowing people to recognize more and more who he was, and he leads his readers along the same path. Thus he curtails the temptation narrative when Jesus vindicates his Sonship before Satan, omits early references to Jesus as Son of God, and uses only the first part of Peter's confession because to record Peter saying at that point "the Son of the living God" would be premature in relation to where Mark has by that time brought his readers.

MARK'S THEMES: CONFLICT AND CHOICE

From a very early point in Mark's Gospel (the beginning of chap. 2), Jesus is shown encountering opposition: concerning his claim to forgive sin, his willingness to eat with tax collectors and sinners, his disciples' (and his own) failure to fast when others did, his disciples' plucking grain on the Sabbath, and his healing on the Sabbath. This culminates in the Pharisees' conferring with the Herodians to plan "how to destroy him" (3:6). Next, he encounters opposition from his own family who want to seize him because he is mad (3:21) and who come seeking him (3:31–35). The scribes now brand him as an emissary of Satan, whose deeds are performed by Satan's power (3:22). The people of "his own country" do not believe in him (6:1–6). When his disciples omit the ritual washing before eating, he is challenged again by the Pharisees and scribes (7:1–23). They argue with him, demanding a sign (8:11–12), and he warns his disciples against them (8:13–22).

In an endeavor to trap him, various groups press him with test questions about divorce (10:2), about his authority (11:28), about paying taxes to Caesar (12:13–15), and about the resurrection (12:18–23). He again warns about the scribes (12:38–40). His enemies are seeking how to accomplish his death (14:1–2) when Judas provides them with a way (14:10–11), and Jesus is duly arrested (14:43–49), tried, condemned, crucified, and buried (15:1–47).

Mark builds up a picture of who Jesus is and shows what he is doing in the world, and he demonstrates how Jesus' presence confronts mankind with a moral dilemma and forces him to make a choice: he is *for* Jesus, or *against* him. The whole thrust of Mark's Gospel, and the manner of its arrangement and presentation, is aimed at facing the reader with the same choice, and thus bringing him to a point of decision and response. The final scenes are quite ironic in this regard; all the influential groups within Jewry combine their skills in an endeavor to trap Jesus in his words and procure his downfall, which they accomplish with the assistance of a traitor from the inner circle. Their final judgment is that he is a blasphemer (14:64), but his executioner, a Roman centurion, is led to exclaim, "Truly this man was the Son of God" (15:39).

The opposition to Jesus is crowned with success and he is (they think) destroyed. But he does not remain dead, and an angel in the empty tomb proclaims the good news, "He has been resurrected! He is not here!" (16:6–7).

WHAT MARK DOES NOT CONTAIN

After our survey of Mark's content and major themes, it is now appropriate to consider what Mark does not contain; that is to say, what part of the Synoptic tradition we would *not* have if Mark were the only one of the Synoptics to come down to us. What we would lack could be briefly stated as follows:

1. all of the birth and infancy stories, including the genealogies;

2. all of John the Baptist's teachings (except for his call to repentance and half of his testimony to the Mightier Coming One);
3. all of Jesus' teachings in the Sermon on the Mount and Luke's equivalents;
4. approximately half of Jesus' charge to the Twelve in Matthew, and Luke's equivalents;
5. approximately half of the Beelzebul controversy as Matthew gives it;
6. five out of the seven parables in Matthew 13;
7. all of the travel narrative in Luke, including a great deal of parabolic and general teaching, some with equivalents in Matthew;
8. most of the denunciations of the scribes and Pharisees;
9. approximately two-thirds of the Olivet Discourse in Matthew;
10. all of Christ's resurrection appearances (or just a brief summary, if the longer ending of Mark is accepted);
11. apart from those already covered above, a considerable number of other parables given on various occasions—Mark gives only four of 32 parables recorded in the Synoptics;
12. ten miracles of healing (two blind men, a dumb demoniac, the centurion's servant, raising the widow's son, a blind and dumb demoniac, a crippled woman, a man with dropsy, ten lepers, the blind and the lame in the temple on Palm Sunday, the severed ear) and two other miracles (the coin in the fish's mouth, the miraculous catch of fish);
13. sundry other teachings and short sayings (e.g., the sinning brother);
14. a number of incidents, some of which are independent and some attached to pericopes that *are* found in Mark—the main ones being the temptations, the Baptist's question and Jesus' testimony to John, the ministering women, Zacchaeus, Jesus before Herod, the death of Judas, on the way to the cross, the two thieves on the cross, the guard at the tomb, and the false report of the theft of Jesus' body.

These incidents and teachings not recorded could be further analyzed as:

1. happenings prior to the baptism of Jesus and after his rising from the dead;
2. a number of miracles, all of which are paralleled in Mark by miracles of the same general kind;

3. a number of incidents that are either paralleled in Mark by incidents of a similar general kind, and/or that do not in themselves add greatly to an overall picture of the person and work of Jesus;
4. most significantly, the greater part of the Synoptic record of the teachings of Jesus.

The earlier question—What would we have and what would we be without, if of the Synoptics we had only Mark?—could be answered by this summary:

If we had only Mark, we would have the story of Jesus from his baptism to his resurrection, including detailed stories of each kind of miracle he performed and (usually) an elucidation of its significance and the response it evinced, and a detailed account of Jesus' predictions of his passion and also of the passion events themselves. In addition we would have a very small record of his sayings and teachings, almost all of these being (1) connected with conflict situations and/or (2) incidents in which people were confronted with the necessity of deciding their response to him and/or (3) discussions of the various responses to his word, challenges to a right response, and warnings about a wrong response (including eschatological teaching).

On the other hand, if we had only Mark we would be without the infancy and post-resurrection narratives, a number of miracles and other incidents that in themselves add little to the picture of the person of Jesus that is given in Mark, and in particular we would be without the substantial bulk of the sayings and teachings of Jesus.

THE NATURE AND PURPOSE OF MARK'S GOSPEL

What can we conclude from our survey of and assessment of what Mark's Gospel does and does not contain? Initially, it invites comparison with the message that was proclaimed by the early church in its evangelism.

In the book of Acts and in the Epistles we are able to find considerable evidence concerning the content of this message that the early church preached to those outside its ranks. The most significant and detailed consideration of this continues to be C. H. Dodd's *The Apostolic Preaching and Its Developments* (1936). He distinguishes the *kerygma*, the apostolic presentation of the Christian message to outsiders, from the *didache*, the teaching within the church for those who are Christians. He then analyzes the speeches of Acts and Paul's statements of the *kerygma* in his epistles, and he draws attention to the common elements in them and the overall pattern of the apostolic *kerygma* that is presented.

This pattern may best be seen in Peter's speech in Acts 10:36–43 where all the elements are included (despite Peter's being interrupted before concluding what he had to say; see v. 44).

F. F. Bruce (1951, 224) says of this speech, "The summary of Peter's address (10:36–43) gives the apostolic Kerygma in a nutshell. . . . The scope of the Kerygma, as outlined here and elsewhere, corresponds to that of Mk." Dodd (56) says of Acts 10:36–43, "The passage is therefore offered explicitly as a form of apostolic preaching. . . . We may perhaps take it that the speech before Cornelius represents the form of *kerygma* used by the primitive church in its earliest approaches to a wider public." This *kerygma* corresponds exactly with Mark's Gospel. Dodd spends several pages (104–17) showing this correspondence, from which we may note (104, 106):

> We can trace in the Gospel according to Mark a connecting thread running through much of the narrative, which has some similarity to the brief summary of the Story of Jesus in Acts 10 and 13, and may be regarded as an expanded form of what we may call the historical section of the *kerygma*. . . . Mark therefore conceived himself as writing a form of *kerygma*, and that his Gospel is in fact a rendering of the Apostolic preaching will become clear from an analysis of the book itself.

Dodd then gives his analysis of Mark in relation to the *kerygma* (117): "Mark then proceeded, according to the formula of the *kerygma* in 1 Cor 15, to record how Christ was buried, and rose again the third day according to the Scriptures. But unfortunately only a fragment of his resurrection narrative has survived; enough, however, to show what the climax of the Gospel was. The story of the saving facts is complete." Dodd (117, 118, 121, 122, 123) then adds (for he accepts Markan priority) that

> the scheme of Gospel writing laid down by Mark became the model on which the other canonical Gospels were composed. We discern, however, in Matthew and Luke a certain departure from the original perspective and emphasis of the *kerygma*. . . . Matthew is, in fact, no longer in the pure sense a "Gospel". It combines *kerygma* with *didache*, and if we regard the book as a whole, the element of *didache* predominates. . . . In Luke the change is more subtle. . . . But again it represents a certain modification of the original perspective.

That is to say, Mark may be recognized as "pure" *kerygma*, while Matthew and Luke are combinations of *kerygma* and *didache*.

C. F. D. Moule (1962, 92) draws attention to the fact that Mark gives a vibrant presentation of the *kerygma* (as distinct from the *didache*) of the early church for proclamation to the "outsider": "Mark is the apostolic *kerygma*—Old Testament evidence and all—built up into a vivid, narrative form." Moule also states (1967, 105), "Then what of Mark? The most significant fact about it, for the present enquiry, is simply its contents, which are not only within the framework of the *kerygma*, but are themselves in the nature of *kerygma*, and *kerygma* is primarily the 'propaedeutic' for the outsider. . . . it is the *preaching* that is primarily the content of Mark: the *kerygma* for unbelievers."

We recognize the nature of Mark: it is the detailed presentation of the *kerygma* of the early church, "the *kerygma* for unbelievers," as Moule calls it. It "proclaims the gospel, peace by Jesus the Messiah—he is Lord of all" (Acts 10:36), and it progressively unfolds the picture of Jesus as Messiah and Son of God, and shows how the prophets bear witness to him, so that the reader may "repent, and believe in the gospel" (Mark 1:15), for "everyone who believes in him receives forgiveness of sins through his name" (Acts 10:43).

Why are the various contents of Mark included in his Gospel? Because they are part of the *kerygma*. Even the lengthy teaching sections of Mark—the parables (chap. 4) and the Olivet Discourse (chap. 13)—are related to aspects of the *kerygma*: the question of response to the message, and the promise of Jesus' return in glory as Judge.

Why are other parts of the Synoptic tradition not included in Mark? Because they are not part of the *kerygma*, or else they are already represented in Mark by similar material.

Mark's fundamental method of procedure was to include every story from Matthew and Luke about what Jesus did, especially if both the Major Synoptics contained it. However, if Matthew and Luke contain different stories of the same kind (e.g., the call of the first disciples) or variant accounts of the same event (e.g., the rejection at Nazareth) he would include one and ignore the other. The only narratives included by both Matthew and Luke and lacking in Mark are the temptation (but Mark gives a summary), the centurion's servant healed, the (blind and) dumb demoniac healed, and John the Baptist's question and Jesus' response.

All the other material common to Matthew and Luke and omitted by Mark consist of shorter sayings and longer blocks of teaching by Jesus. And (except for some selected teaching sections concerned with redemption or eschatology) it was not Mark's purpose to include Jesus' teachings.

The reason for the curtailment of the temptation narrative has been suggested above; the reason for the omission of the centurion's servant healed and the double pericope about John the Baptist's question are discussed in chapter 9 when we look at the framework of, and the sequence of pericopes in, Mark's Gospel.

The very short story of the man with a dumb spirit (Matt 12:22–23//Luke 11:14) is superfluous because Mark gives the very long story of the healing of a boy with a dumb spirit (9:14–29). It is as if Mark chose to include from Matthew and Luke one story of each major class of healing performed by Jesus—fever, deafness, dumbness, blindness, hemorrhage, paralysis, leprosy, deformity, raising of the dead, four exorcisms of very different kinds, with a further story of his own about a blind man (8:22–26) and four general summaries referring to Jesus' other miracles of healing—providing 17 descriptions of healings altogether.

Our careful and detailed inquiry into the contents of Mark has brought us to the point of recognizing that Mark's use of his sources (whatever they were), what his Gospel contains and does not contain, his themes of who Jesus is, and conflict and choice, and a comparison with the preaching of the early church, all point to his Gospel being a record of the church's *kerygma*.

Why is this significant? The conclusion we have reached concerning Mark's purpose—from an examination of the material that he has chosen to include, and its arrangement and wording—is that Mark did not write for the church at all. That is, not, as it were, for the church's *internal use*. He produced a book for the church's *external use*. He put a sourcebook for the church's *kerygma* into the hands of the church's evangelists.

When the church proclaimed, "Believe in the Lord Jesus Christ" and the interested outsider answered, "Who is he, that I should believe in him?" Christians needed to be able to give a clear and accurate answer. Many of those who were preaching the message of Jesus Christ would not themselves have known or heard him in the flesh. Large numbers of the Christians who were witnessing and preaching would be only semiliterate or quite illiterate. How could they respond when asked this question?

Mark perceived this need, and wrote to meet it. Our study has led us to see that he went through the Jesus traditions to which he had access and drew from them the material that expressed the *kerygma* of the church and that Christians could use to answer the questions about Jesus that would be asked by outsiders and new converts.

THE RELEVANCE OF THIS CONCLUSION FOR SYNOPTIC HYPOTHESES

This investigation has been conducted from a neutral stance in relation to Synoptic hypotheses. The conclusion does not clearly select one hypothesis and eliminate another. For example, it is completely compatible with Markan Priority, so that it could be said, "Mark, in accordance with his purpose (as shown above), went through the sources available to him, selected what he considered appropriate to that purpose, and wrote his Gospel. It was later used by Matthew and Luke as the nucleus of the Gospels that they were writing for the church and into which they each inserted their *didache* material."

However, it is of particular interest to assess our conclusion as to the purpose of Mark with regard to its implications for the Markan Dependence Hypothesis, because one of the major objections to that theory is that if Matthew and Luke already existed there would be no point for someone to write a Gospel like Mark.

What follows is an examination of how the writing of Mark could be explained, given the existence of Matthew and Luke. This in no sense *proves* or could prove Markan Dependence; it is not even an argument for that view. It is an attempt to assess the strength of the case that can be made to justify the writing of Mark as the third Gospel.

We start then with the existence of the Gospels of Matthew and Luke. These are Gospels written for and used in the churches—Matthew primarily for the Jewish church and Luke for Gentile Christians, though the boundaries of their use were no doubt flexible. These Gospels, together with oral tradition, were being drawn upon for the proclamation of the *kerygma* and the instruction of converts. But as the church spreads and advances, John Mark perceives the need for a specific preaching tool for use by those who are seeking to win outsiders to Jesus Christ.

The Gospels of Matthew and Luke contain the needed *kerygma* material, but they contain a great deal of other material as well. Moreover, each has relevant pericopes that the other does not. To make copies of *both* Gospels is a lengthy and expensive business. To make a copy even of one is to copy more than is required for the kerygma. The church needed a book containing the *kerygma*, extracted from both Matthew and Luke. This was considerably cheaper to produce, and considerably easier to use.

Barclay (1975, 25) examined the cost of books in the early Christian centuries and concluded that "a properly scribed copy of the four gospels would cost the equivalent of a craftsman's wages for about six weeks." On the basis of Barclay's figures, a copy of Mark's Gospel would cost the equivalent of just over a week's wages for a craftsman—still a substantial financial commitment. But this was considerably less than a copy of Matthew plus Luke (a combined length of approximately three and a half times that of Mark), which works out as four to five weeks' wages. To consider the significance of these figures, take the average weekly wage today and multiply it by one-and-a-fifth to get today's equivalent of the cost of a copy of Mark's Gospel and by four-and-a-quarter to get the approximate cost of a copy of Matthew plus Luke.

There is therefore a clear motive available for the production of Mark's Gospel when the others were in existence: to provide a special-purpose Gospel containing in clear consecutive fashion the *kerygma* of the church, extracted from Matthew and Luke, for use in evangelism. This answers the Irrelevancy Argument against Markan Dependence, advanced by Styler and so many others.

Another major argument put forward—and regarded as decisive by Markan Priorists—is that no author writing after the Major Synoptics would omit the material that Mark's Gospel leaves out. For example, F. C. Grant (1957, 352–54) writes this about the idea that Mark drew the material for his Gospel from Matthew and Luke: "Furthermore, what purpose can be alleged for such an abridgement? Why should anyone wish to substitute Mark's brief narrative, truncated at both ends, for the fuller narratives of Matthew and Luke?" This argument assumes that if Mark wrote third, he must have intended to *replace* the other Synoptics with his account—and why would any writer want to offer such a truncated version as a replacement for such good material as is found in the other two? Further, Streeter (1924, 158) said "only a lunatic would leave out" of his Gospel such material as "Matthew's account of the Infancy, the Sermon on the Mount, and practically all the parables." As Mark was clearly not a lunatic, it was obvious (Streeter concluded) that Mark's Gospel was not written third. But again, this is an objection that only has a point if Mark's purpose in writing was to replace the other two Synoptics.

Mark was not aiming to produce a Gospel to replace Matthew and Luke or to compete with them in any way, but to meet a specific need of a kind that *they* were not designed to meet. He therefore omitted the birth stories and the teaching that was primarily intended for Christians or was of limited usefulness for evangelistic preaching—this, as we know, formed no part of the church's proclamation to outsiders. Frequently, for the same reason, he gives a shortened version of teaching that he does include, sometimes summarizing what he omits.

Mark's omission of the resurrection appearances is puzzling, for the resurrection was the climax of the *kerygma*—but this omission is a puzzle on any Synoptic hypothesis. It is in fact *less* perplexing on the Markan Dependence Hypothesis because if Mark left out the details of the resurrection stories deliberately he at least knew that they were accessible in Matthew and Luke, whereas on the Markan Priority Hypothesis whatever Mark left out was *not elsewhere available at all*. This is a point worth careful noting, for the absence from Mark of a detailed resurrection account is sometimes regarded by advocates of Markan Priority as being a problem for the Markan Dependence view and is referred to by them in such a way as to imply that it poses no problem at all for the Markan Priority Hypothesis. (For example, see F. H. Woods's remarkably effective article referred to above.)

The whole of this attitude about Mark's omissions is totally mistaken. Mark did not produce an expunged edition of Matthew and Luke. He produced a Gospel containing the church's message to outsiders and all the treasures of the teachings of Jesus—and the other material from Matthew and Luke that he did not utilize remained available to the church in those Gospels. This answers the Expurgatory Argument sometimes advanced against Markan Dependence.

But Mark's Gospel is not a simple series of extracts from other books. It is a real work of authorship in its own right, for which the other Gospels are sources. First of all, it is a careful and skillful blending of the stories of Matthew and Luke, taking advantage of the narratives about Jesus that each of them offers, to the extent that Mark judged them appropriate for his purposes. Thus many of the details given in Mark are combined from the accounts of Matthew and Luke. Mark's obvious preference in telling a story was to make his account as full and rich in detail as he could, and much of this is explained by the thesis that he conflated Matthew and Luke. It is not true to say that he used *every* detail that he found in his sources since details can be found in Matthew and Luke that are absent from Mark, but these are somewhat uncommon. He mostly conflated what he found in his two sources.

Moreover, Mark's Gospel is a great treasury of additional information found in neither Matthew nor Luke. Therefore, clearly, these two Gospels were not his *only* sources. While using the stories of Matthew and Luke as his guide and framework (and he recounts very few stories that he did not find in them), he also incorporated into his telling of these stories a whole host of additional details drawn from his own knowledge of the Jesus traditions. Some of this may be from his personal knowledge (e.g., the youth who fled naked in 14:51–52). Most of it would consist of eyewitness details that he heard while listening to eyewitness recountings of these stories. Mark is known to have been a companion and associate of Barnabas, Paul, and Peter. Paul was not an eyewitness of the events of the life of Jesus, and no evidence exists that Barnabas was an eyewitness. But Peter most certainly was.

There is an early, persistent, and widespread tradition that links Peter with Mark and the writing of the Second Gospel. Some scholars have been inclined to dismiss this testimony of the church Fathers. The tradition may have exaggerated the extent of Peter's link with what Mark wrote, but it is difficult to see how the tradition arose at all if there was no link of any kind. Papias said (see Eusebius, *Church History*, 3.39.15–16; Maier 1999, 129–30):

> Mark became Peter's interpreter and wrote down accurately, but not in order, all that he remembered of the things said and done by the Lord. For he had not heard the Lord or been one of his followers, but later, as I said, a follower of Peter. Peter used to teach as the occasion demanded, without giving systematic arrangement to the Lord's sayings, so that Mark did not err in writing down some things just as he recalled them. For he had one overriding purpose: to omit nothing that he had heard and to make no false statements in his account.

Papias is very clear that Mark wrote down what he had heard from Peter. But, if Mark was also drawing upon the Gospels of Matthew and Luke, why does Papias not mention this? A moment's thought reveals two possible reasons: Papias did not know, or he did not care.

If one familiar with the preaching of Peter and with the Gospels of Matthew and Luke were to read Mark, what would it the more remind him of? It would be the preaching of Peter! Mark simply recorded his account of the common gospel of Christians. Further, the language Mark used and the wealth of small points of detail he gave would make the reader think more of the preaching of Peter than of the other two accounts. Unless Mark were able to come up to Papias and say, "In writing this, I made use of Matthew and Luke," such a piece of information would not be self-evident when reading Mark's Gospel.

But, if Papias did know that Mark had made extensive use of Matthew and Luke as well as his knowledge of Peter's preaching, why would he necessarily mention the former? From what we know of Papias, he would most likely consider it of no consequence—he simply did not care. For Papias valued above all the "living voice." He said (Eusebius, *Church History*, 3.39.4–5; Maier 1999, 127):

> Whenever anyone came who had been a follower of the elders, I asked about their words: what Andrew or Peter had said, or Philip or Thomas or James or John or Matthew or any other of the Lord's disciples, and what Aristion and the presbyter John, disciples of the Lord, were still saying. For I did not think that information from books would help me as much as the word of a living, surviving voice.

When we read Papias's opinion comparing "information from books" with the profit that came from "the word of a living, surviving voice," it is really no surprise that what he records about Mark is his association with Peter and his recollection of the ministry of that apostle, and that he says nothing (except perhaps a comment about the question of "order") in relation to other Gospels. Papias's comment by no means, therefore, excludes the possibility that Mark produced his Gospel later than other written Gospels.

Papias mentions the matter of order twice in this paragraph. First, Mark "wrote down accurately, but not in order, all that he remembered," and second, "Peter used to teach as the occasion demanded, without giving systematic arrangement to the Lord's sayings, so that Mark did not err in writing down some things just as he recalled them."

Peter did not—did not attempt to—put his stories about Jesus into any sort of orderly arrangement, but taught about them just as the need of the moment indicated. So Mark received no awareness of a structure, an order, from his source Peter. But things do (of course!) occur in an order in Mark's Gospel.

In his translation and notes on Eusebius's *Church History*, A. C. McGiffert notes (1979, 173) that Lightfoot supposes the mention of a "lack of order" implies the existence of another written Gospel, exhibiting a different order, with which Papias compares it. McGiffert goes on to mention several scholars who believe this other Gospel to be that of Matthew. If one were to compare the first section of Matthew that covers events in the life of Christ with the first chapters of Mark, one of the most significant features that would impact the reader is their divergences in order when recording the same pericopes. However, in differing from Matthew, Mark is not following here an order of his own, for he has no specific knowledge himself in this matter). But the opening chapters of Mark are following *exactly* the sequence of pericopes in Luke!

I show in chapter 9 that Mark's Gospel is in fact assembled on a very simple structure: not having an order of his own, and wishing to avoid the large teaching sections in the Major Synoptics, Mark follows Luke's order of pericopes to 6:14 and Matthew's order thereafter (inserting into each of these two parts four sections derived from the other Synoptic Gospel that he is not following at the time). Further information about the testimony of the early church Fathers is provided in chapter 6.

We have in fact a thoroughly reasonable basis, from this external testimony, for holding that the source of the abundance of extra detail with which Mark enlivened his Gospel was his recollection of how Peter told these same tales that he (Mark) was now drawing from the Gospels of Matthew and Luke. This means that many of the eyewitness touches of Peter's preaching ended up in Mark's Gospel since Mark would have remembered these eyewitness details from Peter. For convenience I sometimes refer to Mark's third source as P—Mark's private source, primarily Peter's preaching. And it was from using the Gospels of Matthew and Luke as sources that Mark drew the framework and order of pericopes in what he wrote.

There is another aspect of Mark's Gospel very likely reflecting his association with Peter: Mark's Gospel portrays Jesus as a man among men. Mark is effective in gaining the attention of people and leading them to see more fully who Jesus is because he started by making clear that Jesus was (and always continued to be) fully man. Furthermore, Mark's message of what Jesus could do for a person is heightened and exemplified if the disciples are not painted as supermen, spiritual giants, but shown to be—as in fact they were—ordinary people, often puzzled and bewildered, frequently bumble-footed and liable to get things wrong and make mistakes, but people who were becoming increasingly aware of the real nature of the Master they were following.

Moreover, the contrast between what the disciples *had been* and what they *became* (and were known to be at the time when Mark wrote) was itself part of the message: this is what Jesus can do in the life of any person who follows him. Quite apart from the fact that Mark's portrayal can be recognized as accurate in its picture of the disciples, it is the more useful way of describing them in the context of evangelistic preaching. In similar fashion, Mark's approach to doctrine is simple and down to earth. And it is beyond any reasonable doubt that the vocabulary and manner of speech used by Peter is reflected in Mark's Gospel. This matter is worth pursuing further.

An important feature of Mark to be noted is his exceedingly colloquial Greek. To Streeter must go the credit, I believe, for first clearly spelling out exactly the nature and extent of this Markan trait. Earlier writers (and not a few since Streeter's time) tend simply to dismiss Mark's style as "bad Greek." Streeter's (1924, 163) penetrating observation is that "the difference between the style of Mark and of the other two is not merely that they both write better Greek. It is the difference which always exists between the spoken and the written language." Similarly, V. Taylor (1952, 52) comments, "Mark's Gospel is written in a relatively simple and popular form of Greek which has striking affinities with the spoken language of everyday life as it is revealed to us in the papyri and inscriptions." Cranfield (1959, 20) also makes this point: "The style of the Gospel is unpretentious and close to the everyday spoken Greek of the time, making up for its lack of the elegance of literary Greek by its simplicity and directness."

The spoken and written forms of a language are distinctively different. A full recognition of this has only come about in recent times, basically since the invention and use of the tape recorder and the development of linguistic science. The present viewpoint is summed up by Palmer (1971, 3): "What is agreed by almost all linguists is that the spoken and written languages should be kept apart in analysis, that for the purpose of linguistic analysis indeed they are essentially two different languages."

Speech normally consists of paratactic constructions, while writing consists of some paratactic constructions and a predominance of subordinating constructions. There are definite reasons for this. Subordinating constructions allow for greater precision in conveying information by facilitating the transmission of the relationships between the different segments or "bits" of information. But this can result in a complexity of structure, with the consequence that the meaning might be seen clearly only if the sentence is written down, where it can be reread if necessary.

On the other hand, speech is uttered in sense units of about a half-dozen words or so, these units being strung together like beads on a string and the relationship between them being conveyed by such specific speech characteristics as stress, intonation, juncture, and emphasis (for which the linguistic term is *suprasegmentals*), or by means of using additional words to state explicitly what the relationships are. Such short sense units are characteristic of speech because they represent what is called the "span of structural attention" for speaker and hearer. Longer units are more difficult for the hearer to grasp as a thought unit, and they are more difficult for the speaker to formulate.

Gleason (1969, 358) points out that in attempting to speak in longer sense units, the speaker may change his grammatical construction "in the middle of sentences in ways that suggest, on careful examination, that the speaker has lost track of what he started to say. Usually, however, any stretch of six or seven words is consistent within itself structurally. The difficulty appears only when longer sequences are considered—sequences beyond the span of structural attention of either the speaker or the hearer." Gleason (359) continues commenting about speech, explaining that "patterns of clause connection are generally simple. From the viewpoint of literary standards they are usually monotonous. *And* is used very heavily. Connectors of greater range, like *nevertheless, moreover, alternatively*, are very rare. . . . This fact is probably associated with the lack of long-span integration in structure." We can easily correlate these comments with features of Mark's Gospel.

But why does the Greek of Mark's Gospel have this character? Streeter decides (1924, 163) that it is "most probable that his Gospel, like Paul's Epistles, was taken down from rapid dictation by word of mouth." But there is another possible explanation for this Markan feature that Streeter has identified. If Mark was indeed producing a sourcebook for preachers, it would need to be in the kind of language that they used. More than likely, Mark's Gospel was not intended just to be *read* so much as *heard*: his stories would be memorized as the vehicle of the Jesus traditions and then retold by the Christians as opportunity offered. Their detailed form, packed with interest, full of the redundancies and repetitions that are not only *characteristic of* spoken language but that are in large measure *needed by* spoken language, are much more suited for storytelling than the drier factual approach of Luke or the (frequently) brief-notes-only version of a pericope in Matthew.

A precise, polished tale told in well-turned phrases and with hardly an unnecessary word may be the better version for circulation in written form. Streeter (1924, 163) says, for instance, that "Matthew and Luke use the more succinct and carefully chosen language of one who writes and then revises an article for publication." Fair comment. But that is hardly the best idiom for use in attracting a crowd on the streets of Rome. For that, you need an account composed in the vernacular of your intended audience. That is what Mark's Gospel is. It speaks in their language.

This then provides an explanation for all the colloquialisms of every kind that have been documented in Mark's Gospel. They may or may not have represented the typical speech of Mark himself. But whether they did or not, these features would be an asset in Mark's Gospel when stories from it were used in outreach that was aimed at interesting outsiders in the message of Jesus Christ.

What was the situation in which Mark's Gospel could be used to best advantage? Professional storytellers were common and popular in the first century. Christians joined their ranks and told stories about Jesus. They would stand in some convenient place where they hoped to attract a crowd—maybe near the entrance to the marketplace—and begin their story. They must launch into their story quickly to gain an audience. They must arouse and maintain a sense of urgency to hold their audience. They must create interest, paint a vivid picture that captures the imagination, awaken an emotional response amongst the listeners, tell a tale of conflict, good against evil, and maintain suspense throughout the telling.

Otherwise their hearers would wander home or head to the market. The requirements are rather different from those for the Gospels of Matthew and Luke, who had as it were a captive audience for the instruction they gave. But if Mark's story flagged in interest, the audience was lost.

These requirements are universal for storytelling. They are the ingredients of any good novel or gripping drama. They are explicitly built into our television serials so that the viewers will tune in again for the next episode. And they are richly present in Mark's stories. When we examine in detail how he tells a story (e.g., the Gadarene demoniac, Jairus's daughter and the hemorrhaging woman, or the demon-possessed lad), we can recognize what an absolutely superb storyteller Mark is.

This does not deny the historicity of the accounts in his Gospel. On the contrary—he had the greatest drama of all time to relate and had no need to embellish the facts, but only to recount them on the basis of his Gospel sources and the additional eyewitness information to which he had access. Nor does this deny the theological purpose of his Gospel. On the contrary—the story was only the vehicle and was quite valueless apart from the truth that it told and the message it conveyed and the Savior it described. Mark's stories were included in his Gospel for specific theological reasons, and he exercised his skill on them to serve, as we have seen, specific theological purposes. But these things are true also of Matthew and Luke. What distinguishes Mark's account is how he achieves these purposes through the telling of a captivating story.

Thus an awareness of all these factors that I have outlined—the purpose of Mark's Gospel as deduced from examining its contents; the testimony of the early church Fathers to Mark's link with Peter; the sequence of the writing of the Synoptics and the date of Mark; the way in which Mark adjusted his sources Matthew and Luke to colloquial speech (the way in which Peter would have presented his teaching)—goes a long way towards answering objections that some people have raised who claim that these things may not be compatible with Markan Dependence. On the contrary: they are all factors that are in concord with and very supportive of my hypothesis in this book.

This then is how Mark's Gospel can be explained from the perspective of Markan Dependence. Such an explanation does not *establish* the case for Markan Dependence. But it does show that a case can be made out for Markan Dependence that explains the data, answers the objections, accords with what is known of the situation in the early church, and has the virtue of being totally credible.

THE CAPERNAUM CENTURION IN A PSEUDO-MARKAN VERSION

The "Impossibility" Argument against Griesbach

In the ongoing debate about the interrelationship between the Synoptic Gospels, there is one argument that surfaces periodically, is affirmed by one group of scholars and denied by another, and has never, it would appear, actually been put to the test.

I refer to the "impossibility" argument. This argument goes back to the article on "The Gospels" by E. A. Abbott in the *Encyclopaedia Britannica* (1879). His rebuttal of the Griesbach view of Markan conflation was then enthusiastically adopted by others, and treated as a settled, unshakeable fact. It is cited by Farmer (1964, 75) and was reaffirmed by many others, including Mitton's (1965, 3) review of Farmer's *The Synoptic Problem*. It was promoted again by D. Hill (1972, 28), who says, "The judgement of E A Abbott . . . still stands," and he then quotes Abbott's assertion (1879, 791), which reads as follows:

> It can be proved by *reductio ad absurdum* that Mark did not copy from Matthew and Luke. For suppose that he did so copy, it follows that he must not only have constructed a narrative based upon two others, borrowing here a piece from Matthew and here a piece from Luke, but that he must have deliberately determined to insert, and must have adopted his narrative so as to insert, every word that was common to Matthew and Luke. The difficulty of doing this is enormous, and will be patent to anyone who will try to perform a similar feat himself. To embody the whole of even one document in a narrative of one's own, without copying it *verbatim*, and to do this in a free and natural manner, requires no little care. But to take two documents, to put them side by side and analyse their common matter, and then to write a narrative, graphic, abrupt, and in all respects the opposite of artificial, which shall contain every phrase and word that is common to both—this would be a *tour de force* even for a skilful forger of these days, and may be dismissed as an impossibility for the writer of the Second Gospel.

This sounds like a convincing reason why the idea of Markan dependence on Matthew and Luke cannot be taken seriously. This assertion has been influential in turning not a few scholars away from the Griesbach Hypothesis. For if Abbott is right, that what it proposed—i.e., Mark had woven together the accounts of Matthew and Luke—could not be done, so that it is in fact *not* readily possible to achieve a text such as Mark contains by conflating the forms of the pericopes found in Matthew and Luke, then this would surely stop the Griesbach Hypothesis dead in its tracks. It is rather pointless pursuing other lines of argument in relation to this hypothesis if in fact it is impossible for the text of Mark to have been derived from the other two Synoptics.

On the other hand, if Abbott is wrong and such a conflating can be achieved fairly simply, then this ought to be noted, and one argument in the armory of opponents of the Griesbach Hypothesis will have been disarmed.

Abbott exaggerates the degree of correspondence between Mark and the others. Mark does not indeed include "every phrase and word that is common to both," but the thrust of Abbott's argument is clear. The force of the argument was defused somewhat by Sanders; he quotes Abbott and then comments (1969, 270):

> It must be pointed out, however, that Abbott's statement of the case is not quite accurate. If Mark had conflated Matthew and Luke, he would not have had to analyze their common matter and labor to include it. He could simply have copied first one then the other, thereby automatically including what was common to them, excluding any chance that they would agree together against him, and also creating agreements with each of them against the other. Whether one attributes conflation to Matthew or to Mark, the matter will be difficult, but not so nearly impossible as Abbott thought.

Numerous scholars have drawn attention to parallels where interweaving and conflation of the kind postulated for Mark is known to have occurred. Dungan (1970, 91–93) refers particularly to Tatian's *Diatessaron* and *The Gospel of Peter* in which Gospel sources were interwoven. Then Longstaff (1977) also examined Tatian, as well as the work of Roger of Hovedon, who wrote a life of Becket combining a work entitled *Passio Sancti Thomae* and the chronicle written by Benedict of Peterborough (which was itself a combination of a life of Becket by John of Salisbury and the *Passio Sancti Thomae*). Dungan and Longstaff see these parallels as providing collateral evidence in support of the belief that Mark could have produced his text from Matthew and Luke as sources.

Tuckett (1983, 41–43) examines Longstaff's analysis and points out that his parallels are inexact:

> In any one given pericope, Tatian's specific aim was (probably) to include every detail of his sources.... The author must have gone through the gospel texts, taking words from each gospel and piecing them together with great care and fidelity to form a new narrative.... However, in the case of Tatian, such a comparison of sources is not surprising. It is in fact demanded by his overall aim. If he was trying to include every detail of his sources, then he must have carefully compared his sources and been eclectic in his choice of words within any one sentence.

But Tuckett notes that "Tatian's method is different from that of . . . Mark on the Griesbach Hypothesis." In regard to the second parallel, Tuckett (1983, 44, 46) adds that

> Benedict's use of his sources is clearly either to copy verbatim, or to omit large accounts, or to abbreviate drastically. . . . The situation is not very different with Roger, for, in most cases, he uses his sources like Benedict, copying them out verbatim. . . . Thus, in all, there is not much evidence that either Benedict or Roger carefully compared their sources and wove them together in an intricate way. Rather, they copied one source at a time, often very exactly. . . . There is nothing comparable to the Dura fragment of Tatian, or to Mark on the Griesbach Hypothesis; that hypothesis has to assume (for Mark) an almost continuous process of "careful comparison", taking one word from here, one from there, and weaving them together. Moreover, there must have been a large number of very small changes in wording etc., which is quite different from the combination of strict copying and very free re-writing (if it is not dependence on a totally different source) which characterises the conflation process in the chronicles of Benedict and Roger.

It is therefore very dubious how much of a contribution is made by these (alleged) parallels to the resolution of Abbott's claim that the Gospel of Mark could not have been derived from the other two Synoptists.

It also needs to be noted that every Synoptic theory that postulates literary interdependence between the Synoptics accepts that conflation has occurred. Thus on the Augustinian view of Successive Dependence, Luke has conflated Matthew and Mark and on the Two-Document/Four-Document Hypothesis Matthew has conflated Mark, Q, and M, while Luke has conflated Mark, Q, and L (cf. Streeter 1924: 201–5, 246–49).

Now this establishes that *any* theory of literacy interdependence requires belief in the occurrence of *some* kind of conflation. But it still does not provide any kind of direct answer to Abbott's dogmatic assertion that the production of the text of Mark's Gospel from Matthew and Luke "may be dismissed as an impossibility for the writer of the Second Gospel." The issue still continues unresolved. Many still believe Abbott's assertion that even a "skilful literary forger" would have trouble producing a Mark out of a Matthew and Luke. So Mark could not have done it because it was impossible to do. So Griesbach was wrong.

Now I make no claim to be a skillful literary forger. But actually this "impossible" exercise is something that I was doing every weekday of my life for a period of several years. I was appointed a member of the Commonwealth Film Censorship Board in Australia. There were nine of us altogether on the Board, and it was our task to undertake the classification (and, on occasion, censorship) of every film and television program coming into Australia. Most of these were straightforward, and only one or two censors were allocated to view them. There were also, of course, quite a number that were borderline for classification categories—usually at least one every day—and more members (up to all nine of us) were then allocated to view them and make a decision.

For this work we sat at desks in a darkened theatrette, with table lamps on and notepads in front of us, and we made extensive notes of everything that took place on screen that had a bearing on the decision to be made about the particular classification, and we recorded the time into the film when that scene or event took place (in case we needed a second viewing of that part of the film). For each film or program, the members who had viewed it met together and discussed what we had viewed, using the extensive notes we had made, and came to a decision. Then one of those members who had seen the particular program or film (we took it in turns) was required to write up a detailed report on that viewing and the classification decision. This report was not like minutes of a meeting. It embodied the notes that each Board member had written about it, interweaving their comments. This report was then confirmed by all those members who had viewed it as embodying the views of the Board. Those reports had a lot in common with what Griesbach said Mark had done. Each day of our working lives we were all engaged in doing something very much like what Abbott informs us cannot readily be done.

So I decided to attempt a Mark-like treatment of a story from Matthew and Luke. I acknowledge that this conflation takes a little thought, a little care—just like my Board member reports—but I would hardly say that it cannot be done. Here then I describe my approach to creating a Markan version of a pericope.

Putting Abbott's Assertion to the Test

The way forward, it seems to me, is to put ourselves into the position that (on the Griesbach Hypothesis) the author of our Second Gospel faced: to take a pericope common to Matthew and Luke and to see whether it is possible to conflate the two versions so as to produce the sort of account that on this hypothesis Mark is postulated to have done.

From the material common to Matthew and Luke, the most appropriate for our purpose would be a piece of narrative. We have a choice of three: the pericopes of the temptation, the Capernaum centurion, and the inquiry of John to Jesus. Of these, the one that seems to me closest to the typical pericope of the Triple Tradition is that of the Capernaum centurion (Matt 8:5–13//Luke 7:1–10), so this is what I have chosen—a pericope that

Mark's plan for using the Major Synoptics took him past, as described in chap. 9.

I shall therefore seek to produce a "Markan Version" of this story by conflating the Matthean and Lukan accounts, using Mark's approach to the handling of his sources.

When Mark compared the two accounts he would find three elements of the story at variance. First, in Matthew the centurion comes to Jesus in person while in Luke he sends elders of the Jews with a message. Second, in Matthew Jesus offers to come to heal him and immediately the centurion asks Jesus only to say the word, while in Luke the first message that the centurion sends is to ask that Jesus come to him and only subsequently does he request, in a second message, that Jesus but say the word to heal his slave. Third, Matthew uses the word "servant" (παῖς) throughout, where Luke prefers the word "slave" (δοῦλος), though using "servant" (παῖς) in 7:7.

Mark's policy was to reconcile differences between Matthew and Luke as far as possible. The first of the above three differences offers no simple opportunity for reconciliation, so Mark would follow Luke since it is the longer and more detailed account. The second difference is easily resolved: by transferring the request to come to the centurion's house from being spoken by the centurion himself to being spoken by the elders. As for the third difference, since Mark is going to draw most heavily upon Luke (for the reason just mentioned), he would adopt the word "slave" throughout, including in the one place where Matthew and Luke agree in using "servant." (Roman society was used to slaves as servants, so this word would have met with a receptive response from Mark's hearers.)

Mark would not use all that he finds in Matthew and Luke. He would omit from Luke "for he loves our nation, and he built us our synagogue" since this has no relevancy to his hearers in Rome, and Mark not infrequently omits things of this kind. Further, he would omit Matt 8:11–12, part of the pronouncement to which in Matthew the story leads. Mark often omits or apocopates the pronouncements of Jesus similar to this with which Matthew's pericopes end. Thus Mark would end the pericope where Luke does and consequently use Luke's (not Matthew's) form of the ending.

Moreover, Mark would use the historic present at certain points in the story, introduce constructions with καί, and add in εὐθύς to heighten the sense of immediacy and urgency. It is probable that Mark would also change the use of "Lord" by Matthew (8:8) and Luke (7:6), most likely to "Teacher." He would then add into the story other details of which he is aware (perhaps—if this were the case—that the slave's name was

Marcellus and that he was the father of Urbanus, who was a member of the church in Rome in Mark's day). Mark would also record the crowd's amazement at this "healing at a distance" and their comments about it, and the consequence of the miracle. More than likely he would change some of Luke's vocabulary—perhaps Luke's "who was sick and at the point of death" (κακῶς ἔχων ἤμελλεν τελευτᾶν) to his own more colloquial term for "at the point of death" (ἐσχάτως ἔχει; cf. Mark 5:23); perhaps also Luke's word for "heal" (διασώζω; cf. Luke 7:3)—a word Mark never employs—Mark would change to σώζω or more probably to θεραπεύω (Matthew's word in 8:7) or possibly ἰάομαι (used in this pericope in Matt 8:8,13; Luke 7:7).

Mark would then blend the two accounts together, conflating those places where they run parallel. Thus a pseudo-Markan version of this pericope would come out something like this:

> [1]And he entered Capernaum and there was a centurion there having a slave who was dear to him and who was paralyzed and at the point of death. [2]And when he heard about Jesus, immediately he calls to him the elders of the Jews and sends them to Jesus. [3]And finding Jesus, the elders besought him earnestly that he would come and heal the slave, saying, [4]"He is worthy to have you to do this for him." And he says to them, "I will come and heal him," and he goes with them. [5]But when he was not far from the house, the centurion sent friends to him saying to him, [6]"Teacher, do not trouble yourself, for I am not worthy to have you come under my roof; [7]therefore I did not presume to come to you. But only say the word, and my slave will be healed. [8]For I am a man set under authority, having soldiers under me; and I say to one man, 'Go,' and he goes; and to another, 'Come,' and he comes; and to my slave, 'Do this,' and he does it." [9]When therefore Jesus heard these things that he said, he marveled at him and turned and said to the multitude of those who followed him, "Truly, I say to you, with no one in Israel have I found such faith." [10]And when those who had been sent returned to the house they found the slave healed. [11]And all the people were amazed, and they questioned among themselves saying, "How has such power been given to men?" And the report of this spread throughout Galilee. [12]Now the name of the slave was Marcellus, the father of Urbanus.

A Markan Priority Hypothesis Explanation

Once such a version existed it would then be possible to explain the accounts on the basis of Markan Priority as follows:

(1) The use in Matthew and Luke of the iterated preposition (in a compound verb, and then repeated in the prepositional phrase that follows) is a favorite idiom of Mark's that Matthew and Luke have here taken over (see Matt 8:5; Luke 7:1,6).

(2) Luke has followed Mark's account for the most part, but Matthew has abbreviated it by having the centurion come to Jesus in person.

(3) Luke has improved Mark's colloquial language, altering his ἐσχάτως ἔχει into better Greek.

(4) Both Matthew and Luke show more reverence for Jesus by altering Mark's "Teacher" to "Lord." Their other agreement against Mark, "servant" for "slave" in Matt 8:8//Luke 7:7 is a minor agreement of no particular significance.

(5) On occasion Matthew has chosen to take one detail and Luke another where Mark contains redundancies. Thus in Mark's "And he says to them, 'I will come and heal him,' and he goes with them," Matthew takes "And he said to him, 'I will come and heal him,'" while Luke takes "And Jesus went with them"; Matthew takes "When Jesus heard him" and Luke "When Jesus heard this" from Mark's "When therefore Jesus heard these things he said"; similar for the words "to the multitude of those who followed him."

(6) There are a number of details in Mark that both Matthew and Luke have chosen to omit.

(7) Mark has "with no one in Israel have I found such faith" and Luke (7:9) has "not even in Israel," while the textual evidence for Matthew (8:10) is divided between the two—the correct text for Matthew is as in Mark, but some manuscripts have assimilated this to be the wording of Luke.

Since there *is* no Markan version of this pericope, these explanations are of course completely invalid. But this pseudo-Markan version shows how such a pericope could have been produced by Mark from the other two, and if it had been written in this kind of way it would possess characteristics identical with those of genuine Markan pericopes, and it would exhibit the same kinds of similarities and differences found between the three Gospels in the Triple Tradition. And it would then be possible to account for all these features from the perspective of Markan Priority along the lines of the explanations that I have just offered.

My pseudo-Markan version has kept pretty close to each one of his sources where that source is unparalleled in the other source (which mostly applies to Luke, as a number of points in Luke are without parallels in Matthew, whereas most of Matthew occurs also in Luke). Mark may well alter further the language of his sources, adapting it more closely to his own style and vocabulary. He may also add-in other details of which he has independent knowledge. Changes of these kinds would not affect the point under consideration: it is not the places where Mark *differed from* Matthew and Luke but where Mark was seen to "contain every phrase and word that is common to both" that Abbott considered constituted "an impossibility for the writer of the Second Gospel."

CONCLUSION

This small exercise has produced a conflation of the pericope of the Capernaum centurion that exhibits characteristics observable in Mark's versions of other pericopes that are found also in Matthew and Luke. Writing it did not require much time at all—and such a conflation of Matthew and Luke would have taken Mark himself even less, since *we* would need to identify Markan characteristics and specifically build them in, whereas this would be for Mark the automatic expression of his own style and purpose in writing.

This pseudo-Markan version of the Capernaum centurion pericope does not prove very much. It does not prove the Griesbach Hypothesis. But it does eliminate one argument from the armory of those who argue against the Griesbach Hypothesis, for it does *disprove* once and for all Abbott's pronouncement that it takes a skillful forger to combine Matthew and Luke and that Mark would not have been capable of doing this.

Frankly, any moderately competent writer could produce a Markan pericope out of a pericope common to Matthew and Luke (plus some extra details from his own independent knowledge). This can be tested very simply. The detailed extension of the temptation narrative and the pericope of John's message to Jesus remain only in Matthew and Luke at the moment. Perhaps someone may now like to try his hand at producing a pseudo-Markan version of one of these.

4 FLESHING OUT THE FACTS AND FIGURES

This chapter provides a great deal of data about the Synoptic Gospels and considers their significance.

> *It is a capital mistake to theorize before one has data.*
> (Sherlock Holmes in "A Scandal in Bohemia"
> by Arthur Conan Doyle)

INTRODUCTION

Most of our discussion so far has been at the level of generalities, the "big picture." But to get a valid grasp of the situation of Synoptic similarities and differences, we need to look carefully at the details in verses and individual words. That is the purpose of this chapter. It is concerned with the facts and figures about the Synoptics, including lots of data and statistics.

In his *Chapters from My Autobiography* (251), Mark Twain quoted former British Prime Minister Benjamin Disraeli's comment, "There are three kinds of lies—lies, damned lies, and statistics." And I think this report is near the mark too: "Over 83% of statistical figures are simply invented. Including this one." But we do want our statistics to be accurate and reliable before we use them, and that is what this chapter is for.

An example of this kind of thing is that scholarly discussions of the Synoptic Problem frequently cite statistics about the Gospels and almost as frequently differ in the statistics that they use. For example, Griesbach stated (1978, 108) that Mark contains 24 verses that are unique to it; Hendriksen (1973, 6) says 31; Streeter (1924, 195) says 32; Albright and Mann (1971,

XL) say 50; and Swete (1913, lxiiif.) says 80. Where other writers refer to the matter, they tend to take over a figure from an earlier writer whose data they accept. My guess is that the most people give a figure between 50 and 56.

Scholars often say something like, "There is very little in Mark that is distinctive. Almost everything he says is also in Matthew or Luke or—more probably—in both. And this fact points to Mark having been written first; and then Matthew and Luke took over what he said, for what we find is just the situation you would expect to find in those circumstances." You may have heard something along these lines. But is it true? This chapter shows you what the facts *are*, and I am confident that these will surprise you.

New comparative and statistical tools have become available in the last five or six decades from which much information relevant to our present purpose can be gleaned. The most useful of these for my research in this chapter were: de Solages (*Greek Synopsis of the Gospels*, 1959); A. M. Honoré ("A Statistical Study of the Synoptic Problem," 1968); W. Farmer (*Synopticon*, 1969); and two sources by R. Morgenthaler (*Synoptic Statistics*, 1971; German, *Statistische Synopse*; and *Statistics of New Testament Words*, 1958, 1972, 1982; German, *Statistik Des Neutestamentlichen Wortschatzes*). While mainly basing this chapter on these Synoptic statisticians, I have supplemented this information in some areas in this chapter from my own research.

Mark does not have a large number of complete pericopes that are unparalleled in the other two Synoptics. But this is a very imprecise measure for such information. If you look at all the unique material in Mark—his *Sondergut*—you will see that it cannot be so easily dismissed. Then, in addition to the wealth of Mark's extra detail, there is the question of all the places that the Synoptics give pretty much the same information but use quite different words for doing it. There are also places where Matthew and Luke did not simply "take over" Mark's material for their own Gospel, as advocates of Markan Priority tend to put it. To determine if data like this is significant, I provide such information and then assess it. Then I try to determine what these statistics indicate to a neutral observer about the direction of literary copying among the Synoptists. This chapter examines the data of the Synoptics and what can be known of the background and circumstances of their writing. This process provides us with a basis on which further assessment and interpretation can proceed in the following chapters.

MATERIAL IN MARK NOT FOUND IN MATTHEW OR LUKE

Verses Unique to Mark

Listed here is the material in Mark of the size of approximately half a verse in length or greater that is not paralleled in Matthew or Luke. [Square brackets indicate words in Mark that are not unique to Mark but that are included here to clarify the context.]

DETAILS	REF	NO.
Mark's Title	1:1	1
The time is fulfilled . . . believe in the gospel	1:15	½
immediately . . . and Andrew, with James and John	1:29	½
and the whole city was gathered together about the door	1:33	1
Simon seeks and finds Jesus	1:36–37	2
Jesus sternly charged the leper to be silent	1:43	1
the leper talked freely about his cleansing	1:45	½
Jesus returned home, and crowds filled the room	2:1–2	2
a paralytic carried by four others	2:3	½
immediately perceiving in his spirit that in themselves, etc.	2:8	½
He went out again beside the sea and taught the crowds	2:13	1
for there were many who followed him	2:15	½
when they saw he was eating with sinners and tax collectors	2:16	½
Now John's disciples and the Pharisees were fasting	2:18	½
As long as they have the bridegroom with them they cannot fast	2:19	½
The Sabbath was made for man, not man for the Sabbath	2:27	1
with anger, grieved at their hardness of heart	3:5	½
And he told his disciples to have a boat ready for him	3:9	1
And whenever the unclean spirits beheld him they fell down	3:11	1
to be with him and to be sent out to preach	3:14	½
whom he surnamed Boanerges, that is, sons of thunder	3:17	½
Jesus' family think that he is beside himself	3:19–21	2½
And the scribes who came down from Jerusalem [said]	3:22	½
And he called them to him and said to them in parables, etc.	3:23	1
for they had said, "He has an unclean spirit"	3:30	1
and looking around on those who sat about him	3:34	½
and in his teaching he said to them, "Listen!"	4:2–3	½
lest they should turn again and be forgiven	4:12	½
Do you not understand this parable? How then will you understand all the parables?	4:13	1
and the desire for other things enter in and	4:19	½
If any man has ears to hear, let him hear	4:23	1
and still more will be given to you	4:24	½

Fleshing Out the Facts and Figures

DETAILS	REF	NO.
Parable of the seed growing secretly	4:26–29	4
with many such . . . [he spoke] as they were able to bear it	4:33	½
but privately to his own disciples he explained everything	4:34	½
On that day, when evening had come, he said to them	4:35	½
And leaving the crowd, they took him with them . . . just as he was. And other boats were with him	4:36	1
in the stern [asleep] on the cushion . . . "Teacher, do you not care if [we perish]?"	4:38	½
no one could bind him any more, even with a chain	5:3	½
and no one had the strength to subdue him	5:4	½
Night and day he was always crying out and bruising himself	5:5	1
and how he has had mercy on you	5:19	½
[to proclaim] in the Decapolis . . . and all men marveled	5:20	½
he crossed again in a boat to the other side, a great [crowd] gathered about him; and he was beside the sea	5:21	½
woman who had suffered much under many physicians	5:26	1
She had heard the reports about Jesus . . . [came] in the crowd	5:27	½
she felt in her body that she was healed of her disease	5:29	½
and he looked around to see who had done it	5:32	1
and when he had entered [he said] to them, "Why do you make a tumult . . . ?"	5:39	½
he took the child's father and mother and those who were with him and [went in] where the child was	5:40	½
he said to her, "Talitha cumi"; which means, "Little girl, I say to you, [arise]"	5:41	½
and . . . she walked (she was twelve years of age)	5:42	½
except that he laid his hands upon a few sick people and healed them. And he marveled	6:5–6	1
and began to send them out two by two	6:7	½
[and preached] that men should repent. And they cast out many demons and anointed with oil many that were sick	6:12–13	1
Herod and John the Baptist	6:14–29	5
Come away by yourselves to a lonely place and rest awhile; etc.	6:31	1
Now many saw them going, and knew them . . . and got there ahead of them	6:33	½
because they were like sheep without a shepherd, and he began to teach them many things	6:34	½
And they said to him, "Shall we go and buy two hundred denarii worth of bread, and give it to them to eat?" And he said to them, "How many loaves have you? Go and see." And when they had found out, [they said]	6:37–38	1
in groups, by hundreds and by fifties	6:40	½
for they all saw him, and were [terrified]	6:50	½

DETAILS	REF	NO.
for they did not understand about the loaves, but their hearts were hardened	6:52	1
and moored to the shore. And when they got out of the boat, immediately	6:53–54	½
[bring the sick] on their pallets to any place where they heard he was. And wherever he came, in villages, cities, or country, they laid the sick in the market places	6:55–56	1½
Eating with unwashed hands	7:2–4	3
Rejecting the commandment of God	7:9	1
which you hand on. And many such things you do	7:13	½
And when he had entered the house, and left the people	7:17	½
[into] a man from outside cannot defile him, since it enters, not his heart, but . . . Thus he declared all foods clean.	7:18–19	1
coveting, wickedness, deceit, licentiousness, envy, [slander,] pride, foolishness. All these evil things come from within	7:22–23	1
And he entered a house, and would not have anyone know it; yet he could not be hid	7:24	½
Now the woman was a Greek, a Syrophoenician by birth. And she begged him to cast the demon out of her daughter	7:26	1
And she went home, and found the child lying in bed, and the demon gone	7:30	1
The healing of a deaf mute	7:31–37	7
In those days, when again a great crowd had gathered, and they had nothing to eat	8:1	½
and some of them have come a long way	8:3	½
And they had a few small fish; and having blessed them he commanded that these also should be set before them	8:7	1
And he sighed deeply in his spirit . . . and getting into the boat again, [he departed] to the other side	8:12–13	1
and they had only one loaf with them in the boat . . .	8:14	½
or understand? Are your hearts hardened? Having eyes do you not see, and having ears do you not hear?	8:15	1
They said to him, "Twelve." [baskets] full of broken pieces . . . and they said to him, "Seven."	8:19	1
The healing of a blind man in Bethsaida	8:22–26	5
But turning and seeing his disciples, he rebuked [Peter]	8:33	½
in this adulterous and sinful generation	8:38	½
intensely [white], as no fuller on earth could bleach them	9:3	½
So they kept the matter to themselves, questioning what the rising from the dead meant	9:10	1
and how is it written of the Son of man, that he should suffer many things and be treated with contempt?	9:12	½

DETAILS	REF	NO.
[when they came to] the disciples, they saw a great [crowd] about them, and scribes arguing with them. And immediately all the crowd, when they saw him, were greatly amazed, and ran up to him and greeted him. And he asked them, "What are you discussing with them?"	9:14–16	3
it dashes him down; and [he foams] and grinds his teeth and becomes rigid	9:18	½
and he fell on the ground and rolled about, foaming at the mouth. And Jesus asked his father, "How long has he had this?" And he said, "From childhood. And it has often cast him into the fire and into the water, to destroy him; but if you can do anything, have pity on us and help us." And Jesus said to him, "If you can! All things are possible to him who believes." Immediately the father of the child cried out and said, "I believe; help my unbelief!" And when [Jesus] saw that a crowd came running together, [he rebuked the unclean spirit,] saying to it, "You deaf and dumb spirit, I command you, come out of him, and never enter him again." And after crying out and convulsing him terribly, [it came out,] and the boy was like a corpse; so that most of them said, "He is dead." But Jesus took him by the hand and lifted him up, and he arose. And when he had entered the house . . .	9:20–28	8
This kind cannot be driven out by anything but prayer	9:29	½
They went on from there, and passed through [Galilee]. And he would not have anyone know it; for he was teaching his disciples	9:30–31	1
and when he was in the house he asked them, "What were you discussing on the way?" But they were silent; for on the way they had discussed with one another	9:33–34	1½
And he sat down and called the Twelve; and he said to them, "If anyone would be first, he must be last of all and servant of all."	9:35	1
for no one who does a mighty work in my name will be able soon after to speak evil of me	9:39	½
because you bear the name of Christ, etc.	9:41	1
And if your [foot] causes you to sin, cut it off; it is better for you to enter life lame than with two feet to be thrown into hell	9:45	1
where their worm does not die and the fire is not quenched	9:48	1
Concerning salt	9:49–50	2
And in the house the disciples asked him again, etc.	10:10–12	2
But when [Jesus] saw it he was indignant	10:14	½
And he took them in his arms and blessed them	10:16	½
And as he was setting out on his journey, a man ran up and knelt before him	10:17	½
And Jesus looking upon him loved him	10:21	½
And the disciples were amazed at his words. But Jesus said to them again, "Children, how hard it is to enter the kingdom of God!"	10:24	1

DETAILS	REF	NO.
now [in this time], houses and brothers and sisters and mothers and children and lands, with persecutions,	10:30	½
and Jesus was walking ahead of them; and they were amazed, and those who followed were afraid	10:32	½
or to be baptized with the baptism with which I am baptized?	10:38	½
and with the baptism with which I am baptized, you will be baptized	10:39	½
And they called the blind man, saying to him, "Take heart; rise, he is calling you." And throwing off his mantle he sprang up and came to Jesus	10:49–50	1½
tied at the door out in the open street	11:4	½
Blessed is the kingdom of our father David that is coming!	11:10	½
and went into the temple; and when he had looked round at everything, as it was already late, [he went out to Bethany] with the twelve	11:11	½
[And seeing] in the distance [a fig tree] in leaf, [he went] to see if he could find anything on it. When he came to it, [he found nothing but leaves,] for it was not the season for figs	11:13	½
"[May no] one [ever] eat [fruit from you again]." And his disciples heard it.	11:14	½
And they came to Jerusalem	11:15	½
And he would not allow anyone to carry anything through the temple	11:16	1
And he taught . . . for all the nations	11:17	½
And as they passed by in the morning, they saw the fig tree withered away to its roots. And Peter remembered [and said] to him, "Master, look! [The fig tree] which you cursed has withered."	11:20–21	2
and does not doubt in his heart, but believes that what he says will come to pass, [it will be done] for him. Therefore I tell you	11:23–24	½
and whenever you stand praying, [forgive,] if you have anything against anyone; so that [your Father also who is in heaven may forgive you] your trespasses	11:25	½
and so with many others, some they beat and some they killed	12:5	½
[And one of the] scribes came up and heard them disputing with one another, and seeing that he answered them well	12:28	½
Jesus answered, "The first is, Hear O Israel: The Lord our God, the Lord is one . . ."	12:29	1
The scribe's response	12:32–34	3
and the great throng heard him gladly. And in his teaching . . .	12:37–38	½
And he sat down opposite the treasury and watched how the multitude [put] their money [into the treasury]. Many rich people put in large sums.	12:41	1
[And he] called his disciples to him, and [said] to them " . . . those who are contributing to the treasury"	12:43	½
opposite the temple, Peter and James and John and Andrew asked	13:3	½

Fleshing Out the Facts and Figures

DETAILS	REF	NO.
But take heed; [I have told you] all things [beforehand]	13:23	½
when the master of the house will [come], in the evening, or at midnight, or at cockcrow, or in the morning—lest he come suddenly and find you asleep. And what I say to you I say to all: Watch.	13:35–37	2½
[ointment] of pure nard, very costly, and she broke the flask . . . "[Why] was the ointment thus [wasted]?"	14:3–4	½
[sold for] more than three hundred denarii . . . And they reproached her	14:5	½
and whenever you will, you can do good to them	14:7	½
She has done what she could	14:8	½
And [the disciples] set out and [went] into the city	14:16	½
[prayed] that, if it were possible, the hour might pass from him. And he said, "Abba, [Father,] all things are [possible] to you; remove [this cup from me]."	14:35–36	1
and they did not know what to answer him	14:40	½
The young man who fled in the night	14:51–52	2
and their witness did not agree	14:56	½
And some stood up and bore false witness against him, saying, "We heard him [say] . . . I will [build] another, not made with hands." Yet not even so did their testimony agree.	14:57–59	2½
And some began [to spit] on him, and to cover [his face]. . . . And the guards received him with blows.	14:65	½
one of the [maids] of the high priest [came]; and seeing Peter warming himself, she looked at him	14:66–67	½
and the whole council held a consultation	15:1	½
And [Pilate] again asked [him], "Have you no answer to make?"	15:3	½
And among the rebels in prison, who had committed murder in the insurrection, there was a man [called Barabbas]. And the crowd came up and began to ask Pilate to do as he was wont to do for them.	15:7–8	1½
And it was the third hour when they crucified him.	15:25	1
[the mother of James] the younger and of Joses, and Salome, who, when he was [in Galilee, followed him,] and ministered to him; and also many other women who came up with him to Jerusalem.	15:40–41	1
And [when evening] had come, since it was the day of Preparation, that is, the day before the Sabbath	15:42	1
And Pilate wondered if he were already dead; and summoning the centurion, he asked him whether he was already dead. And when he learned from the centurion that he was dead	15:44–45	1½
And when [the Sabbath] was past, Mary Magdalene, Mary the mother of James, and Salome bought [spices]; so that they might go and anoint him.	16:1	1

DETAILS	REF	NO.
And they were saying to one another, "Who will roll away the stone for us from the door of the tomb?" And looking up, [they] saw that [the stone was rolled] back, for it was very large.	16:3–4	2
[And they went out] and fled [from the tomb]; for trembling and astonishment had come upon them; and they said nothing to anyone, for they were afraid.	16:8	1
TOTAL of verses unique to Mark:		155

This equivalent of 155 verses represents 23½% of the 661 verses in Mark's Gospel.

Shorter Details Unique to Mark

Some of the more noteworthy of the shorter details found only in Mark are:

1:13 and he was with the wild beasts
1:20 with the hired servants
1:35 and there he prayed
1:41 Moved with pity
2:3 carried by four men
2:9 take up your pallet
2:14 the son of Alphaeus
2:23 as they made their way
2:25 when he was in need
2:26 when Abiathar was high priest
3:6 with the Herodians
4:1 Again he began to teach
4:10 And when he was alone
4:39 "Peace! Be still!"
5:6 from afar
5:13 about two thousand
5:34 and be healed of your disease
6:14 The king
6:17 because he had married her
6:23 even half of my kingdom
6:26 he did not want to break his word to her
6:30 and taught
6:39 by companies upon the green [grass]
6:40 in groups, by hundreds and fifties
6:47 and he was [alone] on the land
8:15 and the leaven of Herod
8:27 on the way
8:32 And he said this plainly

8:35 and for the gospel's [sake]
9:28 into the house
9:36 taking him in his arms
10:19 Do not defraud
10:20 "Teacher"
10:21 looking upon him, loved him,
10:29 and for the sake of the gospel
10:46 Bartimaeus . . . the son of Timaeus
10:52 on the way
11:17 for all the nations
11:25 And whenever you stand praying
12:12 so they left him and went away
12:27 you are quite wrong
12:42 which make a penny
14:6 "Let her alone"
14:36 "Abba"
14:72 [the cock crowed] a second time
15:21 the father of Alexander and Rufus
15:24 what each should take
15:43 [Joseph] took courage and

Correspondence between Mark's Words and Those of Matthew and Luke

After allowing for all of Mark's small details such as those above, which are too short to be included in the list of verses given in the previous section, the proportion of unique material in Mark would amount to more than 25%. That is to say, more than 25% of the actual content of Mark's Gospel is not paralleled in either Matthew or Luke. So far as I am aware, there are no precise statistics available for this information.

Morgenthaler's statistics are not able to assist with this information since he did not analyze his material along these lines. He does give (1971, 165) a figure of 1,033 words as unique to Mark (*Sondergut* words), but in assigning words to this category (33–65) he does not treat as *Sondergut* many that are in Mark and not paralleled elsewhere. For example, in Mark 1:35–38 the *Synopticon* shows that there are 34 words in Mark that do not occur in Matthew or Luke, whereas Morgenthaler does not list even one word from this passage in his Markan *Sondergut*. Mark 2:1–12 contains quite a bit of unparalleled material (see 2:1–2; "carried by four men," 2:3; etc.—the *Synopticon* shows 76 words in this passage unparalleled in either Matthew or Luke), and again Morgenthaler lists this passage as containing no unique material. Mark 3:1–6 contains 25 words unparalleled in the other

Synoptics, and here Morgenthaler lists three words as unique (these are in 3:4c). Mark 3:13–19 contains 39 unparalleled words (including "those whom he desired"; "to be with him and to be sent out to preach"; "whom he surnamed Boanerges, that is, sons of thunder"), but Morgenthaler shows this passage as containing no *Sondergut*.

It is difficult to perceive what has been Morgenthaler's operating principle in deciding what constituted unique material in Mark; in any case, his figures do not provide any assistance in ascertaining how many words Mark contains that are not to be found in the Major Synoptics. Honoré and de Solages give figures that can assist in this (see further, below).

Morgenthaler's figures show how many words are identical between Matthew and Mark, and between Mark and Luke. Morgenthaler (239–41) lists (in the order of percentage of identical words in the two Gospels) the pericopes that Mark and Matthew have in common, and those that Mark and Luke have in common (241–43). He also gives the number of words in Mark's Gospel, and the words in the corresponding passages of Matthew and Luke, and the extent to which Matthew and Luke use words identical with Mark's (68, 163, 166).

However, the material *is* available for comparison in Farmer's *Synopticon*. The *Synopticon* sets out the Greek text of all three Synoptic Gospels, with the identical words marked in distinctive colors and cognate words underlined in the same colors (blue, agreement between all three Synoptics; orange-yellow, agreement between Matthew and Mark; red, agreement between Matthew and Luke; green, agreement between Mark and Luke). A perusal of the *Synopticon* text of Mark's Gospel discloses that the average number of words per page that are neither marked nor underlined in color is well in excess of 25%. (Cf. table 3 below.)

TABLE 1: PERCENTAGES OF IDENTICAL WORDS IN THE SYNOPTIC GOSPELS

The following table sets out Mark's Gospel, with the percentages of identical words in Matthew and Mark, and Mark and Luke. In the table, there are seven columns of numerical information. The first two columns give percentages for Matthew and Luke; the next three give numbers of words for Mark, Matthew and Luke; and the last two give percentages for Markan words in Matthew and Luke. These figures have the following meaning:

The figures in column 3 are the number of words in Mark for each pericope in sequence; the figures in columns 4 and 5 are, respectively, the numbers of words in Matthew and Luke that are identical with words in Mark for that pericope: that is, column 4 gives the number of words that Mark and Matthew have in common, and column 5 gives the number of words that Mark and Luke have in common. These figures are the basis for the two sets of percentage columns.

Columns 1 and 2 give the percentages of the words in Matthew and Luke in each pericope that are identical with words in Mark. That is, these columns give the percentage that the number of identical words in Matthew and Luke (columns 4 and 5) represents of the *total number of words* that Matthew and Luke respectively have employed for that pericope. For example, in Mark 4:10–12 Luke's parallel for this pericope has 18 words identical with Mark (column 5), which is 50% (column 2) of the total number of words for this pericope in Luke since Luke's version of this pericope contains 36 words.

Columns 6 and 7 give the percentages that these words identical in Mark and the other Gospels represent of the *total number of words* that Mark employed for that pericope. For example, in Mark 4:10–12 Luke's parallel for this pericope has 18 words identical with Mark (column 5), which is 35% (column 7) of the total number of words for this pericope in Mark since Mark's version of this pericope contains 52 words.

The first five columns of this table are compiled from the Synoptic statistics given by Morgenthaler. The figures in the last two columns are not given by Morganthaler but are the percentages of columns 4 and 5, respectively, to column 3.

Mark	Pericope	1 % of Matt	2 % of Luke	3 Mark Total	4 Words the same Matt	5 Words the same Luke	6 % of Mark in Matt	7 % of Mark in Luke
1:1–6	The Baptist	51%	55%	96	48	26	50%	27%
1:7–8	John's messianic preaching	45%	63%	30	14	21	47%	70%
1:9–11	The baptism of Jesus	46%	51%	53	27	22	51%	42%
1:12–13	The temptation	43%	35%	30	9	8	30%	27%
1:14–15	First Galilee preaching	29%	50%	35	7	6	20%	17%
1:16–20	Call of first disciples	61%	—	82	54	—	66%	—
1:21–22	In Capernaum synagogue	62%	44%	31	18	13	58%	42%
1:23–28	In Capernaum synagogue	—	50%	92	—	46	—	50%
1:29–31	Peter's mother-in-law	47%	45%	44	14	17	32%	39%
1:32–34	Sick healed at nightfall	39%	29%	46	7	12	15%	26%

Mark	Pericope	1 % of Matt	2 % of Luke	3 Mark Total	4 Words the same Matt	5 Words the same Luke	6 % of Mark in Matt	7 % of Mark in Luke
1:35–38	Jesus prays alone	—	15%	48	—	7	—	15%
1:39	First preaching tour	7%	63%	15	2	5	13%	33%
1:40–44	Cleansing of a leper	60%	49%	69	37	36	54%	52%
1:45E	Leper spreads the news	—	4%	29	—	1	—	3%
2:1–12	Healing of a paralytic	62%	33%	196	71	71	36%	36%
2:13–17	Call of Matthew/Levi	73%	48%	109	61	45	56%	41%
2:18–22	Question about fasting	69%	55%	129	72	71	56%	55%
2:23–28E	Plucking grain on Sabbath	55%	57%	108	51	52	47%	48%
3:1–6	Man with withered hand	59%	30%	94	37	34	39%	36%
3:7–12	Healing the multitudes	48%	26%	103	19	19	18%	18%
3:13–19	Choosing of the Twelve	19%	33%	90	13	25	14%	28%
3:20–21	Madness accusation	—	—	28	—	—	—	—
3:22	Beelzebul accusation	33%	57%	21	6	8	29%	38%
3:23–30	Beelzebul controversy	38%	20%	120	40	16	33%	13%
3:31–35E	Jesus' true family	50%	44%	83	45	24	54%	29%
4:1–9	Parable of the sower	60%	51%	151	79	46	52%	30%
4:10–12	The reason for parables	22%	50%	52	10	18	19%	35%
4:13–20	Interpreting the sower	42%	36%	146	54	39	37%	27%
4:21–25	Five sayings	75%	40%	76	18	27	24%	36%
4:26–29	Parable of growing seed	—	—	60	—	—	—	—
4:30–32	Parable of mustard seed	34%	33%	57	17	13	30%	23%
4:33–34	Jesus' use of parables	27%	—	25	4	—	16%	—
4:35–41E	Stilling of the storm	35%	36%	120	30	34	25%	28%
5:1–21	The healing of legion	38%	40%	346	55	124	16%	36%
5:22–43E	Jairus/woman of faith	36%	37%	353	49	97	14%	27%
6:1–6a	Rejection at Nazareth	55%	—	126	59	—	47%	—
6:6b–13	Sending out the Twelve	29%	31%	106	33	28	31%	26%
6:14–16	Herod's view of Jesus	35%	34%	54	12	18	22%	33%
6:17	Imprisonment of John	79%	18%	24	15	6	63%	25%
6:18–29	The death of John	53%	—	224	62	—	28%	—
6:30–44	Five thousand are fed	52%	31%	236	87	51	37%	22%
6:45–52	Walking on the water	53%	—	139	63	—	45%	—
6:53–56E	Healings at Gennesaret	66%	—	72	29	—	40%	—
7:1–23	Traditions of men	56%	—	359	132	—	37%	—
7:24–30	Syrophoenician woman	22%	—	130	23	—	18%	—
7:31	By the Sea of Galilee	33%	—	20	6	—	30%	—
7:32–37E	Healing of deaf mute	—	—	94	—	—	—	—
8:1–10	Four thousand are fed	54%	—	146	70	—	48%	—
8:11–13	Pharisees seek a sign	34%	21%	47	12	7	26%	15%

Fleshing Out the Facts and Figures 115

		1	2	3	4	5	6	7
					Words the same		% of Mark in	
Mark	Pericope	% of Matt	% of Luke	Mark Total	Matt	Luke	Matt	Luke
8:14–15	Leaven of the Pharisees	40%	19%	31	9	5	29%	16%
8:16–21	Jesus explains	32%	—	74	21	—	28%	—
8:22–26	Healing of blind man	—	—	80	—	—	—	—
8:27–30	Peter's confession	51%	39%	75	39	26	52%	35%
8:31	First passion prediction	44%	76%	30	14	19	47%	63%
8:32–33	Peter's rebuke	60%	—	39	24	—	62%	—
8:34–9:1	Discipleship conditions	70%	74%	135	82	78	61%	58%
9:2–8	The transfiguration	63%	30%	121	76	43	63%	36%
9:9–10	Descending the mountain	58%	15%	36	14	4	39%	11%
9:11–13	The coming of Elijah	34%	—	52	22	—	42%	—
9:14–29	Healing the epileptic	35%	34%	270	39	37	14%	14%
9:30–32	Second passion prediction	43%	33%	47	13	18	28%	38%
9:33–37	Lesson about the child	43%	48%	85	23	24	27%	28%
9:38–41	The stranger exorcizing	50%	66%	77	12	25	16%	32%
9:42	On causing stumbling	59%	45%	27	17	10	63%	37%
9:43–48	The seriousness of sin	49%	—	95	35	—	37%	—
9:49–50E	Concerning salt	75%	69%	25	6	9	24%	36%
10:1–12	Marriage and divorce	53%	—	147	80	—	54%	—
10:13–16	Blessing the children	53%	77%	64	34	44	53%	69%
10:17–22	The rich young man	43%	71%	110	50	65	45%	59%
10:23–27	Riches and discipleship	53%	69%	91	34	37	37%	41%
10:28–31	Leaving and receiving	63%	63%	80	38	35	48%	44%
10:32–34	Third passion prediction	56%	40%	73	30	17	41%	23%
10:35–40	Zebedee's sons' request	54%	—	112	51	—	46%	—
10:41–45	Exercising lordship	81%	19%	79	59	13	75%	16%
10:46–52E	Healing of Bartimaeus	34%	49%	123	27	53	22%	43%
11:1–10	Entry into Jerusalem	48%	36%	164	63	60	38%	37%
11:11	Jesus in the temple	28%	—	21	7	—	33%	—
11:12–14	Cursing of the fig tree	45%	—	55	17	—	31%	—
11:15–17	Cleansing of the temple	82%	84%	65	37	21	57%	32%
11:18–19	Conspiracy against Jesus	—	25%	32	—	9	—	28%
11:20–25	The fig tree withers	34%	—	101	26	—	26%	—
11:26	[Omitted in critical text]							
11:27–33E	Question on authority	66%	58%	125	76	68	61%	54%
12:1–11	Parable of the farmers	44%	46%	161	77	71	48%	44%
12:12	Attempt to arrest him	32%	46%	20	10	12	50%	60%
12:13–17	Question on tribute	50%	44%	106	58	46	55%	43%

Mark	Pericope	1 % of Matt	2 % of Luke	3 Mark Total	4 Words the same Matt	5 Words the same Luke	6 % of Mark in Matt	7 % of Mark in Luke
12:18–27	Question on resurrection	55%	50%	169	90	85	53%	50%
12:28–31	The Great Commandment	30%	—	78	24	—	31%	—
12:32–34	The scribe's reply	19%	20%	75	3	3	4%	4%
12:35–37a	Question on David's Son	50%	62%	56	31	29	55%	52%
12:37b–40	Scribes and Pharisees woe	14%	72%	51	5	34	10%	67%
12:41–44E	The widow's gift	—	55%	75	—	32	—	43%
13:1–4	Destruction of temple	39%	44%	75	28	20	37%	27%
13:5–8	Signs before the end	72%	52%	57	47	37	82%	65%
13:9–13	Persecutions foretold	47%	25%	97	23	22	24%	23%
13:14–20	The desolating sacrilege	70%	27%	115	81	25	70%	22%
13:21–23	False Christs and prophets	71%	—	37	24	—	65%	—
13:24–27	The Son of Man coming	53%	27%	71	49	18	69%	25%
13:28–29	Parable of the fig tree	92%	49%	37	33	19	89%	51%
13:30–32	The time of the coming	80%	89%	49	40	24	82%	49%
13:33–37E	Exhortation to watch	64%	—	65	7	—	11%	—
14:1–2	Jesus' death sought	21%	46%	34	15	11	44%	32%
14:3–9	Anointing in Bethany	57%	—	124	62	—	50%	—
14:10–11	The betrayal by Judas	34%	25%	30	12	11	40%	37%
14:12–16	Passover preparations	54%	51%	99	33	48	33%	48%
14:17–21	The betrayal foretold	74%	28%	84	59	16	70%	19%
14:22–25	The last supper	68%	43%	69	54	29	78%	42%
14:26	To the Mount of Olives	100%	35%	8	8	6	100%	75%
14:27–28	Resurrection foretold	63%	—	27	22	—	81%	—
14:29–31	Peter's denial foretold	62%	31%	52	32	10	62%	19%
14:32–42	Gethsemane	55%	23%	181	107	16	59%	9%
14:43–50	The arrest of Jesus	59%	26%	122	84	32	69%	26%
14:51–52	The young man who fled	—	—	19	—	—	—	—
14:53–54	Peter follows Jesus	49%	10%	43	19	3	44%	7%
14:55–61a	Jesus before Sanhedrin	56%	—	89	31	—	35%	—
14:61b–64	High priest's question	51%	20%	67	41	15	61%	22%
14:65	Ill treatment of Jesus	19%	15%	23	4	4	17%	17%
14:66–72E	Peter's denial	44%	29%	125	51	33	41%	26%
15:1	Delivered to Pilate	25%	13%	23	7	4	30%	17%
15:2–5	The trial before Pilate	40%	74%	48	24	14	50%	29%
15:6–15	Barabbas or Jesus	37%	20%	124	45	21	36%	17%
15:16–20a	The soldiers' mockery	42%	—	63	33	—	52%	—
15:20b–21	The road to Golgotha	40%	47%	25	8	9	32%	36%
15:22–32	The crucifixion	52%	27%	134	80	31	60%	23%

Mark	Pericope	1 % of Matt	2 % of Luke	3 Mark Total	4 Words the same Matt	5 Words the same Luke	6 % of Mark in Matt	7 % of Mark in Luke
15:33	Darkness over the land	69%	53%	13	9	10	69%	77%
15:34–36	"My God, my God, why?"	43%	—	53	27	—	51%	—
15:37–41	The death of Jesus	40%	27%	82	34	16	41%	20%
15:42–47E	The burial of Jesus	32%	23%	101	25	23	25%	23%
16:1–8	The women at the tomb	21%	21%	137	28	23	20%	17%
	TOTALS:	49.4%	39.7%	11,078	4,230	2,675	38.2%	24.1%

When columns 1 and 2 are viewed from the Markan Priority perspective, they provide the answer to the question: What percentages of the words in Matthew and Luke respectively were taken over unchanged from Mark? From the Markan Dependence perspective this question would be, What percentages of the words in Matthew and Luke respectively were taken over from those Gospels by Mark?

When columns 6 and 7 are viewed from the Markan Priority perspective, they provide the answer to the question: What percentages of the words of Mark were taken over unchanged by Matthew and Luke respectively? From the Markan Dependence perspective this question would be: What percentages of the words of Mark were taken over by Mark from Matthew and Luke respectively?

TABLE 2:
OVERALL SYNOPTIC WORD COMPARISONS

DETAILS	MARK	MATT	LUKE
Number of pericopes in common: Mark with		118	96
Number with 75% or more words in common:		8	4
Number with 50% or more words in common:		60	30
Total words in each Gospel:	11,078	18,278	19,404
Words identical with Mark's words:		4230	2675
Percent identical with Mark in whole of Matthew, Luke		23.1%	13.8%
Total words in passages parallel with Mark:		8555	6737
Percent of words in parallels that are identical with Mark		49.4%	9.7%
Percent of Mark's actual words used by Matthew, Luke		38.2%	24.1%

TABLE 3:
WORDS IN MARK IDENTICAL WITH MATTHEW AND LUKE

Morgenthaler does not give a figure for words in Mark that are identical in *both* Matthew and Luke. Honoré (1968, 98) gives this figure as 1,852 and de Solages (1959, 1041) gives it as 1,818; the difference is because they have made slightly differing assessments concerning equivalence. I have averaged these two figures to arrive at 1,835 as the figure for words identical in all three Synoptics. Using the figures in table 2 for Mark (11,078) shown for "Total words in each Gospel" and "Words identical with Mark's words" gives the following:

	MARK	MATT	LUKE
Words identical in Matthew, Mark, and Luke	1,835	1,835	1,835
Words identical in Matthew and Mark only	2,395	2,395	
Words identical in Mark and Luke only	840		840
Total identical words	5,070	4,230	2,675
Total words in Mark *also* in Matthew or Luke	5,070	45.8%	
Total words in Mark *not* in Matthew or Luke	6,008	54.2%	
Total words in Mark	11,078	100%	

	MARK	MATT	LUKE
Mark's words not in Matthew or Luke		6,008	6,008
Mark's words not in Matthew (but in Luke)		840	
Total of Mark's words *not* in Matthew		6,848	
Mark's words not in Luke (but in Matthew)			2,395
Total of Mark's words *not* in Luke			8,403
Total of Mark's words *not* in Matthew	6848	61.8%	
Total of Mark's words *not* in Luke	8403	75.8%	
Total words in Mark	11,078	100%	

Slightly differing word counts by different researchers reflect small differences in the Greek text used and differences of judgment concerning parallels and equivalence. As noted above, this table supplements Morgenthaler's statistics with an average figure (for words identical in all three Synoptics) calculated from Honoré's and de Solages's statistics. Such differences and such mixing of figures do not significantly affect the outcome, and these tables allow us to see the extent to which the Synoptic Gospels use (or do not use) identical words.

Markan Material Lacking in Matthew

The Markan material lacking in Matthew consists of all the material unique to Mark (as noted above) together with what is found only in Mark and Luke. This material is:

(a) Complete Pericopes

1:23–28	Exorcism in Capernaum synagogue
1:35–38	Jesus prays alone
4:21–25	Five sayings [Matthew has somewhat similar sayings in other contexts]
6:30	The return of the Twelve
9:38–40	The stranger exorcizing
12:41–44	The widow's gift

(b) Significant Parts of Pericopes

There are a number of pericopes that are told by Matthew in abbreviated form and at more length by both Mark and Luke, so that a very substantial amount of their material is lacking in Matthew and is common between Mark and Luke. The most noteworthy of these are:

2:1–12	The healing of the paralytic
3:1–6	The healing of the withered hand
5:1–20	The healing of legion
5:21–43E	Jairus's daughter and a woman of faith
6:14–16	Herod perplexed about Jesus

(c) Smaller Sections

1:45	The leper spreads the news
2:26	[not lawful for] any but the priests to eat, and also gave it to
3:2	[they] watched him to see whether he would [heal]
3:3	And he said to the man who had the withered hand, "Come here."
3:4	Is it [lawful on the Sabbath to do good] or to do harm, to save life or to [kill]?
3:7–8	[Jesus withdrew] with his disciples and a great multitude [followed him] from . . . Tyre and Sidon.
3:32	"Your mother and your brothers are outside to see you." [If Matt 12:47 is spurious]
6:11–12	"as a testimony against them"; the departure and ministry of the Twelve.
9:32	The disciples did not understand and were afraid to ask him.
9:37	receiving the one who sent me
10:52	Your faith has made you well.
11:2	[a colt] on which no one has ever sat.
11:18	Conspiracy to destroy Jesus
12:3	sent him away empty-handed

12:40	who devour widows' houses and for a pretense make long prayers. They will receive the greater condemnation. [If Matt 23:14 is spurious]
14:13–15	A man carrying a jar of water will meet you; follow him . . . and he will show you a large upper room furnished and ready.
15:43	Description of Joseph

(d) Words and Phrases

There are a great many other agreements of Mark and Luke where Matthew is lacking, particularly agreements of words and phrases. They are too numerous to list here, and may be found in Farmer's *Synopticon*, the sections of the Synoptic text marked green.

(e) From Luke's Perspective

The above information is given above from Luke's perspective below.

Markan Material Lacking in Luke

The Markan material lacking in Luke consists of all the material unique to Mark (see tables above) together with what is found only in Mark and Matthew. This material is:

(a) Complete Pericopes

4:33–34	Jesus' use of parables
6:17–29	The death of John the Baptist
6:45–52	Walking on the water
6:53–56E	Healings at Gennesaret
7:1–23	Traditions of men
7:24–30	The Syrophoenician woman's daughter
7:31	By the Sea of Galilee
8:1–10	Four thousand are fed
8:14–21	Leaven of the Pharisees [Luke 12:1 is a parallel, in a different context, to the first part of this pericope]
9:9–13	The coming of Elijah
9:42–48	On the seriousness of sin [Luke 17:1–2 is a parallel, in a different context, to the first part of this pericope]
10:1–10	On marriage and divorce
10:35–41	The request of the sons of Zebedee
11:11	Jesus in the temple
11:12–14	The cursing of the fig tree
11:20–25	The withering of the fig tree
14:26–28	On the way to the Mount of Olives [Luke 22:39 parallels the first part of this pericope]

Fleshing Out the Facts and Figures

| 15:16–20 | The mocking by the soldiers |

(b) Pericopes for which a Different Account Is Used

Some Markan pericopes are not paralleled in Luke, but Luke has, in a different context, another account with some points of similarity. These five pericopes are:

1:16–20	[Luke 5:1–11]	Call of the first disciples
6:1–6	[Luke 4:16–30]	Rejection at Nazareth
10:42–45	[Luke 22:25–27]	Exercising lordship
12:28–31	[Luke 10:25–28]	The Great Commandment
14:3–9	[Luke 7:36–50]	The anointing at Bethany

(c) Significant Parts of Pericopes

There are a number of pericopes that Mark has in common with both Matthew and Luke in which some significant part of the material occurs in both Matthew and Mark and is lacking in Luke. The most noteworthy of these are:

1:5–6	Crowds come to John; his food and clothing.
3:33–34	"Who is my mother and my brothers?" And looking around on those who sat about him, he said, "Here are my mother and my brothers!"
4:1–2	He [was] beside the sea. And a very large [crowd] gathered about him, so that he got into a boat. . . . And he taught them many things in parables.
4:5–6	ground where it had not much soil, and immediately it sprang up since it had no depth of soil; and when the sun rose it was scorched, and since it had no root [it withered away].
5:23	"Come and lay your hands on her, so that she may live."
5:28	"If I touch even his garments I shall be made well."
8:32–33	Peter's rebuke of Jesus and Jesus' reply
9:28	The disciples' question concerning their failure to exorcize
9:41	The one who gives a cup of water will not lose his reward.
10:31	The first last and the last first [Luke 13:30 is a parallel, in a different context, to this saying]
11:15b	and those who bought in the temple, and he overturned the tables of the money-changers and the seats of those who sold pigeons.
13	The Olivet Discourse [see especially 13:10,18,19b–24,27,32–37E].
14:22–25	The last supper [If Luke 22:19b–20 is spurious]
14:33–34	[Jesus] took with him Peter, James and John; asked them to watch.
14:39–42	Jesus' second and third prayers
14:49b–50	for the Scriptures to be fulfilled; and they all forsook him and fled.
14:55–61a	Jesus before the Sanhedrin
15:3–5	On trial before Pilate
15:34–36	"My God, my God, why?"

(d) Words and Phrases

There are a great many other agreements of Matthew and Mark where Luke is lacking, particularly agreements of words and phrases. These are too numerous to list here but can be found in Farmer's *Synopticon*, the sections of the Synoptic text marked orange-yellow.

(e) From Matthew's Perspective

The above information is given from Matthew's perspective below.

Mark's "And he said to them..."

On some occasions Matthew and/or Luke contain continuous words of Jesus whereas Mark interrupts the flow of what Jesus said with "And he said." Here are these instances:

MATTHEW		MARK		LUKE	
12:8	–	2:27	And he said to them	6:5	And he said to them
13:9	–	4:9	And he said	8:8	As he said this, he called out
13:18	–	4:13	And he said to them	8:11	–
[5:15	–]	4:21	And he said to them	8:16	–
[7:2	–]	4:24	And he said to them	8:18	–
	–	4:26	And he said		–
10:11	–	6:10	And he said to them	9:4	–
[15:3]	–	7:9	And he said to them		–
16:28	–	9:1	And he said to them	9:27	–

This expression also occurs in Matthew and Luke as well when introducing a new unit of teaching, e.g.:

MATTHEW		MARK		LUKE	
13:31	Another parable he put before them, saying	4:30	And he said	13:18	he said therefore
13:33	He told them another parable		–	13:20	And again he said

In Mark 7:20 the words "And he said" are used when resuming a quote of Jesus after an editorial aside by the author, commenting on what Jesus had just been quoted as saying, "Thus he declared all foods clean." Mark then adds the words "And he said" to indicate clearly the difference between what are the words of the author of the Gospel and what are being quoted of Jesus' words. This may well be the key to understanding the insertion of these words in the other places in Mark. In several of such places, what follows Mark's "And he said [to them]" could otherwise be taken by a listener as a comment by someone else, such as the author of the Gospel or perhaps an exhortation by the person reading or reciting it. Such a misunderstanding would be impossible for a person *reading* the Gospel himself, or if not impossible, at least unlikely. These iterated "and he said" interjections are suggestive of what is done by *someone speaking* to indicate that *he is still continuing with quoting someone else*. If so, they accord with the suggestion in chapter 3 that Mark's Gospel was intended as a tool for oral use. If not this, then it is less easy to see why they should occur in these places in Mark, in the *middle* of a section that quotes Jesus' spoken words. There are numerous discourses recorded in Mark (e.g., Mark 13:5–37E) where there is no insertion of "and he said," but the suggestion offered here does indicate a way of accounting for the insertion when it *does* occur.

The Significance of This Data for Our Present Study

The content of Mark's Gospel for which there is no direct parallel in either Matthew or Luke is in excess of 25%. This figure is higher than that given by other writers because they have listed only complete verses and/or they have left out some of this material from their assessment on the basis of some subjective judgment. For example, Streeter (1924, 195), when listing "The passages of Mark which are absent from both Matthew and Luke ... total, 32 verses" says, "N.B. These lists do not include odd verses which add nothing material to the sense." Some of this unique material represents repetition of ideas expressed elsewhere in the context, or could be described as "purely verbal expansion" (Streeter, ibid., 158); but there would be very little (if any) of it that could not be said to be fulfilling some function in Mark's narrative.

Consideration needs also to be given to the material in Mark paralleled in one other Synoptic only, because on the Markan Priority Hypothesis all this material was before both Matthew and Luke in Mark's Gospel, and was rejected by one or other of them for inclusion in his own Gospel.

When one examines the wording of those places that are parallel in the Synoptic Gospels, it is found that although they may be closely similar in *content* they can differ quite extensively in *wording* (see above), so that (table 3) more than half (54.2%) of Mark's actual words do not occur in either Matthew or Luke. Moreover (table 2), Matthew's parallel passages contain only 38.2% (that is, less than two words in five) of what is in Mark, and Luke's parallel passages contain only 24.1% (that is, less than one-fourth) of the actual words that occur in Mark. That is to say, if Matthew and Luke have used Mark as their source, then in those passages for which Mark is their source, Matthew has ignored or altered three out of every five of Mark's words, and Luke has ignored or altered three out of every four of Mark's words.

COMPARATIVE SYNOPTIC STATISTICS

Verses in the Synoptic Gospels

The number of verses in the Synoptic Gospels (after allowing for those rejected as spurious in modern critical editions) is as follows:

	MATTHEW	MARK	LUKE
Total verses	1,071	678	1,151
Rejected	4	17	3
Net	1,067	661	1,148
Rejected:	17:21	7:16	17:36
	18:11	9:44,46	22:19b–20
	21:44	11:26	23:17
	23:14	15:28	
		16:9–20	

"Total" is that obtained by taking the last verse number of each chapter and adding these figures together. "Rejected" refers to the number of verses for each Gospel rejected as not authentic by modern critical editions of the Gospels. "Net" thus gives the number of verses usually accepted as authentic for each Gospel. The verses in each Gospel usually rejected as not authentic are then listed. (These frequently-cited figures are given here without prejudice to the separate question of whether textual evidence justifies a verdict in favor of the rejection of any of these verses.)

Verses Unique to Matthew

Matthew's *Sondergut* consists of 485 verses, which is 45.5% of his Gospel. The basis of inclusion here has been the judgment (admittedly on a few occasions of a subjective nature) that the material in question could not reasonably be held to be derived directly and exclusively from what appears in either of the other Synoptic Gospels, so that either its source is Matthew himself or it has come from some other source to which Matthew had access. On some occasions the *Sondergut* material consists of several verses or partial verses scattered through a pericope, and the total number of such verses has been given for *Sondergut* in that pericope, rather than listing each separately. Thus Matthew's *Sondergut* comprises:

MATERIAL	MATTHEW	NO.
Matthean infancy narrative	1 and 2	48
John's message of repentance	3:2	1
Those he saw coming to him	3:7	½
Baptism of Jesus	3:13–15	2½
First Galilee preaching	4:12–17	4
First preaching tour	4:23–25	2½
Sermon on the Mount	5, 6, 7	77
Cleansing of a leper	8:1	1
The healing of the centurion's servant	8:5–13	3
The sick at nightfall (prophecy)	8:17	1
Sayings to would-be disciples	8:18–22	1
Healing of the Gadarene demoniacs	8:28–34	1
The crossing to his own city	9:1	1
Such authority given to men	9:8	½
"I desire mercy, and not sacrifice"	9:13	½
And the report of this went through all that district	9:26	1
Two blind men healed	9:27–31	5
Dumb demoniac healed	9:32–34	3
The mission charge	9:35–10:16	6
The fate of the disciples	10:17–25	9
Exhortation to fearless confession	10:26–33	1½
Divisions within households	10:34–36	1½
Conditions of discipleship	10:37–39	3
Conclusion of the discourse	10:40–11:1	4
John hearing about Christ in prison	11:2	½
Jesus' testimony about John	11:7–19	4
Woe to cities of Galilee	11:20–24	2
Comfort for the burdened	11:28–30E	3
Plucking grain on the Sabbath	12:5–7	3
Healing of the withered hand	12:9–14	2
Fulfillment of Isaiah's prophecy	12:17–21	5
Beelzebul accusation	12:22–24	1
Beelzebul controversy	12:25–37	5
Seeking for signs	12:38–42	1½
So shall it be also with this evil generation	12:45	½
That same day Jesus went out of the house and sat	13:1	½
Fulfillment of Isaiah's prophecy	13:14–15	2
Blessedness of the disciples	13:16–17	2
The parable of the wheat and the weeds	13:24–30	7
Fulfillment of what the prophet spoke	13:35	1
The parable of the wheat and weeds interpreted	13:36–43	8
The parables of the treasure and the pearl	13:44–46	3
The parable of the net	13:47–50	4

MATERIAL	MATTHEW	NO.
The parable of the householder	13:51–52	2
And when Jesus had finished these parables	13:53	½
Feeding of the five thousand	14:13–21	1
Walking on the water	14:22–33	5½
Traditions of men: what defiles a man	15:1–20	3½
Healing the Syrophoenician woman's daughter	15:21–28	5
The healing of many	15:29–31	3
The Pharisees seek a sign	16:1–4	3
The leaven of the Pharisees	16:5–12	2
Peter's confession at Caesarea Philippi	16:13–23	5
And then he will repay every man for what he has done	16:27	½
The transfiguration	17:1–8	3
The disciples understood that he referred to John	17:13	1
The healing of the epileptic boy	17:14–20	1½
Payment of the temple tax	17:24–27	4
The lesson about the child	18:1–5	2½
The inevitability of causes of stumbling	18:7	1
The parable of the lost sheep	18:10–14	4
On reproving one's brother	18:15–20	6
On reconciliation	18:21–22	2
The parable of the unmerciful servant	18:23–35	13
On marriage and divorce	19:1–12	4
The rich young man	19:16–30	1½
The parable of the vineyard laborers	20:1–16	16
Mother of sons of Zebedee's request	20:20–21	1
Fulfillment of what the prophet spoke	21:4–5	2
Jesus in the temple	21:10–17	5
When the disciples saw it, they marveled	21:20	½
The parable of the two sons	21:28–32	5
The parable of the wicked farmers	21:33–46E	2
The parable of the marriage feast	22:1–14	14
Then the Pharisees went and took counsel how	22:15	½
The astonishment of the crowd at his teaching	22:33	1
The Great Commandment	22:34–40	2
The question about David's Son	22:41–46E	2½
Woes against scribes and Pharisees	23:1–36	24
Olivet Discourse	24:4–25:46E	55
The conspiracy to kill Jesus	26:1–5	1
Judas betrays Jesus for 30 pieces of silver	26:15	1
Judas's question and Jesus' answer	26:25	1
Jesus' repeated prayer	26:42–44	1
"Friend, why are you here?" Then they came up	26:50	½

Fleshing Out the Facts and Figures

MATERIAL	MATTHEW	NO.
Jesus' rebuke for using the sword	26:52–54	3
I adjure you by the living God	26:63	½
The death of Judas	27:3–10	8
The message from Pilate's wife	27:19	1
Pilate's repeated question; choice of Barabbas	27:21	½
Pilate washes his hands; the crowd's reply	27:24–25	2
Jesus mocked by the soldiers	27:27–31	1
He trusts in God . . . he said, "I am the Son of God"	27:43	1
Earthquake, and bodies of the saints raised	27:51–54	3
and Joseph, and the mother of the sons of Zebedee	27:56	½
The guard at the tomb	27:62–66E	5
The empty tomb	28:1–8	3½
Jesus appears to the women	28:9–10	2
The report of the guard	28:11–15	5
The Great Commission	28:16–20E	5
TOTAL of Matthew's *Sondergut*:	485 (= 45.5% of 1,067 verses)	

Since there are no direct parallels for this material in Luke, no part of Luke could have been derived from it.

Verses Unique to Luke

Luke's *Sondergut* consists of 686 verses, which is about 60% of his Gospel, and comprises:

MATERIAL	LUKE	NO.
Lukan infancy narrative	1 and 2	132
The fivefold date	3:1–2	2
Quotation from Isaiah	3:5–6	2
John's sociological preaching	3:10–14	5
The questioning of the people	3:15	1
Summary of John's preaching	3:18	1
John's imprisonment	3:19–20	2
Genealogy of Jesus	3:23–38E	16
The devil's boast	4:6–7	1
The devil's departure	4:13	1
First Galilee preaching	4:14–15	2
Rejection at Nazareth	4:16–30	12
high fever . . . they besought him . . . and he stood over her and rebuked [the fever]	4:38–39	½
The sick at nightfall	4:40–41	1
A preaching tour	4:44E	1
Call of the first disciples	5:1–11	11

MATERIAL	LUKE	NO.
The arrival of the leper	5:12	½
The aftermath of healing the leper	5:15–16	1½
No one desires new wine after old	5:39	1
The scribes' and Pharisees' fury	6:11	½
A night of prayer; choosing apostles	6:12–13	1
The Beatitudes	6:20–23	1
The woes	6:24–26	3
Do good, bless those who curse you	6:27–28	1
Lending and receiving again	6:34–35	2
Do not condemn; forgive and give	6:37–38	1
The centurion's message to Jesus	7:3–7	4
The raising of the widow's son at Nain	7:11–17	7
John's question; Jesus' healings	7:20–21	2
Comment on Jesus' reply to John	7:29–30	2
Anointed by the woman who was a sinner	7:36–50E	2
The ministering women	8:1–3	3
That those who enter may see the light	8:16	½
Description of the demoniac	8:27	½
The fear of the people of the Gerasenes	8:37	½
About the woman touching Jesus	8:45–47	1
"but who is this about whom I hear such things?" And he sought to see him.	9:9	½
Now it happened that as he was praying alone, [the disciples] were with him	9:18	½
The transfiguration	9:28–36	4
The explanation about the child and the demon	9:38–39	1
Astonishment at the majesty of God	9:43	1
Second passion prediction	9:44–45	1
But when Jesus perceived the thought of their hearts	9:47	½
for he who is least among you all is the one who is great	9:48	½
The Samaritan villagers	9:51–56	6
and as they were going along the road, a man	9:57	½
Sayings to would-be disciples	9:60–62E	2½
Sending out the 70	10:1	1
Instruction to the 70	10:5–11	4
Hearing or rejecting	10:16	1
Return of the 70	10:17–20	4
Then turning to the disciples he said privately	10:23	½
The lawyer's question	10:25–28	4
The parable of the good Samaritan	10:29–37	9
Mary and Martha	10:38–42E	5
Jesus teaches the Lord's prayer	11:1–4	4

Fleshing Out the Facts and Figures

MATERIAL	LUKE	NO.
The friend at midnight	11:5–8	4
An egg or a scorpion?	11:12	1
The Beelzebul controversy	11:14–23	3½
Concerning light	11:33–36	2½
Discourse against Pharisees	11:37–54E	9
Exhortation to fearless confession	12:1–9	2
The Holy Spirit's help	12:11–12	1½
The parable of the rich fool	12:13–21	9
If you cannot do that, why worry about the rest?	12:26	1
Your Father's good pleasure	12:32	1
Sell your possessions and give alms; provide yourselves with purses that do not grow old, with [a treasure] . . . that does not fail	12:33	½
Watchfulness and faithfulness	12:35–46	5
The servant's wages	12:47–48	2
Divisions in households	12:49–56	6
And why do you not judge for yourselves what is right?	12:57	1
The parable of the barren fig tree	13:1–9	9
The healing of the crippled woman	13:10–17	8
Comparison of the kingdom of God	13:20	1
Exclusion from the kingdom	13:22–30	9
Herod the fox	13:31–33	3
The healing of a man with dropsy	14:1–6	6
The parable about humility	14:7–14	8
The parable of the great supper	14:15–24	10
The conditions of discipleship	14:25–35E	11
The parable of the lost sheep	15:1–7	7
The parable of the lost coin	15:8–10	3
The parable of the prodigal son	15:11–32E	13
The parable of the unjust steward	16:1–13	13
The Pharisees reproved	16:14–15	2
Concerning the law	16:16–17	2
Concerning divorce	16:18	1
The story of the rich man and Lazarus	16:19–31E	13
Causing stumbling	17:1–2	2
On forgiveness	17:3–4	2
On faith	17:5–6	2
On unprofitable servants	17:7–10	4
The healing of 10 lepers	17:11–19	9
On the coming of the kingdom of God	17:20–21	2
The day of the Son of Man	17:22–37E	11
The parable of the unjust judge	18:1–8	8
The parable of the Pharisee and tax collector	18:9–14	6

MATERIAL	LUKE	NO.
Third passion prediction	18:31–34	1½
The healing of blind Bartimaeus	18:35–43E	2
Zacchaeus	19:1–10	10
The parable of the pounds	19:11–27	17
The entry into Jerusalem	19:28–39	3
Prediction of the destruction of Jerusalem	19:39–44	6
One day, as he was teaching the people [in the temple] and preaching the gospel	20:1	½
The parable of the wicked farmers	20:9–19	2½
The question about tribute to Caesar	20:20–26	1½
The question about the resurrection	20:27–40	5
Woes against the Pharisees	20:45	1
The predictions of Jesus	21:8–24	6
The coming of the Son of Man	21:25–28	2½
Take heed and watch!	21:34–46	3
Jesus' ministry in Jerusalem	21:37–38E	2
The betrayal by Judas	22:3–6	1
The Passover	22:7–23	5
Arrangements with Peter and John	22:8–9	2
Jesus' desire; the first cup	22:15–17	3
The hand of the betrayer on the table	22:21	1
Questioning one another who it was	22:23	1
Greatness; and Jesus' promise	22:27–30	4
Warning and exhortation to Peter	22:31–33	3
The two swords	22:35–38	4
Prayer in Gethsemane	22:39–42	2
The agony in the garden	22:43–44	2
The arrest of Jesus	22:47–53	3½
Before the Sanhedrin; Peter's denial	22:54–71E	3½
Before Pilate	23:1–5	3
To Herod and back again	23:6–16	11
Pilate's sentence	23:18–25	1½
The road to Golgotha	23:26–32	6
Jesus' crucifixion	23:33–43	7
Jesus' death on the cross	23:44–49	2
Jesus' burial	23:50–56E	2
Jesus' empty tomb	24:1–12	5
Jesus' resurrection appearances	24:13–53E	41
TOTAL of Luke's *Sondergut*:	686 (= 60.2% of 1,148 vv.)	

Since there are no direct parallels for this material in Matthew, no part of it could have been derived from Matthew.

Verses in Matthew and Mark (but not Luke)

With the above must be considered also the material that Matthew shares with Mark but not with Luke, since no part of Luke is derived from it. This material consists of 187 verses, or 17.5% of Matthew, and comprises:

MATERIAL	MATTHEW	NO.
John's food and clothing	3:4	1
John's baptism	3:5–6	1½
John's arrest	4:12	½
Jesus' message	4:17	1
The call of the first disciples	4:18–22	5
Jesus went throughout Galilee, healing	4:23	½
The ruler's request	9:18	½
The woman's thought	9:21	1
The crowd put outside	9:25	½
A cup of cold water to drink	10:42	1
The command not to make him known	12:16	1
Entering a strong man's house	12:29	½
Forgiveness for sin and blasphemy	12:31	½
Who are my mother and my brothers?	12:48–49	2
Jesus gets into a boat and sits there	13:1–2	1½
No depth of soil, no root; scorched	13:5–6	1
Some sixtyfold, some thirty	13:8	½
Some sixtyfold, some thirty	13:23	½
Smallest of seeds to greatest of shrubs	13:32	½
Jesus' use of parables	13:34	1
Rejection at Nazareth	13:53–58	6
That is why these powers are at work in him	14:2	½
The death of John the Baptist	14:3–12	10
To a lonely place by boat; crowds come on foot	14:13	½
Going ashore and seeing a great throng, he had compassion on them	14:14	½
Jesus walks on the water	14:22–27	6
The wind ceases	14:32	1
Healings at Gennesaret	14:34–36	3
The traditions of men	15:1–20	16½
Healing the Syrophoenician woman's daughter	15:21–28	3
The feeding of the four thousand	15:32–39	8
The Pharisees seek a sign	16:1–4	1
The leaven of the Pharisees	16:5–12	6
Peter's confession at Caesarea Philippi	16:13–23	2½
The coming of Elijah	17:9–13	4½
Often in the fire, often in the water	17:15	½

MATERIAL	MATTHEW	NO.
The disciples' private question	17:19	1
On the seriousness of sin	18:8–9	2
Marriage and divorce	19:1–9	9
Jesus lays hands on the children	19:15	1
The first last and the last first	19:30	1
Jesus going up to Jerusalem	20:17	1
The sons of Zebedee's request	20:20–28	9
Jesus in Jerusalem	21:10–17	2
The cursing of the fig tree	21:18–22	5
I will tell you by what authority	21:24	½
Set a hedge around it and dug a winepress	21:33	½
This was the Lord's doing, and it was marvelous in our eyes	21:42	½
Then the Pharisees seek to entangle him in his talk	22:15	½
Jesus answers them; they bring him a coin	22:18–19	½
The Sadducees' ignorance	22:29	1
The Great Commandment	22:34–40	7
As he sat on the Mount of Olives, the disciples came to him privately, saying, "Tell us"	24:3	½
But he who endures to the end will be saved	24:13	1
Worldwide preaching of the gospel	24:14	1
The desolating sacrilege	24:15–22	6
False Christs and false prophets	24:23–28	3
After the tribulation of those days	24:29	½
The angels will gather his elect	24:31	1
Of that day and hour, no one knows	24:36	1
To arrest Jesus by stealth	26:4	½
The chief priests' caution	26:5	1
The anointing at Bethany	26:6–13	8
The betrayal foretold	26:21–24	3
The last supper	26:26–29	1
The way to Gethsemane: Peter's denial foretold	26:30–35	4½
In Gethsemane	26:36–46	7
Judas's betrayal	26:47–56	5
Where the scribes and elders had gathered . . . [Peter followed] as far as the courtyard of the high priest	26:57–58	½
Testimony of the false witnesses; the judgment	26:59–68	8
The accusations of the chief priests	27:12–14	3
Jesus or Barabbas?	27:15–22	2½
The soldiers' mockery	27:27–31	5
They offered him wine; he would not drink it	27:34	1
Jesus derided on the cross	27:39–42	3
The death of Jesus	27:46–49	4
The women at the cross	27:56	1

Fleshing Out the Facts and Figures 133

MATERIAL	MATTHEW	NO.
TOTAL		204½
Less: Adjustment		17½
NET TOTAL of Matthew and Mark (but not Luke)		187 (= 17.5% of 1067 verses)

Concerning the above adjustment: some of the above passages, while of such significance that they merit inclusion, are a little less than a verse or half-verse in size (as the case may be), so that the total is slightly overstated. Thus this adjustment removes the discrepancy that would otherwise occur, and reduces the Total to a more accurate figure.

Verses in Luke and Mark (but not Matthew)

Similarly, the material must be considered also that Luke shares with Mark but not with Matthew, for no part of Matthew is derived from it. This material consists of 54 verses, which is 4.5% of Luke and comprises the following:

MATERIAL	LUKE	NO.
The exorcism in the Capernaum synagogue	4:31–37	7
Jesus prays alone	4:42–43	2
The circumstances of the paralytic's healing	5:17–19	2
The questioning of the scribes and Pharisees	5:21	½
The healed man takes up his bed, etc.	5:25–26	½
[they] watched him to see whether he would [heal]	6:7	½
and he said to the man who had the withered hand, "Come . . . here."	6:8	½
Jesus' question	6:9	½
Jesus heals the multitudes	6:17–19	2
Five sayings	8:16–18	1½
Confrontation with Legion	8:27–31	3
The reaction of the people	8:35–39	4
Jairus's request	8:40–42	1
Jesus' question; the woman comes forward	8:45–47	1½
Report of the girl's death; Jesus responds	8:49–52	2½
After she is raised	8:55–56	2
"A testimony"; departure of the Twelve	9:5–6	1
Views about Jesus; Herod's comment	9:8–9	1½
The return of the Twelve	9:10	½
and [he] spoke to them of the kingdom of God	9:11	½
"Are we to go and buy food?"	9:13	½
"Sit down in companies"; they did so	9:14	½
The healing of the epileptic boy	9:37–43	1
The stranger exorcizing	9:49–50	2

MATERIAL	LUKE	NO.
For they perceived that he had told this parable against them	12:12	½
The comparison of the kingdom of God	13:18	1
The colt's owners' inquiry	19:33–34	2
Conspiracy against Jesus	19:47–48	2
A servant came for some of the [fruit] of the vineyard; they sent him away empty-handed	20:10	½
Woes against the Pharisees	20:45–47E	1½
The widow's gift	21:1–4	4
Persecution predicted	21:12–17	3
Preparation for the Passover	22:7–13	½
Concerning Joseph of Arimathea	23:50–51	½
TOTAL of Luke and Mark (but not Matthew)	54 (=4.5% of 1148 vv.)	

COMMON AND UNIQUE MATERIAL IN THE SYNOPTICS

The following is a diagrammatic summary of unique verses and of the extent of content equivalence between verses in the Gospels, derived from my own count of verses that are or are not equivalent in the Synoptics. The statistical and other data from which these figures are derived has been set out above. Verses are regarded as equivalent where it is reasonable to decide that what is contained in one Gospel could have been derived from another.

MATTHEW (1067 vv)		LUKE (1148 vv)	
in Mt, not in Lk: 672 vv (63%)	in Mt & Lk: 395 vv (37%)	in Lk & Mt: 408 vv (35½%)	in Lk, not in Mt: 740 vv (64½%)
In Mt Only 485 vv (45½%)	not Mk 131 vv (12½%)	not Mk 132 vv (11½%)	in Lk Only 686 vv (60%)
Mt not Mk 616 vv (58%)		Lk not Mk 818 vv (71½)	
Mt/Mk not Lk 187 vv (17½%)	Mt/Mk also Lk 264 vv (24½%)	Lk/Mk also Mt 276 vv (24%)	Lk/Mk not Mt 54 vv (4½%)
Mt also in Mk 451 vv (42%)		Lk also in Mk 330 vv (28½%)	

171 vv (26%) from Mt	275 vv (41½%) from Mt & Lk	60 vv (9%) from Lk	155 vv (23½%) Unique	PETER

In Mt 446 vv (67½)
In Lk 334 vv (50½)
In either Mt or Lk or both 506 vv (76½)
MARK (661 vv)

Fleshing Out the Facts and Figures 135

Average Verse Length

DETAILS	MATTHEW	MARK	LUKE
Verses	1,067	661	1,148
Words (de Solages 1959, 1049)	18,518	11,090	19,587
Average verse length	14.26 words	16.78 words	14.06 words
Words (Morgenthaler 1971, 89)	18,298	11,078	19,448
Average verse length	14.15 words	16.76 words	16.94 words

NOTE: Morgenthaler and de Solages give different figures for the number of words in the Gospels due to minor differences in the text used, and thus in the word count. The statistics of Morgenthaler are the ones adopted in this study.

The Significance of This Data for Our Present Study

This data allows us to know the extent to which, on verse count, the Synoptic Gospels are and are not parallel in content to each other (*parallel* being defined as sufficiently equivalent so that it is reasonable to consider that material in one or two Gospels could be the source for the material in one or both of the others). It is also possible to see the average word length of verses in the three Synoptic Gospels.

COMPARISON OF PERICOPES AND THE WORDS OF JESUS

Mark's Healing Stories

In the following table, Peri indicates the Pericope Number in Aland's *Synopsis* (sometimes the following pericope in his Synopsis is also included in what is given here); REF is the passage reference in Mark; TYPE is the type of miracle recorded; and the NO. OF WORDS gives the word count based on Morgenthaler, with some adjustment where he divides the pericopes differently.

Types of miracles are designated thus:

B	Blind	F	Fever	L	Leper	R	Raising dead
D	Deaf mute	G	General	N	Nature	S	Supply
E	Exorcism	H	Hemorrhage	P	Paralysis	W	Withered hand

No.	Peri	REF	Type	Details of the Disease Healed	NO. OF WORDS		
					Mark	Matt	Luke
1.	35	1:21–28	E	exorcism of unclean spirit	123	29	119
2.	37	1:29–31	F	fever (Peter's mother-in-law)	44	30	38

No.	Peri	REF	Type	Details of the Disease Healed	NO. OF WORDS		
					Mark	Matt	Luke
3.	38	1:32–34	G	crowds of sick, demon-possessed	46	36	52
				[Mark omits "You are the Son of God" and "he was the Christ"]			
4.	40	1:39	G	casting out demons	15	27	8
				[Mark omits the detailed program of Jesus' ministry, and mentions only the preaching and casting out of demons]			
5.	42	1:40–45	L	a leper	98	62	98
				[Mark omits "But he withdrew [to the wilderness] and prayed"]			
6.	43	2:1–12	P	a paralyzed man	196	126	213
				[Mark has no parallel for the unique introduction, Luke 5:17 (36 words); without this, Mark is longer than Luke by 20 words]			
7.	47	3:1–6	W	a man with a withered hand	94	90	115
8.	48	3:10–12	G	many diseases and unclean spirits	41	12	22
9.	137	5:1–20	E	exorcism of unclean spirit (Legion)	325	135	293
10.	138	5:21–34	H	a woman with a hemorrhage	223	85	166
11.	138	5:35–43	R	a dead girl	151	53	114
12.	148	6:53–56	G	the sick	72	44	–
13.	151	7:24–30	E	exorcism of unclean spirit (a girl)	130	139	–
				[Mark omits the disciples' request to send the woman away and Jesus' words "I was sent only to the lost sheep of the house of Israel"]			
14.	152	7:31–37	D	deaf mute	114	63	–
15.	156	8:22–26	B	blind man of Bethsaida	80	–	–
16.	163	9:14–29	E	boy possessed by dumb spirit	270	133	124
17.	264	10:46–52	B	blind Bartimaeus	123	79	108
			Triple Tradition		1,450	868	1,366
			Matthew/Mark Double Tradition		317	247	–
			Mark/Luke Double Tradition		123	–	119
			Mark's *Sondergut*		80	–	
TOTAL WORDS IN MARK'S HEALING STORIES					1,970	1,115	1,485

Mark's Other Miracle Stories

No.	Peri	REF	Type	Details of the Miracle	NO. OF WORDS		
					Mark	Matt	Luke
1.	136	4:35–41	N	stilling the storm	120	85	94
2.	145	6:30–44	S	feeding 5,000	236	168	164
3.	147	6:45–52	N	walking on the sea	139	120	–
4.	153	8:1–10	S	feeding 4,000	146	129	–
5.	272	11:12–14		the fig tree cursed and			
	275	11:20–26	N	the fig tree withering	156	98	–
TOTAL WORDS IN MARK'S OTHER MIRACLE STORIES					797	600	258

Pericope Length and the Words of Jesus

Morgenthaler (33–68) divides Mark's Gospel into 128 pericopes, which he gives with their parallels in the Major Synoptics. He analyzes the words of all three Synoptics in three categories: when Jesus speaks a *logion* (which Morgenthaler designates by L); other words of Jesus in direct speech (discourse/conversation, designated W); and accompanying text (designated B). Thus L and W together give all that Jesus said, while B indicates accompanying narrative (including what others said).

A generalization can be made about the relationship between the length of Jesus' sayings in the three Synoptics, and about narrative in the three Synoptics:

1. In general, in Mark's pericopes, his narrative material is longer than the parallels in either Matthew or Luke.
2. In general, in every account of Jesus' sayings, Mark's record is shorter than either Matthew's or Luke's.

There are a number of pericopes that are approximately the same size in Mark and one or both of the other Synoptics. And in some particular instances Mark's narrative is shorter or his record of the words of Jesus is longer than those in the other Synoptics; but on these occasions it is usually possible to recognize that some special circumstance is operable in the particular pericope in question. For example, in the short pericope of the healing of the leper (Matt 8:1–4//Mark 1:40–45//Luke 5:12–16), Matt 8:1 and Luke 5:12a contain different settings for this healing, and Mark gives his account without commencing with any setting for it. Without including these introductions, which are not paralleled in Mark, Mark's narrative is longer than Luke's, and much longer than Matthew's.

This difference between the Gospels is illustrated by the overall figures, drawn from Morgenthaler's statistics (1971, 89; the reference numbers given below under "REF.#" are to the sections of his material from which they are drawn):

DETAILS	(REF.#)	MARK		MATTHEW		LUKE	
		B	W+L	B	W+L	B	W+L
Triple Tradition	(1.1/1.2)	6,909	4,169	5,096	3,459	4,243	2,494
Mark doublets	(1.3)			19	109		12
Additional	(1.3)				68		30
Matthew/Luke (Q)	(2.1/2.2)			364	3,497	411	3,252
"Q" doublets	(2.3)			29	61		11
Additional	(2.3)						108

DETAILS	(REF.#)	MARK		MATTHEW		LUKE	
		B	W+L	B	W+L	B	W+L
Sondergut	(Matt 4.1; Luke: 4.2)			2,102	3,704	5,167	3,919
				7,610	10,898	9,821	9,826
Less: Double counting				139	71	130	69
TOTALS		6,909	4,169	7,471	10,827	9,691	9,757
Transfer of B material		—	6,909	—	7,471	—	9,691
GRAND TOTAL			11,078		18,298		19,448
Percent of words of Jesus and of other words in each Gospel							
		62.37%	34.53%	40.83%	59.17%	49.83%	50.17%
		[other]	[Jesus]	[other]	[Jesus]	[other]	[Jesus]

The Significance of This Data for Our Present Study

This data shows that in his miracle narratives Mark is almost always the longest account, and in those instances where Mark is not longer a specific reason for this can be noted in some particular element in Matthew or Luke that is not in Mark's account. The exception is the pericope of the healing of the withered hand, where Luke is longer than Mark in each part of the story. Overall, Mark is longer in these accounts than the other two Synoptics.

The figures for pericope length and the division between the words of Jesus and other material throw interesting light on the differences between these three Gospels. In round figures, one third of Mark's Gospel consists of the words of Jesus, and two thirds consists of other words (narrative, editorial/redactional comment, and the words of others); whereas for Matthew the figures are respectively 60% and 40% (that is, six out of ten of the words of Matthew's Gospel are the words of Jesus); and for Luke the figures are 50% each.

LUKE'S TIME AND PLACE NOTES

The Data

Luke contains numerous notes of time or place, and these occur much more frequently in his Gospel than in Matthew as the following chart shows. (The numbers with the pericope titles are the pericope numbers in Aland's *Synopsis*.)

2, 3, 4, 7. Birth Narratives

Matt 1:18; 2:1–19	Luke 1:5–2:4
1:18 Now the birth of Jesus Christ took place in this way. When his mother Mary had been . . .	5. In the days of Herod, King of Judea, there was a priest named Zechariah, of the division of Abijah, and he had a wife . . .
	8. Now while he was serving as priest before God when his division was on duty . . .
	24. After these days his wife Elizabeth conceived, and for five months she hid herself . . .
	26. In the sixth month the angel Gabriel was sent from God to a city of Galilee named Nazareth . . .
	39. In those days Mary arose and went with haste into the hill country, to a city of Judah
	56. And Mary remained with her about three months, and returned to her home.
	57. Now the time came for Elizabeth to be delivered . . .
	59. And on the eighth day they came to circumcise the child . . .
2:1 Now when Jesus was born in of Judea in the days of Herod the king . . .	2:1 In those days a decree went out from Caesar Augustus that all the world should be enrolled. 2. This was the first enrolment, when Quirinius was governor of Syria. 3. And all went to be enrolled, each to his own city. 4. And Joseph also went up from Galilee, from the city of Nazareth, to Judea, to the city of David, which is called Bethlehem, because he was of the house and lineage of David . . . 6. And while they were there the time came for her to be delivered.
9. When they had heard the king they went their way	
13. Now when they had departed an angel of the Lord appeared	
19. But when Herod died, behold an angel of the Lord appeared	

9. Circumcision and Purification

Matt. 2:22-23	Luke 2:21–38
	21. And at the end of eight days . . .
	22. And when the time came for their purification according to the law of Moses, they brought him up to Jerusalem . . .
	24. And inspired by the Spirit he came into the temple; and when the parents brought in the child Jesus . . .
	38. And coming up at that very hour she gave thanks to God . . .
22-23. But when he heard . . . he went and dwelt in a city called Nazareth	39. And when they had performed everything according to the law of the Lord, they returned into Galilee, to their own city, Nazareth.

12. The Boy Jesus in the Temple

	Luke 2:41–46
	41. Now his parents went to Jerusalem every year at the feast of the Passover. 42. And when he was twelve years old, they went up according to custom . . .
	45. and when they did not find him . . .
	46. After three days they found him . . .
	48. And when they saw him they were astonished.

13. The Beginning of Jesus' Ministry

Matt 3:1–2	Luke 3:1–3
1. In those days	1. In the fifteenth year of the reign of Tiberius Caesar, Pontius Pilate being governor of Judea, and Herod being tetrarch of Galilee, and his brother Philip tetrarch of the region of Iturea and Trachonitis, and Lysanias tetrarch of Abilene, 2. in the high-priesthood of Annas and Caiaphas, the
came John the Baptist preaching in the wilderness of Judea,	word of God came to John the son of Zechariah in the wilderness,
	3. and he went into all the region about the Jordan,
2. "Repent . . ."	preaching a baptism of repentance . . .

19. The Age of Jesus

	Luke 3:23
	Jesus, when he began his ministry, was about thirty years of age . . .

20. The Temptation

Matt 4:1–2	Luke 4:1–2
1. Then Jesus was led up by the Spirit into the wilderness . . .	1. And Jesus, full of the Holy Spirit, returned from the Jordan, and was led by the Spirit
2. and he fasted forty days and forty nights . . .	2. for forty days in the wilderness, tempted . . .

30. Galilee Preaching

Matt 4:12	Luke 4:14
Now when he heard that John had been arrested, he withdrew into Galilee.	And Jesus returned in the power of the Spirit into Galilee.

33. Rejection at Nazareth

Matt 13:54	Luke 4:16
And coming to his own country he taught them in their synagogue . . .	And he came to Nazareth, where he had been brought up; and he went to the synagogue, as his custom was, on the Sabbath day . . .

35. In the Synagogue at Capernaum

	Luke 4:31
	And he went down to Capernaum, a city of Galilee.
	And he was teaching them on the Sabbath . . .

34. Healing of Peter's Mother-in-Law

Matt 8:14	Luke 4:38
And when Jesus entered Peter's house . . .	And he arose and left the synagogue and entered Simon's house . . .

38. Healing of the Sick at Nightfall

Matt 8:16	Luke 4:40
That evening . . .	Now when the sun was setting . . .

39. Jesus Prays Alone

	Luke 4:42
	And when it was day he departed and went to a lonely place

40. A Preaching Tour

Matt 4:23	Luke 4:44
And he went about all Galilee, teaching in their synagogues and preaching . . .	And he was preaching in the synagogues of Judea.

41. The Miraculous Catch of Fish

	Luke 5:1
	While the people pressed upon him to hear the word of God, he was standing by the lake of Gennesaret.

42. The Healing of a Leper

Matt 8:1	Luke 5:12
When he came down from the mountain great crowds followed him . . .	While he was in one of the cities, there came a man . . .

43. The Healing of the Paralytic

Matt 9:1	Luke 5:17
And getting into a boat, he crossed over and came to his own city.	On one of those days, as he was teaching . . .

44. The Call of Matthew/Levi

Matt 9:9	Luke 5:27
As Jesus passed on from there . . .	After this he went out . . .

46. Plucking Grain on the Sabbath

Matt 12:1	Luke 6:1
At that time . . .	On a Sabbath (or, On the second Sabbath after the first) . . .

47. The Healing of the Man with the Withered Hand

Matt 12:9	Luke 6:6
And he went on from there . . .	On another Sabbath . . .

49. The Choosing of the Twelve

Matt 10:1	Luke 6:12–13
	12. In these days he went out to the mountain to pray; and all night he continued in prayer to God.
And he called to him his twelve disciples . . .	13. And when it was day, he called his disciples, and chose from them twelve, whom he named apostles . . .

74. The Great Sermon

Matt 5:1	Luke 6:17
Seeing the crowds, he went up on the mountain . . .	And he came down with them and stood on a level place, with a great crowd of his disciples . . .

85. The Healing of the Centurion's Servant

Matt 8:5	Luke 7:1
	After he had ended all his sayings in the hearing of the people, he entered Capernaum.
As he entered Capernaum . . .	

86. The Raising of the Widow's Son

Luke 7:11
Soon afterward [or, Next day] he went to a city called Nain . . .

115. The Ministering Women

Luke 8:1
Soon afterward he went on through cities and villages, preaching . . .

122. The Teaching in Parables

Matt 13:1–3	Luke 8:4
1. That same day Jesus went out of the house and sat beside the sea. And great crowds gathered about him, so that he got into a boat and sat there; and the whole crowd stood on the beach.	And when a great crowd came together, and people from town after town came to him,
3. And he told them many things in parables . . .	he said in a parable . . .

135. Jesus' True Family

Matt 12:46	Luke 8:19
While he was still speaking to the people, behold his mother . . .	Then his mother . . .

136. Stilling the Storm

Matt 8:18,23	Luke 8:22
18. Now when Jesus saw great crowds around him, he gave orders to go over to the other side. . . . 23. And when he got into the boat, his disciples followed him.	One day he got into a boat with his disciples, and he said to them, "Let's go across to the other side of the lake." So they set out . . .

Fleshing Out the Facts and Figures 143

134. The Healing of Legion

Matt 8:28	Luke 8:26
And when he came to the other side, to the country of the Gadarenes . . .	Then they arrived at the country of the Gerasenes, which is opposite Galilee . . .

138. The Raising of Jairus's Daughter

Matt 9:18	Luke 8:40–49
While he was thus speaking to them, behold, a ruler came in	40. Now when Jesus returned, the crowd welcomed him, for they were all waiting for him. 41. And there came a man named Jairus, who was a ruler . . . 49. While he was still speaking, a man . . .

143. Herod's Perplexity Concerning Jesus

Matt 14:1	Luke 9:7
At that time Herod the tetrarch heard about the fame of Jesus . . .	Now Herod the tetrarch heard of all that was done, and he was perplexed . . .

145. The Return of the Apostles

	Luke 9:10a
	On their return the apostles told him what they had done.

146. The Feeding of the Five Thousand

Matt 14:13–15	Luke 9:10b–12
13. Now when Jesus heard this, he withdrew from there in a boat to a lonely place apart. 15. When it was evening . . .	And he took them and withdrew apart to a city called Bethsaida. 12. Now the day began to wear away . . .

158. Peter's Confession at Caesarea Philippi

Matt 16:13	Luke 9:18
Now when Jesus came into the district of Caesarea Philippi, he asked his disciples . . .	Now it happened that as he was praying alone, he disciples were with him; and he asked them . . .

161. The Transfiguration

Matt 17:1	Luke 9:28
And after six days . . .	Now about eight days after these sayings . . .

163. The Healing of the Epileptic Boy

Matt 17:9,14	Luke 9:37
9. And as they were coming down the mountain . . . 14. And when they came to the crowd . . .	On the next day, when they had come down from the mountain, a great crowd met him.

164. The Second Passion Prediction

Matt 17:22	Luke 9:43b
And as they were gathering in Galilee, Jesus said to them . . .	But while they are all marveling at everything he did, he said to his disciples . . .

166. The Dispute about Greatness

| Matt 18:1 | Luke 9:46 |
| At that time the disciples came to Jesus saying, "Who is the greatest in the kingdom . . . ?" | And an argument arose among them as to which of them was the greatest. |

174. The Decision to Go to Jerusalem

| Matt 19:1 | Luke 9:51 |
| Now when Jesus had finished these sayings, he went away from Galilee . . . | When the days drew near for him to be received up, he set his face to go to Jerusalem. |

176. On Following Jesus

| Matt 8:19 | Luke 9:57 |
| And a scribe came up and said to him . . . | As they were going along the road, a man said to him . . . |

174. The Mission of the Seventy

Luke 10:1
After this the Lord appointed seventy others . . .

180. The Return of the Seventy

Luke 10:17
The seventy returned with joy, saying . . .

181. Jesus' Thanksgiving

| Matt 11:25 | Luke 10:21 |
| At that time Jesus declared . . . | In that same hour he rejoiced . . . |

184. Mary and Martha

Luke 10:38
Now as they went on their way, he entered a village, and a woman named Martha . . .

185. Jesus Teaches the Lord's Prayer

Luke 11:1
He was praying in a certain place . . .

188. The Beelzebul Controversy

| Matt 12:22 | Luke 11:14 |
| Then a blind and dumb demoniac was brought to him . . . | Now he was casting out a demon that was dumb . . . |

190. True Blessedness

Luke 11:27
As he said this, a woman in the crowd . . .

191. The Sign of Jonah

| Matt 12:38 | Luke 11:29 |
| Then some of the scribes and Pharisees said to him . . . | When the crowds were increasing, he began to say . . . |

194. The Pharisee's Invitation to Dine

Luke 11:37
While he was speaking, a Pharisee asked him . . .

Fleshing Out the Facts and Figures

195. The Leaven of the Pharisees

Matt 16:5–6	Luke 12:1
5. When the disciples reached the other side, they had forgotten to bring any bread. 6. Jesus said to them . . .	In the meantime, when so many thousands of the multitude had gathered together that they trod upon one another, he began to say to his disciples first . . .

205. Interpreting the Times

Matt 16:1–2	Luke 12:54
1. And the Pharisees and Sadducees came, and to test him they asked . . . 2. He answered them . . .	He also said to the multitudes . . .

204. Repentance or Destruction

Luke 13:1
There were some present at that very time . . .

208. The Healing of the Crippled Woman

Luke 13:10–17
10. Now he was teaching in one of the
14. As he said this, all his adversaries were put to shame . . .

211. Exclusion from the Kingdom

Luke 13:22
He went on his way through towns and villages, teaching and journeying toward Jerusalem.

212. A Warning against Herod

Luke 13:31
At that very hour some Pharisees came . . .

214. The Healing of the Man with Dropsy

Luke 14:1
One Sabbath when he went to dine . . .

216. The Parable of the Great Supper

Luke 14:15
When one of those who sat at table with him heard this, he said to him . . .

214. The Conditions of Discipleship

Luke 14:25
Now great multitudes accompanied him; and he turned and said to them . . .

219. The Parables of the Three Lost Things

Luke 15:1
Now the tax collectors and sinners were all drawing near to hear him.

229. Warnings against Offenses

Luke 17:1
And he said to his disciples . . .

233. The Cleansing of the Ten Lepers
                Luke 17:11
                On the way to Jerusalem he was passing along . . .

234. On the Coming of the Kingdom of God
                Luke 17:20
                Being asked by the Pharisees when the kingdom of God was coming, he answered them . . .

236. The Parable of the Unjust Judge
                Luke 18:1
                And he told them a parable . . .

237. The Pharisee and the Publican
                Luke 18:9
                He also told this parable to some . . .

253. Jesus Blesses the Children

Matt 19:13	Luke 18:15
Then children were brought to him that he might lay his . . .	Now they were bringing even infants to him that he might touch them . . .

262. The Third Passion Prediction

Matt 20:17	Luke 18:31
And as Jesus was going up to Jerusalem, he took the twelve disciples aside, and on the way, he said to them . . .	And taking the twelve, he said to them . . .

264. The Healing of Bartimaeus

Matt 20:29	Luke 18:35
And as they went out of Jericho . . .	As he drew near to Jericho . . .

265. Zacchaeus
                Luke 19:1
                He entered Jericho and was passing through . . .

266. The Parable of the Pounds
                Luke 19:11
                As they heard these things, he proceeded to tell a parable, because he was near to Jerusalem . . .

269. The Triumphal Entry

Matt 21:1	Luke 19:28
And when they drew near to Jerusalem and came to Bethphage . . .	And when he had said this, he went on ahead, going up to Jerusalem. When he drew near to Bethphage . . .

270. Jesus Weeps over Jerusalem
                Luke 19:41
                And when he drew near and saw the city . . .

274. The Chief Priests and Scribes Conspire
                Luke 19:47
                And he was teaching daily in the temple.

Fleshing Out the Facts and Figures

276. The Question about Authority

Matt 21:23	Luke 20:1
And when he entered the temple . . .	One day, as he was teaching the people in the temple and preaching the gospel . . .

284. Woe to the Scribes and Pharisees

Matt 23:1	Luke 20:45
Then said Jesus to the crowds and to his disciples . . .	And in the hearing of all the people he said to his disciples . . .

301. The Ministry of Jesus in Jerusalem

	Luke 21:37–38
	34. And every day he was teaching in the temple, but at night he went out and lodged on the mount called Olivet. 38. And in the morning . . .

305. The Conspiracy to Kill Jesus

Matt 26:1–2	Luke 22:1
When Jesus had finished all these sayings, he said to his disciples, "You know that after two days the Passover is coming . . .	Now the feast of Unleavened Bread drew near, which is called the Passover.

308. Preparation for the Passover

Matt 26:17	Luke 22:7
Now on the first day of Unleavened Bread . . .	Then came the day of Unleavened Bread, on which the passover lamb had to be sacrificed.

330. Gethsemane

Matt 26:36	Luke 22:39
Then Jesus went with them to a place called Gethsemane . . .	And he came out, and went, as was his custom, to the Mount of Olives . . .

331. Jesus Arrested

Matt 26:47	Luke 22:47
While he was still speaking . . .	While he was still speaking . . .

344. The Death of Jesus

Matt 27:45	Luke 23:44
Now from the sixth hour . . .	It was now about the sixth hour . . .

350. The Burial of Jesus

	Luke 23:54,56
	54. It was the day of Preparation, and the Sabbath was beginning. 56. On the Sabbath they rested according to the commandment.

352. The Women at the Tomb

Matt 28:1	Luke 24:1
Now after the Sabbath, toward the dawn of the first day of the week . . .	But on the first day of the week, at early dawn, they went to the tomb . . .

355. The Journey to Emmaus	
	Luke 24:13
	That very day two of them were going . . .
356. Jesus Appears to His Disciples	
	Luke 24:36
	As they were saying this, Jesus himself . . .
365. The Ascension	
	Luke 24:44–51
	44. Then he said to them . . .
	51. While he blessed them, he parted from them and was carried up into heaven.

The Significance of This Data for Our Present Study

For most pericopes, Luke commences with a link of time, place, or circumstance to what has gone before. But in many cases he does not give any information or gives only a vague or generalized comment:

5:12	While he was in one of the cities . . .
5:17	On one of those days as he was teaching . . .
6:1	On a Sabbath
6:6	On another Sabbath
7:11	Soon afterward
8:1	Soon afterward
8:4	And when a great crowd came together
8:22	One day
9:18	Now it happened that as he was praying alone
20:1	One day

And so on. Furthermore, he frequently adds into his narrative details of the age of one of the key figures, or some other description or identification—such as that the rich man was a ruler, that the child was an only son or daughter, or how serious an illness was. Oftentimes, when a pericope is paralleled in Mark, this information is not in Mark and therefore it must have a non-Markan origin.

ASSESSMENT: WHAT ARE WE TO MAKE OF THE FACTS?

Accounting for Mark's Gospel

Author after author has blithely written of how little material there is in Mark that is not found also in Matthew and/or Luke. And, in the opinion of a host of scholars, there is much material not just "paralleled" but "incorporated" (and therein lies quite a difference) into Matthew and Luke, particularly the former.

But those who speak now of most of Mark being "incorporated into Matthew" are simply parroting the erroneous guesses of the past without updating those guesses with the accurate statistics provided for us by the Synoptic statisticians.

I have set out above all the material equal to or greater than about half a verse in length for which there is no equivalent in Matthew or Luke. This totals to 23.5% of the length of Mark. Then I provided the most important of—though by no means all of—the extra detail that Mark has placed in the stories he tells. I have listed 48 of these "extras." Not many of them are very important (though a few of them could be judged significant), but the point is, if we are assessing what part of the total Gospel record is in Mark alone, this material is part of that. When we add these "extras" to the 23.5%, it takes the total of material in Mark that is not paralleled in either Matthew or Luke to more than 25% of Mark's Gospel.

When we examine this unique material in Mark, we see that this is exactly what an eyewitness of these events such as Peter would be likely to include in his account when telling these stories, and exactly what Mark would remember accurately and would include in his Gospel—and this, as we have seen, is exactly what Papias said he did. The amount of Markan *Sondergut*—material unique to Mark and not paralleled in either Matthew or Luke—is more than 25% of Mark: *this* information has not just come to light as the result of any recent research since it has always been there. But more than 67% of Mark's *Sondergut* has been disregarded by those scholars who, on the basis of their inaccurate methodology, have stated instead that Mark only has about 50 to 56 verses (about 8% of the Gospel) that are not in the other Synoptics.

Table 1 shows the total number of words in Mark as 11,078, and of these, 4,230 words, or 38.2% of the words in Mark's Gospel are identical in Matthew's Gospel. Thus we can see that 61.8% of Mark's words are *not* in Matthew. Some of Mark's words are not identical with Matthew because those words are in Markan content that Matthew lacks completely—they are the words of Mark's *Sondergut* (the 25% of Mark's material not paralleled in Matthew or Luke). But in addition there is material in Mark that is found in Luke but not in Matthew (see above), and that is why these Markan words are not in Matthew. I estimate, from this listing, that this is equivalent to around 5% of Mark. So with the 25% Markan *Sondergut*, this adds up to about 30% of Mark not paralleled in Matthew, which indeed would be why those Markan words were not identical with any words in Matthew.

So, if 61.8% of Mark's wording is not identical with Matthew, while 30% of Mark's content is not in Matthew at all, then the balance of 31.8% of Mark's nonidentical wording is in pericopes that *are* parallel in content with Matthew. That is to say, 31.8% of the total of Mark's wording is where Mark and Matthew have the same content (tell the same story) but use different wording to do so.

What is the significance of this data? It is that 31.8% of the *content* of what Mark's Gospel contains is also in Matthew but uses *different words*. This means that almost a third of Mark's wording has been altered in Matthew.

This data is described in different ways by the advocates of the two competing hypotheses. Those adhering to Markan Priority say that Matthew omitted 30% of Mark's content, took over 38.2% of Mark's actual wording, but (for various reasons) changed the other 31.8% of the words he found in Mark. Suggested reasons are (1) to improve Mark's grammar, (2) because Mark is too hard on the disciples, and so forth.

Advocates of Markan Dependence see it differently. They explain that Mark has in front of him the Gospels of Matthew and Luke, but also in his memory he holds the recollections of Peter who told these same stories. This means that 38.2% of the time, the words Mark uses in telling a story are words that also occur in Matthew, but 31.8% of the time, Mark chooses the words that he remembers from Peter instead of Matthew's words. Plus, of the 30% of Mark's content that was not in Matthew, Mark got 25% from Peter (because it is Markan *Sondergut*) and 5% from Peter and/or Luke (because also found in that Gospel).

All of this is somewhat similar for Luke. Luke has only 2,675 identical words with Mark (table 1), i.e., 24.1%, so that 75.9% of Markan words are not identical. When allowance is made for Luke for the equivalent factors mentioned above for Matthew (Mark's *Sondergut* of 25% of his Gospel, and Markan content in Matthew but not in Luke, as described above, estimated as 29%), we could estimate that Markan content not in Luke is 54% (the 25% plus the 29%). Thus Mark's words and Luke's words, which are *different* but in similar *contents*, would be 21.9% (this non-identical total of 75.9% words minus the 54% of words in the Markan content that is not in Luke). This means that Luke's words have been altered from Mark's (or vice versa) on 21.9% of occasions.

I will not swear to the absolute accuracy of my estimates above (5% for Matthew and 29% for Luke); they depend, for instance, on how one treats similar but different pericopes in Mark and Luke. But, these apart, the figures come from the Synoptic statisticians, and when added together they are realistic and not wildly inaccurate. What they tell us is that in sections of identical content, where Mark and Matthew, and Mark and Luke, are recounting the same pericope, Matthew has altered Mark's wording (or vice versa) for almost one-third (31.8%) of Mark's words, and the same for Luke for more than one-fifth (21.9%) of Mark's words.

How then do we account, overall, for Mark? The order of the pericopes in Mark is (as shown in chap. 9) that of Luke down to 6:14, and thereafter is that of Matthew (for Peter, as Papias said, had no "order" in what he taught—he was totally an *ad hoc* preacher). Possibly, the structure of the pericopes owes something to Matthew and Luke also—though possibly not. The vocabulary of Mark (table 2) is 38.2% that of Matthew and 24.1% that of Luke (or Peter also may have used those same words, so that, at least we can say, in those words there is a concurrence of the vocabulary of Peter with that of Matthew and Luke).

But that is only part of the story. For, according to the statistics, 61.8% of Mark's vocabulary is not identical with Matthew, and 75.9% is not identical with Luke. This includes Mark's *Sondergut* of 25%—content (ranging from complete pericopes to a host of minor eyewitness detail) that is not in either of Matthew or Luke. And this Markan vocabulary is vigorous, down-to-earth vocabulary, the vocabulary of the oral, colloquial language of the day, the Greek of Peter and of Mark himself, the spoken language of Peter's sermons rather than the written language of Matthew and Luke. And this is true not of the vocabulary only, but of Mark's grammatical constructions, the entire way he expresses himself.

What Mark did with the accounts in front of him (Matthew and Luke) was to dress them in the language and thought forms of the recollections of Peter, as preached in his ministry. This is the one, single, completely sufficient, explanation of the wording differences of Mark with Matthew and Luke.

In the next chapter we consider the alternative explanations for the language differences in the same pericopes between Mark and Matthew and then between Mark and Luke. To anticipate a little, other "explanations" are not backed by any facts, or even by the probabilities of logic, and are founded on unsupported speculation. But to the contrary: the view I have put to you is not unsupported. Papias and the other early church Fathers tell us that Mark's Gospel goes back to the preaching of Peter. There are no grounds at all for saying that the Fathers did not know what they were talking about.

In particular, this is based on a recognition of the difference between spoken and written language, as pointed out by the linguists Palmer and

Gleason (see chap. 3). If anyone in (say) AD 66, familiar with both the preaching of Peter and the writings of Matthew and Luke, were to hear Mark's Gospel read aloud and were asked to comment, he would have said decisively, "Ah yes, Mark's Gospel is just what we heard from Peter!"

Accounting for the Major Synoptics

It is important to notice what Matthew contains that Luke does not. This comprises: the Matthean *Sondergut* of 485 verses or 45.5% of his Gospel, together with what he has in common with Mark, which is 187 verses or 17.5% of his Gospel, totaling 672 verses or 63% of his Gospel.

Luke's content that Matthew lacks comprises: the Lukan *Sondergut* of 686 verses or 60% of his Gospel, together with what Mark has in common with his Gospel, which is 54 verses or 4.5% of his Gospel, totaling 740 verses or 64.5% of his Gospel. Thus Matthew has 63% of his Gospel *not* in common with Luke, so there is 37% that is; Luke has 64.5% of his Gospel *not* in common with Matthew, so there is 35.5% that is. This means that each of the two Major Synoptics has somewhat more than one-third of their contents in common—and potentially from a common source (and this is the issue currently under investigation).

Now the material in common with Mark could have come from Mark (thus say the Markan Priorists), and the part that the Major Synoptics have in common with each other (but not in Mark) could have come from the postulated Q (so say the advocates of this source). But others (the Farrer Hypothesis advocates and the Two-Gospel view) say that the explanation is that Luke used the completed Gospel of Matthew. My contention is that the explanation most fully in accord with the data is that this material (to the extent to which the examination of the evidence indicates that it does have a common source) consists of material written by Matthew and in circulation in the form of separate notes or documents during the period from the time of Christ on earth to c. AD 60.

Looking at Mark's Healing Stories, and the Words of Jesus

First of all, we need to consider the words used by each Gospel in telling the healing stories about Jesus. In these stories in the Triple Tradition, Mark uses 1,450 words, Luke 1,366 words, and Matthew 868 words. Then additionally there is one such healing story Matthew does not include, and four of them are not in Luke. Luke has an interest in healings: in recounting these, he uses almost as many words as Mark (for every 17 words Mark uses, Luke uses 16). Yet Luke lacks four healing stories that are in Mark, three of which are also in Matthew. If Luke were using Mark as source (Markan

Priority Hypothesis) or Matthew as source (Two-Gospel Hypothesis), why would Luke, with this clear interest in the healing aspect of Jesus' ministry, have omitted these? My suggestion is that these healings were not found among the documents Luke collected in preparation for his Gospel.

By way of contrast, when Luke tells the two other miracle stories that he has in common with Mark, he uses about the same number of words as Matthew but far fewer than Mark: stilling the storm has 94 words compared to Mark's 120, and feeding 5,000 has 164 compared to Mark's 236. Also, of Markan words in the Triple Tradition (11,078), 34.63% are Jesus' words; whereas in Matthew (18,298 words) the figure is 59.17% and in Luke (19,448 words) 50.17%. In round numbers, in Mark less than four words in ten are words of Jesus; in Luke, the figure is five words in ten; in Matthew, six words in ten.

This is consistent with an overall generalization: Mark is less interested than the Major Synoptics in recording what Jesus said, though he very frequently refers to the fact of Jesus teaching. If Mark wrote his Gospel first, this is very surprising. Because of his background generally and in particular his association with the apostle Peter, he would certainly have been familiar with a great deal more of Jesus' teachings (see chap. 3). So why did he record so little of it? The most persuasive answer is because he was producing a Gospel to be used in preaching the *kerygma* in evangelistic outreach and he knew that Christians in the churches already had access to the *didache* of Jesus in those churches. It was no part of his purpose to repeat it.

Luke's Orderly Ways

Luke tells us that he wrote an "orderly" (καθεξῆς) account (see chap. 2), but in what way is it orderly? Earlier in this chapter, we examined the extent to which Luke has recorded details of the time, place, and sequence of the events he narrates. We can note from this data how, throughout his Gospel, Luke shows a constant concern with these questions. Virtually every separate incident he records is linked with the previous one by some note of transition regarding time or place. And where he cannot ascertain this information, he makes a general transition (e.g., 5:12, "While he was in one of the cities"; 5:17, "On one of those days"; 13:10, "Now he was teaching in one of the synagogues on the Sabbath").

Thus the evidence in Luke's Gospel itself indicates to us that he *intended* to write in chronological order to the extent to which, during his investigations, he was able to discover what that order was. It is still a matter open for further investigation and discussion whether he has fully succeeded in this.

There are, however, a few places where I think Matthew's order is clearly to be preferred. For example, Matthew records the call of Matthew Levi, follows it with Jesus' comments about fasting and new wine into old wineskins, and then says, "While he was saying these things to them, behold, a ruler came in and knelt before him" (9:18)—and recounts the story of Jairus. Luke's introduction to the story of Jairus is, "Now when Jesus returned [from his visit to the territory of the Gerasenes], the crowd welcomed him, for they were all waiting for him. And there came a man named Jairus" (Luke 8:40).

Luke 5:27–39 contains the call of Levi and Jesus' comments about fasting and placing new wine into old wineskins, followed by the incident of plucking grain on the Sabbath (paralleling Matt 12:1–8). These are all in totally different sequence. If Luke had had access to Matthew's account—with Matthew's "while he was thus speaking" tying together the two pericopes that Luke gives so far apart—I think it highly likely that Luke would have arranged them differently in his Gospel. I take it that this comment by Matthew is an editorial addition inserted when he was compiling his finished Gospel, information not available to Luke. This explains the lack of any specific situation when Luke is introducing Jairus, which jells strongly with the explanation that Luke included this information whenever he could find it and did not invent it when he could not.

These points are clear from an examination of all the data:

1. Luke was indeed particularly interested in details of time, place, and circumstance for his pericopes and in their relation to other pericopes.

2. Luke aimed at arranging his pericopes in chronological order so far as he could ascertain from his inquiries what this was. This would confirm that his intention was to narrate his story in chronological order (1:3).

3. When Luke had little information about the setting of a pericope, he did not invent one but mentioned what he knew; e.g., that an event occurred on a Sabbath; or simply "Soon afterward"; or even just, "One day."

It has been said by some that Luke was *not* interested in questions of place or circumstance, and in support of this has been cited the fact that he does not mention that Peter's confession took place at Caesarea Philippi, which is in Matthew and Mark (Matt 16:13//Mark 8:27//Luke 9:18). Such a deduction is predicated on the acceptance of Mark as a source for Luke, but an examination of the whole of Luke's Gospel (whether paralleled in Matthew or Mark or not, and thus irrespective of a particular theory of Synoptic relationships) shows that Luke *does indeed* have an interest in such matters. Thus this issue is relevant to the occasions when Mark or Matthew has more information of this kind in a given pericope than does Luke in his parallel. Since it is clear that Luke records this information when he has it, the most valid explanation that "Caesarea Philippi" is not in Luke is that this information was not in his sources. This means that Luke was not using either Mark or Matthew as sources since both these Gospels mention Caesarea Philippi. So, in summary we could say: there is good reason for taking "orderly" in 1:3 to be a statement of Luke's plan and intention to give a *chronological* account so far as he could.

In this we have a good explanation of the basic difference in order between Matthew and Luke. Certain pericopes had been linked together into pericope clusters at some stage during the period prior to AD 60, though we have no information about the reasons this was done. Still joined in these clusters, they became incorporated into both Major Synoptics, but in greatly varying contexts. For Matthew was arranging material on the basis of "like with like" within a general chronological framework, whereas Luke had the expressed intention of writing a chronological account—which he did to the extent that his material and his personal inquiries made possible.

In any future discussion of Synoptic issues, the data now available to us should be taken into account. I trust this chapter provides some further assistance in this regard.

5 THE MARKAN PRIORITY EXPLANATION

This chapter investigates the arguments advanced for Markan Priority and provides the refutation to them all.

> *Despite the alternatives . . . , the vast majority of the introductions and surveys of the Gospels or of the life of Christ, and the major commentaries on each of the Synoptics, along with studies more focused on individual themes or passages within those Gospels, all presuppose that Matthew and Luke each used Mark.*
> —Craig Blomberg (2001, 20)

> *In conclusion, it would seem that we live in the ironic situation where confidence in Markan priority rises to ever new heights despite the fact that, after forty-five years of steady criticism, knowledgeable defenders of the hypothesis have been forced to abandon one basic argument after another, to the point where there are, at present, no formal arguments left that will justify it and the compositional arguments are just as questionable. It has rightly earned the sobriquet "the Teflon hypothesis."*
> —David Dungan (1999, 390)

INTRODUCTION

The vast majority of New Testament scholars are of the opinion that Mark's Gospel was written first and that Mark was the source upon which Matthew and Luke drew for much of their material. In this book I am offering an alternative explanation and providing the evidence for it. Since many scholars consider they have good reason for claiming that Mark was written first, the arguments that have led them to Markan Priority should be considered and examined.

The Markan Priority Explanation

I have identified 21 such arguments used in support of Markan Priority, and in this chapter I examine them all. These arguments have already been assessed by quite a few scholars before me and refuted convincingly, but these convincing and conclusive refutations are constantly ignored or overlooked, and the old discredited arguments continue to be advanced as if they had never been refuted.

Many modern scholars acknowledge that one major reason for this continued dominance of Markan Priority is not because these arguments are strong and problem-free, but because they (or some of them) seem to make better sense than any other alternative. In this book I am submitting what I believe is a far better and more encompassing explanation of the data before us than Markan Priority is. But this chapter examines and refutes the traditional case for Markan Priority.

It is certainly important to assess the strength of the case for Markan Priority. Markan Priority and the use of Mark by Matthew and Luke affect a great many other areas of our thinking about the Gospels and the New Testament generally. One's view of the Synoptic Problem (and the relationship of the Synoptics to John's Gospel) affects how one reads and interprets the Gospels.

The Markan Priority Hypothesis is used as a starting point for much modern study of the Synoptic Gospels and for comments on them (especially in form criticism and redaction criticism). This means that much modern *interpretation* of the Synoptic Gospels is significantly affected by a *hypothesis* about how they are related to each other. Now, if that hypothesis is justified, then it is reasonable to start from it in looking at the Gospels. But if that hypothesis is incorrect, then interpretations based on it will be incorrect also. Indeed, questions of authorship, date, the place of writing, the audience for whom a Gospel was written, the purpose of writing, the perspective of the author on various things he mentions, as well as numbers of questions of interpretation, are all affected by a person's view of Synoptic relationships.

Moreover, the relationship between the Gospels and the Epistles is also connected with this issue. If, because Matthew followed Mark, his Gospel is to be dated late, then that Gospel was written after most of the Epistles and represents a later stage of church tradition than they do. This in its turn affects the interpretation of parts of Matthew and the Epistles (e.g., Jesus' references to "the church"). Thus from every point of view affecting interpretation, Matthew is a different book if based on Mark compared to Matthew if it is one of Mark's sources. Similar issues apply to Mark and Luke.

Thus time spent in the consideration of Synoptic interrelationships is not wasted but is, to quite a considerable extent, foundational to the study of the Synoptics themselves because of the way in which, in practice, our view of the Synoptic Problem provides the spectacles through which we view the Synoptic Gospels themselves. Canon (later Archbishop) Marcus Loane (*A Brief Survey of the Synoptic Problem*, 1945, 4–5), principal of Moore Theological College when I was a student there, made this significant comment about Synoptic studies:

> It has not been easy for students who cherish conservative views of the inspiration and authority of Scripture to know how to relate their convictions to the conclusions which have been announced with an air of certainty by so many Source Critics. It has been a matter of deep surprise to discover that [numbers of conservative scholars] have apparently accepted many of the findings of certain critics as though their case had been proved. But to demand the priority of Mark and the reality of Q, and to deny the Apostolic authorship of the First and Fourth Gospels, are points which conservative scholars cannot allow to go unchallenged. . . . I shall be satisfied if I have been able to show that the advocates of the Four-Document Hypothesis can by no means claim a fool-proof system. I shall be more than satisfied if I have been able to show that old-fashioned Conservatives still have solid grounds for their faith in the authority and inspiration of the Gospels.

The first of Loane's comments sums up his concern at the dominance of the Markan Priority view in Synoptic scholarship and its consequences. His second comment sets out the result of his own study in this field, which he has summarized in his booklet. His booklet and his teaching presented the details of Streeter's Four-Document Hypothesis, analyzed the case for and against it, and looked at alternative approaches. As a result, students left the college well aware of the majority view in Synoptic scholarship, but aware also of its weaknesses and limitations, that it was an unproven hypothesis which should not structure all our thinking about Synoptic relationships, and that it was not the only valid explanation of the data. I have always been very grateful to Principal Loane for his careful and balanced introduction to the Synoptic Problem.

This study of Markan Priority begins with background, which gives a concise history of the development of the Markan Priority Hypothesis. Then we examine the arguments that scholars use or have used to support it. In particular I want to point to the major studies that have refuted these arguments one after the other, and then to determine which of the arguments (if any) has any real substance today. (Chapter 7 describes 17 impossible things one must believe if one would embrace the Markan Priority Hypothesis.)

SOME BACKGROUND ON MARKAN PRIORITY AND Q

Various views have been offered to account for the similarities and differences in the Synoptic Gospels. The Markan Priority Hypothesis is the explanation that Mark's Gospel was the first of the Synoptics to be written and that Matthew and Luke used Mark in writing their Gospels, which explains the sections that are parallel in Matthew and Mark, or Mark and Luke, or all three. But this hypothesis on its own is insufficient to account for all the similarities in the Synoptics, for there are several major passages and a large number of shorter sayings that are absent in Mark but parallel in Matthew and Luke. Most of those who hold the Markan Priority view also accept the hypothesis that Matthew and Luke used a source called Q for the material common to Matthew and Luke but not in Mark.

There is a wide range of opinion about the nature of Q. T. W. Manson, B. H. Streeter, V. Taylor, and others think Q was an actual document, while Styler (1962, 223) considers it better to employ the term Q to denote the material common to Matthew and Luke (but absent from Mark) rather than to denote an actual document. From this perspective, Q was probably a mixture of short documents in Greek and Aramaic and a rather amorphous body of semi-fixed oral tradition. But other scholars accept Markan Priority but do not find the evidence for Q to be convincing and therefore reject this hypothesis. Thus, A. Farrer (1955, 55–86) contends that Luke drew on Matthew, so there is no need for Q. M. Goulder (1974, 452) and M. Goodacre (2001, 122–23; see below and chap. 10 for more details) also hold this position.

The view that Mark and Q are the sources for Matthew and Luke is commonly known as the "Two-Document Hypothesis"—though this term is something of an anomaly for scholars who do not consider Q to be one document but several or who regard Q as having contained oral traditions. The term "Two-Source Hypothesis" is more common today and has the same meaning without carrying any implication about the nature of Q. I am happy to use either term.

Many scholars regard Q as the source for the material that Matthew and Luke have in common but is not in Mark, so Q is the explanation for the similarities between the Major Synoptics that cannot be explained by the use of Mark by Matthew and Luke. Thus the Q Hypothesis is subordinate to the question of Markan Priority. Therefore this chapter focuses entirely on the issue of Markan Priority and Matthew's and Luke's use of Mark as a source.

Q is basically a mathematical abstraction dependent on Markan Priority. Determining all the material Matthew and Luke have in common and subtracting from this all the material that is in Mark as well, the result is a body of material called Q: (Common material in Matthew and Luke) – Mark's material in common with Matthew and Luke = Q.

FROM STORR TO STREETER AND BEYOND

The Markan Priority Hypothesis was first proposed by G. C. Storr in Germany in 1786. It was expounded and developed by C. G. Wilke (1838), C. H. Weisse (1838), H. Holtzmann (1863), and others, and given a solid foundation in Britain by E. Abbott, F. Woods, W. Rushbrooke, and W. Sanday and the members of his Oxford Seminar.

It is beyond question that the main influence in the establishing of British views on the Synoptic Problem was this Oxford Seminar of W. Sanday, Lady Margaret Professor of Divinity at Oxford University. Sanday began this seminar in 1894, and it met several times a year for many years to engage in the study of the Synoptic Gospels with the express intention of addressing the Synoptic Problem and of considering the consequences of the outcome at which they arrived: which was the Two-Document view—that Matthew and Luke drew upon Mark together with a postulated second document called Q. This seminar included many people who made their own personal contribution to New Testament scholarship, including J. Hawkins (see *Horae Synopticae* 1899; rev. ed. 1909), W. C. Allen (author of the influential *ICC* on *Matthew*, 1907; 1965 ed., which I cite numerous times in this book), and B. H. Streeter. These four men were the major contributors to a volume entitled *Oxford Studies in the Synoptic Problem* (1911). In the first words of his contribution to this book, Allen (Sanday 1911, 235) says, "The criticism of the Synoptic Gospels seems to have reached this point. It is very generally agreed that Matthew and Luke have edited and enlarged the Second Gospel. The points still debated in this connexion [sic] are details. The main fact is, as it would seem, undeniable."

B. H. Streeter's *The Four Gospels: A Study of Origins*, published in 1924, summed up and consolidated where the researches of scholarship had reached, and included a very clear and compelling case for the Two-Document Hypothesis. Indeed, Streeter goes further: he suggests that Matthew and Luke each had used written sources for the material peculiar to their respective Gospels (and he designates these sources as M and L)—thus developing the Two-Document Hypothesis into a Four-Document Hypothesis. He hypothesizes further that there was an original draft of

Luke's Gospel (which he terms Proto-Luke) that Luke completed before encountering Mark and into which he then added sections of Mark.

Streeter did not carry many scholars with him in his thesis of Proto-Luke, but quite a few have been willing to adopt the terms M and L—though often these are used as a convenience to designate the material rather than to indicate a commitment to the belief that these symbols necessarily refer to actual documents. Streeter *was* incredibly successful with his presentation of the Two-Document theory, so that his book became for many years the classic statement of the case and every other book written on this topic since then has of necessity had to interact with Streeter's position and with his arguments in favor of his conclusions—books both by those who accept this position and those who oppose it.

Streeter is, as he tells us, the inheritor of a "century of discussion," and he set out to summarize the fruits of this. He says (1924, 157):

> A century of discussion has resulted in a consensus of scholars that . . . the authors of the First and Third Gospels made use either of our Mark, or of a document all but identical with Mark. The former and the simpler of these alternatives, viz. that they used our Mark, is the one which I hope in the course of this and the following chapters to establish beyond reasonable doubt.

In his presentation of what he entitles "The Fundamental Solution," he says (151–52; and also 159–62):

> I will now present a summary statement of the main facts and considerations which show the dependence of Matthew and Luke upon Mark. Familiar as these are to scholars, they are frequently conceived of in a way which tends to obscure some of the remoter issues dependent on them. They can most conveniently be presented under five main heads.

Streeter's five positive arguments (which he thus calls "heads") were followed by two negative arguments. These seven are:

1. The extent of common subject matter in Matthew-Mark and Mark-Luke.
2. The extent of common words in Matthew-Mark and Mark-Luke.
3. In order of incidents, Mark always agrees with Matthew, with Luke, or with both.
4. Mark's more primitive character indicates that this Gospel was prior to Matthew and Luke.
5. The distribution of Markan material in Matthew and Luke points to these authors having used Mark.
6. The material lacking in Mark is inexplicable if Mark was using Matthew (and/or Luke).

7. Other theories display eccentric views about evidence.

This view of Markan Priority (with Q, and perhaps M and L) has not gone unchallenged. In particular J. Chapman (1937; published posthumously) compared Matthew with Mark and came to the firm conclusion that Mark drew upon Matthew rather than vice versa. Chapman supported the Successive Dependence Hypothesis—that Matthew-Mark-Luke is the order of writing and dependence. B. C. Butler (1951) did not accept the Two-Document Hypothesis either. His view is basically the same as Chapman's and follows a similar line of argument.

The work of Chapman and Butler demonstrated that Streeter's first three arguments only established the literary interdependence of the three Synoptics but did not determine who was dependent on whom, indicating that these arguments did not support Markan Priority. The supporters of Successive Dependence (see chap. 10) contend that the facts to which Streeter refers are completely compatible with their view, and the supporters of Markan Posteriority affirm that this data more specifically supports their position than that of Markan Priority (see chap. 6). Thus Streeter's arguments are valid against the Complete Independence Hypothesis only (see chap. 10), but they are not valid against Markan Dependence. Butler also showed that Streeter's fifth "head" is really not an argument for Markan Priority; it is simply an explanation of a feature of the Synoptic Gospels based on belief in Markan Priority.

These books nibbled away very effectively at Streeter's arguments that Matthew used Mark. In his important treatment of the case for Markan Priority, Styler acknowledged the validity of Butler's rebuttal. But Styler (1962, 228–32) developed four more arguments and gave an incisive restatement of one of Streeter's negative arguments. Styler's four additional reasons are:

1. Matthew clarifies what is obscure in Mark.
2. Matthew misunderstands Mark, but thereby shows that he knows Mark.
3. The freshness and circumstantial nature of Mark indicates priority.
4. Matthew's additions tell heavily against his priority.

Styler's restatement of the first of Streeter's negative arguments says (231), "The point may be put like this: given Mk, it is easy to see why Matt. was written; given Matt., it is hard to see why Mk was needed."

E. P. Sanders (1969a) painstakingly examined the implications of Streeter's fourth argument, and Sanders shows in meticulous detail that the presuppositions upon which Streeter's fourth argument is based are without foundation and in fact unjustified. His conclusion (276–79), from an examination of the Synoptic data relied on for this argument, shows that it is inconclusive in support for *any* Synoptic hypothesis and certainly does not favor the Markan Priority Hypothesis over any other.

Streeter's first negative argument (including Styler's restatement of it) is countered if any reasonable explanation can be tendered for Mark to write his Gospel after Matthew or Luke had already written theirs; such an explanation can most certainly be provided (see chap. 3). Streeter's second negative argument is in fact no argument at all but simply reveals his unwillingness to give open-minded consideration to other views that had already been offered by his day. In fact, Farmer demonstrated this in 1964 in considerable detail. Thus by 1969 scholarly consideration of Streeter's arguments had shown that at most they built a solid case against the Complete Independence position, but that they were not valid for establishing a case for Markan Priority as against Successive Dependence or Markan Posteriority.

At the 1970 Pittsburgh Festival on the Gospels J. Fitzmyer (D. M. Miller, ed. 1970, 131ff.) presented a paper on "The Priority of Mark and the 'Q' Source in Luke." This paper aimed to give a detailed reassessment of the arguments for Markan Priority and Q in the light of developments since Streeter's time. Fitzmyer found two initial arguments for the Two-Source Hypothesis: its "appeal," that is, as "a simple statement of fact" the Two-Source view has appealed to the "majority of twentieth-century scholars"; and its "usefulness," that is, the Two-Source view has proven to be a useful "springboard" for further New Testament research.

Fitzmyer set out objections to the Griesbach (Markan Posteriority) position, and then made the case for the Markan Priority position. Farmer (1983, 501–23) has answered Fitzmyer's objections to the Griesbach position and also replied in detail to Fitzmyer's case for vindicating Streeter's main arguments. In fact, it could be said that Fitzmyer does not add anything of substance to or go much beyond Streeter.

More recently, Markan Priority advocates F. Neirynck and C. Tuckett have taken a different line. Their emphasis is less on generalizations and the selective presentation of evidence (as Streeter did) and more upon the detailed consideration of the actual wording of the Synoptics. Tuckett's main concern is with the *coherence* of the alternative explanations offered for the Synoptic data.

In the twenty-first century, Markan Priority continues to have its advocates, together with those who feel that it is a given. For example,

J. Edwards (2002, 2) is content to acknowledge that "the theory of Markan priority, although not uncontested, continues to be held by a majority of scholars today, the present author included." Then Edwards acknowledges that the question of Synoptic relationships "poses one of the most difficult problems in the history of ideas" that nonetheless "cannot be rehearsed in this commentary." Thus he does not discuss this issue further but adds, "The most that can be done in the present volume with respect to Markan priority is to draw attention to the significant number of passages where Mark reasonably can be supposed to precede, and to have influenced, the other Synoptic Gospels, and Matthew in particular." Similarly J. Nolland (2005, 5) writes, "This commentary proceeds on the general assumption that Matthew had available the Gospel of Mark, or something much like it, and that he shared a considerable body of additional common source material with Luke."

Among more detailed advocates of Markan Priority this century we may note writers in these volumes: (1) D. Black and D. Beck, eds., *Rethinking the Synoptic Problem* (2001), contains the papers from the April 2000 Conference of New Testament scholars held at Southeastern Baptist Theological Seminary; (2) M. Goodacre, *The Synoptic Problem: A Way Through the Maze* (2001), advocates the Farrer-Goulder view (see chap. 10 below) that Luke knew and used Matthew as well as Mark; (3) R. Thomas, ed., *Three Views on the Origins of the Synoptic Gospels* (2002), includes contributions from three scholars who advocate, respectively, the Two-/Four- Source View, the Two-Gospel View, and the Independence View, with responses in each case from the other two; (4) M. Williams, *Two Gospels from One* (2006), supports Markan Priority and Matthean Posteriority based on text-critical criteria.

Significantly, the first and third of these publications include explanations that oppose Markan Priority. Two other books this century that reject the Markan Priority Hypothesis are: (1) D. A. Black, *Why Four Gospels?* (2001), expounds and develops B. Orchard's Fourfold-Gospel Hypothesis, which identifies Mark as written third; (2) D. Peabody et al., *One Gospel from Two* (2002), is a detailed exposition of the Two-Gospel case for Mark's use of Matthew and Luke. Each one of these six is discussed at the appropriate place in this and subsequent chapters. In particular, this chapter considers the arguments now regarded in these books as the strongest for the Markan Priority position. So now we examine and assess all the arguments that have been advanced to support Markan Priority.

THE CASE FOR THE MARKAN PRIORITY VIEW

(1, 2, 3) Mark's Similarities to Matthew and Luke

Three arguments based on similarities among the Synoptic Gospels are commonly used to support Markan Priority: (1) common content, (2) common language, and (3) common order. Since these three are so closely related, they can be treated all at once. I could sum them up this way (based on Streeter 1924, 151, 159–62; Stonehouse 1963, 57–77; Martin 1975, 140; Barclay 1975, 87–88; Kümmel 1975, 57–61) to explain the situation:

> To a very considerable degree, the three Synoptic Gospels contain the same material, frequently written in the same language, with the blocks of material following one another in an order of arrangement that is to a large extent the same for all three (and Mark and at least one of Matthew and Luke are always in agreement in sequence). This indicates that Mark was written first and used by the others.

These facts certainly provide evidence that (1) there is *some* kind of written or literary interrelationship amongst the Synoptics, or between some of them, whereby one or two made use of either or both of the others; and that (2) in *some* sense, Mark is the middle link between the other two Synoptics.

Moreover, there is no doubt that the evidence is completely in accord with and is explained by Markan Priority. But it is completely incorrect to think that Markan Priority is the *only* way to explain the evidence. In fact, the evidence is consistent with *all four* of the major theories of literary interrelationship and of the numerous variations on these that have been proposed. Certainly these are not arguments *for* Markan Priority as *against* Markan Dependence, because they equally support the Markan Dependence Hypothesis. Indeed, the evidence from pericope order gives much stronger support to Markan Dependence (see chap. 9), since Markan Priority must depend on coincidence to account for the fact that it never happens that both Matthew and Luke desert Mark's order at the same point.

As I explain more fully later in this chapter, most (though not all) scholars who hold Markan Priority now accept that these first three arguments— as arguments for Markan Priority in distinction from other hypotheses— have been refuted effectively, originally by Chapman and Butler, and more recently by Farmer and his colleagues. In chapter 6 I claim these arguments as providing evidence in support of Markan Dependence.

(4, 5, 6, 7, 8) Matthew's and Luke's Improvements of Mark

Five arguments based on Matthew's and Luke's alleged improvements of Mark are commonly used to support Markan Priority: (4) the overuse of the historic present; (5) the reduction of redundancies; (6) the quoted Aramaic words; (7) the use of Semiticisms; and (8) the improved literary style. These are treated one at a time below. My summary (drawn from Streeter 1924, 152, 162–64; Martin 1975, 140–41; Metzger 1965, 81; Kümmel 1975, 60; Guthrie 1965, 126–27; Barclay 1975, 88–89) explains thus the general basis for all five:

> Mark's Gospel is marked by a roughness of style and grammar, including awkward and ungrammatical sentences, and the frequent use of colloquial terms and words that belonged to vulgar speech, and of Aramaic words and Semitisms. Furthermore, Mark abounds in repetitions and redundancies. Sometimes when these various features are found in Mark they also occur in Matthew or Luke, but whenever there is a difference between Mark and one of the others, that other has the better Greek. That is to say, the Greek of Matthew and Luke, overall, is in all these respects better than that of Mark. It would be contrary to all analogy that well-written documents should be revised so as to produce a cruder one. Thus these features found in Mark indicate that his Gospel is the most primitive and (given that the existence of a literary relationship has been established) that it was used by Matthew and Luke. Thus Matthew and Luke have in large measure changed the colloquial or Semitic text of Mark into better Greek, and done so in the same or similar ways, though on some occasions only one or the other of them make an improvement.

(4) The Overuse of the Historic Present

Barclay (1975, 88) briefly explains this argument: "There are in Mark 151 examples of the historic present. Matthew retains only 21 of them, and Luke retains only one single instance. Matthew and Luke make more literary Mark's vivid colloquial style" (cf. Hawkins 1909, 143–49; Sanders 1969, 242–46; Guthrie 1965, 126–27; Tuckett 1983, 22–25).

The problem here is that it is misleading to imply that the use of the historic present is either poor Greek or an exclusively Markan feature. Hawkins (1909, 213) notes that there are 337 occurrences in the Septuagint, 232 of which occur in the four books 1 and 2 Samuel and 1 and 2 Kings, with the others spread thinly over the balance of the Old Testament. By comparison the New Testament occurrences of the historic present are Matthew, 93; Mark, 151; Luke, 11; John, 162; Acts, 13. It is also frequent in Josephus and in the papyri. (These details are from Hawkins 1909, 143–49, 213; he does not cite statistics for the other books of the New Testament.) Hawkin's data indicates that some writers had a preference for the historic present, some had a tendency to avoid it, and others used it from time to time in what they judged to be appropriate contexts. (This comes out clearly from its occasional use in some Old Testament books in the Septuagint, where there is no question of borrowing from other Old Testament books.) Moreover, some writers accept it in one context and reject it in another: thus Matthew uses it 15 times in parables and 78 other times; Luke uses it 5 times in parables and 6 other times; Mark uses it 151 times but never in a parable (see Hawkins 1909, 148–49). Matthew uses it 23 times when Mark does not (Sanders 1969, 242–46), and on a further 21 occasions Matthew agrees with Mark in using it.

Thus, it is reasonable to conclude that the historic present is a colloquialism, more common in informal speech or writing than in more formal, literary works. In itself, use of the historic present is not evidence of an early document, and its avoidance is not evidence of a later document. If one were to apply frequency of occurrence as a criterion of earliness to the occurrences of this idiom in the Septuagint, the New Testament, the writings of Josephus, and the papyri, one would end up with totally ludicrous results. For example, Sanders (1969, 253) cites Cadbury's note (*The Making of Luke-Acts*, 174) that "Josephus frequently changed a past tense in 1 Maccabees to a historic present." This exactly parallels what is being postulated for Mark if he used Matthew and Luke, and it shows that this view is completely reasonably in the light of the use of the historic present in the first century. It is just as logical to contend that the use of the historic present shows Mark to be prior to Matthew and Luke, and thus to be their source, as it is to say that because Josephus has the historic present where 1 Maccabees has a past tense, Josephus must be the source of 1 Maccabees.

The evidence simply does not support the contention that Matthew and Luke attempted to improve Mark by changing the historic present. Matthew frequently (21 times—approximately 27% of his non-parable usage) uses the historic present at the same point as Mark has it; slightly more frequently (23 times—approximately 29.5% of his non-parable usage) Matthew has the historic present where Mark does not. Then Matthew has this idiom 15 times in parables, but Mark never uses it in parables. On the remaining occasions when Matthew uses the idiom, there is no Markan parallel. Luke has one use of the historic present paralleling Mark (Luke 8:49), and he also uses it five times in parables (Mark has none) and on five other occasions without direct Markan parallels, together with 13 times in Acts. This demonstrates that it is inconsistent with the facts and unsustainable to assert that Matthew and Luke constantly corrected Mark's use of the historic present in view of their own use of this idiom. Also, the data shows no clear correlation with any idea of sources, seeing that (on any source theory) sometimes the author retains the idiom from his own source, sometimes he alters it, and sometimes he introduces it when his source does not have it.

On any theory of Synoptic relationships, Mark was free to use or not use the historic present on each occasion when the option arose, and that he did not always do so establishes only that while this was an idiom he favored, nonetheless it was one he sometimes used and sometimes did not. He was no more compelled to use it on all possible occasions than was the Septuagint translator of 1 Samuel (who also favored the historic present). Each Synoptic author (independent of whether or not it was in his sources) used or changed the historic present according to his own judgment on each occasion.

(5) The Reduction of Redundancies

My summary (drawn from Hawkins 1909, 125–26; Streeter 1924, 163–64; Stonehouse 1963, 81; Barclay 1975, 89) explains this argument thus: "Mark's style is marked by repetition, and the habit of saying things twice. In such cases it not infrequently happens that Matthew retains one expression and Luke the other. On the Markan Priority Hypothesis, this is due to Luke or Matthew, so to speak, tidying up the repetitions and redundancies in Mark."

It must be agreed, irrespective of the question of Synoptic interrelationships, that Mark *did* write his Gospel in this way. Thus Mark did have something of a tendency toward being prolix. But what is really under consideration is (a) whether this points to Markan Priority, on the basis of its being only (or better) explained on the hypothesis that Mark wrote in this way entirely using his own material; or (b) whether, granted a tendency to fullness on Mark's part, it is possible that Mark, if writing third, would have been willing to include in his Gospel similar expressions taken from both Matthew and Luke where each one had analogous but not identical wording.

A tendency to expansiveness of style, through redundancy or greater detail, is not an indicator of priority or posteriority in sequence, or earliness or lateness in date, as Sanders (1969, 183–89, 269–71) has demonstrated. Instead, this is an idiosyncracy of a particular writer's style. In other words, this feature does not point to Markan Priority since exactly the same kind of phenomenon would result if Mark were using Matthew and Luke and conflating them when they had similar expressions or points of detail in a given pericope. Thus, this argument does not support Markan Priority.

(6) Mark's Use of Aramaic Words

Streeter (1924, 164) states thus the argument about Mark's Aramaic words:

> [T]here are eight instances in which Mark preserves the original Aramaic words used by our Lord. Of these Luke has none, while Matthew retains only one, the name Golgotha (xxvii.33), though he substitutes for the Marcan wording of the cry from the Cross . . . the Hebrew equivalent . . . (Mk. xv34=Mt xxvii.46=Ps xxii.1).

This position is supported by (amongst others) Hawkins 1909, 130; Guthrie 1965, 127; and Stonehouse 1963, 82. To summarize their argument:

The priority of Mark is supported by the fact that this Gospel contains these Aramaic words, because the Synoptic evidence is more readily accountable on the supposition that they are original with Mark and were later omitted by Matthew and Luke, rather than that they are Markan additions, for Aramaic words would be more likely to be omitted from, rather than added to, an existing source.

The eight Aramaic expressions that Mark uses, to which Streeter refers, are in 3:17; 5:41; 7:11,34; 10:46; 14:36; 15:22,34—though not all of these are the words of Jesus. And there are certainly other ways to account for them.

First, Mark always gives the Greek interpretation of the Aramaic expressions he uses—he does *not* presume that his readers know them. Thus the expressions are introduced, not because the readers are familiar with them, but for effect—that is, as part of Mark's art as a storyteller to add extra vividness and verisimilitude to the story. This remains true wherever Mark is placed in the chain of Synoptic interrelationships.

Second, Mark does not do this with Aramaic expressions only. In 5:9 he gives a Latin word and its explanation in reporting what the demon-possessed man said: "My name is Legion, for we are many." Luke does the same thing in 8:30.

Third, John's Gospel contains 11 occurrences (eight different ones) of expression-plus-translation (see 1:38,41[= 4:25],42; 5:2; 9:7; 11:16 [= 20:24 = 21:2]; 19:13; 20:16). If the logic that makes Mark a primitive Gospel because of its use of Aramaic expressions is also applied to John, then John should share priority with Mark among the Gospels since it similarly includes Aramaic words. (I do not know anyone who argues for the priority of John on this basis.)

Fourth, Matthew contains seven Hebrew/Aramaic expressions. Two are parallel with Mark (Matt 27:33//Mark 15:22; Matt 27:46//Mark 15:34; a translation is given in all four); of the remaining five, one is translated (1:23, "Emmanuel") and the other four are untranslated (1:21, where the point is that Jesus=Joshua=Savior; 5:22, *Raca*; 16:17, *Bar-Jona*; 27:6, *korbanan*). The fact that Matthew uses such words without giving their Greek interpretation weighs more heavily for Matthew's closer connection with the Aramaic origins of Christianity than does Mark's use of Aramaic words with their unfailing translation accompanying them.

Fifth, parallels to Mark's (and John's) use of expression-plus-translation also occur in the book of Acts (e.g., 1:19; 4:36; 9:36; 13:6–8). Another example is "Maranatha" ("Our Lord, come"), an Aramaic expression that Paul does not bother to translate (1 Cor 16:22).

This survey of the data shows that Mark uses Aramaic words to enhance his storytelling technique, to provide additional impact and interest, and to increase the vividness of his account with these little details—just as he did with a multitude of other minor details that he added. This explanation remains valid on any hypothesis of Synoptic origins. It is a real leap of creative imagination to assert that this feature of Mark indicates that his Gospel is prior to Matthew.

(7) Mark's Use of Semitisms

This argument can be stated thus:

> Semitic coloring in a Gospel narrative usually indicates a fairly early tradition. A scribe would not invent his own "Aramaisms" (that is to say, the tradition did not tend to become more Semitic). There is a positive relationship between Semitisms and the antiquity of tradition. The one indicates the other. The natural tendency over time was to improve the Greek so that Semitisms that offended against good Greek would frequently be changed. Mark contains more such Semitisms than Matthew or Luke. This indicates the priority of Mark. That is to say: Matthew and Luke have frequently altered the popular and semitically-colored text of Mark to better Greek in the same or in different ways.

Sanders (1969, 190–209; 232–33) sets out the support given to this view by various scholars. He has identified and investigated all the Semitisms to which these scholars were referring. His study shows that this argument presumes either that the tendency of the tradition was to become less Semitic and to be written in better Greek (and he shows that this is in fact not always what happens) or that Matthew and Luke had the redactional tendency to avoid Semitisms while Mark had no redactional tendency to add them (233). But it is as valid to argue that Mark changed Matthew's Greek to his preferred style, or in order to reflect Peter's use of such Semitisms in his preaching, as that Matthew changed it the other way. We seem to be dealing here with the personal preferences of an author rather than a decisive proof of relative antiquity (Sanders, 250). Moreover, the evidence concerning Semiticisms in general indicates that Matthew has the highest level of Semitisms in the New Testament (followed by Luke), while Mark has only about 55% as many as Matthew. It is thus very difficult to argue that Matthew and Luke had the redactional tendency of avoiding Semitisms (Sanders, 254–55).

Some of the apparent Semitisms in the New Testament may simply be the result of the influence of the Septuagint. It seems quite clear that some people did write Greek in imitation of the Septuagint. The conclusion to be drawn from this is that Hebraisms in the Gospel tradition that may be paralleled more or less extensively in the Septuagint prove nothing about the antiquity of the traditions in which they occur (Sanders, 199–202).

A further complication is the possibility that Greek flavored with Semitisms may not indicate Aramaic sources but only the use of Jewish Greek. Some scholars are arguing on strictly linguistic grounds that biblical Greek is distinguishable from ordinary *koine*, largely because of direct and indirect Semitic influences on these writings (Sanders, 204–5).

We may fairly accept that the Greek in which John Mark was raised was, in N. Turner's phrase (1964, 45), "a living dialect of Jewish Greek," and that Mark would have been directly influenced by the language of the Septuagint, the standard Bible of the early church. In addition, he had a noticeable preference, as Sanders's study shows, for writing in vernacular Greek, regularly using an abundance of colloquial constructions and expressions. If this was the dialect of Greek that Mark was ordinarily accustomed to use, we may reasonably expect that he would have written his Gospel in that dialect regardless of when he wrote or what sources he used. In other words, Mark's use of Matthew and Luke (if Mark drew his material from them) would *not* have resulted in such a transformation of his normal style that the absence of such a transformation can be argued as a proof of Markan Priority. Of course, if Mark was basing his writing on the preaching of Peter, what we are seeing in his Gospel may simply be more a reflection of Peter's preaching than of Mark's distinctive style.

(8) Improvements of Mark's Literary Style

Based on the explanations of its advocates (Allen 1907, xix–xxx; Hawkins 1909, 141–42.; Streeter 1924, 162–64; Barclay 1975, 88; Guthrie 1965, 126–27; Metzger 1965, 81), the argument of the improvement of Mark's literary style by Matthew and Luke can be stated thus:

> Mark's Gospel is frequently characterized by poor style: the use of slang expressions and of words condemned by the Greek grammarians, the occurrence of Latinisms and redundant double negatives, unusual words, difficult

constructions, and harsh syntax. It is inconceivable that Mark would revise an earlier Gospel or Gospels so as to deliberately introduce poor grammar or replace good literary Greek with colloquialisms and infelicities of expression. It is not merely conceivable but highly probable that Matthew and Luke, finding these elements in the Gospel in front of them, would take the opportunity of improving the Greek in that Gospel.

Stated this way, this argument sounds very convincing. Who indeed would revise a document so as to make it ungrammatical? On what grounds could we deny that the better wording would be the later wording? Given the existence of a literary interrelationship between Mark and the other two Synoptics, this argument seems to show which direction it operated. Yet this argument is based on three unexamined presuppositions. But examining them shows that they are incapable of bearing the weight placed upon them.

The first presupposition is that, if Mark is writing second or third, he is engaged in "revising" the earlier Gospel or Gospels. There is absolutely no necessity, either upon the Successive Dependence or Markan Dependence views, to believe that Mark had any such purpose. He is using one or both of the other Gospels as a source. And to an extent that he himself decided, he altered the wording in the material taken from his source(s) in line with what he saw as his purpose in writing and (inevitably) in accordance with his own habitual way of using Greek. Further, the more probable explanation is that Mark reflects the "slang expressions" (read "colloquial language") and so on of the apostle Peter (his third source).

The second presupposition is that in Matthew and Luke we *do* have better Greek than in Mark, so that they consistently "correct" Mark's "errors." The impression frequently given in this argument is that Mark is often insensitive to good Greek style and vocabulary, and that Matthew and Luke, who *are* sensitive to such matters, make the necessary changes to Mark whenever they come across this "poor Greek" while using Mark's Gospel as a source.

The facts of the case are rather different. It is simply not accurate to state that Matthew and Luke have "better Greek" whenever Mark has "poor Greek." This generalization is a tendentious distortion of the evidence. Matthew and Luke (and other New Testament writings) contain most of the types of "poor Greek" detected in Mark. Matthew and Luke do not contain *as many instances* of this "poor Greek" as Mark, so to that extent it is legitimate to make the generalization that they write "better Greek," but this misses the point. They cannot be regarded as being opposed to the type of Greek usages in question if they are willing on occasion to take over these usages from Mark (upon the presuppositions of the Markan Priority view) and if also *they themselves* introduce some of them into their Gospels without finding them in Mark—as indeed is the case.

We can thus see that it is not a case of wrong Greek being corrected, but of personal preference, so that sometimes the Synoptists use these words or ways of writing and sometimes they do not, and Mark has a greater preference for them or likelihood of using them than the others. Thus it is not a matter of black and white, a case of right and wrong Greek, but a question of *degree* of usage of various idioms.

The third presupposition is that (to some extent anyway) Mark's Greek actually is "poor Greek." This categorization of Mark's style begs the whole question. Mark's Gospel is written in the Greek that was regularly spoken by the people of his day. Streeter (1924, 163) was more accurate in his description of it as *spoken Greek* in contradistinction to the written or literary Greek of Matthew and Luke. I discuss in chapter 3 the recognized difference between spoken and written language. Mark wrote in very colloquial Greek, and the Major Synoptists wrote in Greek that was a little more formal.

Summary of Arguments 4–8

Mark's Gospel clearly has a different style from that of the other two Synoptists, and there is scope for examining more fully what may be the significance of those differences. In particular they show a preference on Mark's part for a less formal and more colloquial way of writing—that is, as Streeter himself noted, for a spoken rather than a literary style.

All of these "improvements" that Matthew and Luke made to Mark are ultimately related to Mark's difference in style. These arguments are based on the assumption that a later document must be couched in "better" Greek than an earlier document, especially if the two stand in some kind of literary relationship. But this is a prejudicial misstatement of the position. Once the real nature of the stylistic difference between the Synoptics is recognized, and once the role of Peter's preaching as Mark's third source is taken into account also, the question at issue can be rephrased thus: "Is a colloquial and more vernacular document earlier or later than a more formal and literary document?" The answer is that it could be either. After examining these issues at some length, Sanders states (1969, 253, 255), "It is not intrinsically more likely that Matthew and Luke avoided the vernacular than that Mark courted it. . . . It certainly suited Mark's redactional style to write vernacular Greek more than it did the style of Matthew and Luke, but we cannot thereby prove Mark to be the earliest of the Gospels."

The Markan Dependence view sees Mark as replacing the somewhat more academic literary language of his predecessors with starker, more abrupt, and more striking "street talk." His Gospel was written to speak the language of his audience and to jolt them and get their attention. Also, as part of this conscious and deliberate transformation process, Mark inserts into Matthew and Luke that host of minor (usually insignificant) details that are so much a recognized feature of his Gospel.

A very significant number of the differences between Mark on the one hand and Matthew and Luke on the other can be seen to be exactly this kind of situation: that is, Mark had in front of him the more literary language of Matthew and Luke, and he changed them to the format of the spoken word in two primary ways: by choosing the more down-to-earth colloquial word alternative; and by changing the longer and more subordinating grammatical construction of the written language to the simpler paratactic format that is customary in speech.

What was Mark's source for this? The tradition of the early church Fathers provides the answer: Mark's knowledge of the preaching of Peter. In the vast majority of the places where we can see Mark departing from the wording and structure of Matthew or Luke, we can hear the voice of Peter. This, in fact, is what we would deduce from the testimony of the Fathers. Of course, it is from Peter that Mark received all his small additions, and they look much like eyewitness details—because they are!

I cannot totally exclude the possibility that on occasion Mark himself is the source of various such changes that he makes to the particular wording or structure of Matthew or Luke—this may well be the case. But if and where it is so, Mark made such modifications using exactly the same vernacular style so that there is a large measure of consistency in his procedure.

Why would he do such a thing? We can recognize two reasons. The first is because of his initial, immediate audience. Again, the church Fathers fill the gap in our knowledge about this, for they say that Mark was responding to requests from those who had heard Peter's preaching. So Peter's preaching is the hallmark of Mark's style.

But there would be a second and wider audience for his Gospel: those preachers of the new faith who wanted—and needed—an economical copy of the *kerygma* they were to preach, drawn from the accounts in Matthew and Luke but cast in the everyday colloquial speech of those they were seeking to reach; that is, a "preacher's Gospel" for missionary and evangelistic work.

Thus the Argument from Improvements is without substance. In fact, it is quite misconceived. The way in which this argument is framed makes it appear logical and reasonable. But penetrating the framing of the words to expose the actual substance of the argument demonstrates that it lacks any real basis.

In reality, this argument is grounded on assumptions that are totally subjective and quite out of touch with the actualities of the real world. When the youth speaker chooses to speak in the style and language of his church youth group, or the Sunday school teacher breaks down the Bible story to the level of understanding of young children, or the preacher explains a theological concept in terms appropriate to his congregation, they will produce (in relation to questions of grammar, vocabulary, and literary style) something that stands in the same relation to their sources as does Mark to Matthew and Luke. Accepting the Arguments from Improvements to Mark would be to reject out of hand without reason (and certainly without arguing the case) the possibility that Mark may have intended to do something along exactly these lines, as discussed in chapter 3.

(9, 10, 11) Doctrinal Modifications of Mark by Matthew and Luke

Three arguments based on Matthew's and Luke's alleged doctrinal modifications of Mark are commonly used to support Markan Priority: (9) increased reverence for Jesus; (10) increased respect for the disciples; and (11) increased doctrinal sophistication. These are treated one at a time below. These arguments claim that a considerable body of evidence in Mark indicates that Mark's Gospel is primitive, and thus earlier than the Gospels of Matthew and Luke. Thus this evidence would offer strong support for the Markan Priority Hypothesis.

(9) Increased Reverence for Jesus

Hawkins (1909, 117–21) lists 26 "passages seeming (a) to limit the power of Jesus Christ, or (b) to be otherwise derogatory to, or unworthy of, Him." For example, Mark 1:32–34 records that the people brought to Jesus *all* who were sick and Jesus healed *many*, but Matt 8:16 (see also Luke 4:40) says they brought to him *many* and he healed them *all*. In Mark, Jesus is almost never referred to as Lord; in Matthew and Luke this is common. In Mark, Jesus is at times unable to perform miracles (6:5), uses "means" in performing a miracle (7:32–37; 8:22–26), and "sighs" as if the miracle is making tremendous demands on him (8:12). In Mark, a miracle may be gradual or in stages (8:22–26; 11:20), but in Matthew (and Luke), Jesus' miracles are always instantaneous and complete. In Mark, the language sometimes suggests that there were things that Jesus wanted to do and could not carry out; this suggestion is removed in the other Synoptics. Mark alone refers to Jesus as being angry or indignant (3:5; 10:14) and portrays him with a full range of human feelings and emotions. Barclay (1975, 91) says, "Matthew and Luke are much less willing than Mark to show Jesus in the grip of strong emotion."

On several occasions, however, advocates of Markan Priority have not presented their evidence fairly, and the conclusion that is drawn is thus not valid. For example, the contrast between Jesus healing *many* and healing *all* ignores Mark 1:33, which gives the total group from whom Jesus healed *many*—it was "the whole city" and not the total number who were sick: the others were not healed because *they were not ill*. In other passages, the idea that Matthew and/or Luke has a wording that shows a greater reverence for Jesus than that of Mark hardly appears justified upon a comparison of the Synoptics, and this higher degree of reverence must be conceded to lie in the mind of the beholder.

But there are other passages that do (or appear to) exhibit the characteristics claimed about them. Granted for the sake of discussion that all this is so, on what basis does one claim that this demonstrates the priority of Mark? This "demonstration" of Markan Priority is based on the assumption that the wording in Matthew and/or Luke is "due to an increasing feeling of reverence for the person of Christ" (Allen 1907, xxxi), which is seen as pointing to the primitiveness of Mark's Gospel and to its use and alteration by Matthew and Luke. This assumption is unsupported by the presentation of any evidence. It is equally possible that the difference in perspective about the person of Jesus (to the extent that it can be shown to exist between Mark and the other Synoptists) is a consequence of Mark's own purpose in writing—his intention of showing Jesus to be a *genuine man*—and of a deliberate desire to recapture the feeling of questioning uncertainty that existed, during the period of which Mark writes, about who (and what) Jesus really was, and thus to avoid the anachronism of reading back into the days of Jesus' earthly ministry the insights of the church's post-Easter faith (for lengthy discussion, see chap. 3). The question of Mark's purpose in writing requires careful consideration, but it can be noted here that the "greater reverence for the person of Jesus" in Matthew and Luke, to the extent to which it does exist (and this seems to be considerably exaggerated by some writers) can quite easily have co-existed with the desire of a different author—Mark—to show Jesus as a man, and to present him as he was seen by his contemporaries during the time of his earthly ministry.

The assumption that a document showing a "greater reverence for Jesus" than that found in another document must be later than that other document remains an *assumption* unsupported by evidence, and moreover such an assumption makes no allowance for a difference in theological perspective and purpose in writing between different Gospel writers.

(10) Increased Respect for the Disciples

Hawkins (1909, 121–22) lists seven Markan passages that seem to "disparage the attainments or character of the Apostles"; Allen (1907, xxxiii-xxxiv) gives another nine; Metzger (1965, 81) adds one more. The 17 Markan passages to which these authors refer are: Hawkins, 4:13,38; 5:31; 6:51; 8:17–18; 9:38; 10:35; Allen, 4:30; 8:29; 9:5,13,19,32,33–34,35; 14:40; Metzger, 14:71.

As also in argument 9 above, exponents of this view have not always fairly presented the Synoptic data. In particular, they regularly fail to mention that, if this explanation is adopted, Matthew and Luke must be regarded as completely inconsistent in the matter. There are many passages in which Matthew or Luke or both have recorded events that are hardly to the credit of the Twelve, and this evidence must be taken into consideration in deciding whether the Synoptic data as a whole establishes that Matthew and Luke are following a policy of altering Mark so as not to speak disparagingly of the apostles. It is certainly relevant that there are quite a few passages which demonstrate—on the basis of the same arguments that are used to establish that the disciples are being favored—that Mark softened or suppressed unfavorable Matthean or Lukan references to the disciples. The following passages could be read as illustrative of Matthew's or Luke's willingness to record stories or sayings that are in rebuke of or unfavorable to the disciples, or could be seen to disparage their attainments or character: Matt 8:26; 14:31; 15:16–17; 16:8–12, 21–23; 17:16–20; 18:1–3; 19:25–27; 20:20–28; 26:31–35,36–45,56,69–75; Luke 8:25; 9:40–41,45,46–48,49–50,54–55; 18:26–28,31–34; 22:24,31–34,38, 39–46,56–62; 24:25,38–41.

But even granting the basic proposition of this argument, it is still unclear how this actually is evidence that Mark was first and was used by Matthew and Luke. Barclay, who earlier (1975, 89–90) used this argument from increased respect, shows (ibid., 122) that it may not be the only explanation for the data: Mark may have had reasons of his own for his "less reverential" treatment of Peter and the other apostles. Barclay's comment is well justified. This argument for Markan Priority depends entirely on the supposition that a less reverential attitude to the apostles would be found in an earlier document, and a more reverential attitude in a later document—as Barclay put it earlier (ibid., 90), "Mark, the argument is, is telling the story simply and naturally, writing in the days before reverential conventions had got into the church; Matthew and Luke are writing in a day when the apostles had become the legendary princes of the church."

There are four major problems with this view. First, no evidence exists for this claim in any of the comparative data on which such an argument can be founded. This progressive increase in reverence for the apostles is an *assumption* of the proponents of this argument, who regard it as self-evident that such a heightening of reverence over time is more probable than any alternative. An assumption about something is not evidence that it is so or even that it is probable.

Second, proponents also assume that it is an attitude in the church as a whole (as distinct from an attitude on the part of an author, or a purpose by the author in relation to this matter) that determines how reverential a given Gospel would be. This, together with the first assumption, means that the attitude of the church as a whole became more reverential over time, and that this attitude at a given point in time was accurately reflected in a Gospel written at that point in time. This assumption is unrealistic since it allows no room for the possibility that one author may differ from another in the degree of reverence in his attitude or the possibility that he may have his own reasons for the degree of reverence that he wishes to introduce into his Gospel.

Third, it is contradictory of all that we know of early church history to believe that by the time Mark wrote (the earliest date for which, on the standard view, would be about AD 65, about the time of the death of Peter), there would *not* be the kind of respect for the apostles supposedly found in Matthew and Luke and supposedly not found in Mark. In other words, if Mark wrote in AD 65 or later, then he did not reflect the respect for the apostles found in the church at that time. Therefore, if the argument is to have any validity at all, the date for the writing of Mark would have to be brought forward into the very early years of the Christian church, and even then its validity would remain highly questionable. Rather, Mark's presentation of the disciples as they were before the Resurrection and Pentecost contrasts sharply with what his readers knew of them at the time he wrote, and this fact underlines dramatically the difference that faith in the risen Jesus brings about in a person (for more on this point, see chap. 3).

Fourth, in our experience, documents outside the New Testament—whether in the early church or today; and whether in the field of religion or any other field—cannot be ranked chronologically according to degree of respect shown towards Christ, or the apostles, or important people about whom they write. Thus it is not realistic to expect that we could do this with the Synoptic Gospels.

(11) Increased Doctrinal Sophistication

Hawkins (1909, 122–25) lists 17 Markan passages that "might cause offence or difficulty," and Allen (1907, xxxiv) cites numbers of alterations that were made to Mark, in his judgment, for doctrinal reasons. Numerous other authors have also written about the alterations that they believe Matthew and Luke have made to the text of Mark when using it as a source, alterations that reflect an increased doctrinal sophistication.

Examination of these passages shows that most of them do not actually provide evidence to support the contention of increased doctrinal sophistication, but that even if it could be established that such a difference exists between Mark and the others, this does not establish or even support Markan Priority. This is the case since, on this argument, Matthew and Luke would have modified their source in this direction *whatever that source had been*. Thus this does not point specifically to Mark as the source. This argument is really just an *explanation* of the Synoptic data offered from the perspective of Markan Priority.

Summary of Arguments 9–11

All these "arguments" provide a reasonable (although not the only) basis on which certain features of the Synoptics could be explained if *on other grounds* the Markan Priority theory had been demonstrated. They do not in themselves provide evidence to support that theory, nor do they offer any evidence that precludes the alternative explanation. This is that the features of the Gospels of Matthew and Luke represent attitudes that those men brought to their writing, while Mark on the other hand could have had an independent attitude that expressed itself in a different treatment of Jesus in recording his earthly life, in a less reverential attitude to the disciples, and in a simpler theological approach. And, with a different attitude in this way, Mark could be contemporaneous with Matthew and Luke, or writing before them, or writing after them. The correlation between his attitude and his priority to Matthew and Luke has not been established.

(12) The Priority of Mark according to Papias

In his comments on the writings of Matthew and Mark, Papias mentions Mark first and at greater length, and then adds a short comment about *ta logia* ("the sayings") of Jesus written by Matthew. It has been urged by some scholars that Papias's comment is referring to the writing of the Gospels of Matthew and Mark, and that the order Mark-Matthew that he gives provides support for the view that Mark was written first. Why otherwise should he mention Mark first? This interpretation of Papias is taken further by Gundry (1982, 613–14), who analyzes the report in Eusebius

(3.39.15–16) about what Papias recorded of what the Elder said concerning Mark and Matthew. Gundry then concludes (620), "That the elder makes Matthew write after Mark and in view of Mark."

Gundry's argument, however, depends totally on the meaning of οὖν ("therefore") in Eusebius 3.39.16. His interpretation of οὖν is far from obvious and far from certain, yet Gundry hangs his conclusion on this very tenuous thread. Even if we were to go the whole way with Gundry and accept that Papias really did mean that Mark was written before Matthew, Papias is still just one testimony from the early Fathers to this sequence, and it is indeed a lone voice in advocating that order of writing. All other patristic testimony—starting with Clement of Alexandria, who said he was recording specifically what he was told by the early Elders who were before him—places Matthew's writing earlier than Mark's.

(13) The Petrine Origin of Mark

H. H. Stoldt (1980, 185) points out that belief in "the Petrine origin of the second Gospel" was "the cornerstone of their source theory" for the early exponents of Markan Priority (for the full argument, see his chap. 11, "Proof from Petrine Origin").

This belief is based on the statements of Papias, together with those of the later Fathers who wrote along the same lines. Some scholars reject the evidence of Papias as worthless, and take the other Fathers to be simply echoing Papias. Griesbach himself was rather dismissive of the patristic testimony about Peter's relationship to Mark's Gospel, but he acknowledged (1978, 134) that Peter could have been a third source (with Matthew and Luke) for Mark's Gospel: "This one thing can perhaps be conceded, namely that Mark received from Peter the circumstantial details with which he enriched throughout the narratives of Luke and Matthew, although even this is not quite certain, for they could also be derived from another source." Farmer holds a similar position to Griesbach, acknowledging the possible role of Peter as a source for Mark's Gospel.

Thus the point must be made that, while patristic testimony about Peter's preaching as a source for Mark's writing is totally consistent with the Markan Priority Hypothesis, there is good reason from the Markan Dependence perspective for recognizing the existence of a third source (Peter) for Mark alongside Matthew and Luke. When the patristic testimony attributes a role to Peter as source for Mark in writing his Gospel, it does not require that Peter was Mark's *sole* source so as to exclude the possibility that he had also known and used the earlier Gospels of Matthew and Luke as well.

The Markan Priority Explanation 181

The recognition of the role of Peter behind Mark does not conflict with Markan Dependence. On the contrary: throughout this entire book I contend very strongly for this recognition of Peter as the third source for Mark, because the evidence of the language and purpose and occasion and rationale of Mark's Gospel points to the role of Peter (see chap. 3 in particular).

Our conclusion then must be that Peter's preaching is one of Mark's sources, which is completely consistent with *both* the Markan Priority and Markan Dependence hypotheses and favors neither over the other. But, from the perspective of Markan Dependence, many features in Mark's Gospel are more easily explained when the influence of Peter's preaching on Mark is recognized.

(14) Statistical Method and Computer Research

A new type of argument for Markan Priority emerged in the second half of the twentieth century, which utilizes modern statistical method and (in recent decades) enlists the support of computer-aided research. The claim here is that statistical analysis of the Synoptic data supports the view that Mark's Gospel was used as a source by Matthew and Luke. The three most thorough statistical analyses of the Synoptic data are those of de Solages (1959 and 1973), Honoré (1968), and Morgenthaler (1971).

Farmer's (1964, 197–98) perceptive comments answered de Solages in careful detail. *Novum Testamentum* published Honoré's research in 1968, but D. Wenham (1972, 17) questioned his methodology by pointing to fundamental weaknesses in Honoré's presentation. In particular, Honoré's work proceeds from some assumptions about what an author would and would not do in using other writings as his sources. His assumptions are demonstrably inapplicable in the case of the Synoptic Gospels, thus invalidating his conclusions about order of writing and dependence.

Morganthaler's *Synoptic Statistics* (*Statistische Synopse*) (1971) also uses statistical analysis of the Synoptic Gospels as a basis for resolving the Synoptic Problem, and he also concludes that such statistical analysis supports Markan Priority. Morgenthaler's work has been carefully and quite fully reviewed and analyzed by Farmer (1973). In his assessment, Farmer shows that Morgenthaler has not found any support in his statistical analysis for his preference for the Markan Priority theory over that of Griesbach's.

The approaches of de Solages, Honoré, and Morgenthaler have two common characteristics, though these characteristics may be true of them to slightly differing extents. First, they have not fully understood the arguments of Griesbach's position in their rejection of it; second, all that their statistics have shown is that Mark is in some sense (which ultimately the statistical approach cannot further clarify) the middle link between Matthew and Luke. Having rejected the Markan Posteriority explanation from consideration (and certainly being unaware of how it accounts for the data), they then find that Markan Priority is the best explanation of that data. But severe methodological weaknesses totally vitiate their conclusion. They have not produced any basis for judging the Markan Priority Hypothesis to be a better explanation of the data than Markan Dependence.

Chapter 4 above makes extensive use of the statistics compiled by these Synoptic statisticians, and the figures set out there indicate that not only do these statistics lend no support at all to the theory of Markan Priority, they also give a solid foundation for many of the conclusions that are reached in this book.

(15, 16, 17, 18, 19, 20) Direction Indicators

At most, the foregoing arguments simply yield probabilities (as Gospel scholars acknowledge). Therefore, Synoptic scholars have been seeking a line of argument that is nonreversible, independent of subjective judgment, demonstrable in easily understandable terms—that is, a line of argument that relates to factors in the text of the Synoptics that can give a clear indication of the direction in which copying has occurred. Six arguments based on direction indicators are commonly used to support Markan Priority: (15) additions to Matthew; (16) doublets; (17) mistakes made by Matthew and/or Luke in using Mark; (18) mistakes in Mark corrected by Matthew and/or Luke; (19) the use of Old Testament passages; and (20) the freshness and circumstantial character of Mark. These are treated one at a time below.

(15) Additions in Matthew

Styler (1962, 232) claims that Matthew's Gospel contains material that are likely additions to Mark's Gospel: "There are also some narrative additions in Matt. which seem to stem from later apologetic, or even from the stock of legendary accretions which are evident in the apocryphal Gospels. . . . The judgement *[sic]* that Matt.'s narratives are late, and sometimes close to the legendary, must be given full weight." The essence of this argument is that a significant part of Matthew's unique material consists of "legendary accretions" that by their nature indicate a late date. They are not found in Mark, so Mark must be earlier than Matthew, thus indicating the direction of copying between Matthew and Mark.

This argument from what is omitted in Mark and inserted in Matthew is very precarious even on its own terms. It must assume that Mark remained unaware of any of the material in question, because if he had known of this material and then omitted it from his Gospel as the result of a deliberate act of selection, then he could have chosen to act that way whether he knew of it from tradition in the early church or from reading it in Matthew. In other words, the absence of this material from Mark might tell us something about what Mark had in mind in making his choice of what to include, but *it would tell us nothing* about whether he knew Matthew or not.

But the basic suppositions of the argument cannot be so quickly accepted as self-evident. The argument is in fact rooted in subjective skepticism. It flows from an opinion that certain material in Matthew is "later apologetic, or even from the stock of legendary accretions." Even if, as an alternative, one were to hold the opinion that Matthean elements could be "early apologetic," the argument is undercut. If one accepts the miraculous and supernatural elements in the Gospels as a part of the authentic Jesus-tradition that goes back to the actual lifetime of Jesus himself, then this argument no longer exists. Thus the argument flows from a *theological attitude* towards material in the Synoptic texts rather than from the material itself.

One could just as easily (and with as little objective justification) decide that certain elements in Mark's unique material should be categorized as "later apologetic" or "legendary accretions," and that Mark should be designated "late," and that on this basis Mark should be assigned to a time after the writing of Matthew. Such views—whichever way they go—are *subjective opinions*. But such opinions have no validity as arguments for a hypothesis. The opinions of Styler (and any who follow a similar line) about the "later apologetic" or "legendary" nature of some of Matthew's unique material offer no actual support for Markan Priority.

(16) Doublets

The argument from doublets claims that passages in Matthew and/or Luke in material paralleled in Mark and that then occur a second time in passages that do not have a Markan parallel show that they have two sources, one of which is Mark and the other Q, and that this in turn points to the priority of Mark and the Two-Source Hypothesis. Stoldt comments (1980, 173) that from "the time of Christian Herman Weisse, the proof from doublets has constituted the main proof for the two-source theory."

This argument was convincingly refuted by Stoldt in his examination of the "Proof from Doublets" (chap. 10; see especially 173–74, 179, 182, 184). He shows that what can be elicited from the argument from doublets depends in considerable measure on how one defines a doublet. Stoldt provides examples where advocates proceed in such a way that "doublets which support the Two-Source theory are explained by the Two-Source theory, and doublets which do not are explained away." Stoldt's assessment (184) is that "the proof from doublets does not stand the test."

The argument from doublets does not support the Two-Source Hypothesis. If one knew *on other grounds* that Mark was the source for Matthew and Luke, one could proceed to explain that "doublets" could be included as one of the "indications for the Q source" (to quote Neirynck [1984] conference notes). But then if one knew on other grounds that Mark was third, not first (i.e., Markan Dependence), then the doublets could be easily accommodated on that view. Thus, as they fit in readily with either hypothesis, doublets do not constitute an argument for the Two-Source view.

(17) Mistakes Made by Matthew and/or Luke in Using Mark

Styler (1962, 228–29) makes this claim about Matthew's use of Mark: "In some passages Mark is suggestive but obscure, and Matt.'s parallel looks like an attempt to leave the reader with an edifying message; but we are left with the suspicion that Matt. has not penetrated to the real sense."

Styler examines a number of passages that he identifies as places where Matthew made mistakes of various kinds. For Styler, the explanation of Matthew's account in such pericopes is found in Matthew's misunderstandings of Mark, his errors, and his forgetfulness. Styler clearly considers that Matthew is quite a dimwit: not only does Matthew repeatedly misunderstand Mark (228), not only does his handling of Mark's account of John's fate call forth Styler's comment that "this must be an error" (229), but Matthew wants (for some reason that Styler does not explain) to prevent it being known that he is familiar with Mark's version of the story and he cannot even manage this successfully: for example, Styler says (229) that "at 14:9 Matt. betrays the fact that he really knows the full version by slipping in the statement that 'the king' was sorry." And to cap it all, Matthew is so incompetent an author that when "Mark quite properly finishes the story, and then resumes his main narrative with a jump, Matt., failing to remember that it was a 'retrospect,' makes a smooth transition to the narrative which follows" (229). This means that Matthew cannot remember he has been telling a flashback even though "Mark quite properly finishes the story, and then resumes his main narrative" and he—Matthew—*has Mark's narrative right in front of him as his source!*

Mark has a connected and coherent context for his stories in 1:21–39; together they comprise "A memorable day in Capernaum," all taking place within a 24-hour period. According to Markan Priority, this what Matthew has done with these Markan stories:

	MARK	MATTHEW
Jesus goes to Capernaum	1:21a	4:13
Jesus enters the synagogue on the Sabbath	1:21b	omitted
Astonishment at his teaching with authority	1:22	7:28–29
Jesus heals the demoniac in the synagogue	1:23–28	omitted
Jesus heals Peter's mother-in-law	1:29–31	8:14–15
Jesus heals the sick at nightfall	1:32–34	8:16–17
Jesus prays alone	1:35–38	omitted
Jesus begins his first preaching tour of Galilee	1:39	4:23

Mark's next story (1:40–45E, Jesus cleanses a leper) Matthew places at 8:1–4, and the following Markan story (2:1–12, Jesus heals a paralytic) Matthew places at 9:1–8. Styler does not notice (or if he does, he does not mention) that *all these pericopes are paralleled in Luke in exactly the same sequence* so that all that is found in Mark is accounted for completely by the Markan Dependence explanation: "Mark here followed Luke for what he included."

Rather, the logical order and coherence of Mark 1 shows (according to Styler's argument) that *Mark* has the original account and that it is Matthew who has split this up and spread the component pericopes around in other contexts. Yet the orderliness of the Sermon on the Mount is seen as an argument for the fact that Matthew's account is secondary to Luke, who has much of this material scattered in smaller fragments. That is, when Matthew is fragmented and disorderly in comparison with Mark, this indicates that Matthew is secondary to Mark; and when Matthew is more orderly and more tightly-knit than Luke, this indicates that Matthew is secondary to Luke! That is, no matter which one is fragmented and which one is orderly—whatever the data—you interpret it in the way that will support your presuppositions.

(18) Mistakes in Mark Corrected by Matthew and/or Luke

To summarize this line of argument: "On several occasions Mark makes mistakes that are corrected in Matthew and/or Luke. This indicates that Mark's Gospel was first and was used by Matthew and Luke" (this summary is drawn from the explanations and assertions made in Hawkins 1909, 122; Allen 1907, xxxv, "changes made for the sake of greater accuracy"; Styler 1962, 228–29).

To consider the implications of these last two arguments, when Mark is wrong and Matthew and Luke do not contain the mistake, this proves Markan Priority. But when Matthew or Luke is wrong and Mark does not contain the mistake, this proves Markan Priority. When Mark has a better structure and context than Matthew or Luke, this proves Markan Priority. And then when Matthew or Luke has a better structure or context than Mark, this proves Markan Priority.

What sort of an argument is that? Is there *any* situation about Mark—where this Gospel is better or worse or more correct or less correct than the others—that does not indicate Markan Priority? This attempt at establishing the direction of copying from direction indicators in the Synoptic Gospels shows traces of a "heads I win, tails you lose" philosophy. Where are the objective criteria that provide the basis on which it can be said that this characteristic or that feature indicates priority or dependence or posteriority?

The whole concept of mistakes that are being corrected or introduced appears, like beauty, to lie in the eye of the beholder. As shown earlier in considering the issues, other factors are involved that provide a more probable explanation than these arguments presume. In the one case where a genuine problem does exist (Mark's Abiathar comment in 2:26), the Markan Priority Hypothesis does not resolve it: if Matthew and Luke had encountered the comment in Mark and considered it to be wrong, they could have altered the wording in very simple fashion to make what they judged to be the correction needed; total excision of the whole remark was not required. Moreover, there is no reason why Mark could not have inserted this comment into his text if he wrote *after* Matthew and Luke. Thus there is no support in this whole line of argument for Markan Priority.

(19) The Use of Old Testament Passages

This argument asserts that the form of Old Testament quotations in the Synoptics points to Markan Priority. Concerning Matthew, Hawkins (1909, 154) says, "It has often been noticed that the quotations which are introduced by the Evangelist himself agree much less closely with the LXX than those which occur in the course of the common narrative." Hawkins follows this with a series of tables classifying Matthew's quotations and comparing Matthew's wording with the Septuagint, and then he draws this cautious conclusion (156): "This is a very broad distinction, and such as suggests prima facie that we have before us the work of more than one author or editor." That is, the "common narrative" quotations and the other quotations in Matthew come from different authors or editors. The argument is summed up thus by D. Wenham (1972, 12):

> [It] depends on observations about the use of the Old Testament in Matthew's Gospel, and in particular on the observation that those quotations which Matthew has in common with Mark are distinct from his quotations in all other parts of his Gospel. Whereas the quotations in Matthew's Q and M material are sometimes close to the LXX, sometimes not very close, and sometimes quite

remote from it, the Marcan quotations stand out as being consistently close to the Septuagintal form. Not surprisingly the distinctiveness of this particular group of quotations has been taken to be an indication of Matthew's use of Mark.

The danger with a generalization that sums up all the instances of a category (here, Old Testament citations in the Synoptics) is that it can so easily oversimplify a situation to the point where distinguishing features of differing aspects of that situation can be ignored, and thus their significance overlooked.

Gundry wrote a very detailed study of Matthew's use of the Old Testament, and his examination shows that the foregoing generalization is *too* general (1975, 147–50). Rather, the data must more accurately be stated this way: Mark does not parallel Matthew's editorially-inserted quotations or "formula quotations" (with the single exception of Mark 1:2–3); where he does parallel Matthew in giving an Old Testament quotation, that quotation is spoken by one of the participants in the narrative, is integral to the narrative, and therefore normally could not be omitted without losing something of (often, the whole of) the point being made by the pericope.

The data is readily explicable from the Markan Dependence perspective. Mark, writing for a predominantly Gentile audience, is not as greatly concerned as Matthew with the fulfillment of Old Testament prophecy as such; therefore, he does not take over any of these quotations from Matthew, with one exception (1:2–3), which he places as the introduction to his entire Gospel. The only Old Testament quotations he uses are those that are integral to pericopes that he plans to include and that come into his text *as part of* that particular pericope, and which are spoken by the participants in that pericope.

Thus this apparently unidirectional argument supporting Markan Priority turns out on more careful examination to be considerably less than conclusive. Markan Dependence can account for this data equally well, and in some respects can do so even better. Actually, the special features of his sole editorially-inserted quotation (1:2–3) constitute strong evidence for Markan Dependence (see chap. 7).

(20) The Freshness and Circumstantial Character of Mark

Styler (1962, 230) claims that "Of all the arguments for the priority of Mark, the strongest is that based on the freshness and circumstantial character of his narrative." As illustrative of the features to which he refers, Styler cites only "touches that might well come almost directly from an eyewitness, e.g. the cushion in the boat, Mark 4:38; and the Aramaic words and phrases, of which Mark preserves more than Matthew." The multitude of small details unique to Mark are presumably the "touches" to which Styler refers.

Styler (1962, 230) sees the source of these "eyewitness . . . touches"—those that are the spring of "the freshness and circumstantial character of his narrative"—in the explanation that "tradition connects his Gospel with St Peter." But Markan Dependence says that Mark must have had *three* sources, not just Matthew and Luke, and the third one would be Peter, all of which accounts for this phenomenon completely (see full discussion in chap. 3 above). If the aspects of Mark to which Styler refers have indeed come from Peter, and if Mark has *combined what he learned from Peter with what he read in Matthew and Luke*, all the data is explicable. Thus the data is completely compatible with a Markan Dependence explanation.

(21) Coherence of Explanation

Tuckett (1983, 12–13) writes,

> Any source hypothesis can in fact be proposed. . . . What then is required, if the hypothesis is to be made credible, is a presentation of the reasons why the later writers made the changes they are alleged to have done. The application of a "criterion of coherence" would then demand that these reasons form a reasonably coherent whole: they must be rational, consistent with each other and also consistent with the facts as they are. . . . Any proposed source hypothesis must then give a reasonably coherent and self-consistent set of reasons why these changes occurred in the way that the hypothesis claims if the theory is to be seriously considered. The extent to which an hypothesis gives a coherent, consistent picture of the total redactional activity of each evangelist will then be a measure of its viability.

Tuckett then assesses the Griesbach Hypothesis and the Two-Document Hypothesis by this criterion to see which of them is shown by it to be the more satisfactory theory. His conclusion (1983, 187) is that, "Insofar as the Two-Document Hypothesis can often apparently give a more coherent and consistent set of explanations of why the later changes were made (i.e., by Matthew and Luke on the Two-Document Hypothesis), that hypothesis is to be preferred."

Tuckett's contention is valid. No hypothesis can legitimately claim the support of scholars unless it meets the tests he proposes. His judgment in this regard is perceptive and irrefutable when he says (7), "Study of the history of research may help one to recognize where the strengths and weaknesses of different hypotheses have been felt to lie, but one must in the end examine the text itself to see which is the best explanation of the source question."

Therefore this is the one argument that is capable of providing a sound basis for belief in Markan Priority. But Tuckett has not succeeded in showing that it does in fact do so. In the passages he selects, the Markan Dependence Hypothesis gives a better explanation than Markan Priority does. And there are multitudes of other passages that, when considered by this criterion, point to Markan Dependence as giving the more coherent explanation.

So this provides a legitimate test by which alternative theories are judged. Chapter 11 presents a detailed examination of the various issues Tuckett raises in putting his case against the Griesbach Hypothesis. He is convinced that Markan Priority passes the test, but I contend firmly that it fails it. Markan Dependence is by far the more coherent explanation. But the reader will have to be the judge.

SYNOPTIC SCHOLARSHIP IN THE TWENTY-FIRST CENTURY

These are the arguments many scholars have used to establish Markan Priority—the basis on which this hypothesis came to dominate the field of Gospel studies and to be found in almost every twentieth-century book on New Testament Introduction. These are the reasons why thoughtful scholars concluded that Markan Priority was the most likely explanation of the relationship between the Synoptics—and indeed why many of these people came to assert with such confidence that this was the one assured result of New Testament scholarship.

But what about now? How do things stand in the twenty-first century? Is it still the case that most scholars, most academics, most pastors and teachers, most students and church members—most anybody who has an opinion—hold firmly to Markan Priority? D. Dungan (1999, 390) sums up how things stand at the outset of the new century:

> In conclusion, it would seem that we live in the ironic situation where confidence in Markan priority rises to ever new heights despite the fact that, after forty-five years of steady criticism, knowledgeable defenders of the hypothesis have been forced to abandon one basic argument after another, to the point where there are, at present, no formal arguments left that will justify it and the compositional arguments are just as questionable. It has rightly earned the sobriquet "the Teflon hypothesis."

The books mentioned at the beginning of this chapter provide a fairly characteristic cross-section of twenty-first-century opinion on this issue. Two of these specifically present the Markan Priority position against alternative options. One of these books comes from Britain, the rest from the USA. Together they are pretty representative of today's views.

The Synoptic Conference Report

Black and Beck's *Rethinking the Synoptic Problem* (2001) is the report on the Synoptic Problem from the 2000 conference at the Southeastern Baptist Theological Seminary. The book contains papers from several adherents of Markan Priority. One of these, C. Blomberg, wrote the introductory article and notes (20) that "Despite the alternatives . . . , the vast majority of the introductions and surveys of the Gospels or of the life of Christ, and the major commentaries on each of the Synoptics, along with studies more focused on individual themes or passages within those Gospels, all presuppose that Matthew and Luke each used Mark." He then proceeds to list what he describes as "the nine most important reasons for this," which he explains in detail in his *Jesus and the Gospels* (1998). I now provide a critique of these nine, and as I do this you may have a strong sense of *déjà vu* since these arguments were considered and answered earlier in this chapter. Thus a brief response to each of Blomberg's points (as he sets them out in Black and Beck 2001, 20) is sufficient.

First, "Mark frequently contains vivid touches, possibly the product of eyewitness testimony, that Matthew and Luke omit" (ibid., 20). Response: If we take note of the testimony of Papias and the other Fathers, and recognize that Mark had *three* sources, not just two, and take into account the role of the preaching of Peter, then this is exactly what we would expect. This is strong evidence in support of Markan Dependence, not Markan Priority, as explained in full in chapter 3.

Second, "Matthew and Luke often seem to smooth out Mark's rougher grammar" (ibid.). Response: While Mark was engaged in making use of the Gospels of Matthew and Luke, he had ringing in his ears the words and expressions he had so often heard from Peter when the apostle recounted these same tales—and Peter's preaching is reflected in Mark's style of writing. Moreover, this is entirely appropriate, as this Gospel had as one of its primary aims to be a handbook for preachers (so to speak) so Mark could do in writing what Peter had been doing verbally: telling the story of Jesus to those outside the Christian family to bring them to faith. This Gospel is intended to be spoken aloud; it is written in the vernacular of the many who would hear it preached. Mark's "rougher grammar" proves, upon careful examination, to reflect the difference between the informal spoken form of a language and its more formal literary equivalent. This distinction (between the two forms of a language, and between the language in Mark on the one hand and Matthew and Luke on the other) has been recognized for years. Again, this is covered in detail in chapter 3.

Third, "Matthew and Luke often omit potentially misleading details in Mark" (ibid). Response: I examined these "errors" or "problems" above and found that they tend to evaporate under inspection. There is no way that arguments about "misleading details" can be used as "direction indicators"—showing which direction Synoptic borrowing occurred (see "Argument from Doctrinal Modifications" earlier in this chapter).

Fourth, "Mark is the shortest of the Synoptics, yet within individual pericopae he is consistently longer than Matthew or Luke, an unlikely result of later abbreviation." Response: Augustine once called Mark the "abbreviator" of Matthew. But when some readers discover that Mark's pericopes are actually *longer* than Matthew's, they conclude that Augustine was wrong and then jump to the conclusion that in some way this disproves the view that Mark wrote after and made use of Matthew—as if Mark's only reason for writing would have been to shorten Matthew's tales. However, the explanation of Mark's longer stories is (1) he had *three* sources (not just two), so his stories regularly contain more detail than do Matthew and Luke *combined* since some details are drawn from Peter's preaching; (2) he invigorates his Gospel with a multitude of little asides and extras that bring it to life for a spoken presentation; and (3) he adds the repetitions and redundancies that are characteristic of speech when compared with a literary writing. This is because people think in shorter word-spans when listening than when reading: they cannot go back and "re-listen" and thus they need "extras" that clarify their understanding (see fuller discussion in chap. 3).

Fifth, "Less than 10% of Mark is nonparalleled; why would Mark have written at all if longer, fuller treatments were already available and he had so little new to say?" (ibid.). Response: This "argument" commences with an erroneous assertion: Mark's *Sondergut* (as set out in chap. 4) is really 25% of Mark (not 10%), not being found in either Matthew or Luke. One can only arrive at a figure of 10% by looking briefly at the other 15% and claiming that it is not important so it doesn't count—and then not counting it. Chapter 3 examines Mark in detail and concludes that it consists of the material of the *kerygma* of the early church, extracted from the mixed *kerygma*-plus-*didache* of the Major Synoptics to produce a special-purpose Gospel for use in missionary and evangelistic preaching to outsiders. Mark frequently indicates a much wider knowledge of material than he includes (especially of Jesus' teaching), and he writes knowing that when an "outsider" becomes an "insider," they are able to hear the *didache* in church from Matthew's and Luke's Gospels.

Sixth, "Comparatively, Matthew and Luke rarely differ from Mark in the same way at the same time, whereas Mark and Matthew much more frequently agree with each other against Luke, as do Luke and Mark against Matthew" (ibid.). Response: There seems to be a complete failure of logic here in calling this a reason for believing in Markan Priority, especially as against the view that places Mark third. If Mark used both Major Synoptics and chose for the moment to adhere more closely to Matthew and at another time to follow Luke more precisely, Blomberg's "proof" of Markan Priority as stated here is *exactly* the result one would logically expect to find. And this pattern of procedure would also mean that, when the two Major Synoptics agreed, then by following one of them Mark would in fact be following both. And the fact that "Matthew and Luke rarely differ from Mark" is the inevitable result of his choice not to depart from them when they are in agreement. The exception, of course, is that Mark does add 25% of his own material from at least one other source, Peter (see chap. 4).

Seventh, "Mark contains the highest incidence of Aramaisms among the Synoptics" (ibid.). Response: Sanders analyzed (1969) the validity of this argument for Markan Priority back in 1969 and showed that it has no substance (see my discussion of this point earlier in this chapter).

Eighth, "There seems to be no reason for Mark's omission of so much of Matthew and Luke that contains many of Jesus' most precious teachings, if Mark knew of them from a source" (ibid.). Response: The clear implication of this argument is that if Mark knew something he would have included it. Anyone who uses this argument must think that the author of Mark's Gospel was some outsider with no real contact with the Christian community. But if the author of Mark's Gospel is identified as the John Mark referred to many times in the New Testament, then the idea that he knew no more than his Gospel contains is simply ludicrous.

When one thinks about this contention carefully, it is clear that whatever Mark omits or includes must be the result of *selection*, not *ignorance*. He omits certain things because they were outside the scope of his purpose, his focus. And his omissions make a great deal more sense if, in leaving things out, he knew that the Christian community would have access to them in the Major Synoptics; but if he were the first one to write, and all that his readers would have is what he included in his Gospel, then why did he omit so much? This is in fact a huge problem for the Markan Priority Hypothesis. But Mark's omission of so much of Matthew and Luke teachings makes perfect sense if Mark knew they were already available to the Church, and he was using these Gospels as sources but for a very different purpose. Thus what he omits is a strong argument for Mark being written third. Accordingly I discuss it in the next chapter among the evidence supporting this hypothesis (see also chap. 3).

Ninth, "When one assumes Markan priority, coherent patterns of redactional emphases emerge in ways that are not true on alternative models" (ibid.). Response: This argument reminds me of a couple driving down the highway at high speed. When the wife attempts to point out to her husband that they are going in the wrong direction and offers him the map, he cuts her off and says, "Don't bother me with that right now—we're making great progress!"

Gospel scholarship is making great progress "when one assumes Markan Priority"—so we must not put this in jeopardy! It is unscholarly to inquire: "But is it headed in the right direction?" What if this basic premise is mistaken? In this present book I am setting out some very cogent reasons to question Markan Priority and to weigh an alternative. As I do this, I can also say that equally "coherent patterns . . . emerge" from the Progressive Publication of Matthew viewpoint/Markan Dependence view, if we care to take note of them.

Blomberg's "most important reasons" closely correspond with those put forward during the twentieth century and discussed earlier, so that my brief responses above are a reminder of points already made in more detail thus far in this book.

Blomberg's conclusion (2001, 32) is: "Finally, as I mentioned above, the major weakness of the Griesbach theory to date is that its proponents have not demonstrated how Markan style and theology emerge more consistently and coherently on their hypothesis than on the alternatives. Until I see such a demonstration, I will remain unconvinced." This downplays the work of other scholars on this matter, particularly the labors of the members of the Two-Gospel school. Perhaps this present book is also a step in the direction of providing what Blomberg requests.

In *Rethinking the Synoptic Problem*, S. McKnight presents an essay on "A Generation Who Knew Not Streeter: The Case for Markan Priority." He draws attention to the role of Sanday's Oxford Seminar, and particularly the work of perhaps B. H. Streeter (its most well-known member) in laying the foundation in Britain and the English-speaking world for acceptance of Markan Priority. He lists (2001, 75–77) Streeter's first three arguments or "heads" (common content, common order, and common words; see discussion above) and says (77), "The most enduring and influential theory of how these phenomena ought to be explained is the Oxford hypothesis." He then acknowledges (80) that what these phenomena have established is simply that "the Synoptics are related to one another" and that "there are various explanations of the three phenomena." He wants a feature that "can adjudicate the matter" and finds it: "I begin right here with the sole logical solution to the Synoptic problem. The Oxford hypothesis is more probable because of the *linguistic phenomena.*"

McKnight is referring (83) to the various linguistic features of the Synoptics: "the foundational argument for Markan priority is the linguistic argument; it is the *only* argument with probative and decisive force." This argument is a development and expansion of Streeter's fourth "head," and McKnight sets out five aspects of it.

First, he commends and draws upon (81) "the text-critical argument by M. C. Williams," that is, "the argument from the most original reading." McKnight gives three examples of this argument (87) where "Mark's grammar [was] 'corrected' by Matthew or Luke." I have explained earlier in this chapter that Mark's "bad grammar" has more to do with his use of material drawn from the preaching of Peter and the inherent difference between spoken and written literary language. Williams gives his own exposition of his argument in the fourth of the collection of recent books we are considering, and I discuss it below.

Second, McKnight endorses Markan Priority and the Oxford Hypothesis (88) as "more probable because of the *theological phenomena.*" This argument has been examined earlier in this chapter also.

And third, McKnight endorses Markan Priority (89) because "the coherency of the theory is an argument in its favor," and he adds, "This argument is really nothing more than an explanation that makes good sense of the data." McKnight is using the "explanatory power" of Markan Priority to explain the observable data. I would dare to suggest that the scenario I have outlined in this book is far more comprehensive in its explanation of the data—with far fewer unexplained problems and "loose ends" left dangling—than Markan Priority (with or without Q).

Next in the conference report, Farmer presents a case for Luke's use of Matthew and then Mark's use of both. In the final essay, G. Osborne sums up the conference and notes (139) that "literary dependence is mandated by the evidence; the only question is the direction of the flow." He recaps the major arguments adduced for Markan Priority in the other papers, expresses himself unconvinced by the Two-Gospel view because of its belief that Luke used Matthew, and questions several features not satisfactorily explained—particularly (142) that "it is difficult to explain the many omissions if Mark used both Matthew and Luke," and (143) that there is no "credible reason why Mark was written" if Matthew and Luke already existed. Thus he concludes (150) "that the evidence points clearly to the modified Streeter theory that Mark was first."

The Farrer Explanation

In *The Synoptic Problem: A Way Through the Maze* (2001) M. Goodacre looks at the Synoptic data and then (58) aims to show that "there are several ways in which Markan Priority explains this data better than does Markan Posteriority." Goodacre considers the material Mark omits and says (59) that "this data does not make sense on the assumption of Markan Posteriority." He then notes (59–60) the "little material that is present in Mark but absent in both Matthew and Luke" and decides that "Markan Priority seems more likely." Goodacre notes (60) statements in Mark that are open to the interpretation that Jesus' power was limited; he comments again (61) on what Mark fails to include; he remarks (62) that the "striking feature of Mark's style" is that "Mark's is the most blatantly colloquial, the most 'oral' in nature" of the Gospels; he mentions Mark's love of adding "visual detail" and concludes that "it would be odd if the most 'oral' of the Synoptic Gospels turned out also to be the third Gospel." Goodacre continues to develop some of these points for several pages more, canvassing several of the other arguments that I have discussed—and answered—earlier in this chapter.

Then Goodacre finds his most convincing argument for Markan Priority (71–76) in his presentation of the idea of "editorial fatigue," claiming (76) that "The most decisive indicator of Markan Priority is evidence of editorial fatigue in Matthew and Luke." Goodacre recognizes the strength of patristic evidence for Matthean Priority but seeks to discount it.

Goodacre compares (65–67) Mark's "harder readings" with Matthew and Luke, since the way they smooth his roughness and correct his errors supposedly indicates that they were subsequent to Mark. Thus, when Matthew and/or Luke has something that (apparently) makes better sense than Mark's version, this points to Markan Priority. Also, Goodacre claims (71–72) that both Matthew and Luke suffer quite a bit from "editorial fatigue" and forget where they are and what they are copying from Mark: "editorial fatigue results in unconscious mistakes, small errors of detail that naturally arise in the course of constructing a narrative." Goodacre believes these elements indicate that Matthew and Luke were (74) "working from a source," that is, Mark. Thus, when Mark's material makes better sense than Matthew's and/or Luke's, this also points to Markan Priority. So whichever way the situation goes, the explanation is Markan Priority! For those attempting to prove Markan Priority and disprove Markan Posteriority, such evidence is always on their side: "Heads I win, tails you lose."

Goodacre's presentation is lucid and contains summary boxes that clarify his points. But he simply summarizes (without developing) the arguments of twentieth-century scholarship for Markan Priority without seriously considering the extent to which they have been affectively answered by advocates of other views. Goodacre himself follows the Farrer-Goulder view (see chap. 10) that Luke knew and used Matthew as well as Mark. It should be noted how, at the commencement of the twenty-first century, Goodacre's textbook for students (9) builds its case for Markan Priority on almost the full spectrum of arguments discussed in this chapter.

Three-Theory Interaction

R. L. Thomas's book *Three Views on the Origins of the Synoptic Gospels* (2002) includes contributions from three advocates of the Two-/Four-Source View, the Two-Gospel View, and the Independence View, with responses in each case from the other two contributors. In the first one, G. Osborne and M. Williams commence by establishing the case for a literary relationship between the Synoptics, and then they add (55), "Streeter's presentation of the evidence for Markan priority remains the 'classic statement.' Indeed, some scholars have said that no 'new' lines of evidence have been suggested since Streeter."

Osborne and Williams then revisit the majority of the Markan Priority arguments analyzed earlier in this chapter and conclude this section (42) with this judgment: "Proponents of Markan priority agree that no single argument of those presented earlier is conclusive; rather the cumulative effect constitutes the probability that the Two-Source Hypothesis is by far the best solution to the problem of synoptic relationships."

I am reminded of the bar room "eloquent" who exclaimed, in clinching his case, "And if those arguments don't convince you, I have another that is just as good." The fact is that $0 + 0 + 0 + 0$ still adds up to zero. Joining a string of unconvincing arguments together does not add up to having a convincing one. Indeed, Osborne and Williams by implication acknowledge this when they proceed to present their main case—a very detailed elaboration and application of Streeter's "fourth head"—with these words (42): "Streeter's fourth head of evidence—that Matthew and Luke improve Mark's more primitive wording—holds great importance. The following discussion is quite extensive because here, *and only here*, is firm evidence that demonstrates Markan priority" (italics in original).

Osborne and Williams then discuss Matthew/Mark textual differences and apply text-critical criteria because (48) "Streeter's fourth head of evidence is, in fact, similar to many of the text-critical criteria. . . . Thus, the following examination applies text-critical principles to the Gospel texts to determine priority." (Williams developed this approach much further and four years later [2006] wrote a book on it, which is considered below in this connection.)

Their method of accounting for differences between the Gospels includes invoking the authors' creative genius in inventing material. Thus about a phrase in Christ's teaching in Matt 23:5 they state (45), "Regardless of whether Matthew used Mark as a source, one must admit that Matthew invented the preceding phrase." That is, they say, whether one places Mark first or last, this phrase in Christ's teaching is Matthew's invention—and we all must admit it! But I don't admit any such thing. I believe Matthew includes this phrase—and the rest of his record of Christ's teaching—because he heard Christ say it.

The other two views presented in this book are discussed later (the Two-Gospel view in the next chapter and the Independence view in chap. 10).

Text-Critical Criteria

Williams (*Two Gospels from One,* 2006) elaborates in detail his thesis—which is explained briefly in *Three Views on the Origins of the Synoptic Gospels* (Thomas 2002)—that (12) "Text-critical criteria clearly and consistently support Marcan priority and Matthean posteriority." Williams cites (28) Streeter's "five heads of evidence for Markan priority" and acknowledges that "heads" 1, 2, 3, and 5 are not very persuasive. Thereafter he focuses on the fourth head, Streeter's linguistic argument, which he develops and applies to the text of Matthew and Mark. If this sounds a bit familiar, it is because it was discussed earlier in this chapter. Indeed, much of Williams's material is taken directly from this earlier book with only occasional minor verbal modifications (and without acknowledgement of source).

Williams surveys various assessments that scholars have made of linguistic differences between Matthew and Mark, including (40) such things as Fitzmyer's essay "on the evidence for Marcan priority based on awkwardness in Mark's grammar" and "grammatical or stylistic improvements to Mark's text by Luke" (in "McKnight's analysis of Luke's redactions of Mark"). But Williams judges (41) that "more objective" criteria are needed "to determine chronological priority in the Synoptic Gospels. Are such criteria available?" Then he reaches his primary thesis: "Because of the similarities between textual criticism and source criticism (both disciplines seek the prior text), text-critical criteria may be applied in an analysis of the gospel texts in order to determine priority." He then points out (42), "Not only did scribes make unintentional errors, they often made intentional changes in the text they were copying." The copyists may have done this for theological reasons at times or because (43) they wanted "to 'improve' the sense of the text" they were copying.

Williams (citing Aland and Hurtado) considers (43) examples of how "scribes have made significant changes to the text," thereby "improving it by their own standards of correctness." He then attempts to determine where one Gospel author has made similar changes to another as if these writing behaviors are parallel, and he concludes Matthew has corrected Mark (because he has "better Greek"), which Williams contends clearly establishes Markan Priority upon an objective basis.

Making intentional changes, however, is not the role of the scribe. Scribes making a copy of a document (any document) were in the nature of the case supposed to be reproducing that document word-for-word. That was their brief. To the extent that they did not do so, they introduced errors of varying degrees of seriousness. The task of text-critical analysis is to identify what occurred so as to arrive at a correct text. It is a total leap of faith—for which there is no evidence at all—to assume that Mark was committed in a similar way to the task of producing an exact copy of parts of Matthew (on the Markan Posteriority views) or Matthew of Mark (on the Markan Priority view). To judge how well one author has fulfilled this role of copying another author's work when this assumption has not first been established is totally illegitimate.

But why must one assume, out of the blue as it were, that one Gospel author had as his purpose to produce an exact copy (with some modifications) of what another author had written? And what sort of a picture materializes if one recognizes (as Streeter and an army of other scholars has recognized) that the difference in language between Mark and the Major Synoptics is the difference between spoken and written language? What sort of picture materializes if instead one takes seriously the explanation of this Markan feature from the early church Fathers, who said, "Mark wrote down what he heard Peter saying"? (See above for fuller discussion.)

Williams's entire thesis depends on an unproven proposition that is contrary to the evidence at hand: that if Mark were third, his aim and purpose would have been to reproduce material verbatim from Matthew and Luke. Since this obviously did not happen, Williams insists that Mark was clearly not third. Once we recognize that Williams's premise is quite invalid, investigating the extent to which Mark did what it was not his intention to do is irrelevant.

Williams, writing on the lack of consensus on a solution to the Synoptic Problem, says (22) that "the Synoptic Problem consists of having the finished product—three Synoptic Gospels—but only clues as to the exact history of how these three gospels were produced. Because of this lack of clarity regarding history, scholars have struggled to reach a consensus for the solution of the Synoptic Problem." This is a widely held view. Williams speaks of having "only clues as to the exact history," resulting in a "lack of clarity," yet it is surprising to see how much history information is being ignored. First, there is Luke's statement that he used apostolic and other eyewitness sources. Second, the comments of Papias are available, and those of several other Fathers, concerning the role of Peter's preaching in providing the material for Mark. Third, the Fathers place Mark after Matthew—and in most cases, after Luke as well. These are, one might say, significant "clues from history"—but Williams himself focuses his investigation so narrowly that they are not allowed into his discussion, while scholars in general do not put them all together and ponder their purpose and their import.

Williams added (44) this cautious explanation: "Although it is true that the methods of scribes and those of the Evangelists differed, it is here proposed that many of the types of changes made by scribes also might have been made by Matthew, if he were using the text of Mark as a source when he composed his gospel, or by Mark, if he were using the text of Matthew as a source." But he is confident (44, 46) that

> The legitimacy of such detailed comparison is all but unanimously agreed upon in literature related to the Synoptic problem.... Despite the minority opinion to the contrary, it is a worthwhile goal to analyze and compare pericope after pericope from the gospels of Matthew and Mark, using the criteria from textual criticism to determine evidence for priority. Such an analysis and comparison is, in essence, an analysis of Streeter's fourth head of evidence: Is the text-critical argument for the priority of Mark a valid argument?

Williams proceeds with discussions of "History of Textual Criticism" (chap. 2) and "Examining Mark's Textual Apparatus" (chap. 3), and then he applies his criteria in "Examining the Textual Difference Between Matthew and Mark" (chap. 4). This application and extension of Streeter's "fourth head" will have wide appeal because of its offer of an "objective" basis on which to assess the "direction" of dependence between two Synoptic Gospels: in the light of the observable difference, which Gospel can be seen to be correcting another?

Hopefully, Gospel scholars will give careful thought to the methodological basis of what Williams is doing in proposing this criterion. There is a fundamental premise here that needs to be carefully considered: the belief that a later Gospel (whichever one) has as a major purpose in writing to correct an earlier one. On this basis it is then pronounced that Matthew does a much better job of correcting Mark than vice versa. The conclusion is then drawn that Matthew must be subsequent to Mark and must have used his Gospel. Thus, again and again the point is that

> Matthew and Mark differ almost entirely in this verse. . . . Matthew's [wording] is much clearer than Mark's awkward [expression]. . . . This difference in wording resulted in a clearer and more precise text in that Matthew states exactly. . . . This precision eliminates the possible misunderstanding. . . . Thus, it is possible that this is an improvement by the later Christian community. . . . The wording of the question in Mark is obtuse and the more difficult reading. . . .

The quotes above come from page 149 in relation to verses discussed there, but the point needs to be made that Williams says that Matthew was correcting Mark and improving his Gospel—and Williams makes such claims on *every* page of his discussion of this issue. And he claims that Matthew's alterations can be recognized as being made for this very purpose.

There are several things wrong with this text-critical approach. First, it is based on a completely invalid premise. This is like the journal *Wind and Waves* giving this product review: "While admittedly good-looking, and with acceptable carrying capacity, its front end will not cut cleanly through the water, its propulsive method is slow and inefficient, it has poor mooring facilities, and it is going to leak." While failing to note that the product reviewed was built to be an automobile, not a boat. Why judge how well a car performs as a boat when that was not its purpose? Similarly, why judge how well one Gospel corrects or improves the other *when that is not the purpose for which the second Gospel (whichever it was) was written?* Such an argument involves a completely gratuitous assumption unsubstantiated by any facts to support it. Williams's conclusion is derived from circular reasoning by starting with what he is supposed to establish. Once we recognize the different purpose for which each Gospel was written, this "objective criterion" is seen for what it is—ludicrous.

Second, the purpose of textual criticism is to discern which textual variants contain errors and modifications in order to determine the original text. Inherent in this criterion, when applied to the Synoptics, is the concept that the Synoptic differences must actually be departures from an original text—one that scholars must attempt to find. But the fact that (on this view) Matthew and Luke realized that Mark "needed fixing" shows that this view is just one step away from saying, "You can't trust Mark's Gospel because it is in need of correction and improvement." This is completely incompatible with any concept of all three Synoptics being the product of the inspiration of the Holy Spirit so that all three are the Word of God.

Third, this criterion provides a basis for identifying "additions" to Mark by Matthew and Luke as inauthentic later inventions, maybe from the "church" that supposedly fathered that Gospel, or directly from Matthew's or Luke's "creative imagination." For many years many Synoptic scholars have used this assumption to support Markan Priority, and now they have this "objective criterion" to undergird these opinions. This is just one step away from concluding that "Mark is the only Gospel you can trust."

The second point and the third point are contradictory—the former says Mark cannot be trusted and the latter says only Mark can be trusted—yet both points are supported by Markan Priority advocates.

Fourth, this criterion implies that the writers of the later Gospels would have had an adversarial attitude to the earlier one, that when they saw that earlier Gospel they would have said to themselves, "This is terrible—I must do something about this!"

Differences in the Gospels are so often differences of perspective, emphasis, or points of view. These differences are not in conflict: they provide additional enriching insights that aid our understanding; they are there for a purpose.

But the presence of such differences in the Synoptics does not mean that they cannot be harmonized. (See chap. 8 in particular in relation to Matthew and Luke since these two Gospels contain not a few such issues.) I agree with Farnell (2002, 267) that what is needed in scholarship is "harmonization not redactional hermeneutics." I am not persuaded to his Independence View, but I am heartily in accord with him in his attitude and his view of the Gospels when he writes that "the Independence View emphasizes traditional harmonization based on inspiration. The Independence View is optimistic that the Gospels lend themselves to harmonization both historically and factually." My view similarly recognizes harmonization—actually, I find that Mark has done quite a bit of this in relation to Matthew and Luke (see chap. 11).

But many adherents of source theories do not find the concept of harmonization to be congenial. To treat the Gospel writers as being at loggerheads with each other—so that a later writer's attitude is like "a scribal reaction against a predecessor's words" (Niemelä 2002, 107, writing against the Williams proposal)—is ghastly. The text-critical criterion is not merely gratuitous; it is also destructive of the attitude that we must have in studying the Synoptic Gospels. It produces a completely unnecessary and wrongheaded dichotomy between a scholarly approach to studying the Gospels on the one hand, and the devotional use of the Gospels where one submits to their teaching and their authority on the other. This view is not merely invalid. It is downright dangerous in its consequences.

Other Perspectives on the Evidence

Markan Priority continues to attract strong support, but alternative explanations continue to be advocated. Two of the above-mentioned books, the Conference Report and the Three-Theory Interaction, also include expositions that opposed Markan Priority and expounded other theories. Additionally, here are two other recent books that reject the Markan Priority Hypothesis: D. A. Black, *Why Four Gospels?* (2001), expounding and developing B. Orchard's Fourfold-Gospel Hypothesis, which identifies Mark as written third; and D. Peabody et al., *One Gospel from Two* (2002), a detailed exposition of the Two-Gospel case for Mark's use of Matthew and Luke. These two books and other writings along these lines are integral to the discussion of Markan Dependence in the next chapter.

Several other books published this century should also be noted. See B. Gerhardsson (1998, *Memory and Manuscript*, originally 1961); Gerhardsson (2001, *The Reliability of the Gospel Tradition*). Gerhardsson stresses the importance of the oral tradition behind our Gospels. D. Neville (1994, *Arguments from Order in Synoptic Source Criticism*) assesses order and examines "How important and how reliable are arguments based on [the order of pericopes], and where might they lead?" Blomberg (2001, 34) comments on this book: "[This is] (a)nother important study ... but in fact aligning itself with no one solution to the Synoptic Problem.... What Neville does show is that the various arguments from the order of Matthew's and Luke's parallels do not consistently support Markan priority." Compare Neville (2002, *Mark's Gospel: Prior or Posterior?*).

Two other books published this century appeal to me as making a significant contribution to Gospel scholarship, but they are constrained by their authors' assumption of Markan Priority—and therefore I discuss them here. R. Bauckham was the editor of the volume *The Gospels for All Christians: Rethinking the Gospel Audiences* (1998), which points out that "information flow was immediate and pervasive in the first-century world, that the gospels must have been authored for the entire church, instead of specialized 'communities.'" Then in 2006 he published *Jesus and the Eyewitnesses*, which examines in some depth the evidence for the Gospels being based directly on eyewitness testimony. In 2007 M. Roberts wrote *Can We Trust the Gospels?* These two latter books are both concerned with the nature of the Gospel genre.

Roberts devotes chapter 7 to a consideration of genre. He says (83), "What are the New Testament Gospels? ... To which genre should they be assigned? ... if we know the genre of the Gospels, this will help us to interpret them appropriately." His conclusion (85) is that "the New Testament Gospels fit quite nicely within the genre of Hellenistic biography," a genre which he has described to us. He cites (85) others who have reached this same conclusion: B. Witherington (*New Testament History*, 2001, 19–24) and R. Burridge (*What Are the Gospels?* 2004). Roberts uses this categorization to account for the verbal differences found in the Synoptics, which he explains (88) this way:

> Moreover, we must remember that the Gospels give us what is technically called the *ipsissima vox* ("his own voice") of Jesus rather than the *ipsissima verba* ("his own words"). Since it's highly unlikely that Jesus did much teaching in Greek, the autographs of Matthew, Mark, Luke, and John did not preserve his original words (except in a few cases). They do, however, authentically capture his voice.

Roberts then asks (91–92):

> Is it possible to trust a biographical or historical writing that offers the *ipsissima vox* rather than the *ipsissima verba*? I believe it is. Of course, this depends on your evaluation of the overall trustworthiness of the writer and the sources at his or her disposal. I've already talked about the sources used by the evangelists and how they contribute to the historicity of the Gospels. ... The Gospel writers functioned in the mode of the biography and history writers of their day. This means they were permitted greater freedom in certain matters than would be granted to modern biographers and historians. Paraphrasing or rephrasing statements and speeches was acceptable, as was arranging events in thematic rather than chronological order.... For example, the Gospels can faithfully represent the *ipsissima vox* of Jesus without reproducing his *ipsissima verba*. Minor variations of wording or a different ordering of events do not mean that we should discount the reliability of the Gospels as sources of genuine knowledge of Jesus.

This is a reasonable view of the relationship between the words of Jesus as given in the Gospels and what Jesus himself actually said. In fact, it is the kind of explanation towards which one is pushed if one rejects (as does Roberts) ideas of late-date invention of words to put into the mouth of Jesus, and opts instead for the reliability of the Gospel record. That is, one can hold that the Gospels as they are now represent substantially what Jesus said, allowing for "paraphrasing or rephrasing statements and speeches" (to quote Roberts) by the authors. However, I have been pointing out in this book that one can have even greater confidence than this in the Synoptic record of Christ's teachings.

Bauckham (2006) refines further the concept of the genre of the Gospels, presenting compelling evidence for recognizing that eyewitness testimony lies directly behind the Gospel records. He writes (479):

> In this book I have followed Samuel Byrskog in arguing that the Gospels, though in some ways a very distinctive form of historiography, share broadly in the attitude to eyewitness testimony that was common among the historians in the Greco-Roman period. These historians valued above all reports of first-hand experience of the events they recounted. Best of all was for the historian to have been himself a participant in the events (direct autopsy). Failing that (and no historian was present at all the events he needed to recount, not least because usually some would have been simultaneous), they sought informants who could speak from first-hand knowledge and whom they could interview (indirect autopsy).

In the life of Jesus, God has broken through into human history. This is a unique event, and it is therefore absurd to attempt to assess it or categorize it in terms of what would be otherwise familiar to us from ordinary human experience. Bauckham explains (500–501):

> All too easily the attempt to connect what happened with the experience and understanding of our ordinary world makes for easy intelligibility at the cost of the uniqueness of the event and therefore also of its power to disclose. When the quest of the historical Jesus discounts what the witnesses claim in the interests of what is readily credible by the standards of historical analogy, that is, ordinary experience, it reduces revelation to the triviality of what we knew or could know anyway.

The witnesses told what they witnessed, but in doing so they recounted (503) "what they remembered, choosing what to include, shaping the narrative, and they would be likely to tell the story again and again in the form they themselves had given it." Thus Bauckham has identified the genre of the Gospels as testimony (505–6):

> The burden of this book is that the category of testimony is the one that does most justice to the Gospels both as history and as theology. As a form of historiography, testimony offers a unique access to historical reality that cannot be had without an element of trust in the credibility of the witness and what he or she has to report. . . . Eyewitness testimony offers us insider knowledge from involved participants. It also offers us engaged interpretation, for in testimony fact and meaning coinhere, and witnesses who give testimony do so with the conviction of significance that requires to be told. Witnesses of truly significant events speak out of their own ongoing attempts to understand. . . . Reading the Gospels as eyewitness testimony differs therefore from attempts at historical reconstruction behind the text. It takes the Gospels seriously as they are; it acknowledges the uniqueness of what we can know only in this testimonial form.

The Markan Priority Explanation 205

Bauckham identifies the author of the Second Gospel as the John Mark of the Acts and the Pauline letters, and he accepts the testimony of Papias (and the other church Fathers) about the role of Peter behind this Gospel (205–21). Thus (210–11) Papias's comment (Eusebius, *Church History* 3.39.4)

> expresses a preference, following good historiographic practice, for reports as close as possible to those of the eyewitnesses themselves. . . . In Mark's case, although Mark was not an eyewitness himself, he was reproducing Peter's testimony as Peter recited it. Papias portrays Mark as no more than a translator scrupulously accurate in reproducing Peter's oral testimony. . . . Short of a text actually written by an eyewitness, Mark's Gospel, as represented by Papias, would be as good a historical source as one could get in the period after all eyewitnesses had died [i.e., in the period late in the first century about which Papias was writing]. . . . Throughout the passage the complementary roles of Peter and Mark are that Peter *remembered* and Mark *heard and wrote*.

Bauckham devotes two chapters (chaps. 7 and 9) to a focus on the role of Peter in relation to Mark and his Gospel.

I myself would not interpret Papias's comments about Peter and Mark to mean, as Bauckham does (206), that Peter "preferred to express himself in his native Aramaic and allow Mark to translate into more accurate and readable Greek." I see Mark's Greek as reflecting the Greek of Peter's preaching, but I do indeed concur in seeing the witness of Peter as represented directly in the writing of Mark.

I also concur in Bauckham's recognition of the oral nature of Mark's Gospel. He suggests (233) either an oral background for Mark's text, or that "Mark composed the narrative in writing, making use of oral techniques because he was writing for oral performance of his text. In any case, it seems clear that the Gospel was indeed composed for oral performance, and that the oral structuring techniques would have assisted such oral performance and aural reception."

Similarly Bauckham holds (29–30) that "Luke received traditions directly from the eyewitnesses. . . . They are disciples who accompanied Jesus throughout his ministry (cf. Acts 1:21) and who were prominent teachers in the early church. They certainly include the Twelve (cf. Acts 6:4) but also others." The eyewitness testimony that Luke referred to and that he collected as the basis of his Gospel was oral, the result of his personal interviews with eyewitnesses when these were possible. But it was not exclusively oral, as Bauckham explains (37–38):

> [T]he language of tradition does not require that an account be handed on orally. It can refer to the writing of recollections. So, when Luke's preface claims that "those who from the beginning were eyewitnesses and ministers of the

word handed on (*paredosan*) to us [the traditions of the events]" (Luke 1:2), the reference could be to or could include written accounts by the eyewitnesses.

Bauckham assumes Markan Priority and the Two-Source explanation of Synoptic relationships (42), and he rejects Matthew as the author of the First Gospel (98, 108–12, 131, 288, 302). He concedes a possible role for the apostle in the pre-history of the Gospel that came to bear his name (288–89): "The old suggestion that, among the Twelve, it would be Matthew the tax collector who would most likely, owing to his profession, be able to write, might after all be a sound guess and a clue to the perplexing question of the role he might have played somewhere among the sources of the Gospel of Matthew."

I would aver that we can accept the basic thesis that Bauckham proposes—that direct eyewitness testimony, oral and written, stands behind the Gospels as we have them. The result (as Bauckham shows) is that the Gospels stand only one step removed, or at most two, from the events they record. This underlines their claim to accuracy and authenticity in all they report. The fruit of Bauckham's scholarship in this regard is highly valuable.

But Bauckham filters his explanation through the grid of Markan Priority and the various consequences that this implies. It is possible to refine his explanation further by removing this filter and accepting the role of the apostle Matthew—both as active author of the First Gospel and also as the source of much of the material that his Gospel has in common with Luke (irrespective of whether it also occurs in Mark).

Clearly, the Markan Priority view still dominates the field in the twenty-first century, though many of its advocates show less confidence than when this view was declared to be "the one absolutely assured result" of New Testament critical investigation. But, Markan Priority is still advocated. It is appropriate now for us to ask why, especially since this chapter demonstrates that all the arguments for Markan Priority fail to deliver when subjected to thoughtful analysis and assessment. Although individual arguments for Markan Priority may now be recognized as having little force, advocates still encourage us to recognize the cumulative power of their case so we can put them all together and see the "big picture."

The Markan Priority Hypothesis reminds me of a painting in a private art gallery exhibition that caused a commotion in London about a century ago. The young up-and-coming artist who was exhibiting his work needed one more painting to hang in the exhibition before the press and art critics were invited to a preview. He came up with it and put it on display. This particular painting attracted quite a bit of interest. There was nothing on it—it looked for all the world like a blank canvas.

A young reporter pointed to it and said to the artist, "I take it that this one isn't finished yet?" "Oh, no, it's finished all right." Puzzled, the reporter said, "What is it then?" "This one," said the artist, "depicts, as the title says, 'A Dramatic Moment in the Story of the Children of Israel Crossing the Red Sea.'" The reporter stared at the canvas thoughtfully and then ventured tentatively, "But where is the Red Sea?" "Driven right back by the mighty hand of the Lord," the artist explained. "And where are the Children of Israel?" "Under the dynamic leadership of Moses, they have successfully made the crossing." "And what about Pharaoh's chariots?" "They are going to arrive on the scene any moment now."

This painting attracted attention in the press, though reports were mixed. One art critic said, "A brilliant concept—it captures the moment wonderfully." Another said, "It pictures the calm before the storm. Sheer genius." The praise of others was a bit more muted, though one paper headlined a brief review as "Much Ado About Nothing." Now individually, each of the artist's answers seems quite reasonable and can, I suppose, account for what we see (or don't see)—but when we look at the "big picture," there is nothing there! And there is, of course, another explanation. The artist simply didn't paint anything on the canvas.

Similarly, when we look behind all the rhetoric about the case for Markan Priority, there is nothing there. So then: if arguments for Markan Priority are illusory, what alternative explanation do we have? That is the subject of the next chapter.

6 THE MARKAN DEPENDENCE EXPLANATION

This chapter provides detailed evidence for Markan Dependence and answers rebuttals against it.

> *It is apparent that St. Mark makes quick and frequent transitions from one evangelist to the other; and blends their accounts, I mean their words, in such a manner as is utterly inexplicable upon any other footing than by supposing he had both these Gospels before him.*
>
> —Henry Owen (1764, 74)

BACKGROUND

Historical Development of the Hypothesis

Markan Posteriority—the view that Mark was written third and drew upon the Major Synoptics as sources in his writing—is an ancient explanation of Synoptic relationship, having a fascinating history. Augustine wrote at length about the Gospels, and at an early stage of his study (Book 1, 2.3–3.6), he espoused the sequence of writing as in our New Testaments: Matthew, Mark, Luke (with the later utilizing the earlier). He says of Mark's relationship to Matthew, "Mark followed him closely, and looks like his attendant and epitomizer." This view has had its advocates down to recent times, the most notable being H. G. Jameson (1922), J. Chapman (1937), and B. C. Butler (1951).

But D. Peabody (1983) draws attention to a further comment by Augustine that points to a change of mind. Peabody describes Augustine's view of Synoptic relationships (from Book 1) and then continues (47):

> From 2.1.2 to 4.3.10 Augustine was involved in a careful comparison of the four gospels. Up to this point in the *De Consensu* [*Harmony*] he had considered all of the parallel material within all four of the gospels and all of the *Sondergut* within Matthew, Mark, and Luke. Therefore, only the *Sondergut* of John remained to be considered when he came to 4.10.11. At this point Augustine made his concluding statement about the gospels in relationship to one another, looking back on his work with the Synoptic Gospels and looking forward to his work with the Johannine *Sondergut*.

Augustine's "concluding statement" (Book 4, 10.11) gives what he calls "the more probable account of the matter," where he says of Mark that "he holds a course in conjunction with both [the other Synoptists]. For although he is at one with Matthew in the larger number of passages, he is nevertheless at one rather with Luke in some others." Peabody points out that, in context, this looks very much as if Augustine has come to the conclusion, after his detailed consideration of the Synoptic writings, that Mark is "at one" with both Matthew and Luke in ways that indicate he was writing after them—that is, Mark's Gospel was written third. This interpretation of Augustine's comment is not beyond contention, but I find it quite convincing. So it appears that the first person to hold the Markan Posteriority view was Augustine, if indeed Peabody is correct in his interpretation of Augustine's later judgment as a result of his more detailed study of the Synoptic Gospels.

This possibility was overlooked in the years that followed Augustine, and the Augustinian Hypothesis has been the title often given to the view of "Matthew then Mark then Luke." This viewpoint is also frequently entitled the Successive Dependence Hypothesis—the title I use (see chap. 10) to avoid uncertainty about which Augustinian view I am referring to.

No further specific thought was given to this issue until the eighteenth century. Then H. Owen (1764) wrote a book in which he made a careful case for recognizing that Mark was written third and made use of Matthew and Luke. Owen himself regarded his Synoptic explanation as strengthening one's confidence in the accuracy of the Gospels at a time when some were calling this into question. He explains (iv):

> Could we truly discover at what time, for whose use, and on what occasion the Gospels were respectively written, we should doubtless be able, not only to understand them more perfectly, but also to read them with more profit, than we have the happiness at present to pretend to. For such a discovery, as it would throw light on the difficult passages, and help us to reconcile the seeming contradictions, that obstruct our progress in these sacred studies, so would it impart an additional lustre, force, and propriety to the several arguments that the Scripture offers for the confirmation and improvement of our faith.

He returns later (83) to this question of "seeming contradictions":

> How, then, came they not to avoid the many contradictions observable among them? These are only seeming contradictions; and vanish most of them, on a close comparison of the several passages: and were we sufficiently acquainted with the circumstances of the facts, the views of the Relators, the turns of their expressions, and the method they used in their computations, the rest would doubtless immediately disappear; and the several Gospels would perfectly correspond with each other.

Owen sums up (74) the work of Mark: "It is apparent that St. Mark makes quick and frequent transitions from one evangelist to the other; and blends their accounts, I mean their words, in such a manner as is utterly inexplicable upon any other footing than by supposing he had both these Gospels before him."

As Owen looked at the Synoptics, thus linked by the literary relationship that he had pointed out, he was strengthened by his studies to recognize (85) them to be "one complete, entire system of Divinity, supported by the strongest proofs that the subject is capable of, and defended against all the objections which either Jews or Gentiles, or even its more dangerous heretical Professors, could make to the truth and certainty of it." Their literary links were an additional sign of their genuineness (110):

> They likewise quoted each other's words, and thereby recommended each other's Histories. A circumstance of great advantage, whatever some may think of it, to the service of the Christian cause. For by this means they became not only mutual Vouchers for the truth of these *genuine* Gospels, but at the same time joint-opposers of all those *spurious* ones that were impiously obtruded on the world. [italics in original]

Owen's book did not create much of an impact in the scholarly world. In 1774 J. J. Griesbach produced the first volume of a new critical text of the Greek New Testament that covered the Gospels, and he arranged the Gospels in the form of a Synopsis. In 1776 he reissued this *Synopsis of the Gospels* as a separate work.

It is not known whether Owen ever encountered Griesbach, the scholar who was to become identified most closely with the Matthew-Luke-Mark thesis. The extent to which Griesbach was aware of the earlier work of Owen is uncertain, but they may well have met when Griesbach visited London in 1769. In any case, Griesbach did have a copy of Owen's book in his library, though he may not have read it since he makes no mention of it. It could be that he reached his conclusions independent of Owen from his own studies.

Griesbach's *Synopsis* places parallel passages in Matthew, Mark, and Luke in adjoining columns, which allows side-by-side comparison. This made possible, for the first time, a careful pericope-by-pericope and verse-by-verse study of the similarities and differences in sequence and content between the first three Gospels, and thus facilitated the investigation of their interrelationships and origins. B. Reicke (1978, 69) comments that "in fact all scholarly discussion of the relations between Matthew, Mark and Luke which has taken place during the last 200 years goes back to Griesbach's publication of his *Synopsis* in 1776." Griesbach thoroughly examines what his *Synopsis* revealed, and concludes that the evidence indicates Mark wrote third and used Matthew and Luke. The first outline of the Synoptic theory that Griesbach adopted was published in 1783. The view that Mark was written third became widely known because of Griesbach's work and consequently is very frequently referred to as the Griesbach Hypothesis or (more recently) the Owen-Griesbach Hypothesis.

G. C. Storr (1786) introduced the theory of Markan Priority and vigorously rejected Griesbach's Hypothesis that placed Mark last among the Synoptics. Griesbach wrote *Commentatio* (1789) a more detailed treatment of his viewpoint, which was reissued later with additions and a reply to Storr's criticisms (1794).

Griesbach wrote in Latin, so his dissertation remained unavailable in English until B. Orchard provided a translation with the title *A Demonstration That Mark Was Written After Matthew and Luke*. It is now accessible in the 1978 Cambridge monograph *J. J. Griesbach: Synoptic and Text-Critical Studies 1776–1976*.

Griesbach was exclusively concerned with the question of the nature of the relationship that exists between the three canonical Synoptic Gospels, and he found this fully explained by the dependence of Mark on Matthew and Luke. He did not investigate the prior stage, that is, what lay behind the canonical Synoptics and how they came into existence. Commenting on this, Orchard says (1978, 17, 129) that Griesbach "established the sequence, first, Matthew and Luke, second, Mark. But he nowhere in this treatise discussed the relationship of Luke to Matthew, though he is aware of the question. . . . Griesbach allows that it is a question that should have an answer, but in fact it would seem that he took no steps to answer it."

However, Griesbach had held a previous opinion on this matter. W. Baird (1987: 35) tells us that

> Griesbach believed that Luke was dependent on the Gospel of Matthew [and} . . . had presented [this thesis] in a paper during the celebration of

Easter as Jena in 1783, eleven years before the publication of his monumental *Commentatio*.

Griesbach's treatment of this thesis was carefully examined by H. H. Stoldt in an appendix to the second German (1986) edition of his *History and Criticism of the Marcan Hypothesis*. Baird (ibid., 38) reports that Stoldt analyzed Griesbach's treatment and concluded, "Griesbach's claim that Luke used Matthew cannot be sustained." It would seem that upon reflection Griesbach himself came to realize this, for (Baird 38):

> Stoldt also observes that Griesbach's secondary hypothesis is found exclusively in his earlier work. After further research on the synoptic problem, and in the course of the ongoing controversy, Griesbach may have been content to let his notion about Luke's as use of Matthew skip into undisturbed silence.

As Orchard has mentioned, Griesbach left the relationship of Luke to Matthew undiscussed—in his *Commentatio* he never tells us *explicitly* what he considered it to be. But he did not leave us entirely without evidence of his new, revised opinion.

Farmer's Two-Gospel school of thought is convinced otherwise. Farmer wrote (1964, 69), "According to Griesbach, Luke first used Matthew, and then Mark combined Matthew and Luke. This means that Mark was combining two Gospels between which there already exists a relationship of literary dependence." This overstates what Griesbach said. The only time Griesbach referred to the relationship of Luke to Matthew in his *Commentatio*, this is what he actually wrote (1978, 131): "Therefore, the question comes back to this: how did it happen that *Luke* arranged parts of his narrative otherwise than Matthew? This is not the place for examining the question, since we are dealing with Mark. We shall only permit ourselves to note that Luke has departed less than Matthew from the true sequence of events."

Griesbach expressly sets on one side any discussion of the question of the relation of Luke to Matthew with the comment, "This is not the place for examining the question, since we are dealing with Mark"; and he does not return to it at any other place. Thus Orchard is quite correct when he says (1976, 17) that Griesbach "nowhere in this treatise discusses the relationship of Luke to Matthew." Although Griesbach's does not *discuss* the relationship of Luke to Matthew, his comment does reveal what he held that relationship to be.

In saying "We shall only permit ourselves to note that Luke has departed less than Matthew from the true sequence of events," Griesbach indicates: "Matthew has departed from the true sequence of events and Luke has not." This means either that Matthew had a plan of arrangement of pericopes that was not as chronological as was Luke's, or that Matthew was less informed about the sequence of events than was Luke, or both. In either case it shows quite clearly that in Griesbach's view Luke was not dependent on Matthew for the sequence of pericopes in his own Gospel. This is the inescapable conclusion to be drawn from the meaning of his words.

Thus Griesbach's comment indicates that Luke had independent knowledge of "the true sequence of events," knowledge that enabled him to give these events in chronologically correct order on occasions when Matthew did not. And this in turn indicates that Luke had *independent knowledge of the pericopes themselves*, for clearly Luke cannot have known the "true sequence" of the pericopes while being ignorant of the pericopes.

Griesbach's comment does not preclude Luke from having known Matthew's Gospel, but it does preclude Luke from having drawn his material and sequence of pericopes exclusively from Matthew in those that they have in common. Furthermore, it shows that Griesbach held the view that Luke was in some significant measure independent of Matthew, had access to chronological information different from (and more accurate as regards "the true sequence of events" than) what is given in Matthew, and that Luke was guided by a different principle of compilation of pericopes than Matthew was. That is, Griesbach did not regard Luke's Gospel as dependent on or drawn from Matthew: Luke was sourced independently.

Among those who espoused Griesbach's theory were W. M. L. de Wette (1826; 6th ed., 1860) and F. J. Bleek (1869) in Germany (each wrote a New Testament introduction). Indeed, for a time the Griesbach Hypothesis was the prevailing viewpoint among German New Testament scholars and had many prominent adherents. The reasons why this view then fell into disfavor and disuse—so that the Markan Priority Hypothesis came to prevail—are investigated by Stoldt (1980). He gives details on the weaknesses of the Markan Priority Hypothesis, and after comparing this view with the Griesbach Hypothesis, he concludes (259): "Henry Owen and Johann Jacob Griesbach correctly recognized that Matthew and Luke formed the textual basis for Mark. And Griesbach in fact proved this with a textual analysis carried out with philological precision." But the Griesbach Hypothesis found little favor in Britain. It was supported by S. Davidson (1882) but strongly opposed by E. A. Abbott (1879) and F. H. Woods (1886).

Abbott asserted (1879, 791) that "it can be proved by *reduction ad absurdum* that Mark did not copy from Matthew and Luke." Abbott's argument consists of a demonstration that it was impossible for a person such as Mark to produce a document such as the Second Gospel by combining the material of the Gospels of Matthew and Luke in the way that the Griesbach

Hypothesis contends occurred. This is certainly a serious assertion: if it could not be done, then clearly Mark did not do it. (In chap. 3 of this book, I responded to Abbott's assertion that such a thing could not be done in the most effective way: by doing it.) Shortly afterward, Woods (1886, 66–67) read a paper on the Synoptic Problem in which he gave four arguments against the Griesbach position:

> 1. We cannot reasonably account for the remarkable omissions which St Mark must continually have made . . .
> 2. It is almost impossible to suggest any method by which St Mark could have made his selection.
> 3. This view would not account for the order of St Mark in several passages . . .
> 4. Lastly, this view leads us into greater difficulties than those it proposes to solve.

His conclusion is (67), "We seem therefore forced to adopt the opposite alternative, viz., that St Matthew and St Luke both made use of a Gospel very nearly agreeing with our present St Mark in its subject matter and the order of its contents." The arguments of Woods and Abbott carried the day. After recording (1964, 63–85) these objections raised against Griesbach's view, Farmer comments in wonderment (84f.),

> The historian of the Synoptic Problem is led to ask anew, "how could it have been possible for the Griesbach hypothesis to have received no more serious attention than was afforded to it by the leading students of the synoptic problem at both Oxford and Cambridge, even granting the powerful influence of the arguments of Woods and Abbott against this hypothesis?"

The criticisms made by Woods and Abbott in Britain were so effective that no voice was raised thereafter in favor of Markan Posteriority. Consequently, the main proponents of Markan Priority during the past century or so have engaged in only very limited rebuttal of the Markan Posteriority position.

But the publication of Butler's careful critique of Markan Priority in 1951 (see chap. 5) caused waves in the scholarly world. Later in the decade following Butler's publication, Farmer encountered it and reached the conviction that Butler had undermined the basis of Markan Priority. As a result of his own study of the issues, Farmer (1964) presented the case for reopening the discussion of the Synoptic Problem and reexamined the Griesbach Hypothesis that Mark was written third and used Matthew and Luke. Farmer's work (and that of his students and followers, who now term their position the "Two-Gospel" view) succeeded in reopening the Synoptic debate. Since the publication of Farmer's book, there has been an increase in the attention paid by writers to the rebuttal (as distinct from the mere rejection) of Mark's dependence on Matthew (and Luke).

Farmer's position has been subjected to detailed challenge. The best-known systematic presentations of the case against the Griesbach Hypothesis (Markan Dependence) are by C. H. Talbert and E. V. McKnight (1972, "Can the Griesbach Hypothesis Be Falsified?"), and J. A. Fitzmyer (1970, "The Priority of Mark and the 'Q' Source in Luke"). The detailed comparison of the Markan Priority and Markan Dependence perspectives for explaining general phenomena and particular passages in the Synoptics has been attempted with great care and thoroughness by C. M. Tuckett (1983, *The Revival of the Griesbach Hypothesis*).

The "Two-Gospel" case has received much attention but has not found widespread acceptance. The two main reasons for this are that (1) the Two-Gospel school holds that Luke used Matthew for his Gospel, and many scholars find convincing reasons why they cannot accept this; and (2) ultimately, the reasons put forward for Mark writing his Gospel when the church already had Matthew and Luke—and the explanations for the way in which Mark would have had to treat these Gospels—have been unconvincing. These and other objections—and the positive case for Markan Dependence—are considered below.

Facing the Factors to Be Considered

I have never believed in Markan Priority. I entered theological college without any firm opinion on the issue, and without any awareness that the relationship between the Gospels mattered all that much. I guess I was kind of an unfocused Independent Gospels adherent if I was anything.

In college I was taught about Markan Priority. But, as stated in the previous chapter, our New Testament lecturer Marcus Loane (later to become Archbishop of Sydney) also made us very aware of the limitations and shortcomings of this theory. I was very impressed with reading John Chapman's *Matthew, Mark and Luke*, and I felt then (as I feel now) that his careful scholarship, with its devastating demolition of the Markan Priority case, has not received the attention it deserved.

I have given quite a bit of my time to the study of this question since then. I first published my thinking on the matter in 1977 in my *The Progressive Publication of Matthew—A New Explanation of Synoptic Origins* (Tyndale Fellowship for Biblical Studies in Australia, Ridley College, Melbourne). I was at Farmer's Synoptic Conferences in Cambridge in 1979 and Jerusalem in 1984. I have been teaching about these matters in theological and Bible colleges for 30 years.

I mention these things to underline the fact that I have been aware of the scholarly currents in this field for a considerable amount of time. This is the context within which I have been assessing, evaluating, and refining my conclusions. I have great respect for the scholars with whom I take issue in this present treatment of the issues. I respect their integrity and academic standing and ability, and their personal faith and godliness. I simply cannot help coming to the conclusion that there are certain aspects of the available data that they have overlooked or given inadequate weight to in their thinking. In the previous chapter, I shared with you how this applied to the Markan Priority question.

In coming now to examine the hypothesis of Markan Dependence, I am at pains to elucidate the ways in which I share common ground with both the Fourfold-Gospel Hypothesis and the Two-Gospel school, and the main areas of disagreement. There is much in their respective positions with which I concur. But there are also some places where I would invite the supporters of both these positions to consider these issues afresh and to reflect further.

In Farmer's revived version of the Griesbach Hypothesis, he has on occasion gone beyond Griesbach in that he (Farmer) derives Luke from Matthew. Farmer's specific form of the theory has therefore been designated by some writers as the Neo-Griesbach Hypothesis, though this term does not appear to have been adopted very widely, and the name of Griesbach continues at times to be attached to the theory as held today by some scholars who do not notice that no one holds this theory today in just the way Griesbach did.

The Farmer school deliberately adopted the designation the Two-Gospel Hypothesis on the grounds that Farmer explains (1983, xxxiv): "The advantage of this way of referring to the view that Mark used both Matthew and Luke is that it makes clear that the basic Gospel tradition of the church can be traced back to two actual Gospels, Matthew and Luke, rather than two hypothetical documents, namely Ur-Marcus and "Q." The school also chose this designation in light of the view held by Farmer and his associates, that Luke derived from Matthew. Farmer explains (1983, xxxv):

> In order to grasp the full significance of the view that Luke used Matthew, and Mark used both Matthew and Luke, one must recognize that this way of understanding the relationship of the Gospels makes it possible to avoid all of the major hypothetical documents that have bedeviled critics for over a century— not merely "Q" and "Ur-Marcus," but "Proto-Luke," "Proto-Matthew," and a

whole series of such hypothetical documents called for in an unending number of multiple-source hypotheses.

Several modern writers refer to this view as Markan Posteriority, in contradistinction to Markan Priority.

My title for the relationship between the Gospels is Markan Dependence, which is a version of the Markan Posteriority view—that is, Mark was written third and drew from the other two Synoptics. But there are three other Markan Posteriority hypotheses, and it would be wise for me to clairfy their similarities and differences.

Some scholars, in particular those of the Jerusalem school, hold the view that Luke was written first (see chap. 10). My views about the Synoptics must be distinguished from others who also hold to Matthean Posteriority, particularly the Two-Gospel position. There are numbers of areas where I have not found the Two-Gospel explanation at all convincing, and the data has led me to quite different conclusions (as this chapter explains). This means that (and I wish to make this point quite clearly) an argument against the Two-Gospel view is *not necessarily* an argument against Markan Dependence and the Progressive Publication of Matthew Hypothesis. Similarly, I wish to clarify the extent to which I agree and disagree with the Fourfold Gospel viewpoint.

Other Markan Posteriority Hypotheses: The Two-Gospel Hypothesis

The Two-Gospel team presented the Two-Gospel Hypothesis (2GH) in detail in a book written by the Two-Gospel team, *One Gospel from Two: Mark's Use of Matthew and Luke* (2002, Peabody et al.). There is a great deal of common ground between Markan Dependence and this viewpoint, but also some specific areas of disagreement, and it is important that these differences be clearly delineated. It is highly possible that numbers of scholars who are currently adherents of the Two-Gospel Hypothesis may feel persuaded by the case that I present for an alternative position on these issues.

First, the Two-Gospel advocates clearly spell out (17–18) their relationship to the originators of the Markan Posteriority viewpoint, H. Owen and J. J. Griesbach:

> [W]e are unsatisfied when we are identified too closely with Griesbach's views because our views differ significantly from Griesbach on several critical points, some of which we will enumerate and discuss further below. . . . As contemporary advocates of the Two Gospel Hypothesis continue to discover, uncover, and recover evidence that the author of the Gospel of Mark used the Gospels of Matthew and Luke as his main sources, they have moved a considerable

distance beyond the methods and conclusions of Johann Jakob Griesbach and Henry Owen.

Fair enough. They are simply asking that their views in the twenty-first century be examined and then stand or fall according to what they say *now*, and not be judged by what eighteenth-century scholars said about the issue. I share this viewpoint with them about my own presentation, which should not simply be labeled "the Griesbach view" and treated as if I were merely echoing Griesbach.

I differ from the 2GH in a number of minor ways, but also in numerous matters of interpretation of Mark's Gospel and its relation to the Major Synoptics. In particular, I differ from the 2GH in the following seven matters.

Luke's Use of Matthew

First, the 2GH team begins (19) with the proposition that "following the composition of the Gospel of Matthew, the next stage was Luke's use of Matthew to compose his gospel." The team asserts (14) that the Griesbach Hypothesis claims Luke used Matthew and "Mark conflated them both." But it is *absolutely incorrect* to claim that the Griesbach Hypothesis includes the idea that Luke used Matthew (as I clarified above). In making this claim, they have certainly "moved beyond" Griesbach!

I completely reject the conclusion that Luke knew or used the finished, canonical Gospel of Matthew, and I devote chapter 8 to an examination of the evidence against this idea. I trace the common material in Matthew and Luke to early documents of Matthean origin that were used by both of them—a very different explanation of the origin of the two Major Synoptic Gospels.

The Role of Peter's Preaching

Second, the 2GH team identifies (35) distinguishing features of Mark that are not in Matthew and Luke as "the Markan Overlay" (see pp. 38–45 for examples).

For the most part I am happy to accept the results of their research in this regard, but with the proviso that quite a good deal of what they include in this category looks to me as if it could be better explained as going back beyond Mark himself to the influence of Peter's preaching. The early church Fathers explained that the preaching of Peter lay behind Mark's Gospel, and there is every support for this in the wording of Mark's Gospel itself: in its language, its wording, and its addition of a multitude of eyewitness details. Markan Dependence points out that Mark depended upon three sources, not just two: Matthew, Luke, *and Peter*.

Mark's Breaking-Up of Matthew's Patterns

Third, the 2GH team claims (20) that "In several pericopae, Matthew presents well-organized argumentation, based upon the interpretation of Scripture. The parallels in Mark, on the other hand, are often fragmented, losing or obscuring the carefully structured logic of the Matthean text. Therefore, we see them as revisions of Matthew."

One problem here is that this is not really an argument for Mark's use of Matthew. It is totally reversible. The adherent of Markan Priority can easily say, "This is how Mark wrote it, and how Matthew found it, and (following his known policy of putting like with like, and imposing order upon his material), Matthew took Mark's jumble and brought order out of chaos." Indeed, when the 2GH team looks at this feature from the two perspectives, they acknowledge (45) that when this sort of thing happens, "There is no clear a priori answer" as to which way it points. But they say that "when the phenomenon occurs with regularity, that line of reasoning [that Matthew improved Mark] becomes untenable." Therefore Mark used Matthew. Another problem is that, on occasion, what is found in Mark could be simply explained by Mark following the lead that he finds in Luke. Finally, and most importantly, the explanation is most likely not that Mark is simply being unthinkingly and wantonly iconoclastic of Matthew's careful structure, but that he is following Peter's treatment of this matter.

This 2GH argument is along the lines: Mark found "a nice piece of writing in Matthew and messed it up something terrible," so this proves Mark is last. This is not my understanding of the situation, and I do *not* see here an argument favoring Markan Posteriority.

The Provenance and Purpose of Mark

Fourth, the 2GH team's treatment of this issue (55–63) makes numbers of helpful points with which I can agree. But not with its main thrust. My presentation in chapter 3 sees a different provenance and purpose for Mark's Gospel which goes well beyond what they assert (which appears to me to be total speculation). My alternative view is, I dare to suggest, much more firmly grounded in what we actually find in the Gospel of Mark itself.

Synoptic Dating

Fifth, the 2GH team do not attempt to tie down the question of dating too tightly. The team says (55) of Mark's date "that this would have been no more than a few decades after the martyrdoms of Peter and Paul in 65–68 CE." And they say (268) about Luke, "Luke, clearly writing post 70 CE, focuses upon Jerusalem being surrounded by the Roman armies."

This dating puts the Synoptics much too late. I have assembled the evidence (see chap. 2) for a date c. AD 60 for both Matthew and Luke, and c. AD 65 for Mark, and these are much better supported than the much later dates of the 2GH team claims.

Synoptic Authorship

Sixth, the 2GH team members do not specifically discuss who the Synoptic authors actually were, but some of their comments indicate that they do not believe the authors to be those traditionally ascribed. They do write at times as if they accept that the author of Mark's Gospel is the John Mark of the New Testament (e.g., 48), but they also say (35):

> On the basis of our assessment of all the relevant evidence known to us, much of which is presented and discussed in this book, we have concluded that the author of Mark most probably composed his Gospel on the basis of the texts of Matthew and Luke. We, therefore, expect that the hand behind these integrated and interrelated features in Mark was most likely that of the author. Hence, we describe all of the categories of evidence that make up this network as *Markan*, intending to give credit for it to the author of this Gospel, whatever the name of that person might have been.

There are, similarly, references to the "authors" of Matthew and Luke, for example (34), "Most critical scholars would agree that Matthew 4:23, 9:35 and 10:1 are the work of the author of Matthew." They thus distance themselves from endorsing the traditional authorship. I have explained my hypothesis of the Progressive Publication of Matthew from the perspective of acceptance of the testimony of church history in this matter. I have argued the case for the Matthean authorship of the First Gospel at some length (see chap. 2), and I have found no reason to question the unanimous testimony of the early church about Synoptic authorship.

Extensive and "Creative" Redaction of the Earlier Gospels

Seventh, the 2GH team's explanations of Mark's treatment of the other Synoptics—and they of each other—frequently involve attributing to the Gospel writers extensive and "creative" redaction of the other Gospels, in which one can see misunderstandings of them and unexplained additions to them (especially in relation to Mark's extra comments). These frequently move beyond actual evidence into speculation that I find unnecessary. Here are two examples of such explanations:

The 2GH team notes (220) that "Luke had already been puzzled by . . . Mt 19:17. . . . Accordingly he rewrote the entire exchange. . . . In so doing, Luke obscured the true topic of the unit." The 2GH team also says (174–75):

Mk 7:18–23 Since Mark has taken the entire pericope to be a discourse on within and without, he revises Matthew's text freely. . . . The quotation from Isaiah, which helps to formulate the whole of Mt 15:1–20, makes it clear that the central issue is what proceeds from the heart, not what goes into it. Mark has missed the point. Mark also concludes his version of these sayings of Jesus with the unparalleled note that "thus [Jesus] made all foods clean." . . . Mark may have found in . . . Acts a warrant for the unique and extraordinary affirmation he places on the lips of Jesus here, "Thus he made all foods clean." This is a far cry from the perspective found in Matthew.

In the view of the 2GH team, Mark here revises Matthew freely; Mark misses the point; Mark places a unique and extraordinary affirmation on the lips of Jesus; and his version of the pericope and its point are a far cry from Matthew.

My understanding of the situation is quite different: Mark has heard this story—and this explanation—told by Peter, and this knowledge is what guides his wording here. Matthew's version is emphasizing Jewish aspects of the incident, while Mark is drawing attention to a consequence of real relevance in a Gentile context.

There are some aspects of the usual Two-Gospel exponents' explanations of what (in their judgment) the Synoptic authors would have done that are not persuasive. For these features, I have different explanations. In these matters I would not want my conclusions to become confused with the judgments of the Two-Gospel school. And as they do not ascribe to Peter's preaching the large and influential role that is to be recognized from the church Fathers, they do not see Peter as the source from which this additional information (and indeed, frequently, this very wording) has come. At this point the Markan Dependence Hypothesis is different, and has more support from the evidence.

These are the seven major areas of disagreement I have with the 2GH team. But we are in agreement on one significant conclusion: Mark was written third and made use of the Gospels of Matthew and Luke.

Other Markan Posteriority Hypotheses: The Fourfold Gospel Hypothesis

An alternative explanation of the Markan Posteriority position is advocated by adherents of the Fourfold Gospel Hypothesis (4GH), particularly B. Orchard, H. Riley, and D. A. Black. The presentation of this view is readily accessible in Black's *Why Four Gospels?* (2001). It shares with the Two-Gospel Hypothesis the proposition that Luke used canonical Matthew, but it differs from the Two-Gospel Hypothesis in some of the points just mentioned above, and in these areas I am in agreement with 4GH.

So how do these authors see the question of authorship and dating? In his 1976 volume *Matthew, Luke and Mark* (note the order), Orchard examines the text of the three Synoptics with a view to ascertaining their relationship without hypothesizing other documents. He says (25), "In other words we are concerned only with the shape of the Gospels we have." His conclusion (121) is that "Matthew is now established as the principal source for the material common to Luke and Matthew," Luke having known and used our canonical Matthew in his own writing.

Orchard insists that this view of the relationship between the Synoptics (i.e., the Markan Posteriority view) is a result of consideration of the evidence and it should be recognized quite independently of any question of dating. He says (121), "This literary nexus between Matthew, Luke and Mark is to be understood as being quite independent of any date that might be credibly assigned to any of them; it simply establishes a mutual, timeless and immutable literary relationship between the three of them."

Orchard and Riley co-authored the book *The Order of the Synoptics: Why Three Synoptic Gospels?* (1987), and then Riley wrote *The Making of Mark* (1989). I find that Riley closely approaches my proposal of the Progressive Publication of Matthew Hypothesis. Riley identifies (245) at least two stages or "editions" of Matthew in circulation, saying that for this hypothesized first edition a date of "about the year AD 50 is probable," and that it would have been known to James (and is reflected in his Epistle) and to Paul when he wrote the Thessalonian Epistles and probably also to Luke, adding (246), "All this is of course in the realm of probabilities, but a consistent picture emerges, with its own evidential value." Matthew's "expanded text" (the canonical version) would have been "already available when Luke and Mark wrote"—and Luke knew both versions (246). Also, Riley explains (249) his dating of Luke and Mark:

> The date of the Third Gospel must be earlier than that of Acts, though it need not have been much earlier. It is reasonable to suppose that if Acts was completed by the year 62 or 63, the Gospel would have been in circulation not later than the year 60. That is consistent with the probable earlier date of Matthew, and with the production by Mark of his Gospel a few years later.

Black says this (9) about his book: "While representing my own conviction about the synoptic problem, it is essentially a popularization of Dr. Orchard's views, written at his behest and with an eye on a hitherto unreached audience." He says this (69) about the date of Matthew: "The formation of Matthew's Gospel probably took place in the first decade of the church's life, that is, before 44, and thus not only before 1–2 Thessalonians and Galatians but probably before Paul's second visit to Jerusalem 'after fourteen years' (Gal 2:1; cf. Acts 11:27–30; 12:25)." He goes on to say that Luke produced his Gospel in 58–60 (91), and Mark a few years later "after the death of Peter" (92).

More generally about this hypothesis, Black writes (52, 72): "The Fourfold-Gospel Hypothesis needs no hypothetical documents to support it, nor any restrictions. It holds that the second evangelist knew the first and that the third knew the other two, and it has practically the total support of the patristic and historical evidence. . . . According to the Fourfold-Gospel Hypothesis, Luke had Matthew before him as his exemplar." Black sums up (94) the position taken by this Hypothesis thus:

> If the Fourfold-Gospel Hypothesis is found to be the correct source-critical theory, then there will be no problem either in the apostle Matthew being the author of his Gospel or in Peter and Paul authenticating the Gospels of Mark and Luke, since it proves that Matthew and Luke were written before Mark, which itself is dated about 62, thus permitting all three Synoptic Gospels to have been written during the life span of Matthew and the "apostolic men."

My explanation does not envisage the production of the complete Gospel of Matthew by the early date proposed by Black, but, rather (a) the production by then of quite a few Matthean documents that indeed could well have reached James and Paul and Luke, and then (b) the subsequent incorporation of these early Matthean documents (possibly together with others from Matthew) by Luke in his Gospel, as well as their being included by Matthew in his "collected edition" (i.e., our canonical Matthew).

I find that the evidence points to the conclusion that Luke did *not* know the complete Gospel of Matthew, as I explain in chapter 8, though in his research Luke would have accumulated a collection of documents produced earlier by Matthew. And I cannot find the rationale for the Gospels of Luke and Mark to lie within a postulated plan by Paul to get their "authentication" from Peter, as set out by Black. My view is that the explanation for Mark is to be found in a recognition, from its contents, of what its purpose was (as I explain in chap. 3). But in other areas—particularly the acceptance of authorship and the dating of the Synoptics by no later than the 60s, and more generally the role of Peter's preaching behind Mark and the patristic testimony—I find that their research and mine have led us to similar conclusions.

EXTERNAL EVIDENCE FOR THE MARKAN DEPENDENCE HYPOTHESIS

The Part Played by Peter's Preaching

Mark's use of Peter's preaching is integral to the Markan Dependence Hypothesis: Peter's preaching is the third source that Mark used in writing his Gospel. The evidence for this is unanimous in Papias and all the other early church Fathers. It may be desirable to weigh their testimony carefully in regard to others matters, but not on this point. They clearly tell us that Mark wrote down what he got from Peter's preaching.

We will need to consider how this information about Peter meshes with Mark's use of Matthew and Luke as sources also, and to inquire what we can learn about that preaching, and about the nature of Mark's use of it. We can ask whether he made notes or wrote information down accurately from memory later. But as to the fact of the matter itself, the testimony of the church Fathers is clear.

Recognition of this evidence enables us to understand Mark's different, colloquial, and oral style of writing, in contrast with the Major Synoptics. Mark reflects both the manner of Peter's speech and his own purpose in carrying on Peter's ministry of evangelism by writing a handbook for preachers containing stories of Jesus (see chap. 3 for details).

Patristic Testimony to Authorship and Order of Writing

In some quarters there is a tendency to denigrate the testimony of the early church Fathers, even to the point of implying that they can be disregarded. Black examined in detail (2001) the contribution of the early church Fathers to Synoptic issues, and this is how he summarizes the present situation (47): "Today the academic guild, both in Europe and North America, assumes that the patristic evidence is basically legendary and unreliable. . . . the patristic testimony is said to be inconsistent, contradictory and insecurely based." Basically, scholars have concluded that the church Fathers contradict each other about Gospel origins, so they cancel each other out. The evidence of the church Fathers is thus removed from serious consideration, primarily because it conflicts with the hypothesis of Markan Priority. This is a very prejudicial and self-serving assessment. However, the 2GH team examined the evidence of the church Fathers and came to this evaluation (54): "Until recent decades, the patristic evidence appeared to be essentially divided. In light of recent research it can be said that, on balance, the patristic evidence strongly supports the Two Gospel hypothesis with regard to the order of the composition of the Gospels."

Black retranslated the church Fathers and assessed carefully what they are saying, distinguishing when they are writing about the authorship of the Gospels (without particular attention to any question of order of writing or relationships) from when *these* issues are the specific focus of what they are saying. Black provides (37–44) a translation of all the relevant passages in the church Fathers and, in his evaluation of their explanations, he emphasizes the trustworthiness of the testimony of their texts. Concerning these texts he says (42), "They have been preserved from the earliest times because they are the witnesses of the most distinguished churchmen of those days, men whose integrity and competence were universally recognized." He also notes (48) that the objections made to their testimony

> need no refutation when we recall the scholarship, intelligence, and integrity of these outstanding churchmen. It is interesting to note that classical Greek and Roman scholars have never shared modern biblical critics' distrust of ancient ecclesiastical writers regarding the authority and authenticity of the Gospels. They have always been willing to give them at least as much credence as they have given to the secular historians of antiquity, and to recognize that the skills of ancient scholars in critical analysis were just as sharp as those of modern critics, even though they worked with less sophisticated tools.

What were the views of the early church Fathers about the writing of the Gospels? Papias does not make any comment about the order the Gospels were written. The early church Fathers record that Mark wrote his Gospel while Peter was still alive and preaching. Eusebius reports (*Church History* 6.14.5–7) what was said by Clement of Alexandria (c. 190) about the writing of the Gospels:

> Again, in the same books [i.e., *Hypotyposeis*], Clement gives the tradition respecting the order of the Gospels, as derived from the earliest elders, as follows: He used to say that those Gospels were written first which included the genealogies, and that the Gospel according to Mark came into being in this manner: while Peter was engaged in preaching in Rome and proclaiming the gospel by the Spirit, numbers of people encouraged Mark, as one who had followed Peter for a long time, and remembered what he had said, to write it down. . . . When Peter learned about this he neither encouraged nor discouraged this endeavour.

Additionally, Eusebius says (*Church History* 5.8.1–4) that Irenaeus (c. 190) wrote that after the death of Peter, "Mark, the disciple and interpreter of Peter, did also hand down to us in writing the things that used to be preached by Peter." If we take this testimony at face value and put all the evidence together, these early church Fathers indicate that Mark was working on his Gospel towards the end of Peter's lifetime, with the Christians in Rome requesting copies, particularly after Peter's death, of Mark's remembrances of what the apostle had preached.

We do not know if Mark completed his Gospel before Peter died or if it was intended for wide and public circulation. Certainly after Peter's death Christians requested that Mark provide his record of what Peter had preached and Mark was not hesitant in "handing over the Gospel to those who had asked for it" (Clement of Alexandria, quoted by Black, 41).

The judgment of Black (85) is that "as long as Peter was alive, it seems to have circulated privately; but after his martyrdom, Mark himself probably published it as an act of *pietas* to the memory of his old master." This information gives AD 65 as the date for Mark, the year Peter was martyred. But when Mark began to write his Gospel in Rome, the other two Synoptics had already been written. (Significantly, the tradition of the earliest elders, reported by Clement, indicates that "those Gospels were written first which included the genealogies.")

Black suggests further (27–28) that Peter himself had been making use of the Gospels of Matthew and Luke in his preaching and teaching. This remains a possibility, though I do not see any evidence for it—or against it, for that matter. I am rather doubtful that Peter would need the memory-jogging of these other Gospels for his preaching in Rome in the sixties, for he had by then already been preaching these stories for some 30 years.

What is more certain is that his colleague Mark had both Gospels in front of him when he came to assemble his notes of Peter's preaching into order for publication. This is clear because Mark follows exactly the sequence of the pericopes of Luke to 6:14 and of Matthew thereafter, but also making four additional insertions each into this framework from the other Gospel (for a full explanation of this, see chap. 9).

There is unanimity in the church Fathers that Matthew was the first Gospel written. None of the Fathers suggests the priority of Mark. There is some uncertainty whether Mark is to be placed second or third.

The one order of writing that is completely consistent with both Clement and Irenaeus, and contradicts nothing in either writer, is the order Matthew-Luke-Mark-John. Their joint testimony also indicates that Matthew and Luke wrote before the death of Peter, and that similarly Mark must have written (or at least, commenced writing) before Peter's death and "handed down" or distributed his Gospel after Peter's death.

Origen uses the order Matthew-Mark-Luke-John, but he does not give any grounds that would suggest that he thought this the *order of writing*. Instead, he appears to be explaining the order into which the Gospels were then being placed in the crystallizing of the New Testament canon, this being the order in which it was most helpful to *read* them. John Chrysostom states that "Matthew was before the rest in entering on the subject" and that Mark and Luke came after him; thus, Chrysostom mentions them in that order but without any express comment as to the order of writing for Mark and Luke.

We have seen earlier that Augustine initially accepted the order Matthew-Mark-Luke-John as being the order of writing, deriving this apparently from Origen and from the order in which the Gospels appeared in the canon of the New Testament. But at a later time, Augustine—as the result of his own studies of the Gospels—apparently came to the view that Mark was the third and used Matthew and Luke.

Therefore, patristic testimony gives support to two—and only two—orders for the writing of the Gospels: Matthew-Luke-Mark-John, and Matthew-Mark-Luke-John. Augustine is the only one who states that the latter was the order of writing, and it would seem that he later reconsidered this matter and altered his view; other references to this order are not to it as being to an *order of writing*. There is clear patristic testimony in support of Matthew-Luke-Mark-John as the order of writing. The church Fathers give no support for Mark or Luke being the first Gospel written. If Mark was the first Gospel published (as the Markan Priority view requires), then it would appear that no church Father knew of this, for every single one of them who mentions the matter at all says that Matthew was written first.

There are no valid grounds for disregarding this testimony or explaining it away. The patristic evidence must not be set aside so casually as advocates of Markan Priority do.

INTERNAL EVIDENCE FOR THE MARKAN DEPENDENCE HYPOTHESIS

Similarity of Contents in the Synoptics

All New Testament scholars—indeed, all readers of the Synoptic Gospels—are aware of the significant extent to which they contain similar material. Most of the contents of Mark's Gospel are paralleled in either or both Matthew and Luke. This is exactly what would result if the author of Mark's Gospel had drawn his material from Matthew and Luke.

Similarity of Wording in the Synoptics

Numerous Synoptic scholars have drawn attention to the significant extent that individual pericopes contain close correspondence between the Synoptic Gospels in vocabulary, points of grammatical construction, and the sequence that events are mentioned. This is exactly what would result if the author of Mark's Gospel had drawn his material from Matthew and Luke.

The Order of Pericopes in the Synoptics

A comparison of the Synoptic Gospels shows that sometimes they agree in the order in which they detail the events that they record, and sometimes they differ among themselves. The overall extent of the agreement in pericope order is quite substantial, but the changes in order between one Gospel and another are also considerable.

A closer examination of the nature of the agreements and disagreements reveals that Mark always agrees with the order of Matthew and Luke where these two agree, and always agrees with the order of *either* Matthew *or* Luke where the two Major Synoptics differ in order. This means that the three Synoptics never display three different orders of events in which they give their pericopes, and Matthew and Luke never agree against Mark in order of pericopes. This outcome is exactly what would result if the author of Mark's Gospel had drawn his material from Matthew and Luke. But could this feature have arisen in any other circumstance?

These three arguments are the same as the first three of the five that Streeter claims establish Markan Priority. When the evidence on which they are based is examined, it can be seen that they decisively rule out the Complete Independence Hypothesis, which does not adequately account for the extent to which similar contents and at times identical wording, phrasing, and grammatical constructions occur in two or all three Synoptics. Furthermore, this hypothesis cannot account for the degree of correspondence in pericope order if the Synoptics were written independently of each other based on oral traditions, since pericopes in oral traditions would not all occur in a fixed order that would then be reproduced in independently written Gospels.

Most New Testament scholars today agree that the explanation of Synoptic similarities and differences is to be found in either a Markan Priority-plus-Q approach (Two-Source) or Markan Posteriority approach. Not *all* scholars agree, for there are those who affirm strongly the Complete Independence of the Synoptics, and also those who hold to the Farrer view (Markan Priority without Q) or the Jerusalem school view (Lukan Priority). I discuss these possibilities in chapter 10.

But for those who have concluded that the most probable answer is either Two-Source or Markan Posteriority, there is a strong tendency to believe that an argument *for* Two-Source is an argument *against* Mark being third. This is not necessarily so.

In particular, Streeter's first two "heads" are also the first two arguments I listed above for Markan Dependence. Specifically, the first two arguments are two main areas where Two-Source and Two-Gospel (and Fourfold Gospel and Markan Dependence) are in agreement. These are in fact areas that distinguish these hypotheses from others and that demonstrate that there must be some kind of literary relationship among the Synoptics, of which "Mark is the middle factor" (McKnight 2001, 77). But the first two arguments are compatible not only with both Markan Dependence and Markan Priority but also with Successive Dependence and with virtually any theory of Synoptic interdependence that has Mark as its middle term.

But the third argument, the question of pericope order, rules out the Successive Dependence view. For on the Successive Dependence Hypothesis, the data of pericope order would require that Luke adhered strictly to Mark's order whenever Mark *differs* from Matthew (because Luke always agrees with Mark where Mark and Matthew diverge), and yet that Luke would feel at liberty to desert Mark's order whenever Mark *agrees* with Matthew (because the only times that Luke differs from Mark's order are when Mark and Matthew agree in order). There is no basis for believing that Luke would adopt such a peculiar procedure.

Furthermore, it is simple to explain the original divergence in order between Matthew and Luke with which Mark was confronted. Both the Major Synoptics use the same general chronological framework for their presentation of Christ's life and ministry, but Luke throughout his Gospel was concerned with the question of order of events (as he says in 1:3). On the other hand, Matthew was very much interested in the teachings of Jesus: of the 18,298 words in Matthew's Gospel, 10,827 (59.17%) are the words of Jesus, that is, six out of ten of the words of Matthew's Gospel are words spoken by Jesus (see chap. 4 for details).

Within a general chronological framework, Matthew's approach is to group together Jesus' teachings in large sections, and similarly to group Jesus' various miracles. Matthew 4:23–25 is not describing what happened *before* any of the events in the following chapters, but is in effect a summary of them and operates virtually as a "table of contents" or outline of his presentation of Jesus' Galilean ministry.

Advocates of the Markan Priority Hypothesis seek to offer individual explanations for each separate instance when Matthew or Luke deserts Mark's order, but have produced no overall explanation of the phenomenon. Again, if Mark is the source for Matthew and Luke, then these two authors are independently deciding either to follow or depart from Mark's order and then when to return to it again—and it *just happens* that while each is thus acting independently for his own reasons, it never turns out that they both leave Mark's order at the same time, seeing that Mark's order is always supported by at least one of them. Thus the Markan Priority view must invoke a very high level of coincidence for the fact that Matthew and Luke, each of whom having departed from Mark's order when he chose, do not *ever* happen both to do so for the same material.

This phenomenon of Synoptic order is easily explained by Markan Dependence: Mark had no knowledge of pericope order apart from what he saw in Matthew and Luke, or alternatively he deliberately chose not to alter their order. He adhered to the order of the Major Synoptics wherever they themselves were in agreement (which is why Matthew and Luke never agree in order against Mark), and when they differed he followed one or the other of them (which is why Mark always agrees in order with at least one other Synoptic).

The argument from order thus weighs very heavily against Markan Priority and is one of the strongest features pointing to Markan Dependence. I have devoted all of chapter 9 to a thorough and detailed consideration of this Synoptic feature.

The Argument from Conflation

There are a large number of places in the Synoptics where Mark has a form of wording or a presentation of details partially paralleled in Matthew and partially paralleled in Luke. The Markan Priority Hypothesis explains this as being due to a Markan tendency to verbosity, with Matthew and Luke sometimes using different ways of cutting down Mark's wordiness. However, the wording of the Synoptic texts is better and more consistently accounted for as due to Mark's policy of melding together what he has before him in the Matthean and Lukan stories. Below is an analysis of some examples of this apparent conflation.

Matt 3:11	Mark 1:7	Luke 3:16
but he who is coming after me is mightier than I	After me comes he who is mightier than I	but he who is mightier than I is coming,
whose sandals I am not worthy to	the thong of whose sandals I am not worthy to stoop down and	the thong of whose sandals I am not worthy to
carry	untie	untie

The Promise of the Coming One (Matt 3:11//Mark 1:7//Luke 3:16)

If Matthew is using Mark, why does he change "stooping down and untying a sandal thong" to "carrying sandals"? Why does Luke omit "after me" and "stoop down"? In the Greek, the accounts of Mark and Luke are identical except that Luke lacks these expressions and has an initial δέ (*de*) that Mark does not need because of his introduction, "And he preached, saying."

But if Mark is using Matthew and Luke, then his procedure is straightforward: he follows Luke closely, but he also adds "after me" from Matthew and "stooping down" as an additional point of detail of his own.

The Rich Young Man (Matt 19:16-30//Mark 10:17-31//Luke 18:18-30)

The accounts of the rich young man in Matthew and Luke differ from each other in a multitude of details of wording, word order, grammatical construction, perspective and viewpoint—but neither of them differs from Mark nearly as much. Stated another way, Mark is in general agreement with both of them when they agree with each other, and almost seems to alternate in agreement with each in those places where they differ. In fact, his account so effectively reconciles the Matthean and Lukan versions that only a careful consideration of their text, with Mark put to one side, allows us to see the extent of their differences. The data points strongly to the explanation that Mark has conflated the accounts of Matthew and Luke.

To consider a specific example, both Matt 19:18–19 and Luke 18:20 give a partial list of the Commandments, but with these differences: In Matt 19:18, the Commandments are given in the form οὐ plus the future, and the order of the first two in the list is, "You shall not kill" and "You shall not commit adultery," and then those from the Decalogue are followed by "You shall love your neighbor as yourself." In Luke 18:20 the Commandments are given in the form μή plus the aorist subjunctive; the order of the first two in the list is, "Do not commit adultery" and "Do not kill"; and the commandment to love one's neighbor is not given.

Mark corresponds with Luke in using μή plus the subjunctive and in the omission of "You shall love your neighbor as yourself," but he agrees with Matthew in the *order* that the Commandments are listed. It is a reasonable explanation that Mark, in using Matthew and Luke and being confronted with their differences, conflates them by adopting the *order* used by Matthew and the *form of words* used by Luke. The alternative (Markan Priority) explanation would be that Matthew, in using Mark, retained Mark's *order* and altered his *form of wording* whereas Luke, also using Mark, chose to do the opposite and altered Mark's *order* but retained his *form of wording*. Which raises a very puzzling question: Why would either of them depart from Mark in these ways? But it is very straightforward to see why Mark, confronted with *existing differences* between his two accounts, should meld them by combining features of each. This disagreement between Matthew and Luke, and the agreement of Mark now with one and now with the other, runs through the whole pericope. Markan Prioritists often cite this pericope as evidence for their view. However, these differences are so numerous (36 in total) and so significant that I have devoted chapter 11 to examining them and accounting for them.

The various differences fall short of being contradictions, and it is easy to conceive of how they could exist in two independent reports of the incident from two different eyewitnesses. What is much more difficult to explain is how they could arise from the redaction of a single account, whether that one account be Mark's or any other. Thus from the data we are led towards the conclusion that the two accounts in Matthew and Luke could not have been derived one from the other or from any common document, but that they are separate accounts deriving independently from the one actual event.

Markan Priority advocates explain this pericope on the basis that Matthew and Luke each made quite a few rather insignificant changes at every level to much of what Mark says but they had frequently acted alternatively in what they each retained from Mark and in what they each altered. This is much less coherent than the Markan Dependence explanation that Mark had in front of him two different accounts from two independent sources and that he combined them in a manner which largely reconciled the differences of detail.

Other Examples of Conflation

There are hundreds of other verses in the Synoptics where Mark's Gospel can be seen to be a conflation of the wording of Matthew and Luke. Here are some of them:

> Matt 3:1–4:17//Mark 1:2–15//Luke 3:1–4:15 (especially
> Mark 1:2–4,7–13)
> Matt 9:1–17//Mark 2:1–22//Luke 5:17–39
> Matt 17:1–7//Mark 9:2–8//Luke 9:28–36
> Matt 17:14–21//Mark 9:14–29//Luke 9:37–43a
> Matt 21:33–46//Mark 12:1–12//Luke 20:9–19

These are examples of a phenomenon that can be observed in varying degrees throughout all the material of the Triple Tradition.

Streeter in 1924 and Tuckett in 1983 looked at some possible instances of conflation where half of something in Mark was paralleled in Matthew

The Markan Dependence Explanation

and the other half in Luke. They pointed out that Matthew and Luke were each shorter than Mark for most of the stories that they had in common. In the nature of things, if Matthew and Luke were using Mark and abridging it, sometimes they would agree in what they left out from Mark (giving rise to agreements against Mark at that point). And sometimes they would differ, one omitting one half of what Mark contained and the other Gospel omitting the remainder of what Mark had (giving rise to the appearance of conflation in Mark whereas it was actually a case of abridgement by Matthew and Luke).

This explanation of conflation sounds reasonable until one examines the actual Synoptic text and observes how in passage after passage Mark contains ideas, details, individual words, and grammatical structures that occur also in *either* Matthew or Luke but *not* in both.

If Mark is prior, then it seems that Matthew and Luke have virtually taken turns in excising or altering things that Mark says. The extent of these differences is exceedingly high. Of the 11,078 words in Mark, Matthew has taken over only 4,230 words (38.2%) in parallel passages; that is, he has omitted or changed 61.8% of Mark's words. Of these 11,078 words in Mark, Luke has taken over only 2,675 words (24.1%); that is, he has omitted or changed 75.9% of the words that he had in front of him in Mark. (See chap. 4, table 2, for details.) Why in these passages Matthew or Luke should both wish to change the text of Mark to this extent, and then in such different ways, is hard to explain.

But the Markan Dependence Hypothesis makes it simple to see what Mark has done. He has in front of him two somewhat different accounts of an event or a saying of Jesus, and he blends the two by taking ideas, details, words, and grammatical structures from each.

Chapter 4 above shows that of the words that Mark has in common with Matthew (4,230) and with Luke (2,675), there are only 1,835 words that Mark has in common with *both* Matthew and Luke. This means that, on the Markan Dependence view, there are 2,395 words (i.e., 4,230 minus 1,835) that Mark drew from Matthew, and 840 (i.e., 2,675 minus 1,835) that he drew from Luke, and 1,835 that occurred in both Matthew and Luke and that Mark took over. In addition, there are ideas, details, and grammatical structures that Mark has in common with Matthew or Luke where identical words were not employed, and that are also evidences of conflation. Mark's total words in common with *either* Matthew or Luke is 5,070, which is 45.8% of his total words, so that 6,008 of his words (54.2%) are unique to Mark and *not* found in *either* Matthew or Luke in parallels. (See chap. 4, table 3, for details.)

This evidence of conflation strongly points to Markan Dependence as the relationship of Mark to Matthew and Luke.

The Argument from Mark's Shorter Accounts

On a number of occasions Mark contains a short version of something (ranging from brief sayings to a lengthy pericope) that occurs in a fuller form in Matthew and Luke. In such cases Mark obviously cannot have been the source for all that is in Matthew and Luke. Here are some examples.

1. Matt 3:11–12//Mark 1:8//Luke 3:16–17. All three contain John's testimony to the Coming One and say, "he will baptize you with the Holy Spirit." Mark stops here, but Matthew and Luke continue: "and with fire. His winnowing fork is in his hand, and he will [Mt]/to [Lk] clear his threshing floor and gather the wheat into his granary, but the chaff he will burn with unquenchable fire."

2. Matt 4:1–11//Mark 1:12–13//Luke 4:1–13. All three record the temptation, but Mark's account is very brief and does not refer to the nature of the temptation. Matthew and Luke give much more detail.

3. Matt 9:20//Mark 5:27//Luke 8:44. Matthew and Luke record that the sick woman touched the "fringe of" Jesus' robe; Mark lacks this and says only that she touched his robe. For the Jew, the fringe of a rabbi's robe had special religious significance (Num 15:37–41; Deut 22:12). If Matthew and Luke were drawing this story from Mark, it is barely possible to see why Matthew might decide to insert *the fringe of*, and it is quite impossible to conceive of any reason why Luke would do the exact same thing. But if Matthew and Luke wrote first, then they included the detail because it *happened*—the fringe was significant to the woman—and Mark omitted the reference to the fringe because this point was meaningless to his intended readership. (See further on this in chap. 7.)

4. Matt 17:17//Mark 9:19//Luke 9:41. Matthew and Luke read, "O faithless and perverse generation"; Mark says only "O faithless generation." It is not immediately apparent why Mark would have omitted the words "and perverse" if they were in the sources that he was following. But that he should do so is more believable than claiming both Matthew and Luke independently chose to insert the word "perverse" at this point. This is not a common word—the term "perverse" (διεστραμμένη) occurs only in this pericope in the Gospels. If then, as Markan Priority holds, the only source for this pericope in Matthew and Luke is Mark, and if Matthew and Luke followed the wording of Mark and did not introduce "perverse" here, then this word would not have occurred at all in the Gospels. Thus, it really stretches the imagination to claim that it would occur independently to

both Matthew and Luke to add it. The difficulty is not overcome by saying that Matthew and Luke include "and perverse" because this is what Jesus actually said. Once this explanation is tendered, then it completely contradicts the fundamental tenet of the Markan Priority Hypothesis, which is that *Mark alone* is the source in this pericope for what is in Matthew and Luke.

The Markan Dependence alternative is much more believable: Matthew and Luke record this saying because *Jesus actually said it*, and, for some reason that is not now known to us, Mark (while using Matthew and Luke as his sources) chose to abbreviate Jesus' words here. (See further on this in chap. 7.)

Alternative Explanations

Instances (1) and (2) and others of similar kind (notably, the Beelzebul controversy, the parable of the mustard seed, and the mission charge to the Twelve) are explained by exponents of Markan Priority as instances of an overlap between Mark and the presumed second source Q. But if this be so, it means that in these cases Mark is not the source for Matthew and Luke for material that is common to all three Synoptics. But whatever argument leads us to postulate in these cases an alternative source (that is, a source other than Mark) could also justify holding that same non-Markan source to be the origin of *other* Synoptic material that also happens to occur in Mark.

Thus, this explanation forces interpreters to call on a source other than Mark to account for the observable data (as described above). Having invoked this source, there is then no basis (other than subjective opinion) on which one can *exclude* the possibility that this other source, Q, could have been known and used by Mark, and thus *that source* could have been the source for the rest of the common material in the Synoptics. Once we open the door for the use of Q to explain Matthew-Luke agreements against Mark, it is very hard to keep it open only for selected instances. Thus, it is impossible to affirm that some pericopes were found in both Mark and Q without simultaneously allowing the Ur-Gospel approach to take over from the Two-Source Hypothesis. For all these pericopes, the Markan Dependence explanation remains as a clear and simple alternative that fully accounts for the Synoptic data.

For examples (3) and (4) above, and all the many others of this kind, the exponents of Markan Priority offer the following explanations: (a) Matthew and Luke in these instances had separate information about the events, information that they each chose here to conflate with Mark (note that this is virtually invoking Q here also); and/or (b) Matthew and Luke each happened to think of and use the same addition at the same point; and/or (c) the agreement between Matthew and Luke is due to the text of the one having here been assimilated to that of the other Gospel. Streeter (1924, 327) advanced the latter view, so that for the question "Who is it that struck you?" (Matt 26:68//Luke 22:64, absent in Mark 14:65), he explains that this was due to the fact that *all the extant manuscripts of Matthew had been corrupted by being assimilated to Luke*. Interestingly, Tuckett does not agree with Streeter's explanation. The Markan Dependence explanation is much more believable.

The Agreements of Matthew and Luke against Mark

The instances just mentioned above are particular instances of a much larger category, the agreements between Matthew and Luke against Mark. It is widely recognized that these agreements constitute a difficulty for Markan Priority, but Markan Priority advocates in general are satisfied with the explanations that have been offered for them. But the number of these agreements is often underestimated. Stoldt (1980, 10–21) has shown that in addition to the five pericopes unique to Mark (the deaf-mute, the blind man from Bethsaida, the seed growing secretly, Jesus thought to be beside himself, and the young man who fled), there are: (a) 180 "passages in the second Gospel in which minor additional details extend beyond the particular text parallels which Mark shares with Matthew and Luke," (b) another 35 "sections in which both Matthew and Luke contain material which goes beyond the parallel text of the second Gospel," (c) another 35 places again where there are "concurrence of the first and third Evangelists in expressions and wording against Mark," and (d) a further 22 cases of "corresponding divergences of Matthew and Luke from Mark . . . each of which involved the use of the same word." That is, there are a total of 277 instances of agreement of Matthew and Luke against Mark. These cannot be so lightly set aside as some scholars apparently wish to do.

If only a few such instances existed, then it would be reasonable to explain them as due to Matthew and Luke hitting on the same additions, deletions, or other alterations to Mark. But the large number and wide scope of these agreements of the Major Synoptics against Mark make this explanation much less convincing.

The more reasonable explanation is that Mark wrote with Matthew and Luke in front of him. In these instances—since he was an independent author and not a mere copyist or compiler, since he had his own independent reasons for producing a Gospel, and since he was also drawing on his knowledge of Peter's preaching—Mark departed from what Matthew and Luke had written.

Mark's Inclusions and Omissions

We have seen several times that Mark's omissions are regularly raised as being an argument for Markan Priority on the grounds that it is hard to see why Mark would omit this information if he had it in front of him in Matthew and Luke. But Mark's inclusions and exclusions indicate that he wrote for a church that already possessed Matthew and Luke—otherwise these inclusions and exclusions are virtually inexplicable. So it is not merely the case (as shown in chap. 3) that this assertion based on what is not in Mark has no substance as an argument for Markan Priority. For if one thinks carefully about this matter and follows the argument to its logical conclusion, it is clear that this point is actually strong evidence in favor of Markan Dependence.

What serious student of the Synoptics is going to assert today that each of the Synoptists recorded all that he knew, and if something is not in their Gospel, it is because of the author's ignorance of that detail or that pericope? If you can find me such a person, I would like to ask him how he considers that the author of Mark could have grown up in a home that was a meeting-place for Christians, become a companion for a time with Paul and Barnabas in their missionary endeavors and a useful helper for Paul in his old age, and be in particular an active associate of the apostle Peter in his preaching and teaching ministry, but somehow never heard more than the things he records? Did Peter *never* mention the Lord's Prayer, the Sermon on the Mount, or others "of Jesus' most precious teachings"—as Blomberg put it in his eighth reason for Markan Priority (see chap. 5)—or any of the resurrection appearances, for instance? The idea that Mark did not know these teachings is one of the impossibilities that Markan Priority advocates ask us to believe (see chap. 7).

Certainly Mark would have known a great deal more than he included in his Gospel. On any view of who Mark was and when he wrote, the content of his Gospel (both what he included and what he omitted) is therefore the result of *selection* and not of *ignorance*, and his content is completely related to his purpose in writing (see chap. 3 for details). His inclusions are those stories about Jesus that conformed to the *kerygma* of the early church. And his omissions make complete sense when one recognizes that these omissions were not regarded as part of the *kerygma* by the early church and that Mark knew believers would have access to them in the other Synoptics.

Markan Priority advocates have to answer a far more difficult question: If Mark was indeed the first one to write, so that the only written information that his readers would have had at that time is what he included in his Gospel, how can you explain (on the basis of Markan Priority) that Mark did not include this other teaching of which—as a member of the Christian community—he must have been aware? Markan Dependence explains this easily: Mark's omissions point clearly to the conclusion that he knew that this information was *already available* in the church in the other Synoptics.

Indeed, there are a number of occasions when Mark specifically mentions items of teaching that he does not himself record. It was encountering these passages when he was looking for them but not expecting to find them that led to J. Chapman's conversion (his term) from Markan Priority to recognizing that Matthew was written first and that Mark was drawing upon him. Reference to these places that convinced Chapman—and they do indeed provide further evidence in support of the hypothesis that Mark used Matthew—are in chapter 10 where Chapman's work is discussed. As chapter 7 demonstrates, it is impossible to read these verses and then say that Mark would *not* have known about this additional teaching when in fact he is telling us in his Gospel that he did.

The Integrity of the Text

To me this is the most important and most convincing argument of all. The others are significant, and they indeed point to Markan Dependence as the explanation of all the data. Other arguments point to Markan Dependence to the exclusion of other hypotheses, or else they indicate that Markan Dependence is far more probable than any other. But this argument is based on the integrity of the text as it stands, meaning that the accounts in the Synoptics record what really happened and that they complement each other—rather than contradict or "correct" or "improve" each other.

When Matthew and Luke are sufficiently similar as to indicate a common source, that source was the apostle Matthew. These accounts are acceptable as they stand because *he* was trustworthy. The redactions in these two Gospels result from fitting their accounts into the respective pattern and purpose of each of those two Gospels. Sometimes their two accounts exhibit differences that are consonant with Matthew having rewritten an episode in Greek that he had originally written in Hebrew/Aramaic, whereas Luke's account is a different translation of that same Hebrew/Aramaic. (Chap. 10 details how the Jerusalem school documents how often Luke seems like such a translation.)

When accounts are so significantly different that they appear to have different sources, it is because they *do* have different sources. Matthew is the source of the version in his Gospel, and Luke has in the course of his investigations obtained the second account from some other eyewitness who was present on the occasion—which he says in his preface he checked out and vouches for. Sometimes the accounts are quite clearly of the same occasion, but they actually have little in common. The pericope of Jesus' visit to Nazareth in these two Synoptics is a very clear example of this. Sometimes the accounts overlap extensively, but with exactly the kind of difference in perspective expected in two reports from different eyewitnesses.

The Synoptic accounts of the rich young man provide an example of conflation. There are 36 differences of detail—most of them of very minor significance—between Matthew and Luke. Their sources were different eyewitnesses: this explanation accounts for these pericopes as they stand. Then Mark came to these two different accounts and melded them marvelously—on 18 occasions following Matthew and on the other 18 following Luke. (A list of these 36 differences and how Mark handles them is provided in chap. 11.)

In this there is a simple, clear-cut, straightforward explanation that accounts fully for what is found in the three Synoptics. But if Mark is first, the explanation is much more difficult. With this common starting point, Matthew altered Mark's account in 18 ways—small and insignificant changes for the most part—so that one can only guess what he was doing. The interpreter often simply has to say, "He just felt like changing it." But then Luke, starting from the same pericope in Mark's Gospel, also makes 18 changes—but all 18 are different! So Matthew and Luke created 36 differences between them although they were using the same source, Mark's Gospel. Markan Priority advocates have much more explaining to do than those who follow Markan Dependence.

So there are two approaches to this pericope in the Triple Tradition: (1) Matthew and Luke between them "corrected" and "improved" Mark's text 36 times, in small points of detail, but in different ways; or (2) Matthew and Luke record two independent eyewitness accounts of the event, and Mark blended the two together seamlessly.

Which of these two alternatives, Markan Priority or Markan Dependence, gives the simpler explanation? Which has the ring of truth? Which respects the integrity of the text as we have them in all three Gospels?

Sometimes the different Synoptic accounts are reports from different sources of similar parables or other teachings that Jesus gave on *different* occasions—for clearly Jesus did not ever give each teaching only once in his three years of ministry. The parable of the lost sheep is an example of this kind, a similar teaching given on two different occasions (see chap. 7).

When I examine pericope after pericope in the Triple Tradition, this explanation fits: taken together with the recognition that a lot of the time Mark drew his wording from three sources not just two, and that third source was Peter—and we can see a great deal of Peter's language (and Mark's!) in Mark. And this explanation accounts fully for the Double Tradition, and also for the places where Mark agrees with just one of the Majors, and for the *Sondergut* in all three Synoptics.

And at all points the integrity of the text is preserved. This means that interpreters do not have to grope for an explanation such as, "This author is correcting that author, or improving him, or creatively adding to him something that is being put into the mouth of Jesus that Jesus in fact did not say!" As the previous chapter shows, Markan Prioritists use all of these arguments and more to explain differences between the Synoptics. But if one believes that Jesus said the things the text says he said and that he did the things the text says he did—in other words, if one accepts as a starting point that the text is accurate as it stands—then the explanation that best accords with this viewpoint is Markan Dependence.

This is not a doctrinaire approach, making the facts fit some prior doctrinal position that I adopt. Rather, it simply asks, Can I account for the text of the Gospels as it stands if I approach it with the attitude of expecting that it is fully accurate unless evidence clearly indicates otherwise? Yes, I can, on the basis of the Markan Dependence Hypothesis. It is not that each Gospel just provides a general idea (more or less) of what occurred, but that it is thoroughly reliable. This is what is meant in saying that Markan Dependence respects the integrity of the text.

I am an academic, a theologian, a scholar, looking now at the text of the Synoptics. But before I was those things, I was simply a believer in Jesus. I became a Christian on the basis of believing the words of Jesus. Now that I am an academic, a theologian, a scholar, do I have to adjust my thinking to take account of the fact that Jesus may not have actually said the words that the Gospels inform me that he did? Not at all! For I find that Markan Dependence allows me to accept the text of the Synoptics as it stands. It is the explanation that I arrive at by taking the Gospel records seriously and at face value, and accepting them as accurate. In their differences they are complementary, not contradictory. These differences can be accounted for in the ways I have mentioned, and on the Markan Dependence Hypothesis they do not involve saying that one Gospel is correcting or improving another or is better or more accurate than another, but rather that they all give us a reliable account of what happened.

Coherence and Purpose

Tuckett (1983, 12–13) makes this point: "Any source hypothesis can in fact be proposed. . . . The extent to which an hypothesis gives a coherent, consistent picture of the total redactional activity of each evangelist will then be a measure of its viability." Similarly, Black writes (2001, 52): "In our view, the source theory that best reflects the actual historical circumstances is most likely to be the true explanation."

Markan Dependence provides a valid, self-consistent explanation of all the data of the Synoptics, an explanation that accords with the situation of the early church as it is known to us. It accounts for all the similarities and differences in wording and order between the Synoptics, and it accepts each Gospel as a work of authorship in its own right, written for a particular readership with precise aims in view and guided by specific criteria concerning what was included and what was omitted.

The Markan Dependence Hypothesis holds all the data together:

- It coheres beautifully.
- It fits the facts.
- It accounts for the data.
- It explains the evidence.
- It answers the difficulties.
- It covers everything.
- It is reasonable, logical, and satisfying.
- It conforms to the information we have about the authors Matthew, Mark, Luke—and Peter; and it fully recognizes this apostle's role as Mark's third source.
- It makes sense of the material in each Gospel and—very important—the material that is *not* there.
- It arises out of the Synoptic data that is available.
- It meshes with the information available from the early church Fathers.
- It allows interpreters to understand what each author—Matthew, Mark, and Luke—did in assembling their respective Gospels.
- It does not leave a host of loose ends and significant unexplained conundrums.
- It causes interpreters again and again to exclaim, "Of course! That is why . . . [this or that piece of evidence or part of the Gospel is what it is]."

- It provides a solid basis for the further investigation of key questions—such as, Can we identify more precisely the early Matthean documents that Matthew and Luke have in common?

It may well raise the question, "Why hasn't anyone come up with this explanation before?" But they have! I point this out all the way through this book. The Progressive Publication of Matthew Hypothesis, which includes Markan Dependence, builds upon what a great many others have recognized down the years. What I have done is to take the pieces of the jigsaw puzzle and join them together to show the "big picture." I have assembled the various parts that others have made into an entire and workable whole. And now I can say, "Look at this—see how it all fits together." Markan Dependence does not require the acceptance of any improbabilities, let alone swallowing all the "impossibilities" that need to be believed on the basis of Markan Priority, as I point out in the next chapter.

But first, I respond to the 18 objections that have been raised against the Markan Posteriority Hypotheses. These objections do not represent a very convincing case against the presentation of the explanation given here.

THE CASE AGAINST MARKAN DEPENDENCE

Numbers of scholars have raised significant objections against the Markan Posteriority explanation of Synoptic relationships. I have collected all of them that I can find and set them out here, together with the answers to these objections.

Fitzmyer's presentation of the case against Markan Posteriority (1970, 131–70) is one of the best of which I am aware. Orchard (1976, 130) calls Fitzmyer's article, "The strongest case so far made out against Farmer's thesis." Fitzmyer tabulates nine arguments against the Griesbach Hypothesis and in particular against Farmer's presentation of this theory. Farmer took Fitzmyer's objections seriously and responded to each of them (1977). Fitzmyer's article may be taken as the most complete and thorough case against the Griesbach Hypothesis (Tuckett's book follows a different approach), so his nine arguments are listed here, together with nine further arguments raised by other scholars.

Seven of Fitzmyer's objections are presented in the form of questions, implying that these questions are unanswerable so that he has demolished Markan Posteriority as a credible hypothesis. Examination of these questions reveals that they are often founded upon an invalid premise that needs to be identified and challenged. Sometimes his objections are directed to aspects of the Farmer version of the Markan Posteriority Hypothesis, so

The Markan Dependence Explanation 243

they do not relate at all to Markan Dependence as I explain it here. To the extent that they are legitimate questions, they are readily answered in this book.

1. **Fitzmyer**: "Why would anyone want to abbreviate or conflate Matthew and Luke to produce from them a gospel such as Mark actually is?"

Answer: Neither Griesbach nor Farmer nor I would say that Mark is an abbreviation of Matthew and Luke. Fitzmyer has shown he does not understand the hypothesis he is supposedly challenging. As to why Mark would "produce from them a gospel such as Mark actually is," this is fully answered in chapter 3.

2. **Fitzmyer:** "Why is so much of Matthew and Luke omitted in the end product? Why is so much important gospel material that would be of interest to the growing and developing churches eliminated by Mark? Why, for example, has he omitted the Sermon on the Mount?"

Answer: Fitzmyer's question assumes that Markan Posteriority advocates assert that Mark intended his Gospel to supersede and replace both Matthew and Luke in their use in the church—a gratuitous assumption for which there is *no evidence whatsoever*. The Two-Gospel team states quite explicitly (2002, 63), "Thus, the two foundational memoirs of Jesus' life, Matthew and Luke, were not to be replaced but to have a capstone, Mark." As I have shown throughout this book, it is integral to understanding Mark's Gospel to see that he presumed the availability and use of both Matthew and Luke in the churches. And Mark omits (not eliminates) the material in question, which was available to the church in the already existing Gospels of Matthew and Luke, because it was not relevant to his aim of providing a handbook for evangelists and preachers of the *kerygma* in the early church (see chap. 3).

Those who raise this as an objection fail to see that it is actually far more devastating to the Markan Priority Hypothesis, for Mark must have known key teachings that he failed to include since he had been living in a home where the early church met and had been part of its missionary outreach, and he was an associate of some of the apostles. The Two-Gospel team (59) cites the comment made in 1976 by the Markan Priority supporter N. Dahl, with respect to the sayings of Jesus: "Since Mark has chosen some sayings and excluded others, the selection must be determined by the evangelist's intention."

So the question of the omissions in Mark is really one for the Markan Priorists to answer. Knowing as he did so much more than he used, why did

Mark not include these other things if his Gospel was (at the time) the only Gospel there was? This question deserves an answer! I use this as an argument *in favor* of Markan Dependence—which it clearly is.

3. **Fitzmyer:** "How could Mark have so consistently eliminated all traces of Lucanisms?"

Answer: Farmer (1977, 275–95) has shown that "It seems doubtful that Mark has eliminated all traces of Lucanisms." Farmer claims that traces of five of Hawkins's list of "seven 'favourite or habitual' expressions of Luke . . . are found in Mark." But no "'favourite or habitual' expressions of Mark appeared in the text of Luke or Matthew" according to Hawkins's list—which is very odd if both Matthew and Luke used Mark's Gospel. "Out of nineteen [Matthean expressions] listed by Hawkins, fourteen appear in Mark."

If, then, no "favourite or habitual" Markan expressions occur in Matthew or Luke, while five out of seven such expressions of Luke (and 14 out of 19 Matthean expressions) can be traced in Mark, it would seem that the evidence from "favourite and habitual expressions" favors the Markan Dependence explanation against that of Markan Priority, and not the other way around, as Fitzmyer implies.

4. **Fitzmyer:** "What would have motivated Mark to omit even those elements in the infancy narratives of Matthew and Luke that are common? His alleged interest in narratives, rather than teaching, would have led him instead to present a conflated harmonized infancy narrative."

Answer: There is no evidence of any kind to suggest that the early church made any use of the infancy narratives in its evangelism. In particular, all the relevant references in Acts and the Epistles commence with the ministry of John the Baptist (see Acts 1:21–22; 10:36–38; 13:23–31; 18:25; 19:1–5). Further, none of the Epistles recount or discuss the infancy of Jesus. That is to say, the infancy narratives clearly formed no part of the *kerygma* of the early church, and thus Mark did not include them in his handbook of its kerygmatic material.

5. **Fitzmyer:** "Mark's resurrection narrative, even if it be limited to 16:1–8, is puzzling. Can it really be regarded as an abbreviation or conflation of the Matthean and/or Lucan accounts?"

Answer: If indeed the text of Mark ends at 16:8 (as I find is usually the view held by those who reject Markan Posteriority), this certainly does bring his Gospel to an abrupt halt. However, the Markan Dependence explanation is simply that the *kerygma* of the early church went up to the *fact* of the resurrection, and when Mark reached this he concluded his narrative.

He knew that his readers could turn to the two Major Synoptics to read about the resurrection and the appearances of the risen Christ. Thus, an abrupt ending at Mark 16:8 therefore tells strongly *for* Markan Dependence and *against* Markan Priority. When someone uses this argument as an objection to Markan Dependence, I want to ask them: "Then you tell me: how do *you* explain this Markan ending if Mark was first-written and thus the only Gospel in existence at the time?" (See the more detailed discussion regarding the resurrection accounts at Impossibility 3 in chap. 7.)

6. **Fitzmyer:** "What sort of early theologian does Mark turn out to be if his account is based on Matthew and Luke? Having behind him the certainly more developed christologies and ecclesiologies of Matthew and Luke, what would be his purpose in constructing such a composition?"

Answer: Putting Mark first in no way resolves this issue. Mark's Gospel was not written before the church had a high view of Jesus' person. Therefore, on *any* Synoptic view it is necessary to explain Mark's Christology.

Matthew and Luke wrote for the church, and therefore they could (and did) assume from the beginning that their readers accepted that Jesus is the Christ, the Son of God. Mark most certainly makes no such assumption. Mark takes his readers (and his hearers—for Mark's Gospel is intended for preaching) along the same road that the disciples had trodden. Mark announces in his title (1:1) that this is where he intends to go with his Gospel—in fact, that title is an outline summary of his Gospel. Thereafter, he does not assume any prior faith or commitment on the part of the readers and hearers of his Gospel, but he reveals who Jesus is through his record of what Jesus does.

Thus Mark's Christology does not *differ* from that of Matthew and Luke, but Mark's revelation of the person of Jesus is *progressive,* initially assuming nothing on the part of the readers and hearers and then leading them step by step in their understanding. Thus he patterns his approach the way Jesus himself progressively led people into a deeper understanding of who he was (see chap. 3 for details).

7. **Fitzmyer:** "It seems to be an argument from order that Farmer ultimately depends on in his attempt to justify the creation of Mark. For the dominant reason of his contention that Mark is a conflation of Matthew and Luke is precisely the agreement, not in subject matter, but in order. If it were true that Mark was composed by a concentration 'on those materials where their [i.e. Matthew's and Luke's] texts bore concurrent testimony to the same

gospel tradition,' then why has Mark not copied at least some of the co-called Double Tradition?"

Answer: This objection appears initially to address the argument from order, but in the event Fitzmyer does not challenge it at all. It asks (as an objection to Markan Posteriority) why Mark has not copied at least some of the Double Tradition.

Actually, Triple Tradition refers to material found in all three Synoptics, and so, whenever Mark chose to make use of the Double Tradition, it became Triple Tradition. So Mark *did* use Double Tradition, seeing that *all* Triple Tradition was Double Tradition that Mark used! So, when you examine Fitzmyer's question, he is really asking, "Why didn't Mark use what he chose not to use?" That is to say, the question is simply another version of those along these lines asked by Fitzmyer earlier, and the Markan Dependence answer remains the same. It is explained in chapter 3.

8. **Fitzmyer:** "No convincing reason has been given why Mark should have omitted the preaching of John the Baptist, which not only is an element to which Matthew and Luke bear 'concurrent testimony,' but even in the same place in the Synoptic tradition."

Answer: The Baptist's preaching is included to the extent (and only to the extent) that it bore testimony to the person of Jesus. John's eschatological comments (Matt 3:11–12//Mark 1:8//Luke 3:16–17) are cut short in Mark either in accord with a general policy of shortening teaching segments (this is paralleled in other similar shortening of Jesus' teachings in Mark) or because including these eschatological comments about Jesus would have seemed premature to Mark at this point in terms of his progressive revelation of the person of Jesus through his Gospel.

9. **Fitzmyer:** "It is 'asking too much' to regard Mark's phrase 'the son of Mary' [Mk 6:3] as a factor weighing in favour of a date for Mark after the idea of the virginal conception of Mary had been accepted in the Church."

Answer: Matthew 13:55 reads, "Is not this the carpenter's son? Is not his mother called Mary?" Luke 4:22 reads, "Is not this Joseph's son?" Here Fitzmyer is objecting to Farmer's point that Mark's departure from the Jewish custom that a person was designated the son of his father (not his mother)—which is also the pattern of Mark's two sources—is consonant with acceptance by Mark of the tradition of the virgin birth of Jesus, and thus consonant also with Mark being written after Matthew and Luke.

Farmer's answer to Fitzmyer was that he [Farmer] raised this matter in *The Synoptic Problem* purely as "a counter argument against those defenders of Marcan priority who wish to develop a theological or christological argument supporting Marcan priority based upon the absence of the birth narratives in Mark." At most, Fitzmyer is countering a minor point made by Farmer, but this is in no way an argument against Markan Dependence.

Extensive though Fitzmyer's list is, it is not exhaustive. Here are nine more objections to the Griesbach Hypothesis mentioned by scholars and my responses.

10. **Grant** (1965, 354): "How does all this fit . . . the widespread tradition of the Roman origin of Mark and its use of Petrine material? These questions are not answered. But they *must* be answered."

Answer: Both Griesbach and Farmer acknowledge the probability that the preaching of Peter was the source of all the additional snippets of information that Mark includes. I agree with them in this, but I see a much greater role for Peter's preaching in influencing the very form and language of Mark's Gospel. So I am in complete agreement with Grant in acknowledging the use Mark made of "Petrine material"—but this does not conflict with Markan Dependence. On the contrary, the role of Peter's teaching is well supported in tradition and is central to my presentation of Markan Dependence (see above, and chap. 3).

Chapter 4 shows that more than 25% of the content of Mark's Gospel is unparalleled in either Matthew or Luke, and where Mark does parallel Matthew and Luke in *content*, much of the wording differs from that used by the Major Synoptics. Of the 11,078 words in Mark's Gospel, 6,008 do not occur in either Matthew or Luke; 840 occur in Luke but not in Matthew, so that a total of 6,848 (61.8%) of Mark's words do not occur in Matthew; and 2,395 occur in Matthew but not in Luke, so that a total of 8,403 (75.8%) of Mark's words do not occur in Luke.

These words that are in Mark but not in Matthew and/or Luke are due to the inclusion in Mark of additional information or wording that is lacking in the Major Synoptics, or to differences in the wording with which Mark and the Major Synoptics tell the same stories. Markan Dependence says that Mark had in front of him the accounts of Matthew and Luke, which already differed from each other in wording to quite a considerable extent, so that to follow the wording of the one would automatically mean differing from the other. However, on many occasions Mark chose to differ from both by altering their wording or by adding extra material. There must have been some other source for the different and additional material in Mark. The explanation from church history is that Mark's third source was the preaching of Peter. So Mark has three sources of information for the material of his Gospel, not two: Matthew, Luke, and Peter. Grant's objection thus does not constitute an argument against Markan Dependence, which fully recognizes the role of Peter's preaching.

11. **Kümmel** (1975, 64): "That Luke took his common material over directly from Matthew is championed again and again. [Here in a footnote Kümmel cites Farmer among a number of others.] This position is completely inconceivable, however. What could possibly have motivated Luke, for example, to shatter Matthew's sermon on the mount, placing part of it in his sermon on the plain, dividing up other parts among various chapters of his Gospel, and letting the rest drop out of sight? How could anyone explain the fact that not once does Luke place material that he has in common with Matthew at the same point in the Markan framework, apart from the baptism texts and the temptation stories in Lk 3:7–9,17, if he took that material from Matthew and was therefore dependent upon the Markan order that is likewise encountered in Matthew? Is it conceivable that Luke would have taken over none of Matthew's additions to the text of Mark? On this question Schmid and Vaganay have shown that Matthew and Luke alternate in offering the original form of the material they have in common, so that with respect to all these arguments the assumption of a direct dependence of Luke upon Matthew must be described as untenable."

Answer: Farmer contends strongly for the view that Luke knew and used Matthew's Gospel as a major source. Kümmel's objection here is to *this* view rather than to Markan Posteriority itself. I discuss this matter in full in chapter 8, but I must say here that I largely agree with Kümmel's arguments against the idea that Luke knew our Matthew. Certainly, this objection does not challenge in any way the basic question of the relationship of Mark to Matthew and Luke.

12. **Metzger** (1965, 81): "In style and language Mark is decidedly less polished than Matthew and Luke, and it would be contrary to all analogy that well-written documents should be so revised as to produce a cruder one."

Answer: This argument is often found in the form, "Why would Mark alter Matthew's and Luke's good Greek to poor Greek?" This is the Argument from Improvements used in support of Markan Priority. It is based on a totally incorrect (and prejudicial) understanding of the nature of the difference between Mark's Greek and that of the Major Synoptics. This argument was answered by Sanders (1969) and others, and I have discussed it in detail in chapter 3 in relation to the nature of the form of Greek that Mark uses and in chapter 5 as an argument in favor of Markan Priority. By the way, it is not "contrary to all analogy" for the language of a more literary document to be recast in the more colloquial language of everyday usage. In fact, it happens all the time. Markan Dependence says that is what has happened here.

13. **Hill** (1972, 28): "Griesbach considered Mark as an epitomizer of Matthew, while Luke was regarded as also earlier than Mark. This theory . . . has been discounted, to a large extent, because it fails to do justice to the literary characteristics and independence of viewpoint found in Mark."

Answer: Neither Griesbach nor Farmer nor I would consider Mark an abbreviator or epitomizer of Matthew, but rather to have expanded those sections of Matthew and/or Luke on which he drew. In this regard Hill has completely misunderstood the view that he criticizes.

Furthermore, the implication in this objection is that Markan Posteriority makes Mark out to be no more than a scissors-and-paste editor or compiler, so that on the one hand this hypothesis destroys the value and purpose of Mark's Gospel while on the other hand the picture it gives of Mark's Gospel is at variance with the freshness and vigor of his Gospel that one finds when reading it.

Quite to the contrary of what Hill has said and implied, the Markan Posteriority view recognizes Mark as no mere compiler or assembler of extracts from predecessors, but as an independent author in his own right, having his own way of writing and his own purposes for producing a Gospel. And he has done this in such a way that his own literary characteristics and independence of viewpoint are clearly stamped on his work. Markan Dependence does not compromise this or call it into question in any way. There is no substance to Hill's objection as an argument against Markan Dependence.

14. **Abbott** (1879, 791): "It can be proved by *reductio ad absurdum* that St. Mark did not copy from St. Matthew and St. Luke. For suppose that he did so copy . . . this would be a *tour de force* even for a skilful literary forger of these days, and may be dismissed as an impossibility for the writer of the Second Gospel."

Answer: Abbott appeals to the impossibility argument mentioned earlier (see chap. 3 for my response). My only reason for mentioning it again here is because many scholars consider this a decisive objection ever since Abbott proposed it.

15. **Goodacre** (2001, 58) states: "If Mark wrote third, using both Matthew and Luke, one will want to know why it is that he omitted so much material from his predecessors." He expects it would be because "Double Tradition pericopae must have been material that was in some way uncongenial to Mark." He finds "places in Mark where the insertion of double-tradition might have been highly conducive to his purposes, both literary and theological." The material he considers here is the Lord's Prayer. Since Mark did not insert it where he might have, Goodacre exclaims (59) that "this data does not make sense on the assumption of Markan Posteriority." This discussion of Mark leads him to this conclusion (65):

> The difficulty, in short, for the Griesbach Theory in dealing with Mark's alleged omissions and additions is that so many contrasting features of Mark are placed into such sharp relief.... Often, on the theory that Mark wrote third, there seems to be a deliberate rejection of the concurrent testimony of Matthew and Luke that on the Griesbach Theory he is supposed to value, in order simply to add almost redundant clarificatory clauses, something that appears to be contradicted by his very careful and subtle work elsewhere.

Answer: Goodacre uses some of the contra-Griesbach objections mentioned above, but his main thrust is different. Basically, Goodacre's point is that Mark does not do what Goodacre thinks the Griesbach Theory says that he should. Goodacre's points are fully answered by the explanation of the "literary and theological" purposes of Mark to be deduced from Mark's Gospel itself (see chap. 3 for discussion).

16. **Blomberg** (2001): Two speakers at the April 2000 Conference on the Gospels argue against the Griesbach/Two-Gospel position (the papers of which are published in the above volume). They represent the critical thinking of evangelicals on the Markan Posteriority position early in the twenty-first century, so it is important that we should note them. First, C. Blomberg begins (31) his critique of the Griesbach Hypothesis in this way:

> The major challenge to the two-(or four-) source hypothesis over the last forty years has been what is increasingly called the two-Gospel hypothesis. Following the lead of the late-eighteenth-century German scholar Johann Jakob Griesbach, this view stands Markan Priority on its head and argues that Mark was the last of the Synoptics to be written. Much like various Greco-Roman historians who substantially abbreviated their sources, Mark is believed to have abridged and conflated both Matthew and Luke.

From this introduction one would hardly suspect that Griesbach's Markan Posteriority view was the earlier, and that Markan Priority is the one that did the head-standing. And again, Blomberg repeats the mistake that Griesbach and the Two-Gospel school believe that Mark simply abbreviated the Major Synoptics. This argument, as I explained earlier, is not only misleading but is simply *not true*.

Blomberg concludes (32) that "the major weakness in the Griesbach theory to date is that its proponents have not demonstrated how Markan style and theology emerge more consistently on their hypothesis than on the alternatives. Until I see such a demonstration, I will remain unconvinced."

Answer: Such a demonstration is set out in chapter 3.

17. **Osborne** (2001): Next, G. Osborne sums up the various Synoptic Gospel presentations at this conference and says (142), "Thus far the two-Gospel hypothesis sounds not only cogent but absolutely convincing. However there are some serious drawbacks to the theory. . . . For one thing, it is difficult to explain the many omissions if Mark used both Matthew and Luke." Osborne then elaborates this point in a fashion that goes back to Streeter (and has been followed by a great many others ever since). We have seen that the explanation lies in the different purpose of Mark in writing (see chap. 3).

Then Osborne considers the patterns of each pair of Gospels agreeing in turn against the third, and finds that this occurs in all possible permutations. He deduces that this data favors neither hypothesis, though "the agreements between Matthew and Luke can be explained in several ways." He suggests (143) that observable features that might favor Markan Dependence "are often due to an overlap between Mark and Q, to those normal differences in style that writers normally make in using sources, or to other oral tradition." Indeed, that both Matthew and Luke were "following a fixed tradition . . . may have occasioned the Matthew/Luke agreements against Mark."

Answer: The issue of the Mark-Q overlap has been addressed above. I consider some of the more significant of the Matthew/Luke agreements against Mark in chapter 7, where I show that these are very difficult to explain away according to Markan Priority and that they strongly favor Markan Dependence.

18. **Osborne and Williams** (2002): In this book each of the proponents of the three views put their case, and the other two then critique the presentation. J. Niemelä argues for the Two-Gospel view, and Osborne and M. Williams respond from the Markan Priority/Two-Source perspective. While they contend against Niemelä's particular presentation and methodology, they advance few arguments against the basic contention that Mark

was third. They do, however, repeat the standard objections, such as (205) "instances where Mark omits contents that appear in both Matthew and Luke," so that they ask (205–6, 208):

> How does this theory explain these omissions, given that Mark normally follows and condenses the material that he finds in the other two Synoptic Gospels? Why Mark omitted the contents of these particular verses is of primary importance in a defense of the Two-Gospel Hypothesis. . . . This last point is perhaps the most significant critique of the Two-Gospel Hypothesis, namely, the failure to explain the textual differences between the Gospels. If Mark used Matthew and Luke on a larger scale, how does one explain his failure to use the Sermon on the Mount, or the Infancy stories, or, given Mark's emphasis on teaching, much of the teaching material?

Then they complain (208) that "One looks in vain for any type of discussion of a specific text of the Gospels in Niemelä's chapter."

Answer: Discussion of specific passages are in this present book. The other comments they make are the same points already noted as "stock-in-trade" objections against Markan Posteriority, and they are answered in chapter 3 (see also chap. 7).

SUMMARY

The last four objections occur in twenty-first-century books. Perhaps you may get the feeling from these that nothing much has been added to the collection of objections advanced—and answered—over the last two centuries. Yes, so do I. And the answers to those objections have been spelled out again (with some elaborations and refinements) in this present volume.

Other objections occur in many of the reviews of Farmer's book, objections that rejected strongly the case for Mark's use of Matthew and Luke that Farmer had made. The review by C. L. Mitton (1965, 1–3) raises a number of objections, including these in particular: (1) "Perhaps the greatest single weakness of Professor Farmer's position is his inability to discover any really convincing purpose for the production of such a book as he claims Mark to have been." He dismisses in this way Farmer's attempt to explain Mark as fulfilling a role in reconciling differences that exist between Matthew and Luke. (2) Mitton quotes with approval Abbott's words (which I have referred to—see objection 14, above) that the conflation of Matthew and Luke as Mark is supposed to have done "may be dismissed as an impossibility for the writer of the Second Gospel." Thus Mitton simply writes off

Farmer's solution to the Synoptic Problem as ascribing an impossibility to Mark.

The review of Farmer by F. C. Grant (1965, 352–54) is entitled "Turning Back the Clock"—a title that is (and was clearly intended to be) indicative of his response to this book. In the course of his review he writes, "Furthermore, what purpose can be alleged for such an abridgement? Why should anyone wish to substitute Mark's brief narrative, truncated at both ends, for the fuller narratives of Matthew and Luke?"

There are basically two distinct issues here in these objections. The first issue is Abbott's assertion that Mark could not have done what Markan Dependence says that he did. Second, even if Mark could have produced such a Gospel, why on earth (as Styler asks) would Mark want to, and even if he did, why (as Grant asks) would he have done it in such a fashion as appears from an examination of his Gospel, leaving so much out?

I have referred several times to how often numerous otherwise careful scholars understand Griesbach and Farmer to mean that Mark's purpose was to abbreviate Matthew. Grant, for instance, in his review (as above) assumes that the Griesbach Hypothesis asserts that Mark was *abridging* Matthew and Luke, and this is also the case in Cutt's review (1966, 225–27). Cutt shows a fair appreciation of Farmer's arguments and of the overall value of his study, but he is apparently unclear on what Farmer's view is about Mark's use of Matthew and Luke: Cutt says, "If Mark is an epitome of Matthew and Luke," and then questions a deduction made from this mistaken premise.

Some scholars, it seems, fail to understand Griesbach's Hypothesis (and Farmer's presentation of it) because they confuse it with the purpose that was postulated for Mark by Augustine in *his* hypothesis (see above). One must comment that the difficulty of combining two documents if one is simultaneously seeking to *abridge* them is of a different degree altogether from the level of difficulty if one is *conflating* what each says, adding in some details of his own, and expanding the length of the story in the process. Mark's narratives—as both Griesbach and Farmer have several times pointed out—are almost invariably longer than the corresponding Matthean or Lukan versions.

Thus the reason for Mark's Gospel being shorter than the other two Synoptics must be sought elsewhere. It is *not* due to Mark's abbreviation of his sources. Is it possible that this oft-repeated misconception of Griesbach's Hypothesis could now be laid to rest? No good purpose is served in scholarly inquiry if one distorts the teaching of a rival hypothesis before replying to it.

These are the matters that need to be addressed, and most of them are answered in chapter 3. Chapter 8 is devoted to the other major issue: a careful consideration of the question of the relationship of Luke with Matthew.

In fact, all of the various arguments against the Markan Dependence Hypothesis have been examined. This chapter shows clearly that:

1. These arguments frequently betray a misunderstanding about, or an unclear perception of the nature of, the Synoptic data; for example, advocates of Markan Priority consistently identify Mark's colloquial, spoken Greek as being "poor Greek."

2. These arguments are often based on subjective or invalid assumptions; for example, if Mark wrote after Matthew and Luke, it could not have been with some different or independent purpose in view, but would have been with the intention of replacing their Gospels with his own.

3. These arguments overlook relevant facts; for example, Grant's argument about Petrine material overlooks how both Griesbach and Farmer recognized Peter's teaching as a third source that Mark drew upon.

4. These arguments are simply in error about the facts; for example, Hill states that "Griesbach considered Mark as an epitomizer of Matthew," and Abbott boldly asserted that to conflate material from Matthew and Luke to produce an account such as Mark's Gospel "may be dismissed as an impossibility."

The foregoing discussion has shown that none of the arguments that has been put forward provides any refutation of the Markan Dependence view propounded in this book.

EVALUATION AND ASSESSMENT

It is very generally agreed by Gospel scholars (e.g., at the AD 2000 Gospel Conference) that the explanation of the Synoptic Problem is almost certainly either Markan Priority or Markan Posteriority. We have looked at the case for Markan Priority and for Markan Dependence, and the objections raised in rebuttal in each case.

It had been my original intention to list the objective arguments I could find that unequivocally and unambiguously support the Markan Priority Hypothesis in distinction from all other alternative hypotheses. These arguments would then be weighed for relative strength against arguments in support of the case for the Markan Dependence Hypothesis

But a list of such Markan Priority arguments cannot be made. I cannot find any. There are *no objective arguments* that unequivocally and unambiguously support the Markan Priority Hypothesis in distinction from all other alternative hypotheses.

Numbers of Synoptic arguments (like those from similarities) are reversible. Other arguments (like those from improvements made to Mark) are based upon subjective assumptions about relevant factors, such as what constitutes evidence that one document is more primitive than another, and upon subjective opinions about what the Synoptic authors would or would not have done. Other arguments are based on opinions about which particular features indicate that one Gospel was prior to or posterior to another, and which elements of a Gospel indicate copying in a given direction.

Other arguments that supposedly support Markan Priority turn out not to be *arguments in support of* Markan Priority at all but *explanations of the redactional procedures of Matthew and Luke* on the prior assumption of Markan Priority. Many of these explanations were in fact first proposed in order to account for what were perceived as *difficulties* faced by the Markan Priority Hypothesis. It is not an objective unequivocal unambiguous argument for a hypothesis being true, in distinction from all other alternatives, that an explanation can be offered for what the parties must have done if that hypothesis *were* true.

I have sought to find rebuttals against earlier versions of the Markan Posteriority position that would also carry weight against the Progressive Publication of Matthew/ Markan Dependence explanation proposed in this book. I was not able to find one such objection that I feel cannot be adequately accounted for by this hypothesis.

Many of those who object to the various forms of the Markan Posteriority position, from Griesbach's version onwards, have misunderstood what it is saying. Indeed, often their (assumed) success in demolishing the case for Griesbach and his successors has been in direct proportion to their misunderstanding of the position they reject.

Yet so many scholars are not taking note of the way in which progressively down the years the various arguments on which Markan Priority is based have been demolished. They still hold tenaciously to it after the support for their viewpoint has disappeared beneath them and even when (as in some cases we have examined in this study) the arguments for it are in fact proven to be illusory. Ultimately, these arguments in support of Markan Priority seem now to come down to asserting, "Markan Priority is a proven and established viewpoint," and thereafter remaining deaf to those who reply, "No it isn't."

It is time to move to some particular passages and to look at the impossibilities that need to be believed by those who remain convinced of Markan Priority.

SEVENTEEN IMPOSSIBLE THINGS BEFORE BREAKFAST

This chapter draws attention to 17 impossible things—and a few improbabilities—that believing Markan Priority involves.

> "I can't believe THAT!" said Alice.
>
> "Can't you?" the Queen said in a pitying tone.
> "Try again: draw a long breath, and shut your eyes."
>
> Alice laughed. "There's no use trying," she said.
> "One CAN'T believe impossible things."
>
> "I daresay you haven't had much practice," said the Queen.
> "When I was your age, I always did it for half-an-hour a day.
> Why, sometimes I've believed as many as six
> impossible things before breakfast."
>
> Lewis Carroll,
> *Through the Looking Glass*, Chapter Five

INTRODUCTION: AN "IMPOSSIBLE" SITUATION

F. W. Beare once stated (1965, 296; his review of Farmer's *The Synoptic Problem*) that "anyone who could imagine any editor at any time or in any place going about his job as Farmer describes Mark as doing would have to make a habit of believing sixteen impossible things before breakfast." To accept Farmer's Synoptic Hypothesis required, in his opinion, a much greater capacity for believing the impossible than that ever attained by the Queen in *Alice in Wonderland*.

As I survey the Synoptic evidence, I find 17 things that are impossible for me to believe and that therefore seem to me significant as "direction indicators" for our present study. These are now explained and critiqued. A business organization that specializes in tackling troublesome projects has as its motto, "The difficult we do at once; the impossible may take just a little longer." Here is my collection for believing 17 impossible things about the Synoptic Gospels. They may be believed before breakfast, or in fact, if one needs a little longer, before any other meal.

MARK'S OMISSIONS

Some of the material omitted by Mark is quite significant when weighing the order and relationships of the Synoptics. Three aspects of Mark's omissions are considered here.

1. Mark Did Not Know the Sermon on the Mount

One of the most well known and widely quoted of Streeter's comments about Mark's omissions is (1924, 158) that "only a lunatic would leave out Matthew's account of the Infancy, the Sermon on the Mount, and practically all the parables, in order to get room for purely verbal expansion of what was retained." Ever since then, Markan Priority advocates have continued to echo Streeter's claim—up to and including writers in the twenty-first century (see the arguments against Markan Dependence in chap. 6).

It should be noted that this is Streeter's *later* view, but his *earlier* view was that Mark was acquainted with Q (1911, 167, 176) and that Q contained not only what is common to Matthew and Luke but also a considerable amount of the material now found only in Matthew or Luke: "Probably therefore much of the peculiar matter of Matthew and a little of the peculiar matter of Luke is from Q" (185). Thus Q would have included (184, 187, 189) the whole of the "Great Sermon" (the Sermon on the Mount in Matthew; the Sermon on the Plain in Luke) and also many of the parables only in one of the Major Synoptics (184, 196–98).

Streeter makes his suggestions very cautiously. For example, he says that "the solutions here suggested are therefore only tentatively put forward, and are of a far more speculative character than anything heretofore" (193); but he still considers them *possible*. Thus in 1911 Mark was considered to be familiar with much of the material that his Gospel lacks (because he was familiar with Q, and this material was in Q), so that Mark would have omitted this material by choice. Yet in 1924 Streeter asserts that Mark was to be classified as a lunatic if he could be shown to have acted in precisely this very way!

The assumption is that if Mark did not have Matthew (and/or Luke) in front of him, then he would not have known Jesus' teachings as contained in the Sermon on the Mount—that is, if he did not get it from Matthew or Luke, then he would not have had access to it at all. Thus the material in Matthew and Luke not found in Mark was unknown in the early church until Matthew and Luke published their Gospels. Are we really to believe that Jesus' teaching in the Sermon on the Mount was not widely known in the church at large, but that its line of transmission to Matthew and Luke (whether per Q or the other postulated sources M and L, or otherwise) was secret—or at any rate, sufficiently secret that none of the Sermon on the Mount (or other teachings of Jesus omitted in Mark) ever became known to Mark? This implication, implicit in Markan Priority reasoning, is preposterous and incredible.

Luke (1:1–4) states that he was recording "the things that have been accomplished among us, just as they were delivered to us by those who from the beginning were eyewitnesses and ministers of the word . . . , that you may know the truth concerning the things of which you have been informed." This is the very opposite of the idea of now publishing for the first time information that hitherto had been hidden from the church and unknown until his Gospel appeared.

Actually, altogether a very considerable amount of Jesus' teachings in Matthew and Luke is lacking in Mark. Are we to believe that Mark was totally unaware of any of it? It is impossible to see how a person so involved in the affairs of the early church as John Mark, and associated with its central figures, could have remained so ignorant of Jesus' teachings.

So some scholars assign a late date to Mark's Gospel and reject the view that it is the work of the John Mark referred to in the New Testament. But to adopt this view of the authorship of the Second Gospel does not in any measure diminish the high probability that the author of Mark's Gospel (whoever he was) knew more of Jesus' teachings than he recorded and, in particular, that he knew the contents of the Sermon on the Mount and other major discourses. A later writer in the church would be *more* likely, not *less* likely, to know a greater amount of Jesus' teaching than is contained in the Second Gospel. Any opponent of this conclusion has a substantial task ahead of him: he would need to explain how the author of this Gospel could know the things that he did know and record, and thus presumably be a member of the Christian community, and yet *not* know at least the more important teachings that his Gospel lacks.

A careful assessment of the situation in the early church, and of the evidence that we have for the way Jesus' teachings were disseminated in the

Christian communities, leads to the conclusion that Mark, being actively involved within the Christian community, was aware of its traditions of the teachings of Jesus (including the Sermon on the Mount, the parables, and so forth) *before any of the Gospels were written*, and quite irrespective of their order. It is impossible to believe that Mark would not have known any of the Sermon on the Mount and other teachings until and unless he read it in Matthew and/or Luke.

Once this is recognized, Streeter's argument is turned on its head. Now, one must examine what Mark did on the assumption that when he wrote his Gospel he was indeed familiar with the Sermon on the Mount. Why then did he omit all this teaching from his Gospel? If Mark was the first Synoptist to write, that question is difficult to answer. Knowing such incomparable teachings of Jesus (which—on this view—were not at that time recorded in any Gospel) and being himself engaged in writing a Gospel, Mark would certainly (we might think) wish to include them. And, in those circumstances, *that he did not do so* is what needs explaining.

However, if Mark was the *last* Synoptist to write, it is quite simple to account for his omission of the Sermon on the Mount (and other teachings of Jesus). Mark did not include the Sermon on the Mount in his Gospel for the very straightforward reason that *it was already available to those for whom it was intended, the church, in the Gospels of Matthew and Luke*—and he had a different purpose in writing. It is far easier to understand Mark's omission of such material as the Sermon on the Mount if he knew that this teaching was already being read in the church than if he deliberately decided to leave it out of his Gospel when his was the first Gospel to be written.

Advocates of Markan Priority must claim that Mark did not know the Sermon on the Mount, because the moment the alternative is accepted—that Mark knew it but left it out—then they are confronted with the fact that this omission was the result of an intentional decision Mark made. They then would have to face the possibility that he omitted it because he knew it was already available in the other Synoptics—meaning that Mark was not the first Gospel. So their only consistent choice is to hold that—impossible as it seems—Mark did not know this sermon.

2. Mark Deliberately Disobeyed the Commandment of Jesus

In Matt 28:20 Jesus instructs his followers to teach their converts to observe all those things that he had commanded. Mark records in very full detail the Gospel pericopes telling all that Jesus did, but he gives rather little of what Jesus commanded or of what Jesus taught. This discrepancy—if that is what it is—between what Jesus commanded and what Mark did is worthy of some consideration.

To reply that Mark would not have known Matt 28:20 because Matthew's Gospel had not yet been written is specious and irrelevant. Jesus' teaching ministry was central to his total ministry, and to be a Christian would be to know this. Mark's Gospel records how often Jesus was addressed as "Teacher" and refers repeatedly to the frequency with which Jesus taught: Jesus is called "Teacher" 12 times in Mark (11 times in Matthew; 15 times in Luke); he is mentioned 15 times in Mark as engaged in teaching (10 times in Matthew; 14 times in Luke); a combined frequency of 21 times in Matthew, 27 times in Mark, and 29 times in Luke. Bearing in mind the different lengths of the Gospels, this is a frequency per 100 verses of 1.97 in Matthew, 4.08 in Mark, and 2.53 in Luke, so that the *relative frequency* that each mentions Jesus as teacher is the highest in Mark's Gospel.

The words of Matthew 28 do not stand alone. The Sermon on the Mount ends with the contrast between the house built on sand and the house built on rock (Matt 7:24–27), illustrating Jesus' intention that his teaching was to become the foundation of men's lives. He taught with authority (Matt 7:29; Mark 1:22,27; Luke 4:32), that is, he expected to be obeyed. To "learn from him" was a requirement for those who would become disciples (Matt 11:29). His trenchant criticism of some who followed him was, "Why do you call me 'Lord, Lord,' and do not do what I tell you?" (Luke 6:46).

This emphasis also occurs in John's Gospel. Repeatedly Jesus stressed that the test and the evidence of true discipleship was obedience to his teachings (John 14:15,21–24; 15:10; 17:8). Obedience to his teaching would be the basis of the judgment to come, and his words would in fact be the judge on the last day because he spoke with the Father's authority (John 12:47–49; 14:10).

The early Christians had no doubt about the importance of Jesus' teachings and their responsibility to teach them to new converts. The members of the Pentecost church "devoted themselves to the apostles' teaching and fellowship, . . . day by day attending the temple together and breaking bread in their homes" (Acts 2:42–46). Similarly Paul declared that his ministry had involved "teaching you in public and from house to house. . . . Therefore be alert, remembering that for three years I did not cease night and day to admonish everyone with tears" (Acts 20:20,31). When Paul taught about divorce, he based his comments on Jesus' teachings, introducing it with the words, "To the married I give charge, not I but the Lord" (1 Cor 7:10).

Examples could be multiplied. So how can it be that Mark gives so little space in his Gospel to the things that Jesus taught? It is impossible that this should be because Mark would deliberately disobey the things that Jesus said or the commands that Jesus gave concerning his teachings, for this would run directly counter to the spirit of all that Mark does say in his Gospel; or because Mark was unaware of Jesus' teachings apart from what he did include; or because Mark did not recognize the importance of Jesus' teachings (which is ruled out when we consider the way in which he so frequently records that Jesus was addressed as "Teacher" and refers to Jesus' teaching ministry).

But advocates of Markan Priority will find, in consequence of that view, that this is an impossibility they are required to believe. But the question still remains: Given then all the factors in the situation, why *would* Mark feel so free to write an account of the life and ministry of Jesus and to include in it so little of His teachings?

The most reasonable explanation is to be found in two related factors. First, recording Jesus' teachings as such, for its own sake, was not part of Mark's primary purpose in writing (a point considered in detail in chap. 3); and second, Mark was free not to record more than he did of Jesus' teachings *because he knew they were already available in the Gospels of Matthew or Luke or both.*

3. Mark Omitted Details of the Resurrection Though He Wrote First

Most early manuscripts of Mark's Gospel contain an account of Jesus' resurrection (16:9–20) which is lacking in some important early manuscripts. Some manuscripts have an alternative ending (frequently referred to as "the shorter ending") and a few have both endings. In light of the significance of Jesus' resurrection in early Christian preaching and Christian theology (as seen in the speeches in Acts and in the Epistles), many New Testament scholars find it difficult to understand how the longer ending was deleted from or lost from these manuscripts if it was part of the original text of the Gospel, or how alternative endings arose.

As I indicated earlier, I want to make it absolutely clear that the Markan Dependence Hypothesis is not tied to any particular view of the ending of Mark's Gospel. If Mark 16:9–20 is authentic, then we have in these verses the same kind of brief Markan summary of pericopes that occur in much greater detail in the other Gospels—such as the temptation, the mission charge, and so on—together with the addition of numerous details that are unique to Mark. There is certainly no difficulty for the Markan Dependence Hypothesis here. It is much more readily possible to account for the three Synoptics on the basis of Mark being written third than that it was written first and that Matthew and Luke expanded Mark's verses into their respective versions.

But many scholars claim that if Mark's Gospel does end at 16:8, then this poses a difficulty for Markan Posteriority. They consider it impossible that Mark would conclude his Gospel at this point if indeed he had Matthew and Luke in front of him as he wrote. If Mark's Gospel does end at 16:8, then how do advocates of Mark Posteriority explain this? This means that Mark's Gospel does not contain any details of the resurrection. As already noted (see chap. 6), Fitzmyer raises this as an objection against Markan Posteriority.

Mark contains an appearance in the tomb of a messenger from God, who says to the women, "Do not be amazed; you seek Jesus of Nazareth, who was crucified. He is risen, he is not here; see the place where they laid him. But go, tell his disciples and Peter that he is going before you to Galilee; there you will see him, as he told you" (16:6–7). Thus Mark's Gospel ends with a very clear statement attesting to the *fact* of the occurrence of the resurrection. But (on the truncated view) the risen Lord himself does not appear in this Gospel. There is an instruction for the women to report what they had seen to "his disciples and Peter," but there is no record that the women obeyed. There is a promise of a meeting in Galilee, but no record of it taking place. There is an implication in the final verse of fear and incredulity, but no record of how this became transmuted into joy and trust.

All in all, 16:8 is a most unexpected way for the Gospel to end. This has led many scholars to postulate a "lost ending for Mark"—a final page of the original codex that became detached and lost, or the last part of the original scroll that became destroyed in some way. It is impossible to prove that such a thing could not have happened; all one can say is that there is absolutely no evidence whatsoever in support of this hypothesis. It is completely speculative, and it leaves a number of other questions for which a convincing answer is not immediately apparent: if the end of one early copy was lost in some way (and assuming that the lack of the ending was as obvious to the people of that day as it is to us), why was this loss not immediately remedied from the original or from another copy that was not incomplete? If it was the original manuscript itself that became damaged in some way, why was Mark not able to rewrite the ending there and then? An explanation *is possible*: Barclay (1975, 146) says that "16:9–20 is almost certainly not a part of the original gospel of Mark. This must mean that at one time there must have existed only one copy of Mark which had lost its last section." There would be only the one copy of Mark because it had not yet been copied and published more widely, or because this Gospel was being neglected and all other copies had perished and the defective one was the only one to survive. Perhaps Mark was unable at this time to rewrite his closing section. Barclay (146) suggests that "it is also remotely possible that what happened was that Mark died before he was able to complete his gospel, or was otherwise prevented from finishing it." These explanations appear like grasping at straws. They are called forth because of the difficulty of Mark's Gospel ending at 16:8. Yet, according to the judgment of many scholars, this appears to be the case.

Psychologically, Mark's Gospel is an impossibility (in its present form) as being the first Gospel written. Unless we are to postulate some such lost ending that redressed this psychological flaw, we must be compelled to place Mark as at least the second Synoptic written and in fact almost certainly the third. The Christian church was founded upon the belief in the resurrection of Jesus Christ—his resurrection was God's seal on his life and ministry—and upon the claims implicit in them about who he was. During the years of Jesus' ministry, his inner core of apostles had been very slow to perceive who he was. This full recognition came only after the resurrection, which was an integral part of the *kerygma* of the early church.

Opinions differ among scholars about the authorship of Mark's Gospel and its provenance. But whoever the author was, and whenever and wherever he wrote, his Christian life was lived within the context of a church that accepted as foundational the resurrection of Jesus Christ and the transformation in the apostles that it produced.

Yet Mark's Gospel only shows the apostles in doubt and weakness; it never shows them in faith and strength. Again and again they miss the point of what Jesus says or they misunderstand his teaching; they exhibit doubt and are rebuked for their lack of faith. At the end they forsake him and flee, and their leader totally denies him three times. All of this also occurs in Matthew and Luke, but there the account is balanced at the end: the apostles encounter the risen Christ, and then they are able to grasp the truth about him. Mark's account also goes up to the resurrection, but the apostles do not meet the risen Christ—they are left in their pre-resurrection ignorance and doubt. The picture Mark's Gospel draws of the apostles is in contrast with the record of the early church in the book of Acts. Thus it is psychologically impossible for anyone who is a part of the early church to write such a Gospel before any other existed—to write as he did about the apostles during Jesus' life on earth, go up to the announcement of Jesus' resurrection, and *leave it there*! If at that time this was the only Gospel that the church had, the impression it created would have been so contrary to the situation known to its readers in the early churches from post-resurrection events that the contrast would have been unacceptable.

It is no answer to say that "here we have the rationale for the Gospels of Matthew and Luke—they were written to set the record straight." This may be thought to account for Matthew and Luke assuming Mark was already written, but it leaves the existence of Mark (in the form in which we have it) as an unexplained enigma of very sizeable proportions. Other explanations along the lines of a negative attitude on the part of the author towards the apostles would still leave unresolved the question of how Mark could leave such a gap between what he records in his Gospel and the post-resurrection experiences of the church—especially since he was an active colleague of the apostle Peter.

Apart from a "lost-ending" hypothesis, with its own inherent problems, there is only one explanation that can make sense of this situation: Mark had a restricted purpose in view in writing, and he did not seek to fill in all the gaps or to link his pre-resurrection presentation to the post-resurrection awareness of the church, because he was fully aware that *the church already had Gospels that did that*. This means that he wrote in a situation where the church already possessed Matthew and Luke (or at least one of them) and that he took for granted the post-resurrection material and perspective that these other Gospels presented. He had one fundamental purpose: to present a picture of the person of Jesus through the record of what he did. The dullness of the disciples was a part of this picture, but Mark's record of Jesus reached its culmination in the *fact* of Jesus' resurrection, and nothing further about the apostles needed to be said in that connection.

Mark's treatment of the apostles in his Gospel, and its conclusion with the appearance of the angel to the women, is psychologically inexplicable if Mark's was the first Gospel, so that it was the only Gospel that the church had at the time it was written. Markan Priority seems an unlikely explanation of the data if the longer ending is authentic, but it is absolutely unbelievable that if it were written first this Gospel could end at 16:8. But if you hold to Markan Priority, it is this impossibility that you are called on to believe.

There is another possibility. Mark's Gospel—and its ending—is much more readily understandable if Mark could take for granted that his readers in the church also had available to them Matthew and Luke.

MATTHEW'S OMISSIONS

If Mark was written first, then we are required to believe that Matthew, the former tax collector, excises financial detail or precise numbers and replaces them with vague generalities. In several parallel passages, Mark contains, and Matthew lacks, specific figures for numbers or amounts of money. There is no reason to believe that Mark was particularly interested in figures, yet his Gospel contains these details. Matthew, who was trained in handling finance and keeping records, puts into his account only vague generalizations *precisely at these points* in the record. If Mark's Gospel were written first, then Matthew had exact figures in his source and he deleted them, substituting a generality.

As any person who has been trained in accounting knows, this is, psychologically, quite unbelievable. I know about this: I trained and practiced as an accountant before entering the ministry. The alternative is that Matthew's account lacked that information because it was a detail not known to him or possibly forgotten (being trained in accounts does not mean that you never forget a figure!), whereas it was a detail that Mark knew from his other source, Peter's preaching, and that he inserted into Matthew's material when drawing on Matthew in writing his own Gospel. But that Matthew had this precise information in front of him in Mark and deliberately made it vague and general? Impossible.

I address three instances of this kind of situation.

4. Matthew Omitted the Ointment or Bread Value Though He Knew Mark

In the account of the anointing at Bethany (Matt 26:6–13//Mark 14:3–9//John 12:1–8), Mark and John mention the value of the ointment used ("three hundred denarii"), but Matthew omits it and gives a general expression instead ("a large sum").

Matthew 26:9	Mark 14:5	John 12:5
For this ointment might have been sold for a large sum and given to the poor.	For this ointment might have been sold for more than 300 denarii and given to the poor.	Why was this ointment not sold for 300 denarii and given to the poor?

Why does Matthew omit the value of the ointment? It is impossible to believe that he begrudged the additional words required. Mark 14:5 uses three words (ἐπάνω δηναρίων τριακοσίων), and Matt 26:9 uses one word (πολλοῦ). It is impossible to believe that Matthew made the change to save *two words*! It is impossible in fact to believe that Matthew had the information about the figure for the value of the ointment in front of him as he wrote.

An additional example of this kind is in Mark 6:37 where Mark gives the value of the bread required to feed the crowd as "two hundred denarii," which is paralleled in John 6:7—but in their parallels both Matthew and Luke omit this piece of information. Again, it is impossible to believe that Matthew would do this if this figure were in front of him.

5. Matthew Omitted the Number of Pigs Though He Knew Mark

In the account of the exorcism of the "Legion" of demons (Matt 8:28–34//Mark 5:1–20//Luke 8:26–39), Mark mentions the number of the pigs that ran down the steep embankment into the water and were drowned ("numbering about two thousand"), but Matthew and Luke omit this.

Matthew 8:32	Mark 5:13	Luke 8:33
and behold the whole herd	and the herd, numbering about two thousand	and the herd
rushed down the steep bank	rushed down the steep bank	rushed down the steep bank

This number was not without its significance in the development of the story. If about 2,000 pigs were destroyed, no wonder the people were upset and begged Jesus to leave their neighborhood!

Why do Matthew and Luke (particularly Matthew) omit this highly relevant detail? It is impossible to believe that he begrudged the additional words required. Mark 5:13 uses two words that Matthew and Luke lack (ὡς δισχίλιοι), while Matt 8:32 uses one word for the size of the herd (πᾶσα). It is impossible to believe that Matthew made the change to save *one word*! It is impossible to believe that Matthew had the information about this figure in front of him as he wrote but omitted it.

6. Matthew Omitted the Widow's Gift Pericope Though He Knew Mark

In recording the events of Passion Week, Mark and Luke record the pericope about the poor widow who put all she had into the treasury (Mark 12:41–44//Luke 21:1–4), but Matthew omits it. In both Mark and Luke this pericope follows their brief account of Jesus' pronouncement of woes upon the scribes. Matthew follows his account of these woes (Matt 23:1–36) with the lament over Jerusalem (23:37–39E) and then proceeds straight to the Olivet Discourse (Matt 24:1ff.//Mark 13:1ff.//Luke 21:5ff.).

The story that Matthew omits is in fact very "Matthean" in character: it concerns money (what other textual material about money is there in Mark that does not have a parallel in Matthew?), it centers on a feature of Jewish temple practice (the collection of gifts for the temple), and it concludes with a saying of Jesus contrasting the relative value of the widow's contribution and the other gifts. There is no parallel to it in Matthew, but it is close in spirit to many items that Matthew does include, ranging from the material on this kind of theme in the Sermon on the Mount to his story of the coin in the fish's mouth. It is not of such length to pose any significant problem for inclusion (75 words in Mark's version; 58 words in Luke's). It is unbelievable that Matthew should have had this pericope in front of him in Mark's Gospel but would have chosen not to use it.

LUKE'S OMISSIONS

7. Luke Omitted the Syrophoenician Woman Pericope Though He Knew Mark

Matthew and Mark record the pericope about the Syrophoenician woman whose daughter was possessed by an unclean spirit (Matt 15:21–28//Mark 7:24–30), but Luke omits it. It occurs in that section of Mark that is sometimes called the "Great Omission" (Mark 6:45–8:26) because Luke does not record any of it.

This story that Luke omits is in fact very "Lukan" in character: it is the only story in which Jesus performs a miracle for the benefit of a Gentile woman when he heals her child. Luke consistently shows great interest in Gentiles, women, children, and healings. This pericope involves all four of these interests, one that (on the Markan Priority Hypothesis) lay before him in Mark's Gospel but that he passed over! This story is not of such length to pose any significant problem for inclusion (130 words in Mark's version), so it is unbelievable that Luke would have had this pericope in front of him in Mark's Gospel but chosen not to use it.

Some advocates of Markan Priority have acknowledged the problem of Luke's Great Omission, so they have proposed the explanation that the absence of all this material from Luke is due to it not being in Luke's copy of Mark: he had either a defective copy or a different, presumably earlier, recension. No one can deny the *possibility* of such a thing, but one can say that it has no supporting evidence of any kind. This conjecture is in fact an expedient to account for a difficulty, because it is incredible that Luke would have omitted all the material of the Great Omission—especially *this* pericope—if he had had it in front of him. This is just an exercise in damage control for advocates of Markan Priority.

The alternative explanation—that Mark wrote third and had this story before him in Matthew—fully accounts for all the data *on the basis of the Gospels as we have them*. Markan Dependence does not require leaps into pure speculation about different recensions or defective copies of the Gospel documents.

8. Luke Discarded Names and Time Notes in Mark

In several parallel passages Mark contains and Luke lacks specific details of place and circumstance (including time notes or connecting links). Yet Mark seems much less interested in such information than Luke, who is the one author who states that he plans to write an orderly (i.e., chronological) account (Luke 1:3), who gives the careful dating of events at the beginning of his Gospel (Luke 3:1–2; cf. 1:5,26,56; 2:1), who alone states Jesus' age (Luke 3:23; cf. 2:21,42), and who shows much interest in times, places, and circumstances (see chap. 4).

If Luke used Mark, then Luke had precise names of places and people in front of him in his source and deleted them on a number of occasions. He also had exact time notes in his source and made them more vague. Given what we can see of Luke as a historian—and noting his interest in and care about such details—this is, psychologically, incredible. The alternative explanation, which adequately accounts for the data, is that Mark used Matthew and Luke, and gained some of these pieces of information from their occurrences in Matthew and some from his remembrance of Peter's preaching. Here are three specific examples.

Luke Discarded Names Occurring in Mark

A. Wright (1903, xvi) states:

> There are many cases where S. Luke's record, and even S. Matthew's, is distinctly inferior to S. Mark's. Take for example the case of Proper Names. There are but few of these in S. Mark, 86 altogether, but 25 of them are absent from S. Luke. Now Proper Names give the assurance of definite information and of historic truth, which no reasonable author can afford to neglect. S. Luke was an historian, and in the Acts of the Apostles shows the instincts of an historian. Is it conceivable that he should have deliberately omitted so many names from his Gospel, if he had them before him in writing? I think not. But let us glance at two test cases. (1) S. Mark writes, "And Jesus went forth and His disciples to the villages appertaining to Caesarea Philippi" (Mk 8:27), for which S. Luke gives, "And it came to pass, as he was praying in a solitary place, His disciples were with Him." (2) S. Mark writes, "Bartimaeus, the son of Timaeus, a blind

beggar" (Mk 10:46), for which S. Luke gives, "A certain blind man." What motive can be conceived for this deliberate preference of the indefinite?

Wright has asked two questions, and they deserve an answer. A common suggestion is that Luke suppressed the names of certain people because of the danger that names represented in times of persecution. But this is not convincing for at least four reasons: (1) Luke's Gospel was published some 30 years after the events it records; (2) Luke records a great many other names without any sign of reluctance, so there is no discernible justification along these lines that can be detected for the names he included and those he left out; (3) in any case the precaution is pointless since these names under discussion occur in Mark's publication; and (4) at best this explanation refers only to personal names and does not cover other details and place names, which Luke often omitted also.

Thus it is impossible to believe that Luke would have in front of him (in Mark's Gospel) specific names and definite information but that he would replace them with indefinite generalities.

Luke Altering the Time Interval before the Transfiguration

In the pericope of the transfiguration (Matt 17:1–9//Mark 9:2–10//Luke 9:28–36), Matthew and Mark give a precise time interval before the event ("after six days"), while Luke has a different time interval and states that it is approximate ("about eight days after these saying").

Frequently Luke uses general time notes of some kind when there is no information of a more precise nature in any Gospel (cf. Luke 6:6//Matt 12:9//Mark 3:1; Luke 8:22//Matt 8:18//Mark 4:35; Luke 9:57//Matt 8:19). In those instances we may say that (on any theory of Synoptic relationships) Luke clearly had no more exact information. So there are situations where Luke gives very precise dating, but on other occasions he clearly does not have precise information, so he uses a generalization. In his account of the transfiguration he gives a generalization, while both Matthew and Mark have a precise time here. It is not believable that Luke had "after six days" in front of him in Mark's Gospel and changed it to the less precise "about eight days after."

The explanation that fully explains the data is that Matthew and Luke had independent traditions of the transfiguration (an impression confirmed by a comparison of the similarities and differences in their accounts) and that Luke's version did not contain a more exact time note. Mark, writing with both accounts before him, preferred to adopt the more precise time given by Matthew rather than Luke's less precise one.

Luke Leaving Out So Much Information about People

Luke lacks a considerable amount of personal information about people that Mark contains, and information of this kind would have been of great interest to Luke based on similar material in his Gospel that includes warm, human content. Including this material would have increased the length of Luke's Gospel by only a few words in each case so that this explanation (the usual one given for Luke's not including this material) hardly seems applicable. (See chap. 4 where this kind of material is identified, though these sections only tabulate what is lacking in *both* Matthew and Luke.) In a large number of these instances, the material in question consists of details that are found in Mark's version of a pericope that also occurs in Luke, so that on the Markan Priority Hypothesis *this information has been deliberately excised by Luke when taking over the story from Mark.*

Omissions that could be considered surprising are references to prayer, to Jesus praying, and to Jesus' compassion towards people. But one group of omissions is worthy of particular notice: the deletion of significant details in relation to healings. An example of this kind is the comment that the hemorrhaging women felt in her body that she was healed of her disease (Mark 5:29; lacking in Luke 8:44).

But quite extraordinary is the absence from Luke of any miracle where Jesus healed a deaf person. This was regarded as a healing of special difficulty because the deaf person could not hear the healing word. Mark records the healing of a deaf mute (7:32–37E), but Luke lacks the entire pericope. Mark 9:14–29 records the healing of a lad who was deaf and dumb (see 9:25), but Luke takes over this story from Mark and *omits this information!* There are thus no healings of the deaf in Luke's Gospel. In Luke 7:22 he quotes Jesus as saying "the deaf hear," but he does not have a single instance of this type of healing on record! Can we really believe that Luke would omit from his Gospel every mention in Mark of Jesus' healing the deaf?

This attitude that is postulated of Luke applies also to Q healings. In numerous instances Luke has been careful to give not merely the nature of an illness but also the extent of its progress: thus, in Matt 8:14//Mark 1:30 Simon's mother-in-law has a fever, but in Luke 4:38 she has a "high" fever; in Matt 8:2//Mark 1:40 Jesus is approached by a leper, but in Luke 5:12 he is "a man full of leprosy." But in the Q story of the Capernaum centurion, Matt 8:5 says that the servant's malady was paralysis, while Luke tells us that he was at the point of death (7:2) but *does not mention the nature of his affliction.* Such an omission is distinctly uncharacteristic of Luke.

Thus the second leg of the Two-Source Hypothesis, the Q source, is also called into question. But primarily we are confronted with the omission from Luke not merely of such pericopes as the Syrophoenician's daughter but of a host of small personal details about Jesus and about people that would have taken so little space to include and that are so much the kind of information that it appears Luke valued, and that he had in front of him in Mark and that *he excised from that account when he utilized it for his Gospel*. These omissions are, psychologically, quite incredible.

The alternative explanation is that Mark was not Luke's source and that this information was not in Luke's sources. Mark obtained this information from Matthew, or (on those occasions when Mark's Gospel alone gives the details) his source was his recollection of these details in Peter's preaching.

MARK AGAINST MATTHEW AND/OR LUKE

9. Matthew and Luke Created Positive Minor Agreements against Mark

In a number of Triple Tradition stories, Matthew and Luke include a detail that Mark lacks. These are called the "positive minor agreements" of Matthew and Luke against Mark. Some of these agreements are considered here.

The Fringe of Jesus' Garment

In the account of the healing of the woman with a hemorrhage (Matt 9:18–22//Mark 5:21–34//Luke 8:40–48), Matt 9:20 and Luke 8:44 mention the detail that the women touched the "fringe" of Jesus' garment, but Mark 5:27 omits it.

Matthew 9:20	Mark 5:27	Luke 8:44
came up behind him	came up behind him in the crowd	came up behind him
and touched the fringe of his garment	and touched his garment	and touched the fringe of his garment

The fringe of a rabbi's robe had special religious significance, so perhaps one can see why it might occur to Matthew to insert this detail into Mark's account, as he was writing for a Jewish audience. Schürer (1979, 2:479ff.) describes the origin of the fringe:

The *zizith* (. . . κράσπεδα in LXX and the New Testament . . .) are the tassels or fringes of blue or white wool prescribed by Num 15:37ff. and Deut 22:12 to be worn by every Israelite at the four corners of his garment. As the passage from Numbers specifies, the purpose of the tassel is that "you may look at it, and remember all the commandments of the Lord, and do them." . . . They are . . . worn, as the Pentateuch directs, and as was still customary at the time of Jesus, on the over-garment.

Schürer (481) also states that later Judaism had exaggerated "the importance attached to them, however, and the care with which everything is ordered down to the smallest detail (the number of threads and knots required in the *zizith*, . . . etc.)." (Schürer gives further details about the fringe in this reference, as does A. Edersheim [1950, 1:277, note 1].) The fringe of the garment was thus accorded special religious significance in itself. In the later pericope about healings at Gennesaret, both Matthew and Mark refer to people touching the fringe of Jesus' garment (Matt 14:36//Mark 6:56). Jesus refers to the practice of the scribes and Pharisees of making "their fringes long" so that they were particularly noticeable, which was part of his attack on their hypocrisies (Matt 23:5). While Mark did not mention the woman touching any particular part of Jesus' clothes, doubtless Matthew would have seen a religious point to be made by mentioning that it was the *fringe* she touched. And his Jewish readership would understand the significance of the detail.

But referring to this detail appears a trifle peculiar even for Matthew. He would not, when writing as a *Christian*, be likely to endorse the peculiarly Jewish concept of the special sanctity of a part of Jesus' clothes, particularly in the light of his later citation of Jesus' criticism of the scribes and Pharisees for their ostentatious lengthening of their fringes (Matt 23:5). So why did Matthew choose to add such an idea into his account about the hemorrhaging woman? Mark supposedly has the original account of this incident, with Matthew using it as his source, but Markan Priority does not provide for Matthew to be inserting this detail on the basis that it is extra information of which he has independent knowledge. So Matthew would have included it in because he thought it *might* have happened, or he thought it was appropriate, or he thought it would heighten the spiritual impact of the story, or something similar. But in fact any such motivation on Matthew's part here appears rather unlikely.

If it is *unlikely* that Matthew invented such a detail and inserted it into Mark's account in front of him, it is quite *impossible* to conceive of Luke doing such a thing. We cannot know whether Luke would be aware of the specific significance of the fringe of a rabbi's robe—the word "fringe" (κράσπεδον) occurs only here in Luke. Even if one assumes that Luke knew about this, one can hardly assume that the significance of the fringe would have been known to a large part of his arguably Gentile readership. It is difficult to explain why Matthew would choose to add "the fringe of" into his source, even though he was writing for a Jewish audience who would recognize the reference; it is impossible to see why it would occur to Luke to insert "the fringe of" when it was absent in his source, seeing that he was writing for Gentiles for whom this detail was meaningless. The claim that *both* Matthew and Luke, using only Mark as their source, independently chose at this same point to add this same detail (and it is part of an eight-word sequence in which Matthew and Luke are identical in the Greek) stretches credulity quite beyond all limits.

Mk:	ἐλθοῦσα ἐν τῶν ὄχλων ὄπισθεν ἥψατο	τοῦ ἱματίου αὐτοῦ
Mt:	προσελθοῦσα ὄπισθεν ἥψατο τοῦ κρασπέδου τοῦ ἱματίου αὐτοῦ
Lk:	προσελθοῦσα ὄπισθεν ἥψατο τοῦ κρασπέδου τοῦ ἱματίου αὐτοῦ

In the same context there are two other minor agreements of Matthew and Luke against Mark that can be noted in a comparison of the Greek.

If we were to accept that Mark is the source for this story in both Matthew and Luke, then in this passage both Matthew and Luke have independently chosen to make these changes in the text of Mark that they had before them: (1) Matthew (9:20) and Luke (8:44) altered ἐλθοῦσα ("came up") in Mark 5:27 to προσελθοῦσα ("came up"); (2) Matthew (9:20) and Luke (8:44) deleted ἐν τῷ ὄχλῳ ("in the crowd") in Mark 5:27 but added τοῦ κρασπέδου ("the fringe"). That both the Major Synoptists should have decided to add "the fringe" is quite unbelievable; that in this same place they should make *two other changes* of a minor nature that are *exactly the same*—so that after these alterations to Mark were independently made, the wording of Matthew and Luke in Greek ends up being *completely identical*—must be rated truly impossible.

But there are some variant readings for Luke 8:44, so the correspondence between the Major Synoptics could be due to the assimilation of the text of Luke to that of Matthew. B. Metzger (1971, 145f.) states, "The words τοῦ κρασπέδου constitute one of the so-called minor agreements of Matthew and Luke against Mark. The Committee regarded this as accidental and decided to follow the overwhelming weight of the external evidence supporting the inclusion of the words." Thus, the Committee responsible for the text of the United Bible Societies' edition of the Greek New Testament gave their attention to the significance of the fact that the inclusion of these words created an agreement between Matthew and Luke against Mark, which could have indicated assimilation of Luke to Matthew, and considered this possibility to be outweighed by "the overwhelming weight of the external evidence supporting the inclusion of the words." There is no textual basis for calling into question the agreement of Matthew and Luke against Mark as explained above.

An alternate suggestion is that Matthew and Luke each had some other source (other than Mark) for this information about the woman touching the fringe, and *this* is why they agree here. This other source must have contained an account of this woman's healing, and obviously it had to contain all the words in this verse where Matthew and Luke agree—indeed it must have had some account of the entire incident. If, following tradition, this other document that is a source for both Matthew and Luke is referred to as Q, then we have here a case where Q and Mark overlap in that they both contain the story of the hemorrhaging woman.

But if this story is in Q, and at least this detail comes from Q, then there is no evidence that in this pericope Mark is the source for the Major Synoptics: Matthew and Luke took the entire pericope from Q. By identical reasoning, similar minor agreements of Matthew and Luke against Mark in other pericopes can lead to the conclusion that most of Mark was paralleled in Q, and that Q rather than Mark is the source of Triple Tradition material; indeed, we will no longer have the Markan Priority Hypothesis but an Ur-Gospel Hypothesis (see chap. 10).

In fact, this reasoning for an overlap here between Q and Mark is a circular argument, and quite invalid. How could anyone know that Q and Mark overlap here? Because Matthew and Luke contain the same details not in Mark. How do you account for Matthew and Luke containing the same details not in Mark? Because Q and Mark overlap here.

On the Markan Dependence view, the explanation of the data is straightforward. The woman *did* touch the fringe of Jesus' garment. This factual detail was contained in the tradition transmitted to both Matthew and Luke. Thus it is included by them in their Gospels because it *happened*. Luke has it in his account because it was in his source, and he did not choose to alter his source—even though this point had little or no meaning for Gentiles. However, Mark *did* omit these words, because they were not relevant for *his* intended audience.

This view of Mark's omission of Jewish details has precedents elsewhere. There are numerous parallels for Mark lacking such details that occur in one or both of the Major Synoptics: the flute players (Matt 9:23); saluting a house, and your peace coming on it (Matt 10:12–13//Luke 10: 5–6); the priests in the temple on the Sabbath (Matt 12:5); the sheep in the pit on the Sabbath (Matt 12:11; cf. Luke 13:15 and 14:5); "I was sent only to the lost sheep of the house of Israel" (Matt 15:24; cf. Matt 10:5–6); "for any cause" (Matt 19:3); the difference between Matt 19:9 and Mark 10:11–12; and most of Matthew 23.

There are three alternate explanations of this data. (1) Both Matthew and Luke independently but simultaneously decided to insert the reference to the fringe, for reasons which are impossible to fathom. (2) There was an overlap between Mark and Q for this pericope, based on evidence which is hardly able to bear such weight and on reasoning which is entirely circular. (3) Matthew and Luke included it because it was part of the tradition of what happened, and Mark deleted it—in line with what he did in numerous other pericopes—because it was a detail from the Jewish background of the events in Jesus' life that was absolutely meaningless to Mark's intended audience.

The Perverse Generation

In Mark 9:19 it is difficult to account fully for either alternative: that Mark should omit what was in both Matthew and Luke, or that Matthew and Luke should both add the same expression to Mark. But one is much more believable than the other.

When Jesus came down from the Mount of Transfiguration and met the epileptic boy whom his disciples had not been able to heal, Matthew and Luke record that he said,

Matthew 17:17	Mark 9:19	Luke 9:41
O faithless and perverse generation	O faithless generation	O faithless and perverse generation

Mark's reason for omitting the words "and perverse" if they were in his sources is not immediately apparent. But that he should do so is far more believable than the alternative—that both Matthew and Luke independently chose to insert the words "and perverse" at this point. This is not a common word. It is the perfect middle/passive participle of διαστρέφω, a word that occurs only seven times in the New Testament. Of those seven occurrences, only four are of this particular form, and the two instances other than those now before us are in Acts 20:30 and Phil 2:15. Thus, the occurrences of this term "perverse" (διεστραμμένη) in the pericope under review are *its only occurrences on the lips of Jesus, and indeed its only occurrence in the Gospels*. If Matthew's and Luke's only source for this pericope is Mark, as Markan Priority would hold to be the case, and recognizing that if Matthew and Luke had followed the wording of Mark and not introduced "perverse" here that this word would not have occurred at all in the Gospels, it really stretches the imagination to conceive of why it would occur to both Matthew and Luke to add this same word.

More than that, Markan Priority here asks us to believe the unbelievable. There is nothing in Mark's text that suggests this word. There is no other place in the Bible where the words "unbelieving" and "perverse" occur together. Why should either Matthew or Luke, looking at Mark's wording, consider it necessary to add *any* word to "faithless," and if for some reason they felt they should, then *out of all the words in the Greek language, why should they both select this same one,* thus giving it its only appearance in the Gospels?

Tuckett (1983, 66) deals with this minor agreement with the comment: "Why should Mark omit καὶ διεστραμμένη in 9:19, when the inclusion of it would provide a good example of duality, which is usually considered a feature of Mark's style? On the assumption of Markan priority, its inclusion by Matthew and Luke could be due to assimilation to the text of Deut 32:5." He then suggests that the textual variant that includes these words in Mark may be correct. This textual variant is so poorly supported that it is not included in the apparatus of the United Bible Societies' text or discussed in Metzger's Textual Commentary. It appears to be a clear case of assimilating the text of Mark to Matthew and Luke in a few manuscripts. The Hebrew and Septuagint texts of Deut 32:5 refer to a "crooked and perverse generation," so Tuckett suggests that the single word "generation" would have caused both Matthew and Luke (who had Mark's Gospel in front of them) to think of the Deuteronomy passage and from it to extract the word "perverse" to add to their accounts. Why would both of them choose *this* word—why not the other word, "crooked"? If they had an inclination to assimilate the words of Jesus to this Old Testament passage, why did not one or the other or both of them drop Mark's "faithless" and adopt *both* descriptive adjectives from Deut 32:5? Why, that is, would the sight of "generation" in Mark inspire *both* Major Synoptists to think of the same Old Testament passage and each to select just *one* descriptive adjective from it, and both of them the *same* adjective?

Moreover, γενεά occurs in Mark on four other occasions: 8:12 (twice); 8:38; 13:30. On none of these occasions was either Matthew or Luke moved to assimilate Mark's γενεά to Deut 32:5. Furthermore, Luke in Acts 2:40 has "this crooked [σκολιά] generation," containing *two* words from Deut 32:5, and yet he was not stirred by this to add there the word "perverse." But Tuckett claims that both he and Matthew were influenced to add this one word into their record when they read γενεά in Mark 9:19! Those who wish to believe impossible things may certainly want to add this opportunity to their collections.

The explanation that Matthew and Luke include "and perverse" because this is what Jesus actually said is really no answer to the difficulty for advocates of Markan Priority. Once this explanation is tendered, then it completely contradicts the fundamental tenet of the Markan Priority Hypothesis, which is that *Mark alone* is the source in this pericope for what is in Matthew and Luke. Instead, this situation demands an appeal to an overlap between Mark and Q to rescue the Markan Priority Hypothesis.

The alternative is much more believable: Matthew and Luke record this saying because *Jesus actually said it*, and for some unknown reason Mark (using Matthew and Luke as his sources) chose to quote only part of Jesus' words here.

The Question in the Mocking of Jesus

When Jesus was mocked by the soldiers, we read:

Matthew 26:67	Mark 14:65	Luke 22:63-64
Then they spat in his face, and struck him	And some began to spit on him, and to cover his face, and to strike him,	Now the men who were holding Jesus mocked him and beat him: they also blindfolded him
and some, slapped him, saying, "Prophesy to us, you Christ! Who is it that struck you?"	saying to him, "Prophesy!" And the guards received him with blows.	and asked him, "Prophesy! Who is it that struck you?"

These words "Who is it that struck you?" are identical in Matthew and Luke but absent in Mark. Adherents of the Markan Priority Hypothesis are faced with the requirement of believing that when Matthew and Luke encountered Mark's "Prophesy!" they each inserted the question "Who is it that struck you?" in identical words. Streeter found this too difficult to believe; instead, he found it easier to believe that *all the extant manuscripts of Matthew had been corrupted by being assimilated here to Luke so that this question in Luke was inserted into Matthew!* There is no textual evidence showing variant readings here for Matthew or Luke. Streeter justifies his view by saying (1924, 327), "Assimilation of parallels is a form of corruption which can result, and, as I have shown, has often actually resulted, in producing an *identical* corruption along more than one *independent* line of transmission. I suggest that for once this has happened along all lines. I should say, rather, all lines for which evidence is extant."

Thus although there is absolutely no textual evidence on the basis of which to call these words into question, Streeter rejects them from Matthew nonetheless. The absence of any variants is to be attributed to *all extant* manuscripts sharing the same corruption—that is, Streeter believes these words were inserted later into Matthew's original text, which lacked these words, by later copyists. This is one way of overcoming a piece of evidence against one's position: suggest that all the manuscripts of the New Testament that contain the troublesome words are unoriginal and corrupted! If the genuineness of words in Luke 8:44 (see above) should be questioned on the slimmest of evidence, these words in Matt 26:68 can be rejected with no evidence at all.

This outrageous alternative from Streeter means that there are now *two* impossibilities here that one may choose to believe: (1) that both Matthew and Luke decided to add these identical words into the text of Mark that they were using; or (2) that these words are not really a part of Matthew's original Gospel at all, although they are in all extant manuscripts.

Other Positive Minor Agreements against Mark

There are several other instances of Matthew's and Luke's agreement against Mark that are not so clear cut and impressive as these three, but that nonetheless are difficult to account for on the basis of Markan Priority. When these are considered together, their cumulative impact makes it impossible to believe that *in all these cases* it just so happened that Matthew and Luke decided on the same changes to make to the text of Mark. For those changes are not so self-evident they would lead us to think that it would have occurred independently to both Matthew and Luke to make them.

In several places Matthew and Luke are in agreement in having a word or a point of detail where it is lacking in Mark—which the Markan Priority Hypothesis requires us to believe occurred to both Major Synoptists simultaneously to insert at this place, even though it was not in the source they were using. A number of these have been treated in detail earlier, and here are two others:

Mt 21:23 διδάσκοντι	Mk:27 [not in Mark]	Lk 20:1 διδάσκοντος
Matthew 13:11	**Mark 4:11**	**Luke 8:10**
ὑμῖν	ὑμῖν τὸ μυστήριον	ὑμῖν
δέδοται	δέδοται	δέδοται
γνῶναι τὰ μυστήρια		γνῶναι τὰ μυστήρια
τῆς βασιλείας	τῆς βασιλείας	τῆς βασιλείας
τῶν οὐρανῶν	τοῦ θεοῦ	τοῦ θεοῦ

10. Matthew and Luke Omitted the Negative Minor Agreements against Mark

The phrase "negative minor agreements" refers to those places where Matthew and Luke are in agreement in omitting material which (on the Markan Priority Hypothesis) they both had in front of them in Mark.

On hundreds of occasions both Matthew and Luke lack information that Mark contains. From the perspective of Markan Priority, this means that the two Major Synoptists have on all these occasions both chosen to delete the same words or expressions from Mark's account, though they are frequently words or expressions that add preciseness or vivid and striking eyewitness detail to the narrative. (The more significant of these occasions are tabulated in chap. 4: "Verses Unique to Mark" and "Shorter Details Unique to Mark.")

The most frequent way to account for the omission of this material in the Major Synoptics is to point out that in quite a number of cases the material lacking in Matthew and Luke (and thus unique to Mark) can be seen to consist of Markan expansions or repetitions. Thus these omissions can be attributed to a desire on the part of the two Major Synoptists to avoid unnecessary and repetitive material. But overall, as can be seen by an inspection of the material in question in chapter 4, most of it is not of this character. This material consists of details that clarify and sharpen the focus of the picture in the narrative.

A second reason is adduced for those omissions that are not of the first kind. Matthew and Luke were both conscious of a pressing need to keep the total length of their respective Gospels within manageable lengths. And yet *they themselves* not infrequently contain repetitions (doublets of words, sayings, or complete pericopes), while the inclusion of many of Mark's vivid details would have meant the addition of just a few words and sentences in various places of their narratives. Much of this material from Mark could have been retained without making any significant difference to the overall length of Matthew or Luke.

It is also maintained that at times both Matthew and Luke could have had doctrinal or other objections to what Mark contained. Such judgments are far from being beyond challenge; but even after allowing the widest latitude for such opinions, there still remain many *Sondergut* comments in Mark that these explanations do not cover. A few representative examples are now considered.

Information about Background and Circumstances

Several of Mark's unique comments are explanations that in one way or another clarify the circumstances being described. Thus Mark informs his readers that "the whole city was gathered together about the door" (1:33) when the sick were healed at nightfall; the explanation of the way in which the crowds filled the entire room (2:2) makes the rest of the story of the healing of the paralyzed man more understandable; the instruction to have a boat ready for him when he should need it (3:9) explains how it happened to be there when Jesus did use it later; a reason for the appointment of the Twelve was that they should be with Jesus (3:14); Jesus sent the disciples out in pairs on their mission (6:7); the Syrophoenician was a Greek (7:26), indicating that Jesus spoke to her in that language; the epileptic demon-possessed boy was both deaf and dumb (9:25); Jesus makes the sublime comment at his anointing, "She has done what she could" (14:8); the women were apprehensive about the size of the stone over the tomb and the difficulty of moving it (16:3–4). These examples are typical of a great number of similar instances.

Minor Descriptive Details of an Event

Mark frequently adds to the reader's ability to "see" the scene by means of a few words that sketch in the background or the circumstances. For example, the paralyzed man was carried by four others (2:3); when Jesus fell asleep in the boat, it was in the stern and on the cushion (4:38); at the feeding of the five thousand, the grass was green (6:39); Jesus took up a young child in his arms (9:36). There are many others.

When one examines the lists in chapter 4 of what Matthew and Luke (on the Markan Priority Hypothesis) chose to omit from Mark when using this Gospel as their source, it is very difficult to conceive why either one of them should exclude any of this information from his Gospel. None of the usual explanations, nor all of them together, can adequately explain it. But when it is a case that they have *both* chosen to leave out *all* of this, it moves quite beyond the realm of the unlikely. It is impossible to believe that Matthew and Luke both had all this information in front of them in Mark, while using Mark as their source, and both rejected all of it from their Gospels.

11. Matthew and Luke Made Transformational Minor Agreements against Mark

On not a few occasions Matthew and Luke changed the nature or form of what lay in front of them in Mark (on the Markan Priority Hypothesis), creating transformational minor agreements. Here are some instances.

Changing "Ran ahead" to "Followed"

The prologue to the feeding of the 5,000, mentions:

Matthew 14:13	Mark 6:33	Luke 9:11
But when the crowds heard it,	Now many saw them going, and knew them, and	But when the crowds learned it.
they followed him on foot from the towns.	they ran there on foot from all the towns, and got there ahead of them.	they followed him.

The similarity here between Matthew and Luke is quite marked, and both are distinctly different from Mark not only in the actual words used but also in the idea expressed. Matthew and Mark concur in "on foot from the towns," but otherwise Mark has nothing in common with Matthew or Luke. Markan Priority says that Mark is the source here for Matthew and Luke, which means that both Matthew and Luke had Mark in front of them but they both changed Mark in the same places: (1) Mark says many *saw* them going, but Matthew and Luke decide to change this direct basis for knowing about the departure of Jesus to *hearing* (Matthew) and *learning* (Luke); (2) both Major Synoptists changed *many* to *the crowds*; (3) Mark's emphasis is on the people *running* so that they *got there ahead of them*, but both Matthew and Luke change this idea and its wording and say "they followed him" (the Greek is identical in both these Gospels—ἠκολούθησαν αὐτῷ).

One puzzles over *why* they would both wish to make such an alteration to Mark, but no reason or justification for it is immediately apparent. Markan Priority claims that Mark is the most primitive Gospel—the closest to eyewitness testimony—so that Mark is the sole source of this pericope for Matthew and Luke. Thus one cannot say that both Matthew and Luke were *correcting* Mark for any reason. And one marvels that, having both decided (for some unguessable reason) to alter Mark's vivid account of how the people ran ahead to get to Jesus' landing point before him, they both opt, in lieu of Mark's wording, for the same bald statement, "they followed him." Perhaps we should adopt here Streeter's solution for similar problems and postulate an overlap of Mark and Q, with Luke adopting Q and Matthew conflating the two?

More preferable is the explanation that both Matthew and Luke reflect the tradition of this narrative as it was transmitted, while Mark follows his third source, Peter. Thus Peter was responsible for the way Mark tells this story: he describes in vivid and exciting language the way that some of the people ran along the seashore faster than Jesus and the disciples could travel in their boat, so that they got to their landing point ahead of them. This is exactly the kind of personal detail that Peter would include in recounting the story of what happened, and it is exactly the kind that would remain in Mark's memory and be used to add further vigor to the story that he had it in front of him in Matthew and Luke. Of course, it is also highly probable that some were not so nimble as those who beat Jesus and the disciples to their destination, so that these people were moving more slowly along the shore, following the progress of Jesus and the disciples in the boat, as Matthew and Luke indicate. So, which explanation of this pericope is more cohesive and believable—Markan Priority or Markan Dependence?

Additionally, this same pericope contains numerous other details unique to Mark that clearly suggest eyewitness recollection: the reason that Jesus sought to withdraw with his disciples to a lonely place (6:31–32); the estimate of how much bread money would be required to feed the crowd (6:37—paralleled in John but not the Major Synoptics); the greenness of the grass (6:39); and the vivid description of the way the crowds sat down, grouped (συμπόσια συμπόσια) as in flower beds (πρασιαὶ πρασιαὶ, 6:39–40). Markan Priority advocates claim that both Matthew and Luke decided to exclude all these details from their accounts. But Markan Dependence sees these details as further touches of eyewitness recollection that Mark included in his Gospel from his knowledge of the way Peter used to tell this story.

Reversal of Moses and Elijah

The pericope of the transfiguration has an example of the small agreements that exist between Matthew and Luke and that often go unnoticed: Matt 17:3 and Luke 9:30 state that "behold . . . Moses and Elijah" appeared and talked with Jesus, while Mark 9:4 lacks "behold" and has "Elijah with Moses." The Markan Priority Hypothesis necessitates that both Major Synoptists decided to add "behold" into their source at this point, and both also decided to change "Elijah with Moses" into "Moses and Elijah." The rationale for such a change is not clear. This pericope is the only place where the names of these two Old Testament saints are linked together in this way, and there is no inherent reason why they should appear in one order rather than the other. Why should *both* Major Synoptists decide to alter their source in these two minor particulars? Perhaps it was because immediately afterwards all three Synoptics record Peter as speaking of making booths for Moses and Elijah (in that order); this is a *possible* but hardly a *compelling* reason for both Matthew and Luke to have changed the order of Mark's wording.

The alternative explanation is that once again Mark chose to omit "behold." He does not use this term very often, and he lacks it on many of the occasions where it occurs in Matthew and/or Luke, so his omission of it here is consistent with what is found elsewhere. Mark speaks of "Elijah with Moses," thus highlighting Elijah slightly because Elijah is mentioned twice in the immediate context of this pericope (Mark 8:28; 9:11–13—Matthew parallels both; Luke only the first one).

Peter "Broke Down and Wept" to "Went Out and Wept Bitterly"

When the cock crowed and Peter remembered Jesus' prediction of his denials, his response was:

Matthew 26:75	Mark 14:72	Luke 22:62
And he went out and wept bitterly	And he broke down and wept	And he went out and wept bitterly
καὶ ἐξελθὼν ἔξω ἔκλαυσεν πικρῶς	καὶ ἐπιβαλὼν ἔκλαιεν	καὶ ἐξελθὼν ἔξω ἔκλαυσεν πικρῶς

If Mark was here the source for Matthew and Luke, then each of the Major Synoptists chose independently to alter "he broke down" to "he went out," changed the form of the verb "wept" from an aorist tense to an imperfect, and added the word "bitterly." There is no apparent reason from the text of Mark why either Major Synoptist should make such an alteration, let alone that both of them should do so simultaneously. The Greek word for "bitterly" (πικρῶς) used here by both Matthew and Luke *occurs nowhere else in the entire New Testament*. That both Matthew and Luke, starting from the text of Mark, should make such alterations and *should as a consequence of their independent alterations to Mark end up with this identical wording* is quite incredible.

Streeter's explanation (1924, 323) here is to draw attention to the absence from Luke's text of this verse in several early Latin manuscripts; he claims that the words are not original in Luke but that this verse in Luke's Gospel was assimilated to the text of Matthew. Something of this sort is virtually forced upon Markan Priority advocates because of the extreme unlikelihood that the words could have been adopted by Matthew and Luke independently if they were working from Mark's text. However, textual critics—even if they personally favor the Markan Priority Hypothesis—have not followed Streeter's judgment here. This is hardly surprising in view of the paucity of support for omitting the verse, which does occur in a great many other early Latin manuscripts, and is found in p[75], all the uncials (with the single exception of 0171, and even its absence there is not certain), the miniscules, and the ancient versions. The suggestion of rejecting this Lukan verse would hardly have been entertained were it not for the difficulty that it poses for Markan Priority.

The alternative explanation is that Mark, using Matthew and Luke, chose to alter their wording ("bitterly") to inform his readers that Peter, in recounting this story, told how he broke down when he wept.

From the Heavens Being Split Apart to Being Opened (Mark 1:10)

The pericope of the baptism of Jesus refers to the opening of the heavens and the descent of the Spirit on Jesus.

Matthew 3:16	Mark 1:10	Luke 3:21-22
καὶ ἰδοὺ ἠνεῴχθησαν οἱ οὐρανοί, καὶ ...ἐπ' αὐτόν	εἶδεν σχιζομένους τοὺς οὐρανοὺς καὶ ...εἰς αὐτόν	καὶ προσευχομένου ἀνεῳχθῆναι τὸν οὐρανὸν καὶ ...ἐπ' αὐτόν

Matthew 3:16 and Luke 3:21 say that the heavens "open" (ἀνοίγω), while Mark 1:10 says the heavens "split apart" (σχίζω). The verb ἀνοίγω is common in New Testament usage (78 occurrences), whereas σχίζω occurs only 11 times. Mark's only other use of this word (the splitting of the temple veil) is paralleled in both Major Synoptics (Matt 27:51//Mark 15:38//Luke 23:45). Matthew uses it also in 27:51 ("the rocks were split"—not in Mark's or Luke's parallel), and Luke has it twice in Jesus' saying about sewing on a patch (5:36— not in Matthew's or Mark's parallel). The word also occurs twice in Acts (14:4 and 23:7). Thus 5 of the 11 New Testament occurrences of σχίζω—approximately half—are in Luke's writings. It does not appear that either Matthew or Luke objected to the word, so if they were working from Mark 1:10 either of them *could* have accepted this word from Mark's account.

So there are two possibilities: (1) Matthew and Luke each simultaneously but independently rejected a word (σχίζω) in Mark that they happily adopted concerning the veil in the temple and that they both introduced into their own accounts elsewhere, choosing here to replace it with a more common and less colorful one. (2) Mark, writing third, introduced a word (σχίζω) into his account of the baptism of Jesus as one more instance of an observable preference for using the vivid and colorful word in his Gospel.

Another interesting element in this passage is that Matthew and Luke agree against Mark in having ἐπ' αὐτόν (Mark has εἰς αὐτόν).

A Network of Transformation (Mark 1:40-42)

The pericope of the healing of the leper (Matt 8:2–3//Mark 1:40–42//Luke 5:12–13) contains, as Farmer commented (1964, 145), "a continuous verbatim agreement between Matthew and Luke of eighteen consecutive words," some of which are also found in Mark, though Mark differs in a number of significant ways.

According to Markan Priority advocates, Matthew and Luke made a succession of changes—inserting, omitting, substituting, and transposing the order of words—that resulted in the two Major Synoptics being *identical in wording and word order for 18 successive words*. Further, Matthew and Luke did this while working independently of each other, each of them using Mark's account as his only source. Impossible.

Other Transformational Minor Agreements against Mark

There are several other agreements between Matthew and Luke against Mark where the same kinds of comments apply as for those just given. In all these cases the question is, Is it more believable that Matthew and Luke independently altered Mark in the same way, producing an identical text, or that Matthew and Luke were already in agreement in their wording when Mark received them, and Mark departed from that wording when writing his Gospel? Two of the more interesting and significant of these situations are Matt 9:7//Mark 2:12//Luke 5:25 and Matt 8:27//Mark 4:41//Luke 8:25. In the first example, Matt 9:7 and Luke 5:25 read ἀπῆλθεν εἰς τὸν οἶκον αὐτοῦ, while Mark 2:12 reads ἐξῆλθεν ἔμπροσθεν πάντων. In the second example, Matt 8:27 reads οἱ δὲ ἄνθρωποι ἐθαύμασαν; Mark 4:41 states καὶ ἐφοβήθησαν φόβον μέγαν; while Luke 8:25 says φοβηθέντες δὲ ἐθαύμασαν.

Other places where Matthew and Luke agree against Mark in the use of a word include:

Matt 4:1//Mark 1:13//Luke 4:2; Matt 9:11//Mark 2:16//Luke 5:30; Matt 9:16//Mark 2:21//Luke 5:36; Matt 12:4//Mark 2:26//Luke 6:4; Matt 12:10//Mark 3:1//Luke 6:6; Matt 9:20//Mark 5:27//Luke 8:44; Matt 10:14//Mark 6:11//Luke 9:5; Matt 14:20//Mark 6:43//Luke 9:17; Matt 16:6//Mark 8:15//Luke 12:1; Matt 16:21//Mark 8:31//Luke 9:22; Matt 16:24//Mark 8:34//Luke 9:23; Matt 17:16//Mark 9:18//Luke 9:40; Matt 20:19//Mark 10:34//Luke 18:33; Matt 20:33//Mark 10:51//Luke 18:41; Matt 21:2//Mark 11:2//Luke 19:30; Matt 22:19//Mark 12:15//Luke 20:24; Matt 22:23//Mark 12:18//Luke 20:27; Matt 22:27//Mark 12:22//Luke 20:32; Matt 22:45//Mark 12:37//Luke 20:44; Matt 24:34//Mark 13:30//Luke 21:32; Matt 26:16//Mark 14:11//Luke 22:6; Matt 26:39//Mark 14:36//Luke 22:42; Matt 26:51//Mark 14:47//Luke 22:50; Matt 27:31//Mark 15:20//Luke 23:26; Matt 27:54//Mark 15:39//Luke 23:47; Matt 27:54//Mark 15:39//Luke 23:47; Matt 27:58//Mark 15:43//Luke 23:52; and Matt 27:59//Mark 15:46//Luke 23:53.

In numbers of places Matthew and Luke agree in having the same form of a word or expression, while Mark has a different form of that word. The more significant of these differences are: Matt 9:17//Mark 2:22//Luke

5:37; Matt 13:9//Mark 4:9//Luke 8:8; Matt 13:11//Mark 4:11//Luke 8:10; Matt 10:1//Mark 6:7//Luke 9:1; Matt 17:22//Mark 9:31//Luke 9:44; Matt 19:20//Mark 10:20//Luke 18:21; Matt 19:27//Mark 10:28//Luke 18:28; Matt 21:2//Mark 11:2//Luke 19:30; Matt 21:3//Mark 11:3//Luke 19:31; Matt 21:8//Mark 11:8//Luke 19:36; Matt 24:2//Mark 13:2//Luke 21:6; Matt 24:29//Mark 13:25//Luke 21:26; and Matt 26:14//Mark 14:10//Luke 22:3.

12. Matthew and Luke Made Transpositional Minor Agreements against Mark

On not a few occasions Matthew and Luke change the position of what lay in front of them in Mark (on the Markan Priority Hypothesis), creating transpositional minor agreements. Here are some passages where this occurs.

Evil [and Adulterous] Generation

Jesus' teaching on conditions of discipleship occurs in the triple tradition (Matt 16:24–28//Mark 8:34–9:1//Luke 9:23–27). Jesus says, "For what can a man give in return for his life? For whoever is ashamed of me and of my words in this adulterous and sinful generation, of him will the Son of man also be ashamed, when he comes in the glory of his Father with the holy angels" (Mark 8:37–38). Most of this is paralleled in either Matthew or Luke or both: Matthew parallels the first sentence; Luke the next section; then Mark is alone in saying "in this adulterous and sinful generation," which is the only occurrence of the word "adulterous" (μοιχαλίς) in Mark; Luke parallels the next section, and both Matthew and Luke the final part. Why did both Matthew and Luke delete, "this adulterous and sinful generation"? But that is not all.

Mark quotes Jesus as saying, "Why does this generation seek a sign?" (8:12), and this is paralleled in Matt 16:4, "An evil and adulterous generation seeks for a sign," and in Luke 8:12, "This generation is an evil generation; it seeks a sign." The word "adulterous" only occurs in Matthew in this verse and in the doublet in 12:39; it does not occur in Luke at all. Both Matthew and Luke here refer to the generation as an "evil" generation.

It seems then (from the Markan Priority perspective) that both Matthew and Luke chose for some reason to remove Mark's "in this adulterous and sinful generation" from 8:38 (these words do not occur in the parallels of Matt 16:26 and Luke 9:26) and *both* of them alter the wording—Matthew to "an evil and adulterous generation" and Luke to "an evil generation," and then they *both* conflate it with Mark 8:12, where Mark has "this generation" without "adulterous" or "sinful" or "evil"! Why did they each independently decide on this transposition of Mark's comment about the generation from where *he* has it, in 8:38, to where they each put it, which is in their parallel of Mark 8:12?

Other Transpositional Minor Agreements against Mark

The most significant other transpositional agreement of Matthew and Luke against Mark is Mark 1:2//Matt 11:10//Luke 7:27, but because of its multifarious significance it is dealt with in detail separately below. In addition to these examples of transpositions to contexts removed from the original pericope in Mark, there are numerous instances where Matthew and Luke agree against Mark in transposing words within the one pericope. Here are two examples: (1) Matt 8:3 and Luke 5:13 agree against Mark 1:41; (2) Matt 9:6 and Luke 5:24 agree against Mark 2:10.

It is not necessary to list the many other instances of this kind. No difference of meaning results, but it is worth noting that (from the Markan Priority perspective) Matthew and Luke have agreed in independently making such transpositions in Mark's text.

Concerning the Minor Agreements

The foregoing is not a complete list of the different types of minor agreements, but I have included here the ones that seem to me the most significant. I selected them from the lists given by Hawkins (1909, 210–11), Streeter (1924, 295–331), Argyle (1961, 19–22), Turner (1959, 223–34), Tuckett (1983, 61–75), and Stoldt (1980, 18–21 and 263–80; his list is the fullest).

Clearly, some of these agreements can be explained from the perspective of Markan Priority (cf. Hawkins, 209) as being "improvements" made by Matthew and Luke to Mark's wording (e.g., φέρετε in 11:2), or else as both Major Synoptists independently choosing to use the same rather obvious alternative to Mark's word (κύριε for Mark's ραββουνί in 10:51). Others consist of less obvious changes and could be due to simple coincidence: Mark's wording differs from that of Matthew and Luke on hundreds of occasions, and if the Markan Priority Hypothesis is the real explanation of what happened, then all these differences must be due to both Matthew and Luke choosing to make frequent alterations to the text of Mark that each had in front of him. Given such an editorial attitude on the part of the two Major Synoptists, it would not really be surprising if in making all these editorial changes they should happen to select the same alternative word or expression on a dozen or two occasions.

But while this line of argument—which is commonly advocated by Markan Priorists (cf. Streeter 1924, 304)—can validly account for many of the minor agreements, there are others such as those above that cannot realistically be attributed to such causes. When Mark has a perfectly acceptable word or expression (especially one that the Major Synoptists themselves use elsewhere in their own Gospels), then it is far from obvious why they would have wanted to change it at all, and it represents a high level of coincidence that they should *both change it for the same word* when other forms of the word and indeed other words were available to them also. Numbers of the differences listed above between Mark on the one hand and Matthew and Luke on the other are of this kind.

Sanday (1911, 20–21) gives these additional explanations of the minor agreements between Matthew and Luke against Mark (his italics):

> And then, allowance may also be made for the possibility ... that we have not yet got back to the true text of one or other of the Gospels, and that when we have done so, the double coincidence against St. Mark will be found to disappear. ...
>
> But I believe that by far the greater number of the coincidences of Mt Lk against Mk are due to the use by Mt Lk—not of an *Ur-Marcus* or older form of the Gospel, but—*of a recension of the text of Mk different from that from which all the extent manuscripts of the Gospel are descended.*

Hawkins (1909, 212) accepts both of these explanations as accounting between them for any minor agreements not resulting from coincidence or deliberate and obvious correcting of Mark's grammatical shortcomings. Streeter (1924, 180) describes Sanday's explanation of Matthew and Luke using a different text of Mark from that now extant as being "the most probable" and expands on the idea:

> It involves no *a priori* difficulties. There would have been several copies of Mark at Rome at a very early date; and it is quite likely that one copyist would have felt free to emend the style a little. From this copy those used by Matthew and Luke may have been made, while the unrevised copies, being in the majority, may yet have determined the text that has come down to us.

Streeter also takes up the other suggestion, that many agreements against Mark exist in Matthew and Luke because of errors in our texts of one or more of the Gospels, and under the heading "Textual Corruption" (1924, 306–8) he removes many of the apparent agreements by choosing an alternative reading from the available textual variants. It should be noted that subsequent textual authorities—even those who themselves hold Markan Priority—have not followed Streeter in changing the text as he advocates, and Sanday's idea of a different recension of the text of Mark is totally speculative and unsupported by data of any kind.

There is another possible explanation for the minor agreements. Markan Dependence advocates would say that the traditions followed by Matthew and Luke were in agreement in their wordings and that Mark on these particular occasions chose not to follow them. Reasons for this are often fairly easy to imagine: (1) he chose a more colloquial expression, one more in line with his intended readership; (2) he chose a more expressive or impactful word (e.g., σχιζομένους); (3) he chose a form of words more in accordance with his own usage; (4) or, since he had *three* sources (not two) to use, he chose the word or expression that he had heard Peter use (perhaps the Aramaic form 'Ισκαριώθ for Judas the traitor rather than the Graecized 'Ισκαριώτης). Thus there are no difficulties in accounting for these passages from the perspective of Markan Dependence, and of course Mark could have had other additional reasons of which we now know nothing.

If one considers these various agreements between Matthew and Luke against Mark, which on the Markan Priority Hypothesis Matthew and Luke must have brought about by changes they made independently to Mark, and if one considers also the degree of improbability attaching to each one on its own and then the likelihood that *all of them* could be made in the course of two independent authors drawing upon Mark, it may be judged by a fair-minded person that here, in what Matthew and Luke must each have done to Mark's wording to produce this result, one indeed has another impossible thing to believe.

13. Q Explains the Major Agreements between Matthew and Luke against Mark

The major agreements of Matthew and Luke against Mark (in contradistinction from the minor agreements) are positive agreements that are more extensive in length. They are often referred to as the "Mark-Q overlaps," because that is the explanation for them given by Streeter and others. Streeter provides (1911, 167–78) a list of eight such passages:

1. John the Baptist's preaching (Mark 1:7–8);
2. the temptation (Mark 1:12–13);
3. the Beelzebub controversy (Mark 3:22–30);
4. five sayings (Mark 4:21–25);
5. the parable of the mustard seed (Mark 4:30–32);
6. the mission charge (Mark 6:7–11);
7. the seriousness of sin (Mark 9:42–50);
8. denunciation of the Pharisees (Mark 12:38–40).

Streeter also suggests a further eight places where he thought it possible that Mark and Q may have overlapped but doesn't discuss them in detail. In *The Four Gospels* (1924), Streeter reaffirms passages 1, 2, 3, 5, and 6 of the above list, adds the baptism of Jesus to this list (188), and then concludes (191), "There remain no other considerable passages where Mark and Q are parallel; for only portions of Mark 4:21–25 and Mark 9:42–50 have their equivalents in Q, and that in scattered contexts."

The passages that come to be placed into this category are ones that by their nature cannot be explained on the basis of Markan Priority, for they contain significant amounts of material not in Mark in which Matthew and Luke agree. If they had no Markan parallel, they could be simply attributed to Q. In these circumstances, however, many believe Mark and Q contained these pericopes. They do indeed merit our careful examination.

Tuckett discusses a number of these passages in some detail, and his conclusion is that these pericopes favor (in varying degrees) the Two-Document Hypothesis over the Griesbach Hypothesis (Markan Posteriority). Thus it is important to examine the basis on which Tuckett reached this conclusion and to determine the extent it is justified by the evidence. I now consider Streeter's comments on these passages and Tuckett's discussion of them.

John's Messianic Preaching

All three Synoptics have very similar content (though with differences of detail and order) in their introduction of John the Baptist (Matt 3:1–6//Mark 1:1–6//Luke 3:1–6). The two Major Synoptics are almost identical in their account of John's preaching (Matt 3:7–10//Luke 3:7–9); Luke then has a unique section (3:10–15); and at this point all three Synoptics record John's announcement of the Coming One and say "he will baptize you with the Holy Spirit." Mark stops here, but Matthew and Luke continue.

Matthew 3:11-12	Mark 1:8	Luke 3:16-17
he will baptize you with the Holy Spirit and with fire; whose winnowing fork is in his hand, and he will clear his threshing floor, and will gather his wheat into the granary, but the chaff he will burn with unquenchable fire.	he will baptize you with he Holy Spirit	he will baptize you with the Holy Spirit and with fire; whose winnowing fork is in his hand to clear his threshing floor, and to gather the wheat into his granary, but the chaff he will burn with unquenchable fire.

Thus John's preaching about the Coming One is in all three Synoptics and yet the pericope cannot be explained on the basis of Markan Priority: it is clear that Mark cannot here be the source for the other two because Matthew and Luke continue beyond Mark for a further 28 words (Matt 3:12//Luke

3:17). So they must have had another source for this material that they have in common.

Streeter commented (1911, 167–68):

> Now Mk 1:7–8 occurs almost word for word in Mt 3:11=Lk 3:16, but it is clear that Matthew and Luke did not derive the verse from Mark but from the same source whence they derived the preceding and following verses. . . .
>
> For (a) Matthew and Luke agree against Mark in ἐγὼ μὲν βαπτίζω for ἐγὼ ἐβάπτισα, in αὐτὸς ὑμᾶς βαπτίσει for αὐτὸς δὲ βαπτίσει ὑμᾶς in placing the announcement of ὁ ἰσχυρότερός between instead of before these two contrasted baptisms, and in the addition of the words καὶ πυρί.
>
> (b) What is still more significant, the subject of the relative οὗ in the verse which follows in Mt and Lk but does not occur at all in Mk (Mt 3:12=Lk 3:17) is contained in this verse which they have in common with Mark. Mt 3:12=Lk 3:17 has no meaning apart from the preceding verse, which therefore must have stood in Q and not have been derived by editors of Mt and Lk from Mark. Thus the verses Mt 3:11–12=Lk 3:16–17, or rather Mt 3:7–12=Lk 3:7–9,16–17, form one connected whole, of which Mk 1:7–8 is a mutilated fragment.

Thus Streeter here attributed what is common to Matthew and Luke to the source Q, so that what is found in all three Synoptics is not here to be explained on the basis that Mark is the source for the others, but that there exists an overlap of Mark and Q. Streeter affirms that this overlap was due to Mark's knowledge of the contents of Q, and his discussion (166–78) of the Mark-Q overlaps is part of his case for "St Mark's knowledge and use of Q" (his title for this essay). This was in 1911.

But by 1924 (*The Four Gospels*) Streeter had changed his mind about Mark's knowledge of Q. How then does he regard the Baptist's messianic preaching? He adheres to his explanation that this is an overlap of Mark and Q (188), but apart from listing the passage in this category—and making the suggestion (206) that Q contained a reference to baptism with fire that Matthew and Luke independently conflated with Mark's "with the Holy Spirit"—Streeter does not deal with this pericope at all in the entire volume.

Tuckett does not deal with the story of the Baptist in Mark 1.

The Temptation

The temptation pericope (Matt 4:1–11//Mark 1:12–13//Luke 4:1–13) is similar to the Baptist's messianic preaching in that it occurs in all three Synoptics, but Mark contains only part of what is found in Matthew and Luke. Thus Q is invoked as the source for the entire accounts in the Major Synoptics, and here again Mark is seen as overlapping with Q. Streeter commented (1911, 168):

Mark's brief allusion to the Temptation, 1:12–13, is less original than the longer account of Q, Mt 4:1–11, Lk 4:1–13. An original tradition is always detailed and picturesque, and would hardly record as does Mark a temptation to do nothing in particular. A later author might well allude to a story whose details were familiar, but which he could not entirely omit to notice in a life of the Master.

Streeter follows this comment with a very perceptive observation (168–69): "Thus at the outset we are struck by the fact that the first thirteen verses of Mark, so unlike his usual picturesque diffuseness, read like a summary of a longer and fuller account, which the author gives because it had become the recognized introduction to a Gospel writing, but which he hurries through in order to get on to his own special matter."

At this point Streeter is only a hair's breadth away from the recognition that (for the so-called "overlap" passages at least) Mark has derived his material from Matthew or Luke or both. Instead, he concludes that Mark derived them from Q, whence also Matthew and Luke obtained these stories.

But years later, Streeter continues to list the temptation with his "overlap" stories (1924, 188, 211), though (as we have seen) he abandons Q as a source for Mark. In view of his analysis of the nature of Mark 1:1–13, one would think that this *must* lead him logically to see Matthew and/or Luke as the source for Mark here. But it doesn't. So how does Streeter account for, as he perceived in 1911, "the fact that the first thirteen verses of Mark, so unlike his usual picturesque diffuseness, read like a summary of a longer and fuller account, which the author gives because it had become the recognized introduction to a Gospel writing"? He doesn't. He avoids facing the implications of his own assessment of Mark. In fact, in *The Four Gospels* he does not discuss the pericopes of Mark 1:1–13 in any detail.

Tuckett contends that Mark's temptation narrative poses "enormous difficulties" for the Griesbach view because of the additional detail that it contains, brief as it is, and because of its difference of perspective. Thus he concludes that overall this indicates "that Mark does not offer here simply an excerpt from Matthew" (1983, 89f.). He maintains (90) that "once again the overlap of two independent sources seems to be the most satisfactory answer to the literary problems here."

To Tuckett we can reply, once again the best explanation of the text is that Mark is working from (and here, significantly abbreviating) Matthew and Luke, and also drawing on some details from his knowledge of source P (Peter). In fact, the best analysis of the situation remains that given by Streeter in 1911 (cited above), which is fully compatible with the Markan Dependence explanation set out in this study.

The Beelzebul Controversy

The setting given for this pericope (Matt 12:22–45//Mark 3:20–30//Luke 11:14–32; see Luke 12:10) in Matthew and Luke is an exorcism (the details differ slightly). The people marvel. But then it is asserted—in Matthew by the Pharisees and in Luke by "some of them"—that Jesus casts out demons by Beelzebul the prince of demons. Jesus, knowing their thoughts, speaks to them.

In Mark the circumstances are different (3:19–21). There is no mention of the exorcism. Jesus goes home, and because of the crowds he cannot find time even to eat. His family, hearing this, go out to seize him, saying, "He is beside himself." Scribes arrive from Jerusalem and say that Jesus is possessed by Beelzebul, and it is by the prince of demons that he casts out demons. Jesus calls them to him and speaks to them in parables. Immediately following Mark's record of Jesus' words Mark adds, "For they had said, 'He has an unclean spirit.'" Mark then describes the arrival of his mother and brothers and their request to speak to him—presumably a follow-up from the earlier reference to their setting out to seize him.

There are numbers of places here where Matthew and Luke have positive and negative agreements against Mark, and overall the two Major Synoptics contain in this context a considerable amount of material lacking in Mark. The pericope is in all three Synoptics, but the data is such that it cannot be explained on the basis that Matthew and Luke used Mark as their source. Thus Streeter explains (1911, 170–71; 1924, 189) this pericope as a Mark-Q overlap.

Tuckett commences his examination of the Beelzebul controversy with this comment (1983, 85):

> But how must Mark have treated his sources if these sources were Matthew and Luke? Initially, Mark must have ignored the context, i.e. the occasion of an exorcism, which is in both his sources. Yet this would be despite the fact that (1) the charge of being in league with, or possessed by, Beelzebub now comes very abruptly in Mark, and (2) Mark is usually very ready to record exorcisms: indeed this is the only non-Markan exorcism in the whole Gospel tradition.

Tuckett seeks to turn a difficulty into an argument: *both* Matthew and Luke have the same exorcism context for this incident. The strength of Tuckett's comment is the unlikelihood that Mark would ignore an exorcism to which the Major Synoptics give concurrent testimony. But the very fact to which Tuckett draws attention can explain the situation. Mark provides his readers with enough evidence for Jesus' performing exorcisms so that he does *not* need a specific example immediately before recording the charge of being in league with Beelzebul. Moreover, to assert that "Mark must have ignored the context" is to write in a subjective way about the situation. What in fact we find is not an *absence* of context in Mark but a *difference* of context, a short pericope found only in Mark: the circumstance that led to Jesus' family setting out to seize him because "they were saying, 'He is beside himself.'"

Thus what is happening here (and Tuckett's comments do *not* make this clear) is that Mark records *two* separate accusations being made against Jesus, one by his family ("he is mad") and the other by "the scribes who came down from Jerusalem" ("he has Beelzebul"). In a sandwich-type pericope arrangement, Mark deals first with the second of these (3:22–30) and then follows this with the arrival of Jesus' family and what happened next (3:31–35). Mark indicates that the scribes from Jerusalem arrived *while his family was traveling to him* and then *they* arrived at the end of his comments on the Beelzebul issues. In this latter detail Mark concurs with Matthew, who records (Matt 12:46) that it was "while he was still speaking to the people" that his mother and brothers arrived. Markan Dependence says that Mark did not see the need to record here a brief exorcism reference, and that is all it is in Matthew and Luke—it hardly constitutes an *account* of the healing. Instead, Mark gives what Matthew and Luke do not: the circumstances that led to Jesus' family arriving to see him at this time.

[Mark uses this same type of arrangement elsewhere. In Mark 6:7–13 the Twelve are commissioned and sent out; in 6:14–29 he says that Herod heard about Jesus, and then explains the circumstances of the Baptist's death; in 6:30 the Twelve return after their mission. The components of this "sandwich" are found in Matthew and Luke; in this form it is unique to Mark. A similar "sandwich" is the story of Jairus's daughter and the woman with a hemorrhage (Mark 5:21–43), which *is* paralleled in Matthew and Luke in this form.]

In discussing this Beelzebul pericope, Tuckett several times makes a point that, on the Griesbach perspective, "Here Mark avoids what is common to his sources" (1983, 86; also 85, 86 again). He cites Streeter (1924, 89): "The verbal resemblances between the two accounts [Mark and Luke] are no more than would be inevitable if they represent two quite independent traditions of the same original incident." This Tuckett agrees with and concludes (89), "Thus the best solution is that Matthew is not a source of the other two accounts, but a later conflation of them. There is thus good reason to believe that there are here, in Mark and Luke, two quite independent versions of the pericope, with Matthew as a later conflation of the two forms."

But there is no basis in the text for preferring this explanation to that of Markan Dependence: here indeed are two independent versions of the pericope, but these independent versions are *Matthew* and *Luke* (note that Luke has sections corresponding to Matthew in the order Luke 11:14–23; 12:10; 6:43–45; 11:16,29–32; 11:24–26). Then Mark drew on Matthew and Luke (primarily Matthew, which he was following here for his order, because the main Lukan parallels are in Luke's central travel and teaching section that Mark has preferred to ignore). Again, Mark combines this material with what he knew from P.

The Parable of the Mustard Seed

In 1911 (173), Streeter comments on the parable of the mustard seed (Matt 13:31–32//Mark 4:30–32//Luke 13:18–19): "There are twelve small verbal coincidences between Matthew and Luke against Mark, which show that their version is not derived from him but from Q. What is more important is the fact that in both Matthew and Luke the Parable of the Leaven is appended. . . . Mark's single parable here is therefore a mutilation of an original pair in Q." In 1924 (190), after his change of heart about Mark knowing Q, Streeter accepts a suggestion that

> in Mark the Mustard Seed does not stand alone; it is paired with the parable of the Seed growing secretly, which is quite as appropriate a twin as the Leaven to illustrate the idea of the gradual growth of the Kingdom. It would seem, then, that the twin-parable argument really cuts the other way, and suggests that in Mark and Q we have two pairs which descended along quite independent lines of tradition.

But Sanders (1973) considers that Streeter's earlier comment continues to be very significant. After quoting it, he says (456):

> Now, one of the important proofs of the priority of Mark is that Matthew and Luke do not place the same Q material in the same place in the Marcan Outline. But the Parable of the Leaven is Q material. In both Matthew and Luke, it follows immediately after the parable of the mustard seed. Thus the parable of the mustard seed *must* have stood in Q as well as in Mark. The only alternative is the establishment of an agreement between Matthew and Luke which cannot be explained away.

Tuckett commences his consideration of the Mark-Q Overlap Passages with this pericope and comments (1983, 79), "Given that Mark has chosen to include this parable, the detailed wording of his version also presents problems for the Griesbach hypothesis." He discusses the differences between the three Synoptic versions of the parable, assessing what changes must have been made by Mark if he were writing last, and says (80–81):

> It is possible that some of these last changes are due to Mark's efforts to make the picture more true to life: a mustard plant is not a tree, and birds might shelter under the shadow of the leafy branches but not in the branches themselves.

But this will not account for all the changes. For the overall picture, if Mark is using Matthew and Luke as his sources, is that Mark has carefully and systematically avoided everything that is common to Matthew and Luke: where they agree, Mark disagrees, and where Matthew disagrees with Luke, Mark follows Matthew closely. Thus Mark appears to have taken an intense dislike to Luke (apart from the form, but not the wording, of the opening double question), and to have gone through Matthew's text, changing it where Matthew and Luke agree, and leaving it alone where they differ. Moreover, the result is, in places, grammatical chaos. This seems such an incoherent redactional procedure, and so inconsistent with Farmer's general thesis about Mark's redactional method ("not to deviate from the text to which his predecessors bore concurrent testimony") that it must place a serious question mark against his overall theory.

There is in fact a strong case to be made for the traditional solution to the problem of literary relationships here. For there is evidence favoring the existence of two independent versions of the parable, namely the Markan one and the Lukan one. The difficulties which the Griesbach hypothesis encounters are due mainly to the fact that Mark and Luke have virtually nothing in common beyond the barest essentials necessary for telling a parable comparing the Kingdom of God to a mustard seed. . . . Apart then from the form (but not the actual wording) of the introduction, there is no point of contact at all between Mark and Luke except what is necessary to tell the story at all. . . .

The result of this analysis is that there is strong evidence for the "existence of obviously different versions" (to use Streeter's terms). There is a non-Markan source here which probably extended to the parable of the leaven too (in view of the very similar introductions). Luke's source cannot be Matthew, as the Griesbach hypothesis would maintain, since Luke would have then changed Matthew's wording in a wholly uncharacteristic way. Rather, Luke's source must be a common source prior to both Matthew and Luke. If one calls this source "Q" (without necessarily postulating what else might belong to it), one must conclude that there is here a "Mark-Q overlap." Further, the Q form of the parable can be seen in Luke, since Luke appears to have copied his source with very little change.

Tuckett's analysis deserves several comments. He has adduced very little evidence here for holding that Matthew could have altered Luke but not vice versa. This evidence (83f.) consists of the claims (1) that "Matthew's version has links with both the other accounts. . . . Since these verbal agreements are so great, some sort of direct literary relationship between Matthew and each of the others is demanded"; (2) that "in some instances, Luke's wording is not characteristic of Luke himself, whilst Matthew's different version is characteristic of Matthew"; and (3) that "certainly it is unlikely that Luke would have wanted to change an original ἀγρός (9 times in Luke, 1 in Acts); on the other hand, a change by Matthew to ἀγρός if κῆπος had stood in his source is quite intelligible given Matthew's liking for this word (he uses it 16 times, and cf. the use of it in verses 24, 27, 44 of this chap.).

Thus again there is evidence of the existence of a pre-Lukan source with Matthew rewriting it in his own idiom."

On the Markan Dependence Hypothesis there is of course another explanation available for (1), as we have seen in this study: some early documents produced by the apostle Matthew containing a pericope or pericopes were incorporated into the Gospels of Matthew and Luke. Tuckett's evidence for (2) consists of a deduction drawn from Luke's use of "the ὁμοιο-root" and ἔβαλεν, a deduction that appears to have as an unstated premise the proposition that if a writer does not use an expression often enough for it to be classified as "characteristic" of him, he obviously would not think of using it at all. Both (2) and (3) are perfectly explicable by Markan Dependence.

Tuckett's proposal is a slim basis on which to conclude that "Luke appears to have copied his source with very little change" while "Matthew has rewritten the source in his own idiom." The belief that Luke uses his sources without making any substantial changes in them may (or may not) be valid from the perspective of Markan Priority explanation of the Synoptic data; it has to be established separately as applicable from the Markan Dependence perspective, and without doing so it cannot be evoked (as Tuckett has done) as a factor in discussions of how redaction would have been carried out from that latter perspective. In fact, as seen in chapter 4 (on words in the Synoptics) it would appear on the basis of available evidence that, even from the perspective of Markan Priority, Luke cannot accurately be said "to have copied his source with very little change" but has substantially rewritten his sources—he has omitted or changed rather more than three out of every four words that he had in front of him in Mark. Perhaps it would be better to say that he used his sources as *sources*—that is, he used them for the information he needed for his own account, and has utilized this information according to his own purposes in writing. Certainly *the evidence does not justify* the claim that his sources were incorporated into his text virtually unchanged. This comment that I have just made (on Luke's willingness to reword his sources), on the basis of Morgenthaler's statistics, remains true under both the Markan Priority and the Markan Dependence perspectives.

More importantly, Tuckett did not adduce any basis for preferring the Markan Priority explanation of the data. In fact, he has offered us a choice of *two* alternative explanations.

The parable of the mustard seed ends thus:

Matt 13:32	Mark 4:32	Luke 13:19b
but when it	yet when it	and it

Matt 13:32	Mark 4:32	Luke 13:19b
has grown it is the greatest of shrubs	is sown it grows up and becomes the greatest of all shrubs	grew
and becomes a tree	and puts forth large branches	and became a tree
so that the birds of the air come and make nests in its branches.	so that the birds of the air can make nests in its shade.	and the birds of the air made nests in its branches.

If Mark is the source for Matthew and Luke, then both the Major Synoptists, with Mark in front of them, decided to omit Mark's reference to putting forth large branches, referring instead to it becoming a tree, and they also both change his final word "shade" into "branches." Streeter says (1924, 209) that the parable of "the Mustard Seed . . . must be assigned to Q" and explains (246ff.) the form of the Synoptic data on the basis of Matthew's conflation of Mark and Q (found in Luke). That is, he considers that Mark and Q overlap for this parable, that Luke has followed Q, and that Matthew has conflated both. This is a tacit acknowledgment of the difficulty of seeing Mark's wording as the source of the other two Synoptics.

We can note Tuckett's explanation (1983, 80) of the agreement here of Matthew and Luke against Mark:

> As for the end-result of the seed's growth, Matthew and Luke agree that it "becomes a tree," γίνομαι and δένδρον being common to both. Mark uses neither of these common words and talks instead of "making great branches." Matthew alone has a ὥστε construction which Mark accepts. Finally Matthew and Luke agree verbatim in having an allusion to Dan 4:21 (Theod.) with the birds nesting in the branches; Mark avoids this and has the birds resting in the shade, probably alluding to Ezek 17:23.
>
> It is possible that some of these last changes are due to Mark's efforts to make the picture more true to life: a mustard plant is not a tree, and birds might shelter under the shadow of the leafy branches but not in the branches themselves. But this will not account for all the changes.

Tuckett then outlines difficulties that he sees overall for the Griesbach explanation.

Tuckett's comments deserve some reflection. Mark says that the mustard seed has become the greatest of all shrubs, putting forth large branches under which the birds can nest. Tuckett suggests, reflecting a comment by Wenham (1972, 35), that this is a reference to Ezek 17:23. In fact, Ezek

17:22–23 speaks of God planting a young twig from a *cedar tree*, which "shall become a mighty cedar, and every bird [ὄρνεον] shall rest [ἀναπαύσεται] beneath it, and every bird [πετεινόν] shall rest [ἀναπαύσεται again] in its shade."

Tuckett's view suggests that both Matthew and Luke—with the text of Mark in front of them—decided to alter it, and they did so by making it an allusion to Dan 4:21, Daniel's interpretation of Nebuchadnezzar's dream: "The tree . . . whose leaves were fair and its fruit abundant, and in which was food for all; under which beasts of the field found shade, and in whose branches the birds of the air dwelt." Tuckett notes that this is not, however, an allusion to the Septuagint version but to the translation of the Old Testament by Theodotion. This translation was made in the second century (c. AD 160). It has been noted concerning the New Testament period that (DNTT, 3:494) "the textual tradition was at that time still fluid. Thus NT citations sometimes show similarities to forms of the text that were later used by Theodotion, Aquila and Lucian as the basis of their translations." Certainly Matthew and Luke did not use Theodotion's translation of the Old Testament—that was not published until perhaps a century later. So (if Tuckett's suggestion is right) both Matthew and Luke must have had access to the same non-Septuagintal form of translation of Dan 4:21 (which later became part of Theodotion's version), and both must have chosen to insert this wording at this same point in Mark's account, in place of his (Mark's) allusion to Ezekiel. Tuckett in the end (85) prefers Streeter's explanation: "one must conclude that there is here a 'Mark-Q overlap.'"

The Markan Dependence explanation is that (as indeed Streeter and Tuckett accept) Matthew and Luke did not follow Mark but they had separate and independent forms of the story. Then Mark drew on each of these (on Matthew here to some extent, and Luke hardly at all) and was also influenced by the form of this story as he knew it from the preaching of Peter. Mark's wording "in their shade" may possibly have been influenced by Ezekiel 17, as Wenham and Tuckett suggest. Or his version of the parable may have been more influenced by the realities of the scene being described: birds could certainly find shade and shelter from a mustard shrub, but they could hardly nest in its branches. Or Mark may have simply recorded the way that Peter used to tell the story, which in its turn may represent what Jesus said on one occasion, while the Matthew-Luke tradition could record the wording of another telling of the parable by Jesus on a different occasion (see below).

In view of the independence here of the versions of Matthew-Luke and Mark—this is common ground, since Markan Priorists do not view Mark here as the source for Matthew-Luke—it must be accepted that Mark has *some* source other than the Matthew-Luke tradition, though Mark could have conflated this source with Matthew-Luke. Granted this, then *that* source could explain why Mark has "shade" rather than "branches."

Thus the problems for the Griesbach Hypothesis that Tuckett thinks are posed by this pericope are nonexistent, if one accepts that Matthew and Luke are similar but independent accounts and that Mark conflates Matthew with his source P. (Luke's version of the parable occurs in his central travel and teaching section, which Mark has preferred to ignore.) Markan Dependence thus offers a totally reasonable and coherent explanation for the data. But Markan Priority is forced to say, "Here is a pericope in the Triple Tradition, but Mark is not here the source for the others—Q is, and then Matthew conflates Mark and Q."

The Five Sayings

Streeter mentions Mark 4:21–25, but does not cover it in detail. Tuckett looks at it and notes that these sayings occur in the same context in Mark and Luke, but differ somewhat in their wording. He considers this to be a difficulty for the Griesbach view because (1983, 91)

> Mark must have switched at this point to following Luke as his main source; but then, in the first two logia, he must have omitted very carefully all those small details which bring Luke's version closer to Matthew. . . . Far from reproducing the "concurrent testimony" of his sources, Mark seems carefully to have avoided doing so at this point. Further, Mark must have made other small changes in Luke which make his version even more unlike Matthew's.

He concludes (92) in regard to this passage, as he has for the other passages he has been discussing, "Thus, in this passage, the analysis above indicates that Mark probably has independent versions of the sayings, and one is justified in talking of an overlap of sources." It needs to be noted here that in Matthew these five sayings are scattered in six other different contexts (one of them occurs twice with slightly different wording) and that in general the wording of Mark is closer to that of Luke than to these sayings in Matthew (the exception is part of Mark 4:24).

The Markan Dependence view says that these sayings are given at this point (after the explanation of the parable of the sower) *because that is where Luke has them*—that is, their position in Luke determines their position in Mark, and their *wording* reflects Mark's familiarity with them as teachings of Jesus that were doubtless quoted and used often in the church (by Peter and/or others). Mark's familiarity with Jesus' teachings current in the Christian church cannot be left out of the discussion of his wording of sayings such as these (see below).

The Mission Charge to the Twelve
(Matt 9:35-10:42//Mark 6:6b-13//Luke 9:1-6)

In the mission charge to the Twelve (Matt 9:35–10:42//Mark 6:6b–13// Luke 9:1–6), Mark's account parallels Matt 9:35–10:14//Luke 9:1–6 (except for Matt 9:35b–38; 10:5–8,12–13, which is not in Mark; and Matt 10:2–4 gives the names of the Twelve, which Mark has at 3:13–19). Mark has a parallel for Matt 10:17–25 in another context (the Olivet Discourse of Mark 13:9–13). Mark has no parallel for Matt 10:15–16,26–42. Thus Mark parallels only a few verses out of a much longer mission charge discourse in Matthew. Some of Matthew's charge to the Twelve is paralleled in Luke's charge to the 70 (Luke 10:1–12).

For this material, Streeter (1911, 175) considered that "Q therefore contained substantially all that Mark gives in much the same language, and in addition six sayings which are intimately connected with them. Again, therefore, Mark's version is a mutilated excerpt of Q." In 1924 Streeter's explanation is (190):

> Mt 10:5–16 is clearly a conflation of the Q discourse, given by Luke as the Charge to the Seventy (Lk 10:1–12), with Mark's discourse on the Mission of the Twelve (Mk 6:7–11). . . . Assuming, then, that Lk 10:1–12 (not being conflate with Mark) represents Q, the differences between Mark and Luke are so great and the resemblances so few that they favour the view that Mark's version is independent, not derived from Q. If Mark did use Q, he must have trusted entirely to memory and never once referred to the written source.

Markan Dependence says that in this entire section Mark follows the order of Luke, and thus lists the Twelve earlier. For the charge, Mark follows Luke's much shorter version, though with a number of minor differences that reflect his practice of adding in details and rewording his material—doubtless influenced by the preaching of Peter.

The Significance of the Major Agreements

From these pericopes (and, to a lesser extent, from the other "overlap" passages mentioned by Streeter) one can see that there are a number of places where all three Synoptics are recounting the same story and where Matthew and Luke contain substantial positive agreements against Mark. If Mark is the source for Matthew and Luke, one is required at such points to believe that Matthew and Luke simultaneously and independently decided to depart from Mark in an identically worded change or series of changes: or else that at these points they were both following some other source. Now the former of these alternatives is clearly an unbelievable explanation for these particular pericopes. But the second is in fact just as fatal to the Markan Priority position.

In such a case, Mark is not the source for Matthew and Luke for material in common to all three Synoptics. But whatever argument leads us to postulate in these cases an alternative source (that is, other than Mark) could also justify holding this non-Markan source to be the origin of other Synoptic material that also happens to occur in Mark.

This means that one is obliged to call on a source other than Mark to account for the observable data (as described above). Having invoked this source, there is then no basis (other than subjective opinion) on which one can thereafter exclude the possibility that this other source, Q, could have been used by Mark and thus could have been the source for the rest of the common material in the Synoptics. Simpson makes (1966, 274) the excellent point that "the more strongly we plead the case for Q as a means of explaining all those resemblances between Matthew and Luke which are not attributable to their common use of Mark, the more we undermine the theory of the priority of Mark." Once we open the door for the use of Q to explain Matthew-Luke agreements against Mark, it is very hard to keep it open only for the major agreements. Streeter also clearly perceived the danger of using Q indiscriminately for resolving agreement problems; he warned (1924, 305):

> Some scholars, however, have laid far too much stress on the bearing of the overlapping of Mark and Q on the problem of the minor agreements. We have no right to call in the hypothesis of the influence of Q for this ulterior purpose except in places where the existence of obviously different versions, or of doublets very distinctly defined, provides us with objective evidence of the presence of Q.

Sanders (1973, 454–55) quotes Streeter's warning and then comments,

> Streeter was quite right to make this stipulation. Those who wish to explain all or most of the agreements between Matthew and Luke against Mark by attributing them to the influence of Q are simply arguing for an Ur-Gospel which very closely resembles Matthew. . . . If Q were made responsible for all these agreements, in addition to the traditional Q material, it would be very much like Matthew. To expand the theory of Mark-Q overlaps much beyond Streeter's bounds is simply to deny the two-source hypothesis.

But once the door is opened at all in this way, Streeter cannot impose limits on how wide it can be opened by means of his exercise of some omnipotent fiat, "Thus far and no further!" Or, to use his actual words, "We have no right to call in the hypothesis of the influence of Q for this ulterior purpose except . . ."—and then he states the limits that appear to him reasonable. But, despite his invocation of "objective evidence," how he defines those limits and where he places them is completely arbitrary and subjective.

The fact is, if Q can be seen as containing some material that is also found in Mark (i.e., the "overlaps"), then there is no basis on which it can be asserted with any confidence or on any objective evidence that *any* particular pericope in Mark could not also have been found in Q. The test for this assertion is simple: name *one Markan pericope* that *could not have also occurred in Q*, and then provide the data and the argument that shows that its occurrence in Q is impossible.

In summary, the whole of Streeter's argument throughout his entire discussion of the Mark-Q overlaps in his 1911 essay is completely consistent with Mark having derived his material from Matthew and/or Luke rather than from Q. It is therefore a very pertinent question for us to ask, rather, Why should one call on the hypothetical Q as a source for Mark when everything in Mark in these pericopes can be explained very well on the basis of known and extant Gospels?

Moreover, if the "sayings source" Q is to be expanded as needed, in order to include all these larger sections of material in which Matthew and Luke have positive agreements against Mark, on what basis (other than pure arbitrariness) can it be decided that Q cannot have included other pericopes in which there are similarly striking and significant (though shorter) positive agreements of Matthew and Luke against Mark?

Streeter shrank from that, for it would result in Q assuming the dimensions of an Ur-Gospel similar in form and contents to Matthew. Instead, he sought for other ways of handling the "minor agreements." And he saw the fundamental danger of his contention that Q was a source for Mark—for if so, then all the material that according to Markan Priority was derived from Mark by Matthew and Luke could have been derived by Mark from Q. Then it was a very small step to dispensing with Markan Priority altogether and accepting that Matthew and Luke drew their material directly from Q: the Ur-Gospel Hypothesis (see chap. 10).

Thus by 1924 Streeter had withdrawn from his position that Mark knew Q. He still held to the Mark-Q overlap explanation of the major agreements of Matthew and Luke against Mark, but in abandoning the thesis that Mark used Q he had also abandoned the strongest part of his case (in his 1911 essay) for the overlaps. In 1911, he built up a substantial edifice on which to hang his "overlaps" case. In 1924, he removed the edifice, leaving his "overlaps" case hanging in the air—like the smile that remained after the Cheshire cat had gone.

What does Tuckett say in weighing these issues? We have noted the four of the so-called Mark-Q overlaps that Tuckett discusses—the parable of the mustard seed, the Beelzebul controversy, the temptation, and the five sayings. His conclusion is (1983, 92–93):

> In all the passages considered in this chapter, the synoptic interrelationships are very difficult to explain by the Griesbach hypothesis in the form advocated by Farmer. Mark's redactional motives cannot be what Farmer claims them to be. Either Mark followed a totally different plan of dealing with his sources in these passages from elsewhere in the tradition, or else the underlying theory of synoptic interrelationships is wrong. In all these passages there is evidence of the existence of two distinct versions, a Markan and a non-Markan, and these two are independent of each other. The best explanation of these passages remains the traditional solution of an overlap of Mark with an independent source lying behind Matthew and Luke. Since, therefore, the Two-Document hypothesis gives a more coherent, and self-consistent, picture of the overall redaction involved than does the Griesbach hypothesis, it must be preferred unless advocates of the Griesbach hypothesis can suggest a more convincing rationale behind Mark's alleged redactional procedure.

Thus Tuckett concludes that the overlap of Mark and Q provides the most coherent explanation of the Synoptic texts. But one must notice carefully what he says. The key clause in Tuckett's conclusion is "the Griesbach hypothesis in the form advocated by Farmer" (1983, 92). This was that Luke's account was derived from Matthew, and that the differences between Matthew and Luke were redactional. But we have seen that when Tuckett argues against Luke's use of Matthew he argues against *Farmer* but not against *Griesbach*, who did not advocate this; and there are fundamental and compelling reasons (see chap. 8) for recognizing the basic independence of the Gospels of Matthew and Luke.

Moreover, one must notice what Tuckett is comparing in coming to his conclusion that a Mark-Q overlap is the better explanation. For example, in the temptation story he says (89), "There are here enormous difficulties for the Griesbach hypothesis, since Mark's account has virtually nothing in common with that of Matthew and Luke, and indeed presents major differences." Thus Tuckett is going outside the three Synoptics to another source (Q) to explain the pericopes, *but he does not allow Griesbach to do so*, and he then concludes that the Two-Document account, i.e., Markan Priority *plus Q*, provides a more coherent explanation than the Griesbach Hypothesis—by which Tuckett means that Mark drew from Matthew and Luke *without reference* to any other source. Yet the nature of Mark is such as to require another source (or sources), and this *is plainly stated by Griesbach as part of his Synoptic theory*. That is, Griesbach recognizes that Mark drew on his own extensive knowledge of the Jesus traditions in the writing of his Gospel—this would include what he knew from Peter as a source, but need not be limited to Peter alone. Griesbach's actual comments are (1978, 110f., 134):

> Mark, I insist, was able to learn many things that could not have been known to everyone, because his mother lived in a house in Jerusalem in which the apostles and other Christians used to hold their meetings (Acts 12:12); moreover he had at one time been the servant and companion of both Peter and Paul and had without doubt learnt from them and their intimate friends many deeds and sayings of the Lord well worth relating; and lastly it was Mark too who enriched the narratives of Matthew and Luke with so many special details . . . , so that it was clear to all that he knew the story of Christ very well and could have told us a great many more anecdotes about him, if he had wished.
>
> This one thing can perhaps be conceded, namely that Mark received from Peter the circumstantial details, with which he enriched throughout the narratives of Luke and Matthew; although even this is not quite certain, for they could also be derived from another source.

This quote clearly shows that Griesbach considered that Markan detail came either from Peter and/or from some other source within Mark's general knowledge of the circumstances of Jesus' life and ministry. Thus Tuckett's comments in this instance hardly constitute fair dealing with a viewpoint from which he differs. He does *not* answer the Griesbach Hypothesis, but gives us instead a bowdlerized version of it. *Tuckett* makes use of an additional source in his explanation, and declines to notice that *so does Griesbach* in *his* Synoptic explanation. And this third source for Mark is also an important element in the Markan Dependence explanation.

If one acknowledges—as the evidence shows is necessary—that Mark had another source or sources on which he drew, then in the cases where Mark was not following Matthew and Luke, he was recording the way this story was told by his other source(s).

Tuckett records the line of argument that leads him (and others) to the conclusion that there was another source, Q, that paralleled Mark to some extent and on which Matthew and Luke drew for some of their material, at times conflating it with Mark. The Markan Dependence view says that *exactly this same evidence* can by *the same line of argument* justify that Mark's private source P "overlapped" with Matthew and Luke and that he drew on it as he chose and conflated his sources when he chose. The significant difference between the two alternative explanations is that Q is a totally speculative source, for which there is no objective evidence of any kind whatsoever, whereas Mark's own involvement in the life of the church, and his association with Peter and others, is attested by the New Testament and by church history, and thus is *not a speculation at all*.

When the alternative hypotheses are put beside each other in their full form—Mark plus Q as the sources of Matthew and Luke, or Matthew, Luke, and P as the sources for Mark—then one can see that (1) Markan Dependence offers the more cohesive explanation of the data, and (2) Markan Dependence explains everything in terms of *known* people and their *attested* activities; it does not need to call on hypothetical documents, while acknowledging that any number of such documents *could* have existed in the period prior to the production of the canonical Gospels by their respective authors, and *may* have been consulted by any of these authors.

As noted throughout this chapter, the explanations provided by Markan Priority are really impossible to believe, while Markan Dependence explains Mark's redactional procedure as very lucid and rational. Therefore, using Tuckett's own criterion, the Markan Dependence explanation is preferred.

I make some further comments in chapter 11 about Tuckett's rebuttal of the Farmer form of the Griesbach Hypothesis. However, here we may note that it is impossible to account for the pericopes in question solely on the basis of Markan Priority because their contents go far beyond what could have been derived from Mark. Further, it is impossible to explain them as due to Mark-Q overlaps and then to set limits (as Streeter wished to do) on which Markan pericopes can be permitted to be attributed also to Q; that is, it is impossible to affirm that some pericopes were found in both Mark and Q without simultaneously allowing the Ur-Gospel approach to supersede the Two-Source Hypothesis. And for all these pericopes the Markan Dependence explanation remains as a clear and simple alternative that fully accounts for the Synoptic data.

14. Matthew and Luke Filled Out Mark's Settings

There are occasions when Matthew and Luke give the setting for one pericope, and after relating that story proceed to tell another story immediately following it that happened at the same time, whereas Mark has the *setting* from the first pericope but, omitting the balance of that story, proceeds immediately to the second story. These are the most noteworthy ones.

The Sermon on the Plain

Both Mark (3:7–12) and Luke (6:17–19,20–49) contain the Sermon on the Plain. Luke's account of the great multitude of people—of whom Jesus healed those who were ill (6:17–19)—provides his setting for the Sermon on the Plain that follows (6:20–49). Mark describes the gathering of the crowds that Luke says Jesus addressed, but gives nothing at all of the Sermon itself. Instead, Mark proceeds to give the choosing of the Twelve (Mark 3:13–19), which Luke gives in the *same context* but *before* the description of the gathering crowds and the healings (Luke 6:12–16). Thus, Mark contains the *setting* of the Sermon on the Plain but none of the Sermon itself.

Sayings to Would-be Disciples

A collection of certain sayings to would-be disciples is part of the Triple Tradition (Matt 8:18–23//Mark 4:35–36//Luke 8:22; 9:57–62). In Matt 8:18–23 Jesus decides to leave the "great crowds around him" and gives orders to go across to the other side in the boat. At that point a scribe approaches Jesus, who then has a discussion with him and with another would-be disciple about following him. Then Jesus and his disciples embark in the boat, and there follows the pericope of stilling the storm. Mark contains the *setting* of the sayings to would-be disciples—Jesus' instruction to go across to the other side—but in Mark's account the sayings themselves are not recorded, and Jesus immediately leaves the crowd and embarks in the boat. Thus, Mark contains the *setting* of the sayings to would-be disciples but not the sayings themselves, and he continues immediately with the following pericope on stilling the storm, so that this setting has in his account become the introduction to the storm pericope, explaining what they were doing on the sea at the time (see chap. 11 for discussion of this pericope).

Coming to Capernaum

Mark contains the setting of the pericope of the coin in the fish's mouth, but not the story itself. The setting is prefixed to the pericope of the lesson about the child, which in Matthew follows the coin pericope and has the same setting.

The coin pericope occurs only in Matthew's Gospel, where it is preceded by the second Passion prediction (parallel in all three Synoptics), and is followed immediately by the lesson about the child pericope (parallel in all three Synoptics). Matthew's story about the coin for the temple tax states that this incident occurred in Capernaum, with the discussion taking place "when he came into the house" (17:25); and in the child pericope that follows Matthew commences, "At that time . . .," thus placing the latter pericope also in Capernaum. Luke does not mention Capernaum or give any specific setting for this account (9:46–48). But Mark places the child pericope in the house in Capernaum, thus giving his account the same setting that it has in Matthew; but in Matthew, that setting is stated *in a pericope that Mark does not contain*.

15. Matthew and Luke Expanded Mark's Teachings

There are several occasions where Mark's Gospel contains a short section of the longer material that is found in the parallel pericopes in Matthew or Luke or both. The most significant of these occasions are the Major Agreements of Matthew and Luke against Mark: the so-called Mark-Q overlaps (discussed above). There are also a number of other noteworthy passages of this kind. And there are also several occasions where Mark's Gospel lacks a record of teaching that occurs at that point in the parallel pericopes in Matthew or Luke or both, and where Mark makes some reference to the fact that he records only part of what Jesus taught at that time. Here are the most noteworthy of these two related kinds.

Summary of Jesus' First Preaching in Galilee

All three Synoptics refer briefly to Jesus' going to Galilee and there engaging in preaching or teaching (Matt 4:12–17//Mark 1:14–15//Luke 4:14–15). Matthew 4:13–16 (Jesus' going to dwell in Capernaum, and the Old Testament quotation) is absent from Mark. Thus, Matthew has (on the Markan Priority view) expanded the Markan reference to Jesus' preaching.

Teaching with Authority

All three Synoptics state that Jesus taught with authority (Matt 7: 28–29//Mark 1:22//Luke 4:32). Mark contains nothing of Jesus' teaching in the Sermon on the Mount. Matthew ends the Sermon with the statement, "And when Jesus finished these sayings, the crowds were astonished at his teaching, for he taught them as one who had authority, and not as their scribes" (7:28–29). Luke has a parallel statement, "And he went down to Capernaum, a city of Galilee. And he was teaching them on the Sabbath; and they were astonished at his teaching, for his word was with authority" (4:31–32). In Luke, this leads into the incident of the healing of the demoniac in the synagogue (lacking in Matthew). Mark parallels Luke's statement that Jesus went to Capernaum and taught, and then the 18 words of Mark 1:22 correspond *exactly* with Matt 7:28–29 (Matthew adds, "the crowds").

Therefore Mark here parallels both Luke and Matthew in turn; at the point where both Major Synoptics refer to the astonishment of the people at the authority of Jesus' teaching, Mark corresponds with Matthew exactly. And this point in Matthew's Gospel is the place where he records the reaction of the people to the Sermon on the Mount. Thus, Mark records the crowd's reaction to Jesus' teaching but omits the teaching.

Summary of Jesus' First Preaching Tour of Galilee

Matthew gives here what is in effect a program for the contents of almost the first half of his Gospel: Jesus went about all Galilee, teaching and preaching, and healing every disease and infirmity (Matt 4:23–25//Mark 1:39//Luke 4:44). Mark mentions only that Jesus preached in their synagogues and cast out demons. Luke refers only to his preaching in synagogues, which Luke places in Judea. Thus, Matthew has (on the Markan Priority view) expanded the Markan reference to Jesus' preaching.

Healings by the Seaside

In the pericope on healings by the seaside (Matt 12:15–21//Mark 3:7–12//Luke 6:17–19), Mark's account parallels Luke's pericope and the first two verses of Matthew; Matt 12:17–21 is an Old Testament citation that is absent from Mark (and Luke). The correspondence of Matthew with Mark here is only approximate; but if it is held that Matthew used Mark, then Matthew added extra material to what Mark has.

Teaching from a Boat in Parables

Both Matthew and Mark state that Jesus sat in a boat and spoke "many things in parables" to the crowds (Matt 13:1–52//Mark 4:1–34//Luke 8:4–18; 13:18–21); then Mark adds "and in his teaching he said to them . . ." Thus, Mark indicates that what he records represents what was spoken by Jesus *in the course of* longer teaching. Mark then recounts three parables (the sower, the seed growing secretly, and the mustard seed) together with some general comments about parables, while Matthew gives seven parables (eight if 13:51–52 is a parable).

After giving his three parables, Mark's concluding paragraph reiterates, "With many parables of this kind he spoke the word to them" (4:33); Matthew's parallel (13:34) states, "All this Jesus said to the crowds in parables" (13:34). Again, Mark's wording indicates that he does not profess to be recording *all* the parables that Jesus had spoken; Matthew's account implies no such kind of limitation.

Perhaps, as Markan Priorists suggest, Matthew had available a supply of suitable parables, and when he came to Mark's comments with their implication that more parables were actually spoken on this occasion than Mark himself recorded, Matthew was able to insert several additional ones from his parable stock—and then of course he removed the Markan implication (in 4:2 and 4:33) that other parables were spoken at the time. Alternatively, it could be that Mark used Matthew here, and his wording (in the way he writes his introductory and concluding statements) reflects the fact that he used only some of the parables found at this point in his source.

The Great Reversal

Matthew and Mark place Jesus' teaching on "the great reversal" in the same context (Matt 19:30//Mark 10:31). At the conclusion of Jesus' teaching on riches and discipleship (Matt 19:23–30//Mark 10:23–31//Luke 18:24–30) Mark has the saying, "But many that are first will be last, and the last first" (10:31). Luke lacks this here, but has a general parallel at 13:30.

Matthew, like Mark, ends the pericope with this saying. Then Matthew includes a unique parable (the workers in the vineyard) that illustrates this saying in a very specific way, and he ends this parable with another form of the same saying, "So the last will be first and the first last" (20:16).

Now if Matthew is using Mark as his main source, then we must suppose that he had a stock of additional material from Q and from M (his own unique material) that he held ready to insert into the Markan framework at appropriate points, so that when he came across this saying in Mark he had available the ideal parable with which to illustrate it and reinforce it. This is very possible, of course. But as we keep coming across more and more cases where Matthew must be thus supposed to have had available, ready at hand, units of material that were so apposite to the Markan contexts, this explanation becomes progressively less likely.

Passion Week Teaching in Parables

All three Synoptics record that Jesus taught in parables during Passion week (Matt 21:33//Mark 12:1//Luke 20:9). Immediately after the question about authority, Luke says, "And he began to tell the people this parable" (20:9), and recounts *one* parable, that of the wicked farmers, following this with the parable on paying tribute to Caesar. Between the question about authority and the pericope on paying tribute to Caesar, Matthew gives *three* parables: the two sons, the wicked farmers, and the marriage feast. At this point, Mark (like Luke) gives only one parable, the wicked farmers—but in introducing it Mark writes in the *plural*: "And he began to speak to them in parables."

It is possible, once again, that Matthew noticed that Mark said Jesus spoke in "parables," plural, while only recording *one* parable, and thus this seemed a very appropriate place to insert others from the supply of special parables that he had. So Matthew added two further parables here, one in front of and the other after the single parable found in Mark.

There are two difficulties with this explanation. The first is what it presumes about the supply of other appropriate teachings from Jesus that Matthew apparently had on hand, lacking only a suitable context into which to place it. The second is the extraordinary aptness of the contexts in Mark into which Matthew was able to insert them; they are so apt as to suggest that they were original in those contexts and actually occurred in the circumstances where Matthew placed them. But this conclusion is excluded by the Markan Priority view, because, as Streeter (1924, 166) puts it:

> Matthew's method is to make Mark the framework into which non-Marcan matter is to be fitted, on the principle of joining like to like. That is to say, whenever he finds in a non-Marcan source teaching which would elaborate or illustrate

a saying or incident in Mark, he inserts that particular piece of non-Marcan matter into that particular context in the Marcan story. . . . So the Marcan saying, repeated in Mt 19:30, 'The first shall be last and the last first,' suggests to him the addition in that particular context of the parable of the Labourers in the Vineyard which points the same moral. Similarly the moral of the Marcan parable of the Wicked Husbandmen, Mt 21:33ff. (which is directed against the Jewish authorities), is reinforced by the addition immediately before and after it of the anti-Pharisaic parables of the Two Sons and the Marriage Feast.

Let us be quite clear about this. Streeter is telling us that, on the Markan Priority explanation of the Synoptic data, none of these teachings found in Matthew but lacking in Mark actually took place in the situation where Matthew placed them: for Matthew had them only as this or that "particular piece of non-Marcan matter." Matthew lacked any knowledge of the actual circumstances of their utterance, so that what he did was that "he inserts that particular piece of non-Marcan matter into that particular context in the Marcan story" solely on the basis of his judgment as to a good fit: "wherever he finds in a non-Marcan source teaching which would elaborate or illustrate a saying or incident in Mark."

So those who hold the Markan Priority viewpoint have no basis for believing that Jesus actually spoke the parable of the two sons or of the marriage feast in the circumstances where they are found in Matthew. They are placed into this context by Matthew purely because Matthew, in using Mark's Gospel, judged that they "would elaborate or illustrate a saying or incident in Mark" at that point.

Yet time after time the context in which Matthew has them appears to be the actual one in which they occurred. Thus the parable of the two sons follows on so appropriately from the question about John the Baptist and authority that the two together form a flowing sequence, for in this parable Jesus continues his discussion of the ministry of John the Baptist begun in the question about authority and confronts the Jewish leaders with the fact that they had rejected John (Matt 21:32).

It is just not possible to believe that Matthew had this parable available as a separate unit in the way Streeter describes, which he could thus insert into Mark at such a point to add further to what Mark records of what Jesus said to the "chief priests and elders of the people" about John (Matt 21:23), and which provided such a fitting reply to the situation as Mark described it. Similarly, Matthew's parable of the marriage feast elaborates the same theme of God's rejection of the Jewish nation. The three parables hang together as a close-knit unit, and *this* context, as Matthew has provided it, is the *right* and *original* context for them.

But if these parables point to the originality of Matthew's account here, so that it was Mark who used Matthew's Gospel (not vice versa), how could it happen that Mark would break up such a unit by leaving two of these three parables out of his Gospel? The answer is that they were very relevant to Matthew's Gospel with its Jewish background and milieu so that they can be accepted as a record of what actually took place at this time, but they were much less appropriate for Mark's readership. Both of the omitted parables dealt with the question of the rejection of the Jews. It is easy to see why further discussion of the ministry of John was not deemed useful by Mark: he recorded only John's testimony to Jesus and the story of John's death, prefiguring in its essentials, as it did, Jesus' own death; he did not include John's general teaching or Jesus' testimony to John. Similarly, the parable of the marriage feast—with its climax based in Jewish custom, the wedding garment—did not advance either of Mark's two purposes of evangelism and Christology. Mark was adequately served by the inclusion of the middle parable, the wicked farmers, which sums up all that needed to be said about the rejection of the Jews and which was especially relevant from Mark's point of view because, in particular, it spoke proleptically of the death of the Son.

Woe to the Scribes

All three Synoptics contain Jesus' woes on the scribes (Matt 23: 1–6//Mark 12:37–38//Luke 20:45); Matt 23:1–36 contains Jesus' lengthy criticism of the scribes and Pharisees. It is paralleled to some extent in Mark 12:37b–40//Luke 20:45–47; these short accounts are much closer to each other than to Matthew. Luke's introduction is general: "And in the hearing of all the people he said to his disciples . . ." Matthew says, "Then said Jesus to the crowds and to his disciples . . ." But Mark states, "And in his teaching he said . . ." That is, Mark states that he is about to record something that Jesus said *in the course of longer teaching on this occasion*. Mark then gives *all* that Luke has on this matter, but *it represents only a small part of what occurs here in Matthew*.

It is possible, as Streeter affirms (254), that Matthew has compiled this discourse by a conflation of Q, M, and Mark. But the explanation that is much more consistent with the data is that Mark used Matthew and Luke, and that by writing "And in his teaching he said" Mark acknowledged that he used only a small part of what Jesus said on this occasion.

The Olivet Discourse

Mark parallels the Olivet Discourse in Matthew and Luke quite closely up to Matt 24:35//Mark 13:31//Luke 21:33. At that point Luke ceases to correspond to Matthew and has instead a short (three-verse) conclusion hinging upon two imperatives: "Take heed to yourselves . . . lest that day come upon you suddenly like a snare" (21:34), and "watch at all times" (21:36). Matthew's discourse continues at some considerable length (24:37–25:46E). Mark's account parallels Matthew's next verse (Matt 24:36//Mark 13:32), and then also terminates with a brief (five-verse) conclusion. But while his wording is unique here, the ideas he expresses in fact summarize what is said in Matthew and Luke. He captures the thrust of Luke's ending with his words (13:33), "Take heed, watch; for you do not know when the time will come." This same thought, amplified by Mark in his next four verses, also reflects the theme of much that is in the remaining sections of Matthew.

The exhortation to watch in Mark's opening, middle, and closing verses (13:33,35,37) occurs at several points in Matthew's account; connected with this is the warning concerning the uncertainty of the time of the Master's return, a point which is made repeatedly in Matthew with an Old Testament citation and several stories. Mark illustrates this factor with a story (13:34) of a man leaving home on a journey, which has ideas (and some words) in common both with the parable of the good and wicked servants and the parable of the talents; the references in Mark 13:35 to the various times of the day or night when the master of the house may return correspond with the times implied in Matthew's stories (any time: Noah and the flood; during daylight hours: the workers in the field and at the mill; during the night: the householder and the thief; and midnight for the cry of the arrival of the bridegroom). The warning about finding them asleep (Mark 13:34) is comparable to the comment that "as the bridegroom was delayed, they all slumbered and slept" (Matt 25:5). Mark's closing verse is a reiteration of the theme of both Matthew and Luke in this section: "And what I say to you I say to all: Watch."

Clearly, Mark 13:33–37 reads like an interpretative summary not only of the essence of Luke's closing three verses, but also of the teaching contained in Matthew after 24:36. Thus, it is a reasonable interpretation of the data that Mark used Matthew's and Luke's Gospels and—rather than including the balance of Matthew's material (given Mark's policy regarding teaching material, this passage was too long to include) or else simply omitting it—Mark instead chose to summarize it in his closing five verses. The alternative is that Luke replaced Mark's ending with other material of his own, and Matthew used the themes and ideas in Mark's last five verses as the basis for inserting here a further 61 verses, which he happened to have available and which happened to correspond in such a striking way with the thoughts in Mark.

The Explanations

All the above passages have in common this factor: they are places where one of the Major Synoptics (usually Matthew, occasionally Luke) has material that is lacking in Mark, and at that point in Mark one finds either (1) the setting in which that material is given in another Gospel; or (2) some lesser part of the material that the Major Synoptic(s) give(s) in greater detail; or (3) some mention of other teaching, the reference being of a kind that indicates that Mark was aware that he was including only part of the teaching of Jesus given on the occasion in question.

This is the data. The alternative explanations of this data are that (1) the Major Synoptist in question (usually Matthew) expanded on Mark's teaching or references to teaching to produce the longer accounts in their respective Gospels; or (2) Mark extracted what he wanted for his Gospel from Matthew and Luke, frequently using only part of what they contained, and at times, at the place where he used only a section of what was available, he wrote in such a way as to indicate this.

Streeter considers (1924, 167) that Luke has arranged his sources so that "Marcan and non-Marcan material alternates in great blocks," and from the Markan Priority perspective he gives this explanation (to which attention was drawn earlier) for how Matthew has handled the material he found in Mark. Though lengthy, it is worth noting (166–67, 190):

> Matthew's method is to make Mark the framework into which non-Marcan matter is to be fitted, on the principle of joining like to like. That is to say, whenever he finds in a non-Marcan source teaching which would elaborate or illustrate a saying or incident in Mark, he inserts that particular piece of non-Marcan matter into that particular context in the Marcan story.... So the Marcan saying, repeated in Mt 19:30, "The first shall be last and the last first," suggests to him the addition in that particular context of the parable of the Labourers in the Vineyard which points the same moral. Similarly the moral of the Marcan parable of the Wicked Husbandmen, Mt 21:33ff. (which is directed against the Jewish authorities), is reinforced by the addition immediately before and after it of the anti-Pharisaic parables of the Two Sons and the Marriage Feast.
>
> Examples of this kind of adaptation of non-Marcan matter to a Marcan context could be indefinitely multiplied. But it is worth while to call special attention to the bearing of this process on the longer discourses in Matthew. All of them are clear cases of "agglomeration," that is, of the building up of sayings originally dispersed so as to form great blocks. Four times, starting with a short discourse in Mark as a nucleus, Matthew expands it by means of non-Marcan additions into a long sermon. Thus the 7 verses of Mark's sending out of the Twelve (Mk 6:7ff.) becomes the 42 verses of Mt 10. The three parables of Mk 4—with one omission—are made the basis of the seven-parable chapter, Mt 13. The twelve verses Mk 9:33–37,42–48, are elaborated into a discourse of 35 verses in Mt 18. The "Little Apocalypse" (Mk 13) is expanded, not only

by the addition of a number of apocalyptic sayings (apparently from Q), but also by having appended to it three parables of Judgement (Mt 25). To some extent analogous is the way in which the Sermon on the Mount, far the longest and most important block of non-Marcan matter, is connected with the Marcan framework. It is inserted in such a way as to lead up, and thus give point, to the Marcan saying, "And they were astonished at his teaching: for he taught them as one having authority, and not as the scribes." Cf. Mk 1:22; Mt 7:29. That the Sermon on the Mount is itself an agglomeration of materials originally separate will be shown later. . . . Mt 10:5–16 is clearly a conflation of the Q discourse, given by Luke as the Charge to the Seventy (Lk 10:1–12), with Mark's discourse on the Mission to the Twelve (Mk 6:7–11). Matthew has additional matter both at the beginning and the end which may possibly come from a third source . . . , but in the central part of his version of the discourse (Mt 10:9–16a) there is hardly a word which is not to be found either in Mk 6:7–11 or in Lk 10:1–12.

Streeter's explanation of how Matthew used what he had in front of him in Mark is a good one—*if on other grounds we knew that Mark was prior to Matthew, and that Matthew used it.* But his explanation assumes this relationship without in any way strengthening the case for it. As an explanation for how Matthew ordered material available to him, it has considerable merit and is particularly useful in accounting for the difference between Matthew and Luke in their distribution of much of the "sayings" material that is common to both of them. But in regard to the relationship between Matthew and Mark, it is *totally reversible*. If on other grounds we knew that Mark used Matthew (and not vice versa), then we could recognize that *all* the material in Matthew to which Streeter refers came from Matthew's sources, including what subsequently became incorporated into Mark's Gospel. When reading Matthew, there is no discernible difference between what is also found in Mark and what is not. And there is no difficulty whatsoever in accepting the view that Mark drew from Matthew such material as he judged appropriate in terms of his own purposes in writing, which is the Markan Dependence explanation. So the explanation that one adopts flows entirely from the relationship that one presupposes.

But there is one important extra factor to consider. Almost all the material that we are examining in these sections of our study has in common that it occurs at a point where Matthew contains more than Mark does, and what Mark lacks and the Major Synoptics include in these passages consists of various kinds of teaching. We noted earlier (see chap. 4 on the statistics and chap. 3 on Mark's purposes in writing) that Mark's policy was to be selective about the teaching he included and to incorporate much less teaching into his account than is found in Matthew or Luke. The Markan Dependence Hypothesis says that Mark carefully went through Jesus' teachings in these passages in Matthew and Luke *and selected from it only those short extracts that accorded with his purposes*, and that when major teaching is not included it is either represented by short extracts, it is summarized, or a statement indicates that Mark only recorded part of what was said in the whole discourse.

So also is found, similarly, the inclusion in apocopated form of occasional other material (i.e., those which are not specific teachings of Jesus such as John's preaching and the temptation): this enables the incident to have a place in Mark's Gospel without slowing down the action and detracting from his main purposes. This is a very reasonable explanation and in accord with Mark's clear general policy.

Streeter's explanation from the Markan Priority viewpoint only covers some of the occasions that have been listed here; it does not touch on the overall pattern, so frequently in evidence, that Mark shows an awareness of Jesus engaging in teaching or giving more teaching precisely at those places where Matthew (and sometimes Luke) *has given* such additional teaching. This may be written off to coincidence in one instance or another; or in some passages it could, with Streeter, be attributed to Matthew using a nucleus of teaching found in Mark as a hook on which to hang non-Markan teaching of similar kinds that he had available. But when we consider the sum total of the passages concerned, it is not really possible to believe that they can together be all dismissed in this way.

16. Matthean Redaction of Mark 9 Could Have Produced Matthew 18

All three Synoptics are parallel at the lesson about the child. Then Matthew has On the Seriousness of Sin and The Parable of the Lost Sheep, where the theme of young children continues (see Matt 18:6,10). Luke goes on a tangent: Jesus says, "Whoever receives one such/this child in my name receives me" (Matt 18:5//Mark 9:37//Luke 9:48), and then Luke records next that "John answered, 'Master we saw a man casting out demons in your name'" (9:49). Mark has *both* the pericopes of the stranger exorcizing and on the seriousness of sin, and in *that order*. That is to say, Mark parallels Matthew's continuation about young children, but he *interrupts* this discussion with the insertion of the stranger exorcizing, in which he parallels Luke. Not only so, but between these two pericopes Mark 9:41 has a saying that occurs in Matthew in another context (Matt 10:42) that Mark has not used. Matthew says, "And whoever gives to one of these little ones even a cup of cold water"; whereas Mark says, "whoever gives you a cup of water."

The redactional procedures of the Synoptists to produce the texts here, according to the different hypotheses of Synoptic scholars, are enlightening. Markan Priority advocates say that Mark produced this sequence without reference to Matthew and Luke (which in their view had not been written at that time). Drawing on his pericope sources, Mark wrote two pericopes relating to young children (the lesson about the child; on the seriousness of sin) and then *inserted* the stranger exorcizing pericope *in between them*, thus interrupting what otherwise would be a continuous unit relating to children. Yet Mark does not state (cf. Luke 9:49) that "John answered" (i.e., responded to) what Jesus had said earlier; Mark merely has, "John said to him." Thus, Mark's pericope of the stranger exorcizing is not tied specifically to what precedes and could in fact have been placed anywhere else he chose—there is no specific reason apparent that shows why Mark would break up Christ's teaching related to young children with this short pericope at this point. (It begs the question to say, It is given here because this is when it actually took place. There are no links to indicate this in the story. It is not generally held by Markan Priorists that Mark's pericopes have their particular order because that is the order in which they all took place.) Why then would Mark place the stranger exorcizing in the middle of Jesus' teachings related to young children?

Mark follows On the Seriousness of Sin with On Marriage and Divorce (10:1–12) and then with another pericope about children, Jesus' blessing of the children (10:13–16). No one can say of Mark what Streeter (1924, 166) says of Matthew, that he works "on the principle of joining like to like"! Instead, Mark has three pericopes about children (9:33–10:16) but separates them from each other by, respectively, the pericopes of the stranger exorcizing and on marriage and divorce.

Markan Priority advocates say that once Mark was written, Matthew and Luke each used it for writing their own Gospels. In addition to minor redactions, Luke excises from Mark's account "for no one who does a mighty work in my name will be able soon after to speak evil of me," together with Mark's climax to the stranger exorcizing, "For truly I say to you, whoever gives you a cup of water to drink because you bear the name of Christ, will by no means lose his reward," together also with the whole of On the Seriousness of Sin and On Marriage and Divorce. Then instead at *this* point Luke introduces into Mark his substantial central teaching section (approximately a third of the length of his Gospel, 9:51–18:14), rejoining Mark (at Mark 10:13//Luke 18:15) with Jesus' blessing of the children.

If these may be judged rather unlikely ways for Luke to handle Mark's text, Matthew's redactional procedure is quite bizarre. He alters substantially the thrust of Mark 9:33–35 (see Matt 18:1)—in fact he omits 9:35, a very relevant comment for the context; he takes over 18:2 from Mark and then adds in 18:3–4 from some other source (and yet it suits *this* context so exactly as to seem original here!); next, he excises 9:37b, "and whoever receives me, receives not me but him who sent me," and then deletes the whole of the stranger exorcizing, except for "For truly, I say to you, whoever gives you a cup of water to drink because you bear the name of Christ, will by no means lose his reward." He changes "you bear the name of Christ" to "he is a disciple," and "gives you" to "gives to one of these little ones" to make it fit better the context about children—and then moves it to 10:42, where it becomes the final saying of the mission charge in a context where there is not one other single mention of "little ones"! Continuing with Mark 9:42, Matthew adds in the "Woe" of 18:7, apocopates the comment about cutting off hand or foot, and deletes Mark 9:48–50. Instead, at this point he continues Jesus' dissertation with the parable of the lost sheep and various other teachings up to the parable of the unforgiving servant (Matt 18:10–35E), being parallel again with Mark at Matt 19:1//Mark 10:1.

The explanation from the Markan Dependence perspective is much simpler. In the lesson about the child, Mark conflates Matthew and Luke. He then confronts the situation that his two sources differ about what to place next, and he resolves to use what each has. Obviously, he cannot follow *both* of his sources in what to put next, so he must choose between them. He does not include any of Luke's central section, with its emphasis on Jesus' teachings. Therefore, notwithstanding that it thus gets placed into a sequence about children, Mark takes Luke's the stranger exorcizing next. At this stage he has completed the use that he plans to make of Luke until Luke again parallels Matthew at 18:15.

Mark is therefore now free to follow Matthew, and in moving from Luke to Matthew he includes the saying about the cup of water. In the next verse that he is to take from Matthew occur the words "one of these little ones" (18:6), which recalls to him the saying regarding a cup of water (in which these same words also occur), which is part of a section of Matthew that he was not using. So he took the verse from there (quite possibly from memory), but in using it as the climax of his version of the stranger exorcizing he omits the reference to "little ones" as not fitting its new context. (There are several examples where Mark's Gospel has parallels with single verses of Matthew, the Matthean context being a pericope that Mark does not contain; the two most well-known are Mark 1:2 and 1:22.) An alternative explanation is that Mark adds 9:41 to this pericope, together with his other insertions in this context, from his recollection of how these stories were told in the preaching of Peter. Mark continues with On the Seriousness of Sin and then omits Matthew's subsequent teachings (in line with his policy of limited use of long teaching sections), paralleling Matthew again for the pericope on marriage and divorce (Matt 19:1//Mark 10:1).

There is nothing inherently unlikely in such a procedure on Mark's part if he were using Matthew and Luke as sources: in fact, it is a very reasonable and logical way of proceeding, and it is consistent with his handling of sources elsewhere. However, the procedure that Markan Priority advocates claim Mark and Luke would have followed is very unlikely, and the redactional behavior required of Matthew is quite illogical and inconsistent. If Matthew knew the saying in Mark 9:41 (whether only as it is in Mark, or in a form that already said "one of these little ones"), then he would most certainly have been expected to have given it *where Mark gives it,* for here it would have been in a most appropriate context, and this position would have harmonized with his recognized practice of adding like to like. Whatever the reason for Matthew's version of this saying being in the context that it has at 10:42, it is mute testimony that *Matthew did not have before him Mark 9:33–42.* The other redactional changes and the deletions (such as Mark 9:35,37b,38–40,48–50) that Matthew has here made to Mark (assuming Markan Priority) range in varying degrees from unlikely to unbelievable.

The way that Mark's use of the stranger exorcizing intrudes into Jesus' talk about children is very odd and requires explanation. The sequence in Mark *cannot* be the order in which these things would be placed in an original composition. The only plausible explanation is that *this pericope occurs where it does in Mark because that is where it is found in Luke* and Mark was engaged in combining the Matthean and Lukan narratives. Overall, the Markan Dependence explanation accounts for the data realistically, while the Markan Priority explanation invites one to believe the impossible.

17. The Order of Synoptic Pericopes Arose from Matthew and Luke Using Mark

The two sections that follow illustrate and discuss the unbelievable idea that the order of synoptic pericopes could arise from Matthew's or Luke's use of the Gospel of Mark.

The Transposed Citation

After his title in 1:1, Mark gives an Old Testament citation (1:2–3). This is unusual in several ways. First, it is the *only* Old Testament quotation in Mark of an editorial/ redactional nature—that is, the only one which comes from the *author* of the Gospel, as distinct from one of his characters quoting the Old Testament. Second, it is the only formula quotation in Mark's Gospel, that is, introduced by the formula "in order that it may be as was spoken by the prophets," or words to that effect. Third, it comes *after* Mark's introduction of it, in a formula that attributes what follows to Isaiah, and *before* Mark's actual quotation of Isaiah (in v. 3), while it itself is *not* from Isaiah. Fourth, it consists of a very unusual form of wording: it is a conflation of wording from Exod 23:20 and Mal 3:1, and its wording is partly taken from the Septuagint and is partly a translation from the Hebrew. These factors mean that it has a quite unique wording, which would never be duplicated independently by someone else citing from the Old Testament, seeing that it is taken from *two* places and *two* versions. Fifth, Mark has the identical wording of Matt 11:10 and Luke 7:27—except that it lacks their "before you" (ἔμπροσθέν σου); these two words do not occur in the Septuagint of either Exod 23:20 or Mal 3:1.

Markan Priority's explanation to account for this data is worth investigating. It is out of character for Mark to include an "editorial" quotation and indeed to use such a formula quotation at all (there are no other instances). It is out of character for him to use a form of Old Testament quotation wording that does not derive from the Septuagint as all his other quotations are (see Gundry 1975, 148). Thus it is reasonable to say that the wording of this citation was hardly original with Mark.

When they came across this quotation in Mark, both Matthew and Luke must have decided that it should indeed be included in their respective Gospels, but not where Mark had it. They applied this quotation to John (as Mark did), but for some reason they did not use it in the introductory material about the Baptist. And both Matthew and Luke had exactly the right place for it somewhere else: they inserted it at precisely the same point into the comments that Jesus made about the Baptist after John sent a message to Jesus from prison. And they both independently decided to add "before you" at the end—even though these words do not occur in Mark or in the Septuagint of either of the conflated Old Testament verses!

Now if this appears altogether too far-fetched, Markan Priority has an alternative. The citation was originally part of Q in the form and in the position that it now has in Matthew and Luke in Jesus' comments about the Baptist. This explains Matthew and Luke. But where did Mark get it? The simplest answer is that he also got it from Q. This answer could accord with Streeter's 1911 views, who at that time attributed the story of the advent and preaching of the Baptist in all three Synoptists to Q. And concerning the quotation from Isaiah in Mark 1:3, Streeter says (1911, 168):

> Seeing that in no other case does the editor of Mark himself introduce a quotation or reference to the Old Testament it is probable that this also occurred in Q.

Mark alone prefixes to it the quotation from Malachi ἰδοὺ ἐγὼ ἀποστέλλω τὸν ἄγγελον, which is applied to John Baptist in Mt 11:10=Lk 7:27, in the account of John's Message from prison, a passage of Q which does not occur in Mark. It looks as if Mark's double quotation in this passage is a conflation of the two quotations applied to John in two different contexts of Q.

Thus, Streeter held that *Mark found this quotation in Q "in the account of John's Message from prison," which he did not himself choose to use, and instead conflated the quotation with the other Q material about the Baptist with which his Gospel commences.* But by 1924 Streeter had repudiated the possibility that Mark used Q, so in *The Four Gospels* this explanation was no longer available to him. But he does not offer an alternative explanation; in fact, he does not refer to the matter at all (neither Mark 1:2 nor Matt 11:10//Luke 7:27 are dealt with in *The Four Gospels*). Tuckett does not deal with the issue (*Revival of the Griesbach Hypothesis*), and neither do Farmer (*The Synoptic Problem*) and Stoldt (*History and Criticism of the Marcan Hypothesis*).

So how can we account for the fact that Mark 1:2//Matt 11:10//Luke 7:27 are identical—except for the addition of the same two further words in Matthew and Luke? And that Mark uses this citation *in a different context*? The unusual structure of the quotation totally precludes the idea that Mark and Matthew-Luke have independently come up with an identical wording. Thus we have available these alternatives:

1. Each Synoptist obtained it from Q.
2. Each Synoptist derived it from the pre-Gospel oral tradition.
3. Each Synoptist obtained it from some other pre-Gospel written tradition that was not Q.
4. Mark found it in Matthew and Luke in a pericope that he did not intend using. He decided that it would be a worthwhile addition to the introduction of his Isaiah quotation about John, so he used it there instead.
5. Matthew and Luke each derived their account from Mark 1:2, and they independently decided (a) to switch it to the pericope about Jesus' comment on John the Baptist, and (b) to add the same two words ("before you") to it.

Those who find option 5 impossible to accept may make their choice among the others. They can reject Streeter's change of mind and choose option 1, Q as the source of the quotation in all three Synoptics. Such an approach does underline the perceptivity of D. L. Dungan's description (1970, 75) of the role of Q: "the real value of the Q hypothesis is that it provides a way for those doing research in the Synoptic Gospels to handle all of the passages which clearly belie the theory of Mark's originality." J. Chapman's comments (1937, 98, 126) on Q are also worthy of note (italics in the original):

> And further, Canon Streeter has shown that certain parts of this unknown document must have overlapped Mk.
>
> Hence we arrive at the absurdity that Q is not only all the heterogeneous resemblances (distant or close) between Mt. and Lk. against Mk., but may include any part of Mk. also (why not the whole of Mk.?) and any part of Mt. peculiar to him and any peculiar to Lk.
>
> Hence *there is no part of the three Synoptic Gospels which may not quite well be derived from Q!* . . .
>
> Consequently these passages have shown that Q, as a source of Mt. and Lk., independent of Mk., is impossible, since it must include Mk.
>
> I hope the absurdity of all this is clear to the reader. It merely means that *the assumption of a common source for Mt. and Lk. always leads us to find this source to be the common source of three Gospels.* This is not a two-document hypothesis, but a one-document hypothesis, and it is simply a *reduction ad absurdum.* . . .
>
> Q is not a collection of discourses, independent of Mk., *but a name to cover any source one meets with*, and might have included any part, or the whole, of Mt., Mk., or Lk. In fact, it might be the whole Bible.

(For a lot more about Chapman, his change of mind, and his significant book *Matthew, Mark and Luke*, see chap. 10.)

A Q like this is, by its very nature, incapable of falsification. Seeing that an authentic copy of Q does not exist, there are no controls. Q is what you make it. It is pliable enough to fit any purpose you may have in mind. Q is an all-purpose, all-weather, one-size-fits-all, kind of explanation. If in non-Markan material Matthew and Luke agree, they are both quoting Q precisely. If they differ a little, one or both have redacted Q to suit their purposes—and often we can even make a stab at hypothesizing which version is the more "original." If they are so significantly different that one can hardly postulate they both came from a common source, then either (choose your explanation) one of them used Q and the other used a differently sourced version, or Matthew used M and Luke used L.

Q indeed becomes an explanation for all seasons, a rescue device for the Markan Priority Hypothesis whenever it is inadequate to describe the data; it is in fact a kind of literary *deus ex machina* that when all else fails can be invoked to step in and save the day. Q may prove to be an excellent standby for such occasions, but *are we really intended to believe that invoking Q in this kind of way is giving a realistic account of something that actually happened?* But you can still go for option 1 if you want to.

But if one accepts Streeter's 1924 rejection that Mark used Q, then option 1 is ruled out. Yet one can still go for option 2, that the quotation had independent currency in the early church, where all three Synoptists got it; or, if its occurrence in Matthew and Luke is still attributed to Q, where Mark got it. However, if one thinks that the problem with this is the *exact correspondence of wording*—perhaps a little *too* exact for oral tradition—then option 3 can solve this: just postulate another written account (other than Q) from which it was taken. The trouble is that we have now adopted a hypothesis of some kind of Ur-Gospel (whether oral or written) to cope with the data, which in this instance would be fulfilling the same kind of explanatory role usually assigned to Q.

The most straightforward explanation is option 4: Mark derived this quotation from Matthew and Luke. This is in fact almost identical with the implications of Streeter's Q explanation (1911) given above. Mark's motivation and procedure is exactly the same under the two explanations: Mark found the quotation in his source(s) in the context of Jesus' words about John, a pericope that he himself did not intend to use; he decided that this would make an excellent introduction to his Isaiah quotation that (together with its formula-introduction) he was taking from Matt 3:3 and Luke 3:4, so he conflated the two, inserting the transferred citation *between* the introductory formula and the words from Isaiah and omitting the last two words to improve the link with the Isaiah quotation. All this is completely in accord with Streeter's 1911 position with the sole difference that instead of invoking a hypothetical Q as the source from which Mark obtained his quotation, this Synoptist is seen as taking it directly from two extant documents—the Gospels of Matthew and Luke.

In the light of the logic and rationality of this explanation of the data, is it still possible to choose one of the *other* options?

The Order of Pericopes

In chapter 9 our examination of periscope order will allow us to see the extent to which Mark's order is supported by only one of the Major Synoptists. If Mark was the first Gospel written and was used by Matthew and Luke, then both the Major Synoptists have chosen to depart from its order on numerous occasions. No overall cohesive explanation has been offered for the abandonment of Mark's order on these occasions. At best, suggestions can be made on a pericope-by-pericope basis. Furthermore, even if these suggestions could be accepted as reasons that they each left Mark's order on a particular occasion, the reasons do not extend to providing an explanation of the specific order that they have each given to the pericopes in their own Gospels.

It seems, upon the basis of the *prima facie* evidence of the fact that both Matthew and Luke change the order given by Mark, that the two Major Synoptists have found fault with (or at least consider that there are some shortcomings in) the Markan order: yet *on not one single occasion have they altered Mark's order in the same way or even at the same place.* This is a strong indication that there must be *some other explanation* for the question of Synoptic pericope order.

Mark's order is always supported by the order of one or both of the other two Synoptics. Of the 80 units into which Mark's Gospel can be divided on the basis of considerations relating to pericope order, 40 units of Mark are supported by only one Gospel. So, if Mark had placed any of those 40 units into his Gospel at a different place, it would not have been true that Mark's order is *always* supported. (See chap. 9 where the full 80 pericope groups are clearly set out.) Since by common consent it is agreed that Matthew and Luke acted independently where they concur with or else depart from Markan order, *no explanation is possible* for why it did not happen that both Matthew and Luke deserted Markan order at the same point: this circumstance can only be put down to coincidence.

Similarly, there can be no collusion about the way that, whenever a Major Synoptist who has been supporting Mark is about to leave Mark's order, the other Major Synoptist always continues adhering to Mark's order if he has been doing so in the previous pericope, or if he has not, he *invariably returns to Mark's order immediately*. This extraordinary timing must, once again, be attributed to coincidence.

That some of these things could occasionally happen is believable. Such coincidences do occur in life. But that Matthew and Luke should come and go in their support of Mark's order as often as they do without there being any discernible reason why either of them should have done so, and that their respective comings and goings should mesh together in the way that occurs in the data, strains credulity beyond acceptance. Thus the view that the existing Synoptic pericope order has arisen as a result of Matthew and Luke each using—and from time to time altering—Mark's order is quite impossible to believe.

FOUR IMPROBABILITIES

There are numbers of other things that, while not totally *impossible* to believe, are certainly somewhat difficult to swallow. Four of these improbabilities are considered.

1. Matthew and Luke Disregarded Mark's Information and Wording

The first improbability is that Matthew and Luke disregarded Mark's information and wording. The impression one gets from reading some writers on the Synoptics is that Matthew and Luke each took over Mark's material virtually unchanged, beyond doing some minor editing to improve his grammar and style, and making small modifications to adapt it more specifically to his own intended readership. For example, throughout his commentary on Matthew, W. C. Allen (1965) refers to the *editor* and not the *author* of this Gospel, since he sees Matthew's editing of Mark's material primarily in terms of such improvements and modifications.

The modern tools of our computer age enable us to reassess this verdict. Morgenthaler (1971, 239–41) sets out the numbers of words used by the three Synoptics for each pericope and the numbers of words in Matthew and Luke that each has in common with Mark. (See chap. 4 for these statistics.) Morgenthaler lists 118 pericopes that Mark and Matthew have in common, and for only eight of these does Matthew have 75% or more of his words in common with Mark (see chap. 4, table 2). That is, in 110 out of 118 pericopes that Matthew drew from Mark, he altered more than a quarter of the words that he found in his source! Furthermore, in the case of half of the pericopes that he took from Mark, Matthew used less than half of the words that are found in Mark's account!

Mark's Gospel contains 11,078 words. In his parallels to Mark, Matthew uses 8,555 words; of these, 4,230 (49.4%) are identical with Mark's words and 4,325 (50.6%) are different (Morgenthaler, 163 and 166). This means that in Matthew's pericopes parallel to Mark (and that on the Markan Priority Hypothesis are derived from Mark), Matthew overall has 49.4% of his words in common with his source, so that 50.6% of Matthew's words are *not* in Mark's parallel pericopes. Matthew's pericopes are shorter than Mark's, yet Matthew has used 4,230 of the 11,078 words that he had in front of him in Mark, or 38.2%—that is, he rewords and reworks and reorders and otherwise revises Mark's Gospel, and actually copies from Mark less than 40% of what Mark contains (see chap. 4, table 2). Overall, Matthew used fewer than 40% of the words that lay in front of him in Mark's Gospel.

In these circumstances it is hardly legitimate to speak any longer of Mark's material being "incorporated" into Matthew. Such extensive changes to the source material constitute a large-scale rewriting, and the reasons hitherto adduced no longer suffice.

The case is similar for Luke. Morganthaler (241–43) lists 96 pericopes that Mark and Luke have in common, and for only four of these does Luke have 75% or more of his words in common with Mark. That is, in 92 out of 96 pericopes that Luke drew from Mark, he altered more than a quarter of the words that he found in his source! Furthermore, for only 30 of these pericopes does he use even half of the words used by Mark. In 66 out of 96 pericopes taken from Mark, Luke uses fewer than half of Mark's words. Overall, Luke uses fewer than 25% of the words that lay in front of him in Mark's Gospel.

In Luke's parallels to Mark, Luke uses 6,737 words; 2,675 of these (39.7%) are identical and 4,062 (60.3%) are different (Morgenthaler, 163 and 166; see above, chap. 4, table 2). Thus, in his pericopes that are parallel to Mark (and that on the Markan Priority Hypothesis are derived from Mark), Luke overall has 39.7% of his words in common with Mark, while 60.3% of Luke's words do not occur in Mark's parallel pericopes. Luke used 2,675 of the 11,078 words that he had in front of him in Mark, which is 24.1%. This means that, when looking at words specifically, Luke copied from Mark *less than 25% of what Mark contained.*

Lest there be some suspicion about the objectivity of Morgenthaler's statistics, I point out that he himself is an advocate of Markan Priority and sees this position as being supported by deductions made from his statistics. But his statistics, which he obtained by means of computer analysis, give facts that are rather far removed from the estimates of Streeter and other previous writers. Streeter's comment (1924, 159–60) is:

> Mark's style is diffuse, Matthew's succinct; so that in adapting Mark's language Matthew compresses so much that the 600 odd verses taken from Mark supply rather less than half the material contained in the 1068 verses of the longer Gospel. Yet, in spite of this abbreviation, it is found that Matthew employs 51% of the actual words used by Mark. . . . If we leave out of account all passages where there is reason to suspect that Luke has used a non-Markan source, it appears on an approximate estimate that about 350 verses (*i.e.*, just over one half of Mark) have been reproduced by Luke. When following Mark, Luke alters the wording in his original a trifle more than Matthew does; on the other hand he retains many details which Matthew omits, and he does not compress the language quite so much. The result is that on an average Luke retains 53% of the actual words of Mark, that is, a very slightly higher proportion than does Matthew.

Some of the word classifications depend on the subjective judgment of the researcher, and there is scope for future workers to modify Morgenthaler's details a little. But the basic situation revealed by his figures is beyond challenge, that is, if Markan Priority is true, then Matthew took over somewhat less than two words out of five that lay in front of him in Mark, and Luke took over rather less than one quarter of the words of Mark!

Streeter made the best possible assessment in these matters with the tools available to him at the time. But these Streeter statistics are still being quoted today as if they were correct, whereas we now know that they are very wrong.

If the Markan Priority Hypothesis is accepted, then it is incumbent on its supporters to consider the significance of this data and to explain the reason for such drastic and extensive changes by Matthew and Luke to their source, and the basis for them, and the nature of the other source(s) for what Matthew and Luke include that they did not derive from Mark and that is contained in pericopes that parallel Mark in the Double and Triple traditions.

Markan Dependence sees the situation quite differently. In relation to the materials of the Markan Double Tradition, Mark has in front of him material that also occurs in Matthew or Luke, as the case may be. He draws on this as it suits his purpose (see chap. 3), supplementing it with his own knowledge of the circumstances of the event or details of the saying—knowledge derived from his close acquaintance with Peter. In the case of materials of the Triple Tradition, Mark has these pericopes before him in both Matthew and Luke. He draws on both of these accounts, together with his knowledge of the teaching and preaching of Peter. And he rewrites his sources to make his Gospel more colloquial in vocabulary and style, to suit his readership and those using the Gospel as a basis for the preaching of the *kerygma* (see chap. 3).

Markan Dependence agrees that Mark made changes to the wording. But there is an explanation on this hypothesis for the low wording correlations, an explanation that does not apply from the perspective of Markan Priority: in many passages Mark found that his two written sources, Matthew and Luke, did not agree with each other in their actual wording, and in incorporating their subject matter into his Gospel he would normally follow the wording of one or the other. So, from the perspective of Markan Dependence, *there is a very greatly reduced amount of change to sources to be accounted for*, since many of the differences are not due to any of the Synoptists altering his source. Rather, they are due to different lines of tradition, with divergent wording, behind Matthew and Luke, so that even if Mark had wholly followed one of them on all such occasions there would thus have been divergences between Mark's Gospel and the other of his sources, except in those places his sources agreed.

Consider the representative case where in a given pericope Matthew and Luke differ in numerous ways and where on the occasions where they differ Mark agrees with Matthew a third of the time, with Luke a third of the time, and is different from both of them a third of the time. Markan Priority must account for when Matthew varies from Mark—which is two-thirds of the time, one third when Mark is the same as Luke and one third when Mark is different from both—because for all this material Matthew is altering Mark. Similarly, Markan Priority must account for when Luke varies from Mark—which is two-thirds of the time, one third when Mark is the same as Matthew and one third when Mark is different from both—because for all this material Luke is altering Mark.

But on the Markan Dependence view it is necessary only to account for the places where Mark differs from *both* Matthew and Luke (i.e., one third of the time, in this example), because the remaining two-thirds of the time he is following either Matthew or Luke and nothing needs explaining since he differs from the other only because Matthew and Luke differ between themselves. To the extent therefore that Matthew and Luke differ and Mark agrees with one or the other (and this is quite frequent), to that extent there is less redactional modification to be explained by Markan Dependence than by Markan Priority. And as for the occasions when Mark differs from both of the others, the most probable explanation is that Mark was influenced by his recollection of how Peter worded this part of the story.

Examples of this situation are below. Chapter 11 sets out several such passages for careful assessment, but one illustration suffices for now (from Morgenthaler, 147):

Matt 23:6–7	Mark 12:38b–39	Luke 20:46
	βλέπετε	προσέχετε
	ἀπὸ τῶν γραμματέων	ἀπὸ τῶν γραμματέων
	τῶν θελόντων	τῶν θελόντων
		περιπατεῖν
	ἐν στολεῖς	ἐν στολεῖς
	περιπατεῖν	
	καὶ	καὶ
φιλοῦσιν		φιλούντων
	ἀσπασμοὺς	ἀσπασμοὺς
	ἐν ταῖς ἀγοραῖς	ἐν ταῖς ἀγοραῖς

Matt 23:6–7	Mark 12:38b–39	Luke 20:46
δὲ τὴν πρωτοκλισίαν ἐν τοῖς δείπνοις καὶ τὰς πρωτοκαθεδρίας ἐν ταῖς συναγωγαῖς καὶ	καὶ πρωτοκαθεδρίας ἐν ταῖς συναγωγαῖς καὶ πρωτοκλισίας ἐν τοῖς δείπνοις	καὶ πρωτοκαθεδρίας ἐν ταῖς συναγωγαῖς καὶ πρωτοκλισίας ἐν τοῖς δείπνοις
τοὺς ἀσπασμοὺς ἐν ταῖς ἀγοραῖς καὶ καλεῖσθαι ὑπὸ τῶν ἀνθρώπων ῥαββί.		

The Triple Tradition Matt 23:6–7//Mark 12:38b–39//Luke 20:46 contains Jesus' woes on Jewish leaders. If in this pericope, while comparing Matthew and Mark, there are those who claim that either of these is derived from the other, then they must hold that the one who copied has made some very substantial rearrangements in the order of material in his source, maintained the form of words for what he did use virtually unchanged, but left out some of the material in his source while introducing other material of his own. Here are the statistics: the number of words in Matthew is 25, in Mark is 24; the number of identical words is 13. Overall, this is quite a low level of correlation for both words and order. But there is almost total agreement between Mark and Luke: they differ in one change of word (Mark, βλέπετε; Luke, προσέχετε), one change of word order (περιπατεῖν after the phrase ἐν στολαῖς in Mark and before it in Luke), and one word in Luke not occurring in Mark (φιλούντων).

Streeter (1924, 253–54) explains this entire pericope of woes on the Pharisees on the basis "that Luke's version of the discourse ... stood in that document [Q] and that Matthew has again conflated a discourse of Q with one on the same topic which came to him in M.... Yet again, Matthew, besides placing the discourse in a Marcan context, adds to it a few words from Mark." This last comment is a peculiar one since there is not *a single word* in common between Matthew and Mark that is not also in Luke—that is, upon Streeter's analysis, in Q. And how then does it happen that Mark and Luke are almost identical? For according to Streeter *Luke is from Q and not from Mark!* Is this *another* overlap between Mark and Q? Is this a piece of evidence for the fact that Mark used Q? Yes, Streeter claims where he lists (*Oxford Studies* 1911, 176) this passage as the eighth in his series of Markan passages derived from or greatly influenced by Q. (On 412 of the same volume N. P. Williams refers the reader to Streeter's proofs of "the use of Q by the author or final redactor of Mark," and among the passages "either drawn from or based upon Q" he lists Mark 12:38–40.) However, by 1924 Streeter had reversed his opinion that Mark used Q. What is his explanation for Mark 12:38–40? He is completely silent upon the point.

Tuckett deals (1983, 134–39) in some detail with the woes against the scribes and Pharisees, and comments (134): "Lk 11:43 is closely parallel to Mt 23:6, and thus forms a doublet with Lk 20:46. On the Two-Document Hypothesis, the presence of such a doublet can be easily explained as due to the presence of the saying in Luke's two sources, Mark and Q. Mt 23:6 is then a conflation of these two sources." Tuckett believes (138) Luke derived 20:46 from Mark, and he comments (139): "It is hard to envisage Mark spoiling Luke's construction by omitting φιλούντων, whereas Luke's addition of the word is an intelligible improvement of Mark's Greek." But it is not so simple. Tuckett's view is that Luke derived this verse from Mark, and Matthew took the words of Mark and substantially rearranged them and then conflated them with a considerable volume of material from Q and/or M—for Matt 23:6–7 is part of a much longer woes section in Matthew not paralleled in either Luke or Mark.

The Markan Dependence explanation is very simple: Mark found in Matthew a long denunciation of the scribes and Pharisees, and a much shorter comment in Luke, which paralleled material included in Matthew but that also differed in numbers of ways. Mark decided to include a short quotation about this matter in his Gospel and therefore adopted Luke as his guide—and *that* is why his wording is so close to Luke and different from Matthew. The divergence between Matthew and Luke goes back to the two independent lines of tradition behind them (see chap. 8).

The same kind of divergences that exist between Matthew and Luke where they parallel Mark can be noted from the statistics for where Matthew and Luke parallel each other but not Mark, the so-called Q material. Morgenthaler (83, 166) gives the passages where Matthew and Luke are similar, comprising a total of 3,861 words in Matthew and 3,663 in Luke, of which 1,851 words are identical in both, totaling 47.9% of Matthew's wording and 50.5% of Luke's. These figures are considerably higher than those for the correspondence of Matthew and Luke with Mark, because narrative predominates in the material of the Markan Double and Triple Traditions, while most of the Q tradition is direct speech (primarily Jesus' teaching), and it is recognized that direct speech is transmitted and copied with fewer alterations than is the case with narrative. Morgenthaler (163) shows that the identical words in the Markan Double and Triple Traditions for his two subdivisions of direct speech, W (conversation) and L (teaching), are 56% and 62% for Matthew and 51% and 52% for Luke of the total words in parallel pericopes. (These are higher than the Q percentages of 47.9% and 50.5% because the latter are affected by the non-direct speech that *does* occur in Q material.)

In summary, the level of divergence between Matthew and Luke appears to be at a fairly similar level in both the material paralleled in Mark and the material not paralleled in Mark, the Q material. The Markan Priority Hypothesis requires that both Matthew and Luke made very considerable alterations to the text of Mark that they had in front of them, Matthew taking over only 38.2% of Mark's material unchanged and Luke taking over just 24.1% of Mark's material unchanged (as noted from table 2). Thus a very high degree of change must have been made by Matthew and Luke to their source if Markan Priority is true. This is not impossible, but it *is* improbable, and now that these figures are known to us from Morgenthaler's research, exponents of Markan Priority have the task ahead of them of explaining why and how and on what basis these extensive changes were made.

The Markan Dependence explanation is much more reasonable: Matthew and Luke already contained differing traditions, with divergent wording and order, when Mark commenced his work. Because of his theological purposes and his intended readership, he made a number of changes to his source material even where Matthew and Luke agreed; but much of the low level of correlation of Mark with his written sources is due to the extent of the initial divergence between Matthew and Luke, so to that extent Mark—by incorporating what *one* of his sources said—would be diverging automatically from his *other* written source. Moreover, in many cases the lack of exact identity of grammar and wording between Mark and Matthew or Luke in parallel pericopes is because when Mark came to conflate them he frequently had to employ a grammatical construction and forms of the words that differed (even if only slightly) from both of them.

Thus an explanation based on Markan Dependence accounts well for why there would be such a relatively low level of word correlation as actually exists between Mark and each of the two Major Synoptics. This explanation contains no improbabilities.

2. Luke Made the Great Omission from Mark

Often called Luke's "Great Omission" (see Hawkins 1911, 61; Streeter 1924, 172), Mark 6:45–8:26 comprises 74 consecutive verses that are completely unparalleled in Luke. This circumstance requires some comment from the perspective of Synoptic theories. Hawkins wrote an essay (*Oxford Studies* 1911, 60–74) on this matter from the perspective of Markan Priority where he notes that prior to and subsequent to this section Luke follows Mark's order closely and omits very little of what he contains— and then in this one section Luke omits one-ninth of the content of Mark's Gospel (62). He then considers the three most common explanations for the Great Omission: (1) this material was missing from the copy of Mark used by Luke; (2) the omission occurred by accidental oversight; and (3) Luke had reasons for the deliberate omission of each of the nine pericopes in the section.

It is possible that Luke may have used an early edition of Mark's Gospel that lacked the passage in question, but Hawkins shows (64) in his essay that the distinctive features that characterize the other eight-ninths of Mark's Gospel "occur in the block of 74 verses here omitted by Luke with as much proportionate frequency as they do in the other 587 verses which . . . were used by him." Hawkins views (66) more favorably the second possibility: "Considerably more probability attaches to a second theory, viz that this division of our Second Gospel was contained in Luke's copy of it, but that he accidentally left it unused. . . . I have long thought this a more than possible solution."

But Hawkins much prefers the third explanation, that Luke intentionally chose not to use any of this material "because its contents seemed to him unsuitable for his Gospel, or at least not so suitable for it as other materials which he had ready for use" (67). He then discusses (67–74) the "nine constituent parts" of the Great Omission and suggests that the miracles of healings (Mark 7:31–37; 8:22–26) were unnecessary because (68) "Luke especially, in his readiness to save space by avoiding repetition, would be content with the more impressive and significant healings of a κωφός and of a blind man which he meant to record further on in his Gospel (11:14 and 18:35–43)."

Hawking says that Luke's desire to avoid unnecessary repetition also accounts for the omission of the feeding of the 4,000 (he includes the 5,000), a second storm on the lake (he records an earlier one), a general account of healings at Gennesaret (he has a somewhat similar account in 6:17–19 based on Mark 3:7–11), and the refusal of a sign (he has something similar in 11:16,29). The omission of the unwashed hands pericope (Mark 7:1–23) is to be attributed to the fact that "another observable tendency in Luke is to limit the amount of anti-Pharisaic controversy which he preserves" (70). For the leaven of the Pharisees pericope, "this omission is the result of Luke's tendency to 'spare the twelve'—to say comparatively little as to their faults and failings" (71). Regarding the pericope of the Syrophoenician woman's daughter, Hawkins concedes (72) that "in this one case it may seem at first sight that the omission of the incident could not be intentional, since the idiosyncracies and prepossessions of the Third Evangelist would incline him to preserve it in his Gospel." But after discussing it further he says (74):

> It would seem then, on consideration of this narrative, that it might be repellent rather than attractive to St Luke's readers so far as it was taken as bearing on the mutual relations of Jews and Gentiles in the Christian Church. . . . We can thus easily understand his omitting this section as well as the other eight, if at this stage of his compilation he began to see the impossibility of compressing his materials within his space, and therefore the necessity of limiting himself to the most important of them.

Hawkins has a most effective way of disarming criticism of his preferred explanation: he sets out the objections to it, thus showing that he knows of these objections and has taken them into account in coming to his final judgment. But doing this does not in any way actually *nullify* these objections. He first explains how closely Luke follows the order and content of Mark both before and after this section, thus encouraging the reader not to meditate on how very peculiar it is, therefore, that *Luke should so totally ignore this entire 74-verse section, if he had it available to him.*

Another significant objection that Hawkins ingenuously mentions is the fact that Luke's Gospel contains many of the very kinds of "repetitions" that (according to Hawkins's arguments) explains Luke's rejection of six out of the nine pericopes in the Great Omission: for example, the two missions sent out (Luke 9:1ff.; 10:1ff.); two leprosy healings (5:12ff.; 17:12ff.); two comparisons of the position of Jesus' mother with that of his disciples (8:19ff.; 11:27ff.); two disputes concerning greatness (9:46ff.; 22:24ff.); and three Passion Predictions (9:22; 9:44f.; 18:31ff.); plus Luke's eleven doublets (*Horae Synopticae* 1909, 99–106). In the light of these repetitions, the bald assertion that Luke omitted six of the pericopes of the Great Omission because he avoided repetitions and for reasons of conservation of space appears less convincing.

Hawkins's reason for Luke's omission of the seventh pericope—the "observable tendency in Luke to limit the amount of anti-Pharisaic controversy which he preserves" (76)—is by no means impossible, but "limit the amount" is a flexible term that can cover whatever in fact is found. And Luke does contain *some* anti-Pharisaic material, so he obviously was being somewhat selective. In other words, *whatever amount* of anti-Pharisaic material occurred in Luke's Gospel, Hawkins could have covered the situation by varying his terminology slightly. Thus his comment here provides no real reason for the absence of the unwashed hands pericope.

His explanation that the eighth "omission is the result of Luke's tendency to 'spare the twelve'" is a similarly flexible comment that can be adjusted to suit what is found, but which does not adequately account for the omission of the pericope. And the fact is that Luke does contain numerous passages where he does not seem concerned about "sparing the twelve."

Finally, Hawkins's explanation of why Luke would leave out the pericope on the Syrophoenician woman's daughter is a case of doing a good job in a difficult situation: one sympathizes with the performer, but one is not convinced by his achievement. (See discussion on this pericope above as number seven of the seventeen impossible things.) Overall, Hawkins's careful and thorough explanations do not in any way demonstrate that he has proven his case.

Streeter speaks (1924, 174) most warmly of aspects of Hawkins's essay on this subject, as he does at other times of Hawkins's work generally. But this is one occasion where Streeter declines to follow Hawkins, though he concedes (175) that his "hypothesis of intentional omission cannot be ruled out." Further, Streeter gives (174–75) weighty reasons against the "two editions of Mark" explanation. His own explanation (175) is "that Luke used a mutilated copy of Mark. The case for this I state, but merely as a tentative suggestion."

Kümmel (1975, 62–63) says:

> That Mk 6:45–8:26 is lacking [in Luke] is admittedly "enigmatic," but at the same time Luke gives evidence that he had read this section. . . . The view that Luke had access to a truncated version of Mark is as unsatisfactory an explanation of the evidence as any hypothesis of an *Urmarkus*. . . . By far the most probable conclusion is that in the form handed down to us Mark served as a source for Matthew and Luke.

In a footnote (62) Kümmel quotes with approval the opinion of Morgenthaler that "Luke recognized the close relationship of some texts with the texts taken over from Mark and wanted to leave room for his own special material."

It can be seen then that the so-called Great Omission proves "enigmatic" (to use Kümmel's word) for advocates of Markan Priority. The explanations suggested cannot be ruled out of court: any one of them is most certainly *possible*. But it is equally certain that they are not *convincing*. If Luke had Mark in front of him, it is definitely improbable that he would move through a section of 74 verses, one-ninth of the length of this Gospel, and find *absolutely nothing at all* in it of which he wished to make any use! The pericope of the Syrophoenician woman's daughter has already been noted, but much else in this section would also be of interest to Luke, and a thoughtful reading of the "omitted" section suggests that these explanations are attempts to explain away a difficulty. That difficulty does not exist on the Markan Dependence reading of the data: Matthew and Luke were written independently of each other, and the material in question occurs in the traditions Matthew recorded but not in what Luke recorded. Mark made use of both Gospels, found this material in Matthew and used it, and also supplemented what Matthew contains from his third source (Peter) for some stories and details.

It is quite improbable that Luke would have made the "Great Omission" from Mark if that Gospel had been in front of him, as Markan Priority postulates. It is very straightforward to account for the data here in all three Gospels on the basis of Markan Dependence. Thus, once again Markan Dependence provides a much more reasonable explanation of what the Gospels actually contain.

3. Jesus Gave Each of His Teachings Only Once

It is a tacit assumption (and sometimes an explicit assertion) by numbers of Markan Priorists that the variant forms of similar teaching by Jesus recorded in the Synoptics are redacted versions of the one saying by Jesus—if indeed a particular teaching is considered genuine.

There are three main points at which this impinges on the discussion of Synoptic relationships: the question of doublets; judgments regarding equivalence between pericopes in different Gospels; and the redaction of Mark and Q by Matthew and Luke.

Doublets are those places where a similar saying occurs twice in a given Gospel. They are referred to or discussed in all detailed studies of the Synoptic Problem. Thus Hawkins provides full lists of doublets (1909, 82–107) and introduces this section of his book (80) by saying:

> The "doublets," or repetitions of the same or closely similar sentences in the same Gospel, are of great value in supplying hints as to the sources and composition of the Gospels, especially when a comparison can be made with parallels in one or two other Gospels, which is fortunately the case in most instances. . . . These doublets will therefore be brought together here, with a few comments pointing out their bearing upon the Synoptic Problem.

The standard assessment of the doublets is that the doublets in Matthew and Luke are derived from two sources, Mark and Q, and these are presumed to be variant forms of what was originally said.

The second issue is that of judgments regarding equivalence between pericopes in different Gospels. Particular pericopes are in view here. Is the parable of the pounds (Luke 19:11–27) a variant version of the parable of the talents (Matt 25:14–30)? Is the parable of the marriage feast (Matt 22:1–14) the same as the parable of the great banquet (Luke 14:15–24)? What is the relationship between the Matthean and Lukan versions of the Lord's Prayer (Matt 6:9–13; Luke 11:2–4) and the parable of the lost sheep (Matt 18:10–14; Luke 15:3–7)? Numerous scholars accept passages such as these as redactional variants of the one teaching.

Numbers of passages in Matthew and Luke differ from each other in specific details while having a general similarity of content. If these passages are not paralleled in Mark, then they are attributed to Q and their differences are the subject of debate: do these differences result from the redactional modification of Q by Matthew or Luke (or both)? Or are the differences due to Matthew and Luke using differing recensions of Q (or possibly an Aramaic versions of Q)? If the passages in question are not only in Matthew and Luke but also paralleled in Mark, then (with the specific exception of the passages that are regarded as Mark-Q overlaps; see above) it is taken that the variation of Matthew and Luke respectively from Mark is due to the alterations made to Mark by Matthew and Luke respectively. Therefore this third issue is thus the question of the redaction of Mark and Q by Matthew and Luke.

Many of these various passages and types of passages are discussed separately in this study in the appropriate places. The point at issue here is the underlying assumption that exists in many scholars' treatment of these issues; this is, such sayings and pericopes have one common origin from which variation has occurred, either during the oral transmission stages (e.g., the variation between the Q and Markan versions of a saying) and/or at the stage of the redaction of Mark and Q by Matthew and Luke.

The one relevant—indeed, vital—consideration that appears to be lacking in the examination of the issue by many scholars is the question of whether *Jesus could have given similar teaching on more than one occasion*. Addressing this issue in the Jowett Lectures, F. C. Burkitt correctly says (1911, 20):

> On the very shortest estimate the length of the Ministry must have extended to about 400 days, and I doubt if our Gospels contain stories from 40 separate days. So that nine-tenths at least of the public life of Jesus remains to us a blank, even if we were to take every recorded incident as historical and accurately reported. And all the recorded sayings of Christ—how long would they take to pronounce? With due gravity and emphasis they might take six hours—hardly, perhaps, so much. In other words, they would take no more than two

great political speeches, and a considerably less time than this present course of Lectures.

Yet the Gospel records tell us that Jesus engaged in preaching and teaching tours in town after town (Mark 1:38; 6:6), preaching in their synagogues (Mark 1:39) and to crowds in the countryside (Mark 1:45; 2:13; 3:7–10; 4:1–2). He often taught for hours at a time (6:34–35) and sometimes for days on end (Mark 8:1–2). He taught many different groups of people in different places on different occasions. Now what did he teach in the course of these many hours of ministry? In particular, are we really to believe that he never said the same thing twice over, never preached the same message in different towns or different synagogues?

The idea is totally ludicrous. One of the most basic principles of effective teaching is judicious repetition. The writers of the New Testament Epistles very frequently repeat themselves in what they say in different letters. This is most clear in Paul's Letters since his are the greatest number of letters available by one author for comparison. Some of Paul's teachings come up only once or twice, but other themes and concepts are constantly repeated. In the case of some matters that are only mentioned on a small number of occasions in the Epistles, they were covered (as his passing comments indicate) in the course of Paul's personal visits. For example, specific explanations about the Lord's Supper are very few in the New Testament, but where this subject does arise in 1 Corinthians 11 Paul also mentions that he had fully explained about it when he was personally present with them (11:23). Paul was quite willing to draw attention to the fact that he was repeating what he had already said to them previously (Phil 3:1), as was Peter (2 Pet 1:12). Any modern-day teacher or preacher knows that he gives the same lessons to different people on different occasions, and indeed, for the sake of revising and reinforcing the lesson, he goes over it more than once with the same group. Why then should it be thought that Jesus would give each teaching only once? There is no evidence in support of this view of Jesus' teaching ministry as revealed in the Gospels, and there is no justification for coming to such a bizarre opinion about Jesus.

If one grants that Jesus did repeat his teachings, is it necessary to claim that the repetition of a specific teaching must be in words identical with those used on the first occasion? Again, there are no grounds for such a peculiar opinion. Like any other effective teacher, Jesus would modify and adjust the thrust of his teaching from one occasion to another to give it maximum relevance for each group to which he spoke, and he would adapt his stories and illustrations from one situation to the next. One can be confident that is the case—not merely because it is what good teachers have always done, and not merely because this is what we see happening in the ministry of Jesus' followers in Acts and the Epistles—but *because this is what we find in the Gospels themselves.*

Gospel scholars have been busy inventing speculative explanations of how the Synoptic pericopes were redacted so as to end up being different from each other. All one has to do is to cease this long enough to look at the actual situations described in the Gospel records. The two versions of the Lord's Prayer are *said* to have been given in quite different circumstances on different occasions. The same parable of the lost sheep is given a different application in two totally different teaching situations. There are some similarities of ideas between the parable of the marriage feast (Matthew) and the parable of the great banquet (Luke), but the introduction to each of them makes it quite plain that they were spoken in completely different circumstances.

It is *possible* that these and other similar "distant parallels" are variants of the one original teaching, and that the context is in each case the invention of a later redactor. But it is *highly improbable*. There is no evidence, there is no line of argument, there is no basis in logical thought, there is no valid ground of any kind, on which to declare that these distant parallels are derived in each instance from the *one* original teaching. Such a perspective requires a commitment to the idea that Jesus would give each teaching only once—a matter of the highest improbability.

What is most probable is that in the history of each Gospel the circumstances of each pericope's setting were transmitted with that pericope, or were known in some other way to the Gospel's author: to Matthew, from his memory of his own involvement and of what he had heard the other apostles say; to Luke, from the traditions he collected during his investigation and from his personal interviews with eyewitnesses; to Mark, from his knowledge of the general traditions of the church and in particular of the preaching of Peter.

When Matthew and Luke record this teaching or that, one incident or another, they reflect and thus represent the separate traditions that to such a large extent lie behind their Gospels. Frequently, their wording of Jesus' teachings will differ *because they are recording what Jesus taught on somewhat similar issues on different occasions, derived from different eyewitnesses*. When Mark's wording differs from both of them—which is usually when he is adding further details—this represents the influence on his Gospel of his third source, the apostle Peter.

This is the evaluation to which one is led by taking the Gospel records at face value, and this is a far more probable general explanation of the observable differences in Jesus' teaching recorded in the Gospels than the alternative: that Jesus would give each teaching only once, or that if he repeated himself it would be in identical words, so that any difference in reports of that teaching were solely due to changes made in the words of his teaching in the course of their transmission, or that if his teaching differed a little from one occasion to another there could be no multiplicity of witnesses to pass on that teaching in its variant forms. The Markan Dependence view is highly preferable to these improbabilities.

4. The Early Church Invented the Teachings of Jesus

Developments in New Testament scholarship in the twentieth century—as detailed and documented earlier in this study—have led to the adoption by many scholars of a very skeptical attitude about the authenticity of the sayings of Jesus and indeed of the entire Gospel narratives. According to this theory, the Gospels in their present form are the result of many decades of development and adaptation by the early church. Occasionally in the Gospels, one has glimpses here and there of the authentic historical Jesus behind the overlay of tradition that has encrusted the record of the facts of his life and very largely hidden the truth. It is not possible, these scholars confidently assure us, to accept the statements of the Gospels as being historically accurate, either in narrative or in their record of Jesus' teachings. Rather, the Gospels contain evidence of the perceived needs of the early church several decades after the time of Christ, for these Gospels were written to meet those needs so that their contents were devised on *that* basis and for *that* purpose. The Gospels that we have are thus the product of the creative writing of the early Christian community.

This viewpoint conveys the implication that it is quite naïve (as well as rather quaint and old-fashioned) to think that the Gospels preserve the actual words and deeds of Jesus. Rather, these scholars are certain that the Gospels simply contain tales about Jesus told in the oral tradition, shaped and molded in the course of transmission, written down in primitive form in Mark (this theory presumes Markan Priority) and in more developed form in Matthew and Luke; and they were then reworked and reworded, expanded, amplified, and supplemented, by the respective authors of Mark, Matthew, and Luke for and in conjunction with their respective Christian communities.

From this belief emerges the "search for the historical Jesus" that seeks to penetrate through these accretions of the later church to whatever substratum of genuine and accurate tradition about Jesus underlies our present Gospels. Q material is held to be early and original, and largely reliable.

Thus scholars must work their way backwards from the present text to its original form. It used to be thought that what was found in Mark could be accepted as historical, with only the additions and modifications of Matthew and Luke being the result of later church adaptation; but many scholars today would not accept this position and regard Mark as being as historically unreliable as the other two. So the three Synoptic Gospels (I do not encroach here into the related but separate field of Johannine studies) are not by any means authentic and reliable records of what Jesus said and did. Instead, they are the fruits of the imaginative redactional manipulations engaged in by the authors of the Gospels of Mark, Matthew, and Luke.

The line of argumentation in support of this theory is quite circular: we know what these community needs were, which the Gospels were written to meet, from examining the contents of the Gospels; and we know that the Gospels were written to meet such needs because those are the matters with which the Gospels are concerned.

Moreover, even if (and this is an "if" of substantial proportions) we had adequate reason to believe that the particular contents of the Gospels were decided and shaped by such needs of Christian communities decades after the events that they record, this in itself in no way automatically impugns the veracity of their contents. It would be perfectly possible for members of the Christian church who were eyewitnesses, or who were taught by eyewitnesses, to write down a record of those parts of the total tradition that were most relevant to those needs of the community and for those accounts of what Jesus said and did to be *true*. There is no justification for the conclusion that those writers would be compelled by lack of suitable material among the authentic Jesus traditions to *invent* things that Jesus said and did.

Nor have we any basis for believing that the other members of these early Christian communities would have been so gullible that they would believe everything that they were told about Jesus, or that they would be so cut off from the mainstream of the traditions as to be unaware of whether such things were part of those traditions or cleverly devised myths. And there is certainly no evidence whatsoever that would suggest that these early Christians would willingly and knowingly embrace fictitious myths and tales, and adopt them as the basis of how to live, and sacrifice and die for what they had thus adopted as their beliefs. It is those who today believe such things about the early church who show great evidence of gullibility.

If such fictions were accepted in the early church, what happened to all the people who knew the life and ministry of Jesus first hand? To the crowds who so frequently heard his teachings and saw his mighty works? To the apostles themselves, specifically chosen and designated by Jesus to be his witnesses and trained for this role?

Moreover, communities are not "creative." *Communities* do not invent and devise stories and tales. *People* do. And if there were people with the ability to create the kind of teaching attributed to Jesus in the Gospels and that has ever after excited the admiration of the world, then people of this kind and caliber would hardly have become anonymous among the members of the early church. And if such people (whoever they were) were the real authors of the teaching attributed in the Gospels to Jesus, then *they* (and not Jesus) are to be recognized as the superb teachers of Christendom—they are greater than Jesus, for *they* said these things and Jesus did not. The disciple has become greater than the Master!

Not only is there absolutely no evidence for the idea of a community that created its own "teachings and deeds of Jesus," but all the evidence that does exist is directly, sharply, and strongly against such a possibility. There is only one saying not attested in the Gospels that in the Acts and Epistles is attributed to Jesus (Acts 20:35). The fact that there is one such saying reminds us that not all that was known in the early church of the sayings of Jesus has become incorporated into our Gospels. But this saying, quoted by Paul, hardly qualifies as a creative invention of the early church. Yet if this theory is correct, there were considerable quantities of "sayings of Jesus" (and "deeds of Jesus") being generated in the early church just as the need arose.

The church had need of divine guidance at numerous points in the period covered by the book of Acts: from the appointment of a replacement for Judas to the appointment of assistants for the apostles in the church's welfare work; from the decisions about ministry to Gentiles to the decisions about obedience to the law of Moses. There is no emergence of appropriate "sayings of Jesus" to cover any of these situations. In each case the church took the next step after prayer and made a decision, while depending on the leading of the Holy Spirit and frequently referring to an Old Testament passage as relevant to the situation. But there were no citations of some "word of Jesus" on the point. Where at this time were the creative inventors of such helpful sayings of Jesus as the theory postulates?

In the Epistles the same situation exists. There are a considerable number of citations of or allusions to Jesus' teachings, but these are restrained, limited, and in concord with the Gospels. The most noteworthy part of the Epistles in this connection is 1 Corinthians 7. In this chapter Paul gives his authoritative pronouncement on an issue (7:10), and then states explicitly that this is the citation of a word of the Lord. At several other points in the discussion, he states a judgment on one issue or another and clearly states that this is given on his own authority in the absence of any word of the Lord Jesus on the matter (see 7:6,8,12,17,25–26,32,35,40). This careful distinction between what was said by the Lord Jesus Christ and cited by Paul, and what was said on Paul's own apostolic authority, is the very opposite of the "creative invention" of sayings of Jesus for all occasions; and it shows in unmistakable fashion that the distinction between what Jesus himself said and what was being taught by his authorized followers was being very carefully preserved.

It is not as if the matter of authenticity was not raised in the early church, so that at that time all things were possible. There were those who were willing to claim to speak in the name of an apostle (cf. 2 Thess 2:2 and 3:17). The possibility that the first Christians had begun to "follow cleverly devised myths when we made known to you the power and coming of our Lord Jesus Christ" is expressly stated and repudiated on the basis that "we were eyewitnesses of his majesty" (2 Pet 1:16). The genuineness of the message of Jesus was explicitly asserted on the ground of specific eyewitness involvement with Jesus (1 John 1:1–4).

The idea of wholesale and large-scale inventions of Gospel material is in fact a complete denial of what Luke himself expressly states to be the case: his Gospel, he declares in very sober tones, is "a narrative of the things accomplished amongst us, just as they were delivered to us by those who from the beginning were eyewitnesses and ministers of the word" (Luke 1:1–2)—and this comment is true of others also who had undertaken the work of compiling such a narrative. Moreover, in writing his own record, Luke had checked out everything carefully and closely from the beginning in order to set down an orderly account that would enable the reader to *know the truth* of the things that had been taught.

If this is correct, then the theory of invention of "words and deeds of Jesus" is incorrect—and vice versa. They are mutually exclusive. In fact, to hold the theory of church invention of what is now found in the Gospel record is to accept pure speculation devoid of the slightest foundation of objective evidence of any kind and to fly in the face of all the evidence that does exist. This theory is totally suppositional and devoid of the slightest piece of actual objective evidence. Who were the members of this "creative community"? When and where did they live? What information do we have about their activities from any historical source? The opinions about these matters are imaginative speculations and are comparable for dependability, authenticity, and accuracy to what you would get in a sci-fi paper on life forms from the planets of Alpha Centauri.

Yet many people accept these "conclusions" as a scholarly extension of the hypothesis of Markan Priority. In fact, that the early church would—or could—invent the teachings of Jesus can be regarded as highly improbable. Why designate this as improbable, rather than place it with the 17 impossibilities listed earlier? Because in the 17 cases, the relevant evidence is all available for investigation. In those instances one was able to compare the data and evaluate the evidence. Here one must compare the reasoning and evaluate the arguments. We do not have enough information about the time of the early church to be able to say that we have all the facts needed as the basis for final judgment. But we do have enough data from which to judge that to accept the reliability of the Gospel accounts of the life and teachings of Jesus, so far from being naïve and unscholarly, is to accept the conclusion to which reason, logic, and all available evidence points, as does the work of sober, careful scholarship that respects the known facts and does not engage in wild conjectures and unsubstantiated speculations.

CONCLUSION

In this chapter I have set out 17 impossible things that the Markan Priority Hypothesis requires that we accept. I realize that in these matters the judgment of one individual differs from that of another, and doubtless there are numbers of people who have less difficulty than I in accepting some of these things. But it must be acknowledged that these various matters do constitute something of a problem for advocates of Markan Priority.

In a few cases, they also constitute something of a problem for the Markan Dependence view (and indeed for any Synoptic relationship view), but it is always *much less* of a problem than it is for Markan Priority. And in the vast majority of cases, the Mark Dependence explanation of the passages in question is very simple and straightforward.

These passages, and the issues raised about them, are therefore direction indicators. Given that the data strongly indicates the existence of *some* kind of literary relationship among all three Synoptic Gospels, the question confronting Synoptic scholarship is to determine which direction that relationship flowed. These passages indicate that the direction of relationship is that Mark used Matthew and Luke rather than vice versa. Those who desire to reject Markan Dependence and espouse Markan Priority will find it requisite to give their attention to the task of providing reasonable explanations for the passages discussed in this chapter. For as things stand, all of these passages are certainly more easily explained on the basis of Markan Dependence. Alternatively, they may emulate the Queen in *Through the Looking Glass* and through practice develop the capacity for believing impossible things before breakfast.

THE RELATIONSHIP BETWEEN LUKE AND MATTHEW

This chapter looks carefully at the evidence for and against the proposal that Luke knew Matthew's Gospel.

> [T]he Two Gospel Hypothesis can give a plausible account of Mark's composition. A logical outcome of our efforts has been the conclusion that neither Matthew nor Luke was composed on the basis of Mark or Q.... The following is a general description of the way Luke utilized his major source Matthew.
> —A. J. McNicol et al.,
> *Beyond the Q Impasse: Luke's Use of Matthew* (1996, 1, 14)

> The Farrer Theory affirms Markan Priority but suggests that Luke also knew and used Matthew.... On the Farrer Theory... we can see Matthew simply presupposing his Markan source and elaborating on it, and subsequently getting followed by Luke.... Indeed, the value of the Farrer Theory is that it is able to point to strong evidence that Luke knew not only Mark but Matthew's version of Mark.
> —Mark Goodacre (2001, 123, 149, 164)

> [T]hat Lk took his common material over directly from Mt is championed again and again. This position is completely inconceivable, however.... [T]he assumption of a direct dependance of Lk on Mt must be described as untenable.
> —W. G. Kümmel (1975, 64)

> The frequent disagreement with the Matthean order in this regard is crucial to any judgement about Luke's dependence on Matthew; indeed, it suggests he does not depend on him at all.
> —Joseph A. Fitzmyer (1981, 75),

DID LUKE KNOW MATTHEW'S GOSPEL?

The similarities and differences between Matthew and Luke require an explanation. The Two-Source Hypothesis says that where Matthew and Luke parallel Mark (the Triple Tradition), then the similarities in Matthew and Luke are due to these two authors closely following Mark as their source, while the differences are due to redactional modifications that one or the other or both have made when drawing upon Mark as a source. But where Matthew and Luke are similar to each other and are not paralleled in Mark, they are following a second source, usually referred to as Q; and where Matthew and Luke are parallel in basic contents but differ in details or wording, this is due to either of (or a combination of) their redactional modifications of Q or their use of different recensions of Q. The issue for investigation in this chapter is whether this is the only valid hypothesis that covers the data.

For the purpose of this investigation, I have set aside the idea of Q and the hypothesis of Mark as a source for Matthew and Luke in order to determine what sense can be made of Matthew and Luke apart from Q or Mark. This investigation may lead to absurdities, compelling us to return to the Two-Source Hypothesis and accept it as the only sensible explanation of the data; or it may lead us to one or more alternative explanations that need to be evaluated alongside the Two-Source Hypothesis.

THE SIMILARITIES BETWEEN MATTHEW AND LUKE

A comparison of Matthew and Luke reveals similarities of essentially the same kind that have been noted when Mark is also involved in the comparison: similarities of content, wording, and order of pericopes.

Similarities of Content

Both Major Synoptics contain the same basic kind of material: they cover Jesus' teachings; they describe his healings and other miracles; they record his temptation, his transfiguration, and so on. They may at times have different accounts that nonetheless cover the same basic material. Thus they have different accounts of Jesus' genealogies, birth narratives, the call of the first disciples, rejection at Nazareth, resurrection appearances, and so on; but they both *do have* accounts of these things, and they portray a basically similar ministry of healing and teaching.

Some claim in response that these similarities simply reflect the traditions in the early church that go back to the deeds and sayings of Jesus, so that if one were going to write a Gospel record at all such things would need to be included. But John's Gospel shows that a very different approach is possible, and this comparison further highlights the similarities of Matthew and Luke. In John's Gospel, Jesus teaches in lengthy discourses; in Matthew and Luke mostly in shorter discourses and conversations, and pithy memorable sayings, and in parables. In John's Gospel Jesus has a ministry in Judea; in Matthew and Luke his ministry is in Galilee until his last journey to Jerusalem. This list could go on. Thus the Major Synoptics agree to a great extent in including the same story, or at least they are similar in that they include the *same kinds of things* even when they do not give identical accounts, and this is a feature that requires explanation.

Similarities of Wording

Not only are the same events described and the same teachings recorded in Matthew and Luke, but quite frequently this occurs in language that is very similar. The degree of similarity varies considerably: (1) from absolute identity extending over a dozen or more words in succession, and general identity (with a few insignificant verbal differences) that may extend over whole paragraphs; (2) to places of broad agreement in sense occurring with quite significant differences in some wording; and even (3) to virtually no similarity of wording at all even though the same event is clearly being described.

The Lord's Prayer (Matt 6:9–13//Luke 11:1–4) is an example of the second category (compare the similarities and differences of wording), and Jesus' rejection at Nazareth is an example of the third category (Matt 13:53–58//Luke 4:16–30; the agreements are negligible and the differences are extensive). The differences can be explained in numerous ways, particularly on the basis of a combination of variant sources and redactional modifications. The prime consideration in this chapter is the extent of the similarities of wording, especially in passages that fall into the first category.

It may be helpful to note some examples of these similarities. They can be found in passages (1) where the similarities are also shared with Mark; (2) that are paralleled in Mark but Matthew and Luke are much more similar in wording to each other than either is to Mark; and (3) that are without any Markan parallel. Here are some of the more striking examples of each of these:

Close Similarity in Matthew and Luke, Shared with Mark

1. The Cleansing of a Leper (Matt 8:2–4//Mark 1:40–45//Luke 5:12–16)

2. The Healing of a Paralytic (Matt 9:1–8//Mark 2:1–12// Luke 5:17–26)
3. Plucking Grain on the Sabbath (Matt 12:1–8// Mark 2:23–28//Luke 6:1–5)
4. The Parable of the Sower (Matt 13:1–9//Mark 4:1–9// Luke 8:4–8)
5. Conditions of Discipleship (Matt 16:24–28// Mark 8:34–9:1//Luke 9:23–27)
6. Blessing the Children (Matt 19:13–15//Mark 10:13–16// Luke 18:15–17)
7. The Question about Authority (Matt 21:23–27// Mark 11:27–33//Luke 20:1–8)
8. The Question about the Resurrection (Matt 22:23–33// Mark 12:18–27//Luke 20:27–38)
9. Signs before the End (Matt 24:4–8//Mark 13:5–8//Luke 21:8–11)
10. The Parable of the Fig Tree (Matt 24:32–36// Mark 13:28–32//Luke 21:29–33)

(For statistics on the extent of agreement in the number of words and in percentages, see these passages in chap. 4, table 1.)

Close Similarity in Matthew and Luke but Mark Is Less Similar

1. John's Messianic Preaching (Matt 3:11–12//Mark 1:7–8// Luke 3:16–17)
2. The Temptation (Matt 4:1–11//Mark 1:12–13//Luke 4:1–13)
3. The Beelzebul Controversy (Matt 12:22–45// Mark 3:22–30//Luke 11:14–32)

Close Similarity in Matthew and Luke and No Parallel in Mark

1. John's Preaching of Repentance (Matt 3:7–10//Luke 3:7–9)
2. On Serving Two Masters (Matt 6:24//Luke 16:13)
3. Sayings to Would-be Disciples (Matt 8:19–23//Luke 9:57–60)
4. The Plentiful Harvest (Matt 9:37–38//Luke 10:2)
5. John the Baptist's Question (Matt 11:2–6//Luke 7:18–23)
6. Jesus' Testimony Concerning John (Matt 11:7–19// Luke 7:24–35)
7. Woe to Cities of Galilee (Matt 11:20–24//Luke 10:12–15)
8. Jesus' Thanksgiving to the Father (Matt 11:25–27// Luke 10:21–22)
9. Jesus' Lament over Jerusalem (Matt 23:37–39//Luke 13:34–35)

Similarities of Order

Not only are the same pericopes found in Matthew and Luke, with wording that is quite frequently very similar and even at times identical, but the general order of pericopes is very similar in the two Gospels. Thus the overall structure of the Major Synoptics is the same, and the extent and significance of the similarities are much greater than that of the relatively few places where a difference of order does exist. Thus the differences of order are not really significant but are simply due to a rearrangement of some of the material at some stage, while the agreement of order *is* significant because it can hardly be accidental or fortuitous. Even when a large block of material is found in two different locations in Matthew and Luke, pericopes that are not in themselves necessarily connected with each other and that certainly do not possess any innate order are given by both Matthew and Luke in the same sequence within that block.

Noteworthy examples of this are the two blocks each of several pericopes that occur in succession in Matthew (crossing the Sea of Galilee, Matt 8:18–9:1; events in Capernaum, Matt 9:2–17), immediately following the pericopes on the healing of Peter's mother-in-law and the sick at nightfall (Matt 8:14–17). These occur in reverse order in Luke and are widely separated (crossing the Sea of Galilee, Luke 8:22–40, with one part of Matthew paralleled in Luke 9:57–60; events in Capernaum, Luke 5:17–39E), and both of them well after the pericopes on the healing of Peter's mother-in-law and the sick at nightfall (Luke 4:38–41).

Orchard avers that the explanation of this data is that Luke has used Matthew's Gospel in writing his own and adopted Matthew's order as his own basic framework. He argues (1976, 45):

> Luke adheres firmly to certain fixed points in Matthew's framework. What is especially clear is that in the very places where Luke's sequence varies from Matthew's ... there still remain a number of fixed points (the First Preaching Tour, the Gathering of the Crowds, the Great Sermon, the Centurion's Slave, the Sending of the Twelve, the Missionary Discourse, Herod's Interest in Jesus) where their joint sequence remains absolutely the same. Thus the units which Luke re-groups in his own way in chapters 4–8 are still grouped round the same fixed points. Moreover Luke retains every one of Matthew's topics, except for those in his Great Omission. The quality and amount of agreement is in fact so high as strongly to urge assent to the conclusion that the one Gospel must be in some real literary dependence on the other, i.e. that Luke has adopted the actual pattern and sequence of Matthew, with the reservations stated.

Orchard then examined in detail the differences of order between Matthew and Luke in the placement of their common material, and he attributes this to Luke's reworking of Matthew's order to suit his own purposes.

After an explanation of how Luke appears to have treated Matthew's order, Orchard comments (53), "These re-arrangements of Luke properly explain what many have thought to be a jumble of clueless transpositions, and show his Gospel to be a purposeful re-editing." It can thus be argued that the substantial agreements between the order of pericopes in Matthew and Luke are evidence of a literary relationship between the two Gospels, and that the best explanation of the nature of this relationship is that Luke made use of Matthew's Gospel.

Conclusions Drawn

There are several sections in Luke, ranging from short sayings to lengthy pericopes, that in content and wording are so similar to parallel sections of Matthew and that occur in such similarity of order that scholars in general conclude that they must have a common source. There are four ways that such similarities could have arisen: (1) Luke used Matthew; (2) Matthew used Luke; (3) both Matthew and Luke used the same earlier material (the Two-Source hypothesis falls into this category, but there are other explanations of this kind, as we will see); (4) both Matthew and Luke used oral traditions that were transmitted in a sufficiently fixed form to account for the similarities.

The first view commands quite strong support and is evaluated in detail below. The second view requires that Matthew's Gospel was written somewhat later than Luke's and necessitates rather complex explanations for how Matthew handled what he found in Luke. While this approach does have some supporters—it is a concomitant of R. L. Lindsey's view (1963, 1992) of Lukan Priority (see chap. 10)—and cannot be dismissed as an impossibility, it is rarely defended and the arguments in its support, though advanced strongly by the Jerusalem school, have not appeared very compelling in the academic world. The difficulties that it faces seem so insurmountable that I have come to agree with others who have reached the same conclusion, and in my judgment this appears the least likely of the possible explanations of the parallels in Matthew and Luke. The third view has had an advocate in H. Koester (see Farmer 1983, xxxv). The fourth view must confront a major obstacle in regard to the matter of order. To assert that the identical order of numerous independent pericopes would be conveyed as an integral part of the oral tradition is to adopt a position that is difficult to sustain logically, and there is absolutely no direct evidence of any kind, internal or external, for this claim. One must concede that this is *possible*, but it is not easy to see why *oral* tradition would have connected together certain pericopes as a single item of transmission, for example, the healing of the paralytic, the call of Levi (Matthew), eating with sinners, and the question of fasting (Matt 9:2–17//Luke 5:17–39E), so that they have become embodied in both Matthew and Luke in just that sequence in each case.

To say that this block and other similar clusters of pericopes are given in just that order because that is the sequence in which the events occurred does not solve the problem, because these blocks as a whole occur *out of order* as between Matthew and Luke. So the question is, Why would oral tradition so carefully preserve this order *within each block* when there is no observable reason for that order having any significance and when the blocks of pericopes are in different order in relation to each other in Matthew and Luke? Similarly, the theory of completely oral transmission also has difficulties in accounting for similarities of content and wording (see chap. 10).

The view that Luke used Matthew has strong support, and some are advocates of Markan Priority who are unconvinced of the existence of Q. Thus A. W. Argyle, "Evidence for the View that St Luke Used St Matthew's Gospel" (1964); A. M. Farrer (1955, 56) says, "We can conceive well enough how St Luke could have both read St Matthew's book as it stands, and written the gospel he has left us. . . . There is no difficulty in supposing St Luke to have read St Matthew" (cf. A. W. Argyle 1964; the Farrer hypothesis is examined in chap. 10). Similarly, Morgenthaler supports (1971, 4:300ff.) both Markan Priority and the view that Luke used Matthew.

Some who advocate the independence of Matthew and Mark also suggest that Luke used Matthew. Thus Albright and Mann (1971, XL) say, "It is only necessary (as some have suggested) to posit that Luke had read Matthew before compiling his gospel . . . to dispense with the mysterious 'Q' altogether." In particular, Farmer and his associates of the Two-Gospel Hypothesis held that Luke used Matthew, as did the Fourfold Gospel school (see chap. 6).

The extent of the similarities between Matthew and Luke demands a literary connection. The simple explanation that Luke used Matthew provides that connection, and this view offers an alternative to the proposition that Matthew and Luke used Q or used Q together with Mark. But these similarities are only part of the observable data.

THE DIFFERENCES BETWEEN MATTHEW AND LUKE

Numerous scholars have assessed the question of whether Luke used Matthew. Some have given explanations of how Luke could have done so, and others have given explanation of why he could not have done so. There is no doubt that Luke's use of Matthew would account for all the phenomena of similarity between the Major Synoptics noted above. The major issue is accounting for the manner in which Luke used Matthew. B. Orchard (1976) gives a detailed presentation of how Luke could have used Matthew in order to produce the Gospel of Luke, as does D. A. Black (2001, 69–76). This view was developed fully by the Two-Gospel team (McNicol, 1996). The team's explanation (14) of Luke's methodology is that after the infancy stories and genealogy,

> Luke did not simplistically adopt the order of Matthew's pericopes from Mt 3 to 18. Rather, he created his narrative by moving forward through Matthew to a certain point and then—still following his own narrative agenda—*went back* to an earlier part of Matthew and proceeded to work his way forward in Matthew again. He repeated this procedure a number of times until he used most of the material in Matthew down to Mt 18 (a speech of Jesus dealing with community discipline). Here Luke stopped his method of successive utilization of Matthew's stories and sayings in order to create a lengthy teaching section loosely set against the backdrop of Jesus travelling towards Jerusalem (Lk 10:1–19:27). Known as the Lukan Travel Narrative, the method Luke followed here was to weave together sayings taken from the major speeches of Jesus in Matthew, mostly in the order in which the sayings occur within each speech in Matthew, around a number of themes appropriate to Christians in the Hellenistic world.

These scholars see Luke as making a series of "sweeps" through Matthew's Gospel, and in each sweep taking from Matthew whatever he wished to use in his own Gospel, without (it would appear) a great deal of regard for the context into which Matthew had placed it. In this manner, Luke was then able (14) "to weave together sayings taken from the major speeches of Jesus in Matthew." In addition to placing some of these in various parts of his Gospel, Luke was also able from these sayings and by this method to construct "a lengthy teaching section," his Lukan Travel Narrative: "Luke's revision of Matthew was guided by a number of considerations which we will identify and explain in due course, but the most important of all was his determination to write a narrative that was 'accurate,' i.e., presented in what he considered to be an appropriate *chronological* order for a literary work" (15).

The very idea that anyone would treat Matthew like this has long been raised as a serious objection against any hypothesis of either Mark or Luke using Matthew's Gospel. In 1924 Streeter raised it as an argument against Matthew's priority to Mark, saying that only a "crank" would dismember Matthew in such a way as Mark would be seen as doing. Kümmel (1975, 64) growls, "What could possibly have motivated Lk . . . to shatter Mt's sermon on the mount, placing parts of it in his sermon on the plain, dividing up other parts among various chapters of his Gospel, and letting the rest drop out of sight." On the basis of these and other arguments—which were based on assuming Markan Priority—Kümmel then asserted that the idea that Luke was dependent on Matthew was "completely inconceivable."

Fitzmyer considers the question of "Luke's Supposed Dependence on Matthew" and gives six reasons (1970; his reasons answered by Farmer 1983, 517–23) for rejecting this possibility. The thrust of several of these various objections is directed primarily against the Farrer Hypothesis, which accepts Markan Priority, and thus these arguments have no relevance for Markan Posteriority. But Fitzmyer also asks, Why would Luke ignore such things as the "fuller form of the Beatitudes" and similar material in Matthew; and like Kümmel, he inquires why Luke would wish to break up Matthew's sermons and discourses, especially the Sermon on the Mount (Farmer 1983, 518). Then he objects (Fitzmyer 1970, 137–38; discussed Farmer 1983, 506, 513–14), "The frequent disagreement with the Matthean order in this regard is crucial to any judgement about Luke's dependence on Matthew; indeed, it suggests he does not depend on him at all."

These comments have cogency. I return to them shortly, but first I want to consider the entire question of Luke's dissimilarities with Matthew. I have noted the similarities of the two Major Synoptics, but to recognize the existence of numerous similarities between Matthew and Luke is to see only part of the issue under consideration. One must also account for the equally striking differences between them. These dissimilarities correspond with the categories of similarities noted above: content, wording, and order. Additionally, there are other kinds of differences between Matthew and Luke.

Dissimilarities of Content

When considering the content of Matthew and Luke, it is not enough to mention that Matthew and Luke have different accounts of the genealogy of Jesus, the birth narratives, and so on, or to say that each of the two Major Synoptics *do have* accounts of such things and then move on—as if such comments adequately cover the issue, or as if the similarity of subject matter was a point of correspondence between Matthew and Luke that strengthens the case for seeing a literary relationship between the two.

Such a conclusion has as an unstated premise: that similarity of subject matter between two pericopes in Matthew and Luke indicates (or at least provides support for) a literary link. But under what circumstances could such a thing be true? There are only two possibilities: (1) where one Major

Synoptist was used by the other one (or where a common original source was used by both Matthew and Luke) and the differences are redactional modifications; or (2) where the fact that the first Major Synoptist had a particular type of pericope prompted the second Major Synoptist to include a different account on the same subject. Neither of these two circumstances applies to pericopes in the category now under consideration. Dissimilarities of content include pericopes that, although similar in subject matter, were clearly not drawn one from the other, and neither did they draw from a common source. Thus it is not believable to say that Luke derived Jesus' genealogy from Matthew's (or vice versa) but was subjected to redactional modification; nor is it believable to say that they have come from a single common source. The following pericopes fall into this category since they certainly have similar subject matters but also have independent origins:

PERICOPE	MATTHEW	LUKE
1. The genealogy	1:1–17	3:23–38
2. The infancy narratives	1:18–2:23E	1:5–2:52E
3. The call of the first disciples	4:18–22	5:1–11
4. The rejection at Nazareth	13:53–58E	4:16–30
5. The parable of the great feast	22:1–14	14:15–24
6. The parable of the talents/pounds	25:14–30	19:11–27
7. The anointing	26:6–13	7:36–50
8. The resurrection appearances	28:1–20E	24:1–53E

There are other pericopes that some scholars hold should be added to this list (such as the Greatest Commandment, the dispute about greatness, and the parable of the lost sheep), but the foregoing instances are sufficient at least to establish the existence of this category of pericope. The different placements of these pericopes in Matthew and Luke are significant. Orchard comments (1976, 49): "We may now note that whenever he has a unit with the same topic as a corresponding Matthean unit but with a different content, Luke never places it in the same absolute or relative sequence with its Matthean counterpart, but always in another context."

It is hard to believe that the existence of a pericope in one Gospel inspired the other Major Synoptist to include in his Gospel a *different* account covering *similar* subject matter. This would be as if Luke thought, "Matthew included a story about the call of the first disciples [or the rejection at Nazareth, or any other of these pericopes]. Therefore I must also include an account of such a thing"—and then in *another* place he included a *different* account that he had available from *some other* source. There is no way that the existence of any of these pericopes in one Major Synoptic can be taken as providing evidence for any kind of literary relationship with the other Major Synoptic. On the contrary, the existence of these two sets of pericopes in Matthew and Luke, which may be called "distant parallels," constitutes an argument for affirming that neither Matthew nor Luke used the other's Gospel, because if either of them had done so, his parallel would hardly have been as distant as it is since it would have shown *some* awareness of the existence of the other account. That is to say, the presumption is that if Luke had used Matthew's account of the rejection at Nazareth, then his own account would have shown some evidence that he was aware of it (and similarly for other pericopes in this category), and the onus would be on the advocate of a contrary view to provide a satisfactory explanation on the basis of that view.

The differences in content between Matthew and Luke refer to passages in the one Gospel for which the source could not be the other Gospel nor a source also used by the other Gospel. The differences in content in these pericopes are so extensive as to constitute a serious objection to the view that Luke used Matthew. If Luke used Matthew, then he chose to make use of 37% (395 verses) of that Gospel, taking at most only 35.5% (408 verses) of his own Gospel from it and 64.5% (740 verses) from other sources. This requires an explanation from those who hold that Luke used Matthew's Gospel. (For these statistics, see chap. 4; this issue is considered further below.)

Dissimilarities of Wording

Matthew and Luke share pericopes that have similarity of wording, which suggests a literary relationship or at least a common source, but dissimilarities of wording also occur. These are of such a nature as to require explanation, if Luke was using Matthew as his source.

There are many cases where it is possible to say that the differences are the product of Luke's redaction of Matthew's material and where this is a completely feasible and adequate explanation. But there are numerous places where (1) at crucial points in the story it seems that Luke's account is the more original and that it is Matthew who has redacted Luke; or (2) Matthew and Luke appear independent in what they say; or (3) it is possible that Luke altered Matthew, but it is very difficult to conceive what his purpose was or what he achieved by the alteration.

An example of (1) occurs in Matt 12:28//Luke 11:20. "The finger of God" in Luke is considered more original and more Jewish than "the Spirit of God" in Matthew, while it is Luke's Gospel overall that highlights the work of the Spirit. If we found "finger of God" in Matthew and "Spirit of

God" in Luke, this would accord with their usual respective interests. But that Luke should find "Spirit of God" in Matthew when using it as a source but alter it to "finger of God" is very unexpected. Thus Marshall says (1978, 475–76):

> There is one significant difference from the wording in Matthew. Luke has δάκτυλος, "finger" (11:46 par. Mt 23:4; Lk 16:24) where Matthew has πνεῦμα. The close verbal agreement in the rest of the verse indicates that one word must be a substitution for the other by the Evangelist or his source (if we are dealing with two rescensions of the same source). The meaning is the same in both versions.... Although the meaning is thus the same, both phrases indicating the action of God, the question remains whether Jesus himself here made one of his rare references to the Spirit in a verse which is generally recognised to be his authentic teaching. A majority of scholars hold that δάκτυλος stood in Luke's source (Schulz, 205 n.218). It is argued that Luke is fond of references to the Spirit, and would hardly remove one that already stood in his source; that Matthew may have been removing an anthropomorphism and assimilating the wording to Mt 12:18,31; that the Spirit is not known as an exorcisor in Jewish sources..., but the "finger of God" may be so attested...; and that "finger" gives a direct allusion to the OT.... On the other hand, it has been argued convincingly by C S Rodd ("Spirit or Finger," Exp.T 72, 1960–61, 157f.) that Luke has no greater predeliction for adding references to the Spirit in the body of his Gospel than Matthew; cf. 20:42 par. Mt 12:36. We need not, therefore, be surprised if Luke has removed an original reference to the Spirit. There is no clear case where Matthew has added a reference to the Spirit to his source. However, he does use πνεῦμα θεοῦ in 3:16 diff. Mk. (Schultz, 205). The case for Matthean alteration thus falls short of proof, but on the whole it remains more likely that this is the case, since no good reason for a change by Luke can be found.

Thus Marshall prefers the explanation of a common source for both the Matthean and Lukan accounts that contained δάκτυλος ("finger") with Matthew having then altered this to πνεῦμα ("Spirit").

Another example is in the Olivet Discourse where Luke says "not to meditate beforehand how to answer; for I will give you a mouth and wisdom, which none of your adversaries will be able to withstand or contradict" (21:15). "I will give you a mouth and wisdom" is a very Semitic type of expression. Plummer (1896, 479) compares the usage with Exod 4:12 and Jer 1:9; G. H. P. Thompson (1972, 248) invites additional comparison with Isa 51:16, Wisdom 10:21, and Ecclus 34:8. Matthew parallels this with "do not be anxious how you are to speak or what you are to say, for what you are to say will be given to you in that hour; for it is not you who speak, but the Spirit of your Father speaking through you" (10:19).

Matthew is certainly not the source for Luke, and many scholars consider Luke's wording "more original" than Matthew's. It should also be mentioned that Mark 13:11 ("do not be anxious beforehand what you are to say; but say whatever is given you in that hour, for it is not you who speak, but the Holy Spirit") is much closer to Matthew than to Luke, and similarly Mark cannot be the source for Luke's wording. It is inconceivable that Luke himself *invented* his statement ("for I will give you a mouth and wisdom"), so he must have received it from *some source other than Matthew or Mark*. Thompson comments (1972, 248), "The omission of reference to the Holy Spirit, together with the difference of language, suggests that Luke is not dependent on Mk 13:11. It is perhaps a sign of Luke's faithfulness to his special sources that, despite his obvious interest in the Holy Spirit, he prefers this version of Jesus' promise."

An example of (2), the apparent independence of Matthew and Luke, occurs in the introduction to the transfiguration. Matthew 17:1 (in concurrence with Mark 9:2) has "after six days," but Luke 9:28 has "about eight days after." "Eight days" is a Jewish way of referring to a week; e.g., John 20:26 has "and after eight days," referring to the same day—Sunday in this case—of the following week (the NEB, TEV, and NIV read "a week later"). Another example is in Matt 19:16–22, where Matthew says twice that the rich man who went away sad was young, whereas Luke 18:18–23 says the man was not young but an elder (ruler) who claimed that he had kept God's commandments from (ἐκ) his youth.

An example of (3), differences that could be due to Luke's redaction of Matthew but for which a reason is difficult to discern, occurs in Matt 20:29–34, which says that Jesus healed two blind men while leaving Jericho; but Luke 18:35 says that Jesus healed one blind man "as he drew near to Jericho" on the way into the city (see 19:1). It is difficult to envisage any possible reason that Luke, using Matthew as his source, would make such an alteration. Another example is in Matt 9:18, which says Jairus's daughter was already dead when the synagogue ruler approached Jesus; but Luke 8:40–56 indicates that she was dying when Jairus came to Jesus and actually died while Jesus stood talking with the woman whose hemorrhage he healed. Another example occurs in Luke's list of the 12 apostles (6:15–16), which is not identical with the list in Matt 10:3–4. Yet another example is that Matthew refers to two demoniacs exorcized (8:28–34), two blind men healed (18:35), and two animals brought to Jesus for his use (21:7); in each case Luke mentions only one.

The first type of dissimilarity of wording is where some difference in emphasis, doctrine, viewpoint, or the like, can be perceived. The second and third types are not mutually exclusive and shade from one into the other. Opinions vary as to whether a given dissimilarity of wording was of the first, second, or third kinds. Here are some examples of the most noteworthy dissimilarities of wording between Matthew and Luke.

MATTHEW	LUKE
4:23 And he went about all Galilee, teaching in their synagogues	4:44 And he was preaching in the synagogues of Judea.
7:9 how much more will your Father who is in heaven give good things to those who ask him!	11:13 how much more will the heavenly Father give the Holy Spirit to those who ask him!
7:16 Are grapes gathered from thorns or figs from thistles	6:44 For figs are not gathered from thorns, nor are grapes picked from a bramble bush.
8:5f. a centurion came forward to him, beseeching him and saying . . .	7:2f. a centurion . . . sent to him elders of the Jews, asking him to come . . .
8:15 and he touched her hand, and the fever left her, and she rose	4:39 And he stood over her and rebuked the fever, and it left her, and she rose
9:9 saw a man called Matthew	5:27 saw a tax collector named Levi
10:9 the laborer deserves his food	10:7 the laborer deserves his wages
10:29 Are not two sparrows sold for a penny?	12:6 Are not five sparrows sold for two pennies?
11:17 we wailed, and you did not mourn	7:32 we wailed, and you did not weep
11:19 wisdom is justified by her deeds.	11:35 wisdom is justified by all her children.
12:27 But if it is by the Spirit of God that I cast out demons . . .	11:20 But if it is by the finger of God that I cast out demons . . .
13:6 and since they had no root they withered away.	8:6 it withered away, because it had no moisture.
13:17 many prophets and righteous men longed to see what you see	10:24 many prophets and kings desired to see what you see
14:13 he withdrew from there in a boat to a lonely place apart.	9:10 And he took them and withdrew apart to a city called Bethsaida.
16:13 Now when Jesus came into the district of Caesarea Philippi, he asked his disciples,	9:18 Now it happened as he was praying alone the disciples were with him, and he asked them,
17:1 And after six days	9:28 Now about eight days after
17:5 This is my beloved Son	9:35 This is my Son, my Chosen
19:20 The young man said to him, "All these I have observed."	18:18 And a ruler asked . . . 18:21 And he said, "All these I have observed from my youth."
23:34 Therefore I send you prophets and wise men and scribes,	11:49 Therefore also the Wisdom of God said, "I will send them prophets and apostles,

MATTHEW	LUKE
some of whom you will kill and crucify	some of whom they will kill and persecute"
24:15 So when you see the desolating sacrilege spoken of by the prophet Daniel standing in the holy place . . .	21:20 But when you see Jerusalem surrounded by armies, then know that its desolation has come near.
26:15 And they paid him thirty pieces of silver.	22:5 And they were glad, and engaged to give him money.
26:50 Jesus said to him, "Friend, why are you here?"	22:48 Jesus said to him, "Judas, would you betray the Son of man with a kiss?"
27:54 Truly this was the Son of God!	23:47 Certainly this man was innocent!
28:10 tell my brethren to go to Galilee, and there they will see me.	24:48 stay in the city, until you are clothed with power from on high.
28:16 Now the eleven disciples went to Galilee, to the mountain	24:52 And they returned to Jerusalem with great joy.

Dissimilarities of Order

Even the most casual reading of Matthew and Luke quickly reveals that while they share a similar framework, they also differ frequently in the order they give pericopes or groups of pericopes. If Luke used Matthew, why should there be this difference in order of events?

In fact, the dissimilarities of order between Matthew and Luke exist at every level: the order of blocks of pericopes; the order of individual pericopes; the order of paragraphs within pericopes; and the order of details or words within paragraphs.

The following table shows the dissimilarities of pericope order. Note that in this table, the numbers in the column to the left of the references for Matthew and Luke are to units of the two Gospels (pericopes, parts of pericopes, or pericope clusters) that are being compared. These numbers are consecutive for each Gospel. Numbers absent in the sequence for each Gospel apply to units that are in one Gospel and not in the other. The center column of numbers headed "Matt" sets out the Matthean unit reference number for each of the units listed for Luke; that is, this column shows where that unit in Luke against which it appears occurs in Matthew's sequence. Thus a comparison of this column with the unit numbers for Luke that appear in the column on its right immediately shows how the Matthew's sequence differs from Luke's for the events or teachings they both record.

The Relationship Between Luke and Matthew

		MATTHEW	Mt	Lk		LUKE
5b	4:12b	Jesus Goes to Galilee	5b	10	4:14	Jesus Goes to Galilee
5c	4:13	Jesus Moves to Capernaum	5d	10	4:15	Jesus Teaches in Their Synagogues
5d	4:17	Jesus Begins to Preach	26	11	4:16–30	Rejection at Nazareth
6	4:18–22	Call of the First Disciples	5c	12	4:31a	Jesus Moves to Capernaum
7a	4:23a	Preaching and Healing Tour	8g	12	4:31b–32	Astonishment at Jesus' Teaching
7b	4:23b–25E	Summary, Galilean Ministry	11a	12	4:38–39	Healing Peter's Mother-in-Law
8	5, 6, 7	The Great Sermon	11b	12	4:40–41	Healing the Sick at Nightfall
8g	7:28–29E	Astonishment at Jesus' Teaching	7a	12	4:44E	First Preaching Tour Begins
9	8:1–4	Healing of a Leper	6	13	5:1–11	Call of the First Disciples
10	8:5–13	Healing Centurion's Servant	9	14	5:12–16	Healing of a Leper
11a	8:14–15	Healing Peter's Mother-in-law	13	15	5:17–39E	Events in Capernaum
11b	8:16	Healing the Sick at Nightfall	20	16	6:1–11	Sabbath Controversies
12	8:18–9:1	Across the Sea of Galilee	17a	17	6:12–16	The Choosing of the Twelve
13	9:2–17	Events in Capernaum	21	18	6:17–19	Lakeside Healings
14a	9:18–19	A Ruler's Request	8	19	6:20–49E	The Great Sermon
14b	9:20–22	Woman with a Hemorrhage	22c	19	6:43–45	Trees and Their Fruit
14c	9:23–26	Raising a Ruler's Daughter	10	20	7:1–10	Healing a Centurion's Servant
16a	9:35	Summary of Galilean Ministry	18	22	7:18–35	Concerning John the Baptist
16b	9:36–38E	The Harvest Is Plentiful	25	24	8:4–18	Teaching in Parables (1)
17a	10:1–4	Twelve Chosen Disciples	24	25	8:19–21	Jesus' True Family
17b	10:5–42E	The Mission Charge	12	26	8:22–40	Across the Sea of Galilee
18	11:1–19	Concerning John the Baptist	14a	27	8:41–42	A Ruler's Request
19a	11:20–24	Upbraiding the Cities	14b	27	8:43–48	Woman with a Hemorrhage
19b	11:25–27	Jesus' Exaltation	14c	27	8:49–56E	Raising a Ruler's Daughter
20	12:1–14	Sabbath Controversies	17b	28	9:1–6	The Charge to the Twelve
21	12:15–21	Lakeside Healings	27a	29	9:7–9	Herod's Perplexity
22a	12:22–30	Beelzebul Controversy	27c	29	9:11–17	Feeding of the 5,000

	MATTHEW		Mt	Lk	LUKE	
22b	12:31–32	Sin against the Spirit	29	30	9:18–36	Confession to Transfiguration
22c	12:33–35	Trees and Their Fruit	30	31	9:37–48	The Mountain to Capernaum
23a	12:38–42	Seeking a Sign			*Together with these parallels in Luke's Central Teaching Section:*	
23b	12:43–45	Return of an Unclean Spirit				
24	12:46–50E	Jesus' True Family	12		9:57–62	
25	13:1–52	Teaching in Parables	16b		10:2	
26	13:53–58E	Rejection at Nazareth	19a		10:12–15	
27a	14:1–2	Herod's Perplexity	19b		10:21–22	
27c	14:13–21	Feeding of the 5,000	25		10:23–24	
29	16:13–17:8	Confession to Transfiguration	8		11:9–13	
30	17:9–18:5	The Mountain to Capernaum	22a		11:14–23	
32	19:13–15	Blessing the Children	23b		11:24–26	
			23a		11:16, 29–32	
			22b		12:10	
			8		12:22–32	
			8		12:33–34	
			8		12:57–59	
			25		13:18–21	
			8		16:13	

At the pericope of blessing the children (Luke 18:15ff.), Luke rejoins Matthew in pericope order after his central teaching section, and thereafter their order corresponds quite closely. The above parallels are of similarity of event or teaching, and are not intended to imply that they are necessarily to be regarded as having a common source. (A number of shorter teachings are not included here.)

Some notable dissimilarities of order occur *within* pericopes; for example, the order of the temptation accounts (Matt 4:4–11//Luke 4:4–13) and the order of the bread and cup (Matt 26:26–29//Luke 22:15–19). There are also several minor differences of order within pericopes, which this pericope illustrates:

MATT 12:34a–35	LUKE 6:45
For out of the abundance of the heart the mouth speaks. The good man out of his good treasure	The good man out of the good treasure of his heart
brings forth good, and the evil	produces good, and the evil

MATT 12:34a-35	LUKE 6:45
man out of his evil treasure brings forth evil.	man out of his evil treasure produces evil; for out of the abundance of the heart the mouth speaks.

Other differences of order within pericopes between Matthew and Luke include these:

MATTHEW	LUKE
8:26a Jesus speaks to disciples 8:26b Jesus rebukes winds and sea	8:24 Jesus rebukes wind and waves 8:25 Jesus speaks to disciples
10:3 Bartholomew Thomas Matthew	6:14-15 Bartholomew Matthew Thomas
11:21 Woe to Chorazin, Bethsaida 11:24 More tolerable for Sodom	10:12 More tolerable for Sodom 10:13 Woe to Chorazin, Bethsaida
12:41 The men of Nineveh will arise 12:42 The queen of the South will arise	11:31 The queen of the South will arise 11:32 The men of Nineveh will arise
12:38-42 Request for a Sign 12:43-45 Return of the Evil Spirit	11:24-26 Return of the Evil Spirit 11:29-32 Request for a Sign
13:11 to know the secrets of the kingdom 13:12 to him who has more will be given 13:13 seeing they do not see	8:10a to know the secrets of the kingdom 8:10b seeing they may not see 8:18b to him who has more will be given
14:18-20 The crowds eat the loaves and fish 14:21 there were about 5,000 men	9:14 there were about 5,000 men 9:15-17 The crowds eat the loaves and fish
18:6a causing one of these little ones to sin 18:6b better to have millstone round his neck 18:7 Woe to man by whom temptation comes	17:1 Woe to him by whom temptations come 17:2a better to have millstone round his neck 17:2b causing one of these little ones to sin

The similarities of order discussed above are certainly significant, and any Synoptic explanation needs to cover this feature if it is to be convincing. Undeniably, a common framework *does* exist for Matthew and Luke. But does this, as Orchard contends (1976, 45), establish literary dependence between Luke and Matthew? There are two fundamental reasons why at times Luke's order of units corresponds with Matthew's.

First, there are some units that inherently must be placed at a particular point in the Gospel account. Thus the pericopes about Jesus' infancy and the preaching of John the Baptist must come first, and the Passion Narrative (from Palm Sunday onwards) has its own intrinsic order dictated by the events themselves. Very few other units have an inherent order, but some (such as the Call of the first disciples) must come early and before certain other events, and others (e.g., passion predictions) are more likely to be later than earlier. There is thus a basic framework in the Gospel narrative that is intrinsic to the nature of the material. If a pile of loose-leaf pages, each containing one Gospel pericope, fell to the floor in chaotic confusion, any editors seeking to put them in order again would find themselves in agreement on the basic framework. Similarly, some pericopes imply that other events came earlier: for example, a reference to Jesus' disciples following him implies an earlier call to do so; Jesus' reference (in his answer to John's disciples) about healings he performed makes it desirable that examples of those healings be included before that point.

Second, there are some events of such importance in the overall narrative that they are part of the framework of the Synoptic story and it could be thought that they would of necessity occur in a specific sequence. In particular, these include the feeding of the 5,000, Peter's confession at Caesarea Philippi, Jesus' first passion prediction, the transfiguration, and the commencement of the last journey to Jerusalem. These represent successive stages in the unfolding of events and therefore they could hardly be given in any other order.

The following is a list of pericopes that have an inherent or relative sequence factor:
1. The Infancy Narratives (and Genealogy)
2. Ministry of John, Baptism and Temptation of Jesus
3. From Judea to Galilee; First Preaching
4. Call of the First Disciples
5. John's Question to Jesus, and Jesus' Testimony to John
6. Peter's Confession at Caesarea Philippi and First Passion Prediction
7. Transfiguration
8. End of the Galilean Ministry; Leaving Galilee for Jerusalem
9. Entry into Jerusalem and Events of Passion Week
10. Crucifixion and Resurrection

Furthermore, some short sequences of a few pericopes may have been linked together in the tradition behind both Matthew and Luke. Thus these clusters of pericopes remain the same in sequence in both Matthew and Luke, and they occur at different points in these two Gospels—even though there is no apparent reason for the grouping of these particular pericopes. This phenomenon requires an explanation.

Apart from the pericopes of the foregoing kinds, there are no inherent reasons that demand individual pericopes should occur in a particular order. And apart from pericopes of the foregoing kinds, there is a very low correlation between the order of pericopes occurring in Matthew and Luke. That is to say, after discounting the pericopes for which sequence is predetermined by their inherent nature or their position within the overall flow of events, the pericopes of Matthew and Luke do not correspond in sequence to an extent that suggests either knowledge of Matthew by the author of Luke (or vice versa) or derivation of the order of both from a common source (such as Mark).

As can be seen from an examination of the Table of Synoptic Pericopes above, the extent of agreement in sequence in Matthew's and Luke's Gospels from the time of Jesus' first preaching tour to his triumphal entry is not sufficiently great to be significant or to offer any real support to the argument that Luke used Matthew.

On the other hand, the *changes of order* that Luke made if he used Matthew constitute a more difficult phenomenon to explain. Orchard offers (1977, 34–36 and 118–19) an explanation for how Luke's Gospel was derived from Matthew, but it involves Luke's combing through Matthew several times and selecting small sections each time. While this can account for what we have in Luke's Gospel, it is very difficult to see any motivation or indeed justification for such a redactional procedure. It is as if Luke took all the major structures in Matthew's Gospel, from the Sermon on the Mount to Matthew's blocks of healing and miracle stories, and systematically dismembered them—disbursing the pieces throughout his own Gospel with many of them scattered throughout his central teaching section.

Moreover, the contexts that these pericopes and pericope blocks have in Matthew (for the most part comprising realistic and logical settings) are very frequently abandoned, or the Lukan parallels are placed in different contexts or without any real setting at all. Thus the Lord's Prayer in Matthew has a fitting and appropriate setting within the Sermon on the Mount (Matt 6:9–13), whereas Luke's version (Luke 11:1–4) occurs in response to the disciples' request that Jesus teach them to pray as John taught his disciples. The context for each one is quite different.

Similarly, the parable of the lost sheep in Matt 18:12–13 is in a context (vv. 10–14) about children ("little ones"), the point of which is, "So it is not the will of my Father who is in heaven that one of these little ones should perish." Luke's version of the parable (15:1–7) is Jesus' response to the circumstance that "the Pharisees and the scribes murmured, saying, 'This man receives sinners and eats with them.'" Luke's version has a rather different ending and application (15:6–7) and is the first of three parables on something lost (15:1–32E).

Then, Matthew gives teaching by Jesus about divorce twice: in the Sermon on the Mount (Matt 5:31–32) and in Perea on his final journey to Jerusalem when the Pharisees questioned him about this matter (19:1–12). Luke's one short comment about divorce (16:18) appears to be a conflation of some parts of Matthew's two different passages. It is very brief compared to Matthew's accounts, and it occurs as a disconnected saying for which Luke provided no specific setting at all.

Is it an adequate explanation that all these differences are due to Luke's alteration of what he found in Matthew? Why should Luke treat Matthew's Gospel in this way? One is quite at a loss to conceive of an adequate reason. But this is not all. Within the pericopes, Luke engaged in frequent rearrangements in order of details. On some occasions one can think of a possible reason for it, though there are no actual grounds for believing that Luke made the change for that particular reason. On many other occasions the change of order appears pointless.

Therefore the explanation that Luke changed Matthew's order portrays Luke as frequently following a most arbitrary and bizarre redactional procedure that (so far as one can ascertain from evaluating what it achieves) is pointless and motiveless, and it destroys the setting and context (usually very appropriate) provided in Matthew. This conclusion contradicts what we know on other grounds about Luke as an author, which should cause interpreters to question very seriously the proposition that Luke used Matthew. If Matthew was Luke's source, it is very difficult to believe that he could have treated that Gospel in this fashion.

Differences in How Much Luke Includes

On many occasions Matthew records a lengthy and detailed passage of teaching or dialogue on a subject, and Luke presents this in only one or two short sayings. Here are a few examples:

The scribes and Pharisees	Matt 15:4–20	Luke 6:39
Reproving one's brother	Matt 18:15–18	Luke 17:3
Divorce and remarriage	Matt 19:1–12	Luke 16:18
The Pharisees' hypocrisy	Matt 23:1–36	Luke 20:45–47

If the full account of Jesus' teaching is in front of Luke in Matthew's Gospel, then those who claim Luke used Matthew need to explain why Luke omits most of it in pericopes like these.

Differences Due to What Luke Omits

There are numerous pericopes in Matthew's Gospel that are absent in Luke, and this points to Luke *not* having known Matthew. This argument operates on two levels: the more general and the particularly surprising. More generally, Luke's stated purpose includes thoroughness and completeness (see 1:1–4), and if he had access to Matthew it is a trifle unexpected to find that the material he has in common with Matthew occupies considerably less than 50% of his Gospel. (This figure is frequently put at just under 50%, but I assess it—see chap. 4—as no more than 395 verses or 37% of Matthew, corresponding with 408 verses or 35.5% of Luke.)

On this issue scholars often claim that there were practical constraints on the length of a Gospel, no matter how complete an author may have wanted his work to be. Thus space limitations (in particular, the maximum practical length of a scroll) placed restrictions on what Luke could use from Matthew. Clearly, the problem of length prevented Luke's use of *all* of Matthew's material, even if he did have it in front of him and even if he had wanted to use all of it in some way in his own Gospel. Luke had to operate on *some* principle of selection, though there is no way to determine today exactly what it was. Moreover it appears that Luke in any case possessed another version for many of these events or sayings, and it is reasonable that he should have chosen to use only one such version when he had two available to him. In numerous cases that version would have been a non-Matthean one.

Luke's accounts of a given pericope are almost invariably longer than Matthew's, but this does not accord with a conscious desire on Luke's part to restrict what he took from Matthew because of considerations of overall length, for he has considerably expanded what he supposedly took from Matthew. Sometimes Luke's additional wording is a purely verbal expansion that adds nothing to the meaning and provides no additional information. It ranges from single words to complete sentences: see the redundancy καὶ εἶπαν λέγοντες πρὸς αὐτόν (Luke 20:2); Luke 7:20, unparalleled in Matthew, which repeats Luke 7:19b//Matt 11:3; Luke 8:47//Mark 5:33 (this section of the pericope is absent altogether in Matthew), where both report that the healed woman fell down before Jesus, yet Mark says simply that she "told him the whole truth," while Luke states at greater length that she "declared in the presence of all the people why she had touched him, and how she had been immediately healed." Instances of this kind occur throughout Luke's Gospel and appear inconsistent with the assertion that Luke took from Matthew all the pericopes he could fit in, but he was prevented from using more only by space restrictions.

If one assumes that Luke's Gospel is close to the maximum possible length, then the explanation may simply be that Luke considered it more worthwhile to include the specific material he had that is not in Matthew than to have to exclude some of this in order simply to repeat what he knew was already in Matthew. This sounds like a reasonable explanation except for three questions: Granted this attitude on Luke's part, (1) why did he include as much as he did from Matthew, drawing between 33% and 50% of his own book from that Gospel? (2) Why did Luke choose, from all that Matthew offered, the particular pericopes that he did include? (3) Why did Luke so frequently expand Matthew's version of a particular pericope rather than simply adhere to Matthew's pericope length, which would have enabled him to use more pericopes overall? (See chap. 4 for a comparison of the word lengths of Matthew and Luke for all the healing stories in which they parallel Mark. The totals for parallel healing pericopes are: Matthew, 868 words; Luke, 1,366 words. It can easily be seen how frequently Luke's account of a pericope is from 50% to 100% longer than Matthew's. For a complete presentation of these comparative statistics, see Morgenthaler [1971, 233ff.])

The advocates of Markan Priority who also hold that Luke used Matthew (i.e., Farrer theory supporters) reply to the first question by claiming that, for much of this material that Luke and Matthew have in common, Luke's source was not Matthew but actually Mark. But this does not fully answer the question because, if Luke used both Matthew and Mark as sources, an explanation is still needed for why—if one argues that Luke was more concerned to include what was *not* already available in Matthew and/or Mark—he chose to use so much that *was* already available (either in Matthew or Mark or both).

Some may claim that Luke included *all* that he had from all his sources other than Matthew and Mark, but *selections only* from the other two Gospels. Apart from it being unlikely that Luke would not have learned of other things—in addition to what he does include, that Jesus said, and that are not in Matthew and Mark—this attributes to him a difference in his use of his sources that is not easy to substantiate. This first question also requires a careful answer from advocates of the Two-Gospel Hypothesis, and questions (2) and (3) above merit answers from all who hold that Luke used Matthew.

Luke included versions of pericopes that are longer than the ones he could have borrowed from Matthew, and he also chose (if he was using Matthew) to omit completely some pericopes that on the face of it are very much more suited to his overall purposes (as best we can judge them) than many stories that he does include. The example par excellence of this is the story of the healing of the Canaanite woman's daughter (Matt 15:21–28), which includes the healing of a child at the plea of a person who was a woman, and a Gentile—a Canaanite, a member of the nation who were Israel's ancient enemies—all simultaneously, and all being people in whom Luke took a special interest (see discussion in chap. 7). This pericope certainly appears to be a more likely candidate for inclusion in Luke than the widow's gift pericope, which is a quite Jewish-oriented story that Luke shares with Mark but Matthew omits!

In summary, the point is that—if Luke was going to restrict himself to the length that his Gospel now is, and if he had known Matthew's Gospel—there are good grounds for believing that his Gospel would have differed in numerous ways from what it now is, omitting some things that it contains and including instead other material taken from Matthew that so clearly fit Luke's purposes.

DIFFERENCES WHEREBY LUKE EXCLUDES WHAT MATTHEW PRESENTS

Matthew and Luke share some pericopes where there is an apparent contradiction between them, and several of these are mentioned above. These apparent contradictions can be reconciled, but some differences are much more significant. In these pericopes Luke does not merely *omit* or *ignore* or *differ* from Matthew, he *shows a total unawareness* of what Matthew wrote. Indeed, at times he even seems to positively exclude what Matthew says. Here are three major occurrences of this kind and their significance.

1. *Luke's infancy narrative shows no awareness of Matthew's account and leaves no room for the Matthean events to have occurred.* The events of Matt 1:18–25 are not given a geographical setting, and from the way that 2:1 continues on (mentioning Bethlehem without any change of venue implied) it seems that Matthew knows nothing about Mary and Joseph having come from Nazareth. Also, Matthew's narrative assumes that they had been living in Bethlehem all along, and after the birth of Jesus they simply continue to do so in their own house (2:11). In fact, Jesus and his parents are still living in Bethlehem when he is upwards of two years old (Matt 2:7,16): Matthew calls Jesus a young child (παιδίον; see Matt 2:8,9,11,13,14), not a baby (βρέφος; see Luke 2:12,16), at the time of the visit of the magi.

After the return from Egypt, Matt 2:22–23 gives the impression that they had not previously lived in Nazareth; in fact, Matthew's reference to the circumstances of their going to Nazareth would convey (if we did not have Luke's account) that this was the first time they had gone there and that they chose this place as being an obscure little hill village outside the territory of Archelaus where they would be safe from any danger from him.

Luke 2:1–7 says Joseph and Mary traveled from Nazareth to Bethlehem where Jesus was born. After eight days Jesus was circumcised, and then after forty days he was taken by Mary and Joseph to Jerusalem "for their purification according to the law of Moses" (2:22; see Leviticus 12); from there they returned immediately "to their own city, Nazareth" (Luke 2:39), where Jesus grew up. Luke's account leaves no room for the visit of the magi and the sojourn in Egypt. The two accounts can be observed to be quite independent. It is left for the readers of the two accounts to see how to reconcile them.

2. *The total independence of Matthew's and Luke's narrative at the beginning of the Gospels also occurs at the end.* Luke's resurrection appearances are different from Matthew's, but seems to indicate that Luke was unaware that Jesus had first appeared to the women, as Matthew says. In Matthew, Mary Magdalene and the other Mary (28:1) meet an angel (28:5) and then Jesus (28:9), who instructs them to tell his disciples to go to Galilee to see him (28:10), which the disciples do (28:16). In Luke, a larger group of women (24:10) meet two men in white (24:4) but do not meet Jesus himself, and there is no instruction for the disciples to go to Galilee. So they do not go to Galilee; most of them remain in Jerusalem, but two set out for Emmaus and meet Jesus on the way (24:13–35) and return to Jerusalem where Jesus meets them all (24:36–43), having just previously appeared to Simon Peter (24:34). Jesus instructs them to continue in the city of Jerusalem until clothed with power from on high (24:49), leads them out as far as Bethany, and there ascends to heaven (24:51). After this the disciples return to Jerusalem (24:52) and remain there (24:53).

Here once again there is very important information in Matthew that Luke lacks: immediately after his resurrection Jesus was seen alive by the women. One explanation is that in those days the evidence of women was little regarded, so Luke did not want the initial report of Jesus' resurrection appearance to be dependent on the claims of some excited women. There could be a measure of truth in this: once the risen Christ had appeared to the apostles and they had begun fulfilling their role as witnesses of the resurrection, that initial appearance to the women appears to have played no part in their testimony: Paul does not mention the women in his list of resurrection appearances (1 Cor 15:3–8). Thus it is conceivable that Jesus' resurrection appearance to women was absent from the traditions of the early church, so it never came to Luke's attention when he was doing research for his Gospel and Acts.

But if Luke used Matthew's Gospel, the whole matter is somewhat different since it then would appear that Luke did not merely ignore this appearance but deliberately *suppressed* it. Luke says that the women saw two men in dazzling apparel (24:4) who reminded them about Jesus' prediction of his resurrection (24:7). This group of women included Mary Magdalene and Mary the mother of James (24:10). After they heard the words of their informants (identified in the account of Cleopas as "a vision of angels"; 24:23), they remembered Jesus' words and returned from the tomb to report about this "vision of angels" to the Eleven and "to all the rest" (24:8–9). But Matthew says that Mary Magdalene and the other Mary (28:1) met Jesus risen from the dead (28:9) and that the risen Lord personally gave them a message for his "brothers" (28:10). In Luke the women only report about seeing angels (24:9,23). Luke's wording of Cleopas's report is "They were at the tomb early in the morning and did not find his body; and they came back saying that they had even seen a vision of angels, who said that he was alive" (24:22–23). How could Luke be content to write thus if he had in front of him Matthew's account that said Mary Magdalene and the other Mary *had actually seen Jesus' body—alive*?

But any suggestion that Luke would have deliberately suppressed the appearance of Jesus to the women is beyond belief, and the alternative that Luke did not think it worthwhile to mention the women's testimony to the resurrection of Jesus because he gives details of *men* meeting Jesus (24:28–51) is equally incredible. Luke's stated intention (1:1–4) is to give a fully detailed account, and *his* Gospel is the one that gives the fullest recognition to the role of women during Jesus' earthly ministry. It would be much more consistent with their styles if it had been *Luke* who recorded the appearance to the women and *Matthew* who did not! The only valid conclusion is that Luke would not have written as he did about the women, restricting them to having seen angels only, if he had access to Matthew's account which said Jesus appeared to the women also. There is absolutely no satisfactory reason for Luke to deliberately suppress or simply omit this piece of information, so this evidence compels me to conclude that Luke did not know Matthew's Gospel when he wrote his own.

3. *The matter of Jesus' appearance to the women is not the only issue that arises here.* There are differences in the information in Matthew and Luke about what happened after the resurrection. In Matthew, the risen

Christ instructs his followers on the day of his resurrection that they are to go to Galilee where he will meet with them (28:10), so they go to Galilee and meet with him there (28:16–20E). In Luke, the risen Christ instructs his followers on the day of his resurrection (24:36) that they are to remain in the city of Jerusalem "until you are clothed with power from on high" (24:49), and after saying this "he led them out as far as Bethany . . . while he blessed them he parted from them, and was carried up into heaven" (24:50–51). Luke's account leaves no recognizable place for the visit to a mountain in Galilee, and it states that on the evening of the day of the resurrection Jesus gives his disciples instructions to the very opposite effect, that is, to remain in Jerusalem. Acts 1:3 throws some light on all this since there were 40 days between Jesus' resurrection and ascension, so it *is* possible to find a reconciliation between the two accounts in Matthew and Luke. However, the point is that what Luke says does not merely fail to mention what Matthew reports, but Luke shows no awareness of it. Thus, once again Luke has written in a way that is most readily compatible with the explanation that he was unaware of what Matthew had written. What is at issue is: if Luke used canonical Matthew, how does it happen that at such a number of points Luke differs from Matthew so that the two accounts are in need of some form of reconciliation?

In Conclusion

All the various passages mentioned in this section constitute cumulatively an assembly of very strong evidence: they make it very difficult to defend the view that Luke used Matthew's Gospel. In the call of the first disciples pericopes, Matthew and Luke have some interesting differences. Matthew pictures two pairs of brother—Simon and Andrew, James and John—working quite separately and independently, the latter two working "in the boat with Zebedee their father, mending their nets," so that their decision to respond to Jesus' call meant that "they left the boat and their father" when they "followed him" (4:18–22). Luke says that together with Simon in the fishing boat were "James and John, sons of Zebedee, who were partners with Simon," and "when they had brought their boats to land, they left everything and followed him" (5:10–11). In Luke, there is no reference to Andrew—which is odd in the light of the implication of Matthew's account that Andrew was Simon's partner and the explicit statement that he also responded to Christ's call—and there is no suggestion that Zebedee was a member of the business partnership or even that he was still alive.

Again, it is easy to reconcile the two accounts, but that is not the point. The point is that Luke himself attempts no such reconciliation of the two accounts, which he could have done if he used Matthew. Rather, it appears that Luke was completely unaware of all that Matthew said in his Gospel. The view that Luke used Matthew means that, of two narratives available to him, Luke chose a particular account as the one to use—and it was not Matthew's—and that he used it totally without reference to Matthew even though it was in front of him.

The situation is similar in relation to all the many other places mentioned above where Luke contains a different version of an event or teaching from Matthew's, and where Luke appears to be completely unaware of what Matthew said in his account. In each of these cases, the "Luke used Matthew" school has to say, Luke had access to two versions of the story, one in Matthew and one from another source, and he chose to use the latter version rather than the former. This was his preferred method rather than conflating the two accounts.

This may well be so, but if it is, then it appears to conflict with Luke's stated intention of writing an exhaustive account that covers everything from the beginning (1:1–4). It is one thing to accept that some of what Matthew records may not have come to Luke's attention; it is another matter to say that Luke had access to all the information in Matthew, and in producing his own account he chose to ignore a considerable amount of it and to write as if he were totally unaware of it.

ASSESSMENT

We have reached an impasse. The first major section in this chapter presents solid and compelling evidence that Luke *must have used* Matthew's Gospel: the similarities of content, wording, and order demand this literary relationship if they are to be accounted for. The second major section of this chapter presents solid and compelling evidence that shows that Luke *could not have used* Matthew's Gospel: the dissimilarities of content, wording, and order—and particularly the differences where Luke excludes what Matthew presents—preclude this literary relationship. How is it possible for this paradox to be resolved?

A careful examination of the passages on which our two conflicting conclusions are based discloses an obvious but significant factor—they are *different parts* of Matthew's Gospel. Properly interpreted, therefore, the evidence does not lead to an impasse: it leads to the recognition that some Matthean material indicates that Luke knew it while other Matthean material indicates that Luke did not know it. That is to say, the evidence leads to the recognition that Luke knew and used *some parts* of Matthew and did not know or use *other parts* of Matthew.

Once this is seen, it is possible to reconcile the apparently conflicting evidence and the deductions based on it. One group of scholars, noting the places that indicate Luke's use of Matthew, has extrapolated that Luke used *all* of Matthew. Another group of scholars, noting the places that indicate Luke was unaware of what was in Matthew, has extrapolated that Luke knew and used *none* of Matthew. Both groups are correct in their perception of the evidence but unjustified in the extrapolations based upon it.

The claim that Luke used an early and shorter edition of the Gospel of Matthew (Proto-Matthew) is not a satisfactory explanation of the evidence. The evidence presented above that Luke did not know Matthew's Gospel extends across too much of Matthew; and if these sections were excluded, what is left could hardly be called a Gospel. There must be another explanation that more adequately accounts for the data.

The explanation that accords best with the data is (1) that Luke wrote his Gospel completely independent of Matthew's Gospel, and (2) those portions of Luke's Gospel best understood as having a common source with the parallel sections of Matthew's Gospel came from a number of separate documents—pericopes or pericope clusters—that circulated separately as short tracts, which Luke encountered and collected during his research, and Matthew also incorporated them into his Gospel when he wrote it in its final form.

These written pericopes that both Matthew and Luke used *could* have been produced by any person in the early church, but there is no need to postulate some anonymous author: the most probable source is the apostle Matthew himself. Jesus appointed the apostles to be his witnesses, and Matthew, the former tax official, would have been the most familiar with making notes and writing up reports. For Matthew to have written down notes and stories about Jesus is entirely logical and reasonable.

Evidence of the hand of the one author is found throughout Matthew's Gospel, both in the places where the Gospel is unparalleled in Mark or Luke and where it is paralleled by Mark or Luke or both (see J. C. Hawkins 1909, 3–8). This supports the conclusion that the author of the tracts under discussion, subsequently incorporated into Matthew's Gospel, was the same person as the author of the rest of this Gospel and who was responsible for its final form.

These short tracts were subsequently re-edited (indeed, even revised) at the time when they were used in Matthew's Gospel. Luke also used many of them, and he supplemented their sparse information with additional details obtained during the course of his investigations (Luke 1:3). Thus the similarities between accounts in Matthew and Luke arise from the use of the same original tracts in both Gospels; differences in Synoptic pericope order result from the use by the authors of these two Gospels of different principles for the arrangement of their respective material; and differences within such pericopes are due to redaction of the accounts at the point of the writing of the respective Gospels—together with some rewriting by Luke as he wove into the account the other information he had discovered.

This proposal is as incapable of final and irrefutable proof as any other suggestions about the origins of the canonical Gospels, but so also is the view that Matthew's Gospel was given its present form in one writing over a short period of time. There is no inherent improbability in, nor any evidence against, the idea that Matthew wrote down various separate stories about Jesus and that these circulated in the churches and came to Luke's attention during the period prior to the writing of the Gospels of Matthew and Luke as we now have them.

This explanation that some parts of Matthew's Gospel were written down and began to circulate separately is not *less likely* than the view that Matthew wrote nothing at all about Jesus prior to the time when he came to produce his complete Gospel. The suggestion that I present here accords with and provides an explanation for the material that is similar in Matthew and Luke—without invoking an anonymous, amorphous, unattested source such as Q.

A valid criticism of the Q hypothesis is explaining how such a source, if it ever existed, completely disappeared without a trace. At first sight, the present suggestion may appear open to the same criticism, but such evidence could be present among our data and simply have gone unrecognized. If such separate stories existed in written form, what would have happened to them eventually? Those churches and individuals who possessed them would be glad to have the complete Gospels when they were eventually published, but since the cost of producing written documents was high in ancient times, so these short tracts would not have been discarded but would have been added to. An early codex manuscript containing passages where Matthew's wording appears to have been assimilated to Luke's may in fact have a different history: the codex may have originated from one (or more) of these early tracts Matthew produced and to which the later Matthean material had been added when it became available. And the apparent assimilation of some wording to Luke would then actually be the *original* wording of the tract, which subsequently was incorporated unchanged into Luke's Gospel but was revised by Matthew when this story took its place in his complete Gospel.

Moreover, it is possible that some of these small tracts or Gospel portions continued to be treasured, preserved, used, and *copied* by those who could not afford the cost of complete Gospels; and it is also possible that some of the Gospel fragments found among our present manuscripts were never in fact part of complete Gospels but rather were part of such smaller gospel portions that were *circulating on their own.*

For a number of the fragments that now exist, there is no real evidence that they *must* have come from a complete New Testament or at the very least a complete Gospel, so that they could not have come from a smaller Gospel segment that circulated on its own. Our assumption about the size of the total document from which only a small fragment has been preserved is frequently unsupported by any internal or external evidence. In some instances such an assumption may be as wide of the mark as would be the conclusion of some future archaeologist that any pages of New Testament material dating back to the present must have come from a complete Bible (or at least a complete New Testament). This would be wide of the mark because publishers today print and circulate separate portions of Scripture. Perhaps the small Gospel manuscript fragments that exist today from the early centuries could be reconsidered with this possibility in mind. Certainly it remains possible that, without our being aware of it, we may have in our possession some surviving pieces from copies of original short tracts of Matthew predating his completed Gospel.

THE INDEPENDENCE OF LUKE

Chapter 4 provides statistics showing that Matthew's *Sondergut* consists of 485 verses (45.5%) of his Gospel; that Matthew shares with Mark (but not with Luke) a further 187 verses (17.5%) of Matthew's Gospel; so Matthew has a total of 672 verses (63%) that have no direct parallel in Luke. This means that Matthew has 395 verses (37%) in common with Luke. These statistics show further that Luke's *Sondergut* consists of 686 verses (60%) of his Gospel; that Luke shares with Mark (but not with Matthew) a further 54 verses (4.5%); so Luke has a total of 740 verses (64.5%) that have no direct parallel in Matthew. This means that Luke has 408 verses (35.5%) in common with Matthew. This points to a high level of independence for Matthew and Luke. But the extent of the independence of Luke and Mark—from the perspective of both Markan Priority and Markan Dependence—needs to be investigated.

The Relationship Between Luke and Matthew

Thus Streeter discusses the overlaps of Mark and Q (1911, 167ff.; 1924, 186) and assigns Lukan material to three sources: Mark, Proto-Luke (Q+L), and the nativity source. The picture based on his allocation (1924, 222) is:

Pericope	Proto-Luke	Vv.	From Mark	Vv.	Other	Vv.
Nativity Stories					1:1–2:52E	132
Baptism, Temptation, etc.	3:1–4:30	68				
Capernaum Healings			4:31–4:44E	14		
Call of First Disciples	5:1–11	11				
Healings and Controversy			5:12–6:13	41		
The Twelve Apostles	6:14–16	3				
The Large Crowds			6:17–19	3		
Preaching and Healing	6:20–8:3	83				
Parables and Mission			8:4–9:50	103		
Luke's Travel Narrative	9:51–18:14	351				
Ministry and Healing			18:15–34E	29		
Zacchaeus and the Pounds	19:1–27	27				
Triumphal Entry (1)			19:28–36	9		
Triumphal Entry (2)	19:37–44	8				
In Jerusalem			19:45–21:17	68		
Not a Hair Will Perish	21:18	1				
The End of the Age (1)			21:19–33	15		
The End of the Age (2)	21:34–36	3				
End (3), Last Supper			21:37–22:13	15		
Passion and Resurrection	22:14–24:53E	167				
Total Verses:		722		297		132
Less: Not regarded as genuine: 17:36; 19:25; 22:19b–20		3				
NET TOTAL		719				

[Luke 22:19b–20 is usually excluded in counts of the verses in Luke, but the arguments for inclusion and exclusion are evenly balanced. It is noteworthy that the Aland/ United Bible Societies Greek Text notes the manuscript support for exclusion, but it includes this passage in its text. Since these verses are often excluded from critical editions of the text and in statistics of verse counts, they are listed here but without prejudice to an opinion on this point. This does not affect the main argument of this chapter.]

Some of Streeter's allocations are questionable (e.g., Luke 21:37–38, which is not paralleled in Mark, is *not* allocated to Proto-Luke [i.e., Q+L], and thus it is left as Markan; an anomaly). But overall this enables us to see that from Streeter's own analysis just under 30% of Luke's Gospel is derived from Mark and more than 70% of it comes from independent sources (including Q in Streeter's view).

My own assessment and allocation of Lukan verses as parallel or not parallel with Mark differs in some particulars from Streeter's, but in this regard our overall figures are surprisingly close. My count shows 28.5% of Luke's Gospel (330 verses) parallels Mark, and thus 71.5% (818 verses) does not parallel Mark (see statistics in chap. 4).

As far as Mark is concerned, Streeter says (1924, 160), "If we leave out of account all passages where there is reason to suspect that Luke has used a non-Marcan source, it appears on an approximate estimate that about 350 verses (i.e., just over one half of Mark) have been reproduced by Luke." Again, notwithstanding some differences of detail, my overall count is quite close to Streeter's figures: I find 335 verses in Mark (50.5%) are paralleled in Luke, of which 41.5% are also paralleled in Matthew (see chap. 4).

Streeter was convinced that the issue is about verses in Mark that Luke used, whereas our present inquiry is whether there is a valid alternative to this explanation. But what is not in dispute is the high degree of independence between Matthew and Luke in regard to their respective contents, and the comparatively small extent of the derivation of Luke from Mark (on the Markan Priority Hypothesis), and the large extent of Luke's material drawn from independent sources, or (on the Markan Dependence Hypothesis) the comparatively small amount of Luke that Mark has used, comprising just half of Mark's total contents.

The present chapter has considered an alternative to Markan Priority for the material where Mark and Luke show close correspondence, which occurs in two situations: (1) where this material *is not* closely paralleled in Matthew, then to that extent this Lukan material is *also* derived by Luke (like his *Sondergut*) from his admittedly extensive independent sources; and (2) where there *is* close correspondence in this material between Matthew and Luke, then it has been derived from a source common to both Matthew and Luke—that is, documents written by Matthew that circulated in the churches and subsequently were incorporated into both of the Major Synoptics. This material also occurs in Mark because (on this Markan Dependence view) Mark used both Matthew and Luke in writing his Gospel.

SUMMARY AND CONCLUSION

A fundamental limitation for the explanatory power of the Markan Priority Hypothesis is that Matthew and Luke contain material not paralleled in Mark. The Markan Priority Hypothesis can be used to explain what

Mark has in common with the other two, but obviously it cannot explain what they do not have in common with Mark. Thus at this point there remain features of the Synoptic data to be explained on some other basis. This chapter began with the usual explanation offered for the parallels of Matthew and Luke that are lacking in Mark: the source Q. But the question was asked, Is this the only valid hypothesis that covers the data?

A solution that is commonly offered is that Luke may have used Matthew's Gospel. We have found that there is good evidence in support of this view, but there are significant arguments against it. It seems to me that there is substance in the objections of Streeter, Kümmel, Fitzmyer, and others against a later Gospel writer (i.e., Luke) dismembering sections of Matthew such as his sermons and discourses and other patterns, or ignoring fuller expositions given in Matthew (e.g., the Beatitudes, the Lord's Prayer).

The question of the overall order of the two Major Synoptics is a real enigma: sometimes, in unexpected sections, a cluster of pericopes occurs in complete agreement in order, and then many times there occurs a great disparity of order of pericopes and pericope clusters. I concur with Fitzmyer who says (1970, 75), "The frequent disagreement with the Matthean order in this regard is crucial to any judgement about Luke's dependence on Matthew; indeed, it suggests he does not depend on him at all." And I remain completely unpersuaded by the arguments of Orchard, Black, and the Two-Gospel Hypothesis school for how Luke's treatment of Matthew can be explained.

I find that the evidence that Luke used Matthew is partial and limited: on the one hand, it provides support for believing that Luke used *some parts* of Matthew's Gospel; but on the other hand, there is overwhelming evidence against believing that Luke knew Matthew's Gospel in anything approximating its canonical form. This evidence thus suggests that Luke was acquainted only with certain sections of Matthew's Gospel, and (in view of the different order in which those sections appear in his own Gospel) suggests also that those sections were not parts of a complete Gospel (that is, some sort of Proto-Matthew) but were in separate circulation prior to being incorporated into the Gospels of Matthew and Luke by their respective authors. Further, the most probable author of this material common to Matthew and Luke is the apostle Matthew, and the links between this material and the other material in Matthew's Gospel are consistent with the view that the same author who wrote the sections that are paralleled in Luke wrote all of the Matthew's Gospel. It should be noted that this conclusion is drawn from *all* the data in Matthew and Luke, and is not restricted to those parts that are not shared with Mark. This hypothesis is thus an alternative, not merely to Q, but to Markan Priority.

This hypothesis may be summed up thus:

1. *Most of the material in the Gospels of Matthew and Luke is not of such a nature as to suggest or require a common source for both Major Synoptics, nor that either one of them used the other.* Material that contains similarities of content is easily explained on the basis of independent oral transmission of Jesus traditions—sometimes of the same event or teaching, sometimes of similar but different events or occasions of teaching—and some of these latter traditions could also have been transmitted in writing. Thus, to a significant extent the Gospels of Matthew and Luke are completely independent of each other, and certainly the evidence points to the conclusion that neither author, while composing his own Gospel, saw the other's finished Gospel.

2. *Some of the material in the Gospels of Matthew and Luke is of such a nature as to indicate that it does* have *a common literary origin.* This material was originally circulating in the churches in the form of separate written pericopes or pericopes clusters and was subsequently utilized by both Matthew and Luke in the writing of their Gospels. The differences between these pericopes in the form in which they occur in the two Gospels are attributable to one or a combination of either (1) separate translations (or rewritings) into Greek of material originally written in Aramaic; (2) revision by Matthew of this material at the time of incorporating it into his Gospel; (3) redaction and expansion of this material by Luke, on the basis of other information that he had obtained, at the time of using it in his Gospel.

The purpose of this chapter, as initially stated, was "to see what sense can be made of Matthew and Luke apart from Q and Mark." It was acknowledged that "our investigation may lead to absurdities, compelling us to return to the Two-Source Hypothesis and accept it as the only sensible explanation of the data." But this did not happen. We have found in fact that a very reasonable alternative view of the data is possible. It remains to offer a brief comparison of the two alternative explanations.

Q is a hypothetical source, postulated on the basis of the Matthew-Luke parallels in order to solve the difficulty of how to explain them. We have no independent, objective knowledge of Q, though some scholars in previous decades and centuries did identify this source with Matthew's *logia* to which Papias referred, but this identification lost support by this century. With the rejection of the identification of Papias's *logia* with the source used by Matthew and Luke, the last objective evidence for such a source has disappeared. Its support is now solely the argument of logic that proceeds from an examination of the parallels in Matthew and Luke and the desire to account for them.

The suggestion that early written documents each containing one or more pericopes were used by both Matthew and Luke is, in a sense, also hypothetical. But it does not invoke some lost source written by some unknown author. The postulated documents can easily be identified as written by the apostle Matthew, and indeed as being the first stage in the production of what eventually became our present canonical Gospel. These documents were not lost; they were incorporated into a greater whole.

It is altogether probable that some such documents were originally written in Aramaic for Aramaic-speaking churches, that these were known to Papias, and that it is to these documents that he refers when he speaks of the *logia* of Matthew written in Hebrew/Aramaic. Are we not justified in declining to invoke an unknown, unsubstantiated source to explain the agreements of Matthew with Luke when a very straightforward explanation is at hand? In his investigations (see Luke 1:1–4), Luke encountered and made use of early documents written by Matthew before that apostle produced his full Gospel of Matthew!

This explanation accounts for all the data; it does not invoke unknown authors or documents; rather, it identifies a preliminary stage in the production of (what became) an existing, canonical Gospel. Q has always been the end product of a circular argument, a hypothesis deduced from another hypothesis, an unsubstantiated and unnecessary hypothesis. It is time to inquire whether, in view of the alternative set out here, Q is now to be seen as an unsound, unjustified, and, ultimately, untenable hypothesis.

 # PUTTING THINGS IN ORDER

This chapter examines the pericope order in the Synoptics, and proposes an explanation to account for it.

> *The manner, however, in which Mark's Gospel is composed, the cycle of events he records, and the order in which he groups them strikingly imply a knowledge on his part of the two other Synoptics. This fact really serves to confirm our opinion that Mark makes use of Matthew and Luke as his main authorities in writing his gospel.*
> —Friedrich Bleek (1870, 266–67)

> *Decisive [for the Markan Priority Hypothesis] is the comparison of the sequence of the accounts in the Gospels: within the material that they have in common with Mk, Mt and Lk agree in sequence only insofar as they agree with Mk; when they diverge from Mk, each goes his own way.*
> —Werner G. Kümmel (1975, 57)

> *It is, however, doubtful if this phenomenon [pericope order] can prove much either way. . . .: the evidence is ambiguous and allows a variety of hypotheses, i.e. any hypothesis which places Mark in a 'medial' position . . . and it is logically fallacious to assume that one and only one hypothesis can adequately explain them.*
> —Christopher M. Tuckett
> (Jerusalem Conference, 1984, 10–11)

AGREEMENTS AND DISAGREEMENTS IN ORDER

So far we have noted on several occasions that sometimes the Synoptic Gospels agree in the order in which they set out the events that they record and sometimes they differ. The overall extent of the agreement in pericope order is quite substantial, but the changes in order between one Gospel and another are also considerable.

Explanations offered for these changes of pericope order are tied to viewpoints held about sources of the Synoptic Gospels. Those who hold to a theory of oral sources for the Synoptics, and thus their literacy independence, have no problems with the differences in the order of pericopes. For them, what requires an explanation is the extent to which the various pericopes, all circulating independently, have come to be arranged in the same order in the Synoptics.

Conversely, those who hold one of the theories of literary interrelationship can expect that as a result of this interrelationship there would be correspondences in pericope order. For them, what requires an explanation is why one author, in copying from another, would at times choose to alter drastically the pericope order of his source.

The purpose of this chapter is to investigate the extent of variation in pericope order in the Synoptic Gospels. As a result of this analysis, it is then possible to suggest a simple explanation with three propositions that are fully capable of explaining all the variations of pericope order that occur.

The present study is primarily concerned with the order of complete pericopes and how this phenomenon can be explained. There are quite a few pericopes that have an internal difference of order between the Synoptics, such as Jesus' temptations (Matt 4:4–11//Luke 4:4–13; see chap. 8), the bread and the cup (Matt 26:26–29//Mark 14:22–25//Luke 22:15–19), the tradition regarding hand washing (Matt 15:3–9//Mark 7:6–13), and Jesus' teaching on divorce and remarriage (Matt 19:4–8//Mark 10:3–9). But this is a separate issue, and *any* Synoptic theory that takes one Gospel to be the source of another must assume that the later writer (whoever he was) altered the order of his source within the pericope so that he could more effectively emphasize certain points in the story.

TABLE OF THE ORDER OF MARKAN SECTIONS AND PARALLELS

The Synoptic Table

Scholars have recognized that (1) almost all the pericopes in Mark also occur in Matthew or Luke or both; that (2) Mark stands in some intermediate position between Matthew and Luke regarding pericope order, since Mark agrees with the order of Matthew or Luke or both; and that (3) Matthew and Luke do not agree in order against Mark. This aspect of the phenomenon of order indicates that the way to present the data for examination is to provide an outline of the pericopes in Mark with Matthew's and Luke's parallels on the left and right of Mark respectively.

To facilitate an overview of all the common Synoptic material, the total length of the chart has been minimized by compressing pericopes that are consecutive in all three Synoptics which contain them into a single section or pericope cluster for placement on the chart. This may result in some loss of detail but does not affect any of the overall statements about Synoptic order. Constructed on this basis, the chart has 80 sections.

One of the most relevant pieces of data for this examination is to see, in relation to each pericope or section, whether at that point Matthew and Mark or Mark and Luke agree in order, or whether all three are in agreement. Therefore, Mark's references are given in three columns. When a Markan reference is placed in the center column, then Matthew and Luke are both *in agreement* with Mark as to order, or else they are in agreement in that both *omit* that particular Markan pericope. When a Markan reference is placed in the left column, adjacent to the Matthew reference, then Mark's order accords with the order of Matthew and Luke's order is different. When a Markan reference is placed in the right column, adjacent to the Luke reference, then Mark's order accords with the order of Luke and Matthew's order is different. A Matthean or Lukan passage that occurs in an order different from Mark's is given in the table in brackets.

Thus it can be seen that the columns in the table have the following significance. When the Major Synoptics are following the order of Mark, their references are given without brackets. When either differs from Markan order, that Gospel's reference is in brackets (or it is a dash, if his difference from Mark is that he omits the episode), and the Markan reference is placed in the column adjacent to the other Major Synoptic. If both Major Synoptics differ from the Markan order at the same point, both their references appear in brackets. When the Markan reference appears in the center column, Mark's order is followed by *both* the Major Synoptics or by *neither* of them; or it is an episode in Mark that is not used by either of them. If the Markan reference appears in the column adjacent to one of the Major Synoptics, then that Gospel and Mark are agreed in order against the other Major Synoptic (which has either omitted the episode or placed it in a different position).

NO	SECTION	MATT	MARK			LUKE
1.	John the Baptist	3:1–17E		1:2–11		3:2–22
2.	The Temptation	4:1–11		1:12–13		4:1–13
3.	Ministry in Galilee	4:12–17		1:14–15		4:14–15
4.	Call of the First Disciples	4:18–22	1:16–20			[5:1–11]

Putting Things in Order 385

NO	SECTION	MATT	MARK	LUKE
5.	Demoniac in the Synagogue	—	1:21–28	4:31–37
6.	Jesus Heals Peter's Mother-in-Law	[8:14–17]	1:29–34	4:38–41
7.	Jesus Prays, Then Departs	—	1:35–38	4:42–43
8.	Preaching Tour	4:23–25E	1:39	4:44E
9.	Cleansing the Leper	8:1–4	1:40–45E	5:12–16
10.	Paralytic/Matthew/Fasting	9:1–17	2:1–22	5:17–39E
11.	Plucking Grain/Withered Hand	12:1–14	2:23–3:6	6:1–11
12.	Lakeside Crowds and Healings	12:15–21	3:7–12	[6:17–19]
13.	Appointment of the Twelve	[10:1–4]	3:13–19	6:12–16
14.	Jesus Thought to Be Mad	—	3:20–21	—
15.	Beelzebul Controversy	12:24–30	3:22–27	[11:15–23]
16.	Blaspheming the Holy Spirit	12:31–37	3:28–30	[12:10]
17.	Jesus' True Family	12:46–50E	3:31–35E	[8:19–21]
18.	The Parable of the Sower	13:1–23	4:1–20	8:4–15
19.	Lamps, Hearing, and Getting	(various)	4:21–25	8:16–18
20.	Parable of the Growing Seed	—	4:26–29	—
21.	Parable of the Mustard Seed	13:31–32	4:30–32	[13:18–19]
22.	Jesus' Use of Parables	13:34–35	4:33–34	—
23.	A Storm and a Demoniac	[8:23–34E]	4:35–5:20	8:22–39
24.	Jairus's Daughter/Sick Woman	[9:18–26]	5:21–43E	8:40–56E
25.	Rejection at Nazareth	13:53–58E	6:1–6	[4:16–30]
26.	Mission of the Twelve	[10:5–16]	6:7–13	9:1–6
27.	Herod's Perplexity about Jesus	14:1–2	6:14–16	9:7–9
28.	Death of John the Baptist	14:3–12	6:17–29	[3:19–20]
29.	The Return of the Twelve	—	6:30–31	9:10a
30.	Feeding of the Five Thousand	14:13–21	6:32–44	9:10b–17
31.	Walking on the Water	14:22–33	6:45–52	—
32.	Healings and Washings Dispute	14:34–15:31	6:53–7:37E	[11:37–41]
33.	Feeding of the Four Thousand	15:32–39E	8:1–10	—
34.	Regarding the Pharisees	16:1–12	8:11–21	[12:1]
35.	Bethsaida Blind Man Healed	—	8:22–26	—
36.	Peter's Confession/Passion (1)	16:13–21	8:27–31	9:18–22
37.	Peter's Rebuke	16:22–23	8:32–33	—

NO	SECTION	MATT	MARK		LUKE
38.	To Deny Oneself	16:24–28E	8:34–9:1		9:23–27
39.	The Transfiguration	17:1–9	9:2–10		9:28–36
40.	The Coming of Elijah	17:10–13	9:11–13		—
41.	An Exorcism, and Passion (2)	17:14–23	9:14–32		9:37–45
42.	True Greatness	18:1–5	9:33–37		9:46–48
43.	The Stranger Who Was Exorcizing	—		9:38–41	9:49–50
44.	Warnings about Offenses	18:6–9	9:42–50E		—
45.	Marriage and Divorce	19:1–12	10:1–12		[16:18]
46.	Blessing Children/Rich Man	19:13–30E	10:13–31		18:15–30
47.	Passion Prediction (3)	20:17–19	10:32–34		18:31–34
48.	Request of the Sons of Zebedee	20:20–28	10:35–45		—
49.	The Healing of the Blind	20:29–34E	10:46–52E		18:35–43E
50.	Entry into Jerusalem	21:1–9	11:1–10		19:28–40
51.	Surveying the Temple	—	11:11		—
52.	Cursing the Fig Tree	21:18–19	11:12–14		
53.	Cleansing the Temple	[21:12–17]		11:15–17	19:45–46
54.	Chief Priests and Scribes Conspire	—		11:18–19	19:47–48E
55.	The Fig Tree Is Withered	21:20–22	11:20–26		—
56.	The Question about Authority	21:23–27	11:27–33E		20:1–8
57.	Parable of the Wicked Farmers	21:33–46E	12:1–12		20:9–19
58.	Questions: Taxes, Resurrection	22:15–33	12:13–27		20:20–40
59.	The Greatest Commandment	22:34–40	12:28–34		[10:25–28]
60.	David's Son; Woes to Pharisees	22:41–23:36	12:35–40		20:41–47E
61.	The Widow's Gift	—		12:41–44E	21:1–4
62.	Eschatological Sayings	24:1–22	13:1–20		21:5–24
63.	False Christs and Prophets	24:23–28	13:21–23		[17:23–37]
64.	Coming of the Son of Man; Watch	24:29–25:46E	13:24–37E		21:25–36
65.	The Plot to Kill Jesus	26:1–5	14:1–2		22:1–2
66.	Jesus Anointed	26:6–13	14:3–9		[7:36–50E]
67.	Betrayal Made/Passover Preparations	26:14–20	14:10–17		22:3–14
68.	Jesus Foretells His Betrayal	26:21–25	14:18–21		[22:21–23]
69.	The Last Supper	26:26–29	14:22–25		22:15–20
70.	Peter's Denial Predicted	26:30–35	14:26–31		22:31–34
71.	Gethsemane; Jesus Arrested	26:36–58	14:32–54		22:39–54
72.	False Witnesses in Sanhedrin	26:59–62	14:55–60		—

NO	SECTION	MATT	MARK	LUKE
73.	Jesus Questioned by Sanhedrin	26:63–66	14:61–64	22:66–71E
74.	Jesus Mistreated/Peter's Denials	26:67–75E	14:65–72E	[22:55–65]
75.	Jesus before Pilate	27:1–14	15:1–5	23:1–5
76.	Jesus or Barabbas?	27:15–26	15:6–15	23:17–25
77.	The Mockery of the Soldiers	27:27–31	15:16–20	—
78.	The Road to Golgotha	27:32	15:21	23:26–32
79.	Crucifixion to the Burial	27:33–61	15:22–47E	23:33–56
80.	The Women at the Empty Tomb	28:1–8	16:1–8	24:1–12
Times when Mark is supported only by Matthew:			27	
Times when Mark is supported only by Luke:				13
Times when Mark has unique material:			4	
Times when Mark is supported by both Matthew and Luke:			36	

Mark Is Always Supported in His Order by Another Synoptic

At any point where Matthew, Mark, and Luke recount the same pericope, there are four possibilities concerning the next pericope: (1) both Matthew and Luke contain Mark's next pericope; (2) Matthew contains Mark's next pericope, and Luke has something else; (3) Luke contains Mark's next pericope, and Matthew has something else; or (4) neither Matthew nor Luke contains Mark's next pericope.

Now, obviously the fourth of these circumstances is going to occur in relation to each instance of a pericope unique to Mark. There are eight such pericopes:

1.	"He is beside himself"	3:20–21
2.	The Parable of the Seed Growing Secretly	4:26–29
3.	The Healing of the Deaf Mute	7:31–37E
4.	The Healing of the Blind Man of Bethsaida	8:22–26
5.	About Salt	9:49–50E
6.	Jesus Looks around the Temple	11:11
7.	Keep Awake	13:33–37E
8.	The Young Man Who Fled	14:51–52

Four of these are unparalleled in the Major Synoptics (3:20–21; 4:26–29; 8:22–26; 11:11), so in the above table, they have a dash alongside them in the Matthew and Luke columns.

Two of these (7:31–37E; 13:33–37E) are in the nature of Markan alternatives with somewhat similar content to what Matthew has at that point. Some scholars include Mark 9:49–50 in this category also. One (14:51–52) is included within a Triple Tradition passage.

Markan Priority advocates claim that all of these are occasions when Matthew and Luke both independently decided not to use a given Markan pericope. On the Markan Dependence Hypothesis these are all occasions when Mark inserted a small pericope of his own into what he was drawing from Matthew and Luke. In no case is the question of Synoptic pericope order involved. As far as the discussion of Synoptic pericope order is concerned, these Markan *Sondergut* pericopes can be set aside.

There are numerous cases where the first of the above four circumstances applies, namely, where Matthew, Mark, and Luke continue in parallel for two or more pericopes in succession. This would be expected on both the Markan Priority and Markan Dependence views. Markan Priority says that at successive points in Mark's narrative, neither Matthew nor Luke would have any reason to leave Mark's order. Markan Dependence says that wherever Mark found that Matthew and Luke had the same order, he also retained that order.

One of the "givens" of our investigation is that on occasion Matthew and Mark, and Mark and Luke, do not agree in order. This means that sometimes Matthew and sometimes Luke is not in agreement with the order of the other two Synoptics—numbers (2) and (3) of the four possibilities listed above. This in fact is the phenomenon under investigation. Both Markan Priority and Markan Dependence are able to account for this: Markan Priority by offering reasons why Matthew or Luke would desert Mark's order on each given occasion; Markan Dependence by the explanation that when Mark came to Matthew and Luke there already were these divergences of order between them, and in each such case Mark followed the order of one or the other.

The major focus of our interest in this present section is the fourth circumstance. We have noted the situation where Matthew and Luke differ from Mark's order at a given point because neither of the Major Synoptics include the pericope. But does it happen that at a particular point in Mark, the next pericope he gives *is* found in one of the Major Synoptics but in a different place and that Mark's order where he gives such a pericope is unsupported by the other Major Synoptic?

Given that Matthew and Luke are each free to differ from Mark's order for reasons that are independent of each other, it is to be expected that they could each choose to do so at the same point. As can be seen from a careful consideration of the above table of Synoptic segments, the fact is that this circumstance *does not occur*. That is, there are numerous occasions when, after a point of threefold agreement in recounting a pericope, the threefold agreement extends to the following pericope also, and there are numerous occasions when the next pericope is found only in Matthew and Mark or only in Mark and Luke; but *there is no occasion* when what is found after a given pericope in Mark is not found next in *either* Matthew *or* Luke but *is* found elsewhere in Matthew's or Luke's sequence. There is *no place* where Mark places a pericope in an independent order of his own, an order that is not paralleled in either Matthew or Luke.

D. G. Murray claims (1983, 101.344: 183) that Mark has two pericopes where "Mark's order lacks support from either Matthew or Luke. [These] are (1) 3:13–19 and (2) 11:11–27." Closer consideration of the texts discloses that these passages do not constitute exceptions to the generalization that Mark is paralleled in every pericope in either Matthew or Luke (or both) by the *next* pericope in that Gospel or those Gospels so that the sequence of pericopes is maintained between Mark and at least one other Synoptic.

In the first situation, Mark 3:1–6 (the withered hand pericope) is paralleled by the other two Synoptics (Matt 12:9–14//Luke 6:6–11), and then Matthew and Luke differ in what they place next: Matt 12:15–21 has the healing of the multitudes (which Luke has deferred to a slightly later position; see 6:17–19), and Luke 6:12–16 has the appointment of the Twelve. Next in Mark is the healing of the multitudes, and in this his order parallels Matthew; then he has the appointment of the Twelve, in which he parallels the next pericope in Luke *after* the point of threefold agreement. This agreement in sequence is not nullified by the circumstance that the previous pericope in which the order of Matthew and Mark corresponds (Matt 12: 15–21//Mark 3:7–12) is also the next-but-one pericope in Luke (6:17–19).

In the second instance cited by Murray, Matthew and Mark have a difference of order: Matthew gives the cleansing of the temple before the cursing of the fig tree, whereas Mark has these two reversed.

A careful consideration of the data shows that it is not the cursing of the fig tree that is out of order between Matthew and Mark (as is often stated), but the cleansing of the temple. This is clearly seen since Matthew has the cleansing of the temple occurring on Day One of Jesus' arrival in Jerusalem, and the cursing and withering of the fig tree both occur on

Day Two, whereas in Mark the cursing of the fig tree and the cleansing of the temple occur (in that order) on Day Two, and the fig tree is noticed on Day Three to have already withered away to its roots (Mark 11:20). Thus Matthew apocopates these events into two days and Mark extends them over three days. Note the occurrence of the elements in the story:

STORY ELEMENT	MATTHEW	MARK	LUKE
	DAY ONE	DAY ONE	DAY ONE
Jesus enters Jerusalem	21:10–11	11:11a	
Jesus enters the temple	21:12a	11:11b	
Jesus cleanses the temple	21:12b–16	—	
Jesus retires to Bethany	21:17	11:11c	
	DAY TWO	DAY TWO	
Jesus returns to Jerusalem	21:18	11:12a	
Jesus curses the fig tree	21:19a	11:12b–14	
Jesus enters the temple		11:15a	19:45a
Jesus cleanses the temple		11:15b–17	19:45b–46
			DAILY
Conspiracy against Jesus		11:18	19:47–48E
They leave Jerusalem		11:19	
		DAY THREE	ONE DAY
The fig tree withered	21:19b–22	11:20–26	
Jesus enters the temple	21:23a	11:27a	20:1a
Question about authority	21:23b–27	11:27b–33	20:1b–8

Note the way in which Mark parallels Matthew for the first few elements in the narrative (11:11–14)—except that he omits the cleansing of the temple that occurs here in Matthew. Then from 11:15–18 Mark parallels Luke and here gives the cleansing of the temple. Thus Mark records (contra both Matthew and Luke in this regard) *two* occasions when Jesus entered the temple, on consecutive days, before the Day of Questions (Mark 11:11b,15a). Luke makes no mention of the cursing or withering of the fig tree, so that in his Gospel the cleansing of the temple thus follows immediately after Jesus' entry into the city.

So Mark's account is an amalgam of correspondences with both Matthew and Luke, but with these clear differences between Mark and Matthew: (1) Mark has the cleansing of the temple on the Second Day and Matthew has it on the First Day; (2) Mark has the noticing of the withered fig tree on the Third Day and Matthew has the withering of the fig tree on the Second Day, immediately after the cursing.

No matter what may be thought about these differences, they are most certainly *not* a case of the simple transposition of the order of two pericopes. What happened is more fundamental than that. We have a less detailed chronological sequence of events in Matthew and a more detailed chronological sequence of events in Mark; this situation has similarities to Matt 9:18//Mark 5:23,35 (see Luke 8:42,49), where the daughter is dead from the beginning in Matthew but in contrast is dying at the beginning of the pericope in Mark (and Luke) and is reported to be dead at a later point in the story. It is this kind of difference that is to be seen between Matthew and Mark in the interrelated pericopes of the cleansing of the temple and the fig tree, rather than a difference of pericope order as such. Moreover, Mark's order is in accord with Luke's in placing the cleansing of the temple immediately before, and as a lead-in to, the pericope on the chief priests and scribes (which Matthew lacks).

Certainly, what we see here is not of such a nature as to disturb the validity of the acknowledged circumstance that Mark's order is always supported by either or both Matthew and Luke. Also, when Mark is paralleled in order with only one of the Major Synoptics, Mark's next pericope *either* continues to be parallel with that same Major Synoptic, *or* it is parallel in sequence with the *next* pericope which that Major Synoptic contains that is also contained in the other Major Synoptic. Thus, in this circumstance also, it remains a valid observation that Mark's order is supported by either or both Matthew and Luke.

The Comparison of Synoptic Order

From the Synoptic table given above, it can be seen that the order of pericopes in Matthew and Mark is the same for most of the pericopes in the two Gospels. However, there are several exceptions to this generalization where the dislocation of order is quite substantial, all of which occur in the first six chapters of Mark and their parallels in Matthew.

The extent to which there is a common Synoptic order is one of the arguments for the existence of a literary relationship between the Gospels. It is difficult to account for this degree of correspondence if Matthew and Mark are considered to have been written from the oral tradition independently of each other, since pericopes in the oral tradition would not all occur in a fixed order that would then be reproduced in independently written Gospels. Therefore, there is some relationship between the Gospels of Matthew and Mark, and one author has followed the order of the other most of the time. But who followed whom?

Markan Priority advocates hold that Matthew used Mark (and similarly, Luke used Mark). On the basis of this hypothesis, it is thus Matthew who has on several occasions deserted Mark's order. The Successive Dependence

(Augustinian) Hypothesis and the Markan Dependence Hypothesis both hold that Mark used Matthew, so it is Mark who deserted Matthew's order from time to time. We must now examine the question of Synoptic order on the basis of each of these three views.

ACCORDING TO THE MARKAN PRIORITY HYPOTHESIS

What Matthew Has Done

We start with how Matthew handled Mark's account on the presuppositions of Markan Priority, and then we examine the explanations of Matthew's treatment that have been offered.

Matthew and Mark differ in what they *include* in some of the following pericopes—a feature that in itself is a matter of significance worthy of further consideration separately—but they are in agreement in the *order* in which they give these pericopes:

1. John the Baptist	Mark 1:2–11	Matt 3:1–17E
2. The Temptation	Mark 1:12–13	Matt 4:1–11
3. Ministry in Galilee	Mark 1:14–15	Matt 4:12–17
4. The Call of the First Disciples	Mark 1:16–20	Matt 4:18–22

It can be suggested that the subject matter itself determines that these pericopes come at this point in each Gospel, and in the order given. Thus, the earliest point at which differences in pericope order could occur would be after Jesus commenced his Galilee ministry. Matthew and Mark have only one pericope in common after this point (the call of the first disciples) before their order diverges:

NO.	MARK	MATT	ORD.	WHAT MATTHEW DOES
1.	1:2–11	3:1–17E	1	
2.	1:12–13	4:1–11	2	
3.	1:14–15	4:12–17	3	
4.	1:16–20	4:18–22	4	
				Mark's "Busy Sabbath in Capernaum" Dismantled
5a.	1:21–22	7:28–29	6	transfers this to end the Sermon on the Mount
5b.	1:23–28	—	—	omits Mark's first healing
6.	1:29–34	8:14–17	8	transfers these to be his third and fourth healings
7.	1:35–38	—	—	omits the circumstances leading to the tour
8.	1:39	4:23–25E	5	the tour now follows the Call of First Disciples
9.	1:40–45E	8:1–4	7	this healing now follows the Sermon on the Mount

Putting Things in Order 393

NO.	MARK	MATT	ORD.	WHAT MATTHEW DOES
10.	2:1–22	9:1–17	10	**Mark's two chapters of Conflict Stories (chapters 2 and 3) have now been split up in Matthew**
11.	2:23–3:6	12:1–14	14	
12.	3:7–12	12:15–21	15	
13.	3:13–19	10:1–4	12	moves this back to an earlier position
14.	3:20–21	—	—	omits Jesus "Thought to Be Mad"
15.	3:22–27	12:22–30	16	
16.	3:28–30	12:31–37	17	
17.	3:31–35E	12:46–50E	18	
18.	4:1–20	13:1–23	19	
19.	4:21–25	5:15; 10:26; 11:15// 13:43; 7:2; 13:12.		broken up into five
20.	4:26–29	—	—	omits Parable of the Growing Seed
21.	4:30–32	13:31–32	20	
22.	4:33–34	13:34–35	21	
23.	4:35–5:20	8:23–34E	9	moves this back to an earlier position
24.	5:21–43E	9:18–26	10	moves this back to an earlier position
25.	6:1–6	13:53–58E	22	
26.	6:7–13	10:5–16	13	moves this back to an earlier position
27.	6:14–16	14:1–2	23	

The numbers on the right of the Matthew reference (under the heading ORD. for order) indicate the order of these pericopes in Matthew's Gospel. These numbers show the extent of the general correspondence between their order in Matthew and Mark, and also the departures occurring from that order on several occasions.

Hereafter Matthew *exactly* follows Mark's order to the end of his account, with the minor difference of reversing the order of the cleansing of the temple and the cursing of the fig tree (see explanation above).

Why Matthew Handled Mark the Way He Did

Following this statement of *how* (on the presuppositions of Markan Priority) Matthew handled Mark's Gospel, we must now inquire *why* he has acted this way. Several explanations of Matthew's alterations have been offered by scholars. I have interacted with four of them: W. C. Allen (1907, xiii–xvii); B. H. Streeter (1924, 161–62, 273–74); N. B. Stonehouse (1963, 66–69); and W. G. Kümmel (1975, 57–60).

Allen's treatment is detailed and thorough, and is accepted by Streeter (161) with the commendation, "The discussion of the relation of Matthew and Mark in this work [Allen's] is the most valuable known to me." It is not infrequently referred to by modern writers as a sufficient treatment of the issues. However, we may note that Allen uses slightly different Matthew/Mark equivalents from the more usual.

Allen regards Mark 1:21a "And they went into Capernaum," as being equivalent to (or more precisely, being substituted by) Matt 4:23–25, Jesus' preaching tour of Galilee and the reports of his increasing fame (xv). This, Allen believes, is where Matthew then inserts the Sermon on the Mount. His comment is (xv):

> Mark 1:21b speaks of teaching in the synagogue. Here, therefore, is an opportunity of inserting an illustration of Christ's teaching, which is to be followed by an illustrative group of His miracles. As an introduction to these two sections of illustration, the editor substitutes for Mark 1:21 a general sketch of Christ's activity (4:23–25), using for this purpose phraseology borrowed from various parts of the second Gospel. The reason why he places his illustrations of Christ's teaching before that of His miracles is no doubt to be found in Mark 1:22, which describes the effect produced by that teaching on the people. The editor therefore inserts the Sermon on the Mount between Mark 1:21 and 22 and closes it with the latter verse.

After acknowledging that "it is not easy to account for" what Matthew has done here, Allen gives suggestions for the omission of some pericopes and the transposition of others. He considers (xv–xvi) that Matthew may have placed the healing of the leper as the first of his group of healings—rather than the demoniac in the synagogue, which he omits; or Peter's mother-in-law and the sick at nightfall, which he places as his third and fourth healing pericopes and which were earlier in Mark—because "leprosy was perhaps the most dreaded of all bodily ailments in Palestine, and its cure forms a fitting introduction to a series of three healings of disease."

Allen suggests (xvi) that Matthew did not use the healing of the demoniac because (1) it "may have been that he wished to form a series of three healings of disease, and that in the Church tradition the healing of the centurion's servant was closely connected with the Sermon"; and (2) "there were features in the story of the demoniac which did not commend it to the editor."

Allen then explains that Mark 1:35–39 (Jesus prays alone then proposes a tour) "would be out of place in a series of miracles, and is therefore omitted." Allen continues (xvi):

> Mark 1:40–45 has been already inserted. The editor, therefore, comes to Mark 2:1–22. This he postpones, perhaps because it occurred on a visit to Capernaum different to that just described. By recording it here the editor would confuse the two visits. Mark 2:23–3:6 he reserves for a controversial section. 3:7–35 contain no miracle. 4:1–34 he reserves for his chapter on parables.

Several similar comments follow on omissions and transpositions, and then Allen says (xvii):

> Having now given illustrations of Christ's teachings and miracles, the editor now proposes to show how this ministry found extension in the work of the disciples. He therefore postpones Mark 6:1–6a, and expands 6b into an introduction to this mission modeled on the similar introduction 4:23–25.
>
> Chapter 10:1 continues with Mark 6:7; but the editor here inserts Mark 3:16–19, which he had passed over. The rest of 10–11:1 is an amplification of Mark 6:8–9. . . .
>
> There now follows a series of incidents illustrating the growth of hostility to Christ on the part of the Pharisees. For these the editor now goes back to Mark 2:23–28ff. . . .
>
> Having already borrowed Mark 3:13–19a he now comes to 19b–21 and 22–30. For this he substitutes a similar but longer discourse introduced by another miracle. . . .
>
> This brings him to Mark 4, which is a chapter of parables. The editor borrows this and adds other parables. . . . As he has already inserted Mark 4:35–5:43 he now comes to Mark 6:1–6a. From this point the editor follows the order of Mark's sections.

The above selection of extracts is representative of all that Allen says. Four things in particular stand out. First, Allen's explanation proceeds on a pericope-by-pericope basis, at times in fact virtually on a verse-by-verse basis, since each omission and deviation requires its own explanation.

Second, much of the time Allen does not actually give any explanation of *why* Matthew ("the editor") has proceeded in a particular way, but only gives a statement of *what* Matthew has done, which assumes Markan Priority is true. Thus he attempts no explanation of some of the major transpositions, such as why (on his view) Matthew would postpone "a series of incidents illustrating the growth of hostility to Christ on the part of the Pharisees."

Third, Allen's explanations are often so general that they could cover Matthew's text *whatever* order he had adopted. The explanations he gives are highly subjective and would fit *any* situation. Thus, as already seen, his explanation of why Matthew brings up the healing of the leper from its position as Mark's *fourth* healing story to become Matthew's *first* healing story is that "leprosy was perhaps the most dreaded of all bodily ailments in Palestine, and its cure forms a fitting introduction to a series of three healings of disease" (xv-xvi). But the cure of leprosy would be equally fitting as the *midpoint* or (especially) as the *climax* of a series of healings. Allen does not offer any explanation for why it is *more fitting* as the first in a series of healings, that is, why Matthew places it where he does. Allen's comment could readily be made to apply to the story *wherever* it had occurred in Matthew. If Matthew had put the healing of the leper last, as the climax of a series of healings, Allen would only have to change one word—"introduction" to "climax"—in his comment and it would still fit the situation. In other words, the most that Allen's comment does is explain the inclusion of this pericope *somewhere* in a group of healing miracles. Thus Allen's comment is an all-purpose explanation readily adaptable to whatever the text happened to contain, so it is not specifically related to what the text actually *does* contain.

Fourth, Allen's explanations frequently depend on Matthew having followed a course of action on some occasions contrary to what he has done on others, so that Matthew's principles of compilation are in fact self-contradictory. For example, Mark 1:35–39 (Jesus prays alone then proposes a tour) was omitted because it "would be out of place in a series of miracles" (xvi). But at exactly the point where Mark places this pericope (after the healing of the sick at nightfall, Mark 1:32–34//Matt 8:16–17), Matthew himself inserts (8:18–22) the pericope on discussions with aspirants to discipleship. It is not immediately apparent why what *Mark* had at this point is "out of place in a series of miracles" whereas what *Matthew himself* inserts at the same point, which also has nothing to do with miracles, is not inappropriate "in a series of miracles."

Again, at a later stage—Matthew 9—Matthew sets out another series of miracles for which (on the Markan Priority view) he uses Mark, and between two miracle pericopes (Matt 9:1–8, the healing of the paralytic; and Matt 9:18–26, Jairus's daughter and the woman with a hemorrhage) Matthew is quite content to leave in position two other non-miracle pericopes that occur at this point in Mark (Matt 9:9–13, the call of Matthew; and Matt 9:14–17, the question about fasting).

The bottom line is that Allen gives no actual reasons for Matthew's changes of order that are not either quite subjective or so general that they would cover anything, or else they are inconsistent with what Matthew is seen to be doing (on the Markan Priority Hypothesis) elsewhere in Matthew 1–13. Certainly the transpositions are not explained on the basis of the outworking of discernible principles of policy or procedure.

As noted earlier, Streeter cites Allen's work with approval. He then adds these comments (273f.):

> It is noticeable that Matthew places the [Mission] Charge much earlier than does Mark, a rearrangement of Mark which is probably due to the influence of the order in Q. . . .
>
> The next item in both [Matthew and Luke] is the pair of parables, the Mustard Seed and Leaven. This brings us into Matthew 13. Now we have observed (161) that up to this point Matthew seems to have rearranged the materials he took from Mark with the greatest freedom; but that from chapter 14 onward he

never departs from Mark's order. We seem to have lighted on the explanation. Matthew's rearrangement of Mark has been, at any rate partly, determined by the necessity of combining Mark with Q. Thus the order of Q has evidently suggested to him to anticipate the place of the Mission Charge in Mark; and the late occurrence of the Mustard Seed and Leaven in Q has led him to postpone Mark's collection of parables of the Kingdom, among which he desired to include this pair from Q and others from M.

In a footnote (to p. 274), Streeter adds, "The endeavour to group together representative miracles seems to have been another motive for rearrangement. Cf. W C Allen, *Commentary on Matthew*, xivff."

Streeter's additional proposal is that accommodation of Markan material to the order of Q explains "at any rate partly" the Matthean rearrangement. At best this is using the uncertain order of material that may have been in Q to account for the changes. However, there is very considerable skepticism (even among those who believe in the existence of Q in some form) that Q was a single document with a fixed order. Thus this proposal is of very limited value in explaining the reason for Matthew's changes to Mark's order of pericopes.

Stonehouse describes (66–69) the sequence of pericopes in the first half of Matthew and compares this sequence with Mark's:

Matthew, following the report of the call of the first disciples, has nothing comparable to the Marcan cycle of events connected with Capernaum but proceeds at once to speak generally of the preaching and healing activity in Galilee (4:23–25). Next Matthew goes on to illustrate the ministry of Jesus in considerable detail, introducing the Sermon on the Mount as an example of his preaching (Mt 5:3–7:27) and many works of healing as instances of the manifestation of his power and mercy (8:1–9:34).

Stonehouse also explains (67) how Matthew does this: "it becomes plain that in chapters 8 and 9 Matthew is mainly concerned to exemplify the miraculous activity of Jesus, as he has previously done with his ministry of teaching. Pursuing this plan, Matthew follows the Sermon on the Mount with the story of the healing of a leper, thus returning to the Marcan framework at the exact point where it had left it to introduce the Sermon."

Thus Stonehouse (who in this regard is representative of a great many others) sees Matthew as following, in the writing of this part of his Gospel, a plan of grouping like things with like: a section of teachings, of miracles, of instruction, of controversies, of parables. In part, a program for this is to be found in the words with which these sections are introduced (4:23–25). Matthew supposedly rearranged Mark's pericopes in accordance with this plan.

However much truth there may be in this as an explanation of the construction of Matthew's Gospel, it is not wholly adequate in accounting for the way Matthew has handled Mark, which is set out in detail in the previous section of the present chapter. This explanation has nothing to contribute, for example, to our understanding of why Matthew mentions Jesus' Galilean tour (Matt 4:23–25//Mark 1:39) and excludes the description of the circumstances that led up to it (Mark 1:35–38); or of why the healing of the demoniac at Capernaum (Mark 1:21–28) is omitted or why the dual pericopes of the healing of Peter's mother-in-law and the sick at nightfall (Mark 1:29–34) are not placed first in Matthew's section of miracles—which is where they occur, after the Capernaum demoniac, in Mark's account—but are placed later than Mark's story of the healing of the leper and the Q story (?) of the centurion's servant. Similarly, no light whatever is shed on why the two linked pairs of pericopes that follow each other in Mark—Jesus calms the storm and the healing of the demoniac (Mark 4:35–5:20); and Jairus's daughter and the woman with a hemorrhage (Mark 5:21–43)—are separated in Matthew by another story block (the healing of the paralytic; the call of Matthew; the question about fasting) that Matthew takes from earlier in Mark (Mark 2:1–22).

Yet Stonehouse is convinced that his explanation is persuasive and moreover that this question of the relative order of Matthew and Mark constitutes an overwhelming argument in support of Markan Priority. His treatment of the question of order concludes with this paragraph (68–69), here reproduced in full:

> On the basis of this comparison of the Matthean arrangement of his subject matter in this section with the Marcan order the acceptance of Matthean priority hardly constitutes as live an option as that of the priority of Mark. In both Matthew and Mark, in spite of the presence of many temporal and geographical details, we note a relative unconcern to set forth the precise temporal sequence of the occurrence of various happenings. In this respect, however, Matthew manifests even less interest than Mark. This has been highlighted in the foregoing survey by the observation that Matthew does not present the Capernaum cycle of events found in Mark 1:21–35. On the other hand, as the manner in which the Sermon on the Mount is presented in chapters 5–7 and the long list of miracle stores in chapters 8 and 9 demonstrate, Matthew's approach is more topical and systematic. Thus Matthew is readily understood as having retained substantially the Marcan framework and as having inserted into this framework additional materials derived from various sources or known to him as personal reminiscences. To the extent that a selecting process is manifest it is clear that Matthew qualifies as the selector rather than Mark. On the other hand, if one should start hypothetically with the Matthean outline of events one would have to adopt the implausible supposition that Mark had chosen more or less at random various largely scattered elements of the Matthean framework and yet that he had introduced greater definiteness and concatenation of events into his outline.

Whether Stonehouse's confidence in his conclusion is justified is an issue presently under consideration in this discussion. But it is worth pointing out now that Stonehouse totally ignores the simple explanation: Mark here exactly follows Luke, with the inclusion of the call of the first disciples and the omission of Jesus' rejection at Nazareth, which Mark later includes using Matthew's version.

Kümmel (1975, 57–60) examines the differences of order among the Synoptics and reaches conclusions similar to Stonehouse. He gives a chart showing only four places in which the respective order of Matthew and Mark diverges: Mark 1:29–34//Matt 8:14–17; Mark 3:13–19//Matt 10:1–4; Mark 4:35–5:20//Matt 8:23–34; Mark 5:21–43//Matt 9:18–26. His chart is introduced thus: "Basically Matthew diverges from the Markan order only in a twofold way." The chart is followed by this explanation of this "twofold way":

> (a) In connection with the first great discourse of Jesus (Mt 5–7), there follows a string of ten miracle stories by way of illustrating 4:23; thus Matthew brings together in chapters 8 and 9 miracles that are scattered throughout the first half of Mark (1:29ff; 4:35ff; 5:21ff).
>
> (b) Matthew attaches to these miracle chapters a mission address (10:5ff), as an introduction to which he has moved forward The Call of the Twelve (Mk 3:13ff).

We have here a generalization that cleverly conceals the problem. First, saying that "thus Matthew brings together in chapters 8 and 9 miracles that are scattered throughout the first half of Mark" is no explanation of *why they are given the order that they have in Matthew*, where, even granted that many of Mark's miracle stores have been collected together into a Matthean "miracles section," in that section they have a *different* order from the one they had in Mark. Kümmel's generalization simply jumps over this question.

Second, no account at all is taken of the omission of a miracle (the healing of the demoniac in Mark 1:21–28) and also the omission of the explanation of the circumstances preceding the Galilean tour (Mark 1:35–38), both of which in Mark are tightly linked to pericopes that Matthew *does* use and transpose.

Third, Kümmel does not include any mention at all of Mark 6:7–13, another Markan passage that is paralleled in Matthew (Matt 10:5–16) and found in a different place in Matthew's order. Similarly, he ignores Mark 1:21–22//Matt 7:28–29 (which Allen considered a significant parallel). Kümmel offers no explanations of these transpositions.

In particular, Kümmel finds support for his conclusions in a detail of Matthew's use of Mark (60): "Here also can be observed in detail Matthew's alteration of Mark's sequence: the two controversy sayings in Mt 9:9–17 are out of place in a cycle of miracles and can be accounted for only on the ground that this is where they occur in Mark."

Thus what we find in the order of pericopes in Matthew (in particular, where he places Matt 9:9–17) is attributed to Matthew's carelessness in carrying through his plan for the structuring of his Gospel. Yet Matthew could so easily have avoided this "inconsistency" in his Gospel's structure. The passage in question is Mark 2:13–22, part of Mark's controversies section. Matthew takes the very next pericopes of Mark (2:23–3:6) and places them into *his* controversies section (Matt 12). Why did he not commence this transfer of material 10 verses earlier, at Mark 2:13 instead of 2:23, and thus avoid these verses getting into the "wrong" section, his miracles section? Carelessness indeed on Matthew's part!

There was another simple alternative open to Matthew. He uses Mark 4:35–5:43 (//Matt 8:23–9:26), but he actually inserts Mark 2:1–22 *into the middle* of this other passage that he takes from Mark (in fact, between Mark 5:21 and v. 22). All Matthew had to do was take over Mark 4:35 to 5:43 as a block as he found it and place Mark 2:1–22 at the *end* of it instead of in the *middle*. Then all Matthew's miracles would be grouped together, and the problem passage of Mark 2:13–22 (which appears in Matt 9:9–17) would thus be at the end of and outside the grouping of miracles. But the placing of this material into the middle of another large block of material taken from Mark indicates a deliberation of intent quite at variance with the carelessness attributed to Matthew by Kümmel. These considerations call into question Kümmel's explanation. Yet Kümmel, like Stonehouse, is convinced that the order of Matthew and Mark is explained on this basis, and that the Markan Dependence explanation as an alternative is ruled out, having been "disproved." Kümmel says (60), "The opposite position—that Mark has altered the sequence of Matthew or Luke—offers no clarification in any of the cases mentioned . . . so that the hypothesis of Griesbach, according to which Mark has excerpted the other two synoptists, is disproved, as well as the theory that Mark has used and abbreviated either Matthew or Luke."

These are the explanations reputable Markan Priority advocates offer for the ways in which Matthew has altered Mark's order, together with some initial comments on the extent to which these explanations do in fact explain the exact features of different order that we observe when we compare these two Synoptic Gospels. There are other explanations, of course, but there is also a tendency for scholars to refer to one or more of these writers whom I have discussed as if they have shown that the phenomenon of Synoptic order had been demonstrated to favor Markan Priority.

For example, R. H. Stein (1988, 70) cites with approval an earlier work that offers "an explanation of why Matthew's and Luke's divergences from the Markan order are more understandable than a Markan divergence from Matthew and/or Luke." He doesn't recognize that there are *no* Markan "divergences from Matthew and/or Luke." Mark *always* follows one or the other! Then Stein adds in a footnote, "For an explanation of these Matthean and Lukan divergences, see Werner Georg Kümmel *Introduction to the New Testament* . . . 57–60."

Tuckett, however, in one of the quotations with which this present chapter commences, asserts that the order of pericopes is not decisive for either Markan Priority or Markan Dependence. Some scholars simply refer in passing to the way in which one or other of the Major Synoptists depart from Mark for his own reasons, without attempting any explanation of what those reasons may have been. G. E. Ladd (1967, 123, 126) is an example of this approach:

> The strongest evidence is found in the order of material in the three Gospels. . . . In their ordering of events, the Gospels do not agree. . . . The order of events is determined not by the order in which these events happened, but by the Evangelists' interests and purpose in writing. . . . Three amazing facts emerge from the comparison of these three Gospels. First, Matthew and Luke follow Mark's order for the most part; second, in numerous specific points, as illustrated above, Matthew and Luke, in pursuing their own particular aims, depart from Mark's order of events; and third, *Matthew and Luke never depart from Mark in the same way.* That is to say, Matthew and Luke never agree in their order of events over against Mark. When they differ, they do so in different ways. If Matthew were the oldest Gospel and had been used by Mark and Luke, there would certainly be places where Luke followed Matthew but Mark did not; but this phenomenon is never found. This fact establishes the priority of Mark with reasonable certainty. The Second Gospel provides the basic outline for the other two. However, since Mark's order is not determined primarily by historical chronology, neither the First nor the Third Gospel follows Mark slavishly; both feel free to vary his order as well as his wording. But Mark clearly provides the key to the problem of Synoptic interrelationship.

Ladd claims that "the strongest evidence [for Markan Priority] is found in the order of material in the three Gospels" and that "this fact establishes the priority of Mark with reasonable certainty," and this method of presentation actually serves to cleverly cover up and conceal fatal flaws in his reasoning and thus in the "reasonable certainty" of his conclusion.

First, he commits the logical fallacy of the "undistributed middle." He says, "If Matthew were the oldest Gospel and had been used by Mark and Luke, there would certainly be places where Luke followed Matthew but Mark did not; but this phenomenon is never found." Therefore, Ladd deduces from this that it is not true that Matthew is the oldest Gospel and was used by Mark and Luke. So Ladd concludes that Mark is the first Gospel, as this is the only other explanation. Ladd does not allow for any other possibilities but that either Luke used Matthew or else that Mark is the first Gospel. He refutes the possibility that Luke used Matthew and therefore concludes that Markan Priority is established. But the hypothesis propounded in this present book—that among the documents circulating in Luke's day, to which he refers (1:1) and which he utilized, were pericopes and pericope clusters written by the apostle Matthew—is totally compatible with the data on the order of pericopes in the Synoptics. This is a completely viable alternative explanation to Markan Priority, as I demonstrate shortly.

Second, Ladd affirms that "the order of events is determined . . . by the Evangelists' interests and purposes in writing," and that "in numerous specific points . . . Matthew and Luke, in pursuing their own particular aims, depart from Mark's order of events" for "both felt free to vary his order." This being so, it would be perfectly possible for *both* of these Major Synoptists to leave Mark's order at the same time, but (as Ladd correctly tells us) in fact *they never do so!* There are 40 occasions when one of the Major Synoptists chooses *not* to follow the pattern of Mark, and *on each one* of those occasions at just exactly that point the other Major Synoptist *does* choose to do so. I identify these 40 occasions below and further discuss this extraordinary coincidence! This feature of the data of Synoptic order is a really large problem for the Markan Priority Hypothesis. It is, however, concealed from view in Ladd's analysis.

Luke's Use of Mark

Luke's order is very close throughout to Mark's, and in most cases where Luke appears to be deserting Mark, Luke is not drawing on Mark as his source at all. Instead, he uses a *similar* story from *another* source. Streeter gives (209f.) an explanation of this factor in Luke's Gospel, explaining that such situations are

> derived from a consideration of the way in which he deals with incidents or sayings in Mark, which he rejects in favour of other versions contained either in the Q or in the L elements of that source. . . .
>
> If we look up these passages in Mark or in a Synopsis of the Gospels and notice the incidents which immediately precede and follow them, we shall see

that Luke reproduces everything else in the neighbourhood from Mark in the original order, but that he simply omits Mark's account of these incidents. The alternative versions which he gives are *always* given in a *completely* different context, presumably, then, their context in the source from which he took them.

Pericopes of this kind and their Markan and Lukan versions are as follows:

	MARK	LUKE
1. The Call of the First Disciple	1:16–20	5:1–11
2. Jesus' Rejection at Nazareth	6:1–6	4:16–30
3. Criticism of Pharisaic Views on Washings	7:1–23	11:37–41
4. The Greatest Commandment	12:28–34	10:25–28
5. Jesus Anointed by a Woman	14:3–9	7:36–50

There are four places where the order of two contiguous pericopes (or groups of pericopes) is reversed in Mark and Luke:

	MARK		LUKE
6. Lakeside Crowds and Healings	3:7–12	X	6:12–16
Appointment of the Twelve	3:13–19		6:17–19
7. Jesus' True Kindred	3:31–35E	X	8:4–18
The Parable of the Sower/Sayings	4:1–25		8:19–21
8. Jesus Foretells His Betrayal	14:18–21	X	22:15–20
The Last Supper	14:22–25		22:21–23
9. Jesus Questioned by the Sanhedrin	14:61–64	X	22:55–65
Jesus Mistreated/Peter's Denials	14:65–72		22:66–71

Kümmel (58) states that "from Mk 6:7 on, Matthew and Luke practically never deviate from Mark's sequence, even though at completely different points they offer substantial supplements to Mark." He then goes on immediately to note that "an exception is Lk 22:21–23,56–66" (i.e., the third and fourth of the four cases listed above), but he does not attempt to *account* for these exceptions (to *mention* something is not to *explain* it).

The first two of these four cases are explained by Kümmel (60): "The call of the twelve (Mk 3:13–19) is placed before the crowding of the people around Jesus (Mk 3:7–12) because in this way Luke has hearers on hand for the sermon on the plain which he inserts at 6:20ff; the transposition of the rejection of Jesus' family (Mk 3:31–35) before the parable speech provides the crowds necessary for the scene."

Here are the other instances where Luke has a parallel to Mark but gives his material in a different place:

	MARK	LUKE
10. The Beelzebul Controversy	3:22–27	11:14–23
11. Blasphemy of the Holy Spirit	3:28–30	12:10
12. The Parable of the Mustard Seed	4:30–32	13:18–19
13. The Fate of John the Baptist	6:17–29	3:19–20
14. Regarding the Leaven of the Pharisees	8:11–21	12:1
15. Marriage and Divorce	10:1–12	16:18
16. False Christs and Prophets	13:21–23	17:23–37

Of this list, there are three cases (numbers 13, 14, 15) where a fairly lengthy episode in Mark is represented by a single saying or quite short comment in Luke. Streeter considers that in some of these cases, the source for Luke's material would not be Mark but Q or L, so they are covered by his comments given above. Kümmel does not mention these transpositions.

THE SUCCESSIVE DEPENDENCE HYPOTHESIS

The Successive Dependence Hypothesis says that Mark used Matthew, following his order most of the time though occasionally departing from it, and Luke used the writings of his predecessors Mark and Matthew. In his exposition of this view and his consideration of the question of pericope order in the Synoptics, B. C. Butler rebuts (1951, 62–71) effectively the contention that pericope order establishes Markan Priority, but he does not come to grips adequately with the difficulties and shortcomings of his own view in relation to Synoptic order.

As already noted, while Matthew and Luke both differ in pericope order from Mark on many occasions, they never differ from Mark *simultaneously*. The Successive Dependence Hypothesis (followed by J. Chapman and Butler) explains this by claiming that while Luke used both Matthew and Mark as sources for the *contents* of his Gospel, Luke took his *order* exclusively from Mark, never Matthew. Thus Chapman (1937, 233) refers to Luke's order as "the framework which he borrows from Mark." Further, this means that when Luke found Matthew and Mark following a different order, he *never* follows Matthew's order, as can be seen in the fact that Matthew and Luke never agree in order against Mark. Moreover, Luke was willing to leave Mark's order himself on 16 occasions (as listed above in this chapter), but *only* when Mark was following Matthew's order at the time.

Thus Luke was willing to desert Mark's order *except* when Mark deserted Matthew's order: i.e., when Matthew and Mark agree on their order, Luke was willing to leave that order; when Matthew and Mark differ on order, Luke adheres to Mark's order and never follows Matthew's order. This can be seen in that none of the bracketed references in the Synoptic table (see above in this chapter)—indicating that one of the other Synoptists is not in agreement with Mark's order at that point—ever occur simultaneously for Matthew and Luke against the same passage in Mark. This is indeed a point to ponder. It is possible to believe that an author like Luke *could* follow such a procedure in writing his Gospel. It is very difficult to see any reason *why* he should choose to do so.

THE MARKAN DEPENDENCE HYPOTHESIS

The Markan Dependence Hypothesis says Mark wrote last and utilized the Gospels of Matthew and Luke. The explanation of Synoptic order from this perspective is that (1) whenever Matthew and Luke agree in their pericope order, Mark *always* follows their common order, resulting in agreement between all three; and (2) whenever Matthew and Luke differ in their pericope order, Mark *always* follows one or the other, resulting in agreement between Matthew and Mark against Luke, or Mark and Luke against Matthew. Thus Mark *never* introduces a divergent order of his own that would have resulted in all three Synoptics diverging in their order for the pericope(s) in question.

The reason that Mark acted thus was that he was interested in the *content* of the Synoptic material he was using and not in its *order*. Either Mark had no independent knowledge of pericope order; or in each case his own information tallied with the order of Matthew or Luke (or both, where they agreed); or else he was consciously engaged in harmonizing their pericope order and scrupulously avoiding introducing at any point a different order of his own. (Papias's explanation for this was that Mark drew his material from Peter, but he had no information about the order of events; see chap. 1.) This is in itself a complete explanation of every occurrence of divergences of order in the Synoptic Gospels and in particular of the reason that Mark would have followed the procedure detailed above.

The Markan Dependence Hypothesis may be contrasted with the quandary experienced by scholars in suggesting reasons for the alterations in pericope order that must have been made: by Matthew and Luke (Markan Priority); or the difficulty in explaining why Mark would have left Matthew's order when he did, and the even greater difficulty in seeing any reason for the very odd way of treating his sources that Luke must have followed (Successive Dependence). H. H. Stoldt (1980, chap. VI, 135–54) gives a very thorough rebuttal of the use of the argument from order as an argument for Markan Priority. Farmer (1964, 221–15) and Orchard (1977, 72–84) demonstrate that the argument from order favors Markan Dependence rather than Markan Priority.

Kümmel's comment (1975, 60) on the Markan Dependence (Griesbach) Hypothesis is that "the opposite position—that Mark has altered the sequence of Matthew or Luke—offers no clarification in any of the cases mentioned . . . , so that the hypothesis of Griesbach, according to which Mark has excerpted the other two synoptists, is disproved." This is a truly amazing assertion from a scholar of Kümmel's caliber, and it must represent a momentary lapse of thought that slipped into print. Markan Dependence says that Mark *never* alters the sequence of Matthew or Luke; rather, when confronted with a part of the narrative where these two written sources differ in order, Mark chose one or the other to follow. This in fact offers complete clarification of the cases Kümmel mentions.

The first of Kümmel's cases mentioned (59) is the way "Matthew brings together in Chapters 8 and 9 miracles that are scattered throughout the first half of Mark (1:29ff; 4:35ff; 5:21ff)." As may be seen in the Synoptic table above, all these pericopes occur in Mark in the *exact* place and in the *exact* order that they occur in Luke. (In his examples, Kümmel fails to indicate that the last two passages that he gives—4:35ff. and 5:21ff.—are in fact all one consecutive block in Mark and are thus hardly "scattered," whereas this block is broken into two segments in Matthew 8–9, with another block of three pericopes inserted between those segments where "Matthew brings [them] together." This is hardly an objective description of the situation.

Kümmel's second case (60) is "a mission address (10:5ff), as an introduction to which he [Matthew] has moved forward the call of the twelve (Mark 3:13ff.)." Matthew combines the appointment of the Twelve (Matt 10:1–4) and the mission charge (Matt 10:5ff.), which Mark places separately in his Gospel (Mark 3:13–19; 6:7–13). But in doing so, Mark follows Luke's procedure *exactly*, and in regard to where he gives them in his Gospel, Mark adheres to Luke's order.

Kümmel's third case is that "the two controversy sayings in Mt 9:9–17 are out of place in a cycle of miracles and can be accounted for only on the ground that this is where they occur in Mark." In all three Gospels, these "sayings" (actually, they also include the call of Matthew/Levi) follow the healing of the paralytic—evidently a linking of pericopes from the pre-canonical Gospel days, made by one of those who "have undertaken to compile a narrative" (Luke 1:1). In this group of pericopes, and in what precedes them and what follows them (in which Matthew differs), Mark follows what Luke includes *exactly*, and Luke's order.

Kümmel's fourth case is "the comparison of the parable chapter, Mk 4:1–34, with Mt 13:1–52." But no question of divergence of order is involved here, as all three Gospels include the parables at the same point. Mark's procedure is easily recognizable. After the initial parable, the sower, which is common to all three Synoptics, Mark follows Luke for the sayings (Mark 4:21–25//Luke 8:16–18; these are not in Matthew at this point). Then Mark inserts the short parable that he alone gives (Mark 4:26–29). Next he follows Matthew for one more parable (the mustard seed, Mark 4:30–32//Matt 13:31–32; elsewhere in Luke) and also for Jesus' use of parables (Mark 4:33–34//Matt 13:34–35) with which he closes his parables section. The Markan Dependence explanation of what Mark has done is clear, straightforward, and logical.

There is no justification for Kümmel's strong assertion that by means of "the cases mentioned, . . . the hypothesis of Griesbach . . . is disproved." On the contrary, Markan Dependence offers a very simple explanation for all these cases. Kümmel's explanations leave one with the impression that in the Markan Dependence view, Mark would be totally dismembering coherent sections of Matthew. But Kümmel failed to point out that Mark's procedure is fully explained by the fact that *Mark simply and consistently followed Luke*. Further, one can similarly see that Stonehouse's strictures against Mark using Matthew (which were quoted earlier) are fully met by the explanation that when not following Matthew's order Mark was *always* (and scrupulously) following Luke's order.

The Markan Dependence Hypothesis can accept that Luke aimed to follow a logical or chronological order of presentation (Luke 1:3), and that Matthew worked on the basis of grouping like with like and assembling material in blocks—a widely accepted view. V. Taylor's judgment (1967, 70) that "Matthew's *love of orderly arrangement* is seen in his treatment of his sources" remains true no matter how one views Matthew's sources.

In such circumstances the pericope order of the two Major Synoptics would at times differ because of their different approaches. However, they would agree in their overall chronological framework and in the order of pericopes within small sections, where that grouping of pericopes already existed in the material that they were incorporating. Then Mark follows the order of one or the other *at all times* in writing his Gospel.

That Mark followed the common order of Matthew and Luke when they agreed and the order of one or the other when they differed provides a complete explanation of every aspect of the pericope sequence of the Synoptics. But an examination of the Synoptic table allows a further significant step to be taken in understanding exactly what Mark did and why from the Markan Dependence perspective, which we now consider further.

MARK'S USE OF MATTHEW AND LUKE

Identifying the Markan Framework

A great many scholars have noted that after Matt 14:1//Mark 6:14, Mark and Matthew coincide completely in their order except for the minor situation where the two contiguous pericopes of the cursing of the fig tree and the cleansing of the temple appear in reverse order in these two Gospels (see discussion above).

What then is Mark's relation to Luke during this section of his Gospel? An examination of the Synoptic table above discloses three features. First, a substantial section of Luke's Gospel (9:51–18:14)—mostly consisting of teaching—is not directly paralleled at this point by anything in Mark, though half a dozen verses or so are paralleled in *other* contexts in Mark, where they occur in the *same* contexts that they have in Matthew, from whom he has drawn them. Second, after 6:14, Mark contains several pericopes for which Luke *has* parallels but that occur in Luke in an order different from Mark's. Third, there are four sections that occur in both Mark and Luke and in the same place in the pericope order of Mark and Luke but that are not paralleled in Matthew. Using the numbers in the Synoptic table above, these are:

		MARK	LUKE
29	The Return of the Twelve	6:30–31	9:10a
43	The Stranger Who Was Exorcizing	9:38–41	9:49–50
54	The Chief Priests and Scribes Conspire	11:18–19	19:47–48
61	The Widow's Gift	12:41–44	21:1–4

This data allows one to see that (1) from Mark 6:14 to the end of his Gospel, Mark follows the order of Matthew's Gospel; and that (2) into this framework Mark inserts four short sections taken from Luke's Gospel. A logical reason for Mark's procedure suggests itself. The study of Mark's Gospel shows that he had a limited interest in recording Jesus' teachings, which makes up a small proportion of his Gospel compared with Matthew and Luke (see chaps. 3 and 4 of this book). Luke's central section consists very largely of Jesus' teachings. Choosing Matthew here as his framework allowed Mark to steer a course around Luke's central section, which was unsuited to his (presumed) purposes. When Luke did contain something that Mark wished to use, he simply inserted it into the Matthean framework at the point where it occurred in Luke's narrative. The number of entries in the Synoptic Table in the left hand Markan column (i.e., adjacent to the Matthew column) shows the extent to which Mark was following Matthew as against Luke throughout this section (Mark 6:14–16:8).

This explanation of Mark's procedure in the second half of his Gospel leads us to examine what has happened in the first half. From the occurrence of the entries in both the left hand ("following Matthew") and the right hand ("following Luke") columns of Mark's three columns in the Synoptic table, it appears at first as if Mark were simply alternating in his choice of whomever he follows. However, a more careful inspection shows that from Luke 3:2 to 6:19 Mark uses all that Luke contains except these three: (1) the genealogy (Luke 3:23–38E) since evidently Mark's purpose in writing meant that he did not need to include either genealogies or nativity narratives (he includes none from either Matthew or Luke); (2) rejection at Nazareth (Luke 4:16–30) since Mark chose instead to use the alternative version of this event given by Matthew, which he places where Matthew puts it in his account (Mark 6:1–6); (3) the call of the first disciples (Luke 5:1–11) since Mark chose instead to use the alternative version of this event given by Matthew, which he places where Matthew puts it in his account (Mark 1:16–20).

This may be summarized by saying that from the end of Luke's nativity section (but omitting the genealogy) up to Luke 6:19, Mark contains *exactly* the pericopes that Luke contains, and in the same order, except for two Lukan stories where Mark substitutes the equivalent Matthean stories and inserts them in his framework in the place they occupy in his source (Matthew). No comparable statement can be made about Matthew's order and contents in relation to Mark for this part of Matthew's Gospel.

Mark includes two pericopes that are found here in Luke and absent from Matthew (the demoniac in the Capernaum synagogue and Jesus praying alone). Large sections of this part of Matthew's Gospel are omitted altogether: chief among them is the Sermon on the Mount, together with healing the centurion's servant, healing two blind men, healing a dumb demoniac, part of Matthew's mission charge, John the Baptist's question and Jesus' answer, Jesus' testimony about John, and some sayings. Some narratives in this section of Matthew (8:14–17,23–34; 9:18–26; 10:1–16) occur elsewhere in Mark, where they are placed according to their position in Luke's Gospel.

As noted above, Mark drew from Matthew as a source for two pericopes that he uses (the call of the first disciples in 1:16–20; and Jesus' rejection at Nazareth in 6:1–6), but clearly he adopted Luke here as the framework for his pericope order. We can even offer a reason for this: the Lukan order allowed Mark to steer around the Sermon on the Mount, which it was not his purpose to use.

One small point can be elucidated here. In following Luke, Mark reverses the order of the pericopes on the appointment of the Twelve (Luke 6:12–16) and lakeside crowds and healings (Luke 6:17–19). An explanation for this can be offered. For the section on plucking grain and healing the withered hand, all three Synoptics are together (Matt 12:1–14//Mark 2:23–3:6//Luke 6:1–11). This is followed in Matthew by lakeside crowds and healings, but in Luke by the appointment of the Twelve and *then* Luke's version of lakeside crowds and healings. Matthew's account of the appointment of the Twelve occurs earlier in his Gospel.

Mark chose to use both what Matthew and Luke each give next, but he was faced with this divergence in the order of his sources. He solved this by taking *first* what comes in Matthew and *then* what comes in Luke after the healing of the withered hand, as 6:17–19 is Luke's equivalent to Matt 12:15–21. This allows Mark to include all of Luke's material up to 6:19 with minimum dislocation of his sources.

Luke 6:20 is the commencement of Luke's Sermon on the Plain, and in keeping with his policy of restricting the teaching that he includes, Mark chose to leave Luke at this point. Continuing from the same position in Matthew (12:22)—but placing at this point two additional verses of his own (Mark 3:20–21)—Mark now inserts into his framework a section from Matthew (12:22–13:23).

This procedure has steered Mark around the Sermon on the Plain (and taken him past some other pericopes as well) and brought him back to a pericope—the parable of the sower—where Matthew and Luke are once again parallel. In the process of thus following Matthew, Mark included the story of Jesus' true family, thus moving it from the end of Luke's parable section (Luke 8:19–21) to a position in front of the parables (i.e., where Matthew has it), where it forms the climax to the verses that Mark himself introduced (3:20–21) about the attitude of Jesus' family towards him.

Mark now follows Luke closely again up to Luke 9:9, using Luke's order as his framework and including in his own Gospel all the pericopes that Luke contains (he has already used Luke 8:19–21) and omitting much that Matthew contains. Into this framework he also inserts the short parable unique to his Gospel, the parable of the growing seed (4:26–29); the parable of the mustard seed, and Jesus' use of parables (4:30–34, from Matthew at this point); and Jesus' rejection at Nazareth (6:1–6); in this regard, as mentioned above, Mark chose to use Matthew's version and he places it in the position that Matthew gives it.

Thus after their parables material, Luke has several miracle stories (8:22–56E) and Matthew has the visit to Nazareth (13:53–58E). Mark uses both sets of material, taking Luke's first and then Matthew's; presumably his choice of this sequence was influenced by the way that the miracles that he took over from Luke give added emphasis to the comment by those at Nazareth, "What mighty works are wrought by his hands!" (Mark 6:2b//Matt 13:54b).

After this, Matthew and Luke are parallel in their order again with the account of Herod's perplexity about Jesus (Matt 14:1–2//Mark 6: 14–16//Luke 9:7–9). Here Mark changes from following the framework of Luke to that of Matthew. Mark follows this story of Herod's perplexity about Jesus with the explanation (from Matthew) about John the Baptist's death (which Luke lacks), and from this point Mark retains Matthew's framework to the end of his Gospel.

Arrangement of the Markan Framework

Mark's framework for his Gospel can thus be arranged in this way:

NO	SECTION	MATT	MARK	LUKE
1.	John the Baptist		1:2–11	3:2–22
2.	The Temptation		1:12–13	4:1–13
3.	Ministry in Galilee		1:14–15	4:14–15
4.	The Call of the First Disciples	4:18–22	1:16–20	—
	Rejection at Nazareth		—	4:16–30
5.	Demoniac in the Capernaum Synagogue		1:21–28	4:31–37
6.	Healing Peter's Mother-in-Law and Others		1:29–34	4:38–41
7.	Jesus Prays Alone, and Then Departs		1:35–38	4:42–43
8.	Preaching Tour		1:39	4:44E
	The Call of the First Disciples		—	5:1–11
9.	Cleansing the Leper		1:40–45E	5:12–16
10.	Paralytic/Call of Matthew/On Fasting		2:1–22	5:17–39E
11.	Plucking Grain/Withered Hand Healed	12:1–14	2:23–3:6	6:1–11
12.	Lakeside Crowds and Healings	12:15–21	3:7–12	[6:17–19]
13.	Appointment of the Twelve		3:13–19	6:12–16
14.	Jesus Thought to Be Mad	—	3:20–21	—
15.	Beelzebul Controversy	12:24–30	3:22–27	
16.	Blasphemy of the Holy Spirit	12:31–37	3:28–30	
17.	Jesus' True Family	12:46–50E	3:31–35E	[8:19–21]

NO	SECTION	MATT	MARK	LUKE
18.	The Parable of the Sower	13:1–23	4:1–20	8:4–15
19.	Sayings: Lamps, Hearing, and Getting		4:21–25	8:16–18
20.	The Parable of the Growing Seed	—	4:26–29	—
21.	The Parable of the Mustard Seed	13:31–32	4:30–32	[13:18–19]
22.	Jesus' Use of Parables	13:34–35	4:33–34	—
	Jesus' True Family		—	8:19–21
23.	Jesus Calms a Storm and Heals a Demoniac		4:35–5:20	8:22–39
24.	Jairus's Daughter/Woman with Hemorrhage		5:21–43E	8:40–56E
25.	Rejection at Nazareth	13:53–58E	6:1–6	[4:16–30]
26.	Mission of the Twelve		6:7–13	9:1–6
27.	Herod's Perplexity about Jesus	14:1–2	6:14–16	9:7–9
28.	Death of John the Baptist	14:3–12	6:17–29	
29.	The Return of the Twelve	—	6:30–31	9:10a
30.	The Feeding of the Five Thousand	14:13–21	6:32–44	9:10b–17
31.	Walking on the Water	14:22–33	6:45–52	
32.	Healings; Controversies Regarding Washings	14:34–15:31	6:53–7:37E	
33.	The Feeding of the Four Thousand	15:32–39E	8:1–10	
34.	Regarding the Pharisees	16:1–12	8:11–21	
35.	Bethsaida Blind Man Healed	—	8:22–26	—
36.	Peter's Confession/Passion Prediction (1)	16:13–21	8:27–31	
37.	Peter's Rebuke	16:22–23	8:32–33	
38.	To Deny Oneself	16:24–28E	8:34–9:1	
39.	The Transfiguration	17:1–9	9:2–10	
40.	The Coming of Elijah	17:10–13	9:11–13	
41.	An Exorcism, and Passion Prediction (2)	17:14–23	9:14–32	
42.	True Greatness	18:1–5	9:33–37	
43.	The Stranger Who Was Exorcizing	—	9:38–41	9:49–50
44.	Warnings about Offenses	18:6–9	9:42–50E	
45.	Marriage and Divorce	19:1–12	10:1–12	
46.	Blessing the Children/Rich Young Man	19:13–30E	10:13–31	
47.	Passion Prediction (3)	20:17–19	10:32–34	
48.	Request of the Sons of Zebedee	20:20–28	10:35–45	
49.	The Healing of the Blind	20:29–34E	10:46–52E	
50	Entry into Jerusalem	21:1–9	11:1–10	
51.	Surveying the Temple	—	11:11	—
52.	Cursing the Fig Tree	21:18–19	11:12–14	
53.	Cleansing the Temple	[21:12–17]	11:15–17	19:45–46
54.	The Chief Priests and Scribes Conspire	—	11:18–19	19:47–48E
55.	The Fig Tree Is Withered	21:20–22	11:20–26	
56.	The Question about Authority	21:23–27	11:27–33E	
57.	The Parable of the Wicked Farmers	21:33–46E	12:1–12	
58.	Questions Regarding Taxes, Resurrection	22:15–33	12:13–27	

Putting Things in Order 413

NO	SECTION	MATT	MARK	LUKE
59.	The Greatest Commandment	22:34–40	12:28–34	
60.	David's Son; Woes to Pharisees	22:41–23:36	12:35–40	
61.	The Widow's Gift	—	12:41–44E	21:1–4
62.	Eschatological Sayings	24:1–22	13:1–20	
63.	False Christs and Prophets	24:23–28	13:21–23	
64.	Coming of the Son of Man; Watch	24:29–25:46E	13:24–37E	
65.	The Plot to Kill Jesus	26:1–5	14:1–2	
66.	Jesus Anointed	26:6–13	14:3–9	
67.	Betrayal Made/Passover Preparations	26:14–20	14:10–17	
68.	Jesus Foretells His Betrayal	26:21–25	14:18–21	
69.	The Last Supper	26:26–29	14:22–25	
70.	Peter's Denial Predicted	26:30–35	14:26–31	
71.	Gethsemane; Jesus Arrested	26:36–58	14:32–54	
72.	False Witnesses before the Sanhedrin	26:59–62	14:55–60	
73.	Jesus Questioned by the Sanhedrin	26:63–66	14:61–64	
74.	Jesus Mistreated/Peter's Denials	26:67–75E	14:65–72E	
75.	Jesus before Pilate	27:1–14	15:1–5	
76.	Jesus or Barabbas?	27:15–26	15:6–15	
77.	The Mockery of the Soldiers	27:27–31	15:16–20	
78.	The Road to Golgotha	27:32	15:21	
79.	The Crucifixion to the Burial	27:33–61	15:22–47E	
80.	The Women at the Empty Tomb	28:1–8	16:1–8	

Explanation of Synoptic Pericope Order

We are now able to provide a fuller explanation of Synoptic pericope order based on where our study of the Gospels has led us. All the phenomena about pericope order in the Gospels can be explained on the basis of three simple propositions.

First, within a general chronological framework, Matthew arranges the order of his Gospel (especially the first half) on the basis of adding like to like; Luke arranges the material in his Gospel logically or chronologically; and Mark uses Matthew and Luke as his written sources, and he *always* follows the pericope order of one or the other.

Second, in adopting a framework for the order of his Gospel, Mark avoids the Sermon on the Mount, the Sermon on the Plain, and Luke's central teaching section. He follows the framework of Luke's Gospel up to Mark 6:14–16, and from there to the end he follows the framework of Matthew's Gospel.

Third, into Mark's Lukan framework he adds four sections from Matthew: two pericopes for which he prefers the Matthean to the Lukan versions (Mark 1:16–20; 6:1–6); a parable and a comment on parables (Mark 4:30–34); and a section that took him around the Sermon on the Plain (Mark 3:22–35E//Matt 12:24–50E). Into Mark's Matthean framework he adds four short sections drawn from Luke, consisting of material not paralleled anywhere in Matthew: the return of the Twelve (Mark 6:30–31//Luke 9:10a); the stranger who was exorcizing (Mark 9:38–41//Luke 9:49–50); the chief priests and scribes conspire (Mark 11:18–19//Luke 19:47–48); and the widow's gift (Mark 12:41–44//Luke 21:1–4). In all cases Mark places these insertions into his narrative at the same point at which they occur in the source (Matthew or Luke) from which he takes them.

It should be noted that if Mark was following Matthew or Luke at a given point, then in the nature of the case it would happen that he was *automatically* in parallel with the other Gospel whenever it agreed in pericope order. There was no need for Mark to take any specific action in order to achieve agreement with the other two Synoptic Gospels (i.e., threefold Synoptic agreement in pericope order).

Not only does the Markan Dependence Hypothesis provide a basic principle by means of which the divergence in Synoptic pericope order can be accounted for, and a rational explanation for why the order of each Gospel is as it stands, but it is also possible to see the great simplicity of the plan that Mark adopts for his framework (following Luke up to Mark 6:14–16 and Matthew thereafter), and of his use of other material (four insertions from Matthew into his Lukan framework and four insertions from Luke into his Matthean framework). Moreover it is straightforward to see in large measure the reason for this procedure (to steer around the Sermon on the Mount, the Sermon on the Plain, and Luke's central teaching section, indicating his policy decision that he would only include certain limited and specific instances of Jesus' teaching).

EVALUATION OF THE MARKAN PRIORITY CASE

The Argument for the Requirement of a Common Source

How does the above explanation of Synoptic pericope order compare in reasonableness, logic, and explanatory power with the Markan Priority alternative? It is common for Synoptic scholars to argue that Matthew and Luke each derive their structure from Mark and that Matthew and Luke would not agree in pericope order to the extent that they do unless they derived their order in large measure from some common source—and this common source is identified as Mark.

Streeter (1924, 208) contends that the structure of Luke's Gospel is that of Proto-Luke, into which the material that Luke takes from Mark has been added in sections—but still in an order corresponding quite closely with that which they have in Mark's Gospel.

As recently as 1988, R. H. Stein said (34) that Synoptic agreement in order is an "impressive" argument for Markan Priority. Similarly in 1981 J. Fitzmyer, in his very detailed and scholarly Anchor Bible Commentary of Luke (vol. 1:63) adopts the Two-Document (Markan Priority) viewpoint, which "maintains the priority of the Greek text of Mark over both Matthew and Luke (mainly because of the order of the common passages)." He adds (66) that

> the sequence of episodes in the Third Gospel closely follows that of Mark, even when Luke otherwise adds or omits something. The relatively same order of pericopes is even more crucially apparent when one considers the sequence of episodes in the Triple Tradition. The episodes which Matthew and Luke have in common with Mark generally agree with the Marcan sequence; when Matthew and Luke depart from this sequence, each differs from the other as well, pursuing an independent course.

Thus where Matthew and Luke agree, they are both following Mark, and where they differ it is because one or other of them has deserted Mark's order. The basic argument is presented along these lines:

> There are extensive agreements in pericope order between Matthew and Luke, yet none that are not also shared with Mark. This points to the fact that Matthew and Luke agree with each other precisely because they agree with Mark, which means that Mark is first, and Matthew and Luke have derived their order from Mark. The only alternatives to this explanation are either that Luke derived his order from Matthew (which is highly unlikely in view of the extent of disagreement in order between these two Gospels when viewed apart from Mark), or that Matthew and Luke are independent (which is ruled out by the extent to which they *do* agree in order, which is too high a level of agreement to result from coincidence and which would not have come to exist if there were no relationship between them). Thus the agreements of order between Matthew and Luke point to Markan Priority, as Mark must be the source of their agreed order.

This can adequately explain the phenomenon of Synoptic order. But it has a number of weaknesses. This is a form of the argument from common order, which was explained and critiqued in chapter 5.

It was not mentioned by Stein or Fitzmyer (or Streeter or others who claim the argument from pericope order points to Markan Priority) that exactly this observed phenomenon of order that we find is *just what would result* in the case of Markan Dependence, that is, if Mark were written third and followed the common order of pericopes where the Major Synoptists agree, and of one or the other of them when they differ. Pericope order therefore does not in itself provide an indicator between Markan Priority and Markan Dependence: for that, one needs to compare how the observed features of order are best explained on each hypothesis.

I provide here a specific response to the contention that Mark's order provides a framework for the additions inserted by the Major Synoptists. The argument rests upon the assumption that the sequence of pericopes in Matthew and Luke is of such a nature that a common source (identified as being Mark) is required in order to account for it. Thus the conclusion is drawn that Mark provided the framework of pericope sequence into which Matthew and Luke each inserted their other material and from which on some occasions they each departed to follow their own specific designs.

The basic weakness of the argument is its assumption that the degree of correspondence in order between Matthew and Luke requires a common source to account for their common order. This argument correctly draws attention to the extreme improbability that correspondences in sequence could all be attributed to such sequential information being transmitted in the oral tradition. But it substantially overestimates the extent of the correspondence in pericope sequence between Matthew and Luke; it underestimates the existence of inherent sequence factors (absolute and relative) in the material; and it ignores the possibility of pericope clusters circulating in the churches in written form.

The material of the common tradition may be categorized as of three kinds: (1) material that contains an absolute dating factor, which determines where it must appear in the overall sequence of Jesus' life; (2) material that contains a relative dating factor, which requires that it appear before or after some other pericope; and (3) material lacking any inherent dating factor, and that therefore is not tied to any point in the chronology of Jesus' life. (Pericopes with an inherent or relative sequence are discussed below and in chap. 8.)

Pericopes can also be categorized on another basis: essential or peripheral. Essential pericopes are those essential to the telling of the total story of Jesus as conceived in the Synoptics, and peripheral pericopes are those that are illustrative of Jesus' ministry in many ways and help to fill out the overall picture of his life and teaching but that are not a basic part of the Synoptic framework. There may be a divergence of opinion concerning the classification of some pericopes as essential or peripheral, but there is general acceptance of the distinction in principle. Thus Peter's confession at Caesarea Philippi is an essential pericope, while the healing of a dumb demoniac is a peripheral one.

A combination of those pericopes with inherent dating and the essential pericopes allows the construction of a rudimentary framework for the Synoptic Gospels. Within this framework in Matthew and Luke are found the pericopes containing no sequential factors, and—with one kind of exception—this material occurs in Matthew and Luke in mostly different places. Certainly there is no high correlation of order between this material in Matthew and Luke such as would require a common source to account for it.

The one exception is the presence in Matthew and Luke of clusters of pericopes that are often unrelated and within which the pericopes have the *same* order, although the clusters as a whole occur in *different* positions in the two Gospels. These clusters can be accounted for as groups of pericopes circulating together in writing prior to the composition of any of the Synoptic Gospels, and they were then incorporated into both Matthew and Luke as a cluster.

This situation is considered in detail below. Here it is sufficient to say that *the nature and extent of agreement in pericope order between Matthew and Luke does not require a common source (such as Mark or Q) to account for it.*

The Weakness of Explanations of Why Matthew and Luke Desert Markan Order

Markan Priority itself does not explain *why* Matthew and Luke would choose to leave Mark's order when they do. Further explanations are offered for this (as already shown), but they do not provide an overall, cohesive principle of explanation that can cover the whole situation. Principles such as "miracles are grouped with miracles" may account (in part) for groupings, but do not account for the actual order of pericopes. Explanations based on divergences in order are needed (and not always forthcoming) on a pericope-by-pericope basis. The *ad hoc* nature and general inadequacy of these explanations are noted above.

The Coincidence that Matthew and Luke Never Leave Markan Order at the Same Point

A further weakness of the Markan Priority explanation is its heavy dependence on coincidence. Markan Priorists say it is totally logical to claim that both Matthew and Luke purposely improved Mark's *wording*, and that in the nature of the case there are times when they would decide on the same change of wording as being an improvement. This explanation is used to downgrade the significance of the numerous places where Matthew and Luke agree against Mark in wording (e.g., see Streeter 1924, 295–97).

Markan Priorists also say that Matthew and Luke purposely improved Mark's order. At any rate, on numerous occasions they each *alter* Mark's order, and it is reasonable to deduce that they consider the alteration an improvement, else they would not make it. Several writers have made a point of agreeing with the judgment of Papias that Mark did not write an orderly Gospel and that Matthew and Luke sought to make it more "orderly." R. Gundry develops this theme (1982, 618–19):

> In his statement quoted by Papias, the elder shows concern over Mark's style, particularly over the disorderly way the single points concerning Jesus' ministry appear in the Gospel of Mark. This concern favors a similar frame of reference in the statement about Matthew, whose writing, by contrast, exhibits orderliness.... Matthew's orderly arrangement of the Lord's oracles makes them easier to understand than those in Mark, where disorder prevails.

Similarly, it is commonly accepted by many that Luke's Gospel has a better order than Mark's. Some 60 years earlier than Gundry, Streeter (1924, 19) interpreted Papias's meaning thus: "Of Mark, Papias, or rather the Elder his informant, says in effect 'the facts are correct—that follows from Mark's connection with Peter—but, as Mark had only his memory to rely upon, he has got them in the wrong order.'"

However, if both Matthew and Luke thus engaged in improving on the order of Mark, then—even if they did not necessarily work from the same presuppositions as to what constitutes an improvement—one would expect that in the nature of the case there would be times when they both decide upon the same change, or at the very least, when they both decided on the *same place* in Mark as needing alteration even if they made the alteration in different ways. But the extraordinary fact is that in *every* place where Matthew changes Mark's order, Luke preserves it, and in *every* place where Luke changes Mark's order, Matthew preserves it. This seems very unexpected and hardly provides supporting evidence for the assertion that there is something defective about Mark's order.

Luke's Great Omission is Matt 14:22–16:12, where Luke does not fully parallel any of these Matthean stories. But Mark parallels *all* of these Matthean pericopes and has them in *exactly* the same order, while differing from Matthew at several points *within* some pericopes (most notably in Matt 15:29–31//Mark 7:31–37).

The links between these pericopes are often very tenuous, frequently—especially in Mark—consisting simply of *kai* ("and"). Further, these pericopes are not all of a comparable kind, nor are they united by any similarity of theme or subject matter. Instead, these are a very disparate bunch of episodes: Jesus walking on the sea, healing many at Gennesaret, arguing at length with the scribes and Pharisees, instructing the people and his disciples, journeying to the district of Tyre and Sidon, exorcizing a demon, healing many others, feeding a crowd of 4,000, responding to the Pharisees' and Sadducees' request for a sign, and warning his disciples against the teaching of the Pharisees.

If Matthew was writing after Mark and was using Mark's Gospel, then in the earlier part of Matthew's Gospel he frequently rearranged successions of Markan pericopes of this very kind, and there would be nothing inherently improbable about him rearranging the order of these pericopes to group the teachings with other teachings, the conflicts with other conflicts, the miracles with other miracles (or even to group them together here in this section).

I am not aware of any specific reason from the Markan Priority explanation that here, instead of adopting this kind of procedure that he has used earlier, Matthew chose instead to follow Mark's order precisely; that reason, whatever it could be conjectured to be, is certainly not related to the fact that Luke is not here using Mark at all—for such a reason would imply deliberate Matthean/Lukan collusion, an idea that is universally rejected. If Matthew *had* departed from Mark's order in any way in this entire section (14:22–16:12), then we would have a place where Mark's pericope order was not supported by either Matthew or Luke.

So wherever Matthew deserts Mark's pericope order, it does so in places where Luke continues to follow it, and that here, in a place where Luke is *not* using Mark's material, Matthew *might well* have departed from Mark's order but does not do so—for a reason (whatever it may be) that is totally unconnected with Luke's use of Mark. The consequence is that Matthew's (unknown) reason for closely following Mark's order here (when Luke is not using Mark) means that Mark's always being supported by at least one of the other Synoptics is due to *coincidence*. It is coincidence—it is not purpose or design, and it is not related to the content of the material—that Matthew does not here, in this lengthy and diverse section, desert Mark's order when Luke was not using him.

Similarly, there is no direct Matthean parallel for Mark between Mark 1:20 and 1:39, or between Mark 4:34 and 6:1; in between these two sets of verses, Mark is closely paralleled in sequence by Luke, but the sections in Matthew that parallel Mark in *content* occur in a different place in his *structure*. If at any point in these sections, or at any other place where Mark is only paralleled in sequence by Luke's Gospel, Luke chose to alter the order that Mark uses, then it would not have been true to say that Mark's order was always supported by at least one of the other Synoptics. And in view of the extent to which Markan Priority advocates claim that Luke *does* transpose or more drastically alter the order found in Mark, it would most certainly have been possible that he could have done so here. What reason or argument can be adduced that would preclude such a possibility? Again then we must invoke *coincidence*. It is coincidence—it is not purpose or design, and it is not related to the content of the material—that Luke did not desert Mark's order when Matthew was not following Mark.

Both Matthew and Luke, then, are found to be in agreement that Mark's order is in need of alteration. But they are in *100% disagreement* concerning the alterations required, so that everywhere Matthew alters Mark's order Luke adheres to it, and everywhere Luke alters Mark's order Matthew adheres to it.

In order to place this in perspective, notice the number of occasions involved: of the 80 sections in the Synoptic Table (see above), there are four separately listed occasions where Mark has a pericope not used by either Matthew or Luke (3:20–21; 4:26–29; 8:22–26; 11:11); there are 36 occasions where Mark is supported in order by both Matthew and Luke; and there are 40 occasions where Mark is supported by only one Major Synoptic—either because the other one omits the pericope or has it in a different place in his narrative. *This means that there are 40 places out of a possible 80 where support for Mark would have failed if the Major Synoptic supporting Mark at that point had chosen to include the material in question at a different place in his structure.* Yet that has not occurred. Since both Matthew and Luke were supposedly engaged in altering Mark in conjunction with their own independent and different schemes of assembling Mark's material in sequence, there are no factors in operation to prevent the one who was following Mark's order from abandoning that order *on any number of those 40 occasions where he was Mark's sole support*. Why did it not happen? It was not purpose; it was not design; it was not an intention to ensure the support of another Synoptic for Mark. Coincidence—on every one of those 40 occasions out of 80!

Matthew and Luke Always Return If the Other Is Deserting Mark's Order

It is not merely that at least one of the Major Synoptics is always found to be supporting Mark, improbable as that is. There is the additional factor of *how* they did it. What we observe is that if only one Gospel is supporting Markan order in a given place and that Gospel is about to desert Mark, then *at that very point* the other Major Synoptic comes back to rejoin Mark's sequence in the nick of time so that Mark's Gospel is never left unsupported. The extent and the way that this happens should be noticed.

It is necessary therefore to look at the first part of the Synoptic table above from the perspective of what Markan Priority claims Matthew and Luke must have done in their use of Mark: that is, when did they omit a pericope that Mark contains, desert Mark's order, or resume following Mark's order after either deserting it or omitting a pericope. In the table below:

- "omits" indicates "omits altogether the pericope that is found in Mark at this point";
- "deserts" means "deserts the pericope order that is found in Mark at this point"; i.e., the Gospel in question *does* contain the pericope that Mark gives here, but in that Major Synoptic this pericope and the previous one do not follow in sequence, as they do in Mark; and
- "resumes" means "resumes following the sequence of Mark's Gospel after not having been parallel with Mark in the previous pericope."

NO		MATT	MARK	LUKE	
1.		3:1–17E	1:2–11	3:2–22	
2.		4:1–11	1:12–13	4:1–13	
3.		4:12–17	1:14–15	4:14–15	
4.		4:18–22	1:16–20	[5:1–11]	Luke deserts
5.	Matt omits	—	1:21–28	4:31–37	Luke resumes
6.	Matt deserts	[8:14–17]	1:29–34	4:38–41	
7.	Matt omits	—	1:35–38	4:42–43	
8.	Matt resumes	4:23–25E	1:39	4:44E	
9.		8:1–4	1:40–45E	5:12–16	
10.		9:1–17	2:1–22	5:17–39E	
11.		12:1–14	2:23–3:6	6:1–11	
12.		12:15–21	3:7–12	[6:17–19]	Luke deserts
13.	Matt deserts	[10:1–4]	3:13–19	6:12–16	Luke resumes
14.	Matt omits	—	3:20–21	—	Luke omits
15.	Matt resumes	12:24–30	3:22–27	[11:15–23]	Luke deserts

NO		MATT	MARK	LUKE	
16.		12:31–37	3:28–30	[12:10]	
17.		12:46–50E	3:31–35E	[8:19–21]	
18.		13:1–23	4:1–20	8:4–15	Luke resumes
19.	Matt deserts	(various)	4:21–25	8:16–18	
20.	Matt omits	—	4:26–29	—	Luke omits
21.	Matt resumes	13:31–32	4:30–32	[13:18–19]	Luke deserts
22.		13:34–35	4:33–34	—	Luke omits
23.	Matt deserts	[8:23–34E]	4:35–5:20	8:22–39	Luke resumes
24.		[9:18–26]	5:21–43E	8:40–56E	
25.	Matt resumes	13:53–58E	6:1–6	[4:16–30]	Luke deserts
26.	Matt deserts	[10:5–16]	6:7–13	9:1–6	Luke resumes
27.	Matt resumes	14:1–2	6:14–16	9:7–9	
28.		14:3–12	6:17–29	[3:19–20]	Luke deserts
29.	Matt omits	—	6:30–31	9:10a	Luke resumes
30.	Matt resumes	14:13–21	6:32–44	9:10b–17	
31.		14:22–33	6:45–52	—	Luke omits
32.		14:34–15:31	6:53–7:37E	[11:37–41]	Luke deserts
33.		15:32–39E	8:1–10	—	Luke omits
34.		16:1–12	8:11–21	[12:1]	Luke omits
35.	Matt omits	—	8:22–26	—	Luke omits
36.	Matt resumes	16:13–21	8:27–31	9:18–22	Luke resumes
37.		16:22–23	8:32–33	—	Luke omits
38.		16:24–28E	8:34–9:1	9:23–27	Luke resumes
39.		17:1–9	9:2–10	9:28–36	
40.		17:10–13	9:11–13	—	Luke omits
41.		17:14–23	9:14–32	9:37–45	Luke resumes
42.		18:1–5	9:33–37	9:46–48	
43.	Matt omits	—	9:38–41	9:49–50	
44.	Matt resumes	18:6–9	9:42–50E	—	Luke omits

Beyond this last pericope (44), this feature of the data continues but is not as marked.

Let us review what is happening (on the Markan Priority perspective). After Mark 1:20 Matthew ceases following Mark's order. But at Mark 1:21, Luke (who has not paralleled Mark for the previous pericope) resumes paralleling Mark and does so down to the pericope cluster 2:23–3:6, which is also in Matthew. Mark 3:7–12 is paralleled by Matthew (12:15–21), but Mark 3:13–19 is not paralleled by Matthew but by Luke 6:12–16. At this point Mark has unique material (3:20–21), but he is picked up again by Matthew (Matt 12:24//Mark 3:22) who continues with Mark to the parable of the sower (Mark 4:1–20), which is also in both Matthew and Luke

(Matt 13:1–23//Luke 8:4–15). Mark 4:21–25 is paralleled by what Luke has next (8:16–18, which is not paralleled here in Matthew). Then there occurs Mark's second unique pericope (4:26–29), and then (4:30–34) Mark is paralleled by Matthew (13:31–35, which is not paralleled here in Luke).

At Mark 4:35 Matthew ceases following Mark's order, and precisely at this verse Luke begins to follow Mark's order again, as far as Mark 5:43E. At that point Luke ceases to parallel Mark, but Matthew starts to do so, down to Mark 6:6. At that point Matthew ceases to parallel Mark, but Luke starts to do so, resuming at the point previously reached (Luke 9:1).

Mark 6:14–16 is paralleled in both Major Synoptics (Matt 14:1–2//Luke 9:7–9), and then Luke ceases following Mark's order, but Matthew parallels Mark 6:17–29, and at precisely this verse Matthew omits what Mark has (6:30–31), but Luke has it.

Matthew 14:13–18:5 parallels Mark 6:32–9:37 (sometimes accompanied by Luke), and Matthew ceases to parallel Mark at Mark 9:38–41, but Luke continues to do so. At Mark 9:41 Luke ceases to parallel Mark, but Matthew now parallels Mark and continues to do so from there on until Mark 11:14, at which point Matthew ceases to parallel Mark. But Luke 19:45–48E resumes and then parallels Mark 11:15–19; then Luke ceases to parallel Mark, but Matt 21:20–22 then parallels Mark 11:20–26, and Matthew and Mark continue in parallel as far as Mark 12:40. At this point Matthew ceases to parallel Mark, but Luke 21:1–4 parallels Mark 12:41–44E, then all three are parallel for Matt 24:1–22//Mark 13:1–20//Luke 21:5–24, then Luke ceases following Mark's order for Mark 13:21–23, but Matthew continues to do so. Thereafter Matthew and Mark have the same order to the end, and this order is for the most part also paralleled in Luke.

It certainly looks on the face of it as if Matthew and Luke are alternating in deserting Mark's order and rejoining it. And on a not insignificant number of occasions, the one rejoins and the other deserts Markan order at precisely the same point. And *never* do both Major Synoptics desert Mark's order at the same time. Yet we cannot seriously entertain the proposition that Matthew and Luke were working in collusion in treating Mark's sequence this way. So there is a very high order of coincidence involved here. Or should one postulate some miraculous supernatural intervention, some bewildering divine purpose, to ensure that each Major Synoptist returned to Markan order just where the other was deserting it, and thus to prevent Markan order being left at any time unsupported by a second Synoptic Gospel?

Numerous writers have referred disparagingly to the Griesbach (Markan Dependence) view of Synoptic order as Mark zigzagging back and forth from following Matthew to following Luke and back again. F. W. Beare dismissed (1965, 296) this aspect of the Griesbach view with the comment, "We are asked to suppose that Mark wiggled back and forth from Matthew to Luke in a fashion that is quite incredible."

What Beare (and those others who have taken a similar line) have not confronted and seriously considered is that this alternating of support for Mark from Matthew and Luke is *there* in the Synoptic Gospels. It is part of the Synoptic data and can be observed from the table of the 80 sections of Mark's Gospel by noting the parallels at each point (or the absence of parallels) in the Major Synoptics. Markan Priority requires us to believe that Matthew and Luke alternate in deserting Mark's order and then rejoining it, and that at each point where one Major Synoptic departs from Markan order, the other one continues to adhere to that order (if already following it) or else returns to support Mark's order (if not already supporting that order in the previous verse). This alternating of support for Mark from the Markan Priority perspective is just as striking and incredible as the "zigzagging" that the Griesbach (Markan Dependence) view says would have occurred.

But there is one major difference. The Markan Dependence view maintains that this correspondence of Mark with first one of the Major Synoptics and then the other is the result of *design*, the execution of a policy by an intelligent mind. It is the result of Mark's choice, who was following a deliberate policy that can be identified. On the other hand, the Major Synoptics' alternation of support for Mark, as Markan Priority demands, cannot be attributed to purpose or intelligence—since neither Matthew nor Luke is held to have acted this way deliberately in order to ensure support for Mark's order at all times—and therefore it can only be attributed to coincidence.

If Mark's zigzag pattern, though the result of a describable policy, is to be termed "incredible," what descriptive term should be used for what Markan Priorists are required to believe about the way in which Matthew and Luke, all unknown to each other, succeed in alternating in their support for Mark's order in such a fashion so that Mark is never left unsupported?

Assessment

During the course of the discussions at the 1984 Jerusalem Symposium, Tuckett agreed that, on its own, Synoptic order does not constitute an argument for Markan Priority (as Streeter had taken it), but he strongly resisted the assertions of the Two-Gospel Hypothesis proponents that pericope order was best accounted for on the basis that Mark used Matthew and Luke. He several times made the point that the argument from pericope order favored no Synoptic theory against the others. The examination of this issue in this chapter does not bring us to the same conclusion as Tuckett. The Markan Priority Hypothesis is clearly an unsatisfactory explanation of the data.

First of all, Markan Priority's basic argument regarding pericope order is weak since it rests on the invalid assumption that a common source (Mark) is required in order to account for the agreements in pericope order between Matthew and Luke. Our investigation has shown that this is not so.

Second, Markan Priority does not explain *why* Matthew and Luke would choose to leave Mark's order when they do. For this, further explanations are offered. There is no overall, cohesive principle of explanation that covers what was happening generally. Principles such as "miracles are grouped with miracles in Matthew" may account (in part) for groupings, but they do not account for the actual order of pericopes; thus explanations of divergences in order are needed (and are not always forthcoming) on a pericope-by-pericope basis. Attention has been drawn to the shortcomings of the explanations that have been advanced.

Third, Markan Priority's explanation depends on coincidence. When Mark's Gospel is divided into sections on the basis of when the Major Synoptics either do or do not parallel it, there are 80 sections (see table above). Of these 80, there are 40 where—if the Synoptic that is supporting Mark for that section had placed that particular section of his Gospel elsewhere (as he does many times for the *other* 40 sections)—it would not have been true that Mark's order is always supported by at least one of the other Synoptics. Matthew and Luke, each writing independently and each deserting Mark's order when he chose, according to his own preferences, could each have left Mark's order at the same point in his structure. Why did this not happen on *any* of these occasions when it could have? There is no explanation available, so this feature of the data must also be called sheer coincidence.

Fourth, Markan Priority does not explain the related feature of the data that when one of the Major Synoptists has been following a different order and the other one is at the point of leaving Mark's order, the first one at that point resumes his support for Mark's order. The way in which one Synoptic ceases to accompany Mark and the other one (whichever one it is) resumes following Mark at *precisely* that same point is one of the most remarkable features of the Synoptic data. That this happens, and then happens again and again as it does, can only be described as incredible.

Fifth and finally, it is worth noting that at best Markan Priority offers to explain pericope sequence in Matthew and Luke. It contributes nothing about the order of Mark. One is left with the comment of Papias that Mark contains no particular order at all. It can hardly be claimed that Markan

Priority is able to go very far in providing a satisfactory explanation of pericope order in the Synoptics. It is an acceptable explanation only if there is nothing better available.

Indeed, theories based on the Complete Independence Hypothesis have not been able to provide a better explanation; and the Successive Dependence Hypothesis requires one to accept quite difficult explanations about how Mark used Matthew, and even more difficult explanations to account for the very peculiar policy of Luke in how he ordered his Gospel.

But the Markan Dependence Hypothesis offers satisfactory explanations for each aspect of the data. And the overall explanation of the observable data is quite simple: through Mark 6:13, Mark follows Luke (with four insertions that Mark drew from Matthew and inserted where Matthew had placed them); and from Mark 6:14 onward Mark follows Matthew (with four insertions that he drew from Luke, and inserted where Luke had placed them).

ACCOUNTING FOR MARKAN OMISSIONS AND INCLUSIONS

Where Matthew and Luke Differ in Order

If indeed Mark used Matthew and Luke, how did he go about the task of including this material in his Gospel? At several points this situation is found: Mark includes material that is common to both Matthew and Luke, and this correspondence is followed in Matthew and Luke by *different* pericopes both of which *do* occur in Mark. This situation necessitated an editorial decision by Mark on how to proceed. In all such cases Mark parallels first one and then the other; that is, the pericope that occurs next in each of Matthew and Luke occurs in Mark at this point, not *somewhere else* in his structure, and these two pericopes are given one after the other:

NO.	SECTION	MATT	MARK	LUKE
9.	Plucking Grain/Withered Hand Healed	12:1–14	2:23–3:6	6:1–11
12.	Lakeside Crowds and Healings	12:15–21	3:7–12	[6:17–19]
13.	Appointment of the Twelve	[10:1–4]	3:13–19	6:12–16
18.	The Parable of the Sower	13:1–23	4:1–20	8:4–15
19.	Sayings: Lamps, Hearing, and Getting	(various)	4:21–25	8:16–18
20.	The Parable of the Growing Seed	—	4:26–29	—
21.	The Parable of the Mustard Seed	13:31–32	4:30–32	[13:18–19]
22.	Jesus' Use of Parables	13:34–35	4:33–34	—
23.	Jesus Calms a Storm and Heals a Demoniac	[8:23–34E]	4:35–5:20	8:22–39
24.	Jairus's Daughter/Hemorrhaging Woman	[9:18–26]	5:21–43E	8:40–56E

Putting Things in Order 427

NO.	SECTION	MATT	MARK	LUKE
25.	Rejection at Nazareth	13:53–58E	6:1–6	[4:16–30]
26.	Mission of the Twelve	[10:5–16]	6:7–13	9:1–6
27.	Herod's Perplexity about Jesus	14:1–2	6:14–16	9:7–9
28.	Death of John the Baptist	14:3–12	6:17–29	[3:19–20]
29.	The Return of the Twelve	—	6:30–31	9:10
42.	True Greatness	18:1–5	9:33–37	9:46–48
43.	The Stranger Who Was Exorcizing	—	9:38–41	9:49–50
44.	Warnings about Offenses	18:6–9	9:42–50E	—
53.	Cleansing the Temple	21:12–17	11:15–17	19:45–46
54.	The Chief Priests and Scribes Conspire	—	11:18–19	19:47–48E
55.	The Fig Tree Is Withered	21:20–22	11:20–26	—

In this way Mark includes what is in both Matthew and Luke. Sometimes he takes first from Matthew, sometimes first from Luke; and this choice was apparently determined by his assessment of the most appropriate order for the subject matter.

Thus if Mark were going to include both Luke 8:16–18 and Matt 13:34–35, it is clear that the Matthew passage rounds off the whole section, so the Lukan one must come before it. Similarly, after Matt 14:1–2 Matthew gives a parenthesis to explain Herod's comment regarding John the Baptist, and at the end of this aside Matthew resumes his narrative (14:13) from where he was (14:2). But Mark was using Luke and thus placed the pericope of Herod's perplexity about Jesus after the story of the sending of the Twelve. Therefore, after including Matthew's parenthesis about John the Baptist, Mark follows Luke in recording the return of the Twelve. This is a very logical way of weaving together what occurs in both Matthew and Luke at this place.

At other points in the various cases listed above, Mark had somewhat more flexibility concerning the order in which he took the pericopes from Matthew and Luke, but he seems still to have been influenced by the appropriateness of the sequence of pericopes that resulted and by the intention of ensuring a smoothly flowing narrative.

The Influence of Mark's Framework on His Inclusions and Omissions

Once having decided on his procedure for the utilization of his two sources, Mark follows this with a high degree of consistency. For those pericopes that he uses, he uses both Matthew and Luke for the contents of what he says; *both* the order of his pericopes *and* the choice of pericopes to be included are very largely determined by his overall plan.

As a simplification that is nonetheless largely accurate, it can be said that Mark follows Luke from the beginning to the start of the Sermon on the Plain, at which point he changes to Matthew, following him from the pericopes of the lakeside crowds and healings to the parable of the sower, switching back to Luke for the section from there to Herod's perplexity about Jesus, and from there following Matthew to the resurrection account. This procedure gives Mark his framework. Mark omits little that he comes to by following this procedure, and he includes little that is not found in these sections of Matthew and Luke respectively.

Thus there is a significant difference between Mark's treatment of teachings that are included in this framework and those that are not. Mark's plan takes him around the Sermon on the Mount, Matthew's mission charge to the Twelve, the Sermon on the Plain, and Luke's central travel and teaching section. So Mark includes *none* of the teachings found in those places except to the extent that it occurs in the other Major Synoptic in a place that *does* fall within his framework. Thus Mark includes Luke's version of the mission charge to the Twelve, which occurs within Mark's framework, and some short passages that occur in Luke's central section, because they also occur in Matthew in a place that is within Mark's framework (see sections 15, 16, and 21 in the Synoptic Table). By way of contrast, however, all the other major teaching sections (apart from those just mentioned) occur in a part of Matthew or Luke (primarily Matthew) that Mark *is* following in his framework, and so instead of being completely omitted they are included in Mark in abbreviated form, normally the first part of each teaching section being given in full and the latter part being summarized or omitted altogether.

Material is also curtailed or omitted that does not focus directly on Jesus, who is always central in what Mark includes. At first sight we might therefore have expected Mark to omit the pericope of the death of John the Baptist, as this centers on John not Jesus. But this pericope shows what happened to John when he clashed with Herod, and it follows the statement that Jesus had just come to Herod's attention—who identified him as "John the Baptist risen from the dead." This narrative is therefore proleptic of the fate that lies ahead of Jesus, and in this connection it has a point to make about Jesus.

Thus Mark 1:2–11 gives a general introduction about John the Baptist, which leads up to and climaxes in John's preaching about the Coming One and then the baptism of Jesus. But Mark omits the other introductory material in Matthew and Luke about John. The only part of Matthew's mission charge to the Twelve (which does not lie within Mark's framework) that Mark includes is the passage also found in Luke in a section (9:1–6) that does fall within Mark's framework.

Mark contains but curtails (in the way outlined above) these teaching sections of Matthew: the Beelzebul controversy; teachings in parables; true greatness and forgiveness; riches and rewards (Matt 19:16–20:16—Mark omits the parable of the vineyard laborers); teaching in parables (Matt 21:28–22:14—Mark has one parable out of Matthew's three); warnings about the scribes and Pharisees (Mark confines himself to recording the very short version of this in Luke); the Olivet Discourse. Mark gives four teaching sections at approximately or just less than their length in Matthew: defilement and the commandment of God (7:1–23); the leaven of the Pharisees (8:11–21); Peter's confession at Caesarea Philippi (8:27–9:1); marriage and divorce (10:1–12). Mark also omits some sections not directly centering on Jesus (e.g., the blessedness of Peter; Peter walking on the water).

In Summary

In chapter 3 we saw that Mark has a much greater interest in recording stories of what Jesus *did* than recording what Jesus *said*. Consistent with this is the fact that when at a given point Mark's account is longer than those of the Major Synoptics, this is almost always because he is including additional details in a narrative account; and when at a given point (either a pericope or a section within a pericope) Mark's account is shorter than those of the Major Synoptics, this is almost always because he has omitted teachings or comments from Jesus (or, occasionally, words spoken by someone else).

It may help to be specific about Mark's approach:

1. Where Luke's account is shorter than Matthew's account for a given teaching, Mark tends to accord with Luke's shorter version.

2. Where teaching occurs in the framework that Mark is following (whether Matthew's or Luke's) and that teaching occurs in both Major Synoptics, Mark is most likely to include it; but where it is given by only one Major Synoptic, Mark is likely to omit it.

3. Where Mark's framework takes him around teaching, that teaching is not given at all in Mark.

4. Into this basic framework Mark inserts a small amount of material from the Gospel he is not following. In addition to his diversion to Matthew to take him around the Sermon on the Plain, where he inserts Matt 12:22–13:23 into an otherwise Lukan framework, he also takes from Matthew a parable and some comments about Jesus' use of parables (Mark 4:30–34),

and two narratives where he prefers Matthew's version to Luke's equivalent, and inserts them where they are placed in Matthew's order (Mark 1:16–20; 6:1–6). And he inserts into Matthew's part of his framework four short pericopes drawn from Luke, placing them at the point where they occur in Luke: the return of the Twelve; the stranger who was exorcizing; the chief priests and scribes conspire; and the widow's gift (9:10a,49–50; 19:47–48E; 21:1–4; see pp. 411–13 for the Markan Framework).

5. Apart from these eight insertions just listed (four each from Matthew and Luke), Mark *only* includes in his Gospel those pericopes, whether of teaching or narrative, that he encounters in his framework:

(a) Seeing that Mark's framework steers him around the Sermon on the Mount, the Sermon on the Plain, and Luke's central travel and teaching section, he has none of this material in his Gospel (apart from the very limited extent to which material from Luke's central section is paralleled in that part of Matthew that Mark is following as his framework).

(b) When Mark's framework from Matthew or Luke includes a section of teaching, that teaching section is included in Mark, but usually in curtailed or abbreviated form; and Old Testament quotations are likely to be omitted.

(c) When Mark's framework includes events and stories about Jesus, these are almost always included in Mark. The apparent exceptions to this are short pieces that are specifically Jewish in interest, that record what some person other than Jesus said or did, or that do not focus primarily on the person of Jesus. These pieces are: Peter walking on the water; payment of the temple tax; the death of Judas; Pilate's wife's dream; Pilate washes his hands; the opened graves; and the guard at the tomb.

(d) When Mark's framework bypasses narratives that occur in Matthew or Luke, these narratives are not included in Mark's Gospel. These narratives are: healing the centurion's servant; healing two blind men; healing the dumb demoniac; a teaching and preaching tour; raising the widow's son at Nain; John the Baptist's question and Jesus' reply; Jesus' testimony about John; washing Jesus' feet with tears; the ministering women.

(e) Whatever Mark contains is also included in the framework that Mark was following at the time, i.e., in that section of Matthew or Luke that Mark has adopted as his framework; and it will be placed within Mark in the position that it occupies in the order of the Gospel from which Mark took it. If in a given instance a pericope in Mark occurs in both Matthew and Luke, its placement in Mark's Gospel corresponds with the position it occupies in whichever of Matthew or Luke that Mark was using as his framework at the time when he came upon this pericope.

(f) Mark's overall treatment of narratives is simple: if he comes to a narrative in Matthew or Luke in the course of following his framework, he includes it in his own Gospel; if a narrative is found elsewhere in Matthew or Luke than in those sections that are part of Mark's framework, then it is omitted in Mark's Gospel.

There is thus a highly significant correlation between what Mark finds in the framework he has adopted from Matthew and Luke and what he utilizes in his Gospel.

ORDER IN MATTHEW AND LUKE

Basic Synoptic Framework

Jesus' genealogy and the stories of the infancy, the ministry of John, the baptism of Jesus, the initial temptations, the commencement of Jesus' ministry, and the call of Jesus' first disciples must in the nature of the case go at the beginning of the Gospel. John's inquiry from prison must go after his imprisonment and before his death. The choosing of the Twelve must precede their engaging in specific ministry at Jesus' behest. Jesus must become sufficiently publicly known to come to Herod's attention before the story of Herod's perplexity can be told. The feeding of the 5,000 appears to be linked to the account of Peter's declaration, and that pericope is specifically linked by a time note to the transfiguration, so these are locked into a sequence. Since Peter's declaration was the occasion for a change in Jesus' ministry, having a greater emphasis on teaching the Twelve and a greater explicitness about the forthcoming Passion, pericopes along these lines occur after the Caesarea Philippi account.

From the time when Jesus begins to journey southwards from Galilee through Perea and via Jericho to Jerusalem, events connected with these places become automatically placed in sequence, while stories set in Galilee must be placed before the point at which Jesus leaves Galilee for Perea. Once Jesus rides into Jerusalem on Palm Sunday, the events themselves structure the overall framework of the narrative with room only for relatively minor variations of order.

Thus these stories themselves, by their nature, provide a basic framework for the two Major Synoptic Gospels. That is, if certain stories are to be included at all, they must be presented in a fixed sequence or at least at approximately the same point in the sequence (though there was some flexibility about where a writer could put a genealogy). This framework exists as a result of the inherent nature of some material, without requiring either that some knowledge of sequence of pericopes had to be transmitted in the oral tradition, or that either of the Major Synoptics knew the order of the other or derived this order from Mark. This means that if they were to use these stories at all, they *had to appear* in more or less this order. Therefore, the minimal framework determined on the basis of the inherent nature of material is as follows according to the content of Matthew and Luke:

MATTHEW		LUKE	
		1:1–4	Preface
1:1–17	Genealogy		
1:18–2:23E	Infancy Narratives	1:5–2:52E	Infancy Narratives
3:1–12	John the Baptist	3:1–18	John the Baptist
		3:19–20	Arrest of John
3:13–17E	Baptism of Jesus	3:21–22	Baptism of Jesus
		3:23–28E	Genealogy
4:1–11	The Temptation	4:1–13	The Temptation
4:12a	Arrest of John		
4:12b–16	Jesus Goes to Galilee	4:14	Jesus Goes to Galilee
4:17	Jesus Begins to Preach	4:15	Jesus Teaches in Their Synagogues
4:18–22	Call of the First Disciples	5:1–11	Call of the First Disciples
11:1–18	The Baptist's Question	7:18–35	The Baptist's Question
14:1–2	Death of John the Baptist	9:9	Death of John the Baptist
14:13–21	Feeding of the 5,000	9:11–17	Feeding of the 5,000
16:13–20	Peter's Confession	9:18–21	Peter's Confession
16:21	First Passion Prediction	9:22	First Passion Prediction
16:24–28E	Conditions of Discipleship	9:23–27	Conditions of Discipleship
17:1–8	The Transfiguration	9:28–36	The Transfiguration
17:14–20	Healing the Epileptic Boy	9:37–43a	Healing the Epileptic Boy
19:13–15	Jesus Blesses Children	18:15–17	Jesus Blesses Children

Pericope Clusters

There are several tightly connected pericope pairs where the link is integral and part of the transmission of the pericopes (e.g., healing Peter's mother-in-law/healing the sick at nightfall; the woman with a hemorrhage/raising Jairus's daughter). The ones that require explanation are other pericope groups lacking these close bonds. Prior to Jesus' blessing of the children, the clusters are:

C1. Across the Sea of Galilee: Orders to Cross the Lake/Stilling the Storm/Healing of Legion/Return (Matt 8:18–9:1//Luke 8:22–40)

C2. Events in Capernaum: Healing the Paralytic/Call of Matthew-Levi/Eating with Sinners/The Question of Fasting (Bridegroom-Old Garment-New Wine) (Matt 9:2–17//Luke 5:17–39E)

C3. Sabbath Controversies: Plucking Grain on the Sabbath/Healing Infirmity on the Sabbath (the Man with the Withered Hand) (Matt 12:1–14//Luke 6:1–11)

C4. Herod's Perplexity; Jesus Withdraws: Herod's Perplexity about Jesus/Death of John/Jesus Withdraws/Feeding the 5,000 (Matt 14:1–21//Luke 9:7–17)

C5. From Confession to Transfiguration: Peter's Confession/First Passion Prediction/Conditions of Discipleship/Transfiguration/Healing of the Epileptic Boy/Second Passion Prediction/True Greatness (Matt 16:13–18:5//Luke 9:18–48).

After the pericope on Jesus' blessing of the children, the accounts chronicle the events of Jesus' journey from Perea to Jerusalem, and thence to the cross. Thus an examination of the overall order of pericopes in Matthew and Luke discloses that there are numerous places where they differ in order, and yet other places where a group of pericopes retains the same relative order in these two Gospels while differing in absolute order. There are four possible explanations for this. (1) This is the order of occurrence of the events, knowledge of which was transmitted with the pericopes. (2) They were early arranged into these clusters in the tradition, and thereafter these pericopes retained their association when they were transmitted. (3) There was some perceived link or connection between the pericopes of such a cluster. (4) The grouping is to be explained by Synoptic literary source: either Matthew and Luke follow Mark's order, or else Luke is following Matthew's order.

The problem with all these explanations is that they are valid only up to a point, but in the last analysis they are all incomplete as explanations, and are therefore invalidated because of the following considerations.

Regarding (1), the order within the clusters may well be the original order of events, but it remains to be explained why the original order has not been preserved in so many other places (e.g., where Matthew and Luke differ in their sequence) and has been retained *only* in these five instances.

Regarding (2) and (3), the perceived link or connection between pericopes in a cluster is no greater (and is sometimes less) than between other pericopes in one Gospel where that link does not exist in the other. Thus there is no perceivable link between the pericopes within C2 (the sequence healing the paralytic/call of Matthew-Levi/the question of fasting in Matt 9:2–17//Luke 5:17–39), while there *is* a close link in Matthew between the question of fasting (Matt 9:14–17) and raising the ruler's daughter (for this link, see Matt 9:18ff.), whereas these two pericopes are widely separated in Luke (5:33–39 and 8:41ff.).

Regarding (4), either Markan Priority or the hypothesis that Luke used Matthew provides an explanation for the agreement in sequence *within the clusters*; what is left to be explained is why this limited agreement of order is all that they share of common sequence, that is, an agreement among pericopes that do not have an absolute or relative position in the Synoptic sequence (and indeed are placed differently).

The most satisfactory—and eminently reasonable—explanation is a fifth possibility. *At an early stage the pericopes in these clusters were set down in writing, and they became associated together then and were transmitted as a cluster.* In a particular instance, this association of pericopes in a cluster was most likely derived from the original author, or it may reflect an early stage of the process (to which Luke refers in 1:1) of compiling the Jesus tradition into a narrative. In any case, this association in pericope clusters in writing antedates the production of the Synoptics, and these clusters were taken over *in toto* by both Matthew and Luke.

However, since each cluster circulated as a separate document, and since there was no inherent or relative order indicated or implied between one such document and another, or between these documents and other material used by Matthew and Luke, these five documents (which contain a cluster of pericopes in identical order) appear in different *places* in Matthew and Luke, and in a different *sequence* within these Gospels.

If these clusters and other pericopes circulated as separate documents (as this evidence seems to indicate), the following picture emerges:

(1) For the writing of his Gospel, Matthew already had on hand copies of a number of documents that he had produced at an earlier time and that had been in circulation separately. Luke collected copies of numbers of these documents when gathering material for his Gospel.

(2) For his Gospel, Matthew followed, within a general chronological framework, a practice of assembling his documents on the basis of *similarity of theme or content*, and he subordinated chronology to this principle without abandoning all concern for the sequence in which events occurred. By contrast, Luke arranged his material *in the order in which events occurred*, so far as he was able to ascertain what this was during his inquiries in Palestine.

(3) Matthew edited these early documents of his into a complete connected narrative for publication, adding connecting links with other pericopes, and expanded and elaborated on some of them.

There is no reason, for instance, for denying that "while he was yet speaking" in Matt 9:18 is a genuine reminiscence of what had happened, but it seems clear that these words did not occur at the beginning of the pericope of raising Jairus's daughter when this came to Luke. That is, the connecting phrase is to be attributed to Matthew's redaction at the time he composed his complete Gospel. Similarly, when Matthew wrote his Gospel, he added the comment in Matt 8:1 that links the pericope of healing the leper to the conclusion of the Sermon on the Mount; the same is true for the comment in Matt 12:46 that appends the visit of Jesus' family to the discourses on the Beelzebul controversy.

Matthew regarded the events described in the document "From Confession to Transfiguration" (C5 above) as the turning-point in Jesus' ministry. In editing this document he adds in the mention of Peter's rebuke, the charge to secrecy, and the coming of Elijah. The document common to Matthew and Luke continues with the connected events that followed immediately upon Jesus' descent from the mountain (healing the epileptic boy/second Passion prediction/true greatness), and Matthew expands the latter with further teaching on connected themes (Matt 18:6–35E). Then Jesus leaves Galilee (Matt 19:1) never to return before his resurrection, so from this point onwards Matthew includes only what happened in Perea and on the way to Jerusalem and the cross. Thus all the other (Galilean) material that he had must in these circumstances be included prior to the "From Confession to Transfiguration" document.

Matthew's pericopes on Jesus' early years, which have to be placed first, end with the call of the first disciples (4:18–22). Matthew follows this immediately (4:23–25E) with what is virtually a table of contents for the Galilee section that follows: "And he went about all Galilee [so this covers the Galilee period], teaching in their synagogues and preaching the gospel of the kingdom and healing every disease and every infirmity among the people. So his fame spread throughout all Syria, and they brought him all the sick, those afflicted with various diseases and pains, demoniacs, epileptics and paralytics, and he healed them. And great crowds followed him from Galilee and from the Decapolis and Jerusalem and Judea and from beyond the Jordan."

Following this, Matthew's Gospel has the stories of the Galilean period, which run from the beginning of Jesus' ministry till C5, the last major document of the period, "From Confession to Transfiguration" that ends the Galilee ministry and is followed by Jesus' leaving Galilee on the journey to Jerusalem and the cross (see 19:1).

I have already documented the pericopes and pericope clusters that Matthew includes here and that are paralleled in Luke (see chap. 8). Here are some important points to note from the table in chapter 8 on the comparison of Matthew and Luke. The sections of their Gospels where Matthew and Luke differ in sequence are only those containing the record of Jesus' Galilean ministry (apart from a few minor transpositions in the Passion Narrative). There is no inherent order within this period. In fact, it could be that the order in which everything took place was largely without significance; it would be quite easy to forget the order and there was no reason or purpose for remembering it.

After Peter's confession and prior to the commencement of Jesus' journey to Jerusalem, Matthew contains only the one connected account—most probably a single document (C5) that was published and circulating prior to the writing of his full Gospel, and into which at that latter time he added some further information. Luke is similar in that his Gospel follows this account (9:18–48) with the commencement of Jesus' journey to Jerusalem (9:51). But there the similarity ends, for Luke then has Jesus weaving back and forth in an itinerary that has him at Bethany near Jerusalem (10:38–42) and then back on the border of Samaria and Galilee (17:9). Into this general framework of a journey, Luke weaves a considerable amount of teaching, much of it Lukan *Sondergut*, and most of what does parallel Matthew is found earlier in Matthew than the "From Confession to Transfiguration" cluster (C5).

Healings and John the Baptist's Group of Emissaries

The double pericope about John the Baptist exercises an influence on the arrangement of material (Matt 11:1–19//Luke 7:18–35). Here Jesus draws the attention of John's messengers to the types of healings he has performed as well as his preaching to the poor. Thus at least one representative healing of each type is given by both Matthew and Luke *prior* to this reference that Jesus makes to them. The signs that Jesus performed (listed in identical order in Matt 11:5 and Luke 7:22) and the Synoptists' record of such events are:

Matt 11:5//Luke 7:22	MATT	LUKE
the blind receive their sight	9:27–30	7:21
the lame walk	[8:5–13; 9:2–8]	[5:17–26]
lepers are cleansed	8:1–4	5:12–16
the deaf hear	—	—
the dead are raised up	9:23–26	7:11–17
the poor have the good news preached	5–7 (cf. 5:3)	6:20–49E (cf. 4:18)

The passages Matt 8:5–13; 9:2–8; Luke 5:17–26 refer to paralysis rather than lameness alone, but the result of the healing was that one who previously could not walk was then enabled to do so. The above table also shows that both Matthew and Luke include the statement "the deaf hear," yet there is no record in either of these two Gospels of such a miracle. We may reasonably believe that if either of these Synoptists had access to the account of such a miracle they would have included it to validate this statement in Jesus' message to John, just as they recorded the other types of miracles Jesus mentions.

But in contrast, Mark has two accounts of Jesus' healing a deaf person. The first one is Mark 7:32, the man who was both dumb and deaf (Jesus put his fingers into his ears)—the crowd acknowledges this miracle in 7:37. Matthew's parallel to this episode (15:31) contains only general statements about healings. The second one is Mark 9:25, the boy Jesus healed when coming down from the Mount of Transfiguration. Both Major Synoptists contain this same pericope, but neither of them includes any mention of Mark's detail that the boy was deaf. If (as Markan Priority holds) both Matthew and Luke drew their accounts from Mark, then they edited his Gospel so as to remove the one reference to a miracle of restoring hearing to the deaf that they would otherwise have in their respective Gospels. This would be a truly incredible thing for them to do. The logical explanation of the data is Mark's use of the Major Synoptists and the apostle Peter. Mark here supplemented his two written sources (as he so often did) with his recollection of details from a story as told by Peter in his preaching.

The material between Matthew's first (preview) summary of Jesus' Galilean ministry and the account of John the Baptist's question can be summarized thus:

4:23–25E	First Summary of Galilean Ministry ("Table of Contents")
5–7	Jesus' Teaching Ministry
8:1–9:34	Jesus' Healing Ministry
9:35	Second Summary of the Galilean Ministry
9:36–38E	Exhortation to Pray for More Laborers
10:1–42E	Instructing the Twelve to Go Out as Laborers to Teach and Heal
11:1	Third Summary of the Galilean Ministry
11:2ff.	Group of Emissaries from John the Baptist

This could be further simplified as:

First Summary
    Jesus' Teachings
    Jesus' Healings

Second Summary
      Jesus' Teachings
   Third Summary

In Matthew's "Jesus' Healings" section (8:1–9:34), what is included consists exclusively of (1) pericopes of healings and (2) two pericope-clusters, C1 and C2, which include a healing together with some nonhealing pericopes.

In our consideration of these pericope clusters earlier we saw that the most reasonable and logical explanation for them is that they existed and circulated as written documents prior to their respective incorporation into the Gospels of Matthew and Luke. This explanation sheds further light on the issue about the inclusion of other (i.e., nonhealing) material in Matthew's "Healings" section: these clusters had become established and fixed before the time of the writing of our Synoptic Gospels, and Matthew had them as two documents (8:18–9:1 and 9:2–17). Each document contained a healing appropriate for inclusion in his "Healings" section. Matthew did not choose to dismember these existing documents so as to take out only the healing; so instead, he placed into his Gospel's "Healings" section the *whole* document as it stood.

In this connection it is highly significant that there are no non-healing pericopes between the end of the "Teachings" section (7:29) and the Summary (9:35) apart from what occurs in these two clusters; and these two clusters were identified by noting what contiguous pericopes had the same relative order in both Matthew and Luke, and then seeking an explanation for this.

Matthew's "Jesus' Healings" section consists of these eight pericopes and pericope clusters:

NO	MATT	PERICOPE UNIT	LUKE
1.	8:1–4	Healing of a Leper	5:12–16
2.	8:5–13	Healing the Centurion's Servant	7:1–10
3.	8:14–17	Capernaum Healings (Double Pericope 1)	4:38–41
4.	8:18–9:1	Across the Sea of Galilee (Cluster 1)	8:22–39
5.	9:2–17	Events in Capernaum (1) (Cluster 2)	5:17–39E
6.	9:18–26	Events in Capernaum (2) (Double Pericope 2)	8:40–56E
7.	9:27–34	Healings on the Way (Double Pericope 3)	—
8.	9:35	Summary of Jesus' Healings and Ministry	8:1

The following comments can be made about the order for these pericope units. Matthew 8:1 says specifically that the cleansing of the leper occurred as Jesus descended from giving the Sermon on the Mount. Even if it is argued (as some believe—and it may well be) that the Sermon on the Mount is an agglomeration of teaching spoken on many occasions, there is no justification for the gratuitous assertion that there was *no discourse at all* on a mountain. There is in fact no reason for rejecting Matthew's words at face value. The healing of the leper is narrated here because, as Matthew says, it occurred when Jesus descended the mountain after the Sermon on the Mount and thus it provides a highly appropriate bridge from his "Teachings" section to his "Healings" section.

Matthew's second and third pericope units (8:5–13,14–17) are both set in Capernaum, which would explain the one following the other. Luke also sets both of them in Capernaum, but he has them in reverse order and widely separated (7:1–10; 4:38–41).

In Matthew, pericope units 4, 5, and 6 (see above) are linked together. After the Capernaum healings of unit 3, Jesus sails from Capernaum across the Sea of Galilee, heals Legion, returns to Capernaum (unit 4, cluster 1) for the events of unit 5 (cluster 2), and then there follow, while he is still in Capernaum, the linked events of the healing of the hemorrhaging woman and the raising of Jairus's daughter (unit 6; i.e., pericope units 5 and 6 are tied closely together by the "While he was thus speaking to them" of 9:18). Luke has pericope units 4 and 6 in consecutive sequence (8:22–39,40–56E) and unit 5 is placed much earlier (5:17–39E).

Why does Matthew place unit 5 where he does? Again, there is no valid case against the face value explanation being accepted: this sequence of events (Matt 9:2–17) is placed here because that is when they occurred. Within this sequence of events is the record of Matthew's own call (9:9). If indeed tradition is correct in ascribing the authorship of the First Gospel to Matthew the apostle (as I affirm), then it is entirely reasonable to believe that he would remember when his call took place. It was after Jesus' return across the lake and the healing of the paralytic, and just before the interlinked events of Jesus' healing the hemorrhaging woman and raising the ruler's daughter from the dead.

The final unit is a double pericope of the healing of two blind men and a dumb demoniac, apparently placed into this "Healings" section in anticipation of Jesus' statement in 11:5, "the blind receive their sight."

These comments do not cover every detail of the order of Matthew's "Healings" section, but they can certainly clarify some sections of it.

From John the Baptist's Group of Emissaries Onwards

Jesus' message to John the Baptist points to his healing and preaching ministry as the signs and the evidence to John that he, Jesus, was indeed the expected Coming One, the Messiah (Matt 11:3–4). From this pericope about John to Herod's perplexity (Matt 14:1), Matthew's grouping of material is a little less clear cut, but there is still evidence of such grouping (particularly in the teaching and discourse sections, 11:7–30E and 13:1–52, as also subsequently in 18:1–35E; 23:1–39E; 24:4–25:46E).

Between these two discourse blocks (11:7–30E and 13:1–52) Matthew places a series of incidents that have a common link: they are to some extent touched with controversy. The first of these is what has been identified earlier (see above) as C3, Sabbath Controversies (12:1–14), the two pericopes of confrontations with the Pharisees over working on the Sabbath (plucking grain in the fields) and healing on the Sabbath (the man with the withered hand). Because of the venomous intensity of opposition now aroused (12:14), Jesus withdraws from there (12:15a) but is followed by large crowds whose illnesses he heals, enjoining silence (12:15b–16). Matthew describes these events in terms of fulfillment of Old Testament prophecy (12:17–21). Then Jesus heals a blind and dumb demoniac, and this becomes the occasion for the confrontation with the Pharisees regarding their accusation that his power came from Beelzebul (Satan), the prince of demons (12:22–45).

The final incident related here is the visit of Jesus' family seeking him (12:46–50E), where Jesus' reply gives an indication that there is tension and conflict here also. This leads immediately and closely (13:1, "that same day") into the lengthy discourse section when Jesus taught in parables (13:1–52). The dominant theme here is a description of those who do and those who do not respond to the message of the kingdom (note how this links with Jesus' words in 12:49–50 about his true family). This in its turn leads into and is followed by Jesus' rejection at Nazareth, when Jesus' comment speaks of himself as "without honor . . . in his own house" (13:57). This links back with the pericope of Jesus' family that Matthew placed (12:46–50E) immediately prior to the parables discourse (13:1–52). Thus the section from the "Emissage of the Baptist to Herod's Perplexity" could be summed up as:

11:7–30E	Jesus' Teachings
12:1–50E	Controversy Stories
13:1–52	Jesus' Teachings in Parables
13:53–58E	Rejection at Nazareth

Next there comes C4, "Herod's Perplexity and Jesus' Withdrawal," leading to "The Feeding of the 5,000" (14:1–2,13–21), a document that also has been used by Luke but into which Matthew inserts (doubtless at the stage of final redaction of this material when he was including it into his full Gospel) the parenthetic explanation (14:3–12) of why Herod reacted as he did to hearing about Jesus (14:2). When Jesus hears about Herod's reaction, he cautiously withdraws to a lonely place (14:13), and when the crowds follow him he feeds them (14:14–21).

The next succession of pericopes (14:22–16:12) is absent in Luke (the "Great Omission"), the explanation for this being either that Luke knew them but chose to use none of them or—far more likely—that they did not come to Luke's attention; quite possibly Matthew recorded them in writing only at the time of composing his Gospel. That Matthew would place these pericopes at this point instead of including the various teachings, controversies, and miracles in his other (especially earlier) blocks of pericopes of these types is good grounds for considering that Matthew was aware that these episodes occurred at this stage in Jesus' ministry, that is, between the time Herod became aware of Jesus and the feeding of the 5,000, and the affirmation of Peter at Caesarea Philippi about who Jesus was.

The fifth pericope cluster that occurs in both Matthew and Luke, "From Confession to Transfiguration," marks a turning point in Jesus' ministry. Now that his disciples have come to grasp who he is, he begins to concentrate on teaching them (see 16:21). The transfiguration is followed in both Matthew and Luke (and thus presumably as part of the same document) by the healing of the epileptic boy, the second Passion prediction, and the lesson about true greatness. Into the framework of this document Matthew inserts the charge to secrecy (17:9), the coming of Elijah (17:10–13), and the temple tax (17:24–27E); at the end of it he adds a considerable amount of Jesus' further teaching on temptation and forgiveness (18:6–35E).

This completes Matthew's record of Jesus' Galilean ministry. He then records (from 19:1) that Jesus left Galilee and journeyed to Jerusalem and thence to the cross. The order of events is in general more significant here than it has been to this point. Pericopes are frequently linked with places, which helps to impose an order on them in the record of the journey. From Palm Sunday onwards the flow of events is largely integral to the story and therefore in general terms the sequence would be the same in any careful record of what occurred. The high level of correlation of order between Matthew and Luke in many places where it could have been different (e.g., the various episodes on the day of questions in Matt 21:23–24:1//Luke 20:1–21:5) suggests that the sequence of events was here a part of the tradition that was transmitted. Into this framework for Passion Week, Matthew and Luke each insert some teaching and some narrative that the other does not have.

A Comparison of Luke with Matthew

Numbers of the pericopes and pericope clusters included by Matthew in his Gospel have also been used by Luke. In some cases the extent of verbal similarity between the Matthean and Lukan accounts indicates that both authors used the same document, in Greek. For other pericopes, the overall identity of subject matter together with small differences of wording between Matthew and Luke might best be explained on the basis of separate Greek translations or rewritings of the one original Aramaic document. And again, those places where there are considerable differences between accounts of the one episode point to the two accounts being independent reports of what happened (e.g., Jesus' rejection at Nazareth).

Quite a number of accounts cannot at first glance be allocated to these categories with certainty. Accounts containing both substantial similarities and significant differences could have arisen from the same original traditions (whether transmitted orally or in writing) that both Matthew and Luke used, but with substantial redactional rewriting by one or both authors when incorporating them into their respective Gospels. Or alternatively, the two accounts could be two different versions independently transmitted (orally or in writing) of the one event or teaching, or of two different but similar events or teaching occasions. This is an area that needs further close study of the available evidence to provide a decision between these alternatives.

The order of pericopes in Luke's Gospel is extensively different from that of Matthew's Gospel. The extent of this difference can be seen from the column of comparison of order between Matthew and Luke (see chap. 8). The express statement by Luke (1:3) that his intention was to write an orderly account, and his manifest interest in questions of chronology, sequence, and connection between pericopes (see chap. 4) strongly suggests that Luke has arranged his pericopes and pericope clusters in chronological order, at least to the extent that he was able to ascertain what that order was. This is an eminently reasonable explanation of Luke's method of procedure and his plan of arrangement, *so long as he did not know Matthew's Gospel.* But assuming that Luke used Matthew, the problem is that in several instances Matthew's Gospel gives a clear and unequivocal statement of sequence or succession or link, but Luke often breaks these and places pericopes elsewhere, sometimes giving them the vaguest of settings. Here are a few examples:

Putting Things in Order 443

MATTHEW	LUKE
4:12 "Now when he heard that John had been arrested, he withdrew into Galilee."	4:31 "And he went down to Capernaum, a city of Galilee." [No link with John's arrest]
8:1 "When he came down from the mountain" [the setting for the healing of a leper, specifically placed after the Sermon on the Mount]	5:12 "While he was in one of the cities" [Luke's very vague, generalized setting for his account of the healing of a leper]
9:1 Jesus recrosses the lake after the healing of Legion.	8:40 Jesus recrosses the lake after the healing of Legion: "Now when Jesus returned . . . there came a man named Jairus" [Luke puts Jairus's request directly after the return from Healing Legion, and has put this much later in his overall sequence. The pericopes of Cluster 1 have been placed much earlier, 5:17–39E, introduced with the unspecific "On one of those days, as he was teaching"]
9:2–17 Matthew inserts here the pericopes of Cluster 1	
9:18 "While he was thus speaking . . ." [Matthew ties the Ruler's Request to the end of the pericope Concerning Fasting]	
12:46 "While he was still speaking to the people, his mother and brothers" [Matthew ties the visit of Jesus' family to the end of the Beelzebul discourse, and follows it with his parables chapter, thus:] 13:1 "That same day Jesus went"	8:19 "Then his mother and his brothers came to him" [Luke's parallels to the Beelzebul Discourse are in his chap. 11; the visit of Jesus' family is preceded (8:4ff.) by his equivalent Parables material]

If Luke had wanted to implement a chronological arrangement of material (as the other evidence indicates), it is difficult to see why he broke apart the two pericope clusters that Matthew joined together in 9:18 with the words "While he was thus speaking." The way that Luke introduces the three pericope clusters (8:22, "One day he got into a boat"; 5:17, "On one of those days"; 8:40f., "Now when Jesus returned . . . there came a man named Jairus") hardly indicates that Luke was acting in the light of compelling chronological factors in pulling out the center one of these three clusters from where it occurs in Matthew (9:2–17), breaking its close links in that Gospel and placing it in his own Gospel much earlier (Luke 5:17–39E) than its preceding and succeeding clusters (Luke 8:22–39, 40–45E).

[Mark here parallels Luke, so if Luke was using Mark (Markan Priority), this accounts for Luke's order at this place. But this approach leaves other difficult questions to be answered about the relationship between Mark and Luke.]

Therefore, those who hold that Luke used Matthew need to find some other explanation for Luke's plan of arrangement for his Gospel. But those who accept the implications here about the issue of order, reinforced by the evidence of content and wording given earlier (see chap. 8) that Luke did not know Matthew's Gospel *as a whole*, then the evidence can be perceived to point to this simple explanation: *Some pericopes and pericope clusters circulated in writing independently during the period prior to the composition of the Synoptics and were incorporated into both the Gospels of Matthew and Luke.* Matthew balanced chronological considerations with his plan of assembling large blocks of material of the same general kind; Luke aimed for the best chronological sequence that he could attain. In one case at least, Matthew's eyewitness knowledge allowed a more chronologically accurate placement of a pericope cluster (Matt 9:2–17) than was achieved in Luke for this material. This is what one would expect since this pericope cluster contains Matthew's own call to follow Jesus.

SUMMARY

Clearly, a very cogent case can be made out for the independence of the Gospels of Matthew and Luke, with the two Synoptists making use of a small number of documents that they had in common. The following is a summary of this case.

First, in the period between the events themselves and the writing of the first complete Synoptic Gospel, the apostle Matthew wrote down short accounts of some of the things that Jesus said and did. These written pericopes began to be copied and circulated in the churches, and some small groups of pericopes became clustered together. The pericopes in these clusters may have become linked together in the course of their circulation in the churches (see Luke 1:1), but more probably the clusters go back to Matthew's original writing down of the events and may therefore represent a record of the sequence in which the events occurred. This is the most likely explanation because the pericopes in a cluster usually have no apparent connection with each other and consist of different types of material; yet they occur together in identical sequence in all three Synoptic Gospels, although the clusters as a whole are placed in different contexts within the structures of these Gospels.

Second, Matthew and Luke produced their complete Gospels independently of each other and at approximately the same time, so that neither saw the finished Gospel written by the other before publishing his own. Each incorporated into his Gospel a number of the pericopes and pericope clusters that were then in circulation in the churches, editing these in conjunction with other information known to them about the stories and teachings in the pericopes.

Third, Matthew's Gospel and Luke's Gospel have a similar framework because of the extent to which much of the material itself indicates where it must be placed in the overall story of Jesus, and because they reflect the basic structure provided by the key events in the life and ministry of Jesus. However, many of the materials in these two Gospels are placed in different contexts within that basic framework since these materials contain no inherent time or sequence factors, and Matthew and Luke worked on the basis of different principles for arranging the order of their materials. Within the overall chronological framework, Matthew grouped like-to-like, while Luke sought to present everything in chronological order to the extent to which he was able to ascertain what this was.

Fourth, when Mark began work on his Gospel, the difference in pericope order in Matthew and Luke already confronted him. In keeping with his particular purpose in writing, Mark sought to restrict the amount of Jesus' teaching he included, confining this to material that he judged directly relevant to his overall aims or to material closely linked with other material that he was using. This intention led Mark to the adoption of the framework that he used for his Gospel: he followed the order of Luke through Mark 6:13 and from 6:14 onward he followed Matthew to the end. By this means Mark was able to steer around the major teaching sections that he did not choose to use. Into this framework Mark added a detour around Luke's Sermon on the Plain, plus a few other small pericopes that he drew from whichever Gospel that he was not using as his sequence source at the time, inserting them in each instance at the place in the structure where they occurred in the Gospel from which he took them.

It is striking to notice how close Streeter (1924, 161f.) came to recognizing these implications from the data:

> A curious fact . . . is that, while in the latter half of his Gospel (chapter xiv. to the end) Matthew adheres strictly to the order of Mark (Mk. vi.14 to the end), he makes considerable rearrangements in the first half. Luke, however, though he omits far more of Mark than does Matthew, hardly ever departs from Mark's order, and only in trifling ways. On the other hand, whenever Luke substitutes for an item in Mark a parallel version from another source, he always gives it *in a different context* from the item in Mark which it replaces.

Streeter has commented on the "curious fact" that from Mark 6:14 Matthew and Mark run parallel to the end, while Luke "hardly ever departs from Mark's order"—which is especially true of Mark up to 6:14. Streeter's comments are made from the perspective of his view that Matthew and Luke use Mark. It is interesting to speculate on the outcome if Streeter had stood back to look at the data without the mental bias of his commitment to Markan Priority, and if he had considered the significance of these facts when seen from the perspective of Markan Posteriority. As stated several times already, the alternative explanation of the observable data is simple. Through 6:13 Mark followed Luke (with four insertions he drew from Matthew and inserted where Matthew had placed them), and from 6:14 onward Mark followed Matthew (with four insertions he drew from Luke and inserted where Luke had placed them). Streeter came so close to seeing this!

CONCLUSION

This conclusion is warranted from the evidence: Mark drew his order from Matthew and Luke, and his procedure resulted in the fact that he was always in agreement in sequence with one or other of the Major Synoptics, and he was in agreement with both of them in all the places where they were in agreement with each other.

The clarity, the simplicity, and the comprehensive explanatory power of this interpretation of the data of Synoptic pericope order can be compared with the Markan Priority explanation.

1. Mark's Gospel is placed first, but Markan Priority offers no explanation for the order of Mark. So one is left with the comment of Papias that Mark contains no particular order at all.

2. Markan Priority does not really explain the order of Matthew or Luke, but it offers an explanation only of those places where they are in concord with Mark's order, and then *ad hoc* supplementary explanations have to be tendered for all of the many places where one of them deserts Mark.

3. Markan Priority does not explain why Matthew and Luke never happen to leave Mark's order at the same time, but one or other of them is *always* found agreeing with that order. This fact is trumpeted by proponents of Markan Priority as supporting their case, but this assertion is wishful thinking or poor logic. Markan Priority advocates do *not* claim that Matthew and Luke were acting in collusion, so the fact that they *appear* to act as if they were in collusion when we know that they were not casts grave doubts on the validity of the theory that leads to such a result. Markan Priority's only explanation of the way that Mark is always supported in sequence by one or both of the others is *coincidence*. The high number of occasions when the only Synoptic supporting Mark might well have also deserted Mark's order but did not do so indicates that coincidence of a very high degree is involved.

4. Markan Priority does not explain the alternating nature of the support given to Mark by the other two Synoptics, so that time after time it happens that just at the point where the one Major Synoptic who is following Mark ceases to do so, the other Major Synoptic appears alongside and takes over the role of being Mark's companion in Synoptic sequence. Impeccable timing. Or, incredible explanation. Truly, the Markan Priority explanation does not explain very much at all.

In contrast, Markan Dependence offers a more complete, more satisfying, and more convincing explanation of every aspect of the data of pericope order in all three Synoptics.

10 A QUICK LOOK AT SOME OTHER IDEAS

This chapter describes other proposed solutions for the Synoptic Problem and their shortcomings.

> [T]he Independence View maintains that each Gospel writer
> worked independently of the other three, each having no need
> to derive information from the other three.
> —F. D. Farnell (2002, 255)

> The Gospels, [Augustine] said, are arranged according to their
> order of composition: Matthew wrote first, then Mark, then Luke
> the companion of Paul, and finally John.
> —D. L. Dungan (1999, 121)

> Matthew and Luke did not copy Mark, but . . . all drew
> from a common source.
> —G. Salmon (1889, 155–56)

> If one were to survey the entire literature from its beginnings
> in the late 18th century, the most popular solution—representing
> the largest percentage of all that has ever been written on the
> subject—would clearly be the Urgospel approach.
> —D. L. Dungan (1970, 81)

INTRODUCTION

There have been various views proposed through the centuries to account for the similarities and differences in the Synoptics. Our treatment thus far in this book has focused on two explanations: the Two-Source

Hypothesis and the Markan Posteriority Hypothesis in its various forms—almost as if these two were the only possible solutions to the Synoptic Problem. But there have been other proposed solutions, and it is appropriate now to examine these. Two of these solutions can be traced back to the early church Fathers, and the others have been developed more recently.

SYNOPTIC VIEWS THROUGHOUT HISTORY

The early church Fathers were not very much interested in the order in which the Gospels were written or in their interrelationships. We saw in chapter 1 that several of the early church Fathers referred to the authors of the Gospels and even discussed the order in which the Gospels were written, but their comments about an order of writing for the Gospels are often vague or incomplete. They do agree in placing Matthew first, though one of them does not distinguish between Matthew or Luke being first; not even one early church Father places Mark first.

However, until Augustine and J. Chrysostom, none of them gave consideration to this question of the *interrelationship* between the Synoptic Gospels—that is, if and how (if at all) any Gospel writer made use of the Gospel(s) of his predecessor(s). These two church Fathers were the first to address the question of any kind of interrelationship between the Gospels, or the use of one Gospel by another author. Augustine and Chrysostom wrote at about the same time (c. AD 400) and expressed different views.

Chrysostom strongly affirmed the independence of the Gospel authors and considered that the nature and extent of their agreements and differences is "a very great demonstration of the truth" (Matthew, Homily I, c. 400, 1978, 2) of what they wrote; this is the Complete Independence Hypothesis. Augustine asserted that the order that the Gospels have in the canon—Matthew-Mark-Luke-John—was the order in which they had been written and that each writer utilized the work of his predecessor(s); this is the Successive Dependence Hypothesis. Thus I begin with these two views and the arguments in their support.

THE COMPLETE INDEPENDENCE HYPOTHESIS

Background

In chapter 5, I referred to F. D. Farnell's book on the Synoptic Problem, which presents the case for the Complete Independence Hypothesis. He says (2002, 255):

> In contrast to historical-critical ideology, the Independence View maintains that each Gospel writer worked independently of the other three, each having no need to derive information from the other three. The writers Matthew, Mark, Luke, and John authored four independent accounts of Jesus' life. The Gospels originated without direct literary interdependency.

This hypothesis is usually referred to simply as the Independence View. But I am affirming the independence of Matthew and Luke, in contradistinction from both the Two-Gospel Hypothesis and the Farrer Hypothesis. Thus to emphasize this distinction I refer to the view that all the Gospels are independent as the Complete Independence Hypothesis (or simply Complete Independence).

Modern proponents of independence hold it to have been the tacit opinion of the earliest Christian writers that the Gospels were independent of each other. Insofar as the question is discussed at all, there is (proponents aver) an uncritical acceptance of the four Gospels as being separate accounts of the life and ministry of Jesus and thus, by implication, as being independent of each other in their testimony.

Some exponents of Complete Independence state that this is the only view to be found in the early church Fathers. Farnell states (237): "The Fathers' writings verify a unanimous consensus that Matthew, not Mark, was the first Gospel written and that the Gospel writers wrote independently of each other." In saying this, these scholars too readily discount the comments of Augustine that the second and third Gospel writers knew and used the Gospel(s) prior to them (as I demonstrate below). Apart from Augustine, the early church Fathers do not discuss the nature of the relationship between the Gospels, so we cannot infer from the fact that something is not discussed by these Fathers that they held the particular view we espouse.

Chrysostom's most explicit statement on the Independence view occurs in his *Homilies on Matthew* that he preached in Antioch of Syria during the latter part of the fourth century. In Homily I.5–6 he says that the Gospel authors wrote independently of each other, that the disagreements between them (while minor) show that they did not act in collusion, and thus that their basic agreement on all essentials "becomes a very great demonstration of the truth." Chrysostom's full comment reads (1978, 2–3):

> And why can it have been, that when there were so many disciples, two write only from among the apostles, and two from among their followers? (For one that was a disciple of Paul, and another of Peter, together with Matthew and John, wrote the Gospels.) It was because they did nothing for vainglory, but all things for use.

A Quick Look at Some Other Ideas 451

> "What then? Was not one evangelist sufficient to tell all?" One indeed was sufficient; but if there be four that write, not at the same times, nor in the same places, neither after having met together, and conversed one with another, and then they speak all things as it were out of one mouth, this becomes a very great demonstration of the truth.
>
> "But the contrary," it may be said, "hath come to pass, for in many places they are convicted of discordance." Nay, this very thing is a very great evidence of their truth. For if they had agreed in all things exactly even to time, and place, and to the very words, none of our enemies would have believed but that they had met together, and had written what they wrote by some human compact; because such entire agreement as this cometh not of simplicity. But now even that discordance which seems to exist in little matters delivers them from all suspicion, and speaks clearly in behalf of the character of the writers.

Subsequently, in Homily IV.1, on Matthew's genealogy, Chrysostom makes two further comments concerning the Gospels: (1) Matthew was followed by Mark and Luke; and (2) the two later ones supplemented the earlier. He says (20):

> "Why then," one may say, "doth not Mark do this, nor trace Christ's genealogy, but utter everything briefly?" It seems to me that Matthew was before the rest in entering on the subject (wherefore he both sets down the genealogy with exactness, and stops at those things which require it): but that Mark came after him, which is why he took a short course, as putting his hand to what had been already spoken and made manifest.
>
> How is it then that Luke not only traces the genealogy, but [traces] it through a greater number? As was natural, Matthew having led the way, he seeks to teach us somewhat in addition to former statements. And each too in like manner imitated his master; the one, Paul, who flows fuller than any river; the other, Peter, who studies brevity.

This comment does not contradict what Chrysostom had said earlier: he is not implying that Mark *utilized* or *copied from* Matthew, nor Luke from Matthew (or Mark), but that Mark was brief because Matthew had already written fully (and also because Peter, the implied source of Mark's information, was one "who studied brevity"); and that Luke in his genealogy traces it through a greater number of ancestors than Matthew because "he seeks to teach us somewhat in addition to former statements" and because he "too in like manner imitated his master, . . . Paul, who flows fuller than any river."

Chrysostom cites no source for his information, so his comment apparently represents his own judgment in the matter. But his comment is an uncritical assessment claiming that the Gospels were not interrelated, but were works of completely independent authorship.

J. Calvin also supported (*Harmony of the Gospels,* 1960, 82) the Independence view. In more recent times the view of independent oral traditions behind the Gospels has been supported by numbers of scholars, including J. G. Herder (1796–97), J. C. L. Gieseler (1817–18), B. F. Westcott (1851; 1860), H. Alford (1849) in his Greek New Testament, A. Wright (1896), and R. O. P. Taylor (1946). This view emphasizes the independence of the sources for the Synoptic Gospels and continued to have advocates up to the present (see below).

Alford was one of the more forceful advocates of Complete Independence. His commentary series on the Greek New Testament was one of the nineteenth century's major publications: the first volume covering the Gospels appeared in 1849 and was reissued in a second edition in 1854 (the seventh edition is still in print today). Alford carefully investigated the relationships between the Synoptics and argued strongly for "their independence of one another." His concern was to concentrate on "the evidence furnished *by the Gospels themselves*," and he addressed the various alternative "mutual interdependence" theories that could be adopted to explain the Gospels as we have them and why they were written. His conclusions are (1968, 1:3–12):

> I cannot then find in any of the above hypotheses a solution of the question before us, *how the appearances presented by our three Gospels are to be accounted for*. I do not see how any theory of mutual interdependence will leave to our three Evangelists their credit as *able* or *trustworthy writers*, or even as *honest men*: nor can I find any such theory borne out by the nature of the variations apparent in the respective texts. . . . It remains then that the three Gospels should have arisen *independently of one another*.

The Nature of the Case

What exactly is the contention of the Complete Independence advocates today? How do they present the case for their view? Farnell's explanation is as follows (257–58):

> The Gospel records are authentic, biographical, and historical accounts of apostolic eyewitnesses, written during the lifetimes of the apostles. Those records present accurately what Jesus said and did. The Gospels, therefore, reflect the only legitimate *Sitz im Leben* (situation in life) of Jesus, that is, accurate historical reports of what Jesus said and did during His life on earth, bearing witness to His death, resurrection, and ascension.

The Complete Independence Hypothesis fully acknowledges the role of Synoptic sources. Farnell notes (224) that "Matthew, Mark, and Luke drew from eyewitness sources, oral and written, in their accounts." He also acknowledges (223) that "the agreements of Matthew and Luke against Mark are smaller in number [than agreements of Mark with one or both of the others], but they are, nevertheless, quite substantial in number and very real. Peter's influence accounts for this phenomenon too." He then adds (224): "Yes, Matthew was written before Luke, but Luke had no knowledge of Matthew's Gospel when he wrote, and the book of Matthew was not among the sources available to Luke in his research." Further, Farnell says (240) that "literary-dependency concepts are absent from the writings of the early church Fathers. Although they had frequent opportunity to mention literary dependence, they never do so." He quotes (241) Chrysostom (1978, 1:5–6; 10:3): "'What then? Was not one evangelist sufficient to tell all?' One indeed was sufficient; but if there be four that write, not at the same times, nor in the same places, neither after having met together, and conversed one with another, and then they speak all things as it were out of one mouth, this becomes a very great demonstration of the truth."

Farnell then cites a number of authors from the twentieth century. I find their explanations of Synoptic sources particularly interesting in light of the view to which the evidence has pointed me (as explained in the first two chapters of this book). Farnell says (242), concerning L. Berkhof's view of sources: "Berkhof explained the synoptic origins on the basis of oral tradition and brief written narratives containing especially the sayings of Jesus. For him, such an origin 'explains in a very natural way most of the agreements that are found in the Synoptics.'" Farnell again (2002, 243): "Henry C. Thiessen . . . also recognized short-written narratives (e.g., Fragmentary Hypothesis [Schleiermacher]) and oral tradition (Westcott) in the early church as possible partial explanations but as inadequate to explain Gospel origins by themselves." Farnell cites (244–45) the writings of E. Linnemann for her strong and recent support of the Independence view. He adds (246), "Robert G. Gromacki (*New Testament Survey*) . . . observes that 'in all cases the [Gospel] writer consulted sources, both oral and written, scrutinized them, selected material, and wrote under the direct influence of the Holy Spirit. These were not merely human compositions: they were the Word of God enscripturated through human penmen.'" Then Farnell (246) notes that M. C. Tenney is an "advocate [of] the Independent View to explain synoptic origins." Tenney gives (1961, 145–46) this explanation:

> 1. The Gospel of Matthew represents the notes that Matthew took on Jesus' teaching, with a framework of narrative that closely—and at times verbally—resembles Mark. The resemblance could be explained on the basis of common tradition and living contact quite as well as by appropriation of written work.
>
> 2. The Gospel of Mark represents the main line of narrative preaching about Jesus. It was reproduced by a man who had contact with the apostles from the very inception of the church, and it was written while some of them, at least,

were still alive. Its content was known at a very early date, whether the actual document had been published then or not.

3. The Gospel of Luke represents the independent account of Paul's traveling companion, who wrote in the seventh decade of the first century, and who incorporated both the narrative framework of apostolic preaching and the results of this own research. . . .

Some other aspects of this question deserve consideration. One is that the dates of composition and publication may be widely separated. Matthew, for instance, could have collected his notes during Jesus' lifetime, but they may not have reached the public in organized form until a long time afterward. If so, they could have been used by others in the interim. . . .

Finally, the purposes of the Evangelists should be taken into account. Granting that they possessed much material in common, they put it to different uses, and organized it into different frameworks under the direction of the mind of the Spirit.

Farnell refers to a number of other writers who have given support to the Independence view. Behind the Gospels lies the concept of divine inspiration, which Farnell explains (265):

The Bible should not be viewed as *equally* the product of human and divine elements. In inspiration, the divine element overshadowed the human element so as to provide a book that is *qualitatively* separate from all other books in its inspiration and inerrancy. Although the Bible was written by men, God's superintendence of those men in the inspiration of His Word supernaturally overshadowed the product so that the Holy Spirit guaranteed the accuracy of what men recorded. Such precision in composition is without parallel in human historiography.

Farnell's "Compositional Factors of the Independence Approach" (272–73) includes the following points:

Simply stated, literary independence accounts for the similarities among the Synoptic Gospels by noting that they were accounts of eyewitnesses whose sharp memories, aided by the Holy Spirit, reproduced the exact wording of dialogues and sermons (John 14:26). Literary independence explains the differences between the Gospels by observing that different eyewitnesses reported the same events in different but not contradictory ways. The writers drew upon this combination of eyewitness accounts, which constitute a nonhomogeneous body of tradition without definable limits.

His explanation includes acknowledging "the probability of brief written sources." He explains (282–83):

Although oral tradition partially explains Gospel origins, short written accounts probably existed very early alongside oral tradition, accounting for synoptic material. The prologue of Luke's Gospel indicates that Luke was aware that many others had composed written accounts. . . . The combination of exacting oral tradition and short written accounts helped not only to ensure the accuracy of the Gospel's records of events and sayings but also to provide a reasonable explanation of why the Synoptics have extensive agreement among themselves.

At this point Farnell anchors his presentation of the Independence view in some very dubious argumentation. First, he notes (284) that the contenders for both the Two-Source (Markan Priority) view and the Two-Gospel (Markan Posteriority) view claim that the question of order in the Synoptics supports their position. This leads him to conclude: "Secondly, if the argument from order is so fluid that both Two-/Four Source advocates and Two-Gospel proponents can tailor the statistics to 'prove' their case, the argument is highly subjective, and the validity of the argument is seriously questionable."

This is equivalent to the proposal that because both genuine and counterfeit coins and notes have been detected in circulation, therefore no coins or notes are trustworthy. This conclusion is a gratuitous *non sequitur*. The right response would be to examine the units in question with a view to assessing which (if any) had a valid claim to be trusted. My thoughts are that it is a total copout to say that "because the proponents of differing views disagree about which way the argument from order points, therefore *there is* no argument from order, and this pretense to an argument can be dismissed from consideration."

In this connection Farnell quotes (285) Linnemann's assertions (1992, 85, 91) which conclude, "In other words, when we set aside the narratives that would be expected to follow a similar sequence [because their sequence is inherently determined by the nature of the events themselves], not even one half of the sections in Mark follow the sequence of the other Synoptics."

In response to Linnemann, I would point out that this is the case if Mark follows Luke's order half the time and Matthew the rest of the time—and these two Synoptics so often differ in order! But Mark *always* follows one of them.

Farnell cannot so readily dismiss the serious strength of the relevance of the order found in the pericopes of the Synoptics (see discussion in chap. 9). Farnell's explanation (290–91) of the similarities between the Gospels is as follows:

> The phenomenon of varying combinations of agreements and disagreements is readily explainable under literary independence but not under any form of dependency. All three synoptic writers worked from stereotyped oral tradition and short written sources, readily explaining such agreements of two against one. ... In all probability, Matthew, Mark and Luke had personal contacts with

each other; therefore, the writers had ample opportunities to exchange information about the life of Christ, especially during the early days of the church in Jerusalem.

Arguments against the Complete Independence View

There are two significant features of the modern explanation of the Complete Independence view. First, see how far removed it is from Chrysostom's view quoted earlier, which attributes the verbal similarities of the Synoptic Gospels to the specific guidance of the Holy Spirit and expressly rules out any contact or collusion or comparison of notes on the part of the Gospel authors. Modern exponents of Complete Independence aver, instead, that indeed that is *exactly* what took place.

Second, see how closely at times these proponents have come to the Progressive Publication of Matthew view that I have expounded, particularly these points: the independence of the Gospels of Matthew and Luke—neither used the other; the role of Matthew's notes of Christ's teaching, actually recorded at the time, and circulating afterwards in some form and to some extent; and the role of Peter behind Mark's Gospel, in both content and wording. Almost I am persuaded to be Completely Independent myself. But not quite. There are two kinds of evidence that totally prevent this.

First of all, there is the evidence at the micro level: the broken sentences exactly the same in two or all three Gospels; the little asides; the wording of some sections of some pericopes in the Synoptics, using unusual expressions or rare words.

Second, there is the evidence at the macro level. With the emergence of modern Gospel scholarship, the possibility of the independence of the Gospels has been subjected to careful critical evaluation. G. Salmon (1889) presented strong arguments against this view well over a century ago. The following summarizes Salmon's three arguments against the Independence view (134–37). (1) The closeness of agreement between the Synoptic narratives shows that they are different versions of a common account. This closeness of agreement extends not only to substance but to form—to the common use of a parenthesis, or a departure from chronological order in telling the story. (2) There are numerous verbal coincidences between the corresponding narratives. Frequently these coincidences include rare or unusual words that different authors would be very unlikely to use independently. (3) The close agreement in order of pericopes between most of the Synoptic accounts in the majority of cases rules out the idea of separate and independent oral sources for the Synoptics.

Salmon sumps up (137) the force of the evidence thus: "I feel bound, therefore, to conclude that the likeness between the Gospels is not sufficiently explained by their common basis, the oral narrative of the Apostles; and that they must have been copied, either one from the other—the later from the earlier—or else all from some other document earlier than any."

These arguments do not point to any particular hypothesis of literary interrelationship, but they do pose serious problems for the view that there was none. They are still put forth in books that cover this issue and are given good coverage by R. H. Stein (1988). Salmon's and Stein's arguments can be identified in the following five categories.

Parenthetical Material

Parenthetical material is the first part of Salmon's first argument, which Stein explains (37) this way:

> One of the most persuasive arguments for the literary interdependence of the synoptic Gospels is the presence of identical parenthetic material, for it is highly unlikely that two or three writers would by coincidence insert into their accounts exactly the same editorial comments at exactly the same place. It is furthermore evident in the example below that we can conclude that the common source of the material was *written*, for both Matthew and Mark refer to the "reader" in the comment.

Stein quotes (37) Matt 24:15//Mark 13:14 where both have the parenthesis "let the reader understand" inserted editorially into what Christ is saying: the address to a "reader" presupposes a written document. He then (38) states:

> The comment—"let the reader understand"—is a most impressive agreement between Matthew and Mark. That such a comment is not "necessary" in this eschatological discourse is evident in that Luke does not have it. Furthermore, that such a comment could not be due to a common oral tradition is obvious, for it does not refer to the "hearer" but rather to the "reader."

Stein moves on to consider Jesus' healing of a paralytic in Matt 9:6//Mark 2:10–11//Luke 5:24. In this pericope all three Gospels include a parenthetical statement: "he said to the paralytic" in Matthew and Mark; "he said to the man who was paralyzed" in Luke. Stein's point is that it is unlikely for three totally independent writers, using independent sources, to incorporate the same parenthetical statement in their account of a miracle at the same point and in the same way. He concludes (40): "The fact that each of the Evangelists has the same comment (Matthew's and Mark's are exactly the same) at the same place argues strongly for their having used a common written source."

A Departure from Chronological Order in Telling the Story

Another type of category (the second part of Salmon's first argument) is where two Gospels break in the same way (and at the same place) from what would be the "normal" chronological flow of telling the story. Salmon (134–35) draws attention to this phenomenon in Mark 5:8//Luke 8:29, where these two Gospel accounts first relate the story of the Gerasene demoniac, his cry to "Jesus, son of the Most High God," and the demon's request that Jesus not torment it. Both Gospels add the information that Jesus had instructed the unclean spirit to come out of the man. Salmon states (135):

> Now, if the story had been told in the chronological order we should first have Jesus' command to the unclean spirit to depart, and then the remonstrance of the demoniac. So when we find Mark (5:7) agreeing with Luke in the minute detail of relating the remonstrance first, and then adding parenthetically that there had been a command, this coincidence alone gives us warrant for thinking that we have here, not the story as it might have been told by two different witnesses to the miracle, but the form in which a single witness was accustomed to tell it.

This added explanatory verse in Mark's and Luke's account of what was said is not in the corresponding record of the miracle in Matthew's Gospel. Stein cites (41–42) another instance of this type in Matt 27:18//Mark 15:10, which contain an added explanation that at the trial of Jesus before Pilate, the governor was aware that "it was out of envy that the chief priests [Matthew has "they"] had delivered him up." (Luke's account omits this explanation.) Pilate's perception of their envy occurred *before* he spoke, but the narrative places it *after* his question.

A Vast Number of Verbal Coincidences between the Corresponding Narratives

This is the first part of Salmon's second argument. It is especially significant to see correspondence of successions of words in narrative or in a comment made by someone other than Jesus. Where such verbal correspondence occurs in conversations or dialogue or teaching involving Jesus, it is legitimate to ascribe this to the fact that these are the actual words spoken or the record of an accurate rendering of the traditional oral transmission of such words (either originally as spoken if in Greek or an early Greek translation from an original Aramaic).

We can readily recognize the ministry of the Spirit in bringing Christ's words to the remembrance of the apostles as he promised (John 14:26). But when such verbal agreement occurs in *narrative*, in connecting and introductory passages, in asides that are made, this raises the very significant issue of whether it is more likely that this corresponding information shared by more than one Gospel was transmitted independently or indicates a literary relationship.

Stein's example (42) of this is when the chief priests and their associates were plotting to arrest Jesus and kill him (Matt 26:5//Mark 14:2): "they said, Not during the feast, lest there be a tumult with the people." (This is not in Luke's parallel.) Stein also mentions (42) as an example the reference in common in Matt 26:14//Mark 14:10//Luke 22:3 to Judas Iscariot, one of the Twelve (cf. Matt 26:47//Mark 14:43//Luke 22:47).

Rare or Unusual Words Different Authors Would Be Unlikely to Use Independently

This is the second part of Salmon's second argument. He says (144–45) that such words must have a common written source:

> [The common source must have been in Greek because] the hypothesis of an Aramaic original does not suffice to explain all the phenomena. For there are very many passages where the Evangelists agree in the use of Greek words which it is not likely could have been hit on independently by different translators. . . . The instances of the use of common words [are] numerous. And in order to feel the force of the argument you need only put in parallel columns the corresponding passages in the different Evangelists: say, of the parable of the Sower or of the answer to the question about fasting (Mk 2:18–22; Mt 9:14–17; Lk 5:33–39), when you will find such a continuous use of common words as to forbid the idea that we have before us independent translations from another language. [Other examples of words in common are: ἀνάγαιον (Mk 14:15; Lk 22:12); δυσκόλως (Mt 19:23; Mk 10:23; Lk 18:24); κατέκλασε (Mk 6:41; Lk 9:16); κολοβοῦν (Mt 24:22; Mk 13:20); πτεγύγιον (Mt 4:5; Lk 4:9); διαβλεψεις (Mt 7:5; Lk 6:42).]
>
> The result is, that if an Aramaic original document is assumed in order to account for the verbal variations of the Gospels, a Greek original (whether a translation of that Aramaic or otherwise) is found to be equally necessary in order to explain their verbal coincidences.

These are all instances of the "micro" approach that looks at the text close up and considers how to explain what is there. In the nature of the way in which traditions are passed on, it is highly unlikely that such identical forms of wording could have been passed on orally so as to end up independently in two or more Gospels. The more reasonable explanation is that it was due to a correspondence between written Gospel sources at this point.

The Close Agreement in Order of Pericopes

This is Salmon's third argument. It is also set out in some detail by Stein (1988, 34–37). Complete Independence advocates tend to dismiss lightly the extent and nature of the Synoptic similarities, especially those in relation to pericope order. Advocates claim that these agreements in order are because that is the order in which things happened. But this ignores in particular the very considerable difference in order between Matthew and Luke up to the pericope of Herod's confusion about Christ. The Synoptic order cannot simply be the order of events because these two Synoptics are totally out of whack here on the order of things. This is true except for the pericope clusters—where things do have the same order in these groups or clusters; but these clusters are in totally conflicting locations in the sequences of those Gospels because Matthew and Luke had totally different goals for their respective order of presentation. Neither is "right" because both are legitimate and both can be recognized as under the Spirit's leading.

Salmon cites (136–37) a particular example of the "order of pericopes" argument:

> It is because we have not only one but a series of stories common to the Synoptics that the difference between documentary and oral transmission comes to have a practical meaning. The latter supposition contemplates a number of stories preserved independently; the former regards them as already embodied in a document which, even if it did not pretend to be a complete Gospel, contained the narration of more incidents than one, disposed in a definite order. Our choice between the two suppositions can be guided by examining whether the Evangelists agree, not only in their way of relating separate stories, but also in the order in which they arrange them. Now, a careful examination brings out the fact that the likeness between the Synoptic Gospels is not confined to agreement in the way of telling separate stories, but extends also to the order of arranging them. Take, for instance, the agreement between Matthew and Mark as to the place in which they tell the death of John the Baptist (Mt 14:1; Mk 6:14). They related that when Herod heard of the fame of Jesus he was perplexed who He might be, and said to his servants, 'This is John whom I beheaded.' And then, in order to explain this speech, the two Evangelists go back in their narrative to relate the beheading of John. Their agreement in this deviation from the natural chronological order can scarcely be explained except by supposing either that one Evangelist copied from the other, or both from a common source. The order of St. Luke deviates here from that of the other two Evangelists. He relates the imprisonment of John in its proper place (3:19), and the perplexed inquiry of Herod later (9:7); but we are not entitled to infer that he did not employ the same source, for the change is an obvious improvement that would suggest itself to anyone desirous to relate the history in chronological order. And we may even conjecture that it was in consequence of Luke's thus departing from the order of his archetype that he has come to omit altogether the direct narrative of the beheading of John.

We have already given careful consideration to this whole question of pericope order in the previous chapter, where a comparison of the disparities between the sequences in Matthew and Luke totally deny the view that they are in this order because this is the sequence in which they happened. On the other hand, the common sequence of pericopes within the pericope clusters—the pericope clusters that are placed in totally different contexts by Matthew and Luke—completely rules out of consideration the explanation that these "happened" to become assembled that way quite independently. This pushes us toward another explanation: these pericope clusters were the result of a common literary heritage, and then—as assembled documents—they became incorporated independently by Matthew and Luke in different places in their Gospels, where they best fit each author's purposes.

In the previous chapter we saw that the evidence indicates how Mark followed initially the order of pericopes that he found in Luke, and subsequently moved over to follow the sequence of Matthew. Overall, this results in a sequence of pericopes that certainly brings out clearly Mark's purpose of showing the disciples' developing understanding of who Jesus was.

Doctrinal Considerations

Some exponents of Complete Independence rule out on dogmatic, even doctrinal, grounds the possibility of literary dependence since it is supposedly incompatible with the Holy Spirit's inspiration of the Gospels and since it implies that the later Gospel(s) must be inferior to the earlier Gospel(s) or vice versa. I am completely at one with these teachers in their high view of Scripture and of its full inspiration and authority and reliability as being historically accurate—no quibbles, no hedging around or "making allowances." And I do acknowledge that all literary dependence views have adherents who have a much looser view of the verbal accuracy of the Gospels than I do. But such an attitude does not go with the territory. This is not the inevitable consequence of literary dependence *per se*. We must acknowledge the literary dependence between 1 and 2 Kings and 1 and 2 Chronicles, and between 2 Peter and Jude. Also, Luke states (1:1–4) that he has checked out everything carefully from the beginning, and that he knew about earlier documents in existence. This carries, it seems to me, a clear implication that he had made himself familiar with what these documents said. And this indicates that the idea of some kind of literary dependence is not ruled out of court from the outset. The view of literary dependence in the Progressive Publication of Matthew Hypothesis is that Luke used numbers of documents of apostolic origin (viz, from Matthew) and that he used them in such a way as to conform with his overall aim—as indeed Luke himself tells us he did. On this hypothesis, he did not use them in any fashion that conflicts with divine inspiration of his work or the total reliability of his Gospel.

Mark then took these two rather different Gospels and wove them together in a manner that largely (and legitimately) minimized the differences (differences due in the main to the independence of eyewitness sources used). And he cast the wording of his whole Gospel into colloquial Greek, reflecting the spoken language both of his third source, the apostolic testimony of Peter on which he drew, and his intended audience, the unconverted of Rome and its Empire. So how is this scenario incompatible with a high view of Scripture and its inspiration?

If indeed (as we firmly hold) the Scripture is inspired and inerrant, then we may certainly investigate what it says (i.e., the data, the evidence) with confidence that all of this data, this evidence—rightly understood—will be in accord with that inspiration of an accurate Gospel account. But we do not start with a presupposition and allow it to drive our investigation. But we most certainly test the outcome of our investigation by the doctrine of biblical inspiration and the promises that the writers would have Spirit-guided memories and understanding of the truth—that is part of the evidence that is to be taken into account. There is no *a priori* reason for concluding in advance, by definition, that the activity of the Spirit could not have included the use of one Gospel by the author of another.

There is no reason why adherents of Complete Independence with a high view of Scripture cannot examine the data and become persuaded by the evidence that, in writing his Gospel, Mark drew not only on the preaching of Peter but also his Synoptic predecessors, Matthew and Luke. The Bible is not like other books and records. It is divinely inspired. But that does not lead us to decide in advance how the Spirit may (or may not) go about his work of inspiring the human authors. We look at what he has *done* to see the evidence of what he intended to do.

After emphasizing the commitment to "the plenary, verbal inspiration and inerrancy of the Gospels" by those who hold to the Complete Independence view, Farnell says (2002, 295–96):

> In contrast, dependency hypotheses are linked to modern views of errancy and views of either partial inspiration or noninspiration of the Gospels. . . . One must hold either to a normative view of inspiration that upholds the orthodox position of divine superintendence of the documents and become a proponent of the Independence View or to literary-dependency theories and abandon a normative view of inspiration. No middle ground exists. . . . Only the Independence View provides the necessary safeguards and reflects the orthodox approach to Gospel origins.

Farnell has thus ruled out of consideration all hypotheses that present an explanation involving literary dependency between any Gospels. This is a one-size-fits-all approach to literary dependency hypotheses that declines to differentiate things that differ. It is my sincere hope (and, dare I say, expectation?) that adherents of the Complete Independence view will consider fairly the explanation that I make of how the Progressive Publication of Matthew Hypothesis, with its Markan Dependence extension, is on the one hand completely compatible with their high view of Scripture while on the other it takes account of all the evidence that has led scholars to look for a solution of the Synoptic Problem in terms of some kind of a literary dependence.

If we are to say, regarding such instances of correspondence between different Gospel accounts in the ways I have shown, that it is not acceptable to put these down to literary relationships but that they are the work of the Spirit in bringing about such close correspondence between Gospels, the question arises: "If this is the purpose and intent of the Holy Spirit in inspiring the Gospels, why only on these occasions? Why not on a great many more? That is, if the accounts are thus made to correspond by the direct intervention of the Spirit in the writing process in this way, why not to a far greater extent? Why not, in fact, throughout each Gospel?"

But a moment's reflection indicates that if, as a result of the Spirit working in this particular way, *all* the differences between the Gospels were obliterated, then we would not have four Gospels at all—we would have four copies of the one Gospel record. It follows then that it is simplistic and contrary to what we see of the working of the Spirit in inspiring the Gospel accounts to ascribe such coincidences of wording and sequence just to "the overriding supervision of the Spirit."

Many of the adherents to the Complete Independence Hypothesis happily accept the role of early written documents of various kinds among the sources of our canonical Gospels (as we noted earlier in this section), and can thus attribute these Gospel similarities to this explanation—to which I will reply, "That is exactly what I am outlining!" Then I will refer them to chapters 2 and 3 of this book for the elucidation in more detail of this explanation.

THE SUCCESSIVE DEPENDENCE HYPOTHESIS

Background

In about AD 400 Augustine provided the first statement of any of the church Fathers that discussed the interrelationships between the Gospels. He says (Book 1, 2.3–3.6):

Now those four evangelists whose names have gained the most remarkable circulation over the whole world, and whose number has been fixed as four . . . are believed to have written in the order which follows: first Matthew, then Mark, thirdly Luke, lastly John. . . .

And however they may appear to have kept each of them a certain order of narration proper to himself, this certainly is not to be taken as if each individual writer chose to write in ignorance of what his predecessor had done, or left out as matters about which there was no information things which another nevertheless is seen to have recorded. But the fact is, that just as they received, each of them, the gift of inspiration, they abstained from adding to their several labours any superfluous conjoint compositions. For Matthew is understood to have taken it in hand to construct the record of the incarnation of the Lord according to the royal lineage, and to give an account of most part of His deeds and words as they stood in relation to this present life of men. Mark follows him closely, and looks like his attendant and epitomizer. For in his narrative he gives nothing in concert with John apart from the others: by himself separately, he has little to record; in conjunction with Luke, as distinguished from the rest, he has still less; but in concord with Matthew, he has a very large number of passages. Much, too, he narrates in words almost numerically and identically the same as those used by Matthew, where the agreement is either with that evangelist alone, or with him in connection with the rest.

On the other hand, Luke appears to have occupied himself rather with the priestly lineage and character of the Lord. . . . Luke, on the other hand, had no one connected with him to act as his summarist in the way that Mark was attached to Matthew. And it may be that this is not without a certain solemn significance. For it is the right of kings not to miss the obedient following of attendants; and hence the evangelist who had taken it in hand to give an account of the kingly character of Christ has a person attached to him as his associate who was in some fashion to follow in his steps. But inasmuch as it was the priest's wont to enter all alone into the holy of holies, in accordance with that principle, Luke, whose object contemplated the priestly office of Christ, did not have any one to come after him as a confederate, who was meant in some way to serve as an epitomizer of his narrative.

The overall consequence of Augustine's comments, in which he simultaneously upheld that the number of the Gospels has been fixed as four and implied dismissively that Mark was of negligible value if one had Matthew, was to lead to a neglect of Mark's Gospel that continued until the development of Synoptic scholarship in the last two centuries or so.

Augustine says nothing of the exact nature of the relationship of Luke or John to those Gospels that were (on this view) written before them, beyond this brief comment: "And however they may appear to have kept each of them a certain order of narration proper to himself [a reference, apparently, to the different order of the pericopes in the Gospels], this certainly is not to be taken as if each individual writer chose to write in ignorance of what his predecessor had done, or left out as matters about which there was no information things which another nevertheless is seen to have recorded." Augustine's primary emphasis in this comment is that Matthew was the first Gospel written and that Mark was Matthew's "epitomizer," so that the second Gospel contains little that is not in the first. This is the only Gospel relationship that is explicitly developed. The final clause just quoted suggests that each writer knew everything that all his predecessors had written, while the clause prior to it refutes the idea of a writer choosing to write in ignorance of what his predecessor had done. Hence this view has been termed the Successive Dependence Hypothesis.

In chapter 6 we noted D. Peabody's examination of Augustine's later comment (Book 4, 10.11) on this question of the order and relationship of the Synoptics—a comment that is regularly overlooked by scholars who confine themselves to what Augustine said at greater length in Book 1 of his *Harmony of the Gospels*. Peabody interprets Augustine's later comment to indicate that, after his careful comparison of the Synoptics, he had come to the conclusion that Mark is literarily dependent on both Matthew and Luke, and thus the Gospel of Mark must have been written *after* the Gospels of Matthew and Luke.

If Peabody's assessment of Augustine is correct—and it appears to me to be very well taken—then when he began writing his *Harmony of the Gospels* Augustine took over what he judged to be Irenaeus's view (the view also of Origin) of the order of the Gospels as Matthew-Mark-Luke-John and understood this also to mean their *order of writing*. Then in the course of his examination of the textual evidence, Augustine was led to consider a second view, which he describes now as "more probable." That is, Augustine placed Luke alongside Matthew as a source for Mark. However, the apparent change in Augustine's view in the course of his Gospel studies, and his comment about his change of mind, went unnoticed by those who continued to endorse Successive Dependence. His name is still being given to his earlier view that places the sequence of the Gospels, and their relationship, as Matthew-Mark-Luke-John, so that writers continue to attribute this to him as the Augustinian Hypothesis.

Jameson and Chapman in Support

For most of the Christian centuries it would seem that the question of the interrelationship of the Synoptic Gospels to each other was of small interest to scholars. While the Markan Priority Hypothesis was growing in acceptance and popularity in Britain under the influence of the Oxford Seminar (see chap. 5), there was the occasional voice raised in protest against this view. In particular H. G. Jameson (1922) criticized the arguments put forward for Markan Priority as being "inconclusive" and advocated the Successive Dependence Hypothesis.

Streeter published his definitive book *The Four Gospels* in 1924. He does not mention Jameson by name or acknowledge the seriousness of Jameson's questioning of fundamental tenets of Markan Priority, but quite clearly he has Jameson's book in view when he writes (157–58, 164):

> The attempt has recently been made to revive the solution first put forward by Augustine . . . , who styles Mark a kind of abridger and lackey of Matthew. . . . But Augustine did not possess a Synopsis of the Greek text conveniently printed in parallel columns. Otherwise a person of his intelligence could not have failed to perceive that, where the two Gospels are parallel, it is usually Matthew, and not Mark, who does the abbreviation. . . . How any one who has worked through those pages with a Synopsis of the Greek text can retain the slightest doubt of the original and primitive character of Mark I am unable to comprehend. But since there are, from time to time, ingenious persons who rush into print with theories to the contrary, I can only suppose, either that they have not been at the pains to do this, or else that—like some of the highly cultivated people who think that Bacon wrote Shakespeare, or that the British are the Lost Ten Tribes—they have eccentric views of what constitutes evidence.

Ouch! This put-down of the work of Jameson was neither fair nor accurate, but it worked. Opposition to Streeter's views was effectively silenced.

Well, not quite. During World War I something unexpected had been happening in the life of army chaplain John Chapman. This is his own account of what was happening (1937, 1–3):

> An apology may be thought necessary for any new attempt to elucidate this well-worn subject, and I see no way to make one except by explaining how I came to my present opinions by a complete reversal of my earlier ones. I must give the history of my conversion, because it will show how violently I was torn away by facts from the views to which I clung. This is the excuse for the otherwise absurd egotism of what follows.
>
> I used to think before 1916 that I knew enough about the Synoptic Problem to have a right to a definite opinion on the subject. I held, rather dogmatically, that our Greek St. Matthew depends on St. Mark, and (with somewhat less certainty) that Q, the matter common to Mt. and Lk., was the other source; so that I roughly believed what is called the 'two-document' theory. . . .
>
> At the end of 1915 I was invalided home from the front, and, when I recovered, was sent for a second time to Salisbury Plain as chaplain to a division with which I soon went out again to France. But on Salisbury Plain I had some idle hours, as one could not be the whole time on foot or horseback, and I procured Rushbrooke's *Synopticon* and a Greek Testament as being the simplest elements for interesting study in a hut.

A Quick Look at Some Other Ideas

> I started thus: "It is never good to assume one's own opinion to be infallible, without being able to appreciate the reasons for the other side. Therefore I must assume it possible that tradition really meant that St. Matthew's Gospel was written, as a whole, before St. Mark, and that St. Mark's Gospel is actually an extract from it, and must see whether this can be quite easily disproved."
>
> The fact stared me in the face at once that the ordinary bases of the "two-document" theory are just as consistent with the view that Mt. was first and Mk. second, provided Luke is third.

After his explanation of his "conversion" (his own term) to the theory of Successive Dependence or, one might say, *away* from the theory of Markan Priority, Chapman explains how the observable data can (in his opinion) be accounted for by the different Synoptic theories, and how he proposed a test to decide between them, expecting that the outcome would be the vindication of the view he held: that is, that his test would "set firmly on its feet the 'two-document' hypothesis which was so simple and satisfying and, as it seemed to me at the time, so clearly true" (4). He describes the test and its basis (5):

> If Mk. abbreviated Mt., omitting much, adding next to nothing, since Mk. is carelessly written, with less literary ability than the other Gospels, wherever it makes long omissions we shall find some signs of the gap—perhaps merely want of sequence, for Mt. is very systematic, or even illogical sequence. If there are no such signs—*and there cannot well be, since nobody has noticed them*—I shall conclude quite securely that Mk. is indeed prior to Mt.

Chapman records the details of his test as he applied it to a series of Synoptic passages in succession. He describes (6) his reaction after studying the first two passages (Matt 13:3//Mark 4:2 and Matt 13:34–35//Mark 4:33–34):

> I wonder whether the reader can imagine my surprise on lighting upon A and B, perfectly familiar passages. *I had proposed a test, and I was already answered.* I had imagined, I suppose, some illogical sequence at most, and I expected to find nothing at all; and I had found (apparently) two definite statements by Mark that he had omitted some outdoor parables and indoor explanations. This was astounding.

He went on to Matt 23:1//Mark 12:38 ("example C"), concerning which he says (7), "This coming immediately after A and B, completely bowled me over. No reply is possible. Mk. tells us once more, 'In the course of His teaching He was saying.' What teaching? Look at Mt.; there it is, shoals of it." He concludes his first chapter with the comment (8), "I now see that any form of the 'two-document' theory is a paradox, unworthy of support. I am much ashamed of having held it to be probable."

The data that converted Chapman from the Two-Document Hypothesis to his view of Successive Dependence can be summarized thus:

1. *In many places where Matthew contains and Mark lacks the record of particular teaching by Jesus, Mark contains a reference at that point to another teaching that Jesus gave that he (Mark) does not record (chap. 1 in Chapman).* Thus in Mark 4:2 and again in Mark 12:38 we read, "And in [the course of] his teaching he was saying to them," which could be paraphrased, "Included in Jesus' teaching to them on this occasion was the following." Mark follows this with *some* of the parables or teaching that occurs at that point in Matthew. The explanation that Mark was using Matthew is much more probable than the alternative that Matthew, while reading Mark's Gospel, noticed that Mark referred to more parables than he recorded or to further teaching by Jesus, "so that Mt. thought this was a splendid place for interpolating a number of additional parables" or other material (1936, 6).

2. *In other places where Matthew contains and Mark lacks the record of particular teaching by Jesus, Mark has a summary of what Matthew gives much more fully (chap. 2 in Chapman).* Chapman cites these examples:

D. Matt 24:37–25:46E summarized in Mark 13:33–37.
E. Matt 21:28–22:14 summarized in Mark 12:1–12. (In fact, Mark here gives one parable where Matthew records three, but Mark refers to Jesus' speaking "to them" on this occasion "in parables" [12:1]. This example would have thus been more suited for inclusion in the first category of examples, which Chapman gives in chap. 1.)
F. Matt 17:24–27 is presupposed by Mark 9:33.
G. Matt 18:15–22 is represented by Mark 9:50b.
H. Matt 16:4b–12 is presupposed by Mark 8:13–21.
(Chapman proposes the last two examples tentatively.)

3. *Mark has the appearance of being "Mt. conversationally retold by an eye-witness and ear-witness of what Mt. had set down" (1937, 21).* The stories in Mark are longer and more detailed than in their parallels in Matthew; it is more convincing, on examining them, to explain this as Mark inserting additional eyewitness details (obtained from Peter's preaching, as patristic tradition affirms) than as Matthew "omitting large chunks" of Mark (33). "Mt. not only omits a quantity of Mk's interesting but unessential detail, but even omits detail which in Mk. is essential and his principal point. A good précis writer does not omit the point" (21).

Among his examples Chapman gives (29) the account of the curing of Legion: "We are calmly asked by the upholders of the priority of Mk.

to perceive that Mt.'s story is obviously a précis of Mk.! Why, he omits almost everything that interested Mk., including the main point: the sudden transformation of a most extraordinary maniac, who was possessed by two thousand devils, into a humble disciple and apostle!" Chapman shows that Matthew's account cannot plausibly be explained on the basis that Matthew made a précis of Mark because Matthew is not a summary of Mark but is like Mark though with sections ("chunks," to use Chapman's word) missing from the story (chap. 3 in Chapman, entitled "Matthew Is Not a Précis of Mark"). It is much more reasonable to explain the relationship on the basis that Mark is Matthew's account with additional information added.

By this point in his book Chapman has given the main factors that persuaded him of the priority of Matthew, and the remaining chapters of Book I are an exposition of his view and an attempt to account for some of the perceived problems. In chapter 8 (the last chapter in Book I) Chapman sums up where his investigation has taken him (1937, 89f.). From his survey of the material, two things stand out for him with crystal clarity:

First, Mark used Matthew's Gospel; Matthew did not use Mark's Gospel. This is the inescapable meaning of the evidence. Second, Peter stands solidly behind Mark, and the apostle's touch is to be seen in point after point in this Gospel.

Book II of Chapman's study treats Luke's Gospel. (Chapters are on "On the Impossibility of Q," "The Centurion and the Talents," "Where Luke Follows Matthew," "Why Luke Omitted Bits of Mark and Left Gaps," "How Luke Dealt with Mark," "Luke's Four Additions to His Marcan Matter," and "How St. Luke Wrote His Gospel.") The material in Book II traces Chapman's initial hypothesis (outlined above). Chapman's view of the relationship of Luke to Mark and Matthew is as follows (1937, 130): "Luke had more complications to deal with, for his sources seem to have been multiple, consisting of (a) Mk., (b) a mass of admirable matter accumulated, we know not how, from various sources, oral or written, (c) our Greek Mt., used after the first draft of Lk's work was complete."

I draw attention again to Chapman's comments on Q (98, 126):

> And further, Canon Streeter has shown that certain parts of this unknown document must have overlapped Mk.
>
> Hence we arrive at the absurdity that Q is not only all the heterogeneous resemblances (distant or close) between Mt. and Lk. against Mk., but may include any part of Mk. also (why not the whole of Mk.?) and any part of Mt. peculiar to him and any peculiar to Lk.
>
> Hence *there is no part of the three Synoptic Gospels which may not quite well be derived from Q!* . . .

> Consequently these passages have shown that Q, as a source of Mt. and Lk., independent of Mk., is impossible, since it must include Mk.
>
> I hope the absurdity of all this is clear to the reader. It merely means that *the assumption of a common source for Mt. and Lk. always leads us to find this source to be the common source of three Gospels*. This is not a two-document hypothesis, but a one-document hypothesis, and it is simply a *reduction ad absurdum*. . . .
>
> Q is not a collection of discourses, independent of Mk., *but a name to cover any source one meets with*, and might have included any part, or the whole, of Mt., Mk., or Lk. In fact, it might be the whole Bible.

Chapman's Book III deals with Matthew's Gospel, presenting his view that it is an original composition, initially in Aramaic, and then translated into Greek prior to its use by Peter and John Mark. He explains that Matthew was written by the apostle Matthew in Jerusalem, primarily for Jews (256), and "his Gospel mainly consists in the teaching he heard and wrote down in his notebooks" (258). Chapman sees Matthew's use of Old Testament quotations as providing strong support for this view.

Chapman's book occupied him for the last eight years of his life and was published posthumously in 1937. So far as I can ascertain, it was never reissued after its initial publication.

Barclay and Stonehouse in Response

In spite of the care and thoroughness with which Chapman elucidated his position, his work made rather little impact on Synoptic scholarship. For example, Kümmel (1977) does not so much as mention Chapman's name or book. Many of the writers who refer to Chapman's work do so in passing in a way that suggests that they are not personally acquainted with it. B. Orchard attempts (1977, 125) to explain this neglect of Chapman's work: "It failed to make any impression, firstly because it was published posthumously (Chapman had died in 1933); secondly because the script had been left in an incomplete state at the author's death; and thirdly because it was assumed to be a Roman Catholic apologetic effort rather than a scientific exposition."

In regard to this neglect, a major exception is W. Barclay in his *Introduction to the First Three Gospels* (1975). Barclay has misread Chapman's position at some major points, but notwithstanding this misreading of Chapman, he gave a very fair survey of Chapman's book, taking 14 pages (172–85) for his summary and assessment of Chapman's position. Barclay was not persuaded and still held firmly to Markan Priority. But his thoughtful conclusion is very fair in its acknowledgment of the strength of Chapman's position. In concluding his evaluation of Chapman, Barclay says (184f.):

> That there is a case to present there is no doubt; that that case has been unduly neglected there is also no doubt. Whether the case is strong enough to overturn the widely accepted arguments for the priority of Mark must remain in doubt. It may in the end be safest to say that the view that Mark is the earliest gospel still holds the field, but it cannot be regarded as a totally closed question.

Although he rejects Chapman's position, Barclay does not attempt a detailed rebuttal of his view. N. B. Stonehouse (1963, 73–77) gives such a reply to Chapman. In his assessment of Chapman, Stonehouse centers his attention on demolishing some minor and unimportant peripheral speculations, which Chapman labeled as such—an example of the old cliché "using a sledgehammer to crack a nut" if I ever saw one. But Stonehouse does not face up to, let alone counter, Chapman's serious explanation of why Matthew, not Mark, must be recognized as prior on the basis of a careful comparison of the text.

Butler in Support

In 1951, 14 years after the publication of Chapman's book, B. C. Butler's book on the Synoptic Problem (*The Originality of St Matthew*) appeared. This book, subtitled "A Critique of the Two-Document Hypothesis," was much shorter than Chapman's volume: 179 pages against the 312 larger-sized pages in Chapman; the actual content of Butler's book is only half the size of Chapman's. Butler also supports Successive Dependence. He takes the same basic view as Chapman did and follows a somewhat similar line of argument for it.

Butler commences with a discussion of the primary problem for those who hold to Markan Priority—that this view *on its own* is inadequate to account for the text of the Synoptic Gospels and has to be supplemented by subordinate theories. His first four chapters are devoted to an assessment of Q against the text of Matthew and Luke, and a comparison of the Q explanation with the idea that Luke knew and used Matthew. Butler's assessment (60) is: "The implication is that the Lucan Q passages are derived from Matthew. In chapters III and IV we have tested this conclusion, first in the Lucan parallels to sections of Matthew's Sermon on the Mount, and elsewhere. We have found abundant support for the theory of direct dependence and little evidence tending against that theory."

Chapter 5, which Butler entitles "The Lachmann Fallacy," considers the five "heads of evidence" or arguments Streeter gives for Markan Priority. In Butler's rebuttal of Streeter's position, he shows that "Mark is necessarily the connecting-link between Matthew and Luke in these passages.... The data adduced by Streeter in the 'heads of evidence' referred to at the beginning of this chapter and by Burkitt in the above quotation are quite incapable of giving any indication leading to a more precise determination of the relations obtaining between the three documents than that [just] stated" (1951, 65f.). He then gives three diagrams showing the three possible relationships, all of which he says could equally account for the evidence to which Streeter and Burkitt refer.

This data shows that either (1) Matthew was used by Mark, which was used by Luke (Successive Dependence with Matthean Priority); or (2) Mark was a source for Matthew and Luke (Markan Priority); or (3) Luke was used by Mark, which was used by Matthew (Successive Dependence with Lukan Priority). Butler does not include as a possibility the relationship that Mark used both Matthew and Luke (Markan Dependence, the Griesbach Hypothesis) since he had already considered this and concluded (3): "This is not a solution, because it does not explain the agreements between *all three* documents, which are part of the assumed data."

Butler further comments (67f.) on Streeter's five "heads of evidence":

> The fifth turns out to contain no evidence in proof of Streeter's theory, but a series of deductions from it, with a rather closer examination than that hitherto attempted in *The Four Gospels* of the placing of the "Marcan tradition" in Matthew and Luke. Thus only the fourth head of evidence contains any argument tending to support the theory of Marcan priority to the exclusion of all other solutions. Not five convergent sets of evidence, but one only.

He then proceeds to his rebuttal of Streeter's fourth argument.

In chapter 6 Butler addresses the question of the priority of Matthew or Mark and a comment made (75) on one of the many passages he considers is representative of his conclusion in relation to them all: "The conclusion must be accepted that Mark is here excerpting from Matthew."

In chapters 7–11 Butler considers a wide range of other points raised in support of Markan Priority. Many of his rebuttals are similar to points I have made in relation to Markan Priority in this present book.

Styler and Stonehouse in Response

Butler's book received more serious attention from scholars than had Chapman's before him. Two of the most careful treatments are those by G. M. Styler (1962) and N. B. Stonehouse (1963), and we shall note their evaluations. Styler writes (223–24):

> After a century or more of discussion, it has come to be accepted by scholars almost as axiomatic that Mark is the oldest of the three synoptic gospels and

A Quick Look at Some Other Ideas

that it was used by Matthew and Luke as a source. This has come to be regarded as "the one absolutely assured result" of the study of the synoptic problem. It has also been usually agreed that, besides Mark, Matt. and Lk. shared another source of material, denoted by the symbol "Q."...

But it came as a shock when in 1951 Dom B. C. Butler published his book *The Originality of St. Matthew*, attacking the Q-hypothesis and the priority of Mark at the same time. In a minutely detailed study he subjected both hypotheses to a severe criticism, and argued strongly for the priority of Matt. Mk., he argued, was dependent on Matt.; Lk. was dependent on Mk. for the material which the two had in common, and on Matt. for the Q-material.

Styler acknowledges (225) that Butler's attack was completely successful in demonstrating that Streeter's first three arguments do not establish Markan Priority: "Now it is obvious that the priority of Mk. will satisfactorily *explain* these phenomena. But its advocates have made a serious mistake in arguing (or assuming) that no *other* hypothesis will explain them. Butler is correct in claiming that they are guilty of a fallacy in reasoning."

Styler considers that the other reasons for accepting Markan Priority remain completely valid, and he is far from being persuaded to Butler's alternative. He carefully evaluates these other reasons and is therefore able to say (224):

In spite of much close and careful reasoning, and the existence of at any rate *some* passages which tell in favour of Butler's conclusion, scholars have not abandoned the usual belief in the priority of Mk. In this Excursus it will not be possible to examine all Butler's arguments and instances one by one. But an attempt will be made to show that the belief in the priority of Mk. is in fact securely grounded, and to make clear the principal arguments on either side, on which the decision must turn.

One of the foundational tenets of Butler's position is that there is no Q, and the material common to Matthew and Luke was derived by Luke directly from Matthew. Styler considers the sources that are needed, on both theories, to account for what is found in the Synoptics, and concludes (231): "Our explanation of *his* favourable cases may be cumbersome; but his explanation of *our* favourable cases is incredible." Styler's Excursus concludes (232) with the judgment, "Until some less incredible explanation is forthcoming, the natural conclusion that Mk is prior to Matt. will continue to hold the field."

There is no doubt that many students of the Synoptics are appreciative of Styler's work and consider it to be an effective reply to Butler. The Styler Excursus is highly regarded and widely quoted.

Almost simultaneously with the publication of Moule's *Birth of the New Testament* containing Styler's Excursus, there appeared—in the following year (1963) in America, and the year after that in Britain—another book that took account of Butler's arguments: *Origins of the Synoptic Gospels* by N. B. Stonehouse, to which I have referred earlier. He shows the implausibility of Butler's view that Luke used Matthew (60–61, 65), and he does discuss (79–83) Butler's treatment of Streeter's "fourth head," but although he refers to Butler more than half a dozen times he never really attempts a detailed rebuttal, especially of Butler's case that Mark used Matthew rather than vice versa. He says (79), in evaluation of Butler's writing, "Although Butler's discussion of these materials is worthy of close attention, it does not seem to me to be necessary to enter upon a detailed treatment of it. In weighing the evidence which he presents one would have to keep in view that he is virtually presupposing the validity of his own theory of Gospel relationships."

We can now therefore proceed to summarize the arguments that scholars have offered in opposition to the Successive Dependence Hypothesis of Chapman and Butler. Chapman's book is a very detailed work of serious scholarship, and it is a matter of some surprise—both when it first appeared and since then—that scholars in general have either ignored it or dismissed it in very cavalier fashion. The reasons for this may well include those listed earlier as suggested by Orchard: it was published posthumously, had been left incomplete at the author's death, and was assumed to be a Roman Catholic apologetic effort. But there is one other major reason to which Barclay drew our attention: at some of the crucial points of his reasoning, Chapman's hypothesis was singularly unconvincing. Butler's arguments against the Two-Document Hypothesis received (as noted above) more serious attention from scholars than those of Chapman; but his presentation of the Successive Dependence alternative proved no more convincing.

The objections taken to these presentations were:

1. Their presentations of why, if he was using Matthew, Mark omitted so much valuable material that Matthew contains is totally unconvincing.

2. The order of pericopes in Matthew, Mark, and Luke cannot be satisfactorily explained on the Successive Dependence Hypothesis.

3. It strains our credulity to conceive of why, upon encountering such well-organized material as contained in the early chapters of Matthew (particularly the Sermon on the Mount), Luke would break up this material and place snippets of it scattered through his own Gospel.

4. Luke has made no use of substantial and significant sections of Matthew, such as the nativity story and resurrection appearances. It is not merely that Luke does not *use* this material from Matthew (it is reasonable to say that it was impractical, from length considerations, for Luke

to use *everything* he saw in Matthew), but rather that he writes his nativity story, resurrection accounts, and numerous other pericopes as if he was *completely unaware* of what was in Matthew. This is a weighty argument that has considerable force and cannot be lightly dismissed.

Assessment

Augustine's initial view of Synoptic interrelationships has continued to be accepted by some scholars down to the last century. In particular, Chapman and Butler expounded this hypothesis and attacked the standard arguments given for Markan Priority and belief in Q. Now, taken together, the various objections that have been described present a strong case for rejecting the second part of Successive Dependence—that Luke knew and used Matthew—as a satisfactory part of a solution to the Synoptic Problem. (See chap. 8 for the reasons that I have rejected this possibility.) But the Chapman-Butler case for rejecting the idea of Mark as being prior to Matthew—and especially Butler's critique of Streeter's arguments for Markan Priority—are to be recognized as very well taken indeed. These scholars have drawn attention to some serious weaknesses in the customary arguments that had been put forward to substantiate the Markan Priority/ Two-Document theory. Numerous Gospel scholars have recognized the force of these criticisms and have adjusted their case for Markan Priority accordingly. Yet those same arguments continue to be advanced in current works of scholarship as if Chapman and Butler had never tackled the issues!

Stonehouse demolished one peripheral and subordinate suggestion by Chapman—as Chapman himself calls it, "a fiction devised to explain one feature of the theory of Matthean priority"—but Stonehouse failed to direct himself to Chapman's careful argument for the view that an examination of the text of Matthew and Mark shows that Mark used Matthew and not vice versa.

A comment by Streeter (1924, 168f.) on "Matthew or Luke purposely omitting any whole section of their source" is worth noting in connection with our present consideration:

> Very often we can surmise reasons of an apologetic nature why the Evangelists may have thought some things less worth reporting. But, even when we can detect no particular motive, we cannot assume that there was none; for we cannot possibly know, either all the circumstances of churches, or all the personal idiosyncrasies of writers so far removed from our own time.

But the plain fact is that Chapman's arguments showing that Mark was subsequent to Matthew and that Mark used Matthew—arguments pointing out how frequently it happens that when Mark omits or abbreviates Christ's teaching he refers to the longer and more detailed records of this teaching which can be found given in Matthew—*have not yet been answered.* Ignored, yes, but not answered.

In chapter 7 I discussed the kinds of material in Mark that made such an impact on Chapman. These points from Chapman should be noted in particular:

1. Chapman has drawn attention to evidence that Mark often summarized material that he did not include but that is found in Matthew; and at other times Mark refers to the fact that he is giving only some of the teaching of Jesus, and at that point Matthew contains further teaching (additional parables, etc).

2. Chapman claims it is more reasonable to explain the extra information in Mark that is lacking in Matthew as "Mark inserting additional eyewitness details from Peter's preaching" rather than as Matthew "omitting large chunks" of Mark.

3. Chapman examines the passages that Matthew and Luke have in common and sees it as far more reasonable to accept that Luke had seen Matthew than that one must invoke, to explain these, an unattested Q that "may include any part of Mk. also (why not the whole of Mk.?) and any part of Mt. peculiar to him and any peculiar part of Lk. Hence there is no part of the three Synoptic Gospels which may not quite well be derived from Q!"

I do not agree that the *best* answer to this situation, in the light of all the evidence, is that Luke used Matthew; but Chapman certainly gives (as quoted above) a trenchant critique of the Q theory!

Butler addresses himself to the standard arguments for Markan Priority, and in particular much of his book is directed to making a case against Q. He asserts that Q is an unnecessary hypothesis that is unsupported by the evidence and contrary to probabilities, which would point to Luke's use of Matthew as the explanation of the non-Markan material that they have in common. His major arguments in support of Successive Dependence are along the same lines as those of Chapman above, and in addition they cover one further area:

4. Butler provides further evidence for concluding that Mark used Matthew rather than that Matthew used Mark.

These four points from Chapman and Butler are worthy of the most careful consideration. However the case for Successive Dependence fails in relation to putting Luke last.

First, it really is impossible to find a coherent explanation of what Luke (as the Successive Dependence Hypothesis claims) would have done in relation to the order of pericopes that he found confronting him in Matthew's and Mark's Gospels. For sometimes they agree and sometimes they do not. He would have had to choose always to follow Mark when his order differed from that of Matthew (thus creating a Mark-Luke agreement in sequence whenever Mark would otherwise have been on his own), while feeling quite free to desert Markan order in those sections—and *only* in those sections— where Mark is adhering to Matthew's order (as there are places where there is a Mark-Matthew agreement in pericope sequence, with Luke departing from it). And Luke is *never* found agreeing with Matthew's order where Mark does not (else there would be a Matthew-Luke agreement against Mark—which there never is) or else going off totally on his own (which also never happens).

This situation could never have arisen by accident; that would be far too improbable to imagine. But the mind boggles to conjecture a reason for such a bizarre procedure as the Successive Dependence Hypothesis requires Luke to have adopted.

Second, also inexplicable is the breaking-up of Matthew's teaching (and, occasionally, ministry) blocks and redistributing the material from them that Luke uses in small snippets in other contexts throughout his Gospel.

Third, the places where Luke shows no awareness of what Matthew says (as I have described in chap. 8) also rule out this theory.

A variant possibility could be that Luke was third and used only Mark, not Matthew. But this leaves all the problems of Matthew-Luke agreements in the so-called Q material and does nothing to solve the enigma of pericope order.

No, these problems are too conclusive. Yes, Mark used Matthew, as this theory says. But Luke cannot be put third and after Mark.

OTHER HYPOTHESES

Surveying the Scene

Since the nineteenth century, just about every combination and permutation of sources that human imagination can devise has been proposed to explain the relationship of Matthew, Mark, and Luke. Apart from those already covered—which have been far and away the most influential— there are several others that should be given consideration for the sake of completeness, and in recognition of those who hold or have held them. And beyond those that I specifically mention, there are other combinations and variations of all these hypotheses, virtually without limit.

The number and variety of these is some indication of the complexity of the Synoptic Problem. The development and exposition of these proposals over the years represents the investment of a very considerable amount of time and effort by a vast army of diligent scholars committed to the search for a convincing answer. It must be remembered that, even when some line of investigation may lead to what is now seen as a dead end, that very fact is itself a valuable contribution to the sum total of our knowledge of the whole matter. Here then are four other explanations that we can agree are worthy of mention, even if ultimately I suggest that they are among the dead ends.

The Farrer Hypothesis

Oxford scholar A. Farrer published an article called "On Dispensing with Q" (1955) that proposed a new Synoptic theory: Q was an unnecessary hypothesis and was contrary to the evidence when that evidence was rightly understood. This theory was developed and further publicized by M. Goulder, and thus it can be referred to as the "Farrer-Goulder Theory." Its most able current proponent is M. Goodacre (*The Synoptic Problem: A Way through the Maze*, 2001). Goodacre comments (22) concerning the Farrer Theory: "Michael Goulder, originally a pupil of Austin Farrer, has become the key advocate for this theory, devoting two books and many articles to arguing the case with vigour. Over the years, the theory has gathered a handful of prominent supporters. In Great Britain it is this thesis that has become the Two-Source Theory's greatest rival." Goodacre explains the theory (123): "Q has no part to play in the Farrer Theory, which is also known as . . . 'Markan Priority without Q.' . . . The Farrer Theory affirms Markan Priority but suggests that Luke also knew and used Matthew, which enables one to dispense with Q."

Goodacre's book sets out first of all to demonstrate the validity of the Markan Priority explanation. Mark is recognized as prior because of its simplistic and less-than-reverential view of both Jesus and the disciples (27, 60), because of its primitive nature (62), and because it would be difficult and unconvincing to seek to explain the contents of this Gospel (both what it contains and what it omits) if it were written after, and drawing on, Matthew (59, 67). Matthew and Luke wrote to improve Mark's language and to correct some errors that Mark contains. Both Matthew and Luke are guilty themselves of "inconsistencies" (74) and "continuity errors" (75)—and these actually disclose the fact that they were "working from a source" (74), that is, Mark.

A Quick Look at Some Other Ideas

The Farrer Theory then investigates the case for Q and finds it lacking. Instead, all the double traditions in Luke can be accounted for readily and simply on the basis of Luke's use of Matthew. Why then is Luke's order so different from Matthew's, particularly in the first half of his Gospel? Goodacre (125) explains:

> The answer is that Luke is highly unlikely to have wanted to follow this more rigid arrangement that we find in Matthew, in which one cannot help thinking that the narrative flow is severely and frequently compromised. From what we know of Luke's literary sensitivity and artistic ability, we are bound to conclude that Luke would not have found Matthew's restructuring of Mark congenial.

Luke similarly dislikes Matthew's "lengthy discourses" and breaks them up. Indeed (127), "on the Farrer Theory... Luke is making it clear that he is critical of his predecessors' work and that his radical reordering of Matthew is in Theophilus's best interests." Furthermore (127), "Matthew provided the direct catalyst for Luke's reworking of Mark. He sees what Matthew has done: he has reworked Mark by adding birth and infancy narratives at one end of the Gospel, a resurrection story at the other end, and added lots of sayings material in the middle. Perhaps, Luke thinks, *he can do the same thing, but do it better.*"

Goodacre clearly states (108) the possibilities as he sees them:

> The Double Tradition material of this kind might be explained in any of three ways:
>
> 1. Matthew used Luke.
> 2. Luke used Matthew.
> 3. Matthew and Luke both used a third document now lost to us.

Goodacre has an "all or nothing" approach to deciding between these options. He says (112), after quoting some Synoptic sections, "And if Luke was ignorant of Matthew in passages like these, he was ignorant of Matthew everywhere, and so the Q hypothesis becomes necessary in order to make sense of the Double Tradition."

But Goodacre sees evidence throughout Luke that the author knew Matthew. Thus the conclusion is drawn that Luke must have known the entire Gospel of Matthew as we now have it. And he must have reworked both it and Mark into his own pattern, as this was "in Theophilus's best interests."

The Farrer theory is refuted in this present book—regarding its dependence on Markan Priority (see chap. 5) and regarding its proposition that

Luke knew the whole Gospel of Matthew (chap. 8)—by the explanation that Luke collected and used early documents written by Matthew.

The Lukan Priority Hypothesis

The first modern explanation of Synoptic relationships to be proposed was H. Owen's (1764) hypothesis that Mark was the third Gospel author to write and that he made use of both Matthew and Luke. Two years later A. F. Büsching advocated the order Luke-Matthew-Mark. Neither of these authors created much of an impact in the scholarly world. Griesbach (1783) began to argue for the Markan Posteriority view, which thereafter became widely popular. But Büsching's hypothesis languished.

Then (this covers almost 200 years!) R. L. Lindsey (1963), a Baptist pastor in Jerusalem, published the outcome of research that led him to the view of the priority of Luke's Gospel. (For the following details I am indebted to information on the Internet.) Lindsey independently reached a solution to the Synoptic Problem. He proposed a theory of Lukan Priority that argues that Luke was written first and was used by Mark. This theory postulates two noncanonical documents that were unknown to the synoptists—a Hebrew biography of Jesus and a literal Greek translation of that original—and two other noncanonical sources known to one or more of the synoptists.

Lindsey arrived at his theory unintentionally. Attempting to replace F. Delitzsch's outdated Hebrew translation of the New Testament, he began by translating the Gospel of Mark since he assumed it was the earliest of the Synoptic Gospels. Although Mark's text is relatively Semitic, it contains hundreds of non-Semitisms, such as the oft-repeated "and immediately," that are not present in Lukan parallels. This suggested to Lindsey the possibility that Mark was copying Luke and not vice versa. After further research Lindsey came to his solution to the Synoptic Problem.

Several scholars in Israel, most prominently D. Flusser of the Hebrew University, have espoused Lindsey's source theory. These scholars, now collaborating as the Jerusalem School of Synoptic Research (JSSR), believe that a Hebrew *Vorlage* lies behind the Greek texts of the Gospels. They maintain that by translating the Greek texts back into Hebrew and interpreting how this Hebrew text would have been understood by first-century readers, one gains a fuller understanding of the original meaning of the text.

The JSSR is actively engaged in developing and promoting its viewpoint of Synoptic Relationships. One of its members, H. Ronning of the Hebrew University, gave a presentation of the JSSR's hypothesis (i.e., Lukan Priority) at the Evangelical Theological Society Annual Meeting in Washington, D.C., in November 2006. The JSSR believes that its studies can make a significant contribution to Synoptic scholarship.

I find that this hypothesis takes an interesting slant on a number of Synoptic passages. I am intrigued by the emphasis of the JSSR on the Hebrew background of the Gospels, for there is indeed room for further research in this matter. I certainly agree with its rejection of the idea of Markan Priority. However, I do not find that it calls into question in any way the hypothesis I am propounding for the origins of the Greek Synoptic Gospels.

The Ur-Gospel Hypothesis

Among the varied proposals put forward in the last decades of the eighteenth century to explain the writing of the Synoptic Gospels was G. E. Lessing's Ur-Gospel Hypothesis. Lessing believed that an original Gospel, an Ur-Gospel (German for "primal gospel"), had existed that was the basis from which our three canonical Gospels have been derived. Lessing identified this Ur-Gospel with the Aramaic *Gospel of the Nazarenes* that Jerome mentioned as known to him. Lessing states (1957, 70–71) that it was in due course "found necessary . . . to make extracts or translations of" the Ur-Gospel in Greek, and "The first of these extracts, the first of these translations, was made, I think, by Matthew." So in turn did Luke, and then Mark. Thus Lessing postulated that there was one original written Gospel behind, and a source for, the three canonical Synoptic Gospels—an original Ur-Gospel.

Others have taken up this basic concept of an Ur-Gospel and explained the idea further. In particular J. G. Eichhorn advanced (1794/1804) a very complicated version of the primal Gospel hypothesis that won little support, and then K. Lachmann developed (1835) the thesis that all three Synoptics are dependent on a common original source, and in particular he believed they drew their order of pericopes from it.

Since Mark's order always accords with that of either Matthew or Luke (or both, where they agree), some claim that this means Mark's is the basic order from which Matthew or Luke may from time to time depart. This indicates that Mark reproduces the order of the Ur-Gospel most exactly, while Matthew and Luke reproduce it most of the time. Mark's order must be the order of the Ur-Gospel, for if Matthew's Gospel reproduces the order of the Ur-Gospel we would be faced with the necessity of saying that when Mark and Luke agree with each other but differ from Matthew, it is because each of them had independently but in identical fashion departed from the

Ur-Gospel order at each such point, and this is not credible. Similarly, if Luke had reproduced the original Ur-Gospel order, we would be required to believe that Mark and Matthew had deserted that order to adopt, quite independently, an identical alternative order. These factors indicate that all three Synoptics derive their basic order from the one original source, an Ur-Gospel, and that this order is now preserved for us in Mark.

But Mark is the connection between Matthew and Luke, not only in pericope order but also in content and wording. An application of the same line of reasoning to this feature demonstrates that Mark similarly preserves best the content and wording of the Ur-Gospel. So in this way the Ur-Gospel has been recognized as an original source used by all three Synoptists but most accurately reproduced in Mark.

G. Salmon avers that the use of such an original Gospel by the three Synoptists would provide a complete explanation of all the similarities in their Gospels. And it would pose no problem to account for the minor differences between them. Salmon explains (1889, 133) these with some care. He sums up his own conclusions in this matter in this way (155f.):

> Does it follow, then, that Mark's was the earliest Gospel of all, and that it was used by the other two Evangelists? Not necessarily; and the result of such comparison as I have been able to make is to lead me to believe that Matthew and Luke did not copy Mark, but that all drew from a common source, which, however, is represented most fully and with most verbal exactness in St. Mark's version.

In the twentieth century numerous scholars took it in hand to respond to this Ur-Gospel Hypothesis and very effectively refuted it. The major objections were:

1. The Ur-Gospel that was proposed was an Aramaic document, but, as H. H. Stoldt points out (1980, 4), the Synoptic correspondence in the New Testament is between Greek documents. And no original Aramaic Gospel has ever been found!

2. The Ur-Gospel Hypothesis can account for Synoptic similarities, but to account for the differences between the Synoptic accounts, very unconvincing complexities have to be introduced. Stoldt (4) explains the nature of this difficulty:

> The main difficulty of the written ur-gospel hypothesis was how to offer a credible explanation of the extensive divergences, which at times cover complete chapters, while still insisting on a *common* written basic text, namely the ur-gospel. If the representatives of this theory were going to solve these manifold problems, there was no other way than to take refuge in numerous auxiliary hypotheses in the form of several assumed revisions or translations of the alleged Aramaic original text. What this ultimately meant was that they had

to construct an artful, ingeniously-reasoned super-structure of hypotheses that embraces about twenty auxiliary theories. With their aid it was then possible to "explain" almost all of the phenomena of concordance and of discrepancy between the individual synoptic Gospels. "Exceptions" were acknowledged which were made to appear harmless, but, due to the real impossibility of the over-refined pyramid of hypotheses, this approach to the problem generated its own *reductio ad absurdum*. Thus research of the previous century rejected both the oral and the written ur-gospel solutions—and justifiably so. They belong to the misinterpretations of the Gospels.

3. The Ur-Gospel Hypothesis requires that this primal Gospel contained many things that were not taken over by each of the Synoptists as in his turn he derived his material from it. H. C. Thiessen makes the point (1979, 103f.) that "the theory cannot account for the omissions in the several Gospels of materials that were pertinent to their evident purpose. If the writers had all these materials before them, why then did they not include all in their source that furthered their objectives?"

4. The supreme objection is how such a comprehensive Gospel as this Ur-Gospel could exist, be utilized as a source by our three Synoptists, but never be described or even actually mentioned by the early church writers, and then completely disappear without a trace. W. Barclay stated (1975, 173): "If there was such a gospel, it would be very odd that there is no trace of it." Thiessen concurred (103): "The theory of an Urevangelium has no historical support and is improbable to a high degree. If our Gospels are but excerpts from this 'source,' why was not the source itself preserved?"

5. The most popular version of the Ur-Gospel Hypothesis was that it was a "first draft" of Mark, or a source from which Mark drew heavily, the Ur-Markus proposal. Kümmel outlines (1975, 61–63) the case for this view and after examining it briefly comes to this conclusion: "Since none of the arguments for an *Urmarkus* or for a document used also by Mk is convincing, by far the most probable conclusion is that in the form handed down to us Mk served as a source for Mt and Lk."

F. C. Burkitt provided (1911, 33–64) the most extensive treatment of the Ur-Gospel (or, specifically, the Ur-Markus) Hypothesis. S. Neill says (1966, 118–19) that the best proof against the Ur-Gospel theory is Burkitt's book. Burkitt's assessment (58) is:

> These passages afford the strongest evidence that can be found against the supposition that Matthew and Luke used our Mark much as it has come down to us. It appears to me that the evidence is extremely weak, and that we are not compelled by it to imagine a hypothetical *Ur-Marcus*, a Gospel very much like our Mark, only slightly different here and there, differing, in fact, very much

as a first edition of a modern book may differ from the second or subsequent editions.

This allows Burkitt to come now to this conclusion (59, 64): "We have looked well over this [material], and found no irresistible argument for an *Ur-Marcus*, for an earlier edition of our Mark.... All these things tend to demonstrate the originality of our Mark, and therefore to shew that 'Ur-Marcus' either never existed or was almost indistinguishable from the Mark we possess."

Thus Burkitt looked for evidence of a difference between our Gospel of Mark and what the Ur-Markus must have been like, and he found none; thus he drew the conclusion that Ur-Markus and Mark are one and the same. This means that canonical Mark is the source of the common material it shares with Matthew and Luke and that there is no original Gospel that was used by all three Synoptists as a source. In this manner Burkitt has moved Gospel scholarship from an Ur-Gospel explanation to Ur-Markus, and then removed the Ur-Markus so that we have ended up with Mark as the source for Matthew and Luke—thus we have arrived at Markan Priority.

In various versions, the Ur-Gospel Hypothesis had a significant following in the eighteenth and nineteenth centuries. D. L. Dungan (1970, 81) remarks, "If one were to survey the entire literature from its beginnings in the late 18th century, the most popular solution—representing the largest percentage of all that has ever been written on the subject—would clearly be the Urgospel approach."

What are we now to say of this theory? There is no doubt that an Ur-Gospel explanation can be given for the phenomena of the Synoptic Gospels. What is not so easy to explain is why, given such an Ur-Gospel, our Synoptic Gospels would be written at all, why such a significant document would not be quoted from or at least referred to, and why it would have been permitted to vanish without a trace. (Lessing's identification of it with the lost *Gospel of the Nazarenes* lacks any evidence to support it.)

In brief, there is no actual evidence in support of the existence of an Ur-Gospel—it is at best a hypothetical possibility—and there are quite a few weighty arguments against this hypothesis. It is only to be expected that, as Stoldt says (4), "research of the previous century rejected... urgospel solutions—and justifiably so. They belong to the misinterpretation of the Gospels."

In view of this modern rejection of the Ur-Gospel or Ur-Markus Hypothesis, one may wonder why this book should pay attention to it at all. The significance of this has been explained in considerable detail by Butler. One of the major arguments that has been propounded in support of the

Markan Priority Hypothesis is the relationship of the order of pericopes in Mark to that of the other two Synoptics. In Lachmann's original exposition of this feature, he showed how the relative order of Matthew, Mark, and Luke could be effectively explained on the basis that all three derived their material from an Ur-Gospel, and that Mark adhered to its order more consistently than the other two. Although modern scholarship has successfully removed the Ur-Gospel from this explanation, many adherents of Markan Priority can be found who continue to hold to the outcome of the argument from order as if the Ur-Gospel were still there.

One is reminded of a farmer's explanation of the mysteries of the telephone and the radio to his young son. The working of the telephone, he explained, is like if you kick a bull at one end, and it bellows at the other. "And radio, dad?" "It's exactly the same, son, only without the bull."

The original theory was that Matthew and Luke did not derive from Mark but rather, with Mark, from an earlier Ur-Gospel that Mark followed more closely than the others. The Synoptic connections were to this original document, *not* to each other. But in the later form of the theory, as we have traced it, Mark is the source for Matthew and Luke, and the separate derivations of all three from a common earlier source have gone. No change in the basic logic of the argument is detected. "It's exactly the same, son, only without the bull." But is it indeed exactly the same?

Butler devotes several pages to a careful explanation that after you identify Ur-Markus and Mark as the same, and then remove Ur-Markus from consideration, you have totally changed the terms—and thus the validity—of the argument. He spells this out in considerable detail (63–65), and this exposé of the faulty logic of this form of the argument from order proved to be a very effective rebuttal of Streeter's claim that the Synoptic order of pericopes pointed to Markan Priority—a point that Styler and all serious Synoptic scholars have acknowledged ever since Butler.

So the Ur-Gospel Hypothesis has been put to rest. But it has left this legacy: the idea that the order of pericopes points to Markan Priority. This error also "belongs to the misinterpretations of the Gospels" (as Stoldt puts it)—and it should also now be put firmly to rest.

The Multiple Sources Hypothesis

The original form of the Ur-Gospel Hypothesis is now regarded as dead in the water. However, in its more developed form its advocates needed, as Stoldt describes (4) it,

> to construct an artful, ingeniously-reasoned super-structure of hypotheses that embraces about twenty auxiliary theories. With their aid it was then possible

to "explain" almost all of the phenomena of concordance and of discrepancy between the individual synoptic Gospels. "Exceptions" were acknowledged which were made to appear harmless, but, due to the real impossibility of the over-refined pyramid of hypotheses, this approach to the problem generated its own *reductio ad absurdum*.

Without these extremes, but having ideas in common, as a variant version of a form of the Ur-Gospel Hypothesis, is a Multiple-Stage or Proto-Gospels Hypothesis, currently advocated by M.-E. Boismard and P. Rolland. There are varieties of multi-source theories or explanations with significant features in common. Boismard postulates (1972, 2:17; this volume is an introduction and commentary on the Gospels) seven hypothetical documents that lie behind the canonical Synoptics, and these documents explain their interrelationships. They comprise four original source documents, together with earlier versions of each of the canonical Synoptic Gospels that Boismard calls Intermediate-Matthew, Intermediate-Mark, and Proto-Luke.

The four original source documents and their interrelationships are:

Document Q: source for Intermediate-Matthew and Proto-Luke;
Document A: source for Intermediate-Matthew, Intermediate- Mark, and Document B;
Document B: source for Intermediate-Mark and Proto-Luke;
Document C: similarly, source for Intermediate-Mark and Proto-Luke;
Intermediate-Matthew: derived from A and Q, and used by Matthew and Mark;
Intermediate-Mark: derived from A, B, and C, and used by Matthew, Mark, and Luke;
Proto-Luke: derived from B, C, and Q, and used by Mark and Luke;
(Canonical) Matthew: derived from Intermediate-Matthew and Intermediate-Mark;
(Canonical) Mark: derived from Intermediate-Matthew, Intermediate-Mark, and Proto-Luke;
(Canonical) Luke: derived from Intermediate-Mark and Proto-Luke.

It can be seen that anything that occurs in Mark can be a source for anything in Matthew or Luke by attributing it to Intermediate-Mark, which was used by Matthew, Mark, and Luke; and this gives the hypothesis some features in common with Markan Priority. But further, it can be seen that anything in Matthew or Luke can be a source for anything in Mark by attributing it to Intermediate-Matthew and/or Proto-Luke, both of which were sources for Mark; and this gives the hypothesis some features in common with Markan Dependence. This makes it possible to encompass in support of this theory virtually anything that has been adduced in support of Markan Priority or Markan Dependence. However, it should be noted that all relationships occur at a Proto-Gospel stage; there are no *direct* relationships between the canonical Synoptics Matthew, Mark, and Luke.

The details of the hypothesis have been worked out in considerable detail by Boismard in his commentary on the Synoptics, but the general scholarly response has been that the theory is too complex (and unnecessarily so), and that it postulates rather specific hypothetical documents for which there is little direct evidence. In response to these criticisms, at the 1984 Jerusalem Symposium, Boismard reduced the complexity of his seven hypothetical documents to a pre-Matthew, a pre-Mark, and a pre-Luke, and underlined its distinctiveness from Markan Priority and Markan Dependence (see further below).

Rolland, a colleague of Boismard's, offered a Proto-Gospel Hypothesis that has a number of significant points of difference from that of Boismard but that overall is basically a simplified version of it. Rolland delineates (1984, 232–44) the differences between his theory and Boismard's. The starting point of Rolland's discussion is the statement in Luke 1:1–3 that others before him had taken it in hand to record Gospel narratives. Rolland shows (25ff.) that Matthew cannot have known Luke or Luke Matthew, so he concludes that this rules out (*inter alia*) the Griesbach view. He also discusses "confluence" (conflation) and says he has noted 82 examples in his article ("Mark, the First Gospel Harmony?"), where he also lists 31 places where Mark contains a combination of two ideas or concepts, one of which is found in Matthew and the other in Luke.

Boismard and Rolland were the two major speakers at the 1984 Jerusalem Symposium presenting the Multiple-Stage or Proto-Gospels viewpoint. These extracts from the first two pages of their opening position paper (in French) can be translated as follows:

> The diverse theories of Multiple Stages have in common the following fundamental principle, by which they are distinguished from both the Two-Gospel and the Two-Source hypotheses: in all the material common to the three Synoptics, the agreements between the Gospels are to be explained, not by direct dependence, but by appealing to older, hypothetical sources from which they are derived. For example, the literary contacts between Matthew and Mark would be explained not by direct dependence of Matthew upon Mark where they agree (the Two-Sources hypothesis) nor of Mark upon Matthew (the Two-Gospel hypothesis), but by dependence upon one or several hypothetical sources that are postulated to have existed, whether a Proto-Matthew, or a Proto-Mark, or some further anonymous documents.

> The Synoptic Problem is a complex problem; it can only be resolved by a complex solution. The Two-Source hypothesis and the Two-Gospel hypothesis are too simplistic to account for *all* the literary data that are to be observed. It is too simple to affirm the absolute priority of Mark in its agreements with Matthew and Luke; it is too simple to affirm the absolute priority of Matthew in its agreements with Luke and Mark. Priority must sometimes be accorded to Matthew, sometimes to Mark, and sometimes to Luke, according as the one or the other of these Gospels will have remained more faithful than the others to their common sources.

When they presented their views at the Jerusalem Symposium, the difference was particularly noticeable between their approach and that of the Two-Source Hypothesis team. F. Neirynck was the leader of the Two-Source team, and C. Tuckett was one of the team's most active and able spokesmen. Neirynck's main 122-page presentation to the Symposium is noteworthy in that only a very small part of it is occupied with general discussion of issues, and he moves as quickly as possible to the consideration of actual pericopes and what can be learned from their comparison: the explanation of differences between two Synoptic authors is to be found in the redaction of one by the other, and at this level of investigation one can learn in which direction the copying and redaction has occurred.

It was interesting that during one of the Symposium discussions between Neirynck and Boismard, one of the participants sitting near me leaned over and commented, "When Boismard sees a difference between two Synoptic passages he cries, 'Different sources!' and when Neirynck comes across a difference he cries, 'Redaction!'"

The Multi Sources approach has not commended itself widely. However, if instead of the range of particular hypothetical documents postulated by Boismard (as above), one were to recognize that the evidence is pointing towards multiple documents from apostolic and other eyewitness sources, one has come very close to the Progressive Publication of Matthew Hypothesis set out in this present book. This is in fact the logical conclusion (and one, moreover, that requires fewer hypothetical sources) of the Multi Source theories. I invite adherents of Multi Source theories to give consideration to this.

CONCLUSION

These different views have played a significant role in the history of Synoptic studies. Some of them, in their variant forms, continue to be strongly advocated in the present day. They cannot be said to be without any basis. They have each derived from some aspect of Synoptic data which has been identified: an area of data which is well and validly explained by this view or that. But in the last analysis these views are all inadequate as an explanation of Gospel relationships, for each of these views leaves too many unexplained problems for it to be accepted as a satisfactory explanation. There are too many aspects of the data that they do not cover or for which they cannot adequately account.

I have shown that those areas where one view or another has duly identified important data needing to be taken into account are equally well explained (indeed in most cases, better explained) by the Progressive Publication of Matthew Hypothesis, including Markan Dependence. And this hypothesis, presented here, is able to clarify and resolve those places where the various other views lead down a blind alley.

The Progressive Publication of Matthew Hypothesis accords with each of these other views where that view includes some valid insight into an aspect of the Synoptic Problem, and it provides a better explanation where these other views are inadequate or unconvincing. In fact, it is possible to say that the hypothesis here presented represents a development of the insights of these other views, a development that offers an explanation of the data where these earlier views have fallen short.

11 NOW TAKE THE CASE OF THE RICH YOUNG MAN

This chapter is a detailed examination of a key pericope and some other passages from the perspectives of both Markan Priority and Markan Dependence.

> Study of the history of research may help one to recognize where the strengths and weaknesses of different hypotheses have been felt to lie, but one must in the end examine the text itself to see which is the best explanation of the source question.
> —Christopher M. Tuckett (1983, 7)

> "It is undesirable to believe a proposition when there is no ground whatsoever for supposing it true."
> —Bertrand Russell
> (quoted by James Reston
> in the *Sydney Morning Herald*, January 25, 1985)

THE SIGNIFICANCE OF THIS EXAMINATION OF THE TEXT

One of the most important contributions to Synoptic scholarship during the past century has been C. M. Tuckett's *The Revival of the Griesbach Hypothesis* (1983). A major part of that importance derives from the way in which this book delineates the specifications of the new battleground where the conflict between the rival Synoptic theories will be decided. Tuckett's position in this regard was clarified and amplified by his contributions to the 1984 Jerusalem Symposium, where he was one of the foremost advocates of Markan Priority. He acknowledges that the "classical proofs" adduced for Markan Priority establish only the existence of a literary interrelationship between the Synoptics without demonstrating which direction that relationship runs, and he holds that the basic question is how well each theory accounts for the observable data in the text—what he calls *the criterion of coherence.*

The wheel has turned full circle from the presentation of Streeter's proofs. As we have seen (primarily in chap. 5), the major proofs on which Streeter relied are still being set forth by some Markan Priority advocates as reasons for adhering to that hypothesis. But—as also seen in chapter 5—those same "proofs" are now acknowledged by experts in the study of the Synoptics and the Synoptic Problem to have no compelling validity in themselves: they would point to Markan Priority only when the other relationships with which they are also consistent can be eliminated on other grounds. The actual comparison of Synoptic passages and the consideration of the explanations advanced for their differences according to the different Synoptic theories—which Streeter included in his treatment of the subject but can hardly be said to have majored on—are now perceived as a crucial issue in deciding the matter. Tuckett explains (1983, 12ff.):

> Any source hypothesis can in fact be proposed. There is no logical law which excludes any theory of synoptic interrelationships with the degree of finality which would be attained if it could be shown that such a hypothesis led to a self-contradiction of the kind $0 = 1$. One can, therefore, postulate any hypothesis and then make a list, in a purely mechanical way, of the changes which the later writer must have made to his source(s). For example, if Luke were prior, Mark second, and Matthew a conflation of both, then one could go through a synopsis showing that Mark must have omitted this from Luke, added that, changed this, retained that, etc.; then Matthew must have taken this from Luke, that from Mark, ignored Luke here, preferred Mark there, etc. What is then required, if the hypothesis is to be made credible, is a presentation of the reasons why the later writers made the changes they are alleged to have done. The application of a "criterion of coherence" would then demand that these reasons form a reasonably coherent whole: they must be rational, consistent with each other and also consistent with the facts as they are. With this in mind, the gospel texts can be examined at a number of different levels: one can consider small grammatical changes, the changes of words and phrases with wider theological implications, and the changes involving the choice and ordering of whole pericopes. Any proposed source hypothesis must then give a reasonably coherent and self-consistent set of reasons why these changes occurred in the way that the hypothesis claims if the theory is to be seriously considered. The extent to which an hypothesis gives a coherent, consistent picture of the total redactional activity of each evangelist will then be a measure of its viability.

Tuckett (193) cites Fee (1978, 168), who says, "The real question is not whether it [the Griesbach Hypothesis] can be falsified, any more than whether the two-source theory can (if indeed either could be; then of course we must look elsewhere). The real question is, which theory best explains the phenomena. . . . Although all things are theoretically possible, not all things are equally probable."

Tuckett concluded that when the actual data is examined in this way, the Two-Source Hypothesis is far superior in explanatory power (the criterion of coherence) than the Griesbach (Markan Posteriority) Hypothesis. Thus he states (186–87):

> In the study of the Synoptic Problem, no conclusions can have complete certainty, and any solution is theoretically possible. One can never prove with mathematical rigour that one solution is right, or that another is wrong. Nevertheless, various phenomena considered in this discussion have suggested that the Griesbach hypothesis is considerably less viable as a solution to the Synoptic Problem than the Two Document hypothesis. . . .
>
> In all this, it is a matter of weighing probabilities. The Griesbach hypothesis can give an explanation of the texts at one level, but it fails to account for the reasons why the changes allegedly made by the later writers (i.e. Luke and Mark) were made in the way in which the hypothesis must assume. Insofar as the Two Document hypothesis can often apparently give a more coherent and consistent set of explanations of why the later changes were made (i.e. by Matthew and Luke on the Two Document hypothesis), that hypothesis is to be preferred. . . .
>
> If the Griesbach hypothesis is to continue to be a serious rival to the Two Document hypothesis as a viable solution to the Synoptic Problem, then its adherents must give a more detailed explanation for Luke's and Mark's behaviour. Clearly Luke and Mark could have done what the hypothesis claims: what is still lacking is a detailed explanation of why they might have done this. Until this is shown convincingly, there seems little reason for reviving the hypothesis. The conclusion of this study, therefore, is that there seems to be no good reason for abandoning the traditional Two Document hypothesis, i.e. the theory of independent use by Matthew and Luke of Mark and Q; in addition, perhaps more attention should be given to the distinctive features of Q than has traditionally been the case in past study of the gospels.

It must be agreed at once that in assessing the claims for acceptance of any particular Synoptic hypothesis, the issue raised by Tuckett—what he calls the "criterion of coherence"—is indeed of primary importance. This is the extent to which that hypothesis can provide a credible, coherent, and self-consistent set of reasons for the text of the three Synoptic Gospels, including why the later writers would have made the changes to their sources that the hypothesis assumes they have.

The purpose of this chapter is to consider the Synoptic texts, to lay out the relevant factors that arise in the various passages, and to make an evaluation of the alternative explanations in terms of their coherence, that is, their explanatory power.

Ideally, this study should encompass the whole text of all three Synoptics. Nothing less could ensure the complete coverage in objective fashion of passages that may be considered to favor one hypothesis against another. Such a detailed study is needed, but it is also a major undertaking and impractical at this point. What I have done in this chapter is to examine in full what may be judged to be a representative pericope; next, to note similar features in other passages (including the passages raised by Tuckett and others); and then to assess what may be learned from this approach.

DETAILED CASE STUDY: THE RICH YOUNG MAN

The Significance of This Pericope

I have provided a detailed examination of the Triple Tradition pericope about the rich young man (Matt 19:16–30//Mark 10:17–31//Luke 18:18–30) since it is so frequently referred to in Synoptic literature and since it is dealt with at some length in N. B. Stonehouse's book on Synoptic origins. This pericope receives frequent mention primarily because of the differences between Matthew and Mark-Luke in the form of the question asked by the man and in Jesus' reply. Stonehouse begins (1963, 93–94) his chapter on this pericope with this introduction:

> This study of the Synoptic accounts concerning the rich young man who, according to Mk 10:18, asked Jesus, "Why callest thou me good?", is initiated because of its supposed bearing upon the subject of the priority of Mark....
>
> [I]t is this passage, along with Mk 6:5 as compared with Mt 13:58, which Streeter singles out as a conspicuous illustration of his claim that Mark used "phrases likely to cause offense, which are omitted or toned down in the other Gospels" [Streeter, 151f.]. Streeter's intent, however, is clearly not to rest his entire case upon these two passages. To say the least, he must have in mind the long list which, according to Hawkins, "may have been omitted or altered as being liable to be misunderstood, or to give offense, or to suggest difficulties," and especially the first main section which lists twenty-two "passages seeming (a) to limit the power of Jesus Christ, or (b) to be otherwise derogatory to, or unworthy of, Him" [Hawkins, 117–25]. The claim cannot be made accordingly that this line of reasoning for the priority of Mark is being adequately weighed here. Nevertheless, I believe that to an extent the argument as usually advanced may be rather fairly tested by the examination of this single passage. In being so selective there is at least the advantage of doing justice to the context in which the crucial supposedly discrepant words are found.

Thus we give our attention to this entire passage so that any (supposed) alterations to parts of it may be seen in relation to the whole context.

This pericope contains a complex net of agreements and disagreements between each pair of the three Synoptics, in every possible combination, together with sections where all three are in agreement and other places where each goes his own way. It commences with the discussion of "good" in which Matthew differs very significantly from Mark and Luke, and which is (as we have noted) much discussed in Synoptic literature. But Mark and Luke agree against Matthew in numbers of other significant places in this pericope as well; and Matthew and Mark also agree against Luke in many elements. There are agreements, too, of Matthew and Luke against Mark, though these consist only of a scattering of words and word-forms.

Advocates of Markan Priority see the difference between the way the story begins in Matthew and in the other two as an example of Matthew smoothing the unacceptable wording of Mark. Thus Allen (1907, xxxii) attributes the change from "Why do you call me good?" to "Why do you ask me about the good?" to a "feeling of reverence." Hawkins (1909, 120), Streeter (1924, 162), V. Taylor (1966, 120), Kümmel (1975, 61), and others follow suit. But what needs to be noted is that this is but one instance of a whole series of occasions in this pericope where Mark agrees *with* one of the Major Synoptics *against* the other.

What has not, it seems to me, been given adequate recognition is the extent to which in this pericope it is Mark, as the common link between the others, who holds the three of them together. Matthew and Luke, when compared with each other, can be seen to have very few points of agreement; and Mark is found to be in agreement with them alternatively. From the Markan Priority perspective, the question that needs an answer is, Why do Matthew and Luke not agree with each other more often in taking the same things from Mark's account? It is almost as if they were operating on the principle that when Matthew agreed with Mark, Luke would feel free to differ, and when Luke agreed with Mark, Matthew would go his own way. There is of course an alternative explanation: Mark used Matthew and Luke as his sources, and when he came to them he found them already differing from each other in most particulars, and he deliberately sought to draw his account from both of them—and he did it in such a way that he has largely succeeded in reconciling those differences and bringing them together.

These are the issues we need to explore through a careful and thoroughgoing examination of the text of this pericope.

The Comparison of Matthew and Luke

The starting point of our examination of the text is to consider the extent of the agreements and disagreements between Matthew and Luke. The text of these two Gospels is arranged in four columns, two for each Gospel, in such a way that when they differ their text is in the outside columns and when they agree their text is placed in adjacent columns.

TABLE 1:
COMPARISON OF THE TEXT OF MATTHEW AND LUKE

Matt 19:16–30		Luke 18:18–30	
Differs from Luke	**Same as Luke**	**Same as Matt**	**Differs from Matt**
16. ἰδοὺ εἷς προσελθὼν αὐτῷ εἶπεν,	Καὶ	18. Καὶ	ἐπηρώτησέν τις αὐτὸν ἄρχων λέγων,
	Διδάσκαλε,	Διδάσκαλε	ἀγαθέ,
	τί	τί	
ἀγαθὸν ποιήσω ἵνα σχῶ			ποιήσας
	ζωὴν αἰώνιον;	ζωὴν αἰώνιον	
			κληρονομήσω;
17. ὁ			
	δὲ εἶπεν αὐτῷ·	19. εἶπεν δὲ αὐτῷ	
			ὁ Ἰησοῦς
	Τί με	Τί με	
ἐρωτᾷς περὶ τοῦ ἀγαθοῦ			λέγεις ἀγαθόν οὐδεὶς
	εἷς	ἀγαθός	
ἐστιν ὁ			εἰ μὴ
	ἀγαθός	εἷς	
			ὁ θεος.
εἰ δὲ θέλεις εἰς τὴν ζωὴν εἰσελθεῖν, τήρησον			
	τὰς ἐντολας.	20. τὰς ἐντολάς	
			οἶδας·
18. λέγει αὐτῷ, Ποίας ὁ δὲ Ἰησοῦς εἶπεν, Τὸ Οὐ φονεύσεις, Οὐ μοιχεύσεις, Οὐ κλέψεις,			Μὴ μοιχεύσῃς, Μὴ φονεύσῃς, Μὴ κλέψῃς,

Matt 19:16–30		Luke 18:18–30	
Differs from Luke	**Same as Luke**	**Same as Matt**	**Differs from Matt**
Οὐ ψευδομαρτυρήσεις, 19.	Τίμα τὸν πατέρα	Τίμα τὸν πατέρα	Μὴ ψευδομαρτυρήσῃς, σου
καί, Ἀγαπήσεις τὸν πλησίον σου ὡς σεαυτόν. 20. λέγει αὐτῷ ὁ νεανίσκος,	καὶ τὴν μητέρα,	καὶ τὴν μητέρα.	21. ὁ δὲ εἶπεν,
	Πάντα ταῦτα ἐφύλαξα	Ταῦτα πάντα ἐφύλαξα	ἐκ νεότητος. 22· ἀκούσας δὲ
τί ἔτι ὑστερῶ; 21. ἔφη	αὐτῷ ὁ Ἰησοῦς,	ὁ Ἰησοῦς αὐτῷ,	εἶπεν Ἔτι ἕν σοι λείπει·
Εἰ θέλεις τέλειος εἶναι, ὕπαγε			πάντα ὅσα ἔχεις
σου τὰ ὑπάρχοντα δὸς	πώλησόν καὶ	πώλησον καὶ	διάδος
	πτωχοῖς, καὶ ἕξεις θησαυρὸν ἐν οὐρανοῖς, καὶ δεῦρο ἀκολούθει μοι.	πτωχοῖς, καὶ ἕξεις θησαυρὸν ἐν οὐρανοῖς, καὶ δεῦρο ἀκολούθει μοι.	
22. δὲ ὁ νεανίσκος τὸν λόγον ἀπῆλθεν λυπούμενος, ἔχων κτήματα πολλά. 23.	ἀκούσας ἦν γὰρ Ὁ δὲ Ἰησοῦς	ἀκούσας ἦν γὰρ ὁ Ἰησοῦς	23. ὁ δὲ ταῦτα περίλυπος ἐγενήθη, πλούσιος σφόδρα. 24. Ἰδὼν δὲ αὐτὸν

Now Take the Case of the Rich Young Man

Matt 19:16–30		Luke 18:18–30	
Differs from Luke	**Same as Luke**	**Same as Matt**	**Differs from Matt**
			περίλυπον γενόμενον
	εἶπεν	εἶπεν,	
τοῖς μαθηταῖς αὐτοῦ, Ἀμὴν λέγω ὑμῖν ὅτι πλούσιος			Πῶς
	δυσκόλως	δυσκόλως	
			οἱ τὰ χρήματα ἔχοντες
εἰσελεύσεται	εἰς τὴν βασιλείαν	εἰς τὴν βασιλείαν	
τῶν οὐρανῶν.			τοῦ θεοῦ εἰσπορεύονται
24. πάλιν δὲ λέγω ὑμῖν,	εὐκοπώτερον	25. εὐκοπώτερον	
			γὰρ
	ἐστιν κάμηλον διὰ	ἐστιν κάμηλον διὰ	
τρυπήματος ῥαφίδος διελθεῖν			τρήματος βελόνης εἰσελθεῖν
	ἢ πλούσιον εἰσελθεῖν	ἢ πλούσιον	
	εἰς τὴν βασιλείαν τοῦ θεοῦ.	εἰς τὴν βασιλείαν τοῦ θεοῦ εἰσελθεῖν.	
			26. εἶπαν δὲ οἱ
	ἀκούσαντες	ἀκούσαντες,	
25. δὲ οἱ μαθηταὶ ἐξεπλήσσοντο σφόδρα λέγοντες,			Καὶ
ἄρα	Τίς	τις	
	δύναται σωθῆναι;	δύναται σωθῆναι;	
26. ἐμβλέψας	δὲ ὁ	27. ὁ δὲ	
Ἰησοῦς			
	εἶπεν	εἶπεν,	
αὐτοῖς,			Τὰ ἀδύνατα

Matt 19:16–30		Luke 18:18–30	
Differs from Luke	Same as Luke	Same as Matt	Differs from Matt
	Παρὰ ἀνθρώποις	παρὰ ἀνθρώποις	
τοῦτο ἀδύνατόν ἐστιν,			
	παρὰ		
δὲ			
	θεῷ		
πάντα			
	δυνατά.	δυνατὰ	
		παρὰ	
			τῷ
		θεῷ	
			ἐστιν.
27. Τότε ἀποκριθεὶς			
		28. Εἶπεν	
			δὲ
	ὁ Πέτρος εἶπεν	ὁ Πέτρος,	
αὐτῷ,			
	Ἰδοὺ ἡμεῖς	Ἰδοὺ ἡμεῖς	
			ἀφέντες τὰ ἴδια
ἀφήκαμεν πάντα καὶ			
	ἠκολουθήσαμέν σοι·	ἠκολουθήσαμέν σοι.	
τί ἄρα ἔσται ἡμῖν; 28. Ἰησοῦς			
	ὁ δὲ	29. ὁ δὲ	
	εἶπεν αὐτοῖς, Ἀμὴν λέγω ὑμῖν ὅτι	εἶπεν αὐτοῖς, Ἀμὴν λέγω ὑμῖν ὅτι	
ὑμεῖς οἱ ἀκολουθήσαντές μοι, ἐν τῇ παλιγγενεσίᾳ, ὅταν καθίσῃ ὁ υἱὸς τοῦ ἀνθρώπου ἐπὶ θρόνου δόξης αὐτοῦ, καθήσεσθε καὶ ὑμεῖς ἐπὶ δώδεκα θρόνους κρίνοντες τὰς			

Now Take the Case of the Rich Young Man

Matt 19:16–30		Luke 18:18–30	
Differs from Luke	Same as Luke	Same as Matt	Differs from Matt
δώδεκα φυλὰς τοῦ Ἰσραήλ.			
29. καὶ πᾶς ὅστις			οὐδείς ἐστιν ὃς
	ἀφῆκεν	ἀφῆκεν	
οἰκίας			οἰκίαν
			ἢ γυναῖκα
	ἢ ἀδελφοὺς	ἢ ἀδελφοὺς	
ἢ ἀδελφὰς			
ἢ πατέρα ἢ μητέρα			ἢ γονεῖς
	ἢ τέκνα	ἢ τέκνα	
ἢ ἀγροὺς			
	ἕνεκεν	ἕνεκεν	
τοῦ ὀνόματός μου,			τῆς βασιλείας τοῦ θεοῦ,
			30. ὃς οὐχὶ μὴ [ἀπο] λάβῃ
ἑκατονταπλασίονα λήμψεται			πολλαπλασίονα
			ἐν τῷ καιρῷ τούτῳ
	καὶ	καὶ	
			ἐν τῷ αἰῶνι τῷ ἐρχομένῳ
	ζωὴν αἰώνιον	ζωὴν αἰώνιον.	
κληρονομήσει. 30. Πολλοὶ δὲ ἔσονται πρῶτοι ἔσχατοι καὶ ἔσχατοι πρῶτοι.			

The text used is that of Aland/United Bible Societies; there are quite a few textual variants in the pericope, but they affect none of the points made here to any material extent, so I have not discussed these variants in detail (though a small number are mentioned below at appropriate points).

A careful comparison of Matthew and Luke in this table makes us aware of the considerable number of differences of every kind between the two accounts. The two main questions to be considered in relation to this pericope are: Does the data suggest that the accounts of Matthew and Luke can readily be explained as derived from Mark by redactional modification? If they did not both derive from Mark, is it possible that one of them has been taken from the other? The extent of the differences between the two Gospels is very evident. It would have taken a very large number of changes to Mark's Gospel by Matthew and Luke (*whatever* the wording of Mark's Gospel) to create such a tally of differences. And the comparison of these two versions, given above, indicates that the similarities between Matthew and Luke in the Greek of the whole pericope (Matt 19:16–30//Luke 18:18–30) are not such as to suggest (and certainly not such as to require) a common literary source for both, or that either one derives from the other. On the contrary, the agreements between Matthew and Luke outside of direct speech are almost non-existent and consist of εἶπεν five times (Matt 19:17,23,26,27,28), δέ four times (Matt 19:17,23,26,28), αὐτῷ twice (Matt 19:17,21), ὁ Ἰησοῦς twice (Matt 19:21,23), and once each for καί (Matt 19:16), ἀκούσας (Matt 19:22), ἀκούσαντες (Matt 19:25), ἦν γάρ (Matt 19:22), ὁ Πέτρος (Matt 19:27), and αὐτοῖς (Matt 19:28).

The significance of this can best be appreciated by looking at the extent to which, in the narrative sections of Matthew and Luke (though they are basically saying the same thing), their wording does *not* agree. For example, a verb of speaking occurs in parallel material in both accounts nine times, and while five times they both use εἶπεν (as above), on the other four occasions (Matt 19:16,20,21,25) they do *not* use the same word. The extent of their verbal agreement is slightly higher in the speech sections but is identical only in one place: Matt 19:21b//Luke 18:22b. The wording is fairly close in Matt 19:24//Luke 18:25 but has significant differences. None of the similarities are of a kind to require literary dependence. The differences speak strongly against such dependence.

First, there are extensive differences of wording even when the same information is being conveyed:

Matthew 19	Luke 18
v. 16 have [eternal life]	v. 18 inherit [eternal life]
v. 17 keep [the commandments]	v. 20 you know [the commandments]
v. 21 [sell] your possessions	v. 22 [sell] all that you have
v. 22 [hearing] the saying	v. 23 [hearing] these things
v. 22 he was sorrowful (λυπούμενος)	v. 23 he was sad (περίλυπος)
v. 22 [for he] had many possessions	v. 23 [for he] was very rich
v. 23 with what difficulty a rich man will enter the kingdom of the heavens.	v. 24 With how much difficulty those who have possessions are going into the kingdom of God.
v. 24 to go through the eye of a needle (τρυπήματος ῥαφίδος διελυεῖν)	v. 25 to go through the eye of a needle (τρήματος βελόνης εἰσελυεῖν)
v. 26 With men this is impossible, but with God all things are possible	v. 27 What is impossible with men is possible with God
v. 27 [we have left] everything	v. 28 [we left] our own things

Matthew 19	Luke 18
v. 29 And everyone who has left . . .	v. 29 there is no one who had left . . .
v. 29 or father or mother	v. 29 or parents
v. 29 [for the sake of] my name	v. 29 [for the sake of] the kingdom of God
v. 29 will receive a hundredfold	v. 30 would receive many times more

There are also numerous differences in word order and grammatical constructions. To list these would require reproducing virtually the whole passage again, so they are best observed by going through table 1 and comparing the two Gospels. But attention should be drawn to one of the most significant of these divergences. In Matt 19:18 the Commandments are given in the form οὐ plus the future, and the first two in the list are "You shall not kill" and "You shall not commit adultery," and then those from the Decalogue are followed by "You shall love your neighbor as yourself." In Luke 18:20 the Commandments are given in the form μή plus the aorist subjunctive, and the first two in the list are "Do not commit adultery" and "Do not kill," while the Commandment to love one's neighbor is not given.

Then there are numerous differences of perspective and viewpoint, and details in Matthew that are not in Luke (and vice versa). Again, these are all best noted by a careful verse-by-verse comparison of the accounts of Matthew and Luke, whether in Greek (as in table 1 above) or in English. These features can be noted in particular:

Matthew 19	Luke 18
The person in the story is a man who is described as "young" (20 and 22)	The person in the story is described as a "ruler" who has kept the commandments *from* (ἐκ) his youth (21)—and thus is no longer young.
He says, "Teacher, what good thing must I do to have eternal life?"	He says, "Good teacher, what thing must I do to inherit eternal life?"
Jesus replies, "Why do you ask me about what is good? One there is who is good."	Jesus replies, "Why do you call me good? No one is good but God alone."
Jesus adds, "If you would enter life, keep the commandments."	[This is lacking; the man is simply reminded, "You know the commandments."]
The man asks, "Which?"; Jesus replies. Jesus adds, "Love your neighbor."	[This is lacking.] [This is lacking.]
The man asks, "What do I still lack?"	Jesus says, "One thing you still lack."
Jesus says, "If you would be perfect . . ."	[This is lacking.]
When he hears what Jesus says, the young man goes away sorrowful.	The man becomes sad, but is *not* said to go away, and apparently remains there.

Matthew 19	Luke 18
Jesus speaks to his disciples.	Jesus speaks, still looking at the man, who is apparently still included in the conversation.
Jesus says, "Truly I say to you . . ."	[This is lacking.]
Jesus says, "Again I tell you . . ."	[This is lacking.]
The disciples are greatly astonished.	"Those who heard it" respond.
Peter says, "What then shall we have?"	[This is lacking.]
Jesus says, " . . . in the new world, when the Son of man shall sit on his glorious throne, you who have followed me will also sit on twelve thrones, judging the twelve tribes of Israel."	[This is lacking.]
" . . . will receive a hundredfold	"who will not receive many times more
[This is lacking.]	in this time, and in the age to come
and inherit eternal life."	eternal life."
"But many that are first will be last, and the last first."	[This is lacking.]

It may be noted that only in Matthew is this man called "young," and only in Luke is he called a "ruler."

These various differences fall short of being contradictions, and it is easy to conceive of how they could exist in two independent reports of the incident from two different eyewitnesses. What is not easy to conceive is how they could arise from the redaction of a single account, whether that one account be Mark's or any other. Thus an examination and comparison of what is said would lead us to conclude that these two accounts *cannot have been derived one from the other or from any common document*, but that they are separate accounts deriving independently from two different eyewitnesses of the actual event. So now we consider how they compare with Mark.

Comparing Mark to Matthew and Luke

When we place Mark's account alongside the versions of this pericope in Matthew and Luke, we can see the extent to which it corresponds with (and differs from) each of them. In table 2, when Mark corresponds with Matthew (in wording or meaning), its wording is positioned to the left, alongside Matthew's column; when it corresponds with Luke (in wording or meaning), its wording is positioned to the right, alongside Luke's column; and when it corresponds with both or neither, its wording is positioned in the center, between Matthew and Luke.

TABLE 2:
COMPARING MARK TO MATTHEW AND LUKE

Matthew 19:16–30	Mark 10:17–31 SIMILAR TO			Luke 18:18–30
	Matthew	Both/Neither	Luke	
16. Καὶ		17. Καὶ		18. Καὶ
		ἐκ πορευομένου		
		αὐτοῦ εἰς		
		ὁδὸν		
		προσδραμὼν		
ἰδοὺ				
εἷς	εἷς			
προσελθὼν				
		καὶ		
		γονυπετήσας		
		αὐτὸν		
			ἐπηρώτα	ἐπηρώτητησέν τις
αὐτῷ			αὐτόν,	αὐτὸν
				ἄρχων
εἶπεν,				λέγων,
Διδάσκαλε,		Διδάσκαλε		Διδάσκαλε
			ἀγαθέ,	ἀγαθέ,
τί		τί		τί
ἀγαθὸν				
ποιήσω ἵνα	ποιήσω ἵνα			ποιήσας
σχῶ				
ζωὴν αἰώνιον;		ζωὴν αἰώνιον		ζωὴν αἰώνιον
			κληρονομήσω;	κληρονομήσω;
17. ὁ δὲ	18. ὁ δὲ			
		Ἰησοῦς		
εἶπεν αὐτῷ,		εἶπεν αὐτῷ,		19. εἶπεν δὲ αὐτῷ ὁ Ἰησοῦς,
Τί με		Τί με		Τί με
ἐρωτᾶς			λέγεις	λέγεις
περὶ τοῦ				
ἀγαθοῦ;		ἀγαθόν;		ἀγαθόν;
		οὐδεὶς		οὐδεὶς
εἷς		ἀγαθὸς		ἀγαθὸς
ἐστιν ὁ			εἰ μὴ	εἰ μὴ
ἀγαθός.			εἷς	εἷς
			ὁ θεός.	ὁ θεός.
εἰ δὲ θέλεις				
εἰς τὴν ζωὴν				
εἰσελθεῖν, τήρησον				
τὰς ἐντολάς.	19. τὰς ἐντολὰς			20. τὰς ἐντολὰς
			οἶδας·	οἶδας·
18. λέγει αὐτῷ,				

Matthew 19:16–30	Matthew	Mark 10:17–31 SIMILAR TO Both/Neither	Luke	Luke 18:18–30
Ποίας; ὁ δὲ Ἰησοῦς εἶπεν, Τὸ Οὐ φονεύσεις, Οὐ μοιχεύσεις, Οὐ κλέψεις, Οὐ ψευδοματυρήσεις,		Μὴ φονεύσῃς, Μὴ μοιχεύσῃς, Μὴ ἀποστερήσῃς,	Μὴ κλέψῃς, ψευδομαρτυρήσῃς,	Μὴ μοιχεύσῃς, Μὴ φονεύσῃς, Μὴ κλέψῃς, Μὴ ψευδομαρτυρήσῃς,
19. Τίμα τὸν πατέρα		Τίμα τὸν πατέρα		Τίμα τὸν πατέρα
			σου	σου
καὶ τὴν μητέρα, καὶ, Ἀγαπήσεις τὸν πλησίον σου ὡς σεαυτόν.		καὶ τὴν μητέρα.		καὶ τὴν μητέρα.
20. λέγει αὐτῷ ὁ νεανίσκος,	αὐτῷ,	ἔφη Διδάσκαλε,	20. ὁ δὲ	21. ὁ δὲ εἶπεν,
Πάντα ταῦτα ἐφύλαξα,		ἐφυλαξάμην μου.	ταῦτα πάντα ἐκ νεότητος	Ταῦτα πάντα ἐφύλαξα ἐκ νεότητος.
τί ἔτι ὑστερῶ;				22. ἀκούσας
		ἐμβλέψας αὐτῷ ἠγάπησεν αὐτὸν καὶ	21. ὁ δὲ Ἰησοῦς	δὲ ὁ Ἰησοῦς
21. ἔφη αὐτῷ ὁ Ἰησοῦς,		αὐτῷ,	εἶπεν	εἶπεν αὐτῷ,
			Ἕν σε	Ἔτι ἕν σοι λείπει·
Εἰ θέλεις τέλειος εἶναι, ὕπαγε	ὑστερεῖ· ὕπαγε			
πώλησον σου τὰ ὑπάρχοντα		πώλησον	ὅσα ἔχεις	πάντα ὅσα ἔχεις πώλησον

Matthew 19:16–30		Mark 10:17–31 SIMILAR TO		Luke 18:18–30
	Matthew	Both/Neither	Luke	
καὶ		καὶ		καὶ
δὸς	δὸς			διάδος
[τοῖς] πτωχοῖς,		[τοῖς] πτωχοῖς,		πτωχοῖς,
καὶ ἕξεις θησαυρὸν		καὶ ἕξεις θησαυρὸν		καὶ ἕξεις θησαυρὸν
ἐν οὐρανοῖς,		ἐν οὐρανῷ,		ἐν οὐρανοῖς,
καὶ δεῦρο		καὶ δεῦρο		καὶ δεῦρο
ἀκολούθει μοι.		ἀκολούθει μοι.		ἀκολούθει μοι.
			22. ὁ δὲ	23. ὁ δὲ
22. ἀκούσας		στυγνάσας		ἀκούσας
δὲ ὁ νεανίσκος				
τὸν λόγον	ἐπὶ τῷ λόγῳ			ταῦτα
ἀπῆλθεν	ἀπῆλθεν			περίλυπος
λυπούμενος,	λυπούμενος,			ἐγενήθη
ἦν γὰρ		ἦν γὰρ		ἦν γὰρ
ἔχων κτήματα	ἔχων κτήματα			πλούσιος
πολλά.	πολλά.			σφόδρα.
		23. Καὶ περιβ-λεψάμενος		24. Ἰδὼν
				δὲ αὐτὸν
23. Ὁ δὲ Ἰησοῦς		ὁ Ἰησοῦς		ὁ Ἰησοῦς
				περίλυπον
				γενόμενον
εἶπεν		λέγει		εἶπεν,
τοῖς	τοῖς			
μαθηταῖς	μαθηταῖς			
αὐτοῦ,	αὐτοῦ,			
Ἀμὴν λέγω ὑμῖν				
ὅτι πλούσιος				
			Πῶς	Πῶς
δυσκόλως		δυσκόλως		δυσκόλως
			οἱ τὰ	οἱ τὰ
			χρήματα	χρήματα
			ἔχοντες	ἔχοντες
εἰσελεύσεται				
εἰς τὴν		εἰς τὴν		εἰς τὴν
βασιλείαν		βασιλείαν		βασιλείαν
τῶν οὐρανῶν.			τοῦ θεοῦ	τοῦ θεοῦ
	εἰσελεύσον-ται.			εἰσπορεύονται·
		24. οἱ δὲ μαθηταὶ ἐθαμβοῦντο ἐπὶ τοῖς λόγοις αὐτοῦ. ὁ δὲ Ἰησοῦς		
24. πάλιν	πάλιν	ἀποκριθεὶς		
δὲ λέγω ὑμῖν,	λέγει αὐτοῖς,			

Matthew 19:16–30	Matthew	Mark 10:17–31 SIMILAR TO Both/Neither	Luke	Luke 18:18–30
		Τέκνα, πῶς δύσκολόν ἐστιν εἰς τὴν βασιλείαν τοῦ θεοῦ εἰσελθεῖν,		
εὐκοπώτερόν		25. εὐκοπώτερόν		25. εὐκοπώτερον γάρ
ἐστιν κάμηλον διὰ τρυπήματος ῥαφίδος διελθεῖν ἢ πλούσιον εἰσελθεῖν εἰς τὴν βασιλείαν τοῦ θεοῦ.	[τῆς] ῥαφίδος διελθεῖν	ἐστιν κάμηλον διὰ [τῆς] τρυμαλιᾶς ἢ πλούσιον εἰς τὴν βασιλείαν	τοῦ θεοῦ εἰσελθεῖν.	ἐστιν κάμηλον διὰ τρήματος βελόνης εἰσελθεῖν ἢ πλούσιον εἰς τὴν βασιλείαν τοῦ θεοῦ εἰσελθεῖν.
25. ἀκούσαντες δὲ οἱ μαθηταὶ		26. δὲ οἱ περισσῶς		26. εἶπαν δὲ οἱ ἀκούσαντες,
ἐξεπλήσσοντο σφόδρα λέγοντες,	ἐξεπλήσσοντο λέγοντες	πρὸς ἑαυτούς,	Καὶ	Καὶ
Τίς ἄρα δύναται σωθῆναι; 26. ἐμβλέψας	27. ἐμβλέψας	τίς δύναται σωθῆναι; αὐτοῖς		τίς δύναται σωθῆναι; 27. ὁ δὲ
δὲ ὁ Ἰησοῦς εἶπεν αὐτοῖς,	ὁ Ἰησοῦς	λέγει,		εἶπεν,
Παρὰ ἀνθρώποις τοῦτο ἀδύνατόν ἐστιν,	ἀδύνατον,	Παρὰ ἀνθρώποις ἀλλ' οὐ		Τὰ ἀδύνατα παρὰ ἀνθρώποις
παρὰ δὲ θεῷ πάντα δυνατά.	παρὰ θεῷ,	πάντα γὰρ δυνατά		δυνατὰ

Matthew 19:16–30	Matthew	Mark 10:17–31 SIMILAR TO Both/Neither	Luke	Luke 18:18–30
		παρὰ τῷ θεῷ.		παρὰ τῷ θεῷ ἐστιν.
27. Τότε ἀποκριθεὶς		28. Ἤρξατο Λέγειν		28. Εἶπεν δὲ
ὁ Πέτρος εἶπεν αὐτῷ,	αὐτῷ,	ὁ Πέτρος		ὁ Πέτρος,
Ἰδοὺ ἡμεῖς ἀφήκαμεν πάντα καὶ ἠκολουθήσαμέν σοι· τί ἄρα ἔσται ἡμῖν;	ἀφήκαμεν πάντα καὶ	Ἰδοὺ ἡμεῖς ἠκολουθήσαμεν σοι.		Ἰδοὺ ἡμεῖς ἀφέντες τὰ ἴδια ἠκολουθήσαμέν σοι.
28. ὁ δὲ Ἰησοῦς εἶπεν αὐτοῖς, Ἀμὴν λέγω ὑμῖν ὅτι ὑμεῖς οἱ ἀκολουθήσαντές μοι, ἐν τῇ παλιγγενεσίᾳ, ὅταν καθίσῃ ὁ υἱὸς τοῦ ἀνθρώπου ἐπὶ θρόνου δόξης αὐτοῦ, καθήσεσθε καὶ ὑμεῖς ἐπὶ δώδεκα θρόνους κρίνοντες τὰς δώδεκα φυλὰς τοῦ Ἰσραήλ. 29: καὶ πᾶς ὅστις	Ἰησοῦς,	29. ἔφη ὁ Ἀμὴν λέγω ὑμῖν,	οὐδείς ἐστιν ὃς	29 ὁ δὲ εἶπεν αὐτοῖς, Ἀμὴν λέγω ὑμῖν ὅτι οὐδείς ἐστιν ὃς
ἀφῆκεν οἰκίας		ἀφῆκεν	οἰκίαν	ἀφῆκεν οἰκίαν ἢ γυναῖκα
ἢ ἀδελφοὺς ἢ ἀδελφὰς ἢ πατέρα ἢ μητέρα	ἢ ἀδελφὰς ἢ πατέρα ἢ μητέρα	ἢ ἀδελφοὺς		ἢ ἀδελφοὺς ἢ γονεῖς

Matthew 19:16–30	Matthew	Mark 10:17–31 SIMILAR TO Both/Neither	Luke	Luke 18:18–30
ἢ τέκνα		ἢ τέκνα		ἢ τέκνα
ἢ ἀγροὺς	ἢ ἀγροὺς			
ἕνεκεν		ἕνεκεν		ἕνεκεν
τοῦ ὀνόματός μου,		ἐμοῦ		τῆς βασιλείας τοῦ θεοῦ,
		καὶ ἕνεκεν τοῦ εὐαγγελίου,		
			30. ἐὰν μὴ λάβῃ	30. ὃς οὐχὶ μὴ [ἀπο]λάβῃ
ἑκατονταπλασίονα	ἑκατονταπλασίονα			πολλαπλασίονα
λήμψεται				
		νῦν		
			ἐν τῷ καιρῷ τούτῳ	ἐν τῷ καιρῷ τούτῳ
		οἰκίας καὶ ἀδελφοὺς καὶ ἀδελφὰς καὶ μητέρας καὶ τέκνα καὶ ἀγροὺς μετὰ διωγμῶν,		
καὶ		καὶ		καὶ
			ἐν τῷ αἰῶνι τῷ ἐρχομένῳ	ἐν τῷ αἰῶνι τῷ ἐρχομένῳ
ζωὴν αἰώνιον κληρονομήσει.		ζωὴν αἰώνιον.		ζωὴν αἰώνιον.
30. Πολλοὶ δὲ ἔσονται πρῶτοι ἔσχατοι καὶ ἔσχατοι πρῶτοι.	31. Πολλοὶ δὲ ἔσονται πρῶτοι ἔσχατοι καὶ [οἱ] ἔσχατοι [πρῶτοι.			

There are 96 words in the center columns of table 1, i.e., words that are common to Matthew and Luke. A comparison with Mark shows that 85 of these words are also found in Mark's Gospel. The words that are not, that is, the 11 words in which Matthew and Luke agree here against Mark, are ἀκούσας and ἀκούσαντες, ὅτι, δέ (three times), and εἶπεν (four times, once with αὐτοῖς).

Table 2 shows the comparison of Mark with the other two Synoptics. In addition to the high level to which the significant words that are common to Matthew and Luke occur also in Mark, the two features that stand out are the additional points or details found in Mark, and the extent to which Mark parallels first one and then the other of Matthew and Luke.

Redactional Procedures according to the Markan Priority and Markan Dependence Hypotheses

Let us compare the redactional procedures followed by Matthew and Luke on the hypothesis of Markan Priority (MP), and by Mark on the hypothesis of Markan Dependence (MD). Each verse of Mark's account (and parallels) is examined in turn from the two perspectives. Verse references are from Mark.

10:17 MP: Both Matthew and Luke ignore Mark's introductory setting, "And as he was setting out on his journey, a man ran up and knelt before him." Luke keeps close to Mark, but changes (a) "a man" to "a certain ruler"; (b) the tense of "asked" from imperfect to aorist; (c) the form of "do" from future indicative to aorist participle; and adds (d) "saying." Matthew changes (a) "ran up" to "came up"; (b) "asked him" to "said to him"; (c) "good" from modifying "teacher" to something to be done; (d) "might inherit" to "might have"; and adds (e) "behold."

10:17 MD: From P (his third source, Peter), Mark adds the circumstances of the man's approach. He omits Matthew's "behold" (Mark never uses this in narrative); follows Matthew's "a man"; follows Luke for "asked him" (but changes the tense to imperfect); follows Luke for "Good teacher"; follows Matthew for the future of "do in order that"; and follows Luke for "inherit."

10:18 MP: Luke corresponds with Mark exactly, but Matthew changes Mark's point completely from "Why do you call me good?" to "Why do you ask me about what is good?"; and "No one is good but God alone" to "There is one who is good." Matthew also adds, "If you would enter life, keep the commandments."

10:18 MD: Mark follows Luke exactly.

10:19 MP: Initially, Luke corresponds with Mark exactly; then Luke alters the order of the first two Commandments on the list, so they are no longer in the order of Exodus 20//Deuteronomy 5; and Luke omits "Do not defraud" (which is not part of the Decalogue). Matthew adds, "He said to him, 'Which?' And Jesus said, . . ."; and changes the form of the Commandments from μή plus the subjunctive to οὐ plus the future (the wording of the Septuagint). However, Matthew deletes Mark's "do not defraud" (which is not part of the Decalogue) and "your" from "Honor your father and mother"—which *is* found in the LXX and the Hebrew of Exod 20:12 and Deut 5:16. Further, Matthew inserts "You shall love your neighbor as yourself" (Lev 19:18).

10:19 MD: Mark follows Luke exactly in his wording for this verse, except that he adopts Matthew's *order* for the Commandments (thus conforming to the order of the Old Testament), and he adds "Do not defraud." (In Mark 7:21–22 he also expands the Matt 15:19 list of sins.)

10:20 MP: Luke follows Mark exactly except for deleting "to him," "Teacher," and "my" (in "my youth"); and changing ἔφη to εἶπεν and ἐφυλαξάμην (middle) to ἐφύλαξα (active). Like Luke, Matthew changes ἔφη (to λέγει), ἐφυλαξάμην to ἐφύλαξα, and omits "Teacher." He also reverses the word order of ταῦτα πάντα, omits the conjunction δέ, and adds "the young man" and "what do I still lack?"

10:20 MD: Mark uses a different word (ἔφη) from the other two for "he said," follows Matthew's "to him" and Luke's initial ὁ δέ construction and Luke's "from my youth," thus rejecting Matthew's "the young man." He changes the voice of ἐφύλαξα to middle and adds "Teacher" (a favored form of address for Jesus) and "my" (in "from my youth").

10:21 MP: Luke deletes "[Jesus] looking upon him loved him," replacing it with ἀκούσας; he deletes "Go" and inserts ἔτι and πάντα; he also makes these changes: (a) he replaces σε ὑστερεῖ with a synonym, σοι λείπει; (b) he replaces δός with the compound form διάδος; and (c) he replaces the singular οὐρανῷ with the plural οὐρανοῖς. Matthew also omits "And [Jesus] looking upon him loved him," together with "One thing is lacking for you" (he earlier has the young man ask, "What do I still lack?"). He adds, "If you would be perfect," and he makes these changes: (a) εἶπεν to its synonym ἔφη; (b) ὅσα ἔχεις to σου τὰ ὑπάρχοντα; and (c) like Luke, the singular οὐρανῷ to the plural οὐρανοῖς.

10:21 MD: Mark adds (from his P source), "[And Jesus] looking upon him loved him"; he has εἶπεν like Luke and ὕπαγε like Matthew; he then follows Luke with ὅσα ἔχεις and Matthew with δός; he has what is common to both of them with "sell" and "to the poor, and you will have treasure in heaven; and come, follow me," except that he departs from both of them in preferring to use the singular οὐρανῷ. The statement "One thing is lacking for you" is given by Mark in the position where it occurs in Luke (spoken by Jesus to the young man) but does not use Luke's word λείπει; instead, he uses Matthew's synonymous verb ὑστερεῖ, but in Matthew this occurs in the words of the young man to Jesus.

10:22 MP: Luke departs from Mark almost totally in this verse. The only words in common are the initial ὁ δέ (a standard construction for marking the transition where the narrator refers again to the other party in a conversation) and ἦν γάρ where the construction is still different (the ἦν is auxiliary in Mark as part of a periphrastic imperfect with ἔχων, but it's a finite verb in Luke). Thus for each point where Luke corresponds with Mark in meaning—"at that saying," "sorrowful," "many possessions"—Luke has a synonym. But Luke does not follow Mark in saying that the man went away. Matthew inserts "the young man," changes Mark's στυγνάσας to ἀκούσας with a consequential change in the case of τῷ λόγῳ. From that point he takes over Mark's wording unaltered.

10:22 MD: Mark omits Matthew's reference to a "young man." Luke says "he became sad," and Matthew has "he went away sad" (using related but different words for "sad"). Mark's account includes both of these points: the first by means of an aorist participle from another word meaning "to be sad or saddened" (στυγνάζω) with a consequential change in the construction for "that saying." Mark then takes over the rest of Matthew verbatim.

10:23 MP: Luke changes Mark's "And looking around Jesus said to his disciples" to "And looking at him Jesus said." In Mark the rich man has departed, but Luke does not say he has left, and apparently Jesus' remarks would still be (and would be intended to be) audible to him—if indeed not still addressed to him. (Some manuscripts read, "And when Jesus saw that he became sad he said," which would also imply the continued presence of the rich man with Jesus at this stage.) Luke and Matthew use εἶπεν here for Mark's λέγει. From this point onwards Luke copies Mark exactly, except that he changes Mark's εἰσελεύσονται to εἰσπορεύονται, that is, a change from future to present tense and from the verb εἰσέρχομαι to εἰσπορεύομαι. Matthew makes these changes: omits "looking around"; adds "Truly I say to you"; retains Mark's "with difficulty" and "will enter εἰσελεύσονται [but changed to singular] the kingdom" but reverses Mark's order to place "will enter" in front of "the kingdom"; changes "of God" to "of the heavens" and "those who have riches/possessions" to "a rich man"; and alters the whole grammatical structure of the sentence by exchanging πῶς for ὅτι.

10:23 MD: Mark takes "looking" from Luke but, while retaining the aorist participle form, changes the verb to "looking around"; he then takes from Matthew "[said] to his disciples" so that this is a conflation of the points made in Luke and Matthew. Next, he copies Luke's wording and order for the balance of the verse, except that he adopts Matthew's verb form "will enter" instead of Luke's "are going in"—but he places it where Luke has his verb rather than where it occurs in Matthew.

10:24 MP: Luke omits entirely Mark's record of the response of the disciples to Jesus' words: "And the disciples were amazed at his words. But Jesus said to them again, 'Children, how hard it is to enter the kingdom of God!'" Matthew turns "But Jesus said to them again" into direct speech, "But again I tell you."

10:24 MD: From his source P, Mark inserts both the reaction of the disciples to Jesus' words and Jesus' further comments.

10:25 MP: Luke takes over exactly the form of this saying, but he substitutes synonyms for three key words: τρήματος for Mark's τρυμαλιᾶς; βελόνης for ῥαφίδος; and εἰσελθεῖν for διελθεῖν. Matthew takes over this saying but makes two alterations to it: he alters the position of "to enter" by placing it in front of "into the kingdom of God," and he changes Mark's τρυμαλιᾶς to the synonym τρυπήματος.

10:25 MD: Mark takes over everything in this saying that is common to Matthew and Luke. He follows Matthew in using ῥαφίδος and διελθεῖν, and Luke in placing εἰσελθεῖν as the last word in the saying. And where Matthew and Luke differ in their word for "eye [of the needle]," he uses his own word (τρυμαλιά).

10:26 MP: Luke omits the great astonishment of the disciples and "to him" after "said," replacing Mark's words with "Those who heard it said," so that it becomes the people in general around Jesus who hear his comments and who respond. The content of what is said is taken over unchanged. Matthew makes Mark's implication explicit by inserting "disciples" as the subject; and like Luke, Matthew also adds ἀκούσαντες. Matthew also changes Mark's περισσῶς for σφόδρα, a word he prefers—περισσῶς occurs only in Matt 27:23 (//Mark 15:14), but σφόδρα occurs seven times in Matthew. Matthew also changes Mark's καί for ἄρα. Apart from this, Matthew takes over Mark's wording.

10:26 MD: Mark, finding here that Matthew attributes what was said to the disciples and Luke to the crowd ("those who heard it"), adopts the neutral "they" as his subject. He changes Matthew's σφόδρα to περισσῶς, but he follows Matthew in speaking of the astonished reaction (ἐξεπλήσσοντο) and in including λέγοντες. He also follows Luke in using καί rather than ἄρα.

10:27 MP: Luke rewords the first part of this verse in Mark, condensing it somewhat (including the omission of "Jesus" as the subject and the fact that Jesus looked at them), but he follows the wording of the second half, "are possible with God." Matthew changes Mark's λέγει to εἶπεν and adds τοῦτο; otherwise, Matthew is close to the first half of Mark's verse but lacks Mark's repetition of "with God."

10:27 MD: Mark conflates Matthew and Luke, taking Matthew as the first part of his verse and Luke as the second part while making some grammatical adjustments so they flow together.

10:28 MP: Luke omits Mark's "began" and "to him" and makes these changes also: (1) from λέγειν to εἰρεῖν; (2) from a perfect indicative to an aorist participle of the verb "we have left"; (3) from πάντα to τὰ ἴδια; and (4) from a perfect to an aorist tense of "we have followed." (The only words in Luke that remain the same as in Mark are ὁ Πέτρος ... ἰδοὺ ἡμεῖς ... σοι.) Matthew changes Mark's λέγειν to εἶπεν, and Mark's perfect tense of "we have followed" to an aorist; he also adds Peter's question, "What then will there be for us?"

10:28 MD: Mark decides to spare Peter by not recording his question ("What then will there be for us?"), and so he rewords Matthew's "Then answering Peter said" to "Peter began to say," that is, "Peter began [ἄρχομαι] by saying"—thus indicating that Mark was recording only the *beginning of* and not *all of* what Peter said. Otherwise, Mark records what is common to Matthew and Luke and follows Matthew where they differ, except that he alters the aorist tense ("we followed") in his two written sources to the perfect tense ("we have followed")—thus underlining the permanent nature of the following and its consequences rather than simply the fact of beginning to follow Jesus. V. Taylor (1966, 433) comments, "The distinction of tenses in ἀφήκαμεν and ἠκολουθήκαμεν is noteworthy; the decisive renunciation in Peter's mind stood out against the permanent following. In Matthew and Luke this detail is lost." The form of Taylor's last sentence reflects his presupposition of Markan Priority. But it is far more likely that Mark *inserted* this additional level of meaning (from his source P) than that Matthew and Luke, both having this detail in front of them in Mark, each independently chose to alter the text to *remove* it.

10:29 MP: Luke and Matthew make these same alterations to Mark: (1) from ἔφη to εἶπεν; (2) adding αὐτοῖς; (3) adding ὅτι; and (4) omitting "and for the sake of the gospel." Further, Luke again omits the subject "Jesus" (as in 18:27//Mark10:27) and also omits "or sisters" and "or fields"; adds "or wife"; and changes "or mother or father" to "or parents," and "for my sake" to "for the sake of the kingdom of God." Matthew inserts a new saying concerning the 12 disciples sitting on 12 thrones judging the 12 tribes of Israel, and he makes these changes: (1) Mark's construction "there is no one ... who will not" to "everyone ... will"; (2) "house" to "houses"; (3) "or mother or father" to "or father or mother"; (4) and "for my sake" to "for my name's sake."

10:29 MD: Mark departs from both Matthew and Luke in these places: (1) using ἔφη rather than εἶπεν; (2) omitting αὐτοῖς; and (3) omitting ὅτι. Using his source P, Mark amplifies the phrase "for the sake of"—which differs between Matthew and Luke—to "for my sake and for the sake of the gospel." He changes Matthew's order "or father or mother" to "or mother or father"—perhaps to highlight "mother" since in the next verse he mentions only "mothers" but not "fathers." For the rest, Mark adopts what is in Matthew or Luke: Luke's "there is no one ... who will not receive" rather than Matthew's different wording, and Luke's "house" rather than Matthew's "houses"; but for the rest he follows Matthew's list of those who have been left.

10:30 MP: Luke alters Mark's way of saying "who will not receive" and changes "a hundredfold" to "many times more"; he omits "now"; he adopts Mark's "in this time" but omits Mark's list of what one will receive, including "with persecutions"; and then he follows Mark verbatim for "and in the age to come, life eternal." Matthew alters Mark's way of saying "will receive" to a simple future; he retains "a hundredfold" but omits "now in this time" and the list of what one will receive, including "with persecutions"; he then follows Mark's "life eternal" but adds "will inherit."

10:30 MD: Mark conflates all three of his sources: he alters Luke's ὃς οὐχὶ μὴ to ἐὰν μὴ and Luke's compound ἀπολάβῃ (if indeed this is the right text: manuscripts B, D, and a few others accord with Mark) to the simple λάβῃ as his way of saying "will not receive"; he takes "a hundredfold" from Matthew and "in this time" from Luke; from his P source, he adds "now ... houses and brothers", etc., and takes verbatim from Luke "and in the age to come life eternal."

10:31 MP: Luke omits Mark's closing saying of Jesus; Matthew adopts it verbatim.

10:31 MD: This saying of Jesus occurs in Matthew but not in Luke; Mark adopts it verbatim.

A Preliminary Consideration: Verbs of Speaking

The words for "speak" in this pericope are noteworthy. Discourse usages are shown in square brackets (see Matt 19:17,23,24,28 and parallels, where applicable).

Matt 19	Mark 10	Luke 18
16: εἶπεν	17: ἐπηρώτα	18: λέγων
17: εἶπεν	18: εἶπεν	19: εἶπεν
[17: ἐρωτᾷς	18: λέγεις	19: λέγεις]
18: λέγει		
18: εἶπεν		
20: λέγει	20: ἔφη	21: εἶπεν
21: ἔφη	21: εἶπεν	22: εἶπεν
23: εἶπεν	23: λέγει	24: εἶπεν
[23: λέγω]		
[24: λέγω]	24: ἀποκριθεὶς λέγει	
25: λέγοντες	26: λέγοντες	26: εἶπαν
26: εἶπεν	27: λέγει	27: εἶπεν
27: ἀποκριθεὶς εἶπεν	28: ἤρξατο λέγειν	28: εἶπεν
28: εἶπεν	29: ἔφη	29: εἶπεν
[28: λέγω	29: λέγω	29: λέγω]

In the nature of the case, this discourse requires the use of a present tense, and in the pericope under review this is always a form of λέγω with the single exception of Matt 19:17 (ἐρωτάω). Setting aside the use in discourse for now, we find the number of times each word for speaking is used in each Gospel is as follows:

	Matthew	Mark	Luke
ἀποκρίνομαι	1	1	—
εἶπον	7	2	8
ἐπερωτάω	—	1	1
λέγω	3	5	1
φημί	1	2	—
Totals	12	11	10

In Luke the story begins with ἐπηρώτησεν λέγων, "[a certain ruler] asked, saying"; from this point onwards, Luke always uses forms of εἶπον in narrative. Matthew has a preference for εἶπον and Mark for λέγω, but each is willing to depart from his preferred form to use others—even without there being any apparent relationship to what either of the other

Gospels uses at a given point. Thus we may note how Matthew and Mark ring the changes:

Matthew 19	Mark 10	Luke 18
20: λέγει	20: ἔφη	21: εἶπεν
21: ἔφη	21: εἶπεν	22: εἶπεν
23: εἶπεν	23: λέγει	24: εἶπεν

Mostly, Matthew and Mark differ from each other in the words they use; once (Matt 19:17//Mark 10:18) they agree in using Matthew's preferred word εἶπον and once (Matt 19:25//Mark 10:26) in using Mark's preferred word λέγω. In Matt 19:18, where the words are not paralleled in either of the other two Gospels, Matthew once uses λέγω and once εἶπον.

On one occasion all three use εἶπον (Matt 19:17 and parallels), but on one occasion all three use a different word (Matt 19:20 and parallels). Matthew and Mark agree against Luke in Matt 19:25 and parallels; Mark and Luke agree against Matthew in Matt 19:16,21 and parallels; and Matthew and Luke agree against Mark in Matt 19:23,26,27,28 and parallels. But these agreements are of no real significance because—since (after his first verse) Luke uses εἶπον in narrative throughout his pericope—they simply represent the places where Matthew and Mark use this word or agree in using some other word.

We are already aware (from our previous consideration of the historic present) of Mark's preference for the present form λέγω, a preference not as fully shared by Matthew and not at all by Luke. This is reflected in our present pericope. But if there is any other pattern, if there is any significance for Synoptic studies, in the use of the verbs of speaking in this pericope, I confess that I cannot detect it. The use of these various words here seems to be completely neutral in relation to the questions of alternative hypotheses of Synoptic relationships. We may therefore turn our attention now to other more significant similarities and differences between the Synoptics in this pericope.

Probing the Markan Priority Explanation of the Differences

Exposition of the pericope from the perspective of Markan Priority occurs in the standard commentaries, such as Allen on Matthew, V. Taylor on Mark, Marshall on Luke, Gundry, and Stonehouse (1963, 93–112). As a generalization, it could be said that the commentaries simply describe the alterations that would have been made to Mark by Matthew or Luke (as the case may be), if indeed they each were using Mark as their source. Only occasionally are explanations attempted for *why* one or the other would have acted as he did.

The first thing that we may note is the *exceedingly extensive amount of explaining to be done*, if it were to be attempted: that is, the very great extent to which Matthew and Luke have departed from what they had before them in Mark. Indeed (we may ask), why should they not do so? They are independent authors, writing from their own perspectives and for their own reasons, and simply drawing on Mark for their information. But this comment, while completely true, does not come to grips with what is at issue. It is legitimate to ask what could possibly have led to this or that alteration being made, and then to look at the overall probability that either Matthew or Luke would have made *all* the alterations that the Markan Priority Hypothesis postulates of them.

All three Gospels give this pericope at the same point, which is after the pericope about Jesus blessing the children. Why would both Matthew and Luke excise Mark's setting and the fact that the man ran up to Jesus and knelt before him to ask his question? Why does Matt 19:16 alter Mark's "asked" into the more general "said"? Mark's word ἐπερωτάω (also used by Luke) is well established in Matthew's vocabulary, being used by him eight times in his Gospel: three times paralleled in Mark (Matt 17:10//Mark 9:11; Matt 22:35//Mark 12:28; Matt 27:11//Mark 15:2); twice paralleled in both Mark and Luke (Matt 22:23//Mark 12:18//Luke 20:28; Matt 22:46//Mark 12:34//Luke 20:40), and three times where Matthew introduces it into his narrative when it does not occur in the parallel in his (presumed) source Mark (see Matt 12:10; 16:1; 22:41). Under these circumstances it is difficult to see any specific reason why Matthew would reject the word here.

Similarly, why does Matt 19:16 change Mark's "inherit" to the more colorless "have" eternal life? This word κληρονομέω is inserted by Matthew at the end of this pericope (Matt 19:29) where it is not used by either Mark or Luke, and is also used by Matthew in 5:5 and 25:34 in passages unparalleled in either of the other Synoptics. "'Inheritance' is a common Jewish metaphor to express participation in the blessings of the future" (Allen 1907, 208). All the stranger then that Matthew, the *Jewish* Gospel, omits this term here while Mark and Luke have it, and doubly strange if Matthew has the term in front of him in his source at the time of writing.

As noted earlier, a theological explanation is offered (see Allen, 208; Taylor, 427) for Matthew's change to Mark's text concerning "good"; and his deletion of Mark's "Do not defraud" has been "explained as assimilation to the wording of the Decalogue" (Tuckett, 166; see Taylor, 428). The first comment is a reasonable one from the Markan Priority perspective.

The second suggestion is possible but fails to explain—if Matthew is concerned for conformity with the Decalogue as such—why he deletes Mark's σου in verse 19 ("your" [father and mother]"), thus moving the wording *away from* the text of the Septuagint, which has this word; or why he *inserts* an addition of his own to the Decalogue with "You shall love your neighbor as yourself" (v. 19). If he were going to make an insertion, would it not be more reasonable that it would be something else from the Decalogue not already in Mark—perhaps one of the first four Commandments or the Tenth? Again, why leave the Fifth Commandment in last position? This explanation is thus not consistent.

There are several places where Matthew altered Mark's text to substitute a synonym, where we again can ask why. Also, why did he change Mark's word order (e.g., εἰσελθεῖν in 10:25), or number (οἰκίαν to οἰκίας in 10:29), or grammatical structure (e.g., "there is no one who . . . will not receive" in Matt 19:23 from "everyone . . . will receive" in Mark 10:29–30)? So also we may question Matthew's motive in those passages in Mark that Matthew omits (including primarily Mark 10:21,24,29,30) and in the additions that Matthew makes to Mark. In the latter case, we may also inquire where Matthew obtains these materials, for the Markan Priority Hypothesis does not supply a source for them.

Now there is no difficulty in accepting that it is *possible* that Matthew did these things to Mark's account when using it. But no purpose seems to be served by most of these alterations so that for the most part one is completely at a loss to see the point of them being made at all.

Furthermore, there is the overall perspective of Mark's account, which says that the rich man has kept the commandments from (ἐκ) his youth (Mark 10:20), thus indicating that he is no longer *in* his youth; whereas (on this view) Matthew altered this perspective by omitting this reference and substituting instead two statements (10:20,22) that the man is still a youth. The significance and the deliberateness of these alterations is explained thus by Gundry (1982, 387ff.):

> Mark's later phrase "from my youth" supplies Matthew with a descriptive identification of Jesus' interlocutor as "the youth." Thus, in the interests of the church's accepting young people, a grown man who looks back on his youth becomes a lad still in his youth. . . . Since Matthew has made the grown-up a youth, "from my youth" naturally falls from the end of the statement "All these things I have kept". . . . That νεανίσκος has a semantic range falling within *modern* boundaries of adulthood in no way makes Matthew's designation compatible with Mark's and Luke's ἐκ νεότητός μου at the historical level; for νεότητός covers the period of being νεανίσκος . . . and Matthew's dropping ἐκ νεότητός μου, inserting νεανίσκος, and adding τέλειος for a contrast with

νεανίσκος shows he intends to reduce the age of the rich man. Correspondingly, in Mark and Luke ἐκ νεότητός μου puts the period of having been νεανίσκος in the past.

The motive that Gundry supplies for Matthew's alteration to the age of the rich man—"in the interests of the church's accepting young people"—is quite fanciful and lacks any support in evidence or logic. But if we are to accept that Matthew based his account on Mark's Gospel, the differences between Matthew and Mark-Luke call for some kind of explanation, and Gundry's imaginative speculation is the type of explanation that one finds that one then has to offer.

In a similar vein, Gundry explains the additional material in Matthew as the composition of the author. For example, on Matt 19:17b, Gundry says, "For further emphasis on keeping the law as doing the good, Matthew composes the sentence 'But if you want to enter into life, keep the commandments.'" And Gundry sees Matt 19:28 as being Matthew's extensive reworking and adaptation of Luke 22:28–30 for insertion here. Gundry's overall judgment of Matthew's redaction is (623): "Matthew's subtractions, additions, and revisions of order and phraseology often show changes in substance; i.e., they represent developments of the dominical tradition that result in different meanings and departures from the actuality of events."

If we pursue the same kind of inquiry concerning Luke's redaction of Mark as a source, we are led to similar questions. Why does Luke substitute synonyms for several of Mark's expressions? (See "many possessions" in 10:22; "are going in" for "will enter" in 10:23; "left our own things" for "left everything" in 10:28; "or parents" for "or mother or father" in 10:29; and "many times more" for "a hundredfold" in 10:30.) Why does Luke delete small details (e.g., "Teacher" in 10:20; "Go" in 10:21; "looking at them" in 10:27; "sisters" and "lands" in 10:29) and some larger points that Mark is making (e.g., the initial setting and the reference to the great astonishment of those who heard Jesus in 10:26; and many others, including Mark's final saying in 10:31)? And why does Luke then add in small details of his own (e.g., "ruler" in 18:18; "all" in 18:22; "or wife" in 18:29)? Why does Luke change "for my sake and for the sake of the gospel" (Mark 10:29) to "for the sake of the kingdom of God"?

The changes in Matt 19:29//Mark 10:29//Luke 18:29 are worthy of further comment overall. In this passage the grammatical construction of Mark and Luke is identical ("there is no one who has left house," etc.) while Matthew has a different construction ("every one who has left houses," etc.); the list of what has been left contains the same items in Matthew and Mark (there is one minor change of order) while Luke's list differs in several ways ("sisters" and "lands" deleted, "parents" substituted for "mother or father," and "wife" added). The Markan Priority view requires us to accept that Luke retained Mark's *grammatical form* but changed numerous details in the list (the only ones identical in Mark and Luke are "house," "brothers," and "children"), while Matthew changed Mark's grammatical form ("there is no one who" to "every one who" and "house" to "houses") but used *all the items on the list!* Compare here the Markan Dependence explanation (see below).

Also, why does Luke reverse the order of the Commandments "Do not kill" and "Do not commit adultery" (Mark 10:19)? I. H. Marshall (1978, 685] states correctly, "Whatever be the right order of the commandments is a matter of indifference." But if so, then it is even more surprising that Luke decided to alter it from what he had in his source.

Some changes in particular leave one wondering. They are so minor as to be insignificant, which makes all the greater the mystery of what the motive for change could have been. Mark uses ὑστερέω ("to be missing, have a lack") only in 10:21, and Matthew uses it only in 19:20. Luke uses it twice (15:14; 22:35), and it occurs elsewhere only 12 times for a total of 16 occurrences in the New Testament. Yet when Luke comes across it in Mark 10:21, he does not accept it here but instead chooses the synonym λείπω—a word that occurs nowhere else in Luke's writings and nowhere else in the Gospels. (The word occurs twice in Titus and three times in James for a total of six in the New Testament.)

When Luke comes to Mark's τρυμαλιᾶς ῥαφίδος ("the eye of a needle")—τρυμαλιά occurs only here in the New Testament and ῥαφίος only here and in the parallel in Matthew—Luke rejects both words and substitutes the synonymous expression τρήματος βελόνης (τρῆμα occurs only here in the New Testament, unless one accepts the variant reading for the parallel in Matt 19:24, and βελόνη only here in the New Testament; neither is used in the Septuagint). Why would Luke make such changes as these? Rare words like these for "lack," "hole," and "needle"—especially in Jesus' sayings—tend to be transmitted in the tradition without change. To change one such word in a saying of Jesus for another equally rare word for no apparent reason is very odd indeed. For it to be done *several times* in one passage calls for explanation. In addition, there are the other changes for a synonym in the pericope.

And then there is "heaven" to "heavens" (Mark 10:21). "Heaven" (οὐρανός) occurs "in classical Greek almost without exception in the singular" (TDNT 5:497). In the Septuagint οὐρανός is used to translate the Hebrew *shamayim*, a dual form. Thus the plural form is a Semitism and especially common in Matthew, where it is found in 58 of the 84 occurrences of οὐρανός (TDNT 5:513). The plural is rare in Mark (found in 5 out of 18 occurrences) and rarer still in Luke (3 out of 37 occurrences; and in Acts, 2 out of 26 occurrences).

[TDNT states that there are 37 occurrences in Luke, 5 of them in the plural; but in Moulton and Geden's *Concordance* (1974) I can only locate 3 in the plural, plus the one in the textual variant at Luke 11:2. Morgenthaler (1971, 127) gives a total of only 34 occurrences of the word in Luke's Gospel.]

Apart from the passage under consideration, the other two plurals in Luke are in 10:20 and 12:33—the latter being a context that also mentions "treasure in the heavens." Neither of these passages has Markan parallels; the second is paralleled in Matt 6:20. (The two occurrences in Acts are 2:34, where Peter discusses David in a context full of Old Testament associations; and 7:56, where Stephen, using wording reminiscent of Matt 3:16, speaks of seeing the heavens opened and the Son of man standing at the right hand of God.) Wherever else Luke parallels οὐρανός used in the plural in Mark or Matthew, he uses the singular.

Why then *in this one instance* should he come across a singular in Mark and alter it to the plural? It is unlikely in the extreme that he would deliberately make a change in this word from a singular to a plural. The only reason that makes sense for Luke to have the plural of οὐρανός here in his Gospel would be *that it was plural in his source*. And as it is singular in Mark, this is a strong indicator that *Mark is not Luke's source*. Matthew has the plural of οὐρανός here also, but this could not be Luke's source for this pericope because of all the differences of wording and viewpoint that prevail throughout the pericope. Therefore Luke's source is L, his private source distinct from Matthew, Mark, or Q.

Finally, why would Luke alter Mark 10:22 so that in his account the man no longer went away but apparently remained in the immediate vicinity during what followed? And why would Luke delete all references to the disciples here in this pericope so that in Luke's account Jesus speaks only to the rich man or to the people in general (see 18:26)?

We can make an attempt at some explanations of these matters. In most cases they are very hard to explain because they make no sense and we can see no point in the change. Therefore, if we adopt the Markan Priority position, there is little more that we can do than echo afresh the words of B. H. Streeter (1924, 169): "But, even when we can detect no particular motive, we cannot assume that there was none; for we cannot possibly know, either all the circumstances of churches, or all the personal idiosyncrasies of writers so far removed from our own time."

Probing the Markan Dependence Explanation of the Differences

According to the Markan Dependence explanation, the accounts in Matthew and Luke differ in all the various ways that they do because *they derive from independent eyewitnesses of the event.* The apostle Matthew is himself the source of all that is found in Matthew's Gospel, and it reflects the way in which the incident impressed itself upon him. Luke's account had come down to him from some other eyewitness—possibly another of the 12 apostles, but more likely not, since the disciples are not mentioned at all in Luke's version of the pericope (except Peter's statement in 18:28).

The difference between the perspective of the two accounts is thus readily understandable. The man is a "young man" in Matthew, and in Luke he is an older man who has kept the commandments from his youth and is now a ruler. This difference could simply reflect the different ages of the eyewitnesses who were the sources of the two accounts; for example, a 40-year-old man may be considered young *or* old depending somewhat on the age of the person making the assessment! Similarly, whether the man went away (as in Matthew's account) or is not said to have done so could also depend on *where the witness himself happened to be standing.* If the man indeed moved away from where he had been standing near Jesus, but hovered nearby, still attempting perhaps to listen to what else was said and still in sight of the witness who was Luke's source, this difference is explained.

Some of the minor differences in the two accounts would be due to the details that impacted the two eyewitnesses—which is why one account would be the only one to contain some particular detail and the second account contains something else not in the first. Other differences may possibly result from the way in which one person and another rendered the incident into Greek from Aramaic, if the original discussion took place in that language. This could well be the explanation for some of the different words used for the same ideas.

The accounts of Matthew and Luke bear the stamp of being two completely accurate and quite independent records of a given incident. But when Mark wrote this story for his Gospel, he drew heavily (and primarily) on the information in Matthew and Luke, but there were some additional details that he had learnt from his source P, and these were interwoven with the others in several places. In many cases Mark found one expression in Matthew and a synonym in Luke's parallel. This hardly lent itself to assimilation or conflation. On two such occasions Mark substituted his own word or phrase (τρυμαλιᾶς in 10:25; ἕνεκεν in 10:29). Mark conflates the two "impossible with men/possible with God" versions (see below), and on the other occasions he chooses to adopt the wording either of Matthew or of Luke. So that what Mark has done can be seen, the list of synonymous wordings is repeated here from above but with Mark's adopted words now given in capitals.

Matthew 19	Luke 18
16. have [eternal life]	18. INHERIT [eternal life]
17. keep [the commandments]	20. YOU KNOW [the commandments]
21. [sell] YOUR POSSESSIONS	22. [sell] all that you have
22. [hearing] THE SAYING	23. [hearing] these things
22. HE WAS SORROWFUL (λυπούμενος)	23 he was sad (περίλυπος)
22. [for he] HAD MANY POSSESSIONS	23. [for he] was very rich
23. with what difficulty a rich man WILL ENTER the kingdom of the heavens.	24. WITH HOW MUCH DIFFICULTY THOSE WHO HAVE POSSESSIONS are going into the kingdom OF GOD.
24. to go through the eye of a needle: (τρυπήματος ραφίδος διελυεῖν)	25. to go through the eye of a needle (τρήματος βελόνης εἰσελυεῖν)
26. With men this is impossible, but with God all things are possible.	27. What is impossible with men is possible with God.
27. [we] HAVE LEFT EVERYTHING	28. [we] left our own things
29. And everyone who has left . . .	29. THERE IS NO ONE WHO HAS LEFT . . .
29. OR FATHER OR MOTHER	29. or parents
29. [for the sake of] my name	29. [for the sake of] the kingdom of God
29. will receive A HUNDREDFOLD	30. would receive many times more

[See further discussion of these points in the comments that follow.]

Mark's attitude about the major points of difference between Matthew and Luke can be observed by inspecting what he has done. He has largely followed the perspective of Luke's account. He adopted completely Luke's form of the opening question and Jesus' reply, and he has taken over Luke's "from my youth" (10:20). But he minimized the difference between the two accounts by leaving out both Matthew's "young man" (19:20,22) and Luke's "ruler" (18:18). In 10:22, Mark conflated the points made by Luke that the man became sad and by Matthew that he went away sorrowful. In 10:23 he included Luke's detail that Jesus "looked" but made it "around" rather than "at" the man, since he followed Matthew in saying that the man had left; he also conflated this with Matthew's "[and] said to his disciples."

Several times Mark takes a word or other detail from Matthew and places this into a phrase from Luke. Thus Mark takes ὑστερωέω from

Matt 19:20 and uses it in place of Luke's λείπω (18:22); he takes εἰσελεύσεται from Matt 19:23 and uses it in place of (and in the same position as) Luke's εἰσπορεύονται (18:24), changing its number from singular to plural to match the new context. He blends the two differing ways in which Matthew and Luke have given the Commandments by adopting Luke's *form* (μή plus the subjunctive) with Matthew's *order* (the Commandment about killing before the Commandment about adultery).

Mark finds two different grammatical constructions and two different lists and two different reasons in the sayings about what the disciples have left, so he forms his own account by using Luke's grammatical form, adopting Matthew's list of what was left, and giving his own double ἕνεκεν (Mark 10:29). Mark's account has concepts similar to both Matthew and Luke, is identical with neither, and could have been adapted from Matthew and Luke but probably reflects his source P.

Another striking example of Mark's conflation is his way of handling the different constructions in Matthew and Luke in the saying about what is impossible (Matt 19:26//Luke 18:27). Here is the wording that confronted Mark (assuming Markan Dependence):

Matthew 19:26	Luke 18:27
παρὰ ἀνθρώποις τοῦτο ἀδύνατόν ἐστιν, παρὰ δὲ θεῷ πάντα δυνατά.	τὰ ἀδύνατα παρὰ ἀνθρώποις δυνατὰ παρὰ τῷ θεῷ ἐστιν.

Taking δυνατά as the central or pivotal word, Mark has taken over both what Matthew has before it and what Luke has after it, as can be seen here:

Matthew 19:26	Mark 10:27	Luke 18:27
παρὰ ἀνθρώποις τοῦτο	παρὰ ἀνθρώποις	τὰ ἀδύνατα παρὰ ἀνθρώποις
ἀδύνατόν ἐστιν,	ἀδύνατόν	
παρὰ δὲ θεῷ πάντα δυνατά.	ἀλλ' οὐ παρὰ θεῷ, πάντα γὰρ δυνατὰ παρὰ τῷ θεῷ	δυνατὰ παρὰ τῷ θεῷ ἐστιν.

Notice how closely what *precedes* δυνατά in Mark corresponds with Matthew, and how closely what *follows* δυνατά corresponds with Luke, even to the use of the singular initially (Matthew says, "this is ... ") and then changing to the plural (Luke is plural throughout the verse, "The things that are ... "). Notice also the absence of the article with θεῷ prior to δυνατά (Matthew does not have the article) and the presence of τῷ with θεῷ after δυνατά (this is what Luke has here). The other words added by Mark make the whole saying function as one smooth, two-part sentence.

Whether this overall blending of Matthew and Luke was the result of a deliberate intention to knit the two accounts together or was simply the result of Mark's making personal choices for each of these features in his two written sources, it is not possible now for us to judge. Certainly it shows a complete integration of Matthew and Luke.

Into the structure of Matthew-plus-Luke, Mark blends in a few other words and details from his source P. And in a few places Mark uses other words—such as ἐφυλαξάμην (10:20), στυγνάσας (10:22), τρυμαλιά (10:25), and in particular the singular οὐρανῷ (10:21)—either from his source P or from his own personal preferences in grammar and vocabulary.

The Question of the Good

But what should be said about the frequent focus of scholarly attention in this story, the difference between Matthew and Mark-Luke regarding the word "good" in their accounts of the rich man's initial question to Jesus and his reply? After outlining these differences in the Synoptic accounts, Taylor comments (1966, 425–27), [see below] "The greater originality of the Markan narrative is manifest. ... The secondary character of the Matthean version of the question is generally recognized. ... Taking exception to the Markan form on doctrinal grounds, Matthew has recast it."

Stonehouse cites (1963, 94–95) Taylor's commentary and agrees with him about the originality of Mark's account (110f.):

> The extensive study of this story as a whole has, in my judgement, presented further support of the view that the Matthean account is more readily understood on the supposition that Matthew knew Mark and utilized his account than that Mark is for the most part an expansion upon Matthew. The latter then streamlines Mark in the interest of a more succinct and somewhat simpler narrative but adds the saying of Mt 19:28.

But Stonehouse argues strongly against the view that Matthew alters Mark for doctrinal reasons (108–10):

> [Matthew] may be understood as having chosen to concentrate at the very beginning upon the foundational theme of obedience to the divine commandments. Recognizing these factors, and keeping in view the broader aspects of interpretation which have been previously considered, one may render the firm judgement that the absence from Matthew of the question, 'Why callest thou me good?', has by no means been established as being due to the factor that Matthew would have found it a stumbling block doctrinally. As has been

emphasized above, the story is not concerned with Christological questions. There is rather a preoccupation with the theme of discipleship as that affects the ultimate issues of eternal life. Moreover, the evangelist Matthew does not present an essentially different view of the relationship of Jesus to the Father from that which appears in Mark. . . .

The bearing of our discussion of the story of the rich young man for the subject of [Markan] priority still remains before us. The general thrust of our discussion, however, can only lead to the conclusion that the argument as presented by Hawkins, Streeter, Taylor and many others that a doctrinal modification has taken place is not established. If one studies such a passage as this one in its own setting and in the broader context of the Gospels it appears to be highly precarious to build a substantial argument for the priority of one Gospel or another upon it.

Thus Stonehouse acknowledges that Matthew has altered Mark's wording—a position he cannot really avoid since he accepts Markan Priority—but he plays down the significance of the alterations, and he rejects forcefully the usual reasons advanced for Matthew's alterations. That is, he accepts that Matthew has made these alterations to Mark, but he downplays their significance and says (101), in regard to Matthew's wording of 19:16–17, that the alterations "do not serve to create a contrary impression with regard to the initial thrust of Jesus' teaching. . . . It is by no means evident that Matthew says anything that is not implicit in the Marcan account." Similarly, regarding Matthew's addition to 19:21a—"Jesus said to him, 'If you would be perfect'"—Stonehouse says (101), "But again the substance of the matter is not affected since the word 'perfect' underscores the fullness of conformity to the will of God which constitutes the central thrust of Jesus' teaching in the three Synoptic accounts." He discusses (104) the Matthean narrative's "introduction of the saying of 19:28" without explaining why Matthew—whose account he describes (103) as marked by "characteristic succinctness"—has chosen to insert an additional 30 or so words or where Matthew obtained them.

Stonehouse's explanation for the changes that Matthew made in regard to the use of "good" in the opening verses of the pericope is as follows (108–9):

The foregoing argument for the integrity of Matthew does not however imply that the evangelist could not have exercised a measure of freedom in his literary composition of the narrative. At other points this liberty appears. For example, Mark and Luke report Jesus as saying to the young man, "One thing thou lackest" (Mk 10:21; Lk 18:22), but Matthew records that it was the young man who said, "What do I still lack?" As another example of such freedom one may recall the differences of Matthew and Luke from Mk 10:29: "for my sake and the gospel's sake." Here Matthew says nothing of the gospel and has simply:

"for my name's sake," while Luke, omitting any specific reference to Christ himself, reads: "for the sake of the kingdom of God." It is obvious therefore than the evangelists are not concerned, at least not at all times, to report the *ipsissima verba* of Jesus. And on this background one must allow for the possibility that Matthew in his formulation of 19:16,17 has not only been selective as regards subject matter but also that he used some freedom in the precise language which he employed. The singular use of the adjective "good" might then be a particularly clear example of his use of that freedom.

To compress this explanation even more: Stonehouse says that Matthew was, as an author, quite entitled to "have exercised a measure of freedom in his literary composition of the narrative," for "the evangelists are not concerned, at least not at all times, to report the *ipsissima verba* of Jesus," and so "Matthew in his formulation of 19:16,17 has not only been selective as regards subject matter but also . . . he has used some freedom in the precise language which he employed." But this explanation (and it is the only one Stonehouse gives) does not in fact attempt to explain *why* Matthew should have made such changes but only asserts the possibility that he did so.

How is the matter viewed from the perspective of Markan Dependence? First, one must recognize a major shift in emphasis between the two ways of looking at the issue. Markan Priority says that Matthew had Mark's account in front of him and must have deliberately altered it. Therefore, (1) there must be some ground for why Matthew objected to what Mark's account says, or at least he must have considered his altered wording to be more desirable for some reason; and (2) we do not have in Matthew an account of what actually took place on this occasion but a reinterpretation and rewriting of it in line with Matthew's overall views and purposes. As Gundry (1982, 623) states, "Clearly, Matthew treats us to history mixed with elements that cannot be called historical in a modern sense. . . . Matthew's subtractions, additions, and revisions of order and phraseology often show changes in substance; i.e., they represent developments of the dominical tradition that result in different meanings and departures from the actuality of events."

On the Markan Dependence view, *no such deliberate alteration of one Gospel by another author occurred*, and we are not required to consider *why* it would have been changed, nor are we obliged to regard one account or the other as, in Gundry's phrase, a "departure from the actuality of events." On the Markan Dependence Hypothesis Mark had in front of him, in Matthew and Luke, two accounts of the event and chose to adopt Luke's. What we have in Matthew and Luke are two traditions of what took place, both going back to the actual occurrence itself. The differences between the wording of Matt 19:16b–17a and Luke 18:18b–19a are the differences that exist between two accounts from two different eyewitness who heard the one conversation.

To assess the extent of emphasis being placed upon "good," and therefore the degree of difference to be accorded to the two versions of this conversation, we need to note the overall theme and sequence of thought in the entire pericope. Jesus in his reply queries the way in which the man was using this word, and Jesus himself uses the word "good" as the springboard for his own answer to the man. The man asks what he must do for eternal life. The answer to this question begins with a recognition that God is the source of all goodness, for only God is truly good. And this God who is good has given the Commandments. There is no need and no justification for taking Jesus' comments about "good" and about the Commandments as being unrelated, as if Jesus is speaking to the man about two totally different matters one after the other. Jesus moves deliberately from the rich man's "good" to the question about the Commandments, and the transition or link between the two is the absolute goodness of God, which is revealed and expressed in the Commandments.

Jesus' reply thus means, "Why do you speak of 'good' in this way?" This leads into the goodness of God and from there into the Commandments that embody that goodness and through which we are enabled to know what it means to live a life of goodness—and that in fact is the nature of eternal life: a life of goodness, a life conformed to the Commandments.

Stonehouse (98) says that the rich man made the "claim that he had kept the whole law." This is not accurate. The man did not claim to have kept the whole law. He was not asked about the whole law. Jesus' reply to the rich man lists the Commandments of the Second Table of the law. He does not refer to the Commandments of the First Table, the first four Commandments—Jesus does not raise them here as an issue. The rich man was reminded of Commandments 5, 6, 7, 8, and 9—that is, all the Commandments of the Second Table, *except the Tenth!* And he said—and Jesus did not question the truthfulness of it—"All *these* I have kept." He could not truthfully say this about the Tenth Commandment because *he was not keeping it.*

That is the whole point of this section of the story. When Jesus says, "There is one that you lack," he is not adding some *further* requirement to those already given in the Commandments, as if the man were already fulfilling what Jesus had said thus far, and so more must now be asked of him. Rather, Jesus deliberately omits the Tenth Commandment from his initial list so that he could now use it to penetrate through the man's pride of achievement to his real problem.

When Jesus says "There is one that you lack," his words mean "There is one Commandment that you are failing to keep"—and he is referring to the Tenth Commandment. It is no coincidence that Jesus' listing of the Commandments of the Second Table leaves out this one only—that after the man says he is keeping all those that Jesus lists, Jesus tells him there is one missing and that from subsequent developments in the story it is clear that the man is beset by covetousness. Jesus' instructions to him are not requirements *additional* to the Commandments, but a way for the rich man to break free of his addiction to covetousness so that he can begin keeping the *one that he is lacking*: the Tenth Commandment.

The thesis of the rest of the discussion is: It was an axiom of the day that the rich were more able to meet the requirements of goodness and godliness because of the increased leisure and opportunities afforded them by their riches, which also were in themselves a sign of God's blessing and favor upon them. Jesus turned this traditional wisdom on its head. Riches, far from being an aid, were a fatal hindrance to entering the kingdom of God. (Attempts to water down the starkness of Jesus' conundrum of a camel and a needle's eye are not only unhelpful but quite miss the point, which was to illustrate the impossible.)

Hence the disciples' amazement. If a rich person (with, as it would appear, all the advantages in his favor) cannot be saved, who then can? Their question now allows Jesus to make his point to his followers. Entering and having eternal life has been stated to consist in living in accord with God's Commandments. Riches are a blockage to entering the kingdom. An impasse is reached: under these circumstances no one can be saved.

So Jesus explains: What is impossible with men is possible with God. That is (as the total context makes plain), living out the Commandments in one's life is impossible by human effort—no matter who one is; but it *is* possible by God's help. Inheriting eternal life—entering the kingdom of God (the context shows that the terms are synonymous)—is possible only by the sovereign grace of God; but the Commandments have not at this stage of the discussion been abrogated as the basis of the life of the members of the kingdom—rather, life lived in conformity with them is recognized as possible only through God's help. It is important to note that (1) this progression of thought is clear in all three Synoptics; (2) this progression is unaffected by the differences in their initial wording, which are unimportant to this thought; and (3) no point is being made in any of the Synoptics about "good" except what is common to them all: the man's question and Jesus' reply are steps towards the point that all goodness has its source in God, and the Commandments are an expression of that goodness.

Thus in Matthew's version, "what good thing?" equals "what is the good that I am to do to have eternal life?" The thought in Jesus' reply is, "You don't need to ask me about the nature of the good—as if I have something new and different to say. Good only has one source, God—and hence it can never change its nature, because God's moral character does not change. The way to the life that is good (eternal life) remains the same as it always has been: live according to the Commandments."

This is not a doctrine of salvation by works: "keep the Commandments and thereby you will earn the right to be permitted to enter eternal life." Rather, it is an explanation of the *nature* of eternal life. Eternal life is life lived in accordance with goodness, life lived in accordance with the will of God—and the will of God is revealed in the Commandments. Goodness has its source in God alone, and his will and character are expressed in the Commandments. To enter (aorist) eternal life therefore is to keep (aorist) the Commandments. Eternal life is life lived in harmony with the will and nature of God.

The same implications come from Luke's version. The man calls Jesus "good." Jesus then asks this: "What do you mean by calling me 'good'?" From here he leads the man to the goodness of God and the Commandments.

Thus the differences in the opening verses are not in contrast or set off against one another. In each version they fulfill *the same role*. They do not arise from any Synoptic author deliberately making alterations to another author's Gospel, whether from doctrinal motives (Hawkins, Streeter, Taylor, and most Markan Priority advocates) or not (Stonehouse). Such magnifying of the difference between the accounts to the level of deliberate purpose elevates it to an importance that it does not have in context. This difference is of the nature of those minor discrepancies between the accounts of independent witnesses to which Chrysostom refers (see quotation in chap. 10) when he says that, if the Gospels "had agreed in all things exactly even to time, and place, and to the very words," then their testimony would be much less convincing for the truth than what is observed, which is "that discordance that seems to exist in little matters."

Both Matthew's and Luke's records of the rich man's initial inquiry and of Jesus' reply represent reports of what transpired, each reflecting the impression of the conversation that was made on the hearer, with each account being a slightly abbreviated record of the event. The explanation of the difference may simply be that the conversation between the rich man and Jesus took place in Aramaic, and Matthew and Luke give two accounts in Greek from two different eyewitnesses: Matthew's tradition understood "good" to be applying to what the man was to do, while Luke's tradition understood "good" to be applying to Jesus himself. In any case, the opening verses are not in contrast in the two accounts, but in each version the opening conversation fulfills exactly the same role of raising for discussion the rich man's use of "good," which Jesus immediately uses to lead the man to the supreme goodness of God, from which the line of thought of the pericope then proceeds.

Assessment

The pericope of the rich young man is frequently cited by scholars as providing support for the Markan Priority Hypothesis. A detailed examination of the pericope in the three Synoptics shows that Markan Priority requires that Matthew and Luke have made a substantial number of changes to Mark—some major and significant, some minor and (as far as we can judge) pointless. A very considerable amount of explanation is therefore required, on the criterion of coherence, for this theory, and it is not easy to suggest a reason for most of the changes involved.

But from the perspective of Markan Dependence, Matthew and Luke are separate accounts from independent eyewitnesses, and Mark conflates the two accounts. In the nature of the case, far fewer changes to sources have been made according to this hypothesis, because where Matthew and Luke differ, Mark is usually in accord with one or the other. What is not drawn from either Matthew or Luke is most readily explained on the basis of Mark's third source P, or (in a number of instances) of Mark's redactional choice, such as his preference for particular tenses.

Thus Markan Priority says that a very considerable amount of redaction has taken place, and therefore there is a great deal of alteration to be explained. But Markan Dependence says that Matthew and Luke are independent accounts from different eyewitnesses, that Mark drew on the two of them for his material that he has carefully woven together, and that there is very little in his account which cannot be attributed to one or the other of the Major Synoptics. This does not call for explanation since Mark does not alter what is in his source(s) but simply chooses between what is in one or the other of them, and he amalgamates them where he finds this to be best. What does not come from either Matthew or Luke is mostly readily explained on the basis of his source P; the existence of at least one source in addition to Matthew and Luke must be accepted because of the extent to which Mark in his Gospel has material that overall goes beyond what is in the two Major Synoptics (see chap. 3).

It may seem that P is being invoked a little arbitrarily to deal with any difficulties where the text of Mark cannot be understood solely on the basis of what is in Matthew and Luke. But part of the very essence of the Synoptic Problem is that it is recognizably not possible to account for all that is in Matthew, Mark, and Luke solely on the basis of relationships between them—the nature of the data is such that there *must* be some other source(s).

The Markan Priority Hypothesis invokes Q for what is in Matthew and Luke and cannot be accounted for by Mark; and somewhat similarly the Markan Dependence Hypothesis invokes P for what is in Mark and cannot be accounted for on the basis of Matthew and Luke. There is, however, this difference. Q is a purely hypothetical source arrived at by deduction (in both senses of the word)—by deducting what is in Mark from what is common to Matthew and Luke, and as a source it is not attested independently in any way. But P represents primarily Peter, a known eyewitness, in known association with John Mark, and whose role as a source for Mark's information is attested in church history. This places P and Q on very differing levels of attestation (see further discussion in chap. 3).

A very small number of word changes are attributable to Mark's redactional choices, and many of these correspond with known trends that occur elsewhere (such as a preference for the imperfect tense and for καί rather than δέ); these can be recognized as Markan preferences quite apart from any particular relational hypothesis. The number of items in Mark that are not covered by the above, and which therefore may remain to be explained, are negligible compared with all that needs to be explained on the basis of the Markan Priority Hypothesis. The Markan Dependence Hypothesis accounts simply and comprehensively for the data of the text in a way that the Markan Priority Hypothesis does not.

To me, the puzzle of the century (last century, that is) is how Stonehouse, and all these various other scholars, could look at the Greek of this pericope and come to the conclusion that it favors Markan Priority. This conclusion flies in the face of the facts. Matthew and Luke have differences between them, on my count, in 36 points of detail. (You can see these in table 2.) But in 18 of these instances, Matthew and Mark are in agreement; in the other 18, Mark and Luke are in agreement. If Markan Priority is correct, then Matthew had Mark in front of him and decided to make 18 minor changes. We can speculate about the motives he might have had for doing this. But that is what it is: plain and unabashed speculation. If Markan Priority is correct, Luke also had Mark in front of him, and he also made 18 minor changes—*but a different 18!* So between them they created the situation of having 36 points of difference between them, but with each only having 18 differences from Mark. Reflect on this, and then explain the fact that in "editing" Mark Matthew and Luke each chose 18 details—different details!—to alter. Compare this with the simple and straightforward Markan Dependence explanation that I have given.

SAYINGS TO WOULD-BE DISCIPLES AND STILLING THE STORM

Differences in the Synoptic Record

Let us turn next to consider the Synoptic pericopes of the sayings to would-be disciples and the stilling of the storm (Matt 8:18–27//Mark 4:35–41//Luke 9:57–62; 8:22–25). Mark 4:35–36 contains the setting into which Matthew places the sayings to would-be disciples (8:18), but not the sayings themselves. Matthew contains two sayings (8:19–22) and follows these with his account of the stilling of the storm (8:23–27). Luke contains both these pericopes but in different contexts and in reverse order, separated by a considerable amount of other material (9:57–62; 8:22–25). Luke has an extension to Matthew's second saying (9:60b) and a third saying in addition to Matthew's two (9:61–62). Luke pericope of the storm occurs in the same position as Mark's (Matthew is out of sequence with Mark-Luke here); he lacks any mention of the crowd, and he records Jesus as giving the instruction to go across to the other side of the lake *after* getting into the boat (8:22). All three Synoptics follow the stilling of the storm with the exorcism of legion and then the return of Jesus across the sea (Matt 9:1//Mark 5:21//Luke 8:40).

From the Markan Priority Perspective

Markan Priority says that Matthew obtained the storm pericope from Mark and, after the instruction to go across to the other side and the mention of the crowds (in which there is a considerable amount of Matthean redaction), he inserts into Mark's story, from Q, the account of the man who came up to talk to Jesus and the discussion that ensued. Thus Matthew's redaction of Mark consists of the following: (1) moving the pericope out of its position in Mark (where it follows the parables pericopes) to a much earlier place; (2) deleting "On that day, when evening had come"; (3) changing the direct speech of Jesus' instruction to go across to the other side into indirect speech; (4) moving Mark's reference to Jesus' "leaving the crowds" to the beginning of the story, so that the crowds become the reason for Jesus embarking in the boat: "Now when Jesus saw great crowds around him"; (5) changing the emphasis on the disciples' concern for Jesus ("they took him with them in the boat, just as he was") into the rather different "And when he got into the boat, his disciples followed him"; and (6) deleting the reference (Mark 4:36b) to other boats being with him. This is *very* extensive redaction by Matthew; there is no part of Mark 4:35–36 that is not affected by it.

Matthew then inserts sayings to would-be disciples between the mention of Jesus' giving orders to cross over and his actually getting into the boat. Why would Matthew wish to insert his block of Q teaching at this point in Mark? There is absolutely nothing in Mark's text to suggest this as a place for such an insertion. And this is out of character for Matthew, who normally agglomerates such material as these sayings into larger accounts, joining like to like, as Streeter (1924, 166–67) pointed out.

Luke's redactional procedure is also quite extensive and similarly puzzling. The reasons for these changes are not immediately apparent. Luke's redaction of Mark consists of the following: (1) moving the pericope about Jesus' true family from the beginning of Mark's parables (which in general he parallels) to the end of them (8:19–21), so that it precedes the storm pericope; (2) changing Mark's specific setting ("On that day, when evening had come") into a very general one ("One day"); (3) deleting all mention of the crowd; (4) moving Jesus' instruction to go across to the other side from before Jesus got into the boat to after it, and adding to it the words "of the lake"; (5) changing the emphasis on the disciples' concern for Jesus ("they took him with them in the boat, just as he was") into the rather different "And when he got into the boat, his disciples followed him"; and (6) deleting the reference (Mark 4:36b) to other boats with him. This is *very* extensive redaction by Luke also; there is no part of Mark 4:35–36 that is not affected by it.

From the Markan Dependence Perspective

Markan Dependence says that Mark omits the sayings to would-be disciples (which is consistent with his overall policy of using only some of Jesus' sayings recorded in the Major Synoptics), he conflates Matthew and Luke, almost always following one or the other, and he adds several minor details from his own knowledge of this story from the preaching of Peter.

Thus Mark's redactional procedure consists of the following: (1) following Matthew in placing the pericope about Jesus' true family immediately prior to the parables rather than where Luke has it; (2) following Luke in placing the storm pericope after the parables rather than where Matthew has it; (3) following Matthew in mentioning the crowd, though Mark refers to it after Jesus gives his instruction about going to the other side; (4) following Luke in giving Jesus' instruction in direct speech (Mark's record of Jesus' words is identical with Luke's except that he omits "of the lake"; like Matthew, Mark considers the lake a given); (5) following Matthew in saying that Jesus gave his instruction before he boarded the boat rather than after; and (6) adding several minor details: the alteration of the emphasis, in that the disciples took Jesus with them in the boat, "just as he was"; "On that day, when evening had come"; and "And other boats were with him." Thus Mark's procedure can be explained entirely in terms of following a pattern noted throughout: he omits some sayings in his sources; he conflates what he finds in Matthew and Luke; and he adds further details from his other source, P.

Then, in Mark 4:35–41, Mark has the *setting* for what is found in Matthew (the sayings to would-be disciples), but the Matthean pericope for which it is the setting is absent, so that it thus becomes instead the setting for the *following* pericope that occurs in Matthew. On the criterion of coherence, Markan Dependence provides a much better explanation of the data than Markan Priority.

C. M. TUCKETT'S DISCUSSION OF MARK-Q OVERLAP PASSAGES

C. M. Tuckett has a detailed study of the passages that are usually explained on the basis of Mark-Q overlap, concerning which he says, "The synoptic interrelationships are very difficult to explain by the Griesbach Hypothesis in the form advocated by Farmer" (1983, 92). Tuckett's case is based on two main arguments: (1) the evidence is against Luke's having known Matthew's Gospel (with this we can concur); and (2) it is frequently difficult to see how Mark's text could be derived from what is in Matthew and/or Luke.

But when assessing the explanatory power of the Griesbach Hypothesis, Tuckett limits himself—as he himself acknowledges—to the version of this view advocated by Farmer, and has not taken account of the third source (Mark's knowledge additional to the Gospels of Matthew and Luke) to which Griesbach himself specifically drew attention (see chap. 7). And Mark's text can readily be explained on the basis of Mark's use of this third source P or of his redaction of his material in accord with his attested preference of particular words and constructions. It is Markan Priority (not Markan Dependence) that has the greater difficulty accounting for such factors in the Synoptic text. (I have analyzed Tuckett's explanations in detail in chap. 7.)

Tuckett's Discussion of Specific Passages

Tuckett gives detailed attention to what he calls "Some Particular Texts." There are two kinds: "Selected Markan Passages" and "The Double Tradition" (i.e., the relationship of Matthew and Luke). In his first section, Tuckett examines seven passages:

1. The Healing of the Man with the Withered Hand (Matt 12:9–14//Mark 3:1–6//Luke 6:6–11)
2. The Synoptic Tradition on Uncleanness (Matt 15:1–20// Mark 7:1–23)
3. Cleansing the Temple (Matt 21:12–13//Mark 11:15–19// Luke 19:45–48)
4. Tribute to Caesar (Matt 22:15–22//Mark 12:13–17// Luke 20:20–26)
5. The Double Commandment of Love (Matt 22:34–40// Mark 12:28–34//Luke 10:25–28; 20:39f.)
6. The Woes against the Scribes and Pharisees (Matt 23:5–7// Mark 12:38–40//Luke 20:45–47)
7. The Widow's Gift (Mark 12:41–44//Luke 21:1–4)

In his second section, Tuckett then considers a number of passages occurring only in Matthew and Luke. In all the passages in this latter group, and also at times in relation to passages in the former group, Tuckett directs his rebuttal to the proposition that Luke is dependent on Matthew. For example, in his discussion of the healing of the man with the withered hand, he states (102): "The Griesbach hypothesis must presumably assert that Luke is dependent upon Matthew here." Such a relationship of Luke to Matthew was *no part* of Griesbach's Hypothesis; it was an extension on Griesbach's view made by Farmer—one with which Markan Dependence does not agree, as shown earlier (see chap. 8).

If we consider what Tuckett says in rebuttal of *Griesbach's* Hypothesis (as distinct from Farmer's extension of it, which I concur with Tuckett in rejecting), then this rebuttal depends primarily on one point: How could Mark's text have derived from Matthew and Luke? To the extent that this can be demonstrated to be difficult, Tuckett considers his point made: the Two-Document view gives a more coherent explanation of the text than does the Griesbach view. For example, regarding Mark 12:15//Matt 22:19//Luke 20:24 (Matthew and Luke, "Show"; Mark, "Bring [me a coin]"), Tuckett says (124) that "there is no clear reason why Mark should have avoided the use of δείκνυμι (or a compound) in both his sources, when he uses the verb twice elsewhere (1:44; 14:15)."

Matthew 22:19 has ἐπιδείκνυμι, which he uses three times and which Luke also uses three times (17:14; Acts 9:39; 18:28). Between them this is six out of the seven New Testament occurrences; the word does not occur in Mark at all. Luke 20:24 uses the simple form δείκνυμι, which occurs three times in Matthew, five times in Luke and twice in Acts—and twice in Mark. One occurrence (Mark 1:44, "go, show yourself to the priest") is in a passage closely paralleled in both Matthew and Luke (in citing the words of Jesus in this verse, Mark's wording corresponds exactly with Matthew and Luke where they agree, and exactly with one or the other in the minor points where they differ—with the sole exception that Mark has ἄ where Matthew has the singular ὅ). The other place (Mark 14:15, "he will show you a large upper room furnished") is paralleled in Luke, and δείξει is one of eight consecutive words in Luke that also occur in Mark. In both these places the context requires "show," and "bring" (φέρω) would hardly be a possible substitute.

But in 12:15 Mark adopts φέρω, a verb more frequent in his own Gospel than in either of the other Synoptics—including its suppletive forms, it occurs four times in Matthew, 15 in Mark, and four in Luke. So in the one context that permits it, Mark replaces δείκνυμι with φέρω, a verb he uses more often. Mark's preference for φέρω thus provides a perfectly valid explanation for Mark's redaction here of Matthew and Luke.

Moreover, Tuckett must face the difficulty, on his own terms, of explaining this passage from the Markan Priority perspective: Why did *Matthew and Luke*, in using Mark, *both* reject Mark's perfectly legitimate use of φέρω, a verb that *they* each use twice as often as does Mark δείκνυμι, and why did they both choose to insert here a form of δείκνυμι? That is, why did they substitute for Mark's φέρω a verb that they use less often than (Matthew), or the same number of times, this passage apart (Luke, four times), as they use Mark's φέρω? Realistically, one must say that what Mark did (on the Griesbach Hypothesis) is much "more coherent and self-consistent" than the explanation that must here be postulated for Matthean and Lukan redaction on the Two-Document Hypothesis.

Tuckett's consideration of these passages merits a much more detailed examination than is required here for our present purposes. It is sufficient for us to note that his conclusion that the Two-Document Hypothesis explanation is more coherent is answered by (1) the earlier discussion concerning P, the other material additional to what is contained in Matthew and Luke that Mark could—and did—draw on in the wording of his Gospel; and (2) a recognition that Mark was engaged in putting the wording of his sources into what was his own more familiar and somewhat more colloquial vocabulary, and that it would seem was also the normal style of Greek of his intended readership.

Assessment of Tuckett

Tuckett has drawn attention to the one fundamental criterion by which Synoptic explanations are to be assessed: Which hypothesis gives the most reasonable and coherent explanation of the pericopes in the Synoptic texts? He has examined a number of passages with the aim of assessing Synoptic explanations by this criterion. The passages he looks at are of three kinds: the so-called Mark-Q overlaps, seven selected Markan passages, and some from the Matthew-Luke (Q) tradition.

In every case Tuckett concludes that the Two-Document Hypothesis offers an explanation of the data equal to or (more usually) superior to any explanation offered by the Griesbach Hypothesis. However, we have had occasion to note that Tuckett makes his comparison (92) with "the Griesbach hypothesis in the form advocated by Farmer." This, one may recall, includes an extension on Griesbach that derived Luke's Gospel from Matthew.

We have considered the comparison of the Two-Document Hypothesis with Markan Dependence, the form of the Griesbach Hypothesis as set out in the present study, which recognizes in particular the following: (1) the independence of the Gospels of Matthew and Luke in their canonical form; (2) the use by both Matthew and Luke of some early documents written by the apostle Matthew and in circulation in the church; and (3) the importance of Mark's P source in influencing his point of view and his wording in how he tells the stories that he parallels in Matthew and Luke. When this comparison is made, the problems that Tuckett perceives for the Griesbach Hypothesis evaporate, and it can be seen that the Markan Dependence Hypothesis provides a more coherent and self-consistent explanation than is possible upon the basis of the Two-Document approach.

In particular, we have found confirmation (see chap. 7) that the so-called Mark-Q overlap theory is not a satisfactory explanation of the passages for which it is used. Moreover, as I said there, once the door is opened by this stratagem there is no way in which the size of Q can be contained, for it can be the source for anything in the Gospels; thus, instead of a Markan Priority or Two-Document Hypothesis, we have instead, *de facto*, an Ur-Gospel explanation.

A very detailed examination in this chapter of one oft-cited pericope, the rich young man, has enabled us to see how much more superior is the explanation of the data provided by the Markan Dependence Hypothesis, and this has also been noted in a briefer consideration of other material. Overall, it can be concluded that the ultimate assessment must be made, as Tuckett perceptively said, on the basis of which hypothesis gives the most reasonable and coherent explanation of the pericopes in the Synoptic texts. And we should note that the hypothesis that consistently provides this better explanation is Markan Dependence.

CONCLUSION

This chapter has noted the comments of quite a few scholars who have asserted that the pericope of the rich young man points strongly to the Markan Priority explanation of Synoptic relationships. But a close and detailed examination of the three Synoptic versions of this periscope show a different picture. If Matthew and Luke were drawing this periscope from Mark, then they have made a very considerable number of alterations to the wording of their source. Moreover, there is no coherent, consistent, logical explanation of their procedure, and considered individually the vast majority of these changes appear unnecessary and pointless.

Markan Dependence, on the other hand, sees Matthew and Luke as two independent accounts from different eyewitness, containing exactly the kinds of differences in describing the same event that would be expected. Then Mark takes those two accounts and blends them skillfully in a way that harmonizes them and minimizes those differences, with on occasion the use of vocabulary and the addition of points of detail that can readily be reckoned as derived from his recollection of Peter's preaching.

Similarly, a careful consideration of "Sayings to Would-be Disciples and Stilling the Storm" encounters redactional puzzles from the Markan Priority perspective but receives a clear and coherent explanation on the basis of Markan Dependence. Indeed, this hypothesis gives a more coherent explanation of all the various passages raised by Tuckett and others.

The pericopes selected for detailed examination are ones that Markan Priority advocates consider to support their hypothesis. It can be recognized that a careful consideration of the actual wording of the text points rather to Markan Dependence as by far the better explanation of the data.

12 IN CONCLUSION

This chapter summarizes this book and explains the conclusions determined from the entire investigation of the Synoptic Problem, Markan Dependence, and the Progressive Publication of Matthew Hypothesis.

> *If I wished to deter you from forming any theory as to the origin of the Gospels, and to persuade you that knowledge on this subject is now unattainable by man, I should only have to make a list for you of the discordant results arrived at by a number of able and ingenious men who have given much study to the subject. Yet patient and careful thought has so often gained unexpected victories that we incur the reproach of cowardice if we too easily abandon problems as insoluble. . . . There is a preliminary caution which is by no means unnecessary to give, viz. that in our choice of a solution we ought to be determined solely by a comparison of each hypothesis with the facts.*
> —G. Salmon (1889, 128–30)

SUMMARY

This book has had two purposes: to set out the hypothesis that sections of the Gospel of Matthew were written and published progressively, before this material was revised, edited, and expanded into its current extant form; and secondly to assess the validity of this hypothesis and its implications in comparison with the alternative theories about Synoptic sources that have been presented over the years. The evidence supporting the Progressive Publication of Matthew hypothesis has been weighed and considered, and the various views about Synoptic sources have been assessed and evaluated. This summary chapter examines which hypothesis presents the most rational, cogent, consistent, coherent, explanation of all available data, both internal and external.

Introductory Statement

Any person who begins to write about the Synoptic Problem is aware, with a sense of awe, of the immense labor that has been expended on this one issue by many great stalwarts of scholarship down through the ages, primarily in the past two to three centuries. Any progress that we can make today is possible in large measure because of the work of our predecessors. The very extent of their differences from one another—and these certainly have been considerable—enables us to refine and clarify our thinking about these specific problems.

Even a pygmy can see further than a giant—when he is standing on the giant's shoulders. So it is not surprising that we can see blind alleys and dead ends into which the work of our predecessors has taken Gospel studies. V. Taylor (1966, 76–77) ends his chapter on "The Markan Sources" with these comments:

> The study of the hypotheses which have been examined is barren if it ends in purely negative results. We may feel compelled to reject all known forms of the Ur-Markus Hypothesis, but there is something unseemly in an investigation which ends with *Requiescat Urmarcus*. The same may also be said of the rejection of redactional and compilation hypotheses. There is no failure in Synoptic criticism, for, if we reject a particular suggestion worked out with great learning and ability, we are compelled to reconsider the evidence on which it is based and seek a better explanation, knowing that a later critic may light upon a hypothesis sounder and more comprehensive still.

Furthermore, from our vantage point today, we are able to see where paths that to our predecessors seemed completely separate and diverging will in fact come together just up ahead and lead forward to a solution of one aspect or another of the overall problem.

This perhaps more than any other is the impression made on me by examining what others have already said about these Synoptic issues. Again and again I have found that solutions to which my research has led me and that I had thought to be original have turned out to be foreshadowed in the writings of some commentator or author whom I subsequently came across.

There is therefore little that is totally new in the proposed solution to the Synoptic Problem presented in this book. But in very many cases it could be said that the insights of many careful students of the Gospels in past decades have not received the thoughtful consideration that they merited, because those insights were overshadowed by difficulties left unresolved or were simply overlooked because they did not easily accord with the currently fashionable theory.

But in quite a few cases a steady accumulation of evidence and attestation has so consistently drawn attention to one issue or another, one proposal or another, that it is not easy for it to continue to be ignored by mainstream research and current Synoptic orthodoxy. These insights from the labors of many scholars may allow us to find the resolution of the perplexities that, for any of the currently held Synoptic theories, still remain.

Historical Survey

Papias's comments do not give attention to the order of the Gospels. (Gundry's case for interpreting Papias as implying the priority of Mark is not a strong one.) Clement of Alexandria says that those Gospels with genealogies were written first and then those without. Irenaeus says that Matthew wrote first, and then Mark and Luke (without an order for these two being specified), and finally John. There is one order (and one only) that accords with both Clement and Irenaeus: Matthew-Luke-Mark-John. Origen mentions the Gospels in our canonical order, but he does not say that he considers this to be the order in which they were *written* and his comments can be taken as implying that this is the order in which they are best *read*. He may be simply reflecting the trend at that time to arrange them in this order, a trend that soon crystallized into this sequence for the canon. Thus he does not speak against Matthew-Luke-Mark-John as being the order of writing. Prior to Chrysostom and Augustine, these are the only early church Fathers who discuss the question of the order of or the interrelationships of the Gospels. However, it should be noted that none of the early church Fathers implies the use by any Synoptic author(s) of any prior Synoptic Gospel.

Chrysostom and Augustine were the first to comment on this question of interrelationships, and they did so at approximately the same time (the end of the fourth century). Chrysostom asserts most emphatically that each of the four Gospels was written completely independently of any of the others. By contrast, Augustine avers that each Gospel writer used the work of his predecessor, in the order Matthew-Mark-Luke-John. After this time, any who refer to the matter of Gospel interrelationships at all accepted the judgment of Augustine, and they did so on his authority. Neither Chrysostom nor Augustine refer to any authorities for their views, and they give no evidence of having any specific basis for them. Augustine adopted the order in which the Gospels were arranged in the canon and appears to have accepted (without evidence or indeed any specific investigation) that this order was intended to, and did, reflect the order of writing. There is no reason for judging that this view is better based than, or should be preferred to, that of Clement and Irenaeus. We must also take into account Peabody's strong argument that by the time Augustine had completed his work on the Synoptics he had altered his earlier opinion in favor of the conclusion that the order of writing was Matthew-Luke-Mark.

Thus the evidence of the church Fathers is not totally conclusive, but insofar as it does point in any specific direction, it is to the order Matthew-Luke-Mark-John—unless one believes there is good (even if unstated) evidence for the first conclusion Augustine reached that supports the canonical order as the order of writing. There is no *stated evidence* at all from any of the early church Fathers bearing on the question of any *interrelationship* between the Synoptics, that is, any use made by any of the Synoptic authors of any one or both of the other Synoptic Gospels.

In the last quarter of the eighteenth century, scholars developed the first formulations of the major explanations of Synoptic interrelationships that have been added to those of Chrysostom and Augustine. These I now consider. It can be noted further, however, that through the past two centuries there have also been many scholars who have held that behind the present Synoptic Gospels were several other written documents of various lengths that were used by the authors of the canonical Synoptic Gospels, in whatever order they were written.

Complete Independence

Some scholars have advocated and further developed Chrysostom's view, that the Gospels were written in complete independence of each other. In particular, they claim that Matthew and Mark were written independently. Careful consideration of this case can lead us to acknowledge that it is persuasive in a number of its criticisms of the theory that Matthew used Mark's Gospel as a source, but it has not established the complete independence of the Synoptics as a satisfactory alternative.

On the grounds given by Streeter in his first three arguments or "heads," and echoed by many others, we must regard as established the existence of *some kind* of literary interrelationship between the three Synoptics, even if we cannot follow Streeter in accepting that these particular arguments establish that the nature of that interrelationship must be Markan Priority. Our investigation confirms the virtually universal recognition that Mark's Gospel is indubitably the link in some way between Matthew and Luke, and the factors considered in chapter 10 led us to the conclusion that the Complete Independence Hypothesis cannot account for Mark's position as the middle term between the Major Synoptics; nor can any Complete Independence theory explain adequately the close similarities that exist between Mark and the others in overall contents, detailed wording, and order of pericopes.

Successive Dependence

The evaluation in chapter 10 of the evidence for Augustine's Successive Dependence Hypothesis led us to the rejection of this theory as an adequate Synoptic explanation. Especially significant here are (a) the inexplicable way in which Mark deals with the contents and order of Matthew if he was using it as his source, and (b) the virtually impossible procedure that must be predicated for Luke in *always following* Mark in sequence where Mark *deserts* Matthew, and in feeling free to *desert* Mark's order himself in those places (and *only* those places) where Mark is *adopting* Matthew's order.

An Ur-Gospel

There is a complete lack of any evidence for an all-embracing Ur-Gospel containing all that is found in the three canonical Gospels. Chapter 10 shows that it cannot be accepted that if such a Gospel had existed it would have been passed over by the church in favor of our Matthew, Mark, or Luke (which on this hypothesis would each be only a partial replica of its contents), and certainly it cannot be accepted that it would have disappeared without mention and without a trace. In any case, while adequate to explain the Synoptic *similarities*, this theory leaves the *differences* as inexplicable. Other versions of an Ur-Gospel theory in which an Ur-Matthew or an Ur-Markus is postulated, cannot be as conclusively eliminated. The crucial issues are why such a theory is needed (is it an unnecessary hypothesis?) and what data can be offered that requires it as an explanation. Its only relevance to the question of Mark as the middle term between the others would be in the form of an Ur-Markus. H. J. Holtzmann had proposed this and later abandoned it; F. C. Burkitt, B. H. Streeter, and V. Taylor have argued strongly and cogently against it.

The Jerusalem School Hypothesis (Lukan Priority) does not really impact the case I am putting forward. The Farrer Hypothesis—a combination of Markan Priority and Luke's use of Matthew—is covered by what is said concerning the Two-Source and Two-Gospel Hypotheses. So this leaves just two theories that are capable of propounding a strong and persuasive explanation of Mark's relation to the other Synoptics: the Markan Priority/Two-Source Hypothesis (see chap. 5) and Two-Gospel/Markan Dependence (see chap. 6).

The Two-Gospel Hypothesis

With his revival and development of the Griesbach Hypothesis, Farmer has been responsible for reopening the active consideration of the Synoptic Problem in the present generation of New Testament scholarship (see chap. 6). However, he has not been very persuasive with his explanation of why, given the existence of Matthew and Luke, Mark would have been written at all. And he has tied his presentation of the view of Markan Posteriority to the assertion that Luke used Matthew as a source, whereas the evidence is completely against Luke having known Matthew in its canonical form (as shown in chap. 8).

Markan Priority

All the arguments of Streeter's classic case for Markan Priority have been completely nullified: Streeter's first three arguments and his fifth, by Chapman and Butler; and Streeter's fourth, in its various ramifications, by Sanders and Stoldt. (See chap. 5 for a careful consideration of all the arguments in support of Markan Priority.)

The only argument that survives this detailed assessment is one that was implied at times by Streeter and his followers but not separately identified or developed by them in detail. This is Tuckett's argument of cohesion: that at the level of pericope-by-pericope and indeed verse-by-verse comparison, Markan Priority is the better explanation. Chapters 7 and 11 consider Tuckett's argument and the grounds for challenging Tuckett's conclusion.

Now it must be emphasized that the rebuttal of the arguments for Markan Priority, as set out above, does not prove that Markan Priority is *impossible* or *incorrect*, and it certainly does not establish any alternative theory. But I have shown that the arguments used to establish Markan Priority (or to simply support it) do no such thing. Insofar as these arguments for Markan Priority are objective (dealing with facts as distinct from interpretations and opinions), they establish no more than the high probability of some kind of literary relationship existing between the Synoptics. Insofar as they are matters of interpretation or opinion, or based on presuppositions that have not been (and cannot be) established (e.g., that better Greek indicates a later document, or that greater frankness about the shortcomings of the disciples indicates an earlier document), they are ways in which different aspects of the data would or could be viewed in the event that Markan Priority had been established on other grounds; that is, they are valuable in showing us what the Synoptic data looks like from the perspective of the Markan Priority Hypothesis. But in themselves they provide no definite or specific evidence for the Markan Priority Hypothesis as against any other hypothesis.

Markan Priority advocates need to face this fact squarely. If one can provide as good a ground for rejecting a particular presupposition as for accepting it, or for adopting an alternative presupposition, then he can legitimately examine what the data looks like when viewed from that perspective, and he then can consider the alternative way in which the data can be interpreted. These other interpretations will be as legitimate as those from the perspective of Markan Priority. But it is of very great importance that we do not confuse opinions and interpretations of this kind with evidence or proof.

This is what seems to have happened: The Augustinian (Successive Dependence) and Griesbach (Markan Posteriority) views were ruled out of consideration from the outset on the grounds that Mark lacks important material that Matthew contains and that these views would require the belief that Mark left it out deliberately. But only a lunatic would act like that (Streeter 1924, 158), and Mark was clearly not a lunatic. Next, the Ur-Gospel theory is rejected as an unnecessary hypothesis. The first three arguments (from content, language, and order) establish that a literary interrelationship exits between the Synoptists, and this rules out the oral hypothesis. Other possible alternatives such as Lukan Priority were then excluded for lack of adequate supporting evidence. So the only hypothesis left is Markan Priority. This is thus accepted on the basis of Streeter's first three arguments, after the other possible hypotheses have been rejected. Then his remaining arguments are adduced as additional support for the proposition that has been established in this way.

Now this approach can be noticed in Streeter himself (151–52) where he marks off the first three arguments on their own, taking it that they establish the position. He says that "this conjunction and alternation of Matthew and Luke in their agreement with Mark as regards (a) content, (b) wording, (c) order, is only explicable if they are incorporating a source identical, or all but identical, with Mark." He then presents his next arguments in language that presumes that Markan Priority has been established and that what follows is providing further evidence for this position: "The primitive character of Mark is further shown by . . ."

Barclay (1975, 86f.) also presents the data, acknowledges the existence of other views, opts for Markan Priority, and then sets out "further arguments" that will "confirm this position":

> This would lead us to the strong possibility that Mark was the basis of the other two gospels. We shall shortly adduce other arguments for this, but it may be laid

down here and now that the priority of Mark is one of the most widely accepted principles of the modern study of the gospels. . . . Let us see what further arguments may be found to confirm this position.

Similarly Metzger (1969, 80–81) presents the data, acknowledges the existence of several possible relationships, opts for Markan Priority, and then sets out the other arguments "in support of this view":

> It is obvious from these data that there is some kind of literary relationship among the synoptic Gospels. Of several possible relationships, the one which has approved itself to most scholars is the priority of Mark. . . . In support of this view it is customary to point not only to the implications of the data set forth above, but also to the following features which suggest the primitive character of Mark's Gospel.

Again, V. Taylor (1930, 38–39) gives first of all the arguments of contents, language, and order and then follows this with an argument in which he states that "instances of *stylistic* or *grammatical* change are also significant." He concludes that "these facts considerably strengthen the argument that Matthew and Luke used Mark as a source." His next argument commences, "Further support is given by instances of what appear to be *conscious alterations* of Markan statements which might be misunderstood or raise difficulties."

A great many further examples could be adduced from other major scholars. But the fact is that this presentation of the case for Markan Priority does not at all establish what it has been almost universally taken to establish. What I am asserting is that this methodology is fundamentally invalid as a means of establishing a conclusion. It *is* acceptable (indeed, it is normal) to test a hypothesis by examining the data from the perspective of that hypothesis, to ascertain if what one sees will disprove the hypothesis. This is the standard procedure of *reductio ad absurdum*, for example, and the method of procedure in many scientific investigations. This approach can determine whether the hypothesis is possible or impossible. If a hypothesis is shown to be impossible, we abandon it and examine another. But if a hypothesis is not shown to be *impossible*, this means it is *possible* but not that it has been *proven* or *established*—or even that it is probable. Methodologically, it is invalid to claim that the data establishes Markan Priority, that all the other arguments support Markan Priority, and therefore that Markan Priority is confirmed as the correct explanation of Synoptic interrelationships.

These arguments either provide grounds for accepting that there is a literary relationship between the three Synoptics *without showing in which direction it traveled*; or they are reversible and can be used for supporting other hypotheses as much as (or possibly even more than) Markan Priority;

or they are matters of subjective opinion without objective supporting evidence; or they are in fact not *arguments for* Markan Priority at all; they are simply *explanations of* how that hypothesis would account for the data if that hypothesis had been established on other grounds. Markan Priority is an opinion unsupported by any identifiable evidence that points unequivocally in that direction.

It also needs to be recognized that the relationship of Markan Priority on its own explains only a relatively small part of the Synoptic data: that is, the material of the Triple Tradition that is sufficiently close in wording and scope so that the form of certain pericopes in Matthew and Luke can legitimately be considered to be derived from Mark. This leaves substantial sections of the Major Synoptics to be explained on the basis of other sources: Q for the areas of agreement between Matthew and Luke that do not occur in Mark, and M and L (however these are conceived) for the unique material (*Sondergut*) in Matthew and Luke. These of course (with Mark) are the sources in Streeter's Four-Document or Four-Source theory. But there are other passages that the above scheme does not cover.

First, there are the pericopes that occur in Mark but in such a form that Mark's account could not have been the source for Matthew and Luke. These are of two kinds: first, where Mark's wording differs from Matthew and Luke but the latter are rather closer to each other (the prime example being the parable of the mustard seed); second, where Mark's account is significantly shorter than Matthew and Luke and where the latter agree in what they add to Mark (the main examples are the preaching of John the Baptist, the temptation, and the Beelzebul controversy). The standard explanation is that in these pericopes there was an overlap of Mark and Q, and that both Major Synoptics made use of the Q account. One alternative approach is that Mark used Q (which in a sense is an explanation of how Mark came to overlap Q); another is that Luke used Matthew.

Another major area of Synoptic data is the passages in which there is significant and often extensive agreement in Matthew and Luke against Mark. Streeter's approach was to identify different types of agreements and discuss them separately, a methodology that—as Farmer and others point out—atomizes the evidence and makes it appear less significant than it is, so that the problem this data poses for Markan Priority is side-stepped rather than dealt with. The Two-Document (or Four-Document) approach does not adequately account for such agreements of the Major Synoptics against Mark, so these agreements must be attributed to such factors as Matthew and Luke lighting upon the same "corrections" to make to Mark, to textual distortion, or to coincidence. Upon examination of numerous occurrences of such agreements against Mark, these explanations appear to provide a pretty flimsy case, particularly in view of the fact that many of these agreements are of a kind that it is difficult if not impossible to see as being redactional modifications made to Mark independently by both Matthew and Luke. In these issues we can identify three specific arguments *against* Markan Priority. These arguments, and two others that we have noted earlier, can be summarized as follows.

1. *The nature, extent, and significance of the agreements of Matthew and Luke against Mark.* These agreements are such that it is highly improbable that they could all have arisen by coincidence or independently of each other. They occur in material that is part of the Triple Tradition, and they point to the existence of a common source for the material in question that is used by Matthew and Luke—a common source that was *not* Mark.

2. *The vagueness, dubiousness, and insubstantial nature of Q.* This hypothesized documentary source is invoked to account for one particular class of Matthew-Luke agreements against Mark: those where Matthew and Luke agree in the inclusion of substantial material not in Mark. There is not (and in the nature of the case, could hardly be) unanimity about the scope and extent of Q, because each scholar decides the contents of Q based on his own criteria. As an article by S. Petrie points out, "Q is only what you make it"—a point numerous others have reiterated. There is a sizeable gap between postulating a Q and adducing any *objective evidence* in support of its existence. And if one depends on logical arguments, then those logical arguments will, if carried through fully and consistently, establish a different conclusion because of the Mark-Q overlaps.

3. *The Mark-Q overlaps.* There are numbers of places where Matthew-Luke positive agreements are so many and so significant in a Markan context that the Two-Source Hypothesis is led to conclude that Q and Mark overlapped at the point; that is, they both contained an account of the same pericope, and accordingly, Matthew and Luke each (in his own way and to varying extents) conflated Q and Mark. But if some events recorded in Mark are thus acknowledged also to have been in Q, on what basis (other than pure arbitrariness) can it be decided that all the various other pericopes in Mark could not also be in Q? In other words, if Q existed at all, on what objective basis can its boundaries be drawn so as to exclude the rest of the Markan corpus? There is no way that Q can be confined to being merely a "sayings source." Once we face the significance of Mark-Q overlaps, we find that carrying the argument for Q to its logical conclusion leads us to Q being a full Ur-Gospel, used by Matthew and Luke. It would seem that the argument for Q "proves" too much! But in any case, it is clearly invalid

to conclude that something cannot have been in Q simply because it also occurs in Mark.

Thus the argument for Q removes the necessity for seeing Mark as a source for Matthew and Luke. *All* the common material in Matthew and Luke can be attributed to the Q source, and not merely material that is not in Mark. Thus the way is open to view Mark as also derived from the Q Ur-Gospel, or from Matthew and Luke. In practice, Q advocates will not follow the logic of their arguments to this conclusion. Rather, they argue for Q from the existence of material that is common to Matthew and Luke but that is not in Mark, without justifying their basis for deciding that other common Matthew/Luke material could not also be in Q if it is also in Mark. The recognized Mark-Q overlaps continue to point to the deficiency in their reasoning.

4. *The order of the pericopes in the Synoptics.* The Markan Priority Hypothesis entails belief in a very high level of coincidence; that is, it did not happen that both Matthew and Luke left Mark's order at the same point, and that when one of them was about to desert Mark's order the other Major Synoptic would always continue with Mark's order (if already following it) or return to Mark's order at that same point (if prior to that point he had been following another order).

5. *The extent to which Matthew and Luke have rewritten Mark.* If Markan Priority is true, then both Matthew and Luke have engaged in a deliberate, extensive, and (so far as we now can judge) frequently quite pointless rewriting of what Mark says, breaking up the pattern and organization of Mark's narrative, making numerous dubious "corrections" to his account, and excising a great deal of the vivid detail with which his Gospel abounds.

ASSESSMENT

Attempting an objective assessment of the evidence on an impartial basis is difficult. The real difficulty is coming to grips with what people perceive as being evidence and why. On the one hand, there are those like Kümmel (1975, 60) who look at the data (in this case, a couple of examples of "the colloquial or Semitic text of Mark" and the "better Greek" of Matthew and Luke) and conclude with seemingly absolute confidence that "in every case Mk is primary cannot be doubted." And I am left still doubting—which is something that I have just been informed by Kümmel that I cannot do. Worse still, I find the data to contain *no argument whatsoever* to support Markan Priority. If this is so, how then can Kümmel be so confident that this same data convincingly demonstrates Markan Priority?

On the other hand, there are those who write in much more restrained fashion. Such writers give a clear and comforting impression of a judge who reaches the right verdict after a careful and thorough examination of all the evidence. Thus Stonehouse says (1963, 82) with judicious caution: "On our part, however, we acknowledge that the linguistic phenomena which have been noted create a strong presumption in favor of the view that the less literary Gospel is the earlier." But there has not been any attempt made to substantiate his basic assumption that invariably a later writer, working from the material of an earlier writer, would employ better grammar and vocabulary than that used by the earlier writer. The data that Stonehouse provides (81–82) immediately before the statement of his judgment in the matter is, "Whereas Mark has frequent repetitions and redundancies and his language and style are relatively obscure and awkward or otherwise bear the marks of living speech, Matthew and Luke are more succinct, use more carefully chosen language and in general are more smooth and polished in their writing."

He acknowledges that "students of the Gospels are likely to continue to differ with regard to the implications of these linguistic data," but he finds that they "create a strong presumption in favor of" the Markan Priority Hypothesis. This seems to be arguing in a circle. I can see no factual grounds of any kind whatsoever for drawing a "strong presumption": the conclusion rests on the unstated, untested, and unverified assumption that a later writer would certainly and inevitably use better Greek than an earlier writer.

Mark is noted for the freshness of his narrative and the wealth of circumstantial detail with which he packs it. Weisse refers (vol. 1, 67; Stoldt 1980, 159ff.) to it as Mark's "own independence and originality . . . the impression of fresh naturalness and appealing liveliness." In this feature Mark is better than Matthew or Luke. This is seen as being a reason for Mark's priority. Styler calls (1962, 230) it "the strongest . . . of all the arguments for the priority of Mk."

Mark is considered to be a unity. Holtzmann, stressing this point, says (347; quoted in Stoldt 1980, 156): "Mark alone provides a continuous, unified portrayal of historical developments," while in Matthew "the original sequence of the individual narratives is broken up." A case in point is Mark 1:16–38 (a pericope on a busy day in Jesus' ministry), which Mark portrays as occurring within one 24-hour period and which in Matthew is "broken up." Another case is Mark 2:1–3:35E (a section on conflicts with Jesus' enemies), which highlight the range of issues in which Jesus was embroiled in conflict, and which are dispersed in Matthew. Thus Mark has greater unity and uniformity. In this feature Mark is better than Matthew or Luke. This, too, is seen as pointing to Markan Priority.

Mark is considered to be full of colloquialisms and grammatical clumsiness; his style abounds in repetitions and redundancies. In all these areas Matthew and Luke improve on Mark's style and grammar. In these features Matthew and Luke are better than Mark. This, too, is seen as a reason for Markan Priority.

Thus there are several ways that Mark is viewed as being better than Matthew or Luke. This is seen as an argument for Markan Priority. In several other ways, however, Matthew and Luke are seen as being better than Mark. And this, too, is seen as an argument for Markan Priority! So whether Matthew and Luke have overlooked or broken up something in Mark and thus lost something that Mark had, or if they have improved on Mark—whether Matthew and Luke are better than Mark or in regard to a particular matter Mark is better than Matthew and Luke—the verdict is always the same. *Every* situation is evidence of Markan Priority. Heads I win, tails you lose.

But the response to this objection might be, "Ah, but it all depends on the issue. In some matters the Gospel that is better would be prior, and in others the Gospel that is better would be a later Gospel." Perhaps so. But where are we to find an objective and impartial scale on which we can measure these things and decide which is which?

There is absolutely no law of literature (or knowledge) that says that freshness and wealth of detail is evidence of priority to (and use by) a document with less of each. There is absolutely no law of literature (or knowledge) that says that a less colloquial style and more formal grammar is evidence of posteriority to (and use of) a document that is more colloquial and less formal.

What then constitutes genuine evidence for a resolution of the Synoptic Problem? Where can we turn to find a firm foundation for a decision as to the order of writing of the Synoptics, and the question of which author(s) used which other document(s)?

Is there in fact no hypothesis that can be found that is able to explain all the observed data of the Synoptics? Are we to accept the opinion voiced by a number of scholars at the Jerusalem Symposium on the Gospels in April 1984, and voiced again at the Southeastern Baptist Seminary's Symposium of New Testament Studies in April 2000, that the question of the interrelationships between the Synoptics is beyond the possibility of now being solved? How could all the labors of so many scholars from around the world over so extended a period lead to so inconclusive a result as this?

But this is *not* the result to which our present study has led. Rather, we are able to recognize that the great majority of scholars who have worked on the Synoptic Problem have been right in *most* of what they have affirmed.

Scholars in Gospel studies have espoused views that in their final form are mutually exclusive, and it is a truism that these scholars cannot all be right. There is no means by which all the various points of view can be fully reconciled.

But the scholars whose work underlies the different Synoptic theories have had many completely valid insights into the nature of the Synoptic phenomena and what those phenomena indicate about what actually happened in the first century. They have reached numerous perfectly accurate conclusions from their study of the evidence. In fact, what has surprised me in my investigation of these various issues is not the extent to which so many learned and dedicated scholars have been *wrong*, but the extent to which they have been *right*. The major problems have resulted from their extension of their insights from particular issues and instances so as to become overall generalizations, when the evidence did not justify this. Where they have come to contradict each other, it is oftentimes in the deductions that they have drawn from the data and in the extrapolations they have proceeded to make in extension of what could be known into "conclusions" that were actually matters of pure speculation.

Chrysostom (see chap. 10) was correct in his assessment of the nature of the similarities and differences among the Synoptics and in his judgment that each of the Synoptists was an independent and valid witness to the truth of what he wrote. It does not follow, though, as he thought, that the independence and veracity of their witnesses would be compromised if they were interrelated in such a way that one (or two) of them used his (or their) predecessor(s) as a source. And Augustine was correct in recognizing that each later writer had known and made use of the work of whoever wrote before him, and this insight has become foundational in Synoptic studies. But Streeter was also correct that Augustine, lacking the tools for Synoptic studies that we have available, was in error regarding Mark as just an epitomizer of Matthew.

Further, Streeter was correct in recognizing the importance of the argument from similarities that provides a strong basis for holding to the existence of *some* form of literary interrelationship between the Synoptics. But he was unaccountably shortsighted—in view of the extent to which the aspects of this argument had been used earlier in support of other theories—in asserting that the argument from similarities pointed to (and only to) Markan Priority. Again, Streeter correctly perceived that the distinctiveness of Mark's style of writing was due to the fact that he used the colloquial spoken Greek of his day, but Streeter was mistaken in concluding that this fact was incompatible with Mark's being anything other than the first Gospel to be written.

The many who have advocated some kind of Ur-Gospel approach were correct in recognizing that *some written document or documents* must lie behind the three Gospels as we have them, but they were mistaken in concluding that such document(s) must be entire Gospel(s) of some kind. Griesbach was correct in perceiving how much of the Synoptic data could be satisfied on the assumption that Mark's Gospel was written third. Chapman was correct in saying that when Mark lacks teaching that is given in Matthew, his Gospel contains at that point some kind of reference to Jesus' other teachings. Schleiermacher, Knox, Guy, and Dufour (and a host of others) were correct in noting the evidence for small written sources lying in the prehistory of the Synoptics. Gundry and Kennedy were correct in their perception of the use of notebooks by Matthew and other eyewitnesses during Jesus' earthly lifetime.

Riesenfeld and Gerhardsson were correct in their explanations about the way in which traditions could be transmitted in fixed form during an oral period. Farmer was correct in his overall assessment of the Synoptic situation and perhaps especially for his presentation of how Mark's use of Matthew and Luke can account for the textual data. Farrer, Parker, Petrie, Dungan, and Albright and Mann were correct for their respective treatments of the shortcomings of the Q hypothesis. Neirynck and Tuckett were correct in their recognition that the most significant argument for Markan Priority or any other theory is its power to explain the data at the level of individual pericopes and indeed verses.

I could go on summarizing the contributions to our knowledge of the issues that have been made by a range of scholars over the last two to three centuries. But overall, these men have not agreed with each other's conclusions. I am reminded of the fable of the investigations of the six blind men:

> It was six men of Indostan, To learning much inclined,
> Who went to see the Elephant (Though all of them were blind),
> That each by observation Might satisfy his mind.
>
> The First approached the Elephant, And, happening to fall
> Against his broad and sturdy side, At once began to bawl:
> "God bless me! but the Elephant Is very like a wall!"

The Second, feeling of the tusk, Cried: "Ho! what have we here
So very round and smooth and sharp? To me 'tis mighty clear
This wonder of an Elephant Is very like a spear!"

The Third approached the animal, And, happening to take
The squirming trunk within his hands, Thus boldly up and spake:
"I see," quoth he, "the Elephant Is very like a snake!"

The Fourth reached out his eager hand, And felt about the knee:
"What this wondrous beast is like Is mighty plain," quoth he;
"'Tis clear enough the Elephant Is very like a tree!"

The Fifth, who chanced to touch the ear, Said, "E'en the blindest man
Can tell what this resembles most; Deny the fact who can,
This marvel of an Elephant Is very like a fan!"

The Sixth no sooner had begun About the beast to grope,
Than, seizing on the swinging tail That fell within his scope,
"I see," quoth he, "the Elephant Is very like a rope!"

And so these men of Indostan Disputed loud and long,
Each in his own opinion Exceeding stiff and strong,
Though each was partly in the right And all were in the wrong!

So, oft in theologic wars, The disputants, I ween,
Tread on in utter ignorance, Of what each other mean,
And prate about the elephant, Not one of them has seen!

John Godfrey Saxe (1816–87)

Which of the blind men came nearest to a true understanding of what an elephant is like? The answer of course, as Saxe says, is that all of them were right within limits and all of them were wrong overall. Each man was right in assessing what his groping had encountered. Where he was in error was in assuming that what he had encountered was in some meaningful way typical or representative of the whole animal, so that all of it was the same as the part of it that he had come to understand. For a total understanding of the elephant, each man needed to add the insights of the others to his own. Then and only then would they all be enabled to understand accurately and in its entirety the nature of the beast. If all they did was generalize and extrapolate exclusively on the basis of what each of them individually had discovered, they were bound to continue at loggerheads in their opinions about elephants and, in terms of their overall understanding of the full facts, all of them were bound to be wrong.

I do not mean to say that it is possible to proceed to devise a convincing (let alone accurate) theory of Synoptic interrelationships by making a compilation out of the views of the scholars who have already worked on this issue—that is most certainly *not* the way in which my conclusions were reached. But it would be reasonable to expect that a fairly comprehensive theory will be needed to cover all the complexities of the phenomena, and that none (or very few) of the constituent elements of such a theory *will actually be new*. If they are genuine deductions and justifiable extrapolations from the data, then it is virtually certain (given the incalculable amount of time that innumerable scholars have spent on the Synoptic Problem) that such insights will also have been perceived by scholars already.

This is not to assert that from the present time onwards we can expect nothing new to emerge in this area; rather, it is a recognition that probably most of what we will ever know about the issues involved in the Synoptic Problem have already been perceived by some scholars. We have all the pieces of the jigsaw puzzle (or if not all, as many as we can realistically expect to get), and it is now our task to put them all together in the right way to see the correct picture that they convey. We have the clues. The evidence is in. Like the detective investigating a crime or tracking down a missing person, like the physicist seeking to understand some aspect of the material world, we need now to interpret the clues aright and discern where the evidence points.

CONCLUSIONS

Mark is recognizably the middle term between Matthew and Luke. The most reasonable explanations of how this has come about are that (1) Mark was first and was used by Matthew and Luke; or (2) Mark was third and was dependent on Matthew and Luke. There are no objective reasons for accepting the priority of Mark, and there are several weighty reasons against this (see chap. 5). In fact, Markan Priority is an invitation to believe quite a few impossibilities (see chap. 7). As explained in the foregoing chapters, the case for Markan Dependence is that (1) there are a number of reasons that favor Markan Dependence; (2) there are many passages of the Synoptics that are most readily and reasonably accounted for on the basis of Markan Dependence; (3) Markan Dependence provides a valid and adequate explanation of all the Synoptic data, there are no places that it is impossible to account for on the basis of this perspective, and it is overall a much better explanation of the wording of the Synoptics as a whole than any other alternative; and (4) there are no compelling arguments against it, and those arguments that have been advanced can be satisfactorily answered.

The most influential arguments against advanced Markan Posteriority (Markan Dependence) have been:

First, *if Mark were writing third, he would not have omitted so much of the valuable material that he would have had in front of him in Matthew and Luke.* Markan Priority advocates claim that the absence from Mark of much of Jesus' teachings and other stories constitutes a strong argument for Mark being first. Indeed, this argument for Markan Priority is accepted everywhere as being so self-evident that it hardly needs to be spelled out, and so convincing that it quite overwhelms alternative theories. But this argument is totally based on two presuppositions, neither of which can stand up to scrutiny. The first is that Mark's purpose in writing, if he wrote third, must have been to *replace* the other Gospels with his own; the second presupposition is that if he knew a story or a teaching (especially such as Matthew and Luke have and he lacks), then he most certainly would have included it in his Gospel.

I answered this argument decisively in chapter 3, where I showed that *whenever* the author of Mark's Gospel wrote, and *whoever* he was, he would have had a knowledge of Jesus' life and (especially) his teaching that went far beyond what is included in the Second Gospel. Once this is acknowledged, one can see that it is far more likely that Mark would omit this material if he knew that it was readily available elsewhere for the church than if there were no other Gospel in existence when he wrote. For in that circumstance he would have been aware that what he knew and did not record would not be available at all (at that time) to the church. Thus the absence of valuable material from Mark is not an argument for Mark being *first*, but for Mark being *last*.

Second, *Mark's Gospel cannot be last, for if Matthew and Luke had already existed there would have been no reason for it to be written at all, since it contains almost nothing that did not already exist in one or both of the other two.* I answered this argument also in chapter 3, where an examination of the nature of Mark's Gospel led to an explanation of its rationale that well accounts for why it would have been written when Matthew and Luke already existed.

Third, *Mark's Gospel cannot be last, for if so this would require that it was a conflation of Matthew and Luke, and it is not possible for Mark to have produced such a conflation.* E. A. Abbott first propounded this argument in an article (1879) that became very influential in dissuading scholars from Griesbach's view. I answered this one also in chapter 3, where I provide a pseudo-Markan pericope of the Capernaum centurion. If this can be written now, by treating the accounts of Matthew and Luke in the way that Markan Dependence indicates Mark has done, it is hardly cogent to argue that it was impossible for Mark himself to have done precisely this from the other two Synoptic Gospels in front of him.

Markan Dependence describes the relationship between the three Synoptic Gospels and shows the grounds for holding that Mark wrote last, using both Matthew and Luke, so that it thus presumes the existence of Matthew and Luke. It therefore remains to explain the nature of the relationship between the two Major Synoptics. The simplest solution, and the one favored by Farmer and his associates, is that Luke used Matthew, for Luke's Gospel contains evidence of a knowledge of Matthew. However, a careful comparison of Matthew and Luke provides evidence that leads us to conclude that Luke could not have known Matthew in its canonical form (see chap. 8). There are innumerable places where in large matters and small Luke writes as if he was completely unaware of what Matthew said—as distinct from simply not choosing to use a pericope or a detail that Matthew includes.

This could suggest a form of Ur-Matthew. However, the part of Matthew that the evidence points to as known to Luke is in fact quite small and would not qualify as a Gospel on any normal definition of the term. Thus the evidence indicates that Luke knew *some parts* of Matthew and not others. The parts of Matthew known to Luke will encompass most of what is commonly assigned to Q (excluding those sections where Matthew and Luke agree in subject matter but are not so close in wording as to indicate copying between them). These parts also include those sections of the Triple Tradition where a comparison of Matthew and Luke gives evidence for holding that one directly used the other.

Those places where Matthew and Luke are similar (whether in Q-sections or Markan-sections) but not so similar as to indicate direct literary dependence are to be attributed to the two lines of tradition used respectively by Matthew and Luke, the similarities between them (in that they fall short of identity between the two accounts) being the result of traditions deriving from independent eyewitness testimony to the same event or teaching of Jesus, and/or to the careful transmission of the traditions within the church from the days of Jesus onwards, and/or to the fact that to the extent that two lines of traditions (or parts of traditions) would become known to the same persons in the church there would be assimilation taking place between them.

The foregoing indicates that the form in which Luke knew Matthean material was not as a short Gospel, a Proto-Matthew, but rather as separate sections or "tracts" of various lengths comprising teaching or narrative or combinations of both. Thus the better explanation of the data is that Luke used such written material that he had collected that subsequently also became embodied in canonical Matthew. This conclusion is indicated by three main factors. First, the sections of Matthew that correspond the most closely with sections of Luke do not in themselves constitute what could be called a "Gospel." Second, these sections taken as entities do not correspond in order in Matthew and Luke, suggesting that when they were received by Luke they came without any inherent information about sequence, that is, they were separate unattached documents. There are a number of places where the areas in common between Matthew and Luke can extend through a number of pericopes; these pericopes would then have been linked together as the one document in that sequence (see chap. 9). Third, Luke tells us explicitly (1:1–4) that many had taken it in hand to compile a διήγησις about Jesus' life and ministry. That Luke would have known that such accounts existed and chosen not to consult them is contrary to his statement that he checked on everything carefully from the beginning. To aver that many would take it in hand to compile such accounts, but that none among the "many" would be from the company of the apostles who were eyewitnesses and ministers of the word from the beginning, is to put too great a strain, quite unnecessarily, upon our credulity. The simple, and most reasonable, explanation is that among the accounts of which Luke knew and used were some that had been written by the apostle Matthew.

Simply stated, there was a progressive publication of Matthew's Gospel. At first there were numerous separate sections that would have varied in length from a few lines to documents of a few pages, originally written down by Matthew most probably not for circulation so much as for use as private notes, but in due course these were added to and made available for the use of new churches that had few (or no) eyewitnesses. Then in due course these documents were supplemented by Matthew with a great deal of other material that he wrote, and this was published as our present Gospel of Matthew.

Luke had collected many of the separate documents produced by Matthew, and then in due course he supplemented these documents with a great deal of other material that he gathered and wrote up, and this was published as our present Gospel of Luke.

Those occasional passages in the two Major Gospels that simultaneously contain evidence that what was in Matthew was known and not known to

Luke can be accounted for by the completely reasonable proposition that in combining some of his earlier pericopes for inclusion in his full-scale Gospel, Matthew made some revisions of what he had previously written and Luke would have known nothing about them. Minor differences between Matthew and Luke in a section where (on this hypothesis) Luke used a Matthean document are explainable on the basis either of Matthew's revision of his original document for his full-scale Gospel or of Luke adapting his source at the point of using it.

There are some things that this hypothesis makes no attempt to explain and that will remain a matter of conjecture. For example, when (among his other διηγήσεις) Luke collected documents that had been written by Matthew, was he or was he not aware of their authorship?

There are other things that remain matters for empirical investigation and appraisal. In particular these include, Which sections of Matthew and Luke that contain common subject matter are to be assigned to Matthean documents used by Luke and which to two similar but independent lines of tradition transmission? The answer will come from the close comparison of Matthew and Luke in these passages—this comparison should not be confused by the question of whether or not there is a Markan parallel—and then a judgment can be made. I have given indications in appropriate places of my own preliminary assessments about several of these passages, but I do not put these forward as the final word. There is room here for differences of opinion and for discussion of such judgments in exactly the same way as there has been discussion of the scope and contents of Q between those who believe in this source.

THE SOLUTION TO THE SYNOPTIC PROBLEM

The evidence has indicated that Mark's Gospel is the middle term between Matthew and Luke and that the three Synoptic Gospels stand in some kind of literary relationship. The two hypotheses that can best account for this situation are Markan Priority (that Mark was written first and was used by the other two Synoptists) and Markan Dependence (that Mark was written third and used the other two Synoptics). The foregoing examination of the evidence and of these alternative explanations offered for that evidence shows that Markan Dependence is better able than Markan Priority to account for the actual data of the Synoptics—their similarities and differences of content, wording, and order, and other features.

The Gospels of Matthew and Luke are largely independent of each other, embodying two separate lines of transmission of the Jesus tradition from earliest times. Behind each of them lie numerous sources, some oral and some written. The oral traditions incorporated in Matthew and Luke agree to a very considerable extent with each other because of the care that was taken in the first century in passing on such information accurately. The differences that occur at times between them are due to combinations of factors, including different lines of tradition about the same event or teaching, with some conflation and/or assimilation of these different lines of tradition; and the redaction of their material by Matthew and Luke in relation to their overall purposes in writing for incorporation of it into their Gospels. Some of the written "tracts" that Luke collected and used in his Gospel were written by the apostle Matthew and were also subsequently incorporated by Matthew into his Gospel when it was published. This accounts for the high degree of correspondence between the wording of some pericopes in these two Gospels (without reference to whether or not they are also in Mark).

Some of these accounts were originally written in Aramaic, and then separately translated by Matthew and Luke for their respective Gospels—or possibly Luke may have come across a Greek translation of an original Aramaic document that had been made previously by someone else. This could explain those places where Matthew and Luke are very close in subject matter but unaccountably different in wording, especially in those places where Luke's version appears more "original" than Matthew's.

Mark then wrote his Gospel, using Matthew and Luke as his main sources. He supplemented these two sources with P—private knowledge, primarily Peter's preaching.

HOW THE GOSPELS WERE WRITTEN

The data and discussion hitherto have been primarily concerned with the relationship between the three Synoptic Gospels and have provided substantial grounds for recognizing this relationship as being: The Gospels of Matthew and Luke were written independently of each other, with Luke making use of material that had been written earlier by Matthew and had been published progressively over a period of time; Mark wrote last and used the Gospels of Matthew and Luke in the composition of his own Gospel. This position is sustainable on the basis of the evidence taken from the Gospels themselves and is quite independent of other considerations such as the authorship of the Synoptics, the reason for their writing, and the date of their composition and publication. It is possible for scholars to differ amongst themselves about these matters and still agree with the basic proposition that, according to the evidence, Markan Dependence is a much more satisfactory explanation of the data than Markan Priority.

However, it is my judgment that various aspects of the evidence do point to particular solutions for these other questions of authorship, date, and provenance. In this section I wish to draw attention to these elements in the evidence and offer an assessment of their significance, thus proposing an overall explanation of how the Gospels were written. This summarizes the Progressive Publication of Matthew Hypothesis.

Stage 1: Early Production of Short Accounts by Matthew

During the time of Jesus' earthly ministry, the apostle Matthew made numerous written notes, particularly of what Jesus taught. Whatever form these notes may have taken, they acted as mnemonics of what that teaching had been, and to this extent they were similar to the notes that in the first century were commonly made by pupils from the teaching of their rabbis. In accordance with the attested practice of the day, other listeners also made similar notes as memory aids for their own use.

As the church spread after Pentecost, representatives from various congregations, visiting Jerusalem, asked the apostles for a record of their teachings that could be taken back to their own churches. Matthew provided them with short written accounts, sometimes of Jesus' teachings, sometimes a narrative of something Jesus did; sometimes very short, sometimes running into some hundreds of words; sometimes (according to the need) in Aramaic and sometimes in Greek. Over the years, Matthew thus produced a considerable number of these separate accounts that were based on his own notes of the life and teachings of Jesus and the recollections of the other apostolic eyewitnesses as these things were discussed together and preached in evangelism and ministry in the early congregations.

Matthew's short accounts—pericopes, as we call them now—circulated in the churches and began to be collected together in some places, and those in Aramaic were translated for the benefit of Greek-speaking Christians, who were less at home than the Hebrews with a tradition of oral transmission. These accounts include the *logia* to which Papias refers, written in Aramaic and being translated into Greek as the occasion required.

Stage 2: Compilation of a Narrative from Various Short Accounts

Numerous such accounts—some written by Matthew and some written down by other eyewitnesses—were being sorted into order by various collectors and were thus made into a connected narrative. Luke 1:1–4 refers to this stage.

Stage 3: Matthew Produces a Complete Gospel

Explanation of Matthew's Procedure

Matthew himself was motivated to assemble together the material he had already written and thus to produce a full account of Jesus' ministry and teaching. In doing this, he added further material that had not circulated separately, and he supplied "heads and tails" for his pericopes—introductions, conclusions, and connecting links—as he judged these expedient. If the original account was written in Aramaic, Matthew translated it into Greek or simply rewrote it in Greek. On occasion he may also have rewritten the wording of some part of what he had said earlier to make it more suited to its place in his overall record.

The apostle Matthew is thus both the author of the original sources used in his Gospel and the redactor of the Gospel as it was finally composed and published. In this respect his position is somewhat analogous to that of a modern scholar who produces a substantial quantity of notes about his subject, publishes some of his material in articles of various lengths, and subsequently rewrites and edits his own material into a connected account suitable for publication as a whole. To postulate this about Matthew is not "reading back" into Matthew's time something that is a distinctive characteristic of the modern world. This kind of procedure is a completely logical way that the process of writing an extensive volume can develop, and it is particularly likely for apostolic times in view of the high cost of writing materials in the first century, the immense labor involved in producing books by hand copying, and the complete continuum that existed between private circulation of records and full-scale publishing.

Explanation of Matthew's Order

Matthew used as his framework the general chronology of Jesus' life with certain pericopes taking their natural position at the beginning or latter part of his Gospel. But after the opening stories and prior to the sequence of events that led up to Passion Week, Matthew assembled his material on the basic principle of connecting like with like. His explanation of what happened during this period of Jesus' life (Matt 4:23–25; cf. 9:35) constitutes in fact the outline of that part of his Gospel. Matthew may have been indifferent to questions of chronology; he may have had no precise recollection or other information about the sequence in which various teachings, healings, and other miracles took place; or he may (and this is the most probable) have judged that for didactic purposes the grouping of like material into the one section would be advantageous. In any case, between Matt 4:25 and 14:1 (some would say 19:12) the primary principle of arrangement is the grouping of similar material. However, this is not to the total disregard of chronology, and where Matthew was aware that other incidents had occurred within context with something else that he was recording, he was willing on occasion to include these at the appropriate point. One example is Matt 8:18–22 ("he gave orders to go over to the other side. And a scribe came up and said to him") where a pericope of short sayings follows, included in a lengthy section of various miracles. Another example is Matt 9:18 ("While he was thus speaking to them") where Matthew knew of a time or sequence factor that linked incidents together and inserted this comment.

Explanation of Matthew's Style

Matthew's style in narration tends toward brevity and at times hints at brief notes made at the time of the event (or shortly afterwards), and minimally expanded when written up. For example, compare Matthew's version with those of the other Synoptic Gospels for these pericopes.

Pericope	Matthew	Words	Mark	Words	Luke	Words
Healing of the Paralytic	9:2–8	115	2:1–12	196	5:17–26	213
The Healing of Legion	8:28–34	135	5:1–20	325	8:26–39	293
Jairus's Daughter and the Hemorrhaging Woman	9:18–26	138	5:21–43	374	8:40–56	280
Death of John the Baptist	14:4–12	117	6:18–29	224	—	
Feeding 5,000	14:13–21	158	6:30–44	236	9:10–17	164
Healing the Epileptic Boy	17:14–20	110	9:14–29	270	9:38–43	110

(Figures derived from Morgenthaler 1971, 33ff., 235.)

Matthew's brevity in these succinct and condensed reports can account for such things as Jairus's daughter being already dead at the beginning of his narrative (Matt 9:18; contrast Mark and Luke) and his general lack of detail. They are consistent with what one would expect from a former government official who was used to producing terse, factual reports that summarized a situation clearly and concisely. However, it should be noted that from the commencement of Jesus' journey to Jerusalem (Matt 19:1//Mark 10:1) the parallel pericopes of Matthew and Mark are much closer to each other in length, and while there are differences in wording between them (frequently matters of style or clarification of meaning) there are few details in one Gospel that are not also in the other.

Stage 4: Luke Writes His Gospel as "Part One" of His History

Explanation of Luke's Procedure

While traveling with Paul, Luke kept a notebook or diary of their experiences, and then at some stage he conceived the idea of writing this as a full record of the expansion of the gospel in the early church, and prefixing it with an account of the life and teachings of Jesus. Luke began collecting information for this projected work. He was in Palestine for two years while Paul was imprisoned at Caesarea, and he was thus in a position to add considerably to his collection of material, both oral and written, and to interview participants and eyewitnesses of the events.

Among the traditions that he collected for this purpose were numerous pericopes and pericope-clusters that had been composed earlier by Matthew; some were written in Greek, some in Aramaic subsequently translated into Greek, and some still in Aramaic that Luke himself translated into Greek.

Explanation of Luke's Order

Luke, according to his announced purpose (Luke 1:1–4), set out to produce an "orderly" (that is to say, a chronological) account of all that had taken place, and assembled his material into chronological order to the extent that this was known to him. This explains why his order differs from Matthew's.

Explanation of Luke's Differences

For much of his material, Luke had received independent accounts of teachings and events that had come down to him through separate lines of tradition, some originally written by Matthew and some coming from other eyewitnesses. Where Luke has included in his Gospel an account from a different eyewitness, the variations between Matthew's and Luke's versions are of the same kind that would be found in any two recollections of the same speech or event, which, while both accurate, will always differ from each other.

All this material Luke edited into a connected narrative, reworking it in line with his purposes in writing, adding extra details or clarifying points in the material he received on the basis of the further information that he was able to obtain from interviewing eyewitnesses with whom he discussed the events and teachings of Jesus' life and ministry. Thus, as he himself informs the reader in his prologue, what is recorded in his Gospel goes back to the apostles and other eyewitnesses, and therefore can be accepted as wholly trustworthy (1:4).

Situations where there are agreements and differences between Matthew and Luke can be easily explained. First, minor verbal differences are due to Lukan editing of a short account originally written by Matthew and collected by Luke, and/or minor rewriting by Matthew of the material when incorporating it into his complete Gospel.

Second, in pericopes containing similarity of subject matter but with numerous verbal differences, Luke made a Greek translation of the Aramaic pericope written by Matthew; or the pericope may have come into Luke's hands in the form of a Greek translation made by his informant. In these pericopes the variations between Matthew's and Luke's versions exhibit the differences that exist between any two translations of the one document.

Third, in cases where there are more extensive differences with greater detail in Luke, the differences between Matthew's account of an incident and Luke's are the result of Luke's discussing the account that had come to him with other people who had been present, so he then expanded the account accordingly.

Fourth, where the accounts in Matthew and Luke have significant differences that are too extensive to be compatible with a common source, the account that Luke used came to him from some other eyewitness source other than Matthew, and the differences between them are those that exist between two independent accounts of the one speech or event.

Fifth, where the subject matter of a pericope is very similar in Matthew and Luke but has differences in the introduction or conclusion or setting, this is an instance of a story that circulated (and that came to Luke) without this information being part of it. Luke has provided the story with such information of this kind as he was able to obtain, bearing in mind its position and purpose in inclusion in his Gospel, while Matthew at the time of producing his complete Gospel has similarly added the "heads and tails" to pericopes that had not hitherto needed them when they were circulating on their own.

However, there would also have been occasions when Jesus repeated parables or other teachings that he had given elsewhere, frequently with differences that reflected the various circumstances in which the teaching was given and audiences to whom it was given. In several instances Matthew's Gospel contains the account of one such occasion and Luke another, and in the nature of the case there are similarities and differences between the accounts of the same kind as there would be if we were to give the same basic talk twice and in different circumstances.

Explanation of Luke's Style

The approach, the detail, and the wording of Luke's pericopes are consistent with what one would expect from a person trained as a physician, a careful observer, and one who was experienced (because of his profession) at questioning people to elicit and elucidate the facts.

Stage 5: Mark Produces His Special-Purpose Gospel

Explanation of Mark's Procedure

Mark drew on both Matthew and Luke when writing his special-purpose Gospel for evangelism, leaving out most of the purely *didache* material that was intended for the edification of Christians and that was already available to the church in the same Gospels that he was using.

Where Mark found Matthew and Luke in agreement in relation to something that he planned to use, he frequently used that agreed material (hence the relatively small number of places where Matthew and Luke agree against Mark). On occasion Mark was willing to depart from both of them to use a word (such as his κράβαττον for "bed") or a construction (such as his preference for the historic present and for paratactic constructions with καί) when this accorded better with his own style or intended readership. He also at times departed from his sources in some places where they had a particularly Jewish interest; for example, Mark omits many of Matthew's references to purely Jewish perspectives, such as "I was sent only to the lost sheep of the house of Israel" (Matt 15:24), "for any cause" (Matt 19:3), and "the fringe of" (Matt 9:20//Luke 8:44).

Where he found Matthew and Luke lacking exact agreement, Mark often wove the two accounts together into one, using the details and ideas from both and thus frequently resolving the apparent differences between the two. On some occasions he simply chose to follow one or the other of his two written sources. This is why Mark's material seems to alternate in agreement with Matthew and Luke, and it also seems very frequently to express the thought that is in each of them.

Explanation of Mark's Additional Detail

The hypothesis of Mark's use of Matthew and Luke is not sufficient to account for the content of the Second Gospel. Chapter 4 shows that more than 25% of the content of Mark's Gospel is not paralleled in either Matthew or Luke. Some of this consists of, to use Streeter's expression (1924, 158), "purely verbal expansion" of what is in the Major Synoptics and thus represents Markan redaction of the tradition found in Matthew and Luke. But a substantial proportion of it could not have been derived in any way from what is in the other two (see chap. 4 again for details). Therefore we are compelled by the data to recognize that if Mark is dependent on Matthew and Luke, he must also have had a third source. That source could have been his own imagination. Lacking any information beyond what is in Matthew and Luke, and wanting to enliven his narrative further, he may have simply invented all the additional detail that his Gospel contains.

This explanation is favored in particular by those scholars who do not accept that the author of the Second Gospel is the Mark of the New Testament and who ascribe a later date to the Gospel. But even if a late date were valid, it would not necessarily follow that the additional material in Mark's Gospel is invention. To have had access to Matthew and Luke, and to have any motivation for and purpose in writing a Gospel at all, the author of Mark must have been a part of the Christian community. So, even if one were to hold that Mark's Gospel was written in the late first century or in the early second century, there would still have been in existence oral tradition of the deeds and sayings of Jesus that contained information not in the two Major Synoptics.

It is quite unrealistic to contend that as soon as the Gospels of Matthew and Luke began to circulate in the churches, all those who were eyewitnesses of the events that are described (the apostles included) thereafter ceased to speak of what they knew from their own experience and henceforth restricted themselves to the story as related in those Gospels. On the contrary, the appearance of such accounts of what had happened would stimulate great discussion among those who had been present on this or that occasion, and there would have been comparisons between their recollections and the new written record. We are aware of this in our own day. If a book is published that tells the story of some military campaign in which we fought, or some political or business drama in which we ourselves were involved, we compare what it says with what we remember and share our comments with others. The publication of the book means that the matter becomes discussed *more*, not *less*. As we tell our tales or recount additional details that are not in the published record, our anecdotes have for a time a currency alongside the book itself so that what we say is passed on by some of our hearers.

Thus, even if the author of the Second Gospel was not Mark, so that someone else wrote it many decades after the events themselves, this person came from within the stream of church life and he heard its traditions. From these he would have been in a position to learn considerable amounts of further (and quite accurate) detail not in Matthew and Luke, just as many a youngster of today can remember numerous details of what his grandfather told him—details not in the official histories—when he began reminiscing: "Now I myself saw General So-and-so do such-and-such, right after the battle of . . ."

However, the strong evidence that points to Mark as author of the Second Gospel has led most commentators to accept his authorship. We have had occasion to note how Mark was in the center of the events of the early church. He would therefore have had knowledge of his own about Jesus to draw on, from the circulating traditions of the church, and in particular he would have constantly heard the preaching of his colleagues, particularly Peter, who was an eyewitness *par excellence*.

There is therefore strong support both in the New Testament and in early church history for holding that Mark would have been in a position to hear Peter's own telling of what Jesus said and did. So when Mark was using the Gospels of Matthew and Luke as sources for the stories that he was including in the Gospel that he was writing, he would have found that their accounts of one incident or another would bring back to his mind recollections of the many times he had heard these same stories told by Peter in the course of his teaching.

So it is hardly wild speculation to imagine that under those circumstances, while working from the written record in front of him, Mark would have recalled details and circumstances, and even specific words and phrases, from what Peter had said. And this would affect his own telling of the tale in numerous ways—vocabulary, grammatical constructions, emphasis, point of view, additional details. To deny this would be to assert that Mark learned nothing and remembered nothing from all of Peter's preaching that he heard during his period of close association with the apostle—a possibility that cannot be rated as very likely nor an easy position to substantiate.

Thus the evidence of the contents of Mark's Gospel compels us to see that if indeed Mark was the third to write and that he used the Gospels of Matthew and Luke as his sources, he had another source or sources for all that he said that did not come from the Major Synoptists. There is no need to attribute this extra information to Mark's imagination, which would imply that Mark lived and worked in an ecclesiastical vacuum—something that is in conflict with all the known evidence. Rather, the main source for the further information that is contained in Mark is the apostle Peter. Thus the vivid touches of extra detail that are so characteristic of Mark reflect his third major source—the teaching ministry of Peter—in which, according to the traditions of the early church, Mark himself played an ancillary part.

That is, Markan Dependence holds that Mark was dependent not only on the Gospels of Matthew and Luke for his material, but also on Peter. For the data requires a third source. That third source was oral tradition, and the evidence points to the main source of that oral tradition as being Peter. Thus

Explanation of Mark's Order

Mark had before him the Gospels of Matthew and Luke, with their different order of pericopes on numerous occasions. His intention was to extract from them the material he wanted and to blend his two sources together. In keeping with this, Mark *always* follows the joint order of Matthew and Luke when they agree, and he *always* follows the order of one or the other when they differ between themselves. His choice of which Major Synoptic's order to follow was guided by which one gave him the best sequence for the material he chose to use and which one did not take him through large teaching sections that he did not intend to include.

Explanation of Mark's Style

Mark's presentation of his material—in form, wording, and content—is consistent with what one would expect from a storyteller who sought to tell his story in vivid and colloquial language so as to capture the interest, stir the imagination, challenge the will, and motivate a decision to respond to the Person upon whom all the stories were centered.

Dating

It is not my purpose to canvass here the evidence for an early or late dating for the Synoptics. It will suffice to say that although the hypothesis of Markan Dependence is completely compatible with either approach to dating, the evidence in favor of early dating and against late dating is very impressive. The treatment by Harnack (1911) is still persuasive, and the more recent studies by J. A. T. Robinson (1976) and E. E. Ellis (1980) complement each other in their examination of the grounds for holding an early date.

In particular, the best explanation for the ending of Acts is that the book was written at the close of the two-year period that it mentions in its final paragraph. Further, there is no need to call into question the patristic tradition that Mark was written at about the time of the martyrdom of Peter and Paul. If neither Matthew nor Luke knew the other's Gospel (as this present study has maintained), this indicates that they were published at approximately the same time in different places. The evidence is best satisfied by the conclusion that Luke completed his Gospel and published it in Rome within the first year after Paul's arrival there, circa AD 60. Acts would then have been written and published at the end of the period it covers, circa AD 62. Matthew's Gospel was published in Jerusalem in the same year as

Luke's, circa AD 60. The publication of Mark's Gospel can be dated circa AD 65.

THE RELIABILITY OF THE SYNOPTIC RECORD

This inquiry has sought to be a rigorous investigation of the Synoptic data and an even-handed assessment of the various hypotheses that have been offered in explanation of that data. Doubtless there are shortcomings in both of these areas. Which of us can fully comply with our own standards? But its purpose has been to see which Synoptic explanation can most adequately and most completely account for that data, and it draws attention to that explanation that seems to account for it very fully indeed.

This view—Markan Dependence—is compatible with late dates for the Synoptics and with the work of form and redaction criticism. (Some of the present conclusions of such studies, however, insofar as they presuppose Markan Priority, would require radical rethinking.) However, it is my personal judgment that (as indicated above) the data points to an early date (pre-AD 70) for all three Synoptics and to their authorship respectively by the apostle Matthew, the John Mark of the Acts and the Epistles, and Luke the physician and companion of Paul. This view gives a best fit to all the details of the New Testament text taken at face value, and in fact this view makes it unnecessary and unjustified to take the data other than at its face value.

The methodology of this inquiry has been totally academic and from a scholarly perspective, not dogmatic or doctrinaire. But now that the inquiry has been completed and the results set forth, their implications can be assessed. In particular, there are four main implications.

First, each Synoptic author is allowed to be his own man. Each had a distinct and in large measure separate purpose in writing. Each author marshaled his data, chose the Jesus traditions he intended to use, and arranged them in the sequence that best fulfilled his purpose in writing. Each Gospel is therefore to be examined on its own, within its own terms, as a work of authorship in its own right. And this examination should precede the assessment of each Gospel's overall contribution to our knowledge of "Jesus Christ, Son of God" (Mark 1:1).

Second, each Synoptic Gospel gives a wholly authentic and reliable account of the life and teachings of Jesus, and where they differ they supplement and do not contradict each other. (1) Matthew's Gospel was written by the apostle Matthew from his own personal experience and that of his fellow apostles, based on notes made by Matthew of what happened and what was said. These notes were taken down at the time these things occurred, and they then provided the guide and stimulus to memory when in due course a fuller account of an incident or a teaching was produced. (2) Luke's Gospel is the ministry and message of Jesus that was known to Paul, supplemented by all that Luke was able to discover in the course of his own thoroughgoing inquiries about everything that had taken place, as he himself explains in his preface (Luke 1:1–4). In every way his account goes back to the testimony of those who were eyewitnesses and ministers of the word, and Luke's records were pieced together in a painstaking investigation of "everything from the beginning." This resulted in an ordered account whose aim was to give complete certainty about these things to those who read his Gospel. Luke's Gospel is largely independent of that of Matthew, although he has incorporated into it several "tracts" written by Matthew in earlier years that circulated in the churches. (3) Mark's account takes the stories of Matthew and Luke, selected according to Mark's own purpose in writing, and retells them in the popular colloquial idiom with an abundance of added insight and detail that came from Mark's own awareness of the content of the Jesus traditions in the church and in particular from the preaching of the apostle Peter, whose associate Mark was. Thus those places where Mark reflects a perspective distinct from Matthew's and Luke's—and although the differences in perspective are usually slight, the places where they occur in Mark are very numerous—represent the distinctive testimony of Peter, whose witness is added to Matthew's and Luke's. Therefore, what Mark says is also authentic and accurate since it derives from Matthew, Luke, and Peter.

Third, the evidence does not require or support any view for any part of the Synoptic text as being the result of subsequent redaction in the church by anyone other than the authors Matthew, Mark, and Luke; nor of rewriting or reworking or imaginative addition by the church of a later time to reflect and meet the needs of its own *Sitz im Leben*; nor of any Synoptic author deliberately altering the writing of one (or both) of the other Synoptic authors so as to correct him or improve him in any way whatsoever. These things are all *possible*, but they are not required by anything that exists in any part of the actual evidence, either in the text of the New Testament itself or in anything known to us from church history. In fact, I believe that saying that these things are highly unlikely is actually understating the direction and strength of the evidence, which I am convinced rules them out altogether. The form of the Synoptics as they came from the pens of the apostle Matthew, John Mark, and Dr. Luke is the form in which those authors recorded what happened, as selected and arranged in the light of their overall purposes in writing (which in no way implies any intention to "correct" one another, nor any distortion of the facts). This is also the form in which the Synoptic Gospels were circulated, copied, and transmitted down the centuries.

Fourth, the main conclusion that has been reached in this investigation of the evidence, viz. Markan Dependence, has as an ancillary conclusion the result that the Synoptics may be accepted as being independent and wholly reliable accounts of what they record. This agrees with the full doctrine of biblical inspiration, but these are two independent and parallel issues. That is to say, we do not come to our conclusions about the relationships between the Synoptics on the basis of or because of or in order to agree with our acceptance of a doctrine of biblical inspiration. To do so would be in some measure to prejudge the outcome of an inquiry and in fact to preclude to that extent the possibility that it is a free inquiry. Similarly, we do not found our doctrine of biblical inspiration on the outcome of investigations into the text of the Bible. To do so would be to make acceptance of a doctrine dependent on the outcome of human investigatory labors: which is *not* the basis on which Christian doctrine is to be accepted. Thus the two—the outcome of investigation and the doctrine of inspiration—are parallel but distinct issues.

It is quite a contrast to consider the implications of the Markan Priority/ Two-Source Hypothesis. The Two-Source theory and the scholarship that has flowed from it have taken the Synoptic Gospels and examined them according to its lights, and handed them back to the church greatly diminished in every way—in historicity, in accuracy, in reliability, in integrity. I find in reading the literature that it has become standard for scholars to see the existence of the Synoptic differences as evidence for the development of these stories over many decades, so that some of these Markan Priority scholars have concluded that the stories owe more to the imagination of the church responding to the needs of the day than to the authentic teachings and deeds of Jesus.

When our thinking is structured by the Markan Priority Hypothesis, we come across a passage that states "Jesus said" and we have to hesitate and say to ourselves, "Did he really say that? Or is this something that was constructed this way by the later church? Or does its wording go back no further than the Synoptic author himself?" We then become very cautious about how much weight we can rest on what the wording of the Gospels actually says. There is engendered a skepticism that has brought us to the place where we are hesitant to accept anything as it stands; we can take nothing at face value. Yet this Book is the source of our faith and the foundation of our lives. There are other books around where we may not accept the author's viewpoint, but we are willing to accept that the author *is* saying what we clearly read he is saying. We do not come with this attitude of skepticism towards other books—ancient or modern—but we are encouraged to develop such an attitude toward the Gospels.

When we ask ourselves why we have this caution or hesitation or uncertainty about accepting the wording in front of us in the Gospels, we find that it is not produced by any actual *evidence* there in front of us; instead, it is the consequence of a theory. And when we examine the foundations of that theory—as we have done in this study—we can see that it rests on the flimsiest and most inadequate grounds and not on solid evidence or sustainable argument. This theory is based on feelings and opinions and circularities; on assertions without justification that cannot stand up to sober, objective scrutiny; on the insubstantial sands of dogmatic theological presuppositions; on assumptions that go well beyond the warrant of the evidence; and on argument that marches around in a circle. Upon *this* basis we have renounced our right to accept as valid and genuine what is said in the Gospel narratives that have been passed down to us. We have sold our inheritance for a mess of pottage. Here are a few examples to consider.

1. The Markan Priority position asks us to believe that Matthew and Luke altered the text of Mark out of motives of increased reverence. Thus on two occasions (Mark 1:32,34; 3:10; and parallels) Mark says Jesus healed "many" and Matthew and Luke say he healed "all." Barclay (1975, 92) comments, "It is significant that regularly Matthew and Luke change Mark's *many* into *all*. Such is their reverence for Jesus that they cannot think of his power as being anything less than totally effective." Barclay claims that Mark's account was deliberately altered by Matthew and Luke to avoid giving the impression of "tentative miracles" (Hawkins 1909, 117), i.e., that out of a great number of attempts at healings Jesus succeeded some of the time. This "interpretation" must be completely rejected, not on dogmatic or doctrinal grounds, but because it contradicts the evidence. It is simply not so. The evidence must control the theory, not vice versa. I discussed these passages in chapter 5, which set them in their context. I showed that Mark was making a different point from the other Synoptists by emphasizing the large size of the total numbers healed. From the perspective of Markan Dependence, one can see what happened. Matthew and Luke show that not one person needing healing went away unhealed. Then Mark, with these accounts in front of him, writes so as to bring out an additional facet of the event by drawing on the description of it that he had heard, probably many times, in the preaching of Peter: the total number healed was very great.

Now what requires our attention here is the attitude to the text of the Gospels that is seen in the comments of Hawkins and Barclay based on Mark Priority. Barclay's explanation is that the text was altered by Matthew and Luke from "many" to "all" *not because it is actually true that all were healed but because Matthew and Luke cannot bear to think that perhaps not all were healed.* Thus the text of Matthew and Luke does not bear witness to *the truth* of what happened but to *the wishful thinking* of the two authors about what they hoped had happened. We have surrendered a reliable Bible, and in its place we have received back from the hands of the Markan Priorists a record of the pious hopes of a couple of later Synoptic writers who amended the text to express their best wishes for what Jesus might have done.

But what exactly is the basis for this conclusion about what Matthew and Luke were doing? It has one basis only. It flows from the belief that Mark wrote first and Matthew and Luke used it. It has no other basis. If this Synoptic view were not governing interpretations, this explanation of how and why Matthew and Luke altered Mark's record of the facts would not be offered, for it does not arise from anything in the text of the Gospels. It arises from Markan Priority only.

2. The data indicates that Matthew does not correspond with Mark for three words out of every five in Mark, and Luke does not correspond with Mark for three words out of every four in Mark. (See chap. 4 for the actual figures on word counts.) When this data is viewed from the Markan Priority Hypothesis, this represents a very substantial rewriting by both Matthew and Luke of their source material.

3. Quite a number of the arguments for Markan Priority (see chap. 5) involve as a presupposition that there are deficiencies and shortcomings in Mark that are in need of correction (or at least improvement) and that the Major Synoptists then go about engaging in this work of correction and improvement.

4. Since Matthew and Luke have Mark as their primary source in the Triple Tradition, a question mark hangs over all the places where they contain additional detail not in Mark. If the amount of extra material in the Triple Tradition is large and/or significant—and especially if the detail under consideration occurs in both Matthew and Luke—this can be attributed to an overlap with Q and thus its authenticity might be preserved. Otherwise, it is highly suspect. For example, many scholars call into question the authenticity of the so-called "exceptive clause" on divorce in Matt 19:9 solely on the basis of its absence from the parallel in Mark 10:11.

However, on the Markan Dependence Hypothesis the position is rather different. Markan Dependence is also a theory of relationship, but the difference is that in itself Markan Dependence does not compel us to any theological position. It does not impose an attitude of skepticism on us; it does not impose a particular interpretation of the text on us. It leaves us free to examine and evaluate all of the text without prejudging for or against the authenticity of any part of it. The hypothesis that places Mark last can be affirmed in conjunction with a total skepticism about the historicity of the Synoptic accounts, such as the Tübingen school's view that Farmer says played a role in causing reaction against the Griesbach Hypothesis. Or it can be held in conjunction with a full acceptance of the Gospels at face value, so that each part of each Gospel can speak to us with total authority and with complete authenticity. The hypothesis explains how this can be so, but the message of the text and its reliability are not at the mercy of the hypothesis. This differs from the Markan Priority position, which (if one may judge on the basis of the writings of many of its advocates) inherently involves a skeptical attitude toward the text of the Gospels.

Now it must be emphasized afresh that this study has not proven Markan Priority wrong. This is most certainly not the case. Such a demonstration is in fact impossible. But it has been shown that (1) there are no objective arguments that point exclusively to Markan Priority as the explanation of Synoptic interrelationships; (2) there are many substantial problems with the explanations that Markan Priority offers for the data; and (3) there is a much better alternative explanation that accords with (a) the data of the Gospel texts, (b) the external evidence, and (c) what is known to us of the situation of the early church. In those circumstances the tacit assumption that our approach to interpreting the Synoptic Gospels should commence from the acceptance of the priority of Mark is unjustified, invalid, and unscholarly.

The Markan Dependence Hypothesis provides a cohesive and unitary explanation, which is simultaneously simple and rational, for the pericope order of the respective Synoptic Gospels, and it also provides a coherent and straightforward basis for explaining the relationship between the actual wording of the text of the three Synoptic Gospels. This hypothesis accounts for all the data, is compatible with the testimony of church history, and can supply credible answers to the arguments that have hitherto been adduced against it. In all these respects it is more satisfactory than the other hypotheses that have been offered. Therefore, there is good reason for accepting that Matthew and Luke were written prior to Mark, and that Mark used them in the writing of his Gospel. And the Progressive Publication of

Matthew Hypothesis explains the similarities and differences in order and content between Matthew and Luke in a way that is completely in harmony with, and indeed drawn from, the evidence we have from the Gospels and from church history.

Agatha Christie's Miss Marple once said (Anne Hart 1985, 137), "If you have a theory that fits every fact—well, then it must be the right one." Yes, I think that's the truth of the matter.

Here then is the Progressive Publication of Matthew Hypothesis for your consideration. The case rests.

BIBLIOGRAPHY

Unless the reference would be ambiguous, titles of commentaries are cited by the name of the book of the Bible on which they are written; e.g., W. C. Allen's *Critical and Exegetical Commentary on the Gospel According to S. Matthew* appears in this bibliography with the simple title *Matthew*.

Abbott, E. A. 1879. "Gospels." *Encyclopaedia Britannica*. 9th ed. Edinburgh: A&C Black. 10: 791ff.
Aland, K. 1975. *Synopsis of the Four Gospels*. Stuttgart: Biblia-Druck, United Bible Societies.
Albright, W. F., and C. S. Mann. 1971. *Matthew*. Anchor Bible. New York: Doubleday.
Alford, H. 1849/1854/1958/1968. *The Greek Testament, Vol. I: The Gospels*. Chicago: Moody Press.
Allen, W. C. 1907/1912/1965. *Matthew*. International Critical Commentary. Edinburgh: T&T Clark.
———. 1911a. "The Book of Sayings Used by the Editor of the First Gospel." In W. Sanday, ed. 1911. *Oxford Studies in the Synoptic Problem*. Oxford: Clarendon.
———. 1911b. "The Aramaic Background of the Gospels." In W. Sanday, ed. 1911. *Oxford Studies in the Synoptic Problem*. Oxford: Clarendon.
Anderson, H. 1976. *Mark*. New Century Bible. London: Oliphants/Grand Rapids: Eerdmans.
Argyle, A. W. 1961. "Agreements between Matthew and Luke." *Expository Times* 73: 19–22.
———. 1964. "Evidence for the View that St Luke Used St Matthew's Gospel." *Journal of Biblical Literature* 83: 390–96.
Arndt, W. F., and F. W. Gingrich. 1952/1957. *A Greek-English Lexicon of the New Testament*. University of Chicago Press/Cambridge: University Press.
Augustine of Hippo. c. AD 400. *The Harmony of the Gospels* (Bk I, Chs II & III). In *Nicene and Post-Nicene Fathers*. First series, vol. 6. Grand Rapids: Eerdmans, 1979.
Barclay, W. 1975. *Introduction to the First Three Gospels*. London: SCM/Philadelphia: Westminster.
Barrett, C. K. 1943. "Q: A Re-examination." *Expository Times* 54: 320–23.
Bartlet, J. 1911. "The Sources of Luke's Gospel." In W. Sanday, ed. 1911. *Oxford Studies in the Synoptic Problem*. Oxford: Clarendon.

Bauckham, R., ed. 1998. *The Gospel for All Christians*. Grand Rapids: Eerdmans.
———. 2006. *Jesus and the Eyewitnesses*. Grand Rapids: Eerdmans.
Beare, F. W. 1965. "Review of Farmer's *The Synoptic Problem*." *JBL* 84: 295–97.
Benoit, P., and M. E. Boismard. 1965/1972/1981. *Synopse des Quartre Evangiles en Français*. 3 vols. Paris: Les Editions du Cerf.
Black, D. A. 2001. *Why Four Gospels? The Historical Origins of the Gospels*. Grand Rapids: Kregel.
———, and D. R. Beck, eds. 2001. *Rethinking the Synoptic Problem*. Grand Rapids: Baker.
Bleek, F. 1869/1870. ET W. Urwick. *Introduction to the New Testament*. Edinburgh: T&T Clark. German title: *Einleitung in das Neues Testament*.
Blomberg, C. L. 1998. *Jesus and the Gospels: An Introduction and Survey*. Nashville: B&H Academic.
——— 2001. "Where We Stand at the Start of a New Century." Pages 17–40 in Black and Beck, *Rethinking the Synoptic Problem*.
Boismard, M. E. 1980. See Benoit and Boismard 1965/1972/1981.
———. 1984. "Théorie des Niveaux Multiples." Paper presented to the 1984 Jerusalem Symposium.
Branscomb, B. H. 1937. *Mark*. Moffatt New Testament Commentary. London: Hodder & Stoughton.
Brown, C., ed. 1975–78. *Dictionary of New Testament Theology*. 3 vols. Exeter: Paternoster/Grand Rapids: Zondervan.
Bruce, A. B. 1897. *The Expositor's Greek Testament: Luke*. London: Hodder & Stoughton.
Bruce, F. F. 1951. *The Acts of the Apostles: The Greek Text*. London: Tyndale Press.
Buchanan, G. W. 1974. "Has the Griesbach Hypothesis Been Falsified?" *Journal of Biblical Literature* 93: 550–72.
Burkitt, F. C. 1911. *The Gospel History and Its Transmission*. 1906 Jowett Lectures. Edinburgh: T&T Clark.
Burney, C. F. 1925. *The Poetry of Our Lord*. Oxford: Clarendon.
Butler, B. C. 1951. *The Originality of St Matthew: A Critique of the Two-Document Hypothesis*. Cambridge: University Press.
Caird, G. B. 1963/1977. *Luke*. Pelican Commentaries. London: Penguin/SCM.
Campenhausen, H. von 1972/1977. *The Formation of the Christian Bible*. ET J. A. Baker, London: A&C Black/Minneapolis: Fortress.
Carpenter, J. E. 1890/1906. *The First Three Gospels*. London: Lindsay Press.
Casey, M. 1998. *Aramaic Sources of Mark's Gospel*. Cambridge: Cambridge University Press.
Chapman, J. 1937. *Matthew, Mark, and Luke*. London: Longmans Green.
Chrysostom, J. c. AD 400. *Homilies on the Gospel of St Matthew*. In *The Nicene and Post-Nicene Fathers*. First series, vol. 10. Grand Rapids: Eerdmans, 1978.
Cope, L. 1976. "The Death of John the Baptist in the Gospel of Matthew; or, The Case of the Confusing Conjunction." *Catholic Biblical Quarterly* 38: 515–19.
Cranfield, C. E. B. 1959. *Mark*. Cambridge Greek Text Commentary. Cambridge: Cambridge University Press.
Creed, J. M. 1930/1953. *Luke*. London: Macmillan.
Cremer, H. 1878/1895/1962. *Biblio-Theological Lexicon of New Testament Greek*. Edinburgh: T&T Clark.
Crook, Z. 2000. "The Synoptic Parables of the Mustard Seed and Leaven." *Journal for the Study of the New Testament* 78: 23–48.
Cutt, S. 1966. "Review of Farmer's *The Synoptic Problem*." *Theology* 69: 225–27.
Danker, F. W., ed. 2000. *A Greek Lexicon of the New Testament*. Chicago: University of Chicago Press.

Dibelius, M. 1919/1971/1987. *From Tradition to Gospel.* Cambridge: James Clarke.
———. 1935. *Gospel Criticism and Christology.* London: Nicholson & Watson.
Dodd, C. H. 1936. *The Apostolic Preaching and Its Developments.* London: Hodder & Stoughton.
Downing, F. G. 1965. "Towards the Rehabilitation of Q." *New Testament Studies* 11: 169–81.
Dungan, D. L. 1970. "Mark—the Abridgement of Matthew and Luke." In D. M. Miller, ed. 1970. *Jesus and Man's Hope.* Vol. 1. Pittsburgh Theological Seminary.
———. 1999. *A History of the Synoptic Problem.* New York: Doubleday.
Edersheim, A. 1883/1950. *The Life and Times of Jesus the Messiah.* London: Longmans Green; Grand Rapids: Eerdmans.
Edwards, J. R. 2002. *Mark.* Pillar Commentaries. Leicester: Apollos/Grand Rapids: Eerdmans.
Ellis, E. E. 1966. *The Gospel of Luke.* New Century Bible. London: Thomas Nelson.
———. 1980. "Dating the New Testament." *New Testament Studies* 26: 487–502.
Eusebius. c. 324. *Ecclesiastical History.* ET C. F. Cruse. London: George Bell, 1894.
———. *Church History.* ET A. C. McGiffert. In *The Nicene and Post-Nicene Fathers.* Second Series, vol. I. Grand Rapids: Eerdmans, 1979.
———. *The Church History.* Ed. and ET P. L. Maier. Grand Rapids: Kregel, 1999.
Evans, C. F. 1968. *The Beginning of the Gospel.* London: SPCK.
Farmer, W. 1964/1976. *The Synoptic Problem.* New York: Macmillan/Western North Carolina Press.
———. 1969. *Synopticon.* Cambridge: University Press.
———. 1973. "A Response to Robert Morgenthaler's *Statistische Synopse.*" *Biblica* 54: 417–33.
———. 1977. "Modern Developments of Griesbach's Hypothesis." *New Testament Studies* 23: 275–95.
———. ed. 1983a. *New Synoptic Studies.* Macon: Mercer University Press.
———. 1983b. "The Patristic Evidence Re-examined." In Farmer, *New Synoptic Studies.*
———. 1984. "A Position Paper for the Two-Gospel Hypothesis." Paper presented to the 1984 Jerusalem Symposium.
———. 2001. "The Case for the Two-Gospel Hypothesis." Pages 97–136 in Black and Beck, *Rethinking the Synoptic Problem.*
Farnell, F. D. 2002. In R. L. Thomas, 2002. *Three Views on the Origins of the Synoptic Gospels.* Grand Rapids: Kregel.
Farrer, A. M. 1955. "On Dispensing with Q." In D. E. Nineham, ed. 1955. *Studies in the Gospels.* Oxford: Blackwell.
Fee, G. D. 1978. "Modern Text Criticism and the Synoptic Problem." In B. Orchard and T. R. W. Longstaff, eds. 1978. *J. J. Griesbach: Synoptic and Text-Critical Studies 1776–1976.* Cambridge: University Press.
Fenton, J. C. 1963/1977. *Matthew.* Pelican Commentaries. London: Penguin/SCM.
Filson, F. V. 1960/1971. *Matthew.* London: A&C Black.
Fitzmyer, J. A. 1970. "On the Gospel of Luke, the Priority of Mark, and the Q Source." In D. M. Miller, 1970. *Jesus and Man's Hope.* Vol. 1. Pittsburgh Theological Seminary.
Focant, C., ed. 1993. *The Synoptic Gospels: Source Criticism.* Bibliotheca ephemeridum theologicarum lovaniensium (BETL) 110. Leuven: Leuven University Press.
France, R. T. 2002. *Mark.* New International Greek Testament Commentary. Carlisle: Paternoster/Grand Rapids: Eerdmans.
———. 2007. *Matthew.* New International Commentary on the New Testament. Grand Rapids: Eerdmans.
Friedrich, G. See Kittel & Friedrich.

Frye, R. M. 1978. "The Synoptic Problems and Analogies in Other Literature." In W. O. Walker, ed. 1978. *The Relationship among the Gospels*. San Antonio: Trinity University Press.

Fuller, R. H. 1978. "Classics and the Gospels: The Seminar." In W. O. Walker, ed. 1978. *The Relationship among the Gospels*. San Antonio: Trinity University Press.

Gaboury, A. 1970. *La Structure des Evangiles Synoptiques*. Leiden: Brill.

Gamba, G. G. 1983. "A Further Re-examination of Evidence from the Early Tradition." In Farmer, *New Synoptic Studies*.

Geldenhuys, J. N. 1950. *Luke*. NICNT. London: Marshall/Grand Rapids: Eerdmans.

Gerhardsson, B. 1961/1964/1998. *Memory and Manuscript*. Lund: Gleerup; Grand Rapids: Eerdmans.

———. 1964. *Tradition and Transmission in Early Christianity*. Lund: Gleerup.

———. 1977/1979. *The Origins of the Gospel Traditions*. London: SCM.

Gleason, H. A. 1969. *Introduction to Descriptive Linguistics*. London: Holt, Rinehart, and Winston.

Godet, F. L. 1886/1971. *The First Epistle to the Corinthians*. 2 vols. Edinburgh: T&T Clark/ Grand Rapids: Eerdmans.

———. 1870. *Commentary on the Gospel of Luke*, vol. 1. Reprint 1957. Edinburgh: T&T Clark.

Goodacre, M. 2001. *The Synoptic Problem: A Way through the Maze*. Edinburgh: T&T Clark.

Goodspeed, E. J. 1959. *Matthew: Apostle and Evangelist*. Philadelphia: Winston.

Gould, E. P. 1896. *Mark*. International Critical Commentary. Edinburgh: T&T Clark.

Goulder, M. D. 1974. *Midrash and Lection in Matthew*. London: SPCK.

Grant, F. C. 1957. *The Gospels: Their Origin and Their Growth*. London: Faber.

———. 1965. "Turning Back the Clock: Review of Farmer's *The Synoptic Problem*." *Interpretation* 19: 352–54.

Grant, R. M. 1963. *Historical Introduction to the New Testament*. London: Collins/New York: Harper.

Greeven, H. 1978. "The Gospel Synopsis from 1776 to the Present Day." In B. Orchard and T. R. W. Longstaff, eds. 1978. *J. J. Griesbach: Synoptic and Text-Critical Studies 1776–1976*. Cambridge: Cambridge University Press.

Griesbach, J. J. 1776. *Synopsis evangeliorum Matthaei, Marci et Lucae*. Halle.

———. 1783/1825. *Fontes unde evangelistae suas de resurrectione Domini narrationes hauserint: Paschatos solemnia*. Jena: Gabler.

———. 1789/1794/1978. *Commentatio*, ET B. Orchard. *A Demonstration that Mark Was Written after Matthew and Luke*. In B. Orchard and T. R. W. Longstaff, eds. 1978. *J. J. Griesbach: Synoptic and Text-Critical Studies 1776–1976*. Cambridge: Cambridge University Press.

Gundry, R. H. 1967/1975. *The Use of the Old Testament in St Matthew's Gospel*. Leiden: Brill.

———. 1982 *Matthew: A Commentary on His Literary and Theological Art*. Grand Rapids: Eerdmans.

———. 2003. *A Survey of the New Testament*. 4th ed. Grand Rapids: Zondervan.

Guthrie, D. 1965. *New Testament Introduction*. London: Tyndale.

Guy, H. A. 1954. *The Origin of the Gospel of Mark*. London: Hodder & Stoughton.

Harnack, A. 1911. *The Date of the Acts and of the Synoptic Gospels*. London: Williams & Norgate; New York: Putnam's Sons.

Hart, A. 1985. *The Life and Times of Miss Jane Marple*. New York: Dodd, Mead & Company.

Hawkins, J. C. 1899/1909/1968. *Horae Synopticae*. Oxford: Clarendon/Grand Rapids: Baker.

———. 1911a. "Probabilities As to the So-called Double Tradition of St Matthew and St Luke." In W. Sanday, ed. 1911. *Oxford Studies in the Synoptic Problem*. Oxford: Clarendon.
———. 1911b. "Three Limitations to St Luke's Use of St Mark's Gospel." In W. Sanday, ed. 1911. *Oxford Studies in the Synoptic Problem*. Oxford: Clarendon.
Head, P. M. 1997. *Christology and the Synoptic Problem*. Cambridge: Cambridge University Press.
Hendriksen, W. 1973. *Matthew*. Grand Rapids: Baker/London: Banner of Truth Trust.
———. 1975. *Mark*. Grand Rapids: Baker/London: Banner of Truth Trust.
———. 1978. *Luke*. Grand Rapids: Baker/London: Banner of Truth Trust.
Hengel, M. 2000. *The Four Gospels and the One Gospel of Jesus Christ*. Harrisburg: Trinity Press.
Hill, D. 1972. *Matthew*. New Century Bible. London: Oliphants/Grand Rapids: Eerdmans.
Honoré, A. M. 1968. "A Statistical Study of the Synoptic Problem." *Novum Testamentum* 10: 95–147.
Hughes, R. K. 1989. *Mark: Jesus, Servant and Savior*. 2 vols. Wheaton: Crossway Books.
Jameson, H. G. 1922. *The Origin of the Synoptic Gospels*. Oxford: Blackwell.
Jeremias, J. 1971. *New Testament Theology, Vol. 1: The Proclamation of Jesus*. London: SCM.
Kennedy, G. 1978. "Classical and Christian Source Criticism." In W. O. Walker, 1978. *The Relationship among the Gospels*. San Antonio: Trinity University Press.
Kistemaker, S. J. 1972/1980. *The Gospels in Current Study*. Grand Rapids: Baker.
Kittel, G., and G. Friedrich, eds. 1964–76. *Theological Dictionary of the New Testament*. 10 vols. Grand Rapids: Eerdmans.
Knox, W. L. 1953, 1957. *The Sources of the Synoptic Gospels*. 2 vols. Cambridge: University Press.
Kümmel, W. G. 1972/1973. *The New Testament: The History of the Investigation of Its Problems*. Nashville: Abingdon/ London: SCM.
———. 1975/1977. *Introduction to the New Testament*. Nashville: Abingdon/London: SCM.
Ladd, G. E. 1967. *The New Testament and Criticism*. Grand Rapids: Eerdmans.
Lane, W. L. 1974. *Mark*. Grand Rapids: Eerdmans.
Leon-Dufour, X. 1963/1968. *The Gospels and the Jesus of History*, first published in a longer version in France in 1963: *Les Evangiles et l'histoire de Jésus*. ET J. McHugh, London: William Collins/New York: Desclée, 1968.
Lessing, G. E. 1957. *Lessing's Theological Writings*. ET H. Chadwick. Stanford, CA: Stanford University Press.
Lightfoot, R. H. 1950/1962. *The Gospel Message of St Mark*. Oxford: University Press.
Lindsey, R. L. 1963. "A Modified Two-Document Theory of the Synoptic Dependence and Interdependence." *Novum Testamentum* 6: 252–57.
———. 1992. "A New Approach to the Synoptic Gospels." *Mishkan* 17.18: 87–106.
Linnemann, E. 1992. *Is There a Synoptic Problem*? Grand Rapids: Baker.
Longstaff, T. R. W. 1975. "The Minor Agreements: An Examination of the Basic Argument." *Catholic Biblical Quarterly* 37: 184–92.
———. 1977. *Evidence of Conflation in Mark?* Missoula: Scholars Press.
Lowe, M. 1982. "The Demise of Arguments from Order for Markan Priority." *Novum Testamentum* 24: 27–36.
Lowe, M., and D. Flusser. 1983. "Evidence Corroborating a Modified Proto-Matthean Synoptic Theory." *New Testament Studies* 29: 25–47.
Ludlum, J. H. 1964. "Review of Farmer's *The Synoptic Problem*." *Christianity Today* 9: 306.
Maier, P. See Eusebius.

Mann, C. S. 1971. See Albright and Mann.
Manson, T. W. 1937/1949/1961. *The Sayings of Jesus*. London: SCM.
Manson, W. 1930. *Luke*. Moffatt's NT Commentary. London: Hodder & Stoughton.
Marshall, I. H. 1970. *Luke: Historian and Theologian*. Exeter: Paternoster.
———. 1978. *Luke*. Exeter: Paternoster.
Martin, R. P. 1972. *Mark—Evangelist & Theologian*. Exeter: Paternoster.
———. 1975. *New Testament Foundations, Vol. 1: The Four Gospels*. Grand Rapids: Eerdmans/Exeter: Paternoster.
McKnight, E. V. 1972. See Talbert and McKnight.
McKnight, S. 1988. *Interpreting the Synoptic Gospels*. Grand Rapids: Baker.
———. 2001. "A Generation Who Knew Not Streeter: The Case for Markan Priority." Pages 65–96 in Black and Beck, *Rethinking the Synoptic Problem*.
McNeile, A. H. 1915. *The Gospel According to St Matthew*. London: Macmillan.
McNicol, A. J., D. B. Peabody, D. L. Dungan, and W. R. Farmer, eds. 1996. *Beyond the Q Impasse: Luke's Use of Matthew*. Harrisburg: Trinity Press.
———. 1984. "The Two-Gospel Hypothesis Under Scrutiny." Paper presented to the 1984 Jerusalem Symposium.
Meeks, W. A. 1978. "Hypomnemata from an Untamed Sceptic." In W. O. Walker, ed. 1978. *The Relationship among the Gospels*. San Antonio: Trinity University Press.
Menzies, A. 1901. *The Earliest Gospel*. London: Macmillan.
Metzger, B. M. 1964/1968. *The Text of the New Testament*. Oxford: Oxford University Press.
———. 1965/1969. *The New Testament: Its Background, Growth, and Content*. Nashville: Abingdon/ London: Lutterworth.
———. 1971. *A Textual Commentary on the Greek New Testament*. London: United Bible Societies.
Miller, D. M., ed. 1970. *Jesus and Man's Hope*. Vol. 1. Pittsburgh Theological Seminary.
Mitton, C. L. 1965. "Review of Farmer's *The Synoptic Problem*." *ET* 77: 1–3.
Morgenthaler, R. 1958/1982. *Statistik des Neutestamentlichen Wortschatzes*. Gotthelf-Verlag.
———. 1971. *Statistische Synopse*. Gotthelf-Verlag.
Morris, L. 1974. *Luke*. Tyndale New Testament Commentaries. London: IVP.
———. 1992. *Matthew*. Pillar Commentaries. Leicester: IVP/Grand Rapids: Eerdmans.
Moule, C. F. D. 1962/1966/1971. *The Birth of the New Testament*. London: A&C Black.
———. 1967/1968. *The Phenomenon of the New Testament*. London: SCM.
Moulton, J. H. 1906/1967. *A Grammar of New Testament Greek*. Vol. 1. Edinburgh: T&T Clark.
———, and J. F. Howard. 1919/1929/1968. *A Grammar of New Testament Greek*. Vol. 2. Edinburgh: T&T Clark.
———. *A Grammar of New Testament Greek*. Vols. 3–4. Edinburgh: T&T Clark. (See N. Turner.)
Moulton, W. F., and A. S. Geden. 1974. *A Concordance to the Greek New Testament*. Edinburgh: T&T Clark.
Murray, D. G. 1983. "Order in St. Mark's Gospel." *The Downside Review* 101.344: 182–86.
Neill, S. 1966. *Interpretation of the New Testament 1861–1961*. Oxford: Oxford University Press.
Neirynck, F. 1975. *The Minor Agreements of Matthew and Luke against Mark*. Leuven: Leuven University Press.
———, and F. Van Segbroeck. 1978. "The Griesback Hypothesis: A Bibliography." In B. Orchard and T. R. W. Longstaff, eds. 1978. *J. J. Griesbach: Synoptic and Text-Critical Studies 1776–1976*. Cambridge: Cambridge University Press.

———. 1984. "The Two-Source Hypothesis: An Introduction." Paper presented to the 1984 Jerusalem Symposium.

———. 1984. "Theoretical Statement—Three Approaches to the Synoptic Problem." Paper presented to the 1984 Jerusalem Symposium.

Neville, D. J. 1994. *Arguments from Order in Synoptic Sources*. Gospel Studies 7. Macon: Mercer University Press.

———. 2002. *Mark's Gospel—Prior or Posterior?* Sheffield: Sheffield Academic Press.

Niemelä, J. H. 2002. In R. L. Thomas 2002. *Three Views on the Origins of the Synoptic Gospels*. Grand Rapids: Kregel.

Nineham, D. E., ed. 1955. *Studies in the Gospels*. Oxford: Blackwell.

———. 1963/1977. *Mark*. Pelican Commentaries. London: Penguin/SCM.

———. 1977. "Review of Farmer's *The Synoptic Problem*." *Journal of Theological Studies* 28: 548–50.

Nolland, J. 2005. *Matthew*. New International Greek Testament Commentary. Exeter: Paternoster/Grand Rapids: Eerdmans.

Orchard, B. 1976/1977. *Matthew, Luke, and Mark*. Manchester: Koinonia Press.

———, and T. R. W. Longstaff, eds. 1978. *J. J. Griesbach: Synoptic and Text-Critical Studies 1776–1976*. Cambridge: Cambridge University Press. (Cited as *Griesbach Studies*)

———, and H. Riley. 1987. *The Order of the Synoptics: Why Three Synoptic Gospels?* Macon: Mercer University Press.

Osborne, G. 2001. "Response." Pages 137–52 in Black and Beck, *Rethinking the Synoptic Problem*.

———. 2002. In R. L. Thomas 2002. *Three Views on the Origins of the Synoptic Gospels*. Grand Rapids: Kregel.

Owen, H. 1764. *Observations on the Four Gospels*. London: St. Martin's.

Palmer, F. R. 1971. *Grammar*. Language and Linguistics Series. Harmondsworth: Penguin.

Parker, P. 1953. *The Gospel before Mark*. Chicago: University of Chicago Press.

Peabody, D. 1983. "Augustine and the Augustinian Hypothesis: A Re-examination of Augustine's Thought." In Farmer, *New Synoptic Studies*.

———, L. Cope, and A. J. McNicol, eds. 2002. *One Gospel from Two*. Harrisburg: Trinity Press.

Petrie, S. 1959. "'Q' Is Only What You Make It." *Novum Testamentum* 3: 28–33.

Plummer, A. 1896/1922/1969. *Luke*. ICC. Edinburgh: T&T Clark.

Powers, B. W. 1977. "The Progressive Publication of Matthew: A New Explanation of Synoptic Origins." Tyndale Paper for March 1977 (Tyndale Fellowship for Biblical Studies in Australia. Ridley College, Parkville, Melbourne, Victoria, Australia).

———. 1980. "The Shaking of the Synoptics." *Reformed Theological Review* 39: 33–39.

Rawlinson, A. E. J. 1925. *Mark*. Westminster Commentaries. London: Methuen.

Reicke, B. 1978. "Griesbach's Answer to the Synoptic Question." In Orchard and Longstaff, *J. J. Griesbach: Synoptic and Text-Critical Studies 1776–1976*.

———. 1978. Introduction to Griesbach's *Commentatio*. In Orchard and Longstaff, *J. J. Griesbach: Synoptic and Text-Critical Studies 1776–1976*.

Riesenfeld, H. 1970. *The Gospel Tradition*. Minneapolis: Fortress/Oxford: Blackwell.

Riley, H. 1989. *The Making of Mark: An Exploration*. Macon: Mercer University Press.

Rist, J. M. 1978. *On the Independence of Matthew and Mark*. Cambridge: Cambridge University Press.

Roberts, M. 2007. *Can We Trust the Gospels?* Wheaton: Crossway.

Robertson, A. T. 1919. *Studies in Mark's Gospel*. New York: Macmillan.

———, and W. H. Davis. 1908/1931/1958/1977. *A New Short Grammar of the Greek Testament*. London: Hodder/Grand Rapids: Baker.

Robinson, J. A. T. 1975. "The Parable of the Wicked Husbandmen: A Test of Synoptic Relationships." *New Testament Studies* 21: 443–61.
———. 1976. *Redating the New Testament*. London: SCM.
Robinson, T. H. 1928/1960. *Matthew*. Moffat NT Commentary. London: Hodder & Stoughton.
Rolland, P. 1982. "Les Prédécesseurs de Marc." *Revue Biblique* 89: 370–405.
———. 1983. "Marc, Première Harmonie Evangélique?" *Revue Biblique* 90: 23–79.
———. 1984. *Les Premiers Evangiles*. Paris: Les Editions du Cerf.
Rushbrooke, W. G. 1880. *Synopticon*. London: Macmillan.
Sadler, M. F. 1882. *Matthew*. London: George Bell.
Sagan, C. 1980/1983. *Cosmos*. London and Sydney: Futura/MacDonald and Co.
Salmon, G. 1889. *A Historical Introduction to the Books of the New Testament*. 4th ed. London: John Murray.
Sanday, W., ed. 1911. *Oxford Studies in the Synoptic Problem*. Oxford: Clarendon.
Sanders, E. P. 1969a. *The Tendencies of the Synoptic Tradition*. Cambridge: Cambridge University Press.
———. 1969b. "The Argument from Order and the Relationship between Matthew and Luke." *NTS* 15: 249–61.
———. 1973. "The Overlaps of Mark and Q and the Synoptic Problem." *NTS* 19: 453–65.
———. 1975. "The Synoptic Problem: After Ten Years." *Perkins School of Theology Journal* 28: 70ff.
Saxe, J. G. n.d. "The Blind Men and the Elephant." In C. R. Watt, n.d. *Chosen for Pleasure*. London: Warne.
Schürer, E. 1885/1979. *History of the Jewish People in the Age of Jesus Christ*. Edinburgh: T&T Clark.
Schweizer, E. 1970. *Mark*. Atlanta: John Knox.
Segbroeck, F. Van. 1978. See Neirynck and Segbroeck.
Sevenster, J. N. 1968. *Do You Know Greek?* Leiden: Brill.
Simpson, R. T. 1966. "The Major Agreements of Matthew and Luke against Mark." *NTS* 12: 273–84.
Solages, Mgr. de 1959. *A Greek Synopsis of the Gospels*. Leiden: Brill.
———. 1973. *La Composition Des Evangiles*. Leiden: Brill.
Stein, R. H. 1987/1988. *The Synoptic Problem: An Introduction*. Leicester: IVP.
Stendahl, K. 1967. *The School of St Matthew*. Lund: Gleerup.
Stoldt, H. H. 1980. *History and Criticism of the Marcan Hypothesis*. Macon: Mercer University Press/ Edinburgh: T&T Clark.
Stonehouse, N. B. 1944/1979. *The Witness of the Synoptic Gospels to Christ*. Grand Rapids: Baker.
———. 1963/1964. *Origins of the Synoptic Gospels*. Grand Rapids: Eerdmans/London: Tyndale.
Streeter, B. H. 1911. "St Mark's Knowledge and Use of Q." In Sanday, *Oxford Studies in the Synoptic Problem*.
———. 1924. *The Four Gospels*. London: Macmillan.
Styler, G. M. 1962. "The Priority of Mark." In Moule, *The Birth of the New Testament*.
Swete, H. B. 1913/1977. *Mark*. London: Macmillan/Grand Rapids: Kregel.
Talbert, C. H., and E. V. McKnight. 1972. "Can the Griesbach Hypothesis Be Falsified?" *Journal of Biblical Literature* 91: 338–68.
Talbert, C. H. 1977/1978. *What Is a Gospel?* Minneapolis: Fortress/London: SPCK.
Taylor, R. O. P. 1946. *The Groundword of the Gospels*. Oxford: Blackwell.
Taylor, V. 1930/1967. *The Gospels*. London: Epworth Press.
———. 1933. *The Formation of the Gospel Tradition*. London: Macmillan.
———. 1952/1966. *Mark*. London: Macmillan.

Tenney, M. C. 1961/1978. *New Testament Survey*. Grand Rapids: Eerdmans/Leicester: IVP.
Thiessen, H. C. 1943/1979. *Introduction to the New Testament*. Grand Rapids: Eerdmans.
Thomas, R. L. 1976. "An Investigation of the Agreements between Matthew and Luke against Mark." *Journal of the Evangelical Theological Society* 19: 103–12.
———. 2002. *Three Views on the Origins of the Synoptic Gospels*. Grand Rapids: Kregel.
Thompson, G. H. P. 1972. *Luke*. New Clarendon Bible. Oxford: Clarendon.
Throckmorton, B. H. 1948. "Did Mark Know Q?" *Journal of Biblical Literature* 67: 319–29.
Trocmé, E. 1963/1975. *The Formation of the Gospel according to Mark*. London: SPCK.
Twain, M. *Chapters from My Autobiography*. BiblioLife, 2009.
Tuckett, C. M. 1979. "The Griesbach Hypothesis in the 19th Century." *Journal for the Study of the New Testament* 3: 29–60.
———. 1980. "The Argument from Order and the Synoptic Problem." *Theologische Zeitschrift* 36: 338–54.
———. 1983. *The Revival of the Griesbach Hypothesis*. Cambridge: University Press.
———. 1984a. "On the Relationship between Matthew and Luke." *New Testament Studies* 30: 130–42.
———. 1984b. "Response to the Two-Gospel Hypothesis Documents." Paper presented to the Jerusalem Symposium.
Turner, N. 1959. "The Minor Verbal Agreements of Mt. and Lk. against Mk." *Studia Evang. Texte und Unters* 73: 223–34.
———. 1963. *A Grammar of New Testament Greek*. Vol. 3. Edinburgh: T&T Clark.
———. 1964. "Second Thoughts: VII. Papyrus Find." *Expository Times*, LXXVI.
———. 1976. *A Grammar of New Testament Greek*. Vol. 4. Edinburgh: T&T Clark.
Tyson, J. B. 1987–88. "Order in the Synoptic Gospels: Patterns." *Second Century* 2: 65–109.
Vaganay, L. 1951. "L'absence du Sermon sur la Montagne chez Marc." *Revue Biblique* 58: 5–46.
———. 1954. *Le Problème Synoptique*. Paris-Tournai.
Walker, W. O., ed. 1978. *The Relationship among the Gospels*. San Antonio: Trinity University Press.
———. 1987–88. "Order in the Synoptic Gospels." *Second Century* 2: 83–97.
Watt, C. R. n.d. *Chosen For Pleasure*. London: Warne.
Weiss, B. 1861. "Zur Entstehungsgeschichte der drei synoptischen Evangelien." *Theologische Studien und Kritiken* 34 (1861): 29–100, 646–713.
Wenham, D. 1972. "The Synoptic Problem Revisited." *Tyndale Bulletin* 23: 3–38.
Wenham, J. 1991. *Redating Matthew, Mark, and Luke: A Fresh Assault*. London: Hodder & Stoughton.
Westcott, B. F. 1851/1860. *Introduction to the Study of the Gospels*. London: Macmillan.
Wette, W. M. L. de. 1826/1842/1848/1860. *Lehrbuch der historisch kritischen Einleitung in die kanonischen Bücher des Neuen Testaments*. Berlin: Reimer.
Williams, M. C. 2002. In Thomas, *Three Views on the Origins of the Synoptic Gospels*.
———. 2006. *Two Gospels from One*. Grand Rapids: Kregel.
Williams, N. P. 1911. "A Recent Theory of the Origin of St Mark's Gospel." In Sanday, *Oxford Studies in the Synoptic Problem*.
Woods, F. H. 1886. "The Origin and Mutual Relation of the Synoptic Gospels." *Studia Biblica et Ecclesiastica* 2: 59–104.
Wright, A. 1896/1903. *A Synopsis of the Gospels in Greek*. London: Macmillan.
Zahn, T. 1909. *Introduction to the New Testament*. 3 vols. Edinburgh: T&T Clark.

NAME INDEX

Abbott, E. A. *94–101, 160, 213–14, 220, 249, 252–54, 557, 578*
Albright, W. F. *9, 11, 37, 40, 51–52, 102, 352, 554, 578, 583*
Alford, H. *452, 578*
Allen, W. C. *23, 33–34, 47, 160, 171, 176–77, 179, 185, 326, 393–97, 399, 494, 516–17, 578*
Anderson, H. *578*
Argyle, A. W. *288, 352, 578*
Arndt, W. F. *578*
Atkinson, B. F. C. *30*
Augustine of Hippo *578*

Barclay, W. *85, 165–66, 168, 171, 176–77, 263–64, 470–71, 474, 483, 546, 574–75, 578*
Bartlet, J. *578*
Bauckham, R. *202–6, 579*
Beare, F. W. *257, 424, 579*
Beck, D. R. *1, 4–6, 164, 190, 579–80, 583–84*
Benoit, P. *579*
Berkhof, L. *453*
Black, D. A. *1, 4–6, 45–46, 164, 190, 202, 221–26, 241, 353, 379, 579*
Bleek, F. *23, 213, 382, 579*
Blomberg, C. *1, 4, 156, 190, 192–94, 202, 237, 250–51, 579*
Boismard, M.-E. *486–88, 579*
Branscomb, B. H. *579*
Brown, C. *579*
Bruce, A. B. *27, 579*
Bruce, F. F. *82, 579*
Burkitt, F. C. *23, 337, 472, 483–84, 544, 579*
Burney, C. F. *579*
Burridge, R. *203*
Büsching, A. F. *480*
Butler, B. C. *3, 162, 165, 214, 404, 471–76, 484, 545, 579*

Caird, G. B. *579*
Campenhausen, H. von *579*
Carpenter, J. E. *579*
Casey, M. *579*
Chapman, J. *162, 165, 208, 215, 238, 323, 404, 466–76, 545, 554, 579*
Chrysostom, J. *227, 449–51, 453, 456, 530, 542–43, 553, 579*
Cope, L. *579, 584*
Cranfield, C. E. B. *90, 579*
Creed, J. M. *8, 579*
Cremer, H. *579*
Crook, Z. *579*
Cutt, S. *253, 579*

Dahl, N. *244*
Danker, F. W. *579*
Davis, W. H. *584*
Dibelius, M. *23, 33, 579*
Dodd, C. H. *81–82, 580*
Downing, F. G. *580*
Dungan, D. L. *23, 95, 156, 189, 322, 448, 484, 554, 580, 583*

Edersheim, A. *273, 580*
Edwards, J. R. *164, 580*
Eichhorn, J. G. *481*
Ellis, E. E. *8, 27, 570, 580*
Evans, C. F. *60, 62–63, 580*

Farmer, W. *6, 11–12, 14, 55, 94, 103, 112, 120, 122, 163, 165, 180–81, 194, 212, 214–16, 242–49, 252–54, 257, 285, 297, 305, 307, 322, 351–52, 354, 406, 535–36, 538, 545, 548, 554, 558, 576, 579–84*
Farnell, F. D. *201, 448–50, 452–55, 462, 580*
Farrer, A. M. *54, 152, 159, 164, 195–96, 228, 346, 352, 354, 368, 450, 478–79, 544, 554, 580*
Fee, G. D. *491, 580*

Fenton, J. C.   48, 580
Filson, F. V.   580
Fitzmyer, J.   163, 197, 215, 242–47, 263, 346, 354, 379, 415, 580
Flusser, D.   480, 582
Focant, C.   580
France, R. T.   580
Friedrich, G.   580, 582
Fuller, R. H.   581

Gaboury, A.   581
Gamba, G. G.   581
Geden, A. S.   521, 583
Geldenhuys, J. N.   581
Gerhardsson, B.   8, 17, 20, 29–30, 202, 554, 581
Gieseler, J. C. L.   452
Gingrich, F. W.   578
Gleason, H. A.   91, 152, 581
Godet, F. L.   26–27, 581
Goodacre, M.   159, 164, 195–96, 250, 346, 478–79, 581
Goodspeed, E. J.   8, 30, 581
Gould, E. P.   59–60, 581
Goulder, M. D.   164, 196, 478, 581
Grant, F. C.   86, 247–48, 253–54, 581
Grant, R. M.   581
Greeven, H.   581
Griesbach, J. J.   15, 53–55, 94, 96, 102, 163, 180–81, 210–18, 242–43, 247, 249–51, 253–55, 293, 295, 297, 299, 301, 305–6, 400, 406–7, 423–24, 480, 487, 492, 535–36, 538, 546, 554, 557, 579–81, 583–86
Gromacki, R. G.   453
Gundry, R. H.   7–8, 30–31, 48, 179–80, 187, 321, 418, 516, 518–19, 527, 542, 554, 581
Guthrie, D.   166, 169, 171, 581
Guy, H. A.   24–25, 35, 554, 581

Harnack, A.   43–44, 570, 581
Hart, A.   577, 581
Hawkins, J. C.   160, 166–69, 171, 175, 177, 179, 185–86, 244, 288–89, 332–36, 374, 493–94, 526, 530, 574–75, 581

Head, P. M.   582
Hendriksen, W.   8, 30–31, 102, 582
Hengel, M.   582
Hill, D.   31, 37, 94, 249, 254, 582
Holtzmann, H. J.   160, 544, 551
Honoré, A. M.   103, 112, 118, 181, 582

Jameson, H. G.   208, 465–66, 582
Jeremias, J.   582

Kennedy, G.   554, 582
Kistemaker, S. J.   582
Kittel, G.   582
Knox, W. L.   16, 24–25, 33–34, 554, 582
Koester, H.   351
Kümmel, W. G.   23, 165–66, 248, 335, 346, 353–54, 379, 382, 393, 399–401, 403–4, 406–7, 470, 483, 494, 550–51, 582

Lachmann, K.   481, 485
Ladd, G. E.   401–2, 582
Lane, W. L.   582
Leon-Dufour, X.   554, 582
Lessing, G. E.   481, 484, 582
Lightfoot, R. H.   89, 582
Lindsey, R. L.   351, 480, 582
Linnemann, E.   453, 455, 582
Loane, M.   158, 215
Longstaff, T. R. W.   22, 95, 580–84
Lowe, M.   582
Ludlum, J. H.   582

Maier, P.   18, 21, 88, 580, 582
Mann, C. S.   9, 11, 37, 40, 51–52, 102, 352, 554, 578, 582
Manson, T. W.   159, 583
Manson, W.   583
Martin, R. P.   57, 72, 165–66, 583
McGiffert, A. C.   89, 580
McKnight, E. V.   215, 229, 583, 585
McKnight, S.   5–6, 193–94, 197, 583
McNeile, A. H.   47–48, 583
McNicol, A. J.   346, 353, 583–84
Meeks, W. A.   583
Menzies, A.   583
Metzger, B.   166, 171, 177, 248, 274, 277, 547, 583

Name Index

Miller, D. M.   *163, 580, 583*
Mitton, C. L.   *94, 252, 583*
Morgenthaler, R.   *103, 111–13, 118, 135, 137, 181, 298, 326–27, 329, 331–32, 335, 352, 368, 521, 564, 580, 583*
Morris, L.   *8, 27, 583*
Moule, C. F. D.   *25, 60, 82–83, 473, 583, 585*
Moulton, J. H.   *521, 583*
Murray, D. G.   *389, 583*

Neill, S.   *483, 583*
Neirynck, F.   *163, 184, 488, 554, 583, 585*
Neville, D. J.   *202, 584*
Niemelä, J. H.   *201, 251–52, 584*
Nineham, D. E.   *60, 580, 584*
Nolland, J.   *164, 584*

Orchard, B.   *22, 164, 202, 211–12, 221–22, 242, 350–51, 353, 355, 365, 379, 406, 470, 474, 580–81, 583–84*
Osborne, G.   *194, 196–97, 251, 584*
Owen, H.   *208–11, 213, 217–18, 480, 584*

Palmer, F. R.   *57, 91, 151, 584*
Palmer, H.   *57*
Parker, P.   *554, 584*
Peabody, D.   *164, 202, 208–9, 217, 465, 543, 583–84*
Petrie, S.   *549, 554, 584*
Plummer, A.   *26–27, 47, 357, 584*
Powers, B. W.   *584*

Rawlinson, A. E. J.   *584*
Reicke, B.   *22, 211, 584*
Riesenfeld, H.   *17, 554, 584*
Riley, H.   *221–22, 584*
Rist, J. M.   *584*
Roberts, M.   *203–4, 584*
Robertson, A. T.   *30, 584*
Robinson, J. A. T.   *44–45, 570, 584*
Robinson, T. H.   *21, 48, 585*
Rolland, P.   *486–87, 585*
Ronning, H.   *480*
Rushbrooke, W. G.   *160, 466, 585*

Sadler, M. F.   *585*
Sagan, C.   *18, 585*
Salmon, G.   *448, 456–60, 482, 540, 585*
Sanday, W.   *160, 193, 289, 578, 582, 585–86*
Saxe, J. G.   *555, 585*
Schleiermacher, F.   *16, 22–23, 453, 554*
Schmid   *248*
Schürer, E.   *272–73, 585*
Schweizer, E.   *585*
van Segbroeck, F.   *583, 585*
Sevenster, J. N.   *7, 585*
Simpson, R. T.   *303, 585*
Solages, de   *103, 112, 118, 135, 181, 585*
Stein, R. H.   *401, 415, 457–59, 585*
Stoldt, H. H.   *16, 23, 180, 183–84, 212–13, 236, 288, 322, 406, 482, 484–85, 545, 551, 585*
Stonehouse, N. B.   *49–50, 165, 168–69, 393, 397–400, 407, 470–72, 474–75, 493, 516, 525–28, 530, 532, 551, 585*
Storr, G. C.   *160, 211*
Streeter, B. H.   *3, 5, 13, 15, 58–59, 86, 90, 92, 96, 102, 123, 158–63, 166, 168–69, 171, 173, 193–99, 228–29, 232, 236, 251, 258, 260, 278–79, 282, 284, 288–97, 299–304, 307, 311–13, 315–18, 321–24, 327–28, 330–32, 335, 353, 377–79, 393, 396–97, 402, 404, 415, 418, 424, 445–46, 466, 469, 471–75, 485, 491, 493–94, 521, 526, 530, 534, 543–46, 548, 553–54, 567, 585*
Styler, G. M.   *2–3, 6, 15, 53, 55, 86, 159, 162–63, 182–85, 187–88, 253, 472–73, 485, 551, 585*
Swete, H. B.   *103, 585*

Talbert, C. H.   *215, 585*
Taylor, R. O. P.   *452, 585*
Taylor, V.   *15, 90, 159, 407, 494, 513, 516–17, 525–26, 530, 541, 544, 547, 585*
Tenney, M. C.   *453, 585*
Thiessen, H. C.   *453, 483, 585*
Thompson, G. H. P.   *357–58, 586*
Throckmorton, B. H.   *586*

Trocmé, E.   *61–62, 72, 586*
Tuckett, C. M.   *95–96, 163, 166, 188–89, 215, 232, 236, 241–42, 277, 288, 291–301, 304–7, 322, 331, 382, 401, 424–25, 488, 490–93, 517, 535–39, 545, 554, 586*
Turner, N.   *171, 288, 586*
Twain, M.   *102, 586*
Tyson, J. B.   *586*

Vaganay, L.   *248, 586*

Walker, W. O.   *586*
Watt, C. R.   *586*
Weisse, C. H.   *160, 183, 551*
Wenham, D.   *57, 181, 186, 299–300, 586*

Wenham, J.   *586*
Westcott, B. F.   *36, 452–53, 586*
de Wette, W.   *23, 213, 586*
Wilke, C. G.   *160*
Williams, M. C.   *164, 194, 196–201, 251, 586*
Williams, N. P.   *331, 586*
Witherington, B.   *203*
Woods, F. H.   *58–59, 87, 160, 213–14, 586*
Wright, A.   *57, 269–70, 452, 586*

Zahn, T.   *586*

SUBJECT INDEX

A

Aramaic 7, 9, 11, 17, 22, 30–32, 37, 39–40, 159, 166, 169–71, 187, 205, 238, 290, 337, 380, 442, 458–59, 470, 481–82, 522, 530, 561–63, 565–66, 578–79
Augustine 191, 208–9, 227, 253, 448–50, 463–66, 542–43, 553, 578, 584

B

Barnabas 62, 87, 237
Bartimaeus 5, 66, 68, 111, 115, 130, 136, 146, 269
Beatitudes 128, 354, 379
Beelzebul 69, 80, 114, 125, 129, 144, 235, 294–95, 305, 349, 361, 385, 404, 411, 429, 435, 440, 443, 548
Bethany 67, 108, 116, 121, 132, 266, 370, 372, 390, 436
Bethlehem 139, 369–70
Bethsaida 66, 68, 106, 136, 143, 236, 359, 363, 385, 387, 412

C

Caesar 43, 67, 79, 130, 139–40, 311, 536
Caesarea 10, 39, 565
Caesarea Philippi 66, 70, 126, 131, 143, 154–55, 269, 359, 364, 417, 429, 431, 441
Cambridge 211, 214–15
Capernaum 7, 28, 30, 47, 63–64, 68, 94, 97, 99, 101, 113, 119, 133, 140, 142, 184–85, 271, 308–9, 350, 361–62, 377, 392, 394, 397–98, 409, 411, 433, 438–39, 443, 558
circular argument 275, 381

Clement 180, 225–26, 542–43
Cleopas 371
cluster 379, 384, 417, 422, 433–34, 436, 438–39, 441, 443–44
codex 29–30, 35–36, 263, 375
coherence 163, 185, 188, 241, 491–92, 531, 535
cohesiveness 7
coincidence 3, 14, 165, 230, 288–89, 317, 325, 402, 415, 417, 419–20, 423–25, 446, 457–58, 529, 548–50
colloquial Greek 90, 173, 462
colloquial language 100, 151, 172, 249, 570
Complete Independence 5, 53, 162–63, 228, 426, 449–50, 452, 456, 459, 461–63, 543
conference 4–5, 64, 164, 184, 190, 194, 202, 250–51, 254, 382

D

deaf 66, 68, 106–7, 114, 135–36, 236, 255, 271, 281, 387, 436–37
didache 13, 81–82, 85, 153, 191, 567
direction indicator 182, 186, 191, 257–58, 344
doublet 183, 287, 331
Double Tradition 136, 240, 246, 250, 328, 479, 536, 582

E

Emmaus 148, 370
enigma 265, 379, 477
Eusebius 9, 18, 21–22, 88, 179–80, 205, 225, 580
explanatory power 2, 4, 6, 15, 194, 378, 414, 446, 492, 535

Expurgatory Argument 87
eyewitness *8, 11–12, 27–28, 34, 37–40, 47–50, 87, 90, 93, 149, 151, 174, 187–88, 190, 199, 202, 204–6, 218, 239, 280, 282–83, 343, 444, 452, 454, 462, 468, 476, 488, 522, 528, 532, 539, 558, 565–66, 569*

F

Father(s), early church *12, 15, 21, 45–48, 50, 52, 88–89, 93, 151, 174, 198, 205, 218, 221, 224–27, 241, 449–50, 453, 463, 542–43*
Fragment Hypothesis *22, 25*
framework *11, 13–14, 47, 61, 83, 87, 90, 155, 226, 229, 248, 311, 315–16, 350, 360, 363–64, 397–98, 404, 407–11, 413–14, 416–17, 427–32, 434, 436, 441, 445, 453–54, 563*

G

Galilee *56, 62–66, 99, 107, 109, 113–14, 120, 125, 127, 131, 139–41, 143–44, 185, 263, 309, 348–50, 359–61, 364, 370, 372, 384, 392, 394, 397, 411, 431–32, 435–36, 438–39, 441, 443*
genealogy *127, 353–55, 364, 409, 431–32, 451*
Gentile *20, 78, 85, 187, 221, 268, 274, 369*
Gethsemane *67, 116, 130, 132, 147, 386, 413*
Griesbach Hypothesis *53, 94–97, 101, 188–89, 211, 213–16, 218, 242, 247, 250, 253, 291, 296–97, 301, 305–7, 322, 406, 472, 490–92, 535–38, 545, 576, 579, 585–86*

H

Hebrew *7, 20, 22–23, 30, 37, 40, 169, 238, 277, 321, 381, 480–81, 510, 520*

Hellenist *9, 18, 20, 29–30, 203*
Herod *69, 80, 105, 110, 119, 129–30, 139–40, 143, 145, 295, 428, 441, 460*
Herodians *64, 79, 110*
high priest *68, 71, 78, 109–10, 132*
historic present *98, 166–68, 516, 567*
Holy Spirit *3, 46, 48, 50, 140, 200, 234, 291–92, 342, 358–59, 385, 404, 411, 453–54, 456, 463*

I

impasse *346, 373, 529, 583*
Impossibility Argument *94, 249*
Irenaeus *225–26, 542–43*
Irrelevancy Argument *86*
Isaiah *77, 127, 221, 321–22, 324*
Israel *46, 70–72, 78, 99–100, 108, 136, 207, 276, 480, 502, 514, 567*

J

Jairus *4, 114, 143, 154, 358, 443*
Jerome *22, 481*
Jerusalem *7–9, 11, 16, 20, 25, 34, 39, 44–45, 62, 64, 66–67, 104, 108–9, 115, 130, 132, 139–40, 144–47, 215, 217, 219, 222, 228, 238, 267, 294–95, 306, 348–49, 351, 353, 360, 364, 366, 370, 372, 377, 382, 386, 389–90, 412, 424, 431, 433, 435–36, 441, 456, 470, 480, 487–88, 490, 544, 552, 562, 564, 570, 579–80, 583–84, 586*
jigsaw puzzle *242, 556*
John Mark *25, 60, 62, 85, 171, 192, 205, 220, 259, 470, 532, 571–72*
John the apostle *21, 40, 58, 66, 76, 88, 108, 121, 169, 372*
John the Baptist *40, 55, 59, 61, 63, 65, 69, 73, 77, 80, 83, 105, 114, 120–21, 125–26, 128, 131, 140, 244, 246, 290–91, 312–13, 321–22, 349, 361, 364–65, 384–85, 392,*

Subject Index

404, 409, 411–12, 427–28, 430–33, 436–37, 439–40, 443, 460, 548, 564, 579
Josephus 166–67
Judea 139–41, 310, 348, 359, 364, 435

K

kerygma 13, 24, 34, 81–86, 153, 174, 191, 237, 243–45, 264, 328

L

Latin 7, 169, 211, 284
Levi 28, 51, 64, 114, 141, 154, 352, 359, 406, 433
linguistic science 91
logia 9, 22–23, 26–28, 39, 46, 59, 61, 179, 301, 380–81, 562
Lord's Prayer, the 128, 144, 237, 250, 337, 339, 348, 365, 379
Lord's Supper, the 116, 121, 132, 338, 377, 386, 403, 413

M

Markan Priority 1, 3–6, 14–15,17, 21–22, 25, 36, 41, 45, 48, 54, 56, 59, 75, 82, 84, 86–87, 99–100, 103, 117, 123, 150, 156–207, 211–56, 257–344, 346, 352, 354, 368, 376, 378, 380, 382–447, 455, 465–67, 470–494, 509, 513, 516–18, 520–21, 526–27, 530–33, 535, 537–39, 543–52, 554, 556–57, 560, 562, 571, 573–76, 582–83
Matthean Priority 195, 398, 472, 475
mistake 102, 185, 250, 473
misunderstanding 15, 71–72, 123, 200, 254–55
Multiple-Sources Hypothesis 54

N

notebook 29–30, 565

O

Oxford 160, 193–94, 214, 330, 333, 465, 478, 578–86

P

Palestine 8–11, 39–40, 43, 51, 62, 394–95, 434, 565
Palm Sunday 77, 80, 364, 431, 441
Papias 12, 16, 18, 21–23, 26, 28–29, 32, 39, 46, 51, 59, 88–89, 149, 151, 179–80, 190, 199, 205, 224–25, 380–81, 418, 425, 446, 542, 562
papyrus 18, 35–36, 586
paratactic constructions 91, 567
Passover 67, 116, 130, 134, 140, 147, 386, 413
Paul 10–11, 19–20, 35, 38–39, 43–44, 46–47, 62, 87, 170, 219, 222–23, 237, 261, 306, 338, 342–43, 370, 448, 450–51, 565, 570–72
Pentecost 39, 178, 261, 562
Peter's preaching 12, 15, 88, 90, 171, 173–74, 180–81, 190–91, 199, 205, 218, 221, 223–24, 226, 237, 247–48, 266, 269, 272, 468, 476, 539, 561, 569
Pharisees 51, 64, 66, 78–80, 104, 114–16, 120, 126, 128–34, 144–47, 273, 290, 294, 313, 330–31, 333, 366, 385–86, 395, 404, 412–413, 419, 429, 440, 536
presupposition 6, 172–73, 462, 513, 546, 557, 575
Proto-Gospel 22, 26, 487
Proto-Luke 161, 216, 377, 415, 486
Proto-Mark 487
Proto-Matthew 216, 374, 379, 487, 559
pseudo-Markan 94, 99–101, 558

Q

Q 3, 14, 22, 24, 36–38, 54, 76, 96, 137, 152, 158–60, 162–63, 183–84, 186,

194, 215–16, 228, 235–36, 251, 258–59, 271–72, 275–76, 278, 282, 290–94, 296–97, 299–307, 309, 311, 313, 316, 321–24, 330–32, 336–37, 340, 346–47, 352, 375, 377–81, 396–98, 402, 404, 417, 466, 469–71, 473, 475–79, 486, 492, 521, 532–35, 538, 548–50, 554, 558, 560, 575, 578, 580, 583–86

R

Rome, Roman   7, 10–13, 18–19, 28–31, 35, 39, 43–44, 50–51, 78–79, 92, 98–99, 204, 219, 225–26, 247, 250, 289, 462, 470, 474, 570

S

Sabbath   42, 64, 66, 77–78, 104, 109, 114, 119, 125, 140–41, 145, 147–48, 153–54, 185, 275–76, 309, 349, 361, 392, 433, 440
sandwich stories   295
Sanhedrin   44, 116, 121, 130, 386–87, 403, 413
scroll   18, 29–30, 263, 367
Seminar   160, 193, 465, 581
Semitisms   166, 170–71, 480
Septuagint, LXX   166–68, 171, 186, 273, 277, 300, 321, 510, 518, 520
Sermon on the Mount   13, 58, 62, 64, 80, 86, 125, 185, 237, 243, 248, 252, 258–61, 268, 309, 316, 354, 365–66, 392, 394, 397–98, 409–10, 413–14, 428, 430, 435, 438–39, 443, 471, 474
Sermon on the Plain   13, 55, 248, 258, 307–8, 354, 403, 410, 413–14, 428–30, 445
shorthand   8, 20, 29–31
Son of God   13, 63, 72–79, 83, 127, 136, 245, 360, 571
Son of Man   67, 70, 77, 106, 116, 129–30, 287, 360, 386, 413, 502, 521
Sondergut   103, 111–12, 124, 127, 130, 136, 138, 149–52, 191, 209, 240, 280, 376, 378, 388, 436, 548
spoken language   90, 92, 151, 462
statistics   102–3, 111, 113, 118, 124, 135, 137, 149, 151, 166, 181–82, 298, 316, 326–28, 330–31, 349, 356, 368, 376–78, 455
subordinating constructions   91, 174
Successive Dependence Hypothesis   53, 162, 209, 229, 404, 426, 449, 465–66, 474, 477, 544
suprasegmentals   91
Symposium   424, 487–88, 490, 552, 579–80, 583–84, 586

Z

zigzag, zigzagging   423–24

SCRIPTURE INDEX

Exodus

4:12 *357*
4:22 *72*
20 *509*
20:12 *510*
23:20 *321*

Leviticus

12 *370*
19:18 *510*

Numbers

15:37 *273*
15:37–41 *234*

Deuteronomy

5 *509*
5:16 *510*
22:12 *234, 273*
32:5 *277*

2 Samuel

7:14 *73*

Esther

4:14 *46*

Psalms

2 *73*
2:6–7 *73*
2:7 *73*

Isaiah

9:6 *72*
42:1 *72*
48:16 *72*

51:16 *357*
64:8 *72*

Jeremiah

1:9 *357*

Ezekiel

17 *300*
17:23 *299*
17:22–23 *299–300*

Daniel

4:21 *300*

Hosea

11:1 *73*

Malachi

3:1 *321*

Matthew

1 *125*
1:1 *71*
1:1–17 *435, 529*
1–13 *486*
1:16 *71*
1:17 *71*
1:18 *71, 167*
1:18–2:23 *355, 432*
1:18–25 *369*
1:21 *170*
1:23 *170*
2 *125*
2:1 *139*
2:1–19 *139*
2:7 *369*
2:8–9 *369*
2:9 *139*

2:11 *369*
2:13 *139*
2:13–14 *369*
2:15 *73*
2:16 *369*
2:19 *139*
2:22–23 *370*
2:23 *139*
3:1 *140*
3:1–2 *140*
3:1–4:17 *232*
3:1–6 *291*
3:1–12 *529*
3:1–17 *432, 392, 421*
3:2 *125, 140*
3:3 *324*
3:4 *131*
3:5–6 *131*
3:7 *125*
3:7–10 *291, 349*
3:7–12 *286*
3:11 *230–31, 291*
3:11–12 *234, 246, 291, 349*
3:12 *291*
3:13–15 *125*
3:13–17 *432*
3:16 *285, 521*
3:17 *74*
3–18 *353*
4:1 *138, 286*
4:1–2 *140*
4:1–11 *234, 292, 349, 392, 421, 432*
4:3 *74*
4:4–11 *362, 383*
4:5 *459*
4:6 *74*
4:12 *131, 140, 357*
4:12–17 *125, 309, 384, 392, 421*

4:12a   *432*
4:12b   *361*
4:12b–16   *432*
4:13   *185, 361*
4:13–16   *309*
4:17   *131, 361, 432*
4:18–22   *131, 355, 361, 372, 384, 392, 411, 421, 432, 435*
4:23   *125, 131, 141, 185, 220*
4:23–25   *125, 229, 309, 385, 392, 394–95, 397–98, 421, 435, 437, 563*
4:23a   *361*
4:23b–25   *361*
4:25   *562*
5   *125, 361*
5:1   *142*
5:3   *436*
5:3–7:27   *397*
5–7   *13, 398–99, 436–37*
5:10–11   *372*
5:15   *122, 393*
5:22   *170*
5:31–32   *366*
6   *125, 361*
6:9–13   *337, 348, 365*
6:20   *521*
6:24   *349*
7   *125, 361*
7:2   *122, 271, 393*
7:5   *459*
7:9   *359*
7:16   *359*
7:24–27   *261, 441*
7:28–29   *185, 309, 361, 392, 399*
7:29   *261, 316, 438*
8:1   *125, 137, 141, 319, 435, 438, 443*
8:1–4   *137, 185, 361, 385, 392, 421, 436, 438*
8:1–9:34   *397*
8:2   *271*
8:2–3   *285*
8:2–4   *348*

8:3   *288*
8:5   *125, 142, 271, 359*
8:5–13   *97, 125, 361, 436–39*
8:8   *98–100*
8–9   *406*
8:10   *100*
8:11–12   *67*
8:13   *99*
8:14   *141, 271*
8:14–15   *185, 361*
8:14–17   *350, 385, 392, 399, 409, 421, 438*
8:15   *359*
8:15–20   *126*
8:16   *141, 175, 361*
8:16–17   *185, 396*
8:17   *125*
8:18   *142, 270, 533*
8:18–9:1   *350, 361, 432, 438*
8:18–22   *125, 396, 564*
8:18–23   *308*
8:18–27   *533*
8:19   *144, 270*
8:19–22   *533*
8:19–23   *349*
8:23   *142*
8:23–9:26   *400*
8:23–27   *654*
8:23–34   *385, 393, 399, 422, 426*
8:26   *177*
8:26a   *363*
8:26b   *363*
8:27   *349*
8:28   *143*
8:28–34   *125, 267, 358, 564*
8:29   *74*
8:32   *267*
9   *396*
9:1   *125, 141, 443, 533*
9:1–8   *185, 349, 396*
9:1–17   *232, 385, 393, 421*
9:2–8   *436–37, 564*

9:2–17   *350, 352, 361, 433, 438–39, 443–44*
9:6   *288, 457*
9:7   *286*
9:8   *125*
9:9   *28, 51, 141, 359, 439*
9:9–13   *396*
9:9–17   *400, 406*
9:11   *286*
9:13   *125*
9:13–30   *386*
9:14–17   *396, 433, 459*
9:16   *286*
9:17   *286*
9:18   *5, 131, 143, 154, 358, 391, 434–35, 439, 443, 564*
9:18–19   *361*
9:18–22   *272*
9:18–26   *385, 393, 396, 399, 409, 422, 426, 438, 564*
9:20   *234, 272, 274, 286, 567*
9:20–22   *361*
9:21   *131*
9:23   *275*
9:23–26   *361, 436*
9:25   *131*
9:26   *125*
9:27–30   *436*
9:27–31   *125*
9:27–34   *64, 438*
9:32–34   *125*
9:35   *220, 361, 437–38, 563*
9:35–10:14   *369*
9:35–10:16   *125*
9:35–10:42   *302*
9:35b–38   *302*
9:36–38   *361, 437*
9:37–38   *349*
10   *315*
10:1   *142, 220, 287*
10:1–4   *361, 385, 393, 399, 406, 421, 426*
10:1–16   *409*

10:1–42 *437*
10:2–4 *302*
10:3 *363*
10:3–4 *358*
10:5 *399*
10:5–6 *276*
10:5–8 *302*
10:5–16 *302, 316, 385, 393, 399, 422*
10:5–42 *361*
10:9 *359*
10:9–16a *316*
10:11 *122*
10:12–13 *275, 302*
10:14 *286*
10:15–16 *302*
10:17–25 *125, 302*
10:20,22 *518*
10:26 *393*
10:26–33 *125*
10:26–42 *302*
10:29 *359*
10:34–36 *125*
10:37–39 *125*
10:40–11:1 *125*
10:42 *131, 317, 319*
11:1 *437*
11:1–18 *432*
11:1–19 *361, 436*
11:2 *125, 437*
11:2–6 *349*
11:3 *367*
11:3–4 *440*
11:5 *436, 439*
11:7–19 *125, 349*
11:7–30 *440*
11:10 *77, 288, 321–22*
11:15 *393*
11:17 *359*
11:19 *359*
11:20–24 *125, 349, 361*
11:21 *363*
11:24 *363*
11:25 *144*
11:25–27 *349, 361*
11:27 *74*
11:28–30 *125*
11:29 *261*

12 *400*
12:1 *141*
12:1–8 *154, 349*
12:1–14 *361, 385, 393, 410–11, 421, 426, 433, 440*
12:1–50 *440*
12:4 *286*
12:5 *336*
12:5–7 *45, 125*
12:8 *122*
12:9 *141, 270*
12:9–14 *125, 389, 536*
12:10 *286, 517*
12:11 *276*
12:14 *440*
12:15–21 *310, 361, 385, 389, 393, 410–11, 421–22, 426*
12:15a *440*
12:15b–16 *440*
12:16 *131*
12:17–21 *125, 310, 440*
12:18 *357*
12:22 *144*
12:22–13:23 *410*
12:22–23 *84*
12:22–24 *125*
12:22–30 *361, 393*
12:22–45 *294, 349, 440*
12:24 *424*
12:24–30 *385, 411, 421*
12:24–50 *414*
12:25–37 *125*
12:27 *359*
12:28 *356*
12:29 *131*
12:31 *131*
12:31–32 *362*
12:31–37 *385, 393, 411, 428*
12:33–35 *362*
12:34a–35 *362–63*
12:36 *357*
12:38 *144*
12:38–42 *125, 361, 363*
12:41 *363*
12:42 *363*

12:43–45 *362–63*
12:45 *125*
12:46 *142, 295, 435, 443*
12:46–50 *362, 385, 393, 411, 422, 440*
12:47 *119*
12:48–49 *131*
12:49–50 *440*
13 *80, 315, 396*
13:1 *125, 440, 443*
13:1–2 *131*
13:1–3 *142*
13:1–9 *349*
13:1–23 *385, 393, 412, 422-23, 426*
13:1–52 *310, 362, 407, 440*
13:3 *467*
13:5–6 *131*
13:6 *359*
13:8 *131*
13:9 *122, 287*
13:11 *279, 287, 363*
13:12 *363, 393*
13:13 *363*
13:14–15 *125*
13:16–17 *125*
13:17 *359*
13:18 *122*
13:23 *131*
13:24 *297*
13:24–30 *125*
13:27 *297*
13:31 *122*
13:31–32 *296, 385, 393, 407, 412, 422, 426*
13:31–35 *423*
13:32 *131, 298–99*
13:33 *122, 314*
13:34 *131, 310*
13:34–35 *349, 385, 393, 407, 412, 422, 426*
13:35 *125*
13:36–43 *125*
13:43 *393*
13:44–46 *125*
13:47–50 *125*
13:51–52 *126, 310*

13:53 *126*
13:53–58 *131, 348, 355, 362, 385, 393, 411–12, 422, 427, 440*
13:54 *140*
13:54b *411*
13:55 *246*
13:57 *440*
13:58 *493*
14:1 *143, 408, 440, 460, 563*
14:1–2 *362, 385, 393, 411–12, 422–23, 427, 432, 440*
14:1–21 *433*
14:2 *131, 427, 441*
14:3–12 *131, 385, 412, 422, 427, 441*
14:4–12 *564*
14:13 *131, 282, 359, 427, 441*
14:13–15 *143*
14:13–18:5 *423*
14:13–21 *126, 362, 385, 412, 422, 432, 564*
14:14 *131*
14:14–21 *441*
14:18–20 *363*
14:20 *286*
14:21 *363*
14:22–16:12 *418–19, 441*
14:22–27 *131*
14:22–33 *126, 385, 412, 422*
14:31 *177*
14:32 *132*
14:33 *74–76*
14:34–15:31 *385, 412, 422*
14:34–36 *131*
14:36 *273*
15:1–20 *126, 131, 221, 536*
15:3 *122*
15:3–9 *383*
15:4–20 *366*
15:16–17 *177*
15:19 *510*
15:21–28 *126, 131, 268, 369*
15:24 *276, 567*
15:29–31 *126, 418*
15:31 *437*
15:32–39 *131, 385, 412, 422*
16:1 *517*
16:1–2 *145*
16:1–4 *126, 131*
16:1–12 *385, 412, 422*
16:4 *287*
16:4b–12 *468*
16:5–6 *145*
16:5–12 *126, 131*
16:6 *286*
16:8–12 *177*
16:13 *143, 154, 359*
16:13–17:8 *362*
16:13–18:5 *433*
16:13–20 *432*
16:13–21 *385, 412, 422*
16:13–23 *126, 131*
16:16 *74–75*
16:17 *170*
16:18 *366*
16:21 *286, 432, 441*
16:21–23 *177*
16:22–23 *385, 412, 422*
16:24 *286*
16:24–28 *287, 349, 386, 412, 422, 432*
16:26 *287*
16:27 *126*
16:28 *122*
17:1 *143, 232, 358*
17:1–7 *232*
17:1–8 *126, 432*
17:1–9 *270, 386, 412, 422*
17:3 *283*
17:5 *75, 359*
17:9 *143, 441*
17:9–13 *131*
17:9–18:5 *362*
17:10 *517*
17:10–13 *386, 412, 422, 441*
17:13 *126*
17:14 *143*
17:14–20 *126, 432, 564*
17:14–21 *232*
17:14–23 *386, 412, 422*
17:15 *131*
17:16 *286*
17:16–20 *177*
17:17 *234, 276*
17:19 *132*
17:21 *124*
17:22 *143, 287*
17:24–27 *45, 126, 441, 468*
17:25 *308*
18 *315, 317, 353*
18:1 *144, 319*
18:1–3 *177*
18:1–5 *126, 386, 412, 422, 433*
18:1–35 *440*
18:2 *319*
18:3–4 *319*
18:5 *317*
18:6 *317, 319, 363*
18:6–9 *386, 412, 422, 427*
18:6–35 *435, 441*
18:6b *363*
18:7 *126, 319, 363*
18:8–9 *132*
18:10–14 *126, 337, 366*
18:10–35 *319*
18:11 *124*
18:12–13 *366*
18:15 *319*
18:15–18 *366*
18:15–20 *126*
18:15–22 *468*
18:21–22 *126*
18:23–35 *126*
18:35 *358*
19 *500, 501, 515–16, 523*
19:1 *144, 319–20, 435, 441, 564*
19:1–9 *132*
19:1–12 *126, 366, 386, 412*

Scripture Index

19:3   *276, 567*
19:4–8   *383*
19:9   *276, 575*
19:13   *146*
19:13–15   *349, 362, 432*
19:13–30   *412*
19:15   *132*
19:16   *500, 515–517, 523*
19:16–17   *526*
19:16–20:16   *429*
19:16–22   *358*
19:16–30   *126, 231, 493, 495–500, 503–8*
19:16b–17a   *527*
19:17   *220, 500, 515–16, 519*
19:18   *231, 501, 515–16*
19:18–19   *231*
19:20   *5, 287, 359, 501, 515–16, 520, 523–24*
19:20–21   *500*
19:21   *500, 515–16, 523*
19:21a   *526*
19:21b   *500*
19:22   *5, 500–501, 523*
19:23   *459, 500, 515–16, 518, 524*
19:23–30   *310*
19:24   *500, 515, 520, 523*
19:25   *500, 515–16*
19:25–27   *177*
19:26   *500, 515–16, 524*
19:27   *287, 500, 515–16*
19:28   *500, 515–16, 519, 525–26*
19:29   *501, 517, 519*
19:30   *132, 310, 312, 315*
20:1–16   *126*
20:16   *311*
20:17   *132, 146*
20:17–19   *386, 412*
20:19   *286*
20:20–21   *126*
20:20–28   *132, 177, 386, 412*
20:29   *5, 146*
20:29–34   *358, 386, 412*
20:33   *286*
21:1   *146*
21:1–9   *386, 412*
21:2   *286–87*
21:3   *77, 287*
21:4–5   *126*
21:7   *358*
21:8   *287*
21:10–11   *390*
21:10–17   *126, 132*
21:12   *390*
21:12–13   *536*
21:12–16   *390*
21:12–17   *386, 412, 427*
21:17   *390*
21:18   *390*
21:18–19   *386, 412*
21:18–22   *132*
21:19a   *390*
21:19b–22   *390*
21:20   *126*
21:20–22   *386, 412, 423*
21:23   *147, 279*
21:23–24:1   *441*
21:23–27   *349, 386, 412*
21:23a   *390*
21:23b–27   *390*
21:24   *132*
21:28–22:14   *429, 468*
21:28–32   *126*
21:32   *312*
21:33   *132, 311–12, 315*
21:33–46   *126, 232, 386, 412*
21:37   *75*
21:42   *132*
21:44   *124*
22:1–14   *126, 337, 355*
22:15   *126, 132*
22:15–22   *536*
22:15–33   *386, 412*
22:18–19   *132*
22:19   *286, 536*
22:23   *286, 517*
22:23–33   *349*
22:27   *286*
22:29   *132*
22:33   *126*
22:34–40   *126, 132, 386, 413, 536*
22:35   *517*
22:41   *517*
22:41–23:36   *386, 413*
22:41–46   *126*
22:45   *286*
22:46   *517*
23   *276*
23:1   *147, 467*
23:1–6   *313*
23:1–36   *126, 267, 313, 366*
23:1–39   *440*
23:4   *357*
23:5   *197, 273*
23:5–7   *537*
23:6   *331*
23:6–7   *329-31*
23:14   *120, 124*
23:34   *359*
23:37–39   *349*
24:1   *267*
24:1–22   *386, 413, 423*
24:2   *287*
24:3   *132*
24:4–8   *349*
24:4–25:46   *126, 440*
24:13   *132*
24:14   *132*
24:15   *360, 457*
24:15–22   *132*
24:22   *459*
24:23–28   *132, 386, 413*
24:29   *132, 287*
24:29–25:46   *386, 413*
24:31   *132*
24:32–36   *349*
24:34   *286*
24:35   *384*
24:36   *75, 132, 314*
24:37–25:46   *314, 468*
25   *315*
25:5   *314*
25:14–30   *337, 355*
26:1–2   *147*
26:1–5   *126, 386, 413*
26:4   *126*

26:5   *132, 459*
26:6–13   *132, 266, 355,
   386, 413*
26:9   *266*
26:14   *287, 459*
26:14–20   *386, 413*
26:15   *126, 360*
26:16   *286*
26:17   *147*
26:21–24   *132*
26:21–25   *386, 413*
26:25   *126*
26:26–29   *136, 362, 383,
   386, 413*
26:30–35   *132, 386, 413*
26:31–35   *177*
26:36   *147*
26:36–45   *177*
26:36–46   *132*
26:36–58   *386, 413*
26:39   *286*
26:42–44   *126*
26:47   *147, 459*
26:47–56   *132*
26:50   *126, 360*
26:51   *286*
26:52–54   *127*
26:56   *177*
26:57–58   *132*
26:59–62   *474, 506*
26:59–68   *132*
26:63   *75, 127*
26:63–66   *387, 413*
26:64   *75*
26:67   *278*
26:67–75   *387, 413*
26:68   *236, 279*
26:69–75   *177*
26:75   *284*
27:1–14   *387, 413*
27:3–10   *127*
27:6   *170*
27:8   *45*
27:11   *517*
27:12–14   *132*
27:15–22   *132*
27:15–26   *387, 413*
27:18   *458*

27:19   *127*
27:21   *127*
27:23   *512*
27:24–25   *127*
27:27–31   *127, 132, 387,
   413*
27:31   *286*
27:32   *387, 413*
27:33   *169*
27:33–61   *387, 413*
27:34   *132*
27:39–42   *132*
27:43   *127*
27:45   *147*
27:46   *169*
27:46–49   *132*
27:51   *285*
27:51–54   *127*
27:54   *75, 286, 360*
27:56   *127, 132*
27:58   *286*
27:59   *286*
27:62–66   *127*
28   *261*
28:1   *147, 370–71*
28:1–8   *127, 387, 413*
28:1–20   *355*
28:5   *370*
28:9   *370–71*
28:9–10   *127*
28:10   *360, 370–71*
28:11–15   *127*
28:15   *45*
28:16   *360, 370*
28:16–20   *127, 372*
28:20   *261*

Mark

1   *223, 292*
1:1   *74–75, 77–78, 104,
   245, 571*
1:1–6   *113, 291*
1:1–13   *293*
1:2   *288, 319, 322*
1:2–3   *187, 320*
1:2–4   *232*
1:2–11   *384, 392, 411,
   421, 428*

1:2–15   *283*
1:3   *321*
1:5–6   *121*
1:7   *230*
1:7–8   *113, 290, 292, 349*
1:7–13   *232*
1:8   *234, 246, 291*
1:9–11   *113*
1:10   *285*
1:11   *74*
1:12–13   *58, 113, 234,
   290, 292–93, 349,
   384, 392, 411, 421*
1:13   *110, 286*
1:14–15   *62, 113, 309,
   384, 392, 421, 516*
1:15   *83, 104*
1:16–20   *13, 113, 121,
   384, 392, 403,
   409–11, 414, 421,
   430*
1:16–38   *551*
1:20   *110, 419, 422*
1:21   *394, 422*
1:21–22   *113, 392, 399*
1:21–28   *68, 135, 385,
   398–99, 411, 421*
1:21–35   *398*
1:21–39   *184*
1:21a   *185, 394*
1:21b   *185, 394*
1:22   *69, 185, 261, 309,
   316, 319, 394*
1:23–28   *113, 119, 185,
   392*
1:24   *63, 74*
1:27   *68, 261*
1:29   *104, 399, 406*
1:29–31   *113, 135, 185*
1:29–34   *385, 392,
   398–99, 411, 421*
1:30   *271*
1:32   *574*
1:32–34   *68, 113, 136,
   175, 185, 396*
1:33   *104, 176, 281*
1:34   *63, 69, 74, 574*
1:35   *136*

Scripture Index

1:35–38 *111, 114, 119, 185, 385, 392, 398–99, 411, 421*
1:35–39 *394, 396*
1:36–37 *104*
1:38 *338*
1:39 *68–69, 114, 136, 185, 309, 338, 385, 392, 398, 411, 419, 421*
1:40 *271*
1:40–42 *285*
1:40–44 *114*
1:40–45 *136, 137, 185, 348, 385, 392, 394, 411, 421*
1:41 *110, 288*
1:43 *104*
1:44 *536*
1:45 *104, 114, 119, 338*
2:1–2 *104, 111*
2:1–3:35 *551*
2:1–12 *111, 114, 119, 136, 185, 232, 349*
2:1–22 *232, 385, 393–94, 398, 400, 411, 421*
2:2 *62, 281*
2:3 *104, 110–11, 281*
2:7 *68–69*
2:8 *104*
2:9 *110*
2:10 *286*
2:10–11 *457*
2:12 *286*
2:13 *104, 338, 400*
2:13–17 *114*
2:13–22 *400*
2:14 *28, 51, 110*
2:15 *104*
2:16 *104, 286*
2:18 *104*
2:18–22 *114, 459*
2:19 *104*
2:21 *286*
2:22 *286*
2:23 *110*
2:23–3:6 *385, 393–94, 400, 410–11, 421–22, 426*
2:23–28 *114, 349, 395*
2:25 *110*
2:26 *110, 119, 186, 286*
2:27 *104, 122*
2:28 *77*
3 *64*
3:1 *270, 286*
3:1–6 *111, 141, 119, 136, 389, 536*
3:2 *119*
3:2–4 *69*
3:3 *119*
3:4 *119*
3:5 *68, 104, 175*
3:6 *64, 79, 110*
3:7 *62*
3:7–8 *119*
3:7–10 *338*
3:7–11 *333*
3:7–12 *68, 114, 292, 307, 310, 385, 389, 393, 403, 411, 421–22, 426*
3:9 *68, 104, 281*
3:10 *64, 69, 574*
3:10–12 *136*
3:11 *63, 74–75, 104*
3:13 *399, 406*
3:13–14 *8*
3:13–19 *112, 114, 302, 307, 385, 389, 393, 399, 403, 406, 411, 421*
3:13–19a *395*
3:14 *70, 104, 281*
3:16–19 *395*
3:17 *104, 169*
3:19–21 *104, 294*
3:19b–21 *395*
3:20 *68*
3:20–21 *114, 385, 387–88, 393, 410–11, 420–22*
3:20–30 *294*
3:21 *79*
3:22 *79, 104, 114, 422*
3:22–27 *385, 393, 404, 411, 421*
3:22–30 *69, 290, 295, 349, 395*
3:22–35 *13, 414*
3:23 *104*
3:23–30 *114*
3:28–30 *385, 393, 404, 411, 422*
3:30 *104*
3:31–35 *79, 114, 295, 385, 393, 403, 411, 422*
3:32 *119*
3:33–34 *121*
3:34 *104*
4 *315, 395*
4:1 *68, 110*
4:1–2 *121, 338*
4:1–9 *114, 349*
4:1–20 *385, 393, 412, 422, 426*
4:1–23 *63*
4:1–25 *403*
4:1–34 *310, 394*
4:2 *310, 467–68*
4:2–3 *104*
4:3–9 *62*
4:5–6 *121*
4:9 *122, 287*
4:10 *110*
4:10–12 *113–14*
4:10–20 *67*
4:11 *279, 287*
4:12 *104*
4:13 *65, 68, 104, 122, 177*
4:13–20 *114*
4:17 *65*
4:19 *104*
4:21 *65, 122*
4:21–25 *114, 119, 290–91, 301, 385, 393, 407, 412, 422–23, 426*
4:23 *104*
4:24 *104, 122, 301*

4:26 *122*
4:26–29 *62, 65, 105, 114, 385, 387–88, 393, 407, 410, 412, 420, 422–23, 426*
4:30 *122, 177*
4:30–32 *62, 65, 114, 290, 296, 385, 393, 404, 407, 412, 422, 426*
4:30–34 *13, 411, 414, 423*
4:32 *299*
4:33 *65, 105, 310*
4:33–34 *62, 67, 114, 120, 385, 393, 407, 412, 422, 426, 467*
4:34 *8, 105*
4:35 *105, 270, 399–400, 406, 423*
4:35–5:20 *385, 393, 398–99, 412, 422, 426*
4:35–5:43 *395, 400*
4:35–36 *308, 533–34*
4:35–41 *69, 114, 136, 533, 535*
4:36 *105*
4:36b *534*
4:38 *68, 105, 177, 187, 281*
4:39 *110*
4:41 *68, 70, 286*
5:1–20 *68, 119, 142, 267, 536*
5:1–21 *114*
5:3 *105*
5:4 *105*
5:5 *105*
5:6 *110*
5:7 *63, 74*
5:8 *458*
5:9 *169*
5:13 *110, 267*
5:19 *131*
5:19–20 *77*
5:20 *105*
5:21 *105, 399–400, 406, 413, 533*

5:21–34 *136, 272*
5:21–43 *119, 295, 385, 393, 398–99, 412, 422, 423, 564*
5:22–43 *114*
5:23 *5, 99, 121, 391*
5:26 *105*
5:27 *105, 234, 272, 274, 286*
5:28 *121*
5:29 *105, 271*
5:31 *177*
5:32 *105*
5:33 *367*
5:34 *110*
5:35–43 *136*
5:39 *105*
5:40 *105*
5:41 *105, 169*
5:42 *105*
5:43 *518*
6:1–6 *13, 79, 121, 385, 393, 395, 403, 409–12, 414, 422, 427, 430*
6:1–6a *114, 395*
6:2 *68*
6:2b *411*
6:3 *246*
6:4 *69*
6:5 *175, 493*
6:5–6 *105*
6:6 *68, 338, 423*
6:6b–13 *114, 302*
6:7 *105, 281, 287, 386, 315, 395, 403*
6:7–11 *290, 302, 316*
6:7–13 *70, 295, 385, 393, 399, 406, 412, 422, 427*
6:8–9 *395*
6:10 *122*
6:11 *286*
6:11–12 *119*
6:12–13 *105*
6:13 *426, 445–46*

6:14 *13, 68, 89, 110, 151, 226, 408, 426, 445–46, 460*
6:14–15 *69*
6:14–16 *114, 119, 377, 385, 393, 411–14, 422–23, 427*
6:14–16:8 *409*
6:14–29 *105, 295*
6:17 *110, 114*
6:17–29 *120, 385, 404, 412, 422–23, 427*
6:18–29 *114, 564*
6:23 *110*
6:26 *110*
6:30 *110, 119*
6:30–31 *13, 385, 408, 412, 414, 622–23, 427*
6:30–32 *70*
6:30–44 *69, 114, 136, 564*
6:31 *68, 105*
6:31–32 *283*
6:32–9:37 *423*
6:32–44 *385, 412, 422*
6:33 *105, 282*
6:33–34 *70*
6:34 *105*
6:37 *267, 283*
6:37–38 *105*
6:39 *110, 281, 283*
6:39–40 *283*
6:40 *105, 110*
6:41 *459*
6:43 *286*
6:45–8:26 *41, 268, 332, 335*
6:45–52 *69, 114, 120, 136, 385, 412, 422*
6:47 *110*
6:50 *105*
6:51 *75–76, 177*
6:52 *106*
6:53–7:37 *385, 412, 422*
6:53–54 *106*
6:53–56 *68, 114, 120, 136*

6:55–56   *106*
6:56   *69, 273*
7:1–23   *79, 114, 120, 333, 403, 429, 536*
7:2–4   *106*
7:6–13   *383*
7:9   *106, 122*
7:11   *169*
7:13   *106*
7:16   *124*
7:17   *106*
7:18–19   *106*
7:18–23   *221*
7:20   *122*
7:21–22   *510*
7:22–23   *106*
7:24   *65, 106*
7:24–30   *68, 114, 120, 136, 268*
7:26   *106, 281*
7:30   *106*
7:31   *114, 120*
7:31–37   *106, 136, 333, 387, 388*
7:32   *437*
7:32–37   *114, 175, 271*
7:34   *169*
7:37   *437*
8:1   *106*
8:1–2   *338*
8:1–10   *69, 114, 120, 136, 385, 412, 422*
8:2   *68*
8:3   *106*
8:7   *106*
8:11–12   *67, 79*
8:11–13   *114*
8:11–21   *385, 404, 412, 422, 429*
8:12   *175, 277, 287–88*
8:12–13   *106*
8:13–21   *468*
8:13–22   *79*
8:14   *106*
8:14–15   *115*
8:14–21   *120*
8:15   *106, 110, 286*
8:16–21   *115*

8:17–18   *177*
8:19   *106*
8:21   *68*
8:22–26   *68, 84, 106, 115, 136, 175, 333, 385, 387–88, 412, 420*
8:27   *69, 110, 154, 269*
8:27–9:1   *429*
8:27–30   *70, 115*
8:27–31   *385, 412, 422*
8:28   *284*
8:29   *74–75, 177*
8:31   *66, 70, 115, 286*
8:31–33   *71*
8:32   *110*
8:32–33   *115, 121, 385, 412, 422*
8:33   *106*
8:34   *286*
8:34–9:1   *115, 287, 349, 386, 412, 422*
8:34–38   *66*
8:35   *111*
8:37–38   *287*
8:38   *106, 277, 287*
9   *317*
9:1   *122*
9:2   *358*
9:2–8   *115, 232*
9:2–10   *270, 386, 412, 422*
9:3   *106*
9:4   *283*
9:5   *177*
9:7   *75*
9:9–10   *115*
9:9–13   *120*
9:10   *106*
9:11   *517*
9:11–13   *115, 284, 386, 412, 422*
9:12   *106*
9:13   *177*
9:14–16   *107*
9:14–29   *68, 84, 115, 136, 232, 271, 564*
9:14–32   *386, 412, 422*
9:18   *107, 349*

9:19   *177, 234, 276–77*
9:20–28   *107*
9:25   *271, 281, 437*
9:28   *111, 121*
9:29   *107*
9:30–31   *107*
9:30–32   *115*
9:31   *66, 287*
9:32   *71, 119, 177*
9:33   *468*
9:33–10:16   *318*
9:33–34   *107, 177*
9:33–35   *319*
9:33–37   *115, 315, 386, 412, 422, 427*
9:33–42   *320*
9:35   *107, 177, 319–20*
9:36   *111, 281*
9:37   *119, 317*
9:37b   *319–20*
9:38   *177*
9:38–40   *119, 320*
9:38–41   *14, 115, 386, 408, 412, 414, 422–23, 427*
9:39   *107*
9:41   *107, 121, 317, 319–20, 423*
9:42   *115, 319*
9:42–48   *120, 315*
9:42–50   *290–91, 386, 412, 422, 427*
9:43–48   *115*
9:44   *124*
9:45   *107*
9:46   *124*
9:48   *107*
9:48–50   *319–20*
9:49–50   *66, 107, 115, 387*
9:50b   *468*
10   *515*
10:1   *319–20, 564*
10:1–10   *120*
10:1–12   *115, 318, 386, 404, 412, 429*
10:2   *79*
10:3–9   *383*

10:10–12 *107*
10:11 *575*
10:11–12 *276*
10:13 *318*
10:13–16 *115, 318*
10:13–31 *386, 412*
10:14 *68, 107, 175*
10:16 *107*
10:17 *107, 509, 515*
10:17–22 *142*
10:17–31 *281*
10:18 *515–16*
10:19 *111, 509–10, 520*
10:20 *5, 111, 287, 510, 516, 518–19, 523, 525*
10:21 *68, 107, 111, 510, 515–16, 518–20, 525–26*
10:22 *511, 519, 521, 523, 525*
10:23 *459, 511, 515–16, 519, 523, 642*
10:23–27 *115*
10:23–31 *310*
10:24 *107, 512, 515, 518*
10:25 *512, 518, 522, 525*
10:26 *512, 515–16, 519*
10:27 *513, 515, 519, 524*
10:28 *287, 513, 515, 519*
10:28–31 *115*
10:29 *111, 513–14, 515, 518–19, 522, 524, 526*
10:29–30 *518*
10:30 *108, 514, 519*
10:31 *121, 310, 514*
10:32 *108*
10:32–34 *115, 386, 412*
10:34 *286*
10:35 *177*
10:35–40 *115*
10:35–41 *120*
10:35–45 *386, 412*
10:38 *114*
10:39 *114*
10:41–45 *115*
10:42–45 *121*

10:46 *5, 111, 169, 270*
10:46–52 *68, 115, 136, 386, 412*
10:49–50 *134*
10:51 *286, 288*
10:52 *111, 119*
11:1–10 *386, 412*
11:2 *119, 286–87, 288*
11:3 *77, 287*
11:4 *108*
11:8 *287*
11:10 *108*
11:11 *108, 115, 120, 386–88, 412, 420*
11:11–14 *390*
11:11–27 *389*
11:11a *390*
11:11b *390*
11:11c *390*
11:12 *68*
11:12–14 *115, 120, 136, 386, 412*
11:12a *390*
11:12b–14 *390*
11:13 *108*
11:14 *108, 518*
11:15 *108*
11:15–17 *115, 386, 412, 427*
11:15–18 *390*
11:15–19 *423, 536*
11:15a *390*
11:15b *390*
11:15b–17 *390*
11:16 *108*
11:17 *108*
11:18 *119, 390*
11:18–19 *14, 115, 386, 408, 412, 414, 427*
11:19 *390*
11:20 *175, 390*
11:20–21 *108*
11:20–25 *115, 120*
11:20–26 *69, 136, 386, 390, 412, 423, 427*
11:23–24 *108*
11:25 *108, 111*
11:26 *115, 124*

11:27–33 *67, 115, 349, 386, 412*
11:27a *390*
11:27b–33 *390*
11:28 *79*
12:1 *311, 468*
12:1–11 *115*
12:1–12 *232, 386, 412, 468*
12:3 *119*
12:5 *108*
12:6 *75*
12:12 *111, 115*
12:13–15 *79*
12:13–17 *115, 536*
12:13–27 *386, 412*
12:15 *286, 536*
12:18 *286, 517*
12:18–23 *79*
12:18–27 *116, 349*
12:22 *286*
12:27 *111*
12:28 *108, 517*
12:28–31 *116, 121*
12:28–34 *386, 403, 413, 536*
12:29 *108*
12:32–34 *108, 116*
12:34 *517*
12:35–37a *116*
12:35–40 *386, 413*
12:37 *286*
12:37–38 *108, 313*
12:37b–40 *116, 313*
12:38 *467–68*
12:38–40 *79, 290, 331, 536*
12:38b–39 *330*
12:40 *120, 423*
12:41 *108*
12:41–44 *14, 116, 119, 267, 386, 408, 413–14, 423, 536*
12:42 *111*
12:43 *108*
13 *59, 119, 315*
13:1 *267*
13:1–4 *116*

13:1–20 *386, 413, 423*
13:2 *287*
13:3 *108*
13:5–8 *116, 349*
13:5–37 *123*
13:9–13 *116, 302*
13:10 *121*
13:11 *358*
13:14 *457*
13:14–20 *116*
13:18 *121*
13:19b–24 *121*
13:20 *459*
13:21–23 *116, 386, 404, 413, 423*
13:23 *109*
13:24–27 *116*
13:24–37 *386, 413*
13:25 *287*
13:27 *121*
13:28–29 *116*
13:28–32 *349*
13:30 *277, 286*
13:30–32 *116*
13:31 *313*
13:32 *75, 314*
13:32–37 *121*
13:33 *314*
13:33–37 *67, 116, 314, 387–88, 468*
13:34 *314*
13:35 *314*
13:35–37 *109*
13:37 *314*
14:1–2 *79, 116, 385–86, 393*
14:2 *459*
14:3–4 *109*
14:3–9 *116, 121, 266, 386, 403, 413*
14:5 *109, 266*
14:6 *68, 111*
14:7 *109*
14:8 *109, 281*
14:10 *287, 459*
14:10–11 *79, 116*
14:10–17 *386, 413*
14:11 *286*

14:12–16 *116*
14:13–15 *120*
14:15 *459, 536*
14:16 *109*
14:17–21 *116*
14:18–21 *386, 403, 413*
14:22–25 *116, 121, 383, 386, 403, 413*
14:26 *116*
14:26–28 *120*
14:26–31 *386*
14:27–28 *116*
14:29–31 *116*
14:32–42 *116*
14:32–54 *386, 413*
14:33–34 *121*
14:33–42 *68*
14:35–36 *109*
14:36 *111, 169, 273*
14:39–42 *121*
14:40 *109, 177*
14:43 *459*
14:43–49 *79*
14:43–50 *116*
14:47 *286*
14:49b–50 *121*
14:51–52 *87, 109, 116, 387*
14:53–54 *116*
14:55–60 *386, 413*
14:55–61a *116, 121*
14:56 *109*
14:57–59 *109*
14:61 *68, 71*
14:61–62 *71*
14:61–64 *387, 403, 413*
14:61b–64 *116*
14:62 *75*
14:64 *79*
14:65 *109, 116, 236, 278*
14:65–72 *387, 403, 413*
14:66–67 *109*
14:66–72 *116*
14:71 *177*
14:72 *111, 284*
15:1 *109, 116*
15:1–5 *387, 413*
15:1–47 *79*

15:2 *517*
15:2–5 *116*
15:3 *109*
15:3–5 *121*
15:6–15 *116, 387, 413*
15:7–8 *109*
15:10 *458*
15:14 *512*
15:16–20 *121, 387, 413*
15:16–20a *116*
15:20 *286*
15:20b–21 *116*
15:21 *111, 387, 413*
15:22 *169*
15:22–32 *116*
15:22–47 *387, 413*
15:25 *109*
15:28 *124*
15:33 *117*
15:34 *169*
15:34–36 *117, 121*
15:37–41 *117*
15:38 *285*
15:39 *75, 79, 286*
15:40–41 *109*
15:42 *109*
15:42–47 *117*
15:43 *111, 120, 286*
15:44–45 *109*
15:46 *286*
16:1 *109*
16:1–8 *117, 244, 387, 413*
16:3–4 *110, 281*
16:5–7 *56*
16:6 *78*
16:6–7 *79, 263*
16:8 *55, 110, 244–45, 263–64*
16:9–20 *124, 262–63*

Luke

1 *127*
1:1 *9, 32, 402, 407, 434*
1:1–2 *343*
1:1–3 *487*
1:1–4 *8, 26, 32, 259, 367, 371, 373, 381, 432,*

461, 559, 562, 565,
     572
1:2   8, 22, 206
1:3   42, 154–55, 229, 269,
     375, 407, 442
1:4   565
1:5   42, 139, 269
1:5–2:4   139
1:5–2:52   355, 432
1:8   139
1:23   42
1:24   139
1:26   269
1:32   74
1:39   139
1:56   139, 269
1:57   139
1:59   139
2   127
2:1   139, 269
2:1–7   370
2:2   139
2:3   139
2:4   139
2:6   139
2:11   71
2:12   369
2:16   369
2:21   139, 269
2:21–38   139
2:22   139
2:24   139
2:26   71
2:38   139
2:39   139, 370
2:41   140
2:41–46   140
2:42   269
2:45   140
2:46   140
2:48   140
3:1   140
3:1–2   42, 127, 269
3:1–3   140
3:1–4:15   232
3:1–6   291
3:1–18   432
3:2   140, 409

3:2–22   384, 411, 421
3:3   140
3:4   324
3:5–6   127
3:7–9   248, 291–92, 349
3:10–14   127
3:15   127
3:16   230–31, 292
3:16–17   234, 246,
     291–92, 349
3:17   248, 292
3:18   127
3:19–20   127, 385, 404,
     422, 427, 432
3:21   285
3:21–22   285, 432
3:22   74
3:23   140, 269
3:23–28   432
3:23–38   127, 355, 409
4:1–2   140
4:1–13   234, 292–93, 349,
     384, 411, 421, 432
4:2   286
4:3   74
4:4–13   362, 383
4:6–7   127
4:9   74, 459
4:13   127
4:14   140, 361, 432
4:14–15   127, 309, 384,
     411, 421
4:15   361, 432
4:16   140
4:16–30   121, 127, 348,
     355, 361, 385, 403,
     409, 411–12, 422,
     427
4:18   436
4:22   246
4:31   140, 443
4:31–32   309
4:31–37   133, 385, 411,
     421
4:31a   361
4:31b–32   361
4:32   309
4:34   74

4:38   141, 271
4:38–39   127, 361
4:38–41   350, 385, 411,
     421, 438–39
4:39   359
4:40   141, 175
4:40–41   127, 361
4:41   74
4:42   141
4:42–43   133, 385, 411,
     421
4:44   127, 141, 309, 359,
     361, 385, 411, 421
5:1   141
5:1–11   121, 127, 355,
     361, 377, 384, 403,
     409, 411, 421, 432
5:12   42, 128, 141, 148,
     153, 271, 334, 443
5:12–13   285
5:12–16   137, 348, 361,
     385, 411, 421, 436,
     438
5:12a   137
5:13   288
5:15–16   128
5:17   42, 136, 141, 148,
     153, 443
5:17–19   133
5:17–26   349, 436–37,
     564
5:17–39   232, 350, 352,
     361, 385, 411, 421,
     433, 438–39, 443
5:21   133
5:24   288, 457
5:25   286
5:25–26   133
5:27   28, 51, 141, 234
5:27–39   154
5:30   286
5:33–39   434
5:36   286
5:37   287
5:39   128
6:1   141, 148
6:1–5   349

6:1–11 *361, 385, 410–11, 421, 426, 433*
6:4 *286*
6:5 *122*
6:6 *141, 148, 270, 286*
6:6–11 *389, 536*
6:7 *133*
6:8 *133*
6:9 *133*
6:11 *128*
6:12–13 *128, 142*
6:12–16 *308, 361, 385, 389, 403, 410, 411, 421–22, 426*
6:14–15 *129, 363*
6:15–16 *358*
6:17 *142*
6:17–19 *133, 307, 310, 333, 361, 377, 385, 389, 403, 410–11, 421, 426*
6:17–49 *13*
6:19 *409*
6:20 *403, 410*
6:20–23 *128*
6:20–49 *307, 361, 436*
6:24–26 *128*
6:27–28 *128*
6:34–35 *128*
6:37–38 *128*
6:39 *366*
6:42 *459*
6:43–45 *296, 361*
6:44 *359*
6:45 *362*
6:46 *261*
7:1 *99, 142*
7:1–10 *97, 361, 438–39*
7:2 *359*
7:3 *99*
7:3–7 *128*
7:6 *98–99*
7:7 *98–100*
7:9 *100*
7:11 *142, 148*
7:11–17 *128, 436*
7:18–23 *349*
7:18–35 *361, 432, 436*
7:19b *367*
7:20 *367*
7:20–21 *129*
7:21 *436*
7:22 *271, 436*
7:24–35 *349*
7:27 *77, 288, 321–22*
7:29–30 *128*
7:32 *359*
7:36–50 *121, 128, 355, 386, 403*
8:1 *142, 148, 438*
8:1–3 *128*
8:4 *142, 148, 443*
8:4–8 *349*
8:4–15 *385, 412, 422–23, 523*
8:4–18 *379, 443, 494*
8:6 *359*
8:8 *122, 287*
8:10 *279, 287*
8:10a *363*
8:10b *363*
8:11 *122*
8:12 *287*
8:16 *122, 128*
8:16–18 *133, 385, 407, 412, 422, 423*
8:18 *122*
8:18b *363*
8:19 *142, 334, 443*
8:19–21 *361, 385, 403, 410–12, 422, 534*
8:22 *142, 148, 270, 308, 443, 533*
8:22–25 *533*
8:22–39 *385, 412, 422, 426, 438–39, 443*
8:22–40 *350, 361, 432*
8:24 *363*
8:25 *177, 286, 363*
8:26 *143*
8:26–39 *267, 564*
8:27 *128*
8:27–31 *133*
8:28 *74*
8:29 *458*
8:33 *267*
8:35–39 *133*
8:37 *128*
8:39 *77*
8:40 *154, 443, 533*
8:40–42 *133*
8:40–45 *443*
8:40–48 *272*
8:40–49 *143*
8:40–56 *358, 385, 412, 422, 426, 438, 564*
8:41–42 *361*
8:42 *5, 391*
8:43–48 *361*
8:44 *234, 271–72, 274, 279, 286, 567*
8:45–47 *128, 133*
8:47 *367*
8:49 *167, 391*
8:49–52 *133*
8:49–56 *361*
8:55–56 *133*
9:1 *287, 334, 423*
9:1–6 *302, 361, 385, 412, 422, 427*
9:4 *122*
9:5 *286*
9:5–6 *133*
9:7 *143*
9:7–9 *361, 385, 411–12, 422–23, 427*
9:7–17 *433*
9:8–9 *133*
9:9 *128, 410, 432*
9:10 *133, 359, 427*
9:10–17 *564*
9:10a *143, 385, 408, 412, 414, 422, 430*
9:10b–12 *143*
9:10b–17 *385, 412, 422*
9:11 *133, 282*
9:11–17 *361, 432*
9:13 *133*
9:14 *133, 363*
9:15–17 *363*
9:16 *459*
9:17 *286*
9:18 *128, 143, 148, 154, 359*

9:18–21   432
9:18–22   385, 422
9:18–36   362
9:18–48   433, 436
9:20   74
9:22   286, 334, 432
9:23   286
9:23–27   287, 349, 386, 422, 432
9:26   287
9:27   122
9:28   143, 358–59
9:28–36   128, 232, 270, 386, 422, 432
9:30   283
9:35   75
9:37   143
9:37–43   133
9:37–43a   232, 432
9:37–45   386, 422
9:37–48   362
9:38–39   128
9:38–43   564
9:40   286
9:40–41   177
9:41   234, 276
9:43   128
9:43b   143
9:44   287, 334
9:44–45   128
9:45   107, 177
9:46   144, 334
9:46–48   177, 308, 386, 422, 427
9:47   128
9:48   128, 317
9:49   317
9:49–50   133, 177, 386, 408, 412, 414, 422, 427
9:51   144, 436
9:51–18:14   318, 377, 408
9:51–18:15   13
9:51–56   128
9:54–55   177
9:57   128, 144, 270
9:57–60   349–50
9:57–62   308, 362, 533
9:60–62   128
9:60b   533
9:61–62   533
10:1   32, 128, 144, 334
10:1–12   302, 316
10:1–19:27   353
10:2   349, 362
10:5–6   275
10:5–11   128
10:7   359
10:12   363
10:12–15   349, 362
10:13   363
10:16   128
10:17   144
10:17–20   128
10:21   144
10:21–22   349, 362
10:22   74
10:23   128
10:23–24   362
10:24   359
10:25–28   121, 134, 386, 403, 536
10:29–37   128
10:38   144
10:38–42   128, 436
11   443
11:1   144
11:1–4   128, 348, 365
11:2   521
11:2–4   337
11:5–8   129
11:9–13   362
11:12   129
11:13   359
11:14   84, 144
11:14–23   129, 296, 362, 404
11:14–32   294, 349
11:15–23   385, 421
11:16   296, 333, 362
11:20   356, 359
11:24–26   296, 362–63
11:27   144, 334
11:29   144, 333
11:29–32   296, 362
11:31   363
11:32   363
11:33–36   129
11:35   359
11:37   144
11:37–41   385, 403, 422
11:37–54   129
11:43   331
11:49   359
12:1   120, 145, 286, 385, 404, 422
12:1–9   129
12:6   359
12:10   294, 296, 362, 385, 404, 422
12:11–12   129
12:12   134
12:13–21   129
12:22–32   362
12:26   129
12:32   129
12:33   129
12:33–34   362
12:35–46   129
12:47–48   129
12:49–56   129
12:54   145
12:57   129
12:57–59   362
13:1   145
13:1–9   129
13:10   42, 153
13:10–17   129, 145
13:15   276
13:18   122, 134
13:18–19   296, 385, 404, 412, 422, 426
13:18–21   310, 362
13:19b   299
13:20   122, 129
13:22   145
13:22–30   129
13:30   121, 310
13:31   145
13:31–33   129
13:34–35   349
14:1   145
14:1–6   129

14:5   276
14:7–14   129
14:15   145
14:15–24   129, 337, 355
14:25   145
14:25–35   129
15:1   145
15:1–7   129, 366
15:1–32   366
15:3–7   337
15:6–7   336
15:8–10   129
15:11–32   129
15:14   520
16:1–13   129
16:13   349, 366
16:14–15   129
16:16–17   129
16:18   129, 336, 386, 404
16:19–31   129
16:24   357
17:1   145, 363
17:1–2   120, 129
17:2a   363
17:2b   363
17:3   366
17:3–4   129
17:5–6   129
17:7–10   129
17:9   436
17:11   146
17:11–19   129
17:12   334
17:14   537
17:20   146
17:20–21   129
17:22–37   129
17:23–37   386, 404
17:36   124
18   500–2, 515–16, 523
18:1   146
18:1–8   129
18:3   334
18:9   146
18:9–14   129
18:15   146, 318, 362
18:15–17   349, 432
18:15–30   386

18:18   359, 500, 519, 523
18:18–23   358
18:18–30   231, 493, 495–500, 503–8
18:18b–19a   527
18:19   495, 503, 515
18:20   231, 496, 501, 503, 523
18:21   5, 287, 496, 502, 504, 515
18:22   496, 514, 504, 515, 519, 524, 526
18:22b   500
18:23   496, 500, 505, 523
18:24   459, 496–97, 505, 515, 523–24
18:24–30   310
18:25   497, 500, 506, 523
18:26   498, 507, 516
18:26–28   177
18:27   498, 500, 507, 516, 523
18:28   287, 498, 500, 507, 516, 522–23
18:29   498, 501, 507, 516, 519, 523
18:30   499, 501, 508, 523
18:31   146, 334
18:31–34   130, 177, 386
18:33   286
18:35   5, 146, 358
18:35–43   130, 386
18:41   286
19:1   146, 358
19:1–10   130
19:11   146
19:11–27   130, 337, 355
19:28   146
19:28–39   130
19:28–40   386
19:30   286–87
19:31   77, 287
19:33–34   134
19:36   287
19:39–44   130
19:41   146
19:45–46   386, 412, 427
19:45–48   423, 536

19:45a   390
19:45b–46   390
19:47   146
19:47–48   134, 386, 390, 408, 412, 414, 427, 430
20:1   130, 147–48
20:1–8   349, 386
20:1–21:5   441
20:1a   390
20:1b–8   390
20:2   367
20:9   311
20:9–19   130, 232, 386
20:10   134
20:13   75
20:20–26   130, 536
20:20–40   386
20:24   286, 537
20:27   286
20:27–38   349
20:27–40   130
20:28   517
20:32   286
20:39   536
20:40   517
20:41–47   386
20:44   286
20:45   130, 147, 313
20:45–47   134, 313, 366, 536
20:46   329–31
21:1–4   134, 267, 386, 408, 413–14, 423, 430, 536
21:5   441
21:5–24   386, 423
21:6   287
21:8–11   349
21:8–24   130
21:12–17   134
21:15   357
21:20   360
21:25–28   130
21:25–36   386
21:26   287
21:29–33   349
21:32   286

21:33 *313*	22:62 *284*	**John**
21:34 *314*	22:63–64 *279*	
21:34–46 *130*	22:64 *236*	1:34 *73*
21:36 *314*	22:66–71 *387, 403*	1:38 *169*
21:37–38 *130, 147, 377*	22:67 *75*	1:41 *169*
21:38 *36*	22:70 *75*	1:49 *73*
22:1 *147*	23:1–5 *130, 387*	4:25 *169*
22:1–2 *386*	23:6–16 *130*	4:42 *169*
22:3 *287, 459*	23:17 *124*	5:2 *139*
22:3–6 *129*	23:17–25 *387*	6:7 *267*
22:3–14 *386*	23:44 *147*	7:53 *36*
22:5 *360*	23:44–49 *130*	9:7 *169*
22:6 *286*	23:45 *285*	11:16 *169*
22:7 *147*	23:47 *75, 286, 360*	12:1–8 *154*
22:7–13 *134*	23:50–51 *134*	12:5 *266*
22:7–23 *130*	23:50–56 *130*	12:47–49 *261*
22:8–9 *130*	23:52 *286*	14:10 *261*
22:12 *459*	23:53 *286*	14:15 *261*
22:15–17 *130*	23:54 *147*	14–16 *50*
22:15–19 *362, 383*	23:56 *147*	14:21–24 *261*
22:15–20 *387, 403*	24:1 *147*	14:25–26 *48*
22:19b–20 *121, 124, 377*	24:1–12 *130, 387*	14:26 *50, 454, 458*
22:21 *130*	24:1–53 *355*	15:10 *261*
22:21–23 *387, 403*	24:4 *370*	15:15 *8*
22:23 *130*	24:7 *370*	15:26–27 *48*
22:24 *177, 334*	24:8–9 *370*	15:27 *8, 28*
22:25–27 *121*	24:9 *370*	16:13 *48*
22:27–30 *130*	24:10 *370*	17:8 *261*
22:28–30 *519*	24:13 *148*	19:13 *169*
22:31–33 *130*	24:13–35 *370*	19:19–20 *19*
22:31–34 *177, 386*	24:13–53 *130*	20:16 *169*
22:35 *520*	24:22–23 *371*	20:24 *169*
22:35–38 *130*	24:23 *370*	20:26 *358*
22:38 *177*	24:25 *177*	21:2 *169*
22:39 *120, 147*	24:28–51 *371*	
22:39–42 *130*	24:34 *370*	**Acts**
22:39–46 *177*	24:36 *148, 371*	
22:39–54 *386*	24:36–43 *370*	1:1–5 *43*
22:42 *286*	24:38–41 *177*	1:3 *372*
22:43–44 *130*	24:44 *148*	1:6 *72*
22:47 *147, 459*	24:44–51 *148*	1:8 *8, 28*
22:47–53 *130*	24:45 *49*	1:15 *33*
22:48 *360*	24:48 *8, 28, 360*	1:19 *170*
22:50 *286*	24:49 *370–71*	1:21 *205*
22:54–71 *130*	24:50–51 *371*	1:21–22 *244*
22:55–65 *387, 403*	24:51 *148, 370*	2:40 *277*
22:56–62 *177*	24:52 *360, 370*	2:42 *8*
22:56–66 *403*	24:53 *370*	2:42–46 *261*
		2:46 *34*

Scripture Index

4:13 *30*
4:36 *170*
6:2–4 *8*
6:4 *205*
8:20–22 *72*
9:15 *46*
9:36 *170*
9:39 *537*
10 *82*
10:36 *83*
10:36–43 *82*
10:37 *24*
10:43 *83*
11:27–30 *45, 223*
12:12 *306*
12:12–17 *62*
12:25 *45, 62, 223*
13 *82*
13:5 *62*
13:6–8 *170*
13:13 *62*
13:24 *24*
13:33 *73*
14:4 *285*
15:19–23 *20*
15:30–31 *20*
15:37–39 *62*
18:28 *537*
20:20 *262*
20:30 *276*
20:31 *262*
20:35 *342*
21:15–16 *8*
21:17 *39*
21:20 *8*
22:14–15 *47*
23:7 *285*

23:26 *19*
24:27 *10, 39*
25:26 *19*

1 Corinthians

7 *342*
7:6 *343*
7:8 *343*
7:10 *261, 342*
7:12 *343*
7:17 *343*
7:25–26 *343*
7:32 *343*
7:35 *343*
7:40 *343*
11 *338*
11:23 *338*
15 *82*
15:3–8 *371*
16:22 *170*

Galatians

2:1 *45, 223*

Ephesians

6:21–22 *19*

Philippians

2:15 *276*
3:1 *338*

Colossians

4:7–8 *19*
4:10 *62*

2 Thessalonians

2:2 *343*
3:17 *343*

Hebrews

1:5 *73*
5:5 *73*

2 Peter

1:12 *338*
1:16 *343*

1 John

1:1–4 *343*

www.ingramcontent.com/pod-product-compliance
Lightning Source LLC
Chambersburg PA
CBHW051551230426
43668CB00013B/1816